FUNDAMENTALS *of* HUMAN RELATIONS

Applications for Life and Work

Fundamentals of
HUMAN RELATIONS

Applications for Life & Work

Ralph D. Wray, Ed.D.
Professor Emeritus
Business and Marketing Education
Illinois State University

Roger L. Luft, Ed.D.
Professor
Business Education and
Administrative Information Systems
Eastern Illinois University

Patrick J. Highland, Ph.D.
Director of Vocational Education
Iowa City Community School District

South-Western Educational Publishing

I(T)P
International Thomson Publishing
South-Western Educational Publishing is a division of International Thomson Publishing Inc. The ITP trademark is used under license.

ISBN: 0-538-71396-8

Editor in Chief:	*Peter McBride*
Project Manager:	*Laurie Wendell*
Production Coordinator:	*Tricia Boies*
Editor:	*Alan Biondi*
Senior Designer:	*Elaine St John-Lagenaur*
Photo Editor:	*Alix Roughen*
Marketing Manager:	*Carolyn Love*

4 5 6 7 8 9 VH 03 02 01 00

Printed in the United States of America

Preface

Students preparing for careers in today's world need to develop three kinds of competencies. First of all, they have to acquire a basic body of knowledge encompassing the principles and practices of their chosen career fields. Secondly, students must acquire the critical thinking and decision-making skills they will need to apply on a day-to-day basis. Finally, students must develop and refine their human relations skills if they are to achieve success in a work environment that is characterized by greater cultural diversity, more work performed by self-directed work teams, and greater emphasis placed on quality relationships within organizations.

Fundamentals of Human Relations: Applications for Life and Work gives students an opportunity to understand the complexities of human interactions and their applications in contemporary organizations. It conveys the excitement, relevance, and challenge found in the sociocultural environment with regard to communications, ethics, personal and organizational values and attitudes, social structures, and customs and taboos. The book is written in a lively style and conversational, easy-to-understand language, without complicated abstract terminology.

Rationale for the Text

Rationale for this textbook was derived from a report titled *Learning a Living: A Blueprint for High Performance,* released by the Secretary's Commission on Achieving Necessary Skills (SCANS), U.S. Department of Labor. A careful analysis of the workplace competencies and foundation skills advocated within the SCANS report revealed concern for the development of social (relationship) competencies and work (relationship) competencies that have been addressed in this textbook.

The authors have designed the text to make contributions toward the development of the three foundational skill areas: basic skills (primarily communications), thinking skills, and personal qualities (individual responsibility, self-esteem and self-management, sociability, and integrity). Likewise, the textbook makes contributions to at least four of the five categories of workplace competencies:

► resources (allocation of time and staff)

► interpersonal skills (working in teams; teaching others; serving customers/clients; leading, negotiating, and working with people from culturally diverse backgrounds)

► information (acquiring and evaluating data, interpreting, and communicating)

► systems (understanding social, organizational systems; monitoring correct performance)

► In addition, the authors believe that an interdisciplinary course in human relations (drawing upon the disciplines of psychology, sociology, communications, management, ethics, among others) is compatible with contemporary educational reforms—the integration of academic/vocational subjects, implementation of tech-prep models, preparing students for school-to-work transitions, and redesigning curriculum around skills.

Organization of the Text

Fundamentals of Human Relations: Applications for Life and Work features four units, each highlighting important and related aspects of human interactions in contemporary organizations. Unit 1 provides students with an overview of the human relations movement and introduces them to human relations in organizations and work groups. Students are then exposed to the essentials of human relations as they encounter the challenges of interpersonal and organizational communications, human needs and motivation, and job satisfaction and employee morale in Unit 2. The third unit brings students face-to-face with the realities of the workplace and the problems inherent in modern workplace settings. The final unit focuses upon improving practices in human relations from both leader and follower perspectives.

Throughout *Fundamentals of Human Relations,* numerous real-life examples are provided to illustrate the theories and concepts being presented. These examples show the importance of human relations skills in conducting every-day social and business activities. Special attention has been given to the importance of adherence to ethics in all interactions with people. Likewise, emphasis has been placed upon the need to develop a strong sensitivity to diversity and multicultural customs and traditions prevalent in today's global business community.

Pedagogical Features

The authors have incorporated a number of pedagogical features into *Fundamentals of Human Relations* to enhance the teaching/learning processes.

- *Student-learner objectives* appear at the beginning of each chapter and specify important learning outcomes.

- *Chapter opening scenarios* relate real-world happenings at the beginning of each chapter. The scenarios, while evoking students' interests, may be used to trigger discussions.

- *Practical applications and illustrations,* related to both on-the-job and personal life uses of the concepts and ideas presented, appear throughout the text.

- *Contemporary themes,* Customs and Traditions and Ethical Dimension to Human Relations, appear in each chapter.

- *Key point summaries* are provided at the end of each chapter to reinforce major concepts, principles, and ideas. These summaries may also be valuable for review purposes.

- *Key terms* appear in alphabetized format at the end of each chapter and provide students with the opportunity to recall and use the human rela-

tions vocabulary they have learned. The terms, along with their definitions, also appear in the margins providing quick reference.

- *Discussion questions,* at the end of each chapter, may be used as the basis for both large- and small-group discussions of human relations concepts.

- *End-of-the-unit applications* are succinct descriptions of human relations problems that require students to analyze facts, make decisions, and apply concepts which they have learned.

- *End-of-the-unit cases* provide more detailed presentations of actual human relations-related problems that occur in contemporary work-places.

- The *Glossary,* containing key terms and their definitions, provides a quick reference source.

Supporting Materials

Three supporting products have been developed by the authors for use by students and instructors.

Workbook to Accompany Fundamentals of Human Relations: Applications for Life and Work

Instructor's Manual for Fundamentals of Human Relations: Applications for Life and Work

Computerized Test Bank for Fundamentals of Human Relations: Applications for Life and Work

The workbook is designed to enrich the students' learning experiences. It contains practice test questions including matching vocabulary exercises, true-false items, and multiple-choice items. Additional projects, applica-tions, and cases are provided along with answer keys.

The Instructor's Manual contains an introduction to the text and work-book and suggestions for planning the course. It also contains a list of stu-dent-learner objectives for each chapter, teaching suggestions, keys for end-of-the-chapter discussion questions, and keys for end-of-the-unit applica-tions and cases. Finally, the *Instructor's Manual* contains a test bank and key featuring over 1,200 test items.

The computerized test bank contains 70 objective questions—comple-tion, true-false, and multiple choice—for each chapter.

Acknowledgements

A book of this nature requires the cooperation of many people at Delmar Publishers and South-Western Educational Publishing. The authors are grateful to these individuals for their contributions.

The authors also thank Nina Newberry, Tulsa Technology Center, and Arleen White, Texas State Technical College, for reviews of the manuscript and for their feedback and valuable suggestions. Dennis Schrag, Howard R.

Green Company, also reviewed a portion of the manuscript and provided feedback from an organizational setting.

The authors extend their appreciation to other authors and publishers who gave us permission to quote from their works. Their ideas and concepts have added significantly to our work.

Finally, we owe a debt of gratitude to individuals who carried out a variety of clerical tasks including Rozel White and Susan Pope, Illinois State University; Beverly Luft, Charleston, Illinois; and Christine Huntziner, Iowa City Community School District.

To all others who contributed to the development of this book, the authors are grateful.

Ralph D. Wray, Bloomington, Indiana

Roger L. Luft, Charleston, Illinois

Patrick J. Highland, Iowa City, Iowa

Contents

Unit 1

An Introduction to Human Relations

Chapter 1 • Orientation to Human Relations   2

Interpersonal Relations   2
Human Relations in the Work Environment   3
Human Relations Movements   4
Human Relations as a Field of Study   17
Understanding Human Behavior   18
Practicing Good Human Relations   24
Classic Advice   27

Chapter 2 • Human Relations in Organizations   32

Organizations Defined   32
The Concept of Line and Staff   33
Basic Organizational Concepts   35
Tall and Flat Organizational Structures   38
Centralized and Decentralized Organizations   40
Organizational Environments   42
Bureaucratic Organizations   47
Organizational Effectiveness   50
Organizational Cliques   57
Organizational Development   58

Chapter 3 • Human Relations in Work Groups   63

Joining a Work Group   64
Social versus Formal Work Groups   71
Size and Composition of Groups   74
Work Group Conformity   79
Directed versus Self-directed Work Groups   80
Building the Work Group   84
Work Group Participation   92

Chapter 4 • Human Relations and External Groups   96

External Groups   96
The Community   97
Building Goodwill   105
The Human Factor   105

Avoiding Self-sabotaging Behavior   128
Ethics in Business   129

Applications & Cases   133

Unit 2

The Essentials of Human Relations

Chapter 5 • Interpersonal Communication   144
A Communication Problem   144
A Communication Model   146
Modes of Communication   148
Communication Challenges   164

Chapter 6 • Organizational Communication   168
Organizational Structure   168
Formal Communication   171
Written Communication   175
Informal Communication   181
Electronic Communication   182
Organizational Groups and Communications   186

Chapter 7 • Human Needs and Motivation   192
Individual Differences   192
A Look at "Self"   193
Motivation   195
Maslow's Hierarchy of Needs   196
Herzberg's Motivation-Hygiene Theory   202
Achievement Motivation Theory   204
Equity Theory   210
The Expectancy-Valence Theory   210
Individual Needs and Drives   212

Chapter 8 • Job Satisfaction and Employee Morale   217
Job Satisfaction   217
Understanding Job Satisfaction   218
Determining Job Satisfaction   222
The Individual and Job Satisfaction   224
Job Satisfaction and Performance   229
Improving the Job Environment   231
Company Options to Improve Productivity   237
Pay and Job Satisfaction   243

Applications & Cases   248

Unit 3

Problems in Human Relations

Chapter 9 • Counseling, Rewarding, and Disciplining Workers   256

The Substance of Worker Attitudes   256
Attitudes That Affect Work Performance   257
The Importance of Attitudes   259
Employee Counseling and Coaching   260
Employee Discipline   264
Performance Appraisal   266
Rewarding Employee Behavior   272
Reinforcing Positive Performance   277

Chapter 10 • Coping with Employees' Personal Problems   281

Personal Problems at Work   281
Substance Abuse—Alcoholism and Drug Concerns   282
Drug Abuse   285
Health-Related Personal Problems   288
Family Problems   290
Financial Problems   293
Counseling   296
Time Away from Work   300
Employee Turnover   306

Chapter 11 • Stress in the Workplace   311

What Is Stress   312
Burnout   317
Employee Assistance Programs   320
Violence in the Workplace   325
Confidentiality and Worker Privacy   328
Conclusion   332

Chapter 12 • Managing Time   335

Time Management   335
Analyzing Your Time   335
Gaining Control of Your Time   339
Setting Priorities   346
Time Intrusions   349

Chapter 13 • A Workplace of Mutual Respect 360

Diversity 360
Employer Responsibilities 364
Discrimination 366
Harassment in the Workplace 372
The Disabled Worker and the ADA 378
Age Discrimination 383
Conclusion 385

Chapter 14 • A Rapidly Changing World of Work 388

The Speed of Change 389
Implementing Change 390
Resistance to Change 400
Teams and Change 404
Reengineering with Technology 408
Conclusion 410

Applications & Cases 413

Unit

4

Improving Practices in Human Relations

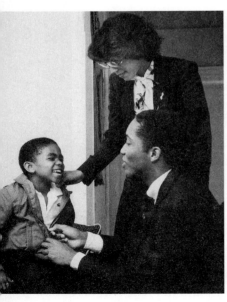

Chapter 15 • Developing a Leadership Lifestyle 422

What Is Leadership 422
Leadership Characteristics 424
Theories of Leadership 426
Leadership and Quality Management 437
Multicultural Leadership 441

Chapter 16 • Understanding Power and Politics 446

Organizational Power 447
Strategies for Acquiring Power 450
The Trend Toward Empowerment 455
Exceptions to an Empowered Workforce 465
Perceptions and Impressions of Power 465

Chapter 17 • Applying Personal Values, Business Ethics, and Social Responsibility 471

Understanding Attitudes and Personal Values 471
Development of Personal Values 473
Relationship of Attitudes, Beliefs, and Values 477
Modification of Values 479

Organizational Values 482
Shared Values in Organizations 483
Conflicting Values in Organizations 484
Business Ethics Defined 487
Ethical Dilemmas 488
Codes of Ethics 491
Whistle Blowers 494
Organizations and Social Responsibilities 495
Other Social Responsibilities 497

**Chapter 18 • Professionalism—The Key to Human
                    Relations**   **501**
Professionalism Defined 501
The Marks of a Professional 505
Equation for Professional Behavior 522
The Professional at Work 522

Applications & Cases   **526**

Glossary   **536**
Index   **545**

Unit 1

An Introduction to Human Relations

Chapter 1
Orientation to Human Relations

Chapter 2
Human Relations in Organizations

Chapter 3
Human Relations in Work Groups

Chapter 4
Human Relations and External Groups

Applications & Cases

Learning Objectives

Upon completing this chapter, you should be able to:

- Provide contemporary definitions for the terms *human relations* and *interpersonal relations.*

- Trace the human relations movement from the early 19th century to the present.

- Identify Maslow's hierarchy of needs.

- Distinguish among the concepts of Theory X, Theory Y, and Theory Z.

- Describe the concept of management by objectives.

- Explain the concepts of job rotation, job enlargement, job enrichment, and job sharing.

Orientation to Human Relations

Aaron was uncomfortable in the situation in which he found himself. The 20-year-old college junior believed he was being treated unfairly by his business communications instructor. He sat in the department head's office peering across the cluttered desk at the chairperson and nervously sought words to explain convincingly how the instructor had rudely embarrassed him on several occasions in front of his classmates. Aaron complained that the instructor returned graded writing assignments about five minutes before the end of the period and then hurriedly collected them before the students had an opportunity to review their mistakes. Also, the instructor had refused to approve any marketing-related problem statements for a major research project. As a marketing major, Aaron was critical of this practice. Finally, the student pointed out that he was an A or B student; yet, for business communications, he anticipated receiving a D. "I have gone to the instructor's office for help, but to no avail," stated the student. "I feel mistreated and cheated; I really haven't learned much in this class."

*I*nterpersonal Relations

As an aspiring young professional, Aaron was groping for answers to some difficult questions. Why do difficult people behave as they do? Are there effective ways to communicate with difficult people? As Aaron launches his career, he will cope with several specific types of difficult people, including yes-people, no-people, know-it-alls, chronic complainers, passives, maybe-people, think-they-know-it-alls, and nothing-people. Aaron is also likely to encounter gossips, saboteurs, liars, and cynics. Some of his coworkers may be complainers, slobs, grumps, bullies, and deadweights. He is likely to encounter different types of leadership styles—authoritarian, democratic, laissez-faire, and combination. In a general sense, the interactions which occur among and between people, whether harmonious or conflicting, may be referred to as **interpersonal relations**. Interpersonal relations occur in social settings and as people conduct personal business activities. Human relations is primarily concerned with the way two or more people behave toward each other within organizations where they work.

Human Relations in the Work Environment

Owners and managers of both profit and nonprofit organizations define **human relations** as fitting people into work situations in such a manner as to motivate them to work together harmoniously and to achieve high levels of productivity, while experiencing economic, psychological, and social satisfaction. It should be noted that such concerns are relatively recent occurrences. Until the 1930s, **arbitrary** methods, which are based upon discretion rather than reason, and **authoritarian** methods, requiring workers to submit to demands, dominated the relationships between owner-managers and workers. Prior to the industrial revolution in the late 18th century, the workplace was characterized by long hours, low pay, and unsafe conditions. In some cases, workers were paid a given amount per unit (piece rate) for all acceptable production. If their work was unacceptable, they were fired. Fortunately, as technology was introduced into the workplace many managers gradually became enlightened about the need for improved relationships with employees.

interpersonal relations-the interactions which occur among and between people

human relations-fitting people into work situations in such a manner as to motivate them to work together

arbitrary-based upon discretion rather than reason

authoritarian-requiring workers to submit to owner-manager demands

The term human relations *has received more attention in recent years as businesses strive to understand how to motivate employees, boost workplace morale, and maximize employees' productivity and creativity.*

Chapter 1·Orientation to Human Relations

By the end of the Great Depression in 1939, the significance of human relations in the organization began to be recognized. Human relations began to emerge as an area of study that was primarily concerned with finding the best way to work and deal with people in organizations. The phrase *with people in organizations* is important because it distinguishes human relations from public relations. As shown in Figure 1.1, people within an organization also deal with people outside the organization—customers or clients, vendors, financial institutions, government agencies, the general public, and other constituencies. Public relations can be vital to an organization. However, **public relations** is concerned with activities and communications intended primarily to obtain goodwill or prestige for an organization.

public relations-activities and communications intended primarily to obtain goodwill or prestige

Figure 1.1 **Relationships Inside and Outside the Organization**

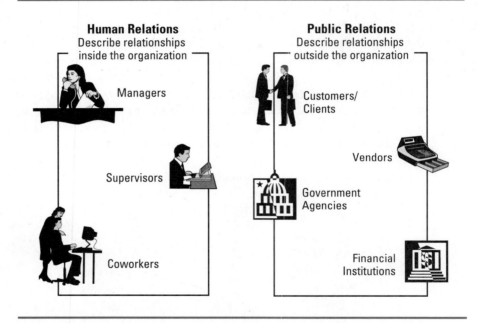

Human Relations Movements

Although some managers continue to practice authoritarian approaches in dealing with employees, most enlightened managers and supervisors reject the ideas that workers should be manipulated or used as tools without concern for their personal well-being. The recognition that a need existed for improved relationships with employees was responsible for the human relations movement that began in the 19th century and continues today.

Paternalism

The early 19th century was characterized by attempts of some factory owners to alleviate the plight of the working class. These employers believed that if they could improve the health and morals of employees, they would produce more. **Paternalism,** as practiced during this time, revealed employers in positions of authority attempting to regulate the behavior of employees much like parents attempt to regulate the behavior of their children. One example of such paternalism was the Lowell System, named for a New England textile mill owner who provided dormitories for his employees. These living arrangements provided Lowell with an opportunity to review many aspects of his workers' private lives. Church attendance, personal conduct, and training in domestic duties for young women were given careful scrutiny. Unfortunately, such practices brought about a profound difference of viewpoints between wage earners and wage payers.

Paternalism, as it evolved in the human relations movement, has been based on the view that the average worker is dull and lazy and must be prodded and disciplined and even protected against personal foolishness. Few, if any, practices in modern organizations are overtly paternalistic. Dress codes, drug abuse testing, formal and informal employee behavior, and other regulatory practices considered appropriate for the employee's position within the firm are examples of indirect paternalism practiced today.

paternalism-an attempt to regulate the behavior of employees

Figure 1.2 **The Concept of Paternalism**

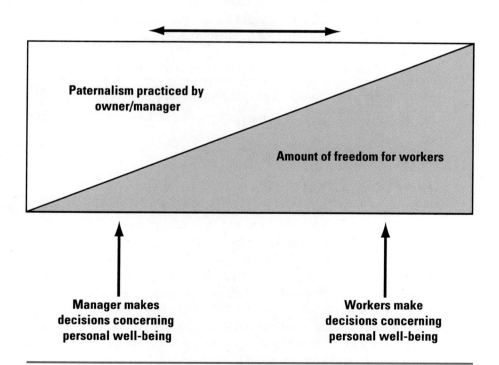

Paternalism practiced by owner/manager

Amount of freedom for workers

Manager makes decisions concerning personal well-being

Workers make decisions concerning personal well-being

Scientific Management

Frederick Taylor, Frank and Lillian Gilbreth, and Henry L. Gantt became recognized as management experts because of their efforts to improve the efficiency of individual workers during the early part of the 20th century. Their approach, which became known as **scientific management,** began with a scientific analysis of jobs during which each work task was identified and narrowed to its most elementary function. A worker was then assigned a very specialized task; the management experts believed that as a result of training and constant repetition, the workers would become highly productive. By dividing the overall work process into specialized tasks and training workers to perform the specialized tasks, increased productivity was envisioned. The final step was to establish workers' performance standards and to determine incentive wages which could be used to encourage individual workers to meet or exceed the standards.

The result of scientific management, as viewed by many workers, was the creation of boring, repetitive tasks which provided little challenge for an ambitious individual eager to advance in an occupational field. Henry Ford, however, liked the approach and was able to replace the hand-crafted method of producing automobiles with mass production. To attract workers to his fast-moving assembly lines, Ford not only trained the workers but he paid them five dollars a day, more than double the prevailing rates of pay in similar industries, disturbing other American industrialists. Today, most human resources experts recognize that inadequate wages create human relations problems which are manifested in excessive employee turnover, poor morale, and inefficient production. As shown in Table 1.1, a satisfactory compensation scheme should attract well-qualified workers, keep them satisfied in their jobs, and inspire them to produce.

Table 1.1 **Elements of a Satisfactory Compensation Plan**

- ► Attracts well-qualified employees
- ► Keeps employees satisfied in jobs
- ► Motivates employees to produce

Labor Unions

While scientific management concepts and the industrial revolution brought the advantages of specialization and increased output, workers often were unhappy with their lives. At the end of the 19th century, the workweek typically was 60 hours, and in some industries it was 72 or even 84 hours—seven 12-hour days a week. Safety standards were nonexistent and working conditions were often bad. Young boys and girls joined the workforce to earn a few pennies that were needed to help their families. When recessions or depressions came, the workers were unemployed. Unemployment insurance did not exist. Poorhouses operated by municipalities were often havens for unemployed workers.

During the industrial revolution in the late 19th century, safety standards were nonexistent and working conditions were often bad. Young boys and girls joined the workforce to earn a few pennies to help their families.

Workers gradually learned that by forming **labor unions,** that is, banding together and bargaining as a unified group, they could win better wages, shorter hours, safer working conditions, and job security. They also learned that as a group they could influence legislation, such as the passage of the Fair Labor Standards Act (1938), which established a federal minimum wage and overtime pay. Labor unions have experienced success in improving the plight of workers in blue-collar industries and trades. The history of organized labor, however, is dominated by disputes between unions and the owner-managers of business and industry. When disagreements occur, employer and employees are placed in adversarial positions.

labor unions-workers who have banded together to achieve common goals

Recognition

In the late 1920s, Elton Mayo and other researchers from Harvard University initiated what has become known as the Hawthorne Studies at the Hawthorne plant of Western Electric Company near Chicago. The purpose of the investigation was to explore the relationship between changes in physical working conditions and employee productivity. Specifically, Mayo and his colleagues were interested in the effect of different intensities of light on employee output. In one experiment, ample lighting was provided to a group of six female workers. Later, the amount of lighting was significantly reduced, and instead of productivity decreasing as expected, it actually increased.

The researchers attributed the phenomenon to what has since become known as the **Hawthorne effect,** that is, employees who participate in scientific studies may become more productive because of the attention they receive from the researchers. This discovery has become important in the human relations movement because it has been interpreted to mean that when employees feel important and recognized, they exhibit greater motivation to excel in their work activities.

Hawthorne effect-employees become more productive because of the attention received from researchers

Motivation

Gene Carlson works as a copywriter for an advertising agency. He can often be found alone in his office late at night working on copy for a client's advertising campaign. Cheryl Rawlings, a corporate attorney, takes legal documents home each evening for further study and review. Why do these people behave in this manner, when other workers call in and report a nonexistent illness or evade job tasks and the acceptance of responsibilities?

In 1943, psychologist Abraham Maslow published a theory of motivation in which he proposed that workers' behavior is determined by a wide variety of needs. According to this theory, motivation starts when an individual experiences a need which he or she desires to satisfy. The individual formulates a goal, which upon achievement will reduce or eliminate the need.

Gene Carlson wants his clients, coworkers, and supervisors to respect both the quality and quantity of his work. This need for respect leads to goal-directed behavior. He will work more hours, when necessary, to achieve higher quality or a larger volume of output. The motivation to achieve the goal will be rewarded by the respect he earns from clients, coworkers, and supervisors.

Maslow arranged his identified needs in a hierarchy and he indicated that lower level needs must be satisfied, at least in part, before an individual begins to recognize and strive to satisfy needs at higher levels. The five levels of needs set forth by Maslow, from lowest to highest levels, include:

▶ **Physiological needs** are the basic needs for food, shelter, and clothing. A hungry person is driven to obtain food before devoting attention to other needs. Minimum wage laws have forced wages upward; since many families can afford to satisfy their basic needs, higher order needs are likely to play more significant roles in workers' motivation.

▶ **Safety needs** are needs for job security, protection from physical harm, and avoidance of the unexpected. Such needs are often alleviated by seniority provisions in labor agreements, occupational health and safety legislation administered by the Occupational Safety and Health Administration (OSHA), and various forms of insurance.

▶ **Social needs** are needs for acceptance by others (belonging), and for giving and receiving love. Formal and informal work groups may help meet workers' social needs. Quality circles, which are small groups of workers in the same work area who meet periodically to find solutions to quality and related problems, have been used by Japanese, as well as United States firms, to foster a sense of belonging.

▶ **Esteem needs,** which are usually more difficult to satisfy, are needs to feel a sense of accomplishment and achievement and respect from

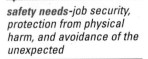

physiological needs-basic needs for food, shelter, and clothing

safety needs-job security, protection from physical harm, and avoidance of the unexpected

social needs-acceptance by others, and for giving and receiving love

esteem needs-to feel a sense of accomplishment, achievement, and respect from others

others. Just as some students are motivated to achieve superior grades, some workers' perceptions of their self-worth are derived from praise and recognition coming from managers and others in the firm.

▶ **Self-actualization needs,** which appear at the top of Maslow's hierarchy, are needs for fulfillment, for living up to one's potential, and for reaching one's fullest potentialities and capabilities. For Sam Walton, self-actualization may have meant being the most successful retailer in the United States. For Wendy Swan, it may mean being named employee of the month at Proctor Hospital.

self-actualization needs-fulfillment, living up to one's potential, and reaching one's fullest capabilities

Figure 1.3 illustrates the hierarchy of needs as conceptualized by Abraham Maslow. Social scientists, for the most part, agree that people are motivated to perform work activities to satisfy their needs. Therefore, to motivate employees, managers and supervisors should provide them with opportunities to satisfy their needs as a result of performing work activities within the organization. A group of accountants, for example, might be asked to collaborate on an auditing report and during the process satisfy the social need associated with belonging or being accepted by others.

Figure 1.3 Needs Which Are the Origin of Motivation

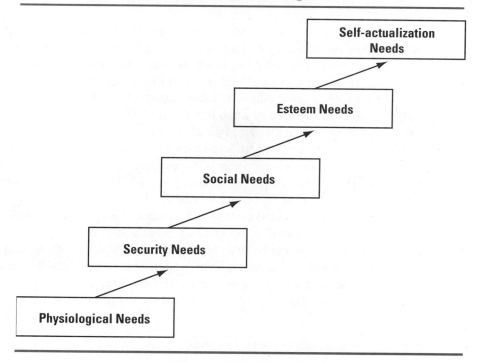

Job Satisfaction

Another psychologist, Frederick Herzberg, examined sources of worker satisfaction and dissatisfaction. Herzberg cited achievement, recognition, work itself, responsibility, advancement, and growth as **job satisfiers** and

job satisfiers-factors that motivate workers

as factors that motivate workers. A job with multiple satisfiers should motivate workers to effective performance. The absence of satisfiers, however, does not necessarily lead to dissatisfaction and poor performance. Instead, it may mean that employees are not motivated to accomplish more than they are presently achieving.

Herzberg further concluded that certain aspects of the job environment which he referred to as **job maintenance factors** are necessary to maintain the desired level of worker satisfaction. They include company policy, supervision, working conditions, interpersonal relations, salary and benefits, and security. While job maintenance factors rarely motivate workers, they may be essential.

Jackie Kenningston enjoyed her job at Seven Continents Travel Agency. She had completed her eighth year of employment at the firm when new owners took over. Soon after resigning her position, she said, "My new supervisor and I were on different planets. She and I are about as different as day and night. She is the by-the-book technocrat and if I, through no fault of my own, couldn't make 'her planes fly on time,' there was mayhem to pay. She and her ego have trouble squeezing into the same room."

As shown above, good manager-employee relationships, for example, may keep employees at a job but won't cause them to work harder. Poor manager-employee relationships, however, may cause them to quit.

While Herzberg's theories and research findings, for the most part, have been widely supported, some labor management experts disagree that salary should be classified as a job maintenance factor instead of a job satisfier. They point out that other researchers have found that employees in many occupations view monetary rewards as sources of job satisfaction.

Job maintenance factors are important considerations in many firms which experience high employee turnover. A company has high **employee turnover** when the number of employees hired to replace those who have left the organization divided by the total number of employees is high. Job satisfiers are likely to lead to high morale. Job maintenance factors, if perceived to be unacceptable by workers, may lead to high employee turnover. There are, of course, other factors which contribute to high employee turnover rates: job burnout, anger and frustration, stress, impending job transfer, lack of an expected promotion, and inadequate directions from supervisors.

Worker Attitudes

The attitudes of workers may influence the way workers interact with coworkers and with the management staff. Douglas McGregor, a student of Maslow, studied the attitudes of workers; as a result of his studies, he formulated some basic assumptions about the attitudes of workers.

Table 1.2 Job Satisfiers and Job Maintenance Factors

Job Satisfiers (Motivate Workers)	Job Maintenance Factors (Retain Workers)
► Achievement	► Company policy
► Recognition	► Supervision
► Work itself	► Working conditions
► Responsibility	► Interpersonal relationships
► Advancement	► Salary and benefits
► Growth	► Security

Theory X. One set of basic assumptions, which McGregor labeled Theory X, includes the following:

1. The average person has an inherent dislike for work and will avoid it if possible.
2. Because people don't like to work, they must be controlled, directed, or threatened with punishment to get them to put forth enough effort to achieve organizational objectives.
3. The average person prefers to be directed, avoids responsibility, is relatively unambitious, and wants security above all.

Managers who accept the above assumptions usually behave in an authoritarian manner. Chris Lane, a swing shift manager at a fast-food restaurant, exemplifies the authoritarian approach as he describes the behavior of college students who work part time at the fast-food outlet.

"These kids are lazy and intend to exert only the efforts that they absolutely must. They are often tardy and they almost always abuse breaks by reporting back late. They're really only here for the paycheck."

Theory Y. McGregor recognized that such assumptions were counter to what Maslow and others had found to be the actual attitude of most workers. Moreover, he believed that if managers viewed workers as irresponsible, lazy individuals, that would be exactly the way the workers would behave. McGregor then formulated another set of assumptions, which described workers with different attitudes, that he labeled Theory Y. The assumptions of Theory Y include:

1. People do not inherently dislike work. In fact, work is as natural as play or rest.

2. Given some freedom, the average individual will work on his own toward the organization's objectives without controls or threats from bosses.

3. How deeply individuals are committed to the organization's objectives depends on "the rewards associated with their achievement." The primary and most important rewards are those that satisfy the worker's ego and provide self-actualization.

4. The average worker learns, under proper conditions, not only to accept but to seek responsibility.

5. Many individuals are capable of a high degree of inventiveness and creativity.

6. Nevertheless, under modern work conditions, the intellectual potential of the average human being is only partly utilized.

Assumptions linked to Theory Y suggest that people will work to achieve objectives without threats from supervisors.

Managers who accept the Theory Y assumptions see workers as desiring challenge and willing to work on their own. These managers are more inclined to create a work environment within which workers can assume responsibility, exhibit creativity, and assume self-direction while performing work activities. When Kelly Nussbaum, owner of Nussbaum Main Street Florist, talked about a new employee, it was obvious that she adhered to the assumptions associated with Theory Y.

I never have to worry about Susan. If she isn't busy with customers, she's using her talents creating fresh floral arrangements, balloon bouquets, or silk flower arrangements. She doesn't have to be told to check the adequacy of our inventory—ribbons, baskets, styrofoam retainers, cards, etc. She's a real asset to this firm.

Theory Z. William Ouchi, a west-coast management scholar, advocates a leadership style labeled Theory Z. This approach combines United States and Japanese business practices into an organizational framework which emphasizes

▶ moderate specialization

▶ individual responsibility

▶ group decision-making

▶ relatively informal control

▶ long-term employment

▶ slow promotions

▶ concern for workers.

When Theory Z is adopted, new employees are given information about all aspects of the business, such as production, marketing, pricing, and competitors. Short-term and long-term organizational goals are revealed so that workers can see where the firm is headed. Employees are encouraged to react openly to production goals and techniques that directly or indirectly affect their jobs. Workers are encouraged to seek creative solutions on their own when problems arise. Managers are encouraged to listen to workers, and decisions seem less like an order and more like group consensus. Firms adopting Theory Z retain management staffs; however, workers participate in decisions and solve problems that had been left to managers in the past. While managers continue to supervise and evaluate workers, less manager/worker friction is likely to exist.

Workers' relationships with coworkers are also influenced by Theory X, Y, and Z leadership styles. Such relationships are examined in Chapter 7.

Morale

Owners and managers of contemporary business organizations have introduced a number of innovations to improve worker morale. **Morale** is usually viewed as the mental attitude of employees toward their employers and/or their jobs. Poor morale is often the cause of high absenteeism and employee turnover. Conversely, good morale is associated with high productivity and employee loyalty.

Management by Objectives. Among the innovations is **management by objectives** (MBO), a process in which a manager and a worker confer together in determining the goals which the worker will achieve.

▼
morale-the mental attitude of employees toward their employers and jobs

▼
management by objectives-process in which a manager and worker confer to establish the worker's goals

The MBO approach may improve workers' morale by permitting them to participate in setting their own goals, letting them know how they will be evaluated, and basing their performance evaluations upon their progress toward achieving agreed upon goals. The process usually involves the following steps:

1. Each worker discusses his or her job description with the supervisor or manager.

2. Together, they establish short-term performance goals.

3. Regular conferences are scheduled during which the worker and the manager or supervisor discuss the progress made toward the achievement of the goals.

4. At the end of the agreed upon time period, the worker and the manager or supervisor jointly evaluate the worker's efforts.

While the MBO approach is advocated by many management experts including Peter Drucker, a respected writer and consultant, it is not an answer to all problems of morale. Some workers are not goal-oriented, and because the MBO approach stresses achievement, workers who do not have morale problems and are content simply to do their jobs may feel distressed or pressured. Used judiciously with consideration for the employees' capabilities and needs, the MBO approach can improve workers' morale and output.

Job Rotation. Some executives have looked at job design as a set of strategies for keeping employee morale at high levels. One such strategy is **job rotation;** it allows employees to move from one job to another, relieving the boredom of performing dull, repetitive work tasks. An employee spends a specified time at a particular job and then moves to a different job. Eventually, the worker returns to the initial job and starts the cycle again. Executives in firms such as Ford Motor Company and Bethlehem Steel experimented with job rotation because they believed workers would encounter greater challenges.

job rotation-allows employees to move from one job to another

Job Enlargement. A strategy closely related to job rotation is **job enlargement;** it involves adding tasks to a job instead of treating each task as a separate job. General Mills, IBM, and Maytag employees have found that their jobs are more satisfying as the number of tasks performed by each worker increases.

job enlargement-involves adding tasks to a job

Kathy McKinny is a cashier at a local family restaurant. Paul Ryder works as a host in the same establishment. Both made angry comments after the manager told them that their job descriptions were being changed. They were directed to alternate between seating patrons and performing cashier duties. In addition, their new assignment—answering the telephone—was a joint responsibility. After one month, both Kathy and Paul expressed greater satisfaction with their jobs. "It's fun to greet customers when they enter the restaurant, chat with them informally, and handle reservations, rather than always asking them if everything was all right and taking their money," said Kathy.

Job Enrichment. **Job enrichment,** a strategy which gives workers more tasks within the job and more control and authority over the job, may also lead to improved morale. This strategy was successfully implemented at AT&T. Installers of telephone switching systems participated with managers in defining the nature of the job. They also helped decide what is acceptable or unacceptable performance.

job enrichment-adds tasks to a job and gives workers more control and authority

Job Sharing. **Job sharing** occurs when two people assume one job. One person, for example, may work from 8:00 A.M. until 12:30 P.M. and the second person may report at 12:30 P.M. and work to 5:00 P.M. Job sharing gives both employees an opportunity to work as well as providing time for other obligations, such as parenting or caring for an elderly parent. Many employees appreciate job sharing, and the employer benefits by gaining the skills of two people for one job.

job sharing-occurs when two people assume one job

Quality Circles. **Quality circles,** voluntary groups of seven to ten people from the same work area who meet on a regular basis to define, analyze, and solve quality and related problems in their work area, is a Japanese concept which has been borrowed by a growing number of

quality circles-small groups of workers in the same work area who meet to find solutions to quality and related problems

Quality circles not only address problems related to quality, but they are also useful in eliciting solutions to operational problems.

United States firms and government units. Based upon the philosophy that a firm's workforce is perhaps the group most qualified to identify and solve work-related problems, workers may experience higher levels of morale simply because they are viewed as being capable of addressing issues and providing input to managers. Human relations become important in quality circles as members of the groups interact with each other. Quality circles meet regularly, typically once a week, and either a supervisor or worker serves as team leader to facilitate discussions and inform managers of the group's progress.

Total Quality Commitment. Relationships in the workplace have also been shaped by the quest for quality. W. Edwards Deming, an American statistician, stressed that the commitment to quality must be a companywide philosophy and a continuing process. His lectures were largely ignored by American business leaders during the competition-free, post-World War II years but were listened to by Japanese business leaders. As a result, Japanese products gained a reputation for outstanding quality and made inroads into American and world markets. During the 1980s, many United States firms, eager to restore their long-held images as producers of high-quality products, embraced Deming's principles. Managers were trained to be flexible advisors and coaches. Employees were treated as partners in the drive to produce on-time, error-free products. Japan's most coveted industrial award, the Deming Prize—given to the company which achieves the most significant gains in quality—has now an American version, The Malcolm Baldrige National Quality Award, named after the late secretary of the U.S. Department of Commerce.

Collaboration. One of today's buzzwords that describes joint endeavors by two or more workers is **collaboration.** Group efforts permeate almost all functional and support areas of today's business and organizational environments. The human relations dimension becomes an important concern as people work together in all types of settings—the surgical team performing open-heart surgery; police partners pursuing an armed robber; the Channel Three news team planning the ten o'clock evening news program; or a copywriter, illustrator, and layout specialist working together to create a new advertisement for Royal Copenhagen, a spray cologne for men.

collaboration-joint endeavors by two or more workers

Quality of Work Life. Many of the contemporary strategies which have been adopted and implemented to keep employee morale high have also contributed to the quality of work life (QWL). **Quality of work life** programs encompass approaches used in making jobs more pleasant for workers. Such programs are based upon the recognition that employees are unique individuals capable of providing valuable input related to all phases of their jobs and workplaces. Appropriate communication channels are essential in every organization if such inputs are to be transmitted from worker to worker and from worker to supervisor or manager.

quality of work life-factors that make jobs more pleasant for workers

Human Relations as a Field of Study

Human relations is an interdisciplinary field because the study of human behavior in organizational settings draws upon the fields of communications, management sciences, psychology, and sociology, shown in Figure 1.4. It is an important field of study because all workers—top managers, middle managers and supervisors, and rank and file or operative employees—engage in human relations activities. As illustrated in Figure 1.5, operative employees are required to refine their technical skills; that is, their knowledge of and ability to perform specialized work activities, such as operating a milling machine or a word processor. Top managers—owners and executives—are expected to refine their conceptual skills, that is, their ability to diagnose problems and develop creative solutions. Middle managers and supervisors should possess both technical and conceptual skills, although to lesser degrees of proficiency than top managers. At all three levels human relations skills are essential.

Figure 1.4 **The Interdisciplinary Field of Human Relations**

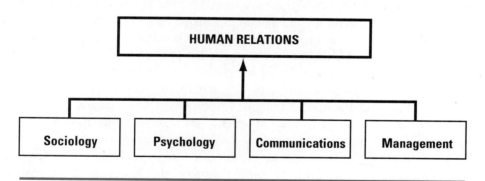

Figure 1.5 **Skills Required in the Workplace**

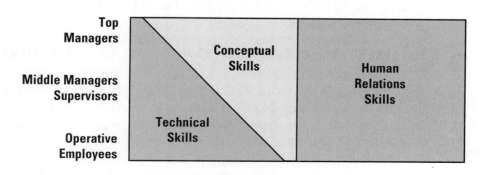

Understanding Human Behavior

The human relations movement demonstrates to an extent how managers and supervisors have tried to shape human relations into a modern tool of management. This is a difficult task because each individual is a unique person whose reactions may be influenced by mental, physical, and/or social dimensions. Consider, for example, the following scenario:

Lois Nevers, owner of a large retail/wholesale carpet outlet, had just received an order for carpet to be installed in a new home. Wanting repeat orders, Lois turned to Ty Lawson, a young installation crew supervisor—well-liked by all members of his work group, who seemed to take pride in the quality work performed by his crew. "Ty, I'm assigning this work to you and your crew. Take special care to turn out a good job on this one, will you?" In an instant, Ty replied, "Why me? Try giving it to one of the other crew leaders for a change." Lois was somewhat surprised by her young subordinate's reaction since it seemed so out of character.

Why did Ty's reaction vary so much from his normal one? Was Ty's reaction triggered by the mental dimension of human behavior? Perhaps he perceived that his crew was being assigned a disproportionate share of difficult work. Another plausible reason for Ty's response might be traced to the physical dimension of human behavior. The assignment may have occurred at the end of a perplexing day during which Ty faced a number of tough, challenging problems. Not only was Ty extremely fatigued, but he also had a cold and felt miserable. Yet another explanation for Ty's response may have been related to the social dimension of human behavior. Perhaps Ty believed that as a result of the request, "Take special care to turn out a good job on this one," the owner was being critical of past work performances.

This incident illustrates the complexity of human behavior. Interactions between individuals are complicated because each individual reacts to stimuli according to unique perceptions related to mental, physical, and social dimensions of behavior.

Mental Dimensions of Behavior

Mental perceptions, for example, are influenced by everything that has passed through an individual's mind. Specifically, that includes all of an individual's experiences, knowledge, biases, emotions, values, and attitudes. Obviously, no two people have identical perceptions because no two people have precisely the same experiences, knowledge, biases, and such.

Mental perceptions may sometimes lead to conflict. Each individual, for example, has formed mental perceptions relating to a number of contro-

Unit 1 · An Introduction to Human Relations

versial issues—abortion, euthanasia, capital punishment, DNA research, and the ethics of transplant surgery among others. When proponents and opponents clash in voicing mental perceptions of controversial issues, conflict occurs. If the issue is one pertinent to the workplace, such as affirmative action, discarding toxic wastes, or abusing a site license for a computer program, different perceptions or values have the potential to lead to human relations problems.

ethnocentrism-a belief that one's own group is superior

Customs and Traditions: Watching for the Global Difference

Mismatches and Embarrassing Moments

When super-neatnik Felix and slovenly, careless Oscar were house-mates in the television comedy "The Odd Couple," their mismatch provoked laughter. In real life, however, such mismatches are not so funny. Everyone, whether sloppy or neat, has felt the frustration of dealing with a person who is "the other way."

While people residing in different countries may, likewise, be mis-matches, no country can isolate itself from the rest of the world. The future prosperity and growth of any country is directly tied to the future prosperity and growth of the rest of the world. About 20 per-cent of the total capital invested in United States manufacturing is in facilities outside the United States. Furthermore, major commercial banks and brokerage houses (firms that sell stocks and bonds) do a similar proportion of their total business through foreign exchanges. Caterpillar, based in Peoria, Illinois, sells over half of its tractors and other heavy equipment to overseas buyers. Boeing, an airplane manu-facturer, gets 58 percent of its business from other countries. Many of the products people in the United States enjoy come from overseas—TV sets, CD players, camcorders, computers, and so forth.

As American workers and workers in other countries interact, they may resemble "The Odd Couple." Different countries have very differ-ent ways of conducting business and, for the most part, such differ-ences can be traced to the diverse cultures of people residing in differ-ent countries. A few years ago, a book titled *The Ugly American* con-demned Americans for their attitudes of "Let 'em do it our way or not at all." **Ethnocentrism,** a belief that one's own group is superior, hin-ders communication, understanding, and goodwill between individu-als engaged in international business.

Embarrassing moments caused by cultural differences can be han-dled without losing face if individuals are aware of those differences. Kenneth Malito was a private real estate investor with many Japanese clients. On a trip to Japan, one of his clients gave a lavish banquet in his honor. Malito reciprocated by throwing a bigger and more expen-sive party for his client. When his phone calls were not being

CONTINUED

returned, Malito discovered that he had offended his customer by out-doing him. Only after several months of casual visits to his client's office to display his friendliness and courtesy did Malito regain the customer's trust. The Japanese call this "selling face," and it can also be used as a way of reminding a Japanese businessperson about a pending deal without appearing to be too brash or bold.

Sources: From HOW TO WORK FOR A JAPANESE BOSS by Jina Bacarr. Copyright © 1993 by Jina Bacarr. Published by arrangement with Carol Publishing Group.

Reprinted from THE OFFICE PROFESSIONAL with permisssion of Professional Training Associates, Inc., 210 Commerce Blvd., Round Rock, TX 78664, 800-424-2112.

Nickels, McHugh, and McHugh, UNDERSTANDING BUSINESS, Richard D, Irwin, Inc., © 1993, pp. 36–37. Reprinted with permission.

Ellen Carothers is responsible for managing the computer laboratories at a community college in the southwestern region of the country. As the number of machines loaded with a database program reached the maximum number allocated under the site-licensing agreement, Ellen approached the dean of her division and requested permission to renegotiate the contract. The dean told Ellen to continue to load machines with the program even though such practice represented a violation of the contract. Ellen turned in her resignation.

ethics-moral rules or values governing the conduct of a person or group

It should be obvious that the above scenario is of an ethical nature. **Ethics** refers to moral rules or values governing the conduct of a person or group. Perhaps more than anything else, an individual's adherence to values or principles related to what is morally right determines the respect that others hold for that individual. Lack of respect for an individual is likely to lead to poor human relations. Ethical dimensions to human relations are so important they will be presented throughout this text.

Social Dimensions of Behavior

personality-the totality of complex characteristics, including behavioral and emotional tendencies, personal and social traits, self-concept, and social skills

The social dimension of behavior is determined by a person's personality, attitudes, needs, and wants. An individual's **personality** is the totality of complex characteristics, including behavioral and emotional tendencies, personal and social traits, self-concept, and social skills. The objective of many personality development courses for employees and supervisors is directed toward improving a person's ability to get along with others. Some employees are perceived to have desirable personalities; others are judged to possess displeasing personalities. Certainly, a person's personality has a major impact on human relations skills.

Rob Weiss and Elaine Burbank are front desk clerks at the Riverfront Inn, a large hotel that often is booked for regional conferences and conventions. The manager, Beth Higgins, has instructed reservations employees to overbook the hotel by six percent when possible, since cancellations and no-shows often reach six percent of total reservations.

Recently, a regional conference was booked at the hotel by the Senior Corps of Retired Executives (SCORE) and the hotel was overbooked by six percent. Thirty-six people had to be referred to other area hotels by Rob and Elaine.

When Rob met an irritated customer, he responded by saying, "Don't take your frustrations out on me, I just work here. If you want to blame someone, go talk to Miss Higgins. She is the one who instigated the stupid policy of overbooking the hotel."

When Elaine was confronted by an incensed customer, she said, "I don't blame you for being disappointed, and I am sorry that we are slightly overbooked. We have made reservations for you in a very nice nearby hotel, and the hotel's free shuttle service will be available to take you to locations within the metropolitan area. We value your patronage and we

Ethical Dimensions to Human Relations

Which Comes First, Moral Citizens or Moral Institutions?

Christina Hoff Sommers, a professor of philosophy at Clark University in Worchester, Massachusetts, is critical of the way ethics is being taught in American colleges. She believes there is an overemphasis on social policy questions, with little or no attention being paid to topics related to private morality, such as hypocrisy, self-deception, and cruelty.

One of Sommers's colleagues had a different opinion. This colleague felt it best to focus on the larger issues of social injustice, oppression of minority groups, corruption in big business, multinational corporations and their transgressions in the Third World without addressing issues of personal morality. The colleague said, "You are not going to have moral people until you have moral institutions. You will not have moral citizens until you have a moral government."

At the end of the semester, the colleague entered Professor Sommers's office carrying a stack of exams and looking very upset. It turned out that more than half the students in her ethics class had copied long passages from the secondary literature.

Educators disagree on the issue of teaching morals, but the fact remains that there have been major cheating scandals at many of our best universities. A recent survey reported in the *Boston Globe* claims that 75 percent of all high school students admit to cheating; for col-

CONTINUED

lege students the figure is 50 percent. A *U.S. News and World Report* survey asked college-aged students if they would steal from an employer; 34 percent said they would.

Because of these statistics and others, an increasing number of educators uphold Professor Sommers's position and believe teachers should insist on basic decency, honesty, and fairness in the classroom as in the workplace. When employees cheat and steal, they jeopardize the trust that customers and clients have in the business as well as the trust that employers and employees need to have in each other.

Reprinted from Christina Hoff Sommers, "Teaching the Virtues," Chicago Tribune Magazine, September 12, 1993.

will make every effort to ensure that the alternative lodging arrangements are satisfactory. In addition, I would like to give you complimentary guest tickets for you and your guest for dinner in our dining room."

One of Miss Higgins's responsibilities as manager of the Riverfront Inn is to evaluate the performance of employees for the purposes of (1) giving them reasonable objectives and adequate feedback concerning performance; (2) improving performance by identifying areas of needed training which will help employees modify behavior in a positive manner; and (3) gathering data from which to make decisions about future job assignments, promotions, demotions, wage and salary increases, and dismissal of incompetent employees. Personality, as revealed by Rob and Elaine, may be an important factor in evaluating human relations skills.

A Human Relations Code of Words

The six most important words . . . *"I admit I made a mistake."*

The five most important words . . . *"You did a good job."*

The four most important words . . . *"What is your opinion?"*

The three most important words . . . *"If you please..."*

The two most important words . . . *"Thank you."*

The one most important word . . . *"We"*

The least important word . . . *"I"*

Author unknown

Introverts are best suited to occupations which call for work of an individualized nature. They usually are more productive and more comfortable when working alone. Extroverts do well working in jobs involving interaction with people, since they gain gratification from sharing thoughts and ideas.

Elaine and Rob reveal very different attitudes through their personalities. An **attitude** is a mental position one possesses with regard to a fact, issue, or belief. Elaine believes that it is her responsibility to provide the customer with the best service possible, even if the hotel is overbooked. Rob believes that the customer's frustrations are not his responsibility. Attitudes which often present problems in the workplace concern controversial issues and biased and prejudiced viewpoints. Generally, employees who possess positive attitudes and who are open minded about controversial issues are judged to have more desirable personalities than those with negative attitudes who hold biased and prejudiced viewpoints.

The social dimension of behavior is also revealed through one's state of introversion or extroversion. An **introvert** is an individual who is more comfortable with his or her own thoughts and feelings and prefers not to interact with others. Other individuals tend to be **extroverts,** that is, they enjoy interacting with others and they gain gratification from sharing thoughts and ideas with others. An extrovert may be more effective when working with colleagues than an introvert. An extrovert, in most cases, is better able to work harmoniously with others to achieve high levels of productivity. An introvert, on the other hand, may achieve high levels of productivity when performing tasks of an individualized nature.

▼
attitude-a mental position one possesses with regard to a fact, issue, or belief

▼
introvert-an individual who is more comfortable with his or her own thoughts and feelings

▼
extrovert-an individual who enjoys sharing thoughts and ideas with others

Physical Dimensions of Behavior

The physical dimension of behavior is composed of many complex components including alertness, fatigue, stress, basic needs (physiological and security), and state of health. When an individual has been deprived of sleep or is feeling ill, that individual may react differently during interactions with supervisors or other employees than if he or she were fresh and alert. Hunger, poor health, and stress may also influence behavior adversely.

Figure 1.6 **The Complex Dimensions of Human Behavior Interact to Influence Behavior**

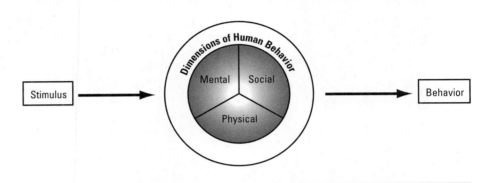

As illustrated in Figure 1.6, the dimensions of human behavior are complex. An understanding of human behavior must include the results of research studies conducted in several social and physical sciences if it is to be coherent. Students of human relations should be aware that much remains to be discovered about human behavior and why people react as they do.

Practicing Good Human Relations

A review of the complexities of human behavior may lead to the question: How can I deal effectively with individuals who exhibit diverse behavior? While there is no simple answer, the development of human relations skills will certainly be helpful. Each chapter of this book addresses topics that can help develop desired human relations skills. It is essential that a person who practices good human relations be able to

▶ empathize with others,

▶ communicate effectively with others,

▶ motivate himself or herself and others,

▶ exercise responsibility in a satisfactory manner,

▶ cope successfully with workplace problems,

▶ exhibit ethical and professional behavior.

Empathy

Empathy is the ability to put oneself in someone else's place and to understand that person's point of view.

As Scott Maltz slowly turned the screwdriver to tighten the clip holding the polished mirror over the bathroom vanity, he heard a crack and the tinkle of broken glass falling onto the marble vanity top. His supervisor was furious. "Maltz," he shouted, "do you know how much that mirror cost?" Scott felt sick. He had only recently been hired as the newest member of the construction crew and his desire to succeed was evident. Later Max Dowling, the senior member of the construction crew and an outstanding crafts technician, tried to reassure Scott. "Accidents happen in this line of work, young man. Don't let it get you down. I've had the same thing happen to me." Suddenly, Scott felt much better. While he had previously respected Max Dowling for his ability to produce quality work, he now considered him to be a friend.

An important human relations practice is the ability to put oneself in someone else's shoes, as Max does in the scenario above, and to understand the person's problems and feelings. It is also important to understand that not everyone has this ability, including some supervisors.

Communication

Perhaps the single most important aspect of designing any work environment is the plan that links all workers and supervisors with channels of communication. Good communication may be cited as the most important aspect of sound human relations. Despite the recognition of the importance of communication, it presents one of the most difficult and perplexing problems faced in modern organizations.

Even in small organizations, where only a few people are involved, sound communication is difficult to establish. When an organization expands in numbers, as well as diversity among its members, the establishment of communication channels which facilitate the transfer of information and understanding becomes even more difficult. This is true regardless of the direction that messages are sent—upward or downward in the organization or horizontally among workers or supervisors.

The communication process will be examined in greater detail in Chapter 5. At this point, however, the following suggestions are offered regarding communications.

1. Make sure messages are accurate. Incorrect information can undermine the confidence the receiver of the message has in the sender of the message. Errors in facts or figures may also lead to other inaccuracies and create conflicts.

2. Analyze the characteristics of the receivers. Choose words that the receiver is likely to understand.

3. Avoid the use of "gobbledygook." Often simple messages are distorted because the sender is trying to impress someone with his or her vocabulary. Choose words with precise meanings which the receiver of the message will understand.

4. Make communications timely. Communicate with other employees or supervisors when the topic is important to them. It makes little sense, for example, to inform a coworker that a particular vendor is offering a lower price for supplies after the purchase has been made.

Motivation

When people are joined together in some type of organization to perform work activities, they relate to each other in specific ways because they are driven by motivating forces. Sometimes people are able to recognize the source of motivation for themselves or others. Perhaps praise, recognition, or approval is the motive. In other cases, unconscious motivators are said to exist, and such motives may not be easily identified or labeled. Never-the-less, motives are the fuel for action and as such are the reasons for behavior. They stimulate, sustain, and determine the general direction of behavior. When one knows the motives of a worker, it is easier to understand the resulting behavior. Likewise, an understanding of what motivates workers can be a useful tool for supervisors and managers.

Responsibility

All workers, whether employed in operative or supervisory capacities, must accept responsibility for their own behaviors. Such behaviors may include diverse personal problems, such as absenteeism, alcohol or drug abuse, discriminatory actions, sexual harassment, stress, job burnout, and racial and intercultural conflicts. Responsibility, in such situations, is the obligation of an employee to be accountable to an employer.

In situations involving work activities, responsibility becomes an obligation after an employee has been delegated the authority to take action. If Todd Carvell, manager at 20-20 Window Cleaning Service, tells Patrick Alexander to take a crew of three workers to a corporate building and clean the atrium windows, he is delegating authority. If Patrick accepts the authority, he must assume responsibility for the job. In such a situation, Patrick would also be accepting responsibility for the human relations function, that is, communicating with and motivating the workers to harmoniously complete the work.

Workplace Problems

Today's workplace is characterized by the prevalence of complex problems. Unfortunately, personal problems encountered by many individuals accompany them to their jobs. Worker fatigue, monotony, or boredom may be reflected in labor turnover, absenteeism, carelessness that leads to accidents, or reduced levels of productivity. Stress and tension created by job pressures or from nonworkplace pressures are the reality in most job environments. In fact, Unit 3 of this book is devoted to problems that must be dealt with if human relationships on the job are to prosper. Most employees are not trained to cope successfully with such problems. As with empathizing, communicating, motivating, and exercising responsibility, coping successfully with workplace problems is a pervasive theme that reappears throughout this book.

Ethical and Professional Behavior

Certainly no one commands more respect and admiration than the worker who adheres to ethical principles and exhibits professional behavior. Some specialists in the field of human resource development have suggested that human relations is doing to others what you would have them do to you. Others have suggested that human relations is doing to others what they would have you do to them. In either case, you or they should expect nothing less than coworkers or supervisors who behave in an ethical, professional manner.

Classic Advice

Dale Carnegie in his book written in 1936, *How to Win Friends and Influence People,* provided the following tips for his readers. The book has become a classic, and the tips are as valid today as they were 60 years ago.

1. Develop an interest in other people. Do things for others—things that require time, energy, unselfishness, and thoughtfulness.

2. Smile. You must have a good time working with people if you expect them to have a good time working with you. If you don't feel like smiling, force yourself to smile. Act as if you were already happy, and that will tend to make you happy.

3. Say a name. When you are introduced to someone, remember that person's name and call it easily; by doing so you pay the person a subtle and very effective compliment. Forget or misspell the name and you place yourself at a sharp disadvantage.

4. Listen carefully. Encourage others to talk about themselves. The people you talk to are likely to be more interested in themselves and their wants and problems than in you and your needs. To be an interesting conversationalist, act interested and be an attentive listener.

5. Talk about topics that interest the person you are addressing. Talk to people about their likes and interests and they will listen to you for hours and probably become your friends.

6. Make the other person feel important—and do it sincerely. Almost everyone you meet feels superior to you in some way. A sure way to other people's hearts is to let them realize you sincerely recognize their importance in their little world.

Key Points Summary

- Human relations may be defined as fitting people into work situations in such a manner as to motivate them to work together harmoniously and achieve high levels of productivity while experiencing economic, psychological, and social satisfaction.

- The concept of human relations is primarily concerned with the way two or more people behave toward each other within organizations where they work. The concept of public relations is concerned with activities and communications intended primarily to obtain goodwill or prestige for an organization.

- The recognition that a need existed for improved relationships with employees was responsible for the human relations movement that began in the 19th century and continues today.

- In the early 19th century, the human relations movement began and was characterized by employers' attempts to improve the health and morals of employees. This practice was labeled paternalism.

- Scientific management, introduced by Frederick Taylor, Frank and Lillian Gilbreth, and Harry Gantt, began with an analysis of jobs during which each work task was identified and narrowed to its most elementary function. A worker assigned a very specific task would as a result of training and constant repetition become highly productive.

- Workers, banding together and bargaining as a unified labor union, were able to win better wages, shorter hours, safer working conditions, and job security, as well as the elimination of oppressive child labor practices.

- The Hawthorne Studies, conducted by researchers from Harvard University in the 1920s, demonstrated that workers may become more productive as the result of increased attention.

- Abraham Maslow devised a theory of motivation within which needs were arranged in a hierarchy starting with physiological needs and moving to safety needs, social needs, esteem needs, and finally to the highest level—self-actualization needs. According to the theory, lower level needs must be satisfied, at least in part, before an individual begins to recognize and strive to satisfy higher level needs.

- Certain job-related factors, such as salary, working conditions, and job security, have been called maintenance factors. They must be present in order to prevent worker dissatisfaction. They do not, however, serve as strong motivators. Job motivation factors, called job satisfiers, include achievement, recognition, work itself, responsibility, advancement, and growth.

- The traditional Theory X manager views workers as being lazy, disliking work, and requiring close and constant supervision. Theory Y assumptions are that employees want to satisfy social, esteem, and self-actualization needs through work as well as through other activities.

- A leadership style labeled Theory Z combines United States and Japanese business practices into an organizational framework which emphasizes (1) moderate specialization, (2) individual responsibility, (3) group decision-making, (4) relatively informal control, (5) long-term employment, (6) slow promotions, and (7) concern for workers.

- Management by objectives (MBO) is a process in which a manager and a worker confer to determine the goals which the worker will achieve.

- Job rotation is a strategy which permits employees to move from one job to another, relieving the boredom of performing dull, repetitive work tasks.

- Job enlargement involves adding tasks to a job instead of treating each task as a separate job.

- Job enrichment is a strategy which gives workers not only more tasks within the job but more control and authority over the job.

- Job sharing occurs when two people assume one job.

- Quality circles, made up of voluntary groups of seven to ten people from the same work area, meet on a regular basis to define, analyze, and solve quality and related problems in their work area.

- Quality of work life is a concept that gives all members of an organization some say about the design of their particular jobs and the general work environment.

- Human relations is an interdisciplinary field because the study of human behavior in occupational settings draws upon the fields of communications, management sciences, psychology, and sociology.

- Interactions between individuals are complicated because each individual reacts to stimuli according to unique perceptions related to mental, social, and physical dimensions of behavior.

- An attitude is a mental position one possesses with regard to a fact, issue, or belief.

- An introvert is an individual who is more comfortable with his or her own thoughts and feelings and one who prefers not to interact with others.

- Extroverts tend to enjoy interacting with others and gain gratification from sharing the thoughts and ideas of others.

- Empathy is the ability to put oneself in someone else's place and to understand that person's point of view.

- Communication messages and channels to relay messages effectively present one of the most difficult and perplexing problems faced in modern organizations.

- In situations involving work activities, responsibility becomes an obligation after an employee has been delegated the authority to take action.

Key Terms

arbitrary

attitude

authoritarian

collaboration

empathy

employee turnover

esteem needs

ethics

ethnocentrism

extrovert

Hawthorne effect

human relations

interpersonal relations

introvert

job enlargement

job enrichment

job maintenance factors

job rotation

job satisfiers

job sharing

labor unions

management by objectives

morale

paternalism

personality

physiological needs

public relations

quality circles

quality of work life

safety needs

scientific management

self-actualization needs

social needs

Discussion Questions

1. Based upon Maslow's hierarchy of human needs, which needs are being addressed in the following situations?

   a. Gina Koons has just been issued a permit to park in the executive parking lot at Meridian Mutual Insurance Company.

   b. Ken Love, President of Bank One, was named President of the East Chapter of the Institute of Management Accountants.

   c. The entry-level job at Baker's Square will be filled by an individual who will earn minimum wage for the first six months.

   d. Grant Lewis and other employees at Hometown Lawn Service received an invitation to the firm's annual summer picnic.

   e. Carnival Cruise Lines initiated a training program designed to reduce the number of employee accidents.

2. Identify examples of good human relations practices that you have observed within an organization with which you have been associated.

   Identify incidents you have observed within the organization which revealed a lack of sensitivity to the importance of human relations.

3. Review the assumptions associated with Theory X and Theory Y. Under which set of assumptions do you prefer to work? Is your current supervisor a Theory X or Theory Y manager? Explain by associating your supervisor's behavior to the assumptions underlying Theory X or Theory Y.

4. Explain what is meant by "human relations" in the context of the workplace.

   How does human relations differ from interpersonal relations? Public relations?

5. Some future jobs may be filled by employees working at workstations within their homes. Workers will be linked to organizations via state-of-the-art computers, telephone modems, facsimile machines, and high-density color printers by fiber-optic cables. In such employment settings, will human relation skills be needed? Explain.

6. Identify situations in which another individual empathized with you. Identify situations in which you have empathized with another person.

Chapter 2

Learning Objectives

Upon completing this chapter, you should be able to:

- Distinguish between line and staff positions.

- Recall the four basic concepts which are inherent in the unification of individuals into an organization.

- Differentiate between tall and flat organizational structures and cite the advantages and disadvantages of each.

- Explain the concepts of centralized control and decentralized control and recognize the questions to be considered when choosing a centralized or decentralized plan.

- Understand the rigid rules of bureaucracy.

- Recognize the multiple interests of external and internal stakeholders and how such interests may conflict.

- Develop planned strategies designed to improve overall organizational effectiveness.

▼

organization-two or more people whose combined abilities make the accomplishment of goals possible

Human Relations in Organizations

Becky Miller was envious, perhaps even a little jealous. Her friend and former college classmate, Tracy Millsap, had just told her that she had been promoted to manager of the word processing center at St. Francis Hospital.

Becky and Tracy became good friends three years ago when they were both top performers in a word processing class at Illinois Central College in East Peoria, Illinois. After earning their associate of applied science degrees in business information systems, Becky accepted a position in the word processing department at Gramm's corporate headquarters. Tracy found a similar position at St. Francis. Now, just a year later, Tracy was promoted to a management position. As a result, she had more authority and her paychecks were larger.

When Becky originally accepted the position at Gramm, she thought her future opportunities would be better than Tracy's. After all, Gramm was a larger organization in terms of the number of employees and locations. It was a profit organization as opposed to St. Francis. The beginning pay was better, and the people in the personnel department appeared to react favorably to Becky's ambitions.

Now, Becky wasn't so sure. Perhaps smaller organizations and nonprofit entities provided better opportunities after all. Maybe comparisons of unlike organizations should not be attempted. Regardless, Becky was now more determined than ever to advance to a higher level position.

Organizations Defined

When a youngster attempts to lift a heavy object and discovers that he or she lacks the strength and enlists the help of a friend, an organization is formed. That is, organized efforts are engaged to accomplish the task or achieve the goal. In simple terms, an **organization** is composed of two or more people whose combined abilities make the accomplishment of goals possible. As the tasks and goals become more complex, additional people with more diverse talents are needed. Organizational structure differs from one type of business corporation to another, such as IBM or a real estate agency located in Charlotte, North Carolina. It may differ between two similar types of businesses located within the same city, for example, Bank One and First of America Bank.

Organizations are created in various environments to achieve goals. Some organizations are social in nature, for example, Sigma Chi Fraternity. Others exist in religious environments, the First Presbyterian Church; recreational settings, the YMCA; benevolent endeavors, Eli Lilly Foundation; sports environments, the Chicago Bulls; and for special interest groups, the American Association of Retired Persons. Organizations may be created by profit-oriented owners, such as Holiday Inns; they may be created as nonprofit entities to serve the needs of society; or they may be governmental agencies, such as a municipal police department.

An examination of organizations is important in the study of human relations because all work groups and most work activity exist within organizations. Because organizations bring people together, the need for human relations skills is created and the necessity to resolve human relations problems becomes apparent.

The Concept of Line and Staff

Organizational theory incorporates the concept of line and staff positions. **Line positions** are involved in, or contribute directly to, the main business activity of a firm. In a bank, for example, savings counselors, tellers, and real estate loan specialists hold line positions. **Staff positions** are filled by individuals who perform specialized activities that are indirectly related to the main business activity; however, people in staff positions assist people in line positions. An attorney's advice, for example, may be required by several employees holding line positions within a bank. The placement of staff positions varies with a particular organization, but usually they can be identified on an organization chart by broken lines connecting them with the main lines of authority and responsibility. (See Figure 2.1.) The broken lines indicate that the person in the staff position does not have authority over line positions. Instead, individuals filling staff positions advise, suggest, assist, or serve the people in line positions to enable them to perform their activities more efficiently.

line positions-are filled by individuals who contribute directly to the main business activity of a firm

staff positions-are filled by individuals who perform specialized activities that are indirectly related to the main business activity

Trevor Morgan holds a staff position in an auto assembly plant. As an employee in the personnel department, Trevor interviews potential new employees, reviews their resumes, checks their references, and administers preemployment tests. Employees filling line positions are involved in the assembly of new automobiles.

Gwyn Kieser holds a staff position in 14 West Virginia school districts. Gwyn specialized in school law as she completed her studies and prepared to become an attorney. Now, she does the legal work and provides legal advice to the 14 local boards of education who employ her on retainers. Gwyn's work, while not directly related to the education of children, is nevertheless essential to the operation of schools.

Vance Bryson is an internal auditor at a brewery in Milwaukee. His staff position requires that he check the accuracy of accounting records, giving special attention to cash flow, inventories, securities, accounts payable, and other places where there is a possibility for fraud.

Figure 2.1 **A Simple Line and Staff Organization**

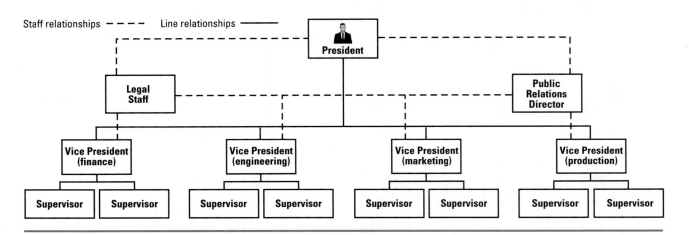

Staff relationships ─ ─ ─ ─   Line relationships ─────

President

Legal Staff

Public Relations Director

Vice President (finance)

Vice President (engineering)

Vice President (marketing)

Vice President (production)

Supervisor   Supervisor   Supervisor   Supervisor   Supervisor   Supervisor   Supervisor   Supervisor

Sometimes the staff position can be filled by a single individual, such as the position that Gwyn Kieser fills. Other times the staff functions may require several employees. Seven people, for example, hold positions in the personnel department where Trevor Morgan works.

The potential for human relations problems between staff employees and line employees is always present. Therefore, it is important to examine features that characterize line and staff relationships.

► A staff employee is primarily an extension of the line employee or employees who would carry out the specialized responsibility if time was available or if the necessary abilities were possessed. People normally assume that a staff employee is sufficiently close to line employees to reflect accurately the view of such employees. If on occasion a staff employee expresses his or her own views, which may be opposite those of the line employees, care should be taken to make the distinction clear.

Unit 1·An Introduction to Human Relations

► A staff employee must often rely on persuasion to get ideas put into effect. Because the staff employee occupies a position outside the power of command, the person must build confidence in his or her ideas and opinions to win acceptance.

► People holding staff positions must in some situations be prepared to submerge their own personalities and their own desires for recognition. The person must be an ardent teamworker, recognizing that a line manager or operating executive will get credit for ideas or work for which he or she was responsible.

When staff functions require multiple employees, a staff unit (department or division) may be created. One of the staff members may be selected as head of the unit, creating superior and subordinate relationships as well as subordinate and subordinate relationships.

Basic Organizational Concepts

Traditional organization theory suggests that four basic concepts are inherent in the unification of individuals into an organization. These basic concepts may be stated as follows:

► A common set of goals or objectives binds the members of an organization together.

► There must be a division of labor organized around functions to achieve organizational objectives.

Ethical Dimensions to Human Relations

Ethics and the Issue of Pay Equity

Ethical issues can be complex. Answers to ethical questions about flagrant violations are clear, at least we normally think they are. The transgressions of an Ivan Boesky or perhaps a Michael Milken are classified as felonies. But ethical concerns are not limited to situations in which people are involved, directly or indirectly, in illegal acts. Ethics is broadly concerned with how persons or organizations act or should act in relations with others.

A number of colleges and universities use the following phrase on their stationery and on announcements seeking faculty candidates for vacant positions: "An affirmative action/equal opportunity institution." Yet, the differential between what male faculty members are paid and what female faculty members are paid is indeed profound.

Chapter 2 · Human Relations in Organizations

Despite the Equal Pay Act of 1963, which requires equal pay for equal work, today women earn about 72 percent of what men earn. (However, the disparity varies considerably by profession.) Some authorities believe that a plausible explanation is that many women try to work as well as care for their families and, as a result, accept more flexible jobs that pay less. But others argue that the disparity can be traced to discrimination.

The question of whether it is fair to pay men more than women may on occasion be reversed. Modeling, for example, is one profession in which men get paid less than women for comparable work, where they have to accept being mere backdrops for women superstars—but it's not a bad life. At rates ranging from $1,200 to $1,500 for catalog shots to $2,000 for runway shows and $5,000 to $6,000 for top advertising campaigns, the biggest male stars can make in excess of $200,000 in a year, but the top women easily pull in more than $500,000.

Another difference is that unlike women models, men don't have to boast the perfect face. What might be a flaw in a woman is a strong point for a man. A scar on a man, if it's in the right place, adds character to a picture.

Sources: Associated Press, "Male Models Earn Half Their Female Counterparts." The Pantagraph (Bloomington, Ill.). January 23, 1994, E3.

Hall, William D. Making the Right Decision. New York: Wiley, 1993, 3.

Nickels, William, James McHugh, and Susan McHugh. Understanding Business. Homewood, Ill.: Irwin, 1987, 611–13.

▶ Division of labor requires that there be coordination of activities.

▶ To coordinate activities, a hierarchy of authority must be established within the organization.

A Common Set of Goals

Many companies have prepared organizational creeds or statements, usually intended for employees and the general public. They express the company's role in providing goods or services and its desire to earn a reasonable profit and to fulfill its obligation to employees, consumers, and the public. While such goals are laudable, perpetuation of the company is obviously a primary goal and the profit motive serves as the means of achieving the goal. Members of the organization strive to earn a profit to perpetuate the company. In some instances, certain employees may be in opposition to the goals. Perhaps they believe that the products produced are harmful or that profits are exorbitant. When such conflicts exist, human relations problems are likely to emerge.

Division of Labor

Opinions vary about how activities should be divided and assigned to workers. Most frequently, however, functions that are closely related are grouped together. This enables employees to be assigned to work in a particular functional area that is most suited to their skills, needs, and interests. A person who wants to work in production does not have to sell, and a person who wants to sell does not have to work in production. This division of labor works well until the people in different organizational units encounter a lack of agreement or communication. People in production may find their work interrupted because people in the purchasing area failed to secure adequate materials. Salespeople may object if they believe that people in the credit approval area are too conservative in extending credit. Such conflicts may lead to human relations problems and unforeseen interpersonal disagreements.

Coordination of Activities

Obviously, if members of units established as a result of a plan for the division of labor proceeded in a helter-skelter fashion with little or no regard for others, the achievement of common objectives would be jeopardized. Thus, **coordination,** or plans to control the timing and sequence of activities, becomes essential. Diamond Star Motors, the Japanese-owned assembly plant that produces the Mitsubishi Eclipse and Eagle Talon, operates on a "just-in-time" plan for inventory needs. The just-in-time concept means that materials and component parts used in the assembly of the autos arrive just in time for production. Failure by production personnel to communicate with purchasing personnel could stop production when this concept is applied. In this aspect of coordination, unit supervisors play essential roles. Accurate communications are mandatory in improving the teamwork necessary to coordinate organizational activities.

coordination-plans which are implemented to control the timing and sequence of activities

Hierarchy of Authority

The unified efforts of either a small group or large group of workers will break down if one individual disregards the activities of others. According to traditional concepts of organization, the use of authority is the best way to ensure coordination. The arrangement of organizational authority is known as the **chain of command.** It determines who reports to whom. Everyone in a workplace reports to someone, with the possible exception of the individual or individuals at the top of the organizational chart. An individual owner, **proprietor,** or individual owners, **partnership,** occupy the top spot on an organization chart and may be responsible only to themselves. In a corporation, the board of directors occupies the top spot on the organizational chart. They report to the stockholders, who are the owners.

chain of command-the arrangement of organizational authority

proprietor-an individual business owner

partnership-two or more individual business owners

The introduction of managers and supervisors with authority over other workers creates potential human relations problems. Such problems may arise as a result of disagreements, personality conflicts, different values, and various other reasons.

All he really wanted was a yes man, rationalized Wade Carlson. Wade had just quit his job at the Northwest TeleCable Company. The truth was, Wade's immediate manager, Bill Powell, resented the speed with which "youngsters with a college diploma" were moving into positions that were equal to his own. As a result, Wade met a cold reception when he was assigned as a management trainee to Bill Powell. Wade had been surprised with Mr. Powell's continued expressions of disapproval of his work. One night after a week of particularly trying relations with his new boss, Wade announced that he was leaving Northwest TeleCable.

Tall and Flat Organizational Structures

tall organizations-characterized by few people reporting to each manager

flat organizations-characterized by many people reporting to each manager

Some organizations are referred to as **tall organizations;** others are identified as **flat organizations.** In tall organizations, few people report to each manager. In flat organizations, many people report to a given supervisor or manager. Figure 2.2 illustrates a simplified view of organization within tall and flat organizations.

Figure 2.2 **A Simple Line and Staff Organization**

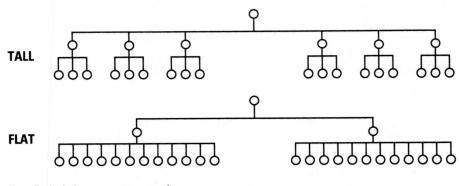

Note: Each circle represents one worker.

Tall organizations bring managers and supervisors into close contact. Flat organizations, on the other hand, reduce the interactions between managers or supervisors and workers. In flat organizations, self-directed work groups are more likely to flourish; while in tall organizations, the role of the manager or supervisor receives greater emphasis.

Research has been conducted to determine the optimum span of control. In the management sciences, the concept of **span of control** refers to the number of employees who report to a supervisor or manager. Even though organizations vary, most findings indicate that one person can effectively supervise 12 to 21 workers at the operative levels. If most workers are performing similar tasks, a manager can supervise several people. As attention is focused at higher levels within an organization, however, the span of control is reduced. The president of a company, for instance, may be able to supervise effectively only six vice presidents representing accounting, marketing, finance, production, personnel, and research. It should be obvious that flat organizations depend upon self-motivated workers who like to work independently with minimum supervision. If the workers are unable to function without close supervision, problems will quickly develop.

Tall organizations increase the problems associated with effective communications. Because messages must be relayed from one level to another—both upward and downward—the possibilities for communication breakdowns are inherent. Not only does it take longer for messages to be relayed through the various levels, but misinterpretations also are always a possibility.

To summarize, tall organizations have the advantage of fewer people reporting to each manager or supervisor. Flat organizations may have fewer communications problems since messages pass through fewer levels and distortion is not as likely to occur. Table 2.1 compares the characteristics of tall and flat organizations.

span of control-refers to the number of employees who report to a supervisor or manager

Table 2.1 A Comparison of Characteristics Between Tall and Flat Organizations

Characteristic	Tall	Flat
Span of Control	Small	Large
Supervision	Close	Reduced
Work Groups	Manager-directed	Self-directed
Communication	Less Effective	More Effective
Decision-making	Slower	Faster
Worker Motivation	Greater	Lesser

Some advocates of flat organizations believe that by eliminating several layers of management, there is a substantial cost savings. They also point out that a decision can be made more quickly since fewer people are required to review and approve the decision. On the other hand, advocates

Chapter 2 · Human Relations in Organizations

of tall organizations believe that it is difficult for managers in flat organizations to develop close relationships with their employees—there are simply too many. In addition, because the organization has fewer levels, there may be less incentive to strive for promotions. As a result, the workers' motivation levels may be less.

Centralized and Decentralized Organizations

▼

centralized control-decisions are made by relatively few high-ranking officials

▼

decentralization-occurs when decision-making is allowed to filter down to lower ranks

Some firms follow principles of **centralized control** where decisions are made by relatively few high-ranking officials. Other companies have experienced success by practicing **decentralization;** that is, decision-making is allowed to filter down into the lower ranks of the organization's hierarchy.

Centralization works well in small companies and in organizations in which operations are not very diversified. In such cases, there is usually close personal contact between upper level managers and other organizational members. In today's business environment, the use of computers and management information retrieval systems makes decision-making faster and more scientific than was ever thought possible. A centralized system, however, may foster frustration on the part of the middle managers and supervisors. They may perceive their roles as lacking authority and responsibility.

Decentralization allows decisions to be made on the spot by managers and personnel at operative levels in an organization.

Decentralization distributes authority to managers and other personnel at operative levels. In organizations with multiple geographic locations, decisions may be made on the spot, rather than waiting for a decision from headquarters.

Midwest Produce distributes fresh fruit and vegetables to supermarkets, restaurants, and specialty food stores in three midwestern states—Illinois, Indiana, and Michigan. Each day, representatives of the firm visit wholesale auctions in Chicago, Indianapolis, and Detroit. These representatives have been given authority to make buying decisions on the spot, rather than calling the company's headquarters.

In determining whether to follow a centralized or decentralized plan, the following questions should be considered.

1. Who has the information or knows the facts upon which the decision will be based? Sometimes a purchasing agent, salesperson, production worker, or operative employee has all the facts needed to make a decision. In other cases, only the chief executive officer possesses the needed information.

2. Who has the capacity to make sound decisions? Clearly, if employees at lower levels lack the ability and experience to make a wise decision on a given problem, decision-making authority should be withheld from them. On the other hand, an auto mechanic may have greater capacity to make a decision concerning an auto repair than the owner of an auto dealership.

3. Must speedy, on-the-spot decisions be made to meet local conditions? The salesperson in a department store may be required to render a quick decision to satisfy an irate customer rather than waiting for the store manager.

4. Must the decision concerning an activity be coordinated with decisions relating to other activities? Laying out a national sales promotion program, for example, requires that activities in several areas be synchronized.

5. How significant is the decision? A decision that will increase or decrease profits by only one or two dollars may be left to an operative employee. A decision that will have a major impact on the profits or losses incurred by the firm is more likely reserved for a senior executive.

6. How busy are the managers who might be assigned decision-making tasks? A manager may already have so many duties that additional assignments would result in an overload.

7. If a decision is made to decentralize, will increased morale and initiative be significantly improved?

Decentralization is compatible with the principles of human relations because it allows greater participation by members of the organization. In organizations in which decentralization is practiced, capable and motivated people who want to accept responsibility for decision-making are essential. In some organizations, employees may not wish to accept responsibility and, in fact, they may lack the necessary skills to make sound decisions.

Organizational Environments

The structure of an organization surrounds an environment characterized by formal rules, job descriptions, and communication networks in which people function during working hours. This environment may satisfy needs or block them; it can contribute to the development of good or bad attitudes. It determines, in part, how people interact, how motivated they become, and whether they are cohesive, harmonious members of the organization. Therefore, the organizational environment is highly important. In the following sections, a variety of environmental factors which may contribute to or detract from the satisfaction of human needs will be explored.

Small Units

If many workers are needed for an operation, social satisfactions will be greater when workers are assigned to small groups of perhaps three to ten. For example, a large financial institution's word processing center of perhaps 60 workers is too large to function as a social group. The workers would form small informal friendship groups, but their socializing would probably occur apart from their work. If the workers were organized into small units, the workers, to some extent, could satisfy social needs while engaged in assigned work. Then, too, a sense of belonging would probably be fostered in the smaller group. If group output were measured, it might be found that the workers possessed a greater sense of achievement.

Jeffrey Tompkins processes health care claims at Medicare, an agency of the Health Care Financing Administration (HCFA). "There are so many claims and so many processors that no one identifies with the work performed," Jeffrey told his supervisor. "If mistakes are made, the attitude seems to be, 'What do you care? You don't pay anyhow.' But we all pay for such errors." Jeffrey's supervisor agreed to pilot a revamped organizational structure which would assign specific claims to small units of processors. A record of the number of mistakes for each unit would be established with hopes that each unit would take pride in maintaining a low ratio of errors.

Isolated Workers

As social needs of workers are considered, a manager or supervisor should be wary of isolating an individual.

In considering the social needs of workers, a manager or supervisor should be wary of isolating an individual.

The personal secretary to the president of a Fortune 500 company confessed that she was not as happy as she was before she got promoted to the position. "Oh, I enjoy the plush office surroundings, the power and the prestige of the position," she said. "But the door is always closed, and we're so busy in here I never have a minute to chat with the other secretaries like I used to do." When a worker is separated from other workers, the term **organizational isolation** is used to describe the setting.

Some organizational isolation may be necessary. The work may be so specialized and the volume of work so small that only one person is assigned to the task and that person may lack opportunity to interact with other workers.

organizational isolation-occurs when a worker is separated from other workers

Melissa Jansen is responsible for making travel arrangements for executives at Tulane Industries. Her job duties include booking flights, reserving hotel rooms, and arranging auto rentals. Melissa is the only employee with this responsibility. The executives fill out a form specifying details of their travel needs and send it to Melissa for processing.

In this situation, Melissa must either sacrifice social satisfaction during working hours or misuse company time for conversations irrelevant to her job.

As an alternative, Tulane Industries might include Melissa in a unit of workers who also perform administrative support work. She would probably derive social satisfaction from interacting with colleagues. Most organizations recognize that socializing is inherent and does not cause serious interruptions. Workers, however, should recognize that excessive socializing reduces productivity and peak efficiency.

Two-Way Communication

If social needs are to be satisfied, relationships must be reciprocal. People resent always giving and never receiving, as well as one-way conversations. For these reasons, the exchange of information should be somewhat equal and reciprocal.

The give-and-take concept is difficult to establish when one manager or supervisor tells other people what to do and when and how to do it.

Brian Bennet majored in horticulture at Big Bend Community College located in Moses Lake, Washington. Soon after graduation, Brian found a position at Lakeview Lawn and Garden Center and was told that he would be given responsibility for flowers and ornamental plants. John Mays, a longtime employee, supervised all landscaping work for the firm. When a new job was contracted, John told Brian which plants he had chosen for the landscape. Brian was not involved in the planning process and was not consulted concerning the appropriateness of the plants chosen. As might be expected, the position did not meet Brian's expectations, and he started looking around for other opportunities.

If the owner or manager of Lakeview Lawn and Garden Center would have modified the model of operation, involving Brian in the planning process, Brian's feelings and social satisfactions would have been quite different. One organization change that might have brought this about would have been for the owner or manager to set up planning meetings involving John, Brian, and other employees with landscaping expertise. If the meetings were properly conducted, they would provide for a maximum exchange of ideas through give-and-take communication.

The purpose of conducting planning meetings is not merely to keep employees satisfied. In fact, if employees perceive that the purpose of such meetings contributes little or nothing toward the achievement of company goals, such meetings may actually have an adverse effect on of employee morale. Employees may believe that such meetings are a waste of time and take them away from other important work activities. If the work, however, is suited to a reciprocal exchange of ideas, an important by-product is social satisfaction.

Perceived Status

A common expression is: "Forget the title, just give me money." While money is important, most people also aspire to important positions within an organization. They take pride in reporting to a high-level executive. It enhances their self-perceived status and perhaps impresses their colleagues.

Organizational theorists, however, recognize that adding a supervisory level into an organizational structure cuts into the perceived status satisfactions of those who report to the new supervisor. In one company, for example, the department head of sales promotion and the department head of advertising resigned when a new manager of external relations was named. Previously, they had reported directly to the vice president of marketing. The two department heads perceived themselves to have been demoted, even though their work assignments and pay remained the same.

Perceived status is also related to job titles. Titles are significant because they may influence perceptions about the importance of a person, both within the organization and externally. Titles generally help people understand the hierarchy of an organization and in most cases describe where a job fits into an organizational structure. Managers, however, have recognized the ingenuity of devising attractive titles that lead to greater employee satisfaction. The philosophy that says, "Let's give this employee a better title instead of a raise" has been successful on occasion because it led to greater job satisfaction.

Breadth of Job Assignments

Narrow, highly specialized jobs often lead to worker dissatisfaction. An assembly line worker who spends hour after hour and day after day tightening a specific bolt on a component part as it moves along the assembly line has a menial, routine, monotonous job. In most cases, this worker leaves at the end of the day with little sense of achievement.

Narrow specialization also affects an individual's opportunity for growth. Perhaps this is one reason why many employers have embraced the concept of job enlargement (see Chapter 1).

Paul Sanders and Robin Viorst hold jobs in a small manufacturing plant in Savannah, Georgia, that processes and bottles food flavoring products. Robin opens cartons of new, empty bottles and pushes them onto the line. An automatic server squirts 12 fluid ounces of food flavoring into each bottle, which is then capped and labeled as it moves on down the line. The bottled food flavors move off the line onto a turntable where Paul picks them up and recases them into the empty cartons discarded by Robin.

One day, during a 15-minute break, Paul and Robin were bemoaning how boring and unchallenging their jobs were. Suddenly, Robin had an idea. "Why don't we ask our supervisor, Nate Walsh, if we can trade off every hour," Robin said. Mr. Walsh agreed to allow the two to try the switch-offs. Job satisfaction has improved and both Paul and Robin have demonstrated greater interest in their jobs.

Instead of restricting each worker to one end of the assembly line, each worker was able to work both ends. The jobs became more challenging than under the former setup; each worker became aware of a natural completeness or wholeness of their work; and each worker felt a greater sense of accomplishment.

Independence

Opportunity for independence is of concern to workers and supervisors in organizations. This freedom affects the fulfillment of self-expression needs. At one extreme are specific guides and rules defining worker behavior.

The freedom of independence is of importance to workers and supervisors in organizations and affects the fulfillment of self-expression needs.

Courtney McCollum works as a telefund solicitor for the foundation at a large northwestern university. Courtney's job requires that she call alumni and solicit gifts to support university needs and scholarships. Courtney would like greater latitude in the way she approaches and interacts with alumni and friends of the university. The rules, however, are very strict. Courtney must repeat a standard solicitation presentation which she has memorized from the foundation's manual. The same presentation is given to every prospect.

At the other extreme is almost complete freedom.

Sean Macpherson, who studied sales promotion and public relations at Lorain County Community College in Elyria, Ohio, is the special events manager at College Hills Mall. Sean, who works for the Mall Association, is responsible for booking special events in the mall which will likely attract large audiences. Craft shows, new auto shows, boat shows, musical performances, and other events which will attract crowds are Sean's responsibility. The underlying premise is that once people come to the mall, they will do some shopping, which will increase revenues for members of the Mall Association. Sean has almost complete freedom. Last February, for example, he arranged a chili cook-off contest.

The higher the degree of freedom, the more satisfaction an employee can expect from asserting ideas. The employee who believes that he or she is "running the show" will experience satisfaction from achievements. Freedom caters to self-expression needs. It should be recognized, however, that the employee must be able to handle freedom in an adept manner. Not all employees are able to do this and not all organizational leaders are willing to let them try.

Bureaucratic Organizations

Max Weber, a German sociologist, used the term *bureaucracy* to describe an ideal mechanistic structure. His book, *The Theory of Social and Economic Organizations,* was introduced in the United States in the late 1940s and has become a classic. Weber's concept of a **bureaucratic organization** consisted of three layers of authority: (1) top managers who are the decision-makers, (2) middle managers who develop rules and proce-

bureaucratic organization-consists of three layers of authority: top managers, middle managers, and workers

Figure 2.3 **Bureaucratic Organization with Layers of Supervisors and Managers**

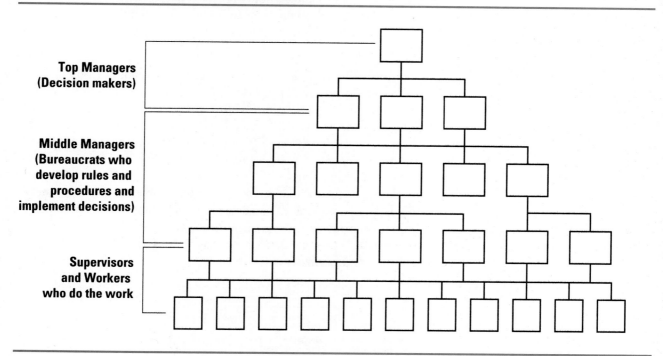

Top Managers
(Decision makers)

Middle Managers
(Bureaucrats who
develop rules and
procedures and
implement decisions)

Supervisors
and Workers
who do the work

dures for implementing the decisions, and (3) workers and supervisors who perform the work.[1] Weber envisioned a pyramid-shaped organization structure similar to that depicted in Figure 2.3. Weber's philosophy, which has been rejected by many scholars in the field of human behavior today, separated decision-making from workers. Weber was a strong proponent of specific rules, procedures, regulations, and policies. Today the word *bureaucracy* has negative connotations and is usually applied to organizations with many managers who seem to have nothing to do but formulate rigid rules. Rigid rules often bog down the organization and lead to inefficiency.

Jan Erickson, a teller at First National Bank, was experiencing high frustration and low job satisfaction. Since the bank's cashier established a new policy, Jan encountered one irate customer after another. Located in a midwestern city which is the home of a large state-supported university, the bank served many students with small savings and checking accounts. Often, the students would withdraw money from their savings accounts, leaving only two or three dollars. They would then leave for the summer or graduate and leave the money in the bank. "Nickel and dime accounts" was the phrase the bank's cashier used to describe the accounts. Since First National was required to continue servicing the accounts, including preparing income statements for tax purposes, the cost of servicing the small accounts exceeded the revenues generated. As a result, the cashier established a new policy; a service charge was assessed to each account which had been inactive for six months. Long-standing customers with thousands of dollars in their accounts objected angrily. "By creating a policy that addresses a problem created by only a percentage of the customers, the cashier has made my life and our customers' lives miserable," Jan complained.

The cashier at First National might benefit from reading Craig Cantoni's book, *Corporate Dandelions: How the Weed of Bureaucracy Is Choking American Companies and What You Can Do to Uproot It*. Cantoni believes the way to cut bureaucracy and create vibrant companies is not to lay off people, but rather to simplify operations, refocusing on the heart of the business and dropping practices that foster rigidity, hierarchy, narrow thinking, and paper pushing.[2]

Formulating decisions that address complex problems is an extremely slow process in a bureaucracy. The delay occurs because layers of supervisors, middle managers, and top managers have to concur before a final decision is reached. In some cases, minor as well as major decisions are reached slowly as described next.

---

[1] Max Weber. *Economy and Society: An Outline of Interpretive Society.* New York: Badminster, 1968 (originally published in 1925), 956–58.

[2] Craig Canton. *Corporate Dandelions: How the Weed of Bureaucracy Is Choking American Companies and What You Can Do to Uproot It.* New York: Amacom, 1993.

Unit 1·An Introduction to Human Relations

Anthony Carmichael is a purchasing agent at American Fluorochrome. Tony orders materials used in the manufacturing process as well as supplies needed at the plant. Seven months ago, Mary Moynihan complained about the liquid soap in the washroom. "My skin is sensitive and the liquid soap is simply ruining my hands. They are just raw," she said as she held up her red hands for his inspection. "Some of my coworkers are also seeing a dermatologist. How about giving us a break and ordering some milder soap?" Tony took the request to his supervisor, who, in turn, forwarded a request to a manager. Now, seven months later, Tony received approval to order the milder liquid soap.

As bureaucracies grow into large organizations, they usually are characterized by inefficiency and confusion. While it is recognized that large organizations are needed to carry out large-scale tasks, there is also recognition that small organizations or small subunits within a large organization are more efficient.

The rigid rules of a bureaucracy which are applied uniformly do not allow for exceptions based on individual circumstances.

Universities, like other organizations, are sometimes characterized by bureaucracy. A large Pac-Ten university enacted a new policy covering course withdrawals. Students withdrawing from a course with a WX designation, (withdrawal before a grade could be determined), were required to sign the withdrawal card in the registration office by the end of the tenth day of classes. Mark Johnson enrolled in a computer science course and discovered that he lacked prerequisite skills and knowledge. Before he could withdraw, he was called home due to the death of his grandmother. Upon return to campus, he was told that withdrawal from the course would yield a WF (withdrawal, failed) grade because the tenth day of classes had passed.

In 1969, Laurence J. Peter and Raymond Hull coauthored a book, *The Peter Principle.* The often quoted **Peter Principle** in essence states, "In a hierarchy, every employee tends to rise to his or her level of incompetence."[3] What the authors were really saying was, many people get promoted once too many times. While an employee may be competent at one level, he or she may prove to be incompetent at a higher level. Incompetent people in decision-making positions often add to the bureaucracy.

In some organizations, attempts are being made to drop practices that foster bureaucracy. People who take action to kill bureaucracy are being rewarded. They may receive public praise, be cited in a company newsletter, or be given an award for the best antibureaucracy idea of the month.

Peter Principle-implies that in a hierarchy, every employee tends to rise to his or her level of incompetence

---

[3]Lawrence J. Peter. *The Peter Principle.* New York: William Morrow, 1969, 26.

Organizational Effectiveness

Most authorities probably agree that the assessment of organizational effectiveness is related to the achievement of organizational goals. However, achievement of stated goals cannot be the only basis for judging the effectiveness of an organization, because not everyone agrees what the stated goals of an organization should be.

Organizational Goals

The owners of a corporation (stockholders) may believe the primary goal of the organization is to earn a profit. A customer or client may view organizational effectiveness in terms of the quality of the products or services which the organization produces. Managers and supervisors may look at various factors as measures of organizational effectiveness, such as productivity, motivation and morale of employees, and the absenteeism rate or turnover rate of employees. Rank and file employees may evaluate organizational effectiveness in terms of job satisfaction, conflict/cohesion within work groups, opportunity for participation in decision-making, and other humanistic concerns. Environmentalists may judge organizational effectiveness by the prudent use of natural resources, adherence to nonpollution guidelines, and overt actions directed at a clean, nonhazardous environment. A government agency might view an organization's effectiveness by its affirmative action and equal employment opportunity programs. As a result, the following definition has been provided for organizational effectiveness:

> **Organizational effectiveness** refers to human judgments about the desirability of the outcomes of organizational performance from the vantage point of various constituencies (stakeholders) directly and indirectly affected by the organization.[4]

This definition recognizes the interests that various stakeholders, including the owners, have in an organization. It also recognizes that effectiveness is judged by different groups using varying criteria, rather than by absolute or natural criteria. Thus, organizational effectiveness is not reflected in the achievement of a single goal.

Stakeholders

Stakeholders are members of the organization (owners, managers, supervisors, employees) and outsiders who have a direct or indirect interest in the organization. Outsiders, or external stakeholders, who have an interest in the organization, either directly or indirectly, may vary from one organization to another. In addition to customers and clients, external stakeholders may include competitors, suppliers, investors, and society in general. Figure 2.4 illustrates the two types of stakeholders.

▼
organizational effectiveness-human judgments about the desirability of the outcomes of organizational performance

▼
stakeholders-members of the organization and outsiders who have a direct or indirect interest in the organization

---

[4]Raymond F. Zammuto. "A Comparison of Multiple Constituency Models of Organizational Effectiveness." *Academy of Management Review.* 9 (1984), 606–16.

Figure 2.4 **Stakeholders of the Organization**

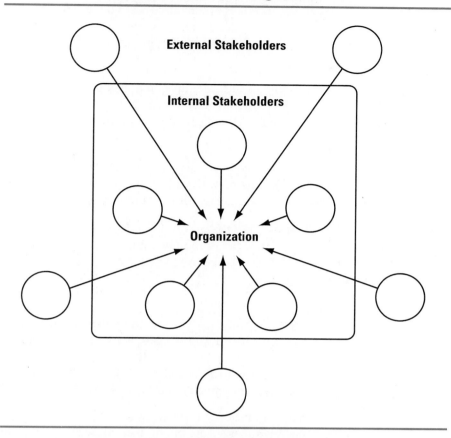

In some cases, the interests of stakeholders may conflict with one another. Consider the following example.

The Illinois Department of Transportation (IDOT) is considering the construction of a new interstate highway providing a direct route from Peoria to Chicago. Economic developers in the Peoria Metropolitan Area and in the towns and cities along the proposed route are excited about the news. Frequent travelers between the cities also welcome the prospects of a new highway which will cut travel time. Farmers along the proposed route, however, have reacted with anger to the proposal because a new highway will add more pavement over the rich black soil. Environmentalists, too, have voiced objections to plans which may endanger some prairie plants and wildlife species. Political leaders in towns and cities along the existing alternate route have also indicated resistance.

This scenario illustrates how stakeholders with varying interests are influenced by differing concerns.

The application of human relations skills becomes increasingly important when internal stakeholders find themselves to be in opposition.

Imagine the following scenario: A group of executives in a firm which owns a national chain of motels are huddled around a table trying to make a decision on whether to acquire a site and build a new motel in a rapidly growing city located in the New England region.

Vice President of Research:

Our preliminary studies indicate this could be a profitable move for us. Getting established in this city within the next year would show the industry that we're the leaders, not the followers.

Vice President of Marketing:

I'm worried about occupancy rates. We are not well known in the New England states, and after the fall vacation season ends, I'm afraid we could be sitting there with a lot of empty rooms.

Vice President of Accounting:

Our projected cash flow is not too favorable. Can we cost this project a little lower? I would like to hear what contractors say on construction costs.

Vice President of Acquisitions:

This is certainly a poor time to start worrying about cash flow and occupancy rates. If we had gotten bogged down on such details two years ago, we wouldn't have our successful units in the upper Midwest. This location is right for us and we will have the market to ourselves until our major competitors follow us like they always do.

In the above interactions, each executive presents a specific viewpoint and tries to convince the others of its importance. Based upon the validity of the viewpoints, compromises between the internal stakeholders (vice presidents) will lead to a decision or course of actions. In an effective organization, varying views are accepted. An ineffective organization is often characterized by the intolerance to or rejection of points of view.

Both external and internal stakeholders exert pressures on the organization, and balancing these pressures to achieve effectiveness is a challenge.

Internal Stakeholders. What do these people have in common?

► Mary has just graduated from college where she studied organizational behavior and has just been hired as a management trainee.

► Doug has received his MBA from a prestigious Ivy League school.

► Michael has been an American expatriate for five years and has just returned to the United States.

► Mohammed, an Egyptian who was educated in Britain, has lived in the United States for three years.

► Maria, a Hispanic high school graduate, was recently recruited under her employer's affirmative action plan.

Each of these people work in the same organization. Each of them will contribute to the organizational culture which is manifested in values, attitudes, beliefs, myths, rituals, performance, and myriad other ways. In such organizational cultures, members must develop coping skills and adaptive strategies to become successfully integrated into the group. Today's workers, more than ever before, encounter coworkers with multicultural backgrounds.

Customs and Traditions: Watching for the Global Difference

Arab Business Customs and Protocol

Arab businesspeople are not all the same. Yet there are some common traits among Arabs. An Arab is any individual whose native language is Arabic, considers himself or herself Arab, and has some heritage that may be traced to Saudi Arabia.

Arabs tend to be warm, hospitable, friendly, and courteous. By tradition Arabs are expected to extend hospitality for up to three days for a guest. Arabs have the reputation of being very emotional and sentimental. They have a strong sense of justice and they become morally outraged by historical events and any individual's behavior that goes against their sense of justice.

Arab society demands a high degree of conformity. Honor, social prestige, and a secure place in society are brought about when conformity is achieved. If one fails to conform, such behavior is considered to be damning, and leads to a degree of shame. The shame, while linked to the lack of conformity, is compounded by having others discover the transgression. An individual committing an act that brings shame loses power and influence.

To an Arab, commerce is a most blessed career. For a Moslem, Mohammed the Prophet was a man of commerce and he married a lady of commerce. Thus business, trade between people, is highly respected. Arab businesspeople have reputations of being sound, shrewd, and knowledgeable in the art of making money. Negotiating and bargaining are considered normal and commonplace. Bargaining is a Middle Eastern art, and the visiting businessperson must be prepared for some intense "haggling." Establishing rapport, mutual trust, and respect are essential for a successful business relationship. An Arab does business with the person, not with the company or organization.

A Western businessperson's belief is that one is in control of time. Adherence to that belief will lead to frustration when dealing with Arabs. *Burka insha Allah* is an Arab expression that is difficult for Westerners to understand and accept. It means, "tomorrow if God wills." Business travelers who expect Arabs to conform to their time

CONTINUED →

Chapter 2 • Human Relations in Organizations

will be disappointed. Being on time for appointments or even keeping appointments is unusual.

The foreign business representative may be forced to wait a long time before seeing the host. The meeting may not be private and may be subject to frequent interruptions by other visitors. Refreshments are offered as a gesture of hospitality, and this offer should always be accepted. Business cards are essential and exchanged at the first meeting. Business cards should be presented with English on one side and with Arabic on the other. The Arabic side of the card should be face up in the presentation. The first business visit should be approached as a leisurely getting to know each other process. Conversation may not turn to business for several days, and it is considered rude for the visiting person to press the issue.

The Arab handshake may feel limp when compared with the firm clasp of most Westerners. Kissing on the cheeks is commonplace when men greet each other and women greet each other. When an Arab businessperson meets a stranger for the first time, eye contact may be averted. Once acquaintanceship has been established, eye contact is much more intense and may exceed comfortable limits for the Westerner.

Among the list of "don'ts" recommended for Western visitors are the following:

▶ DON'T bring up business before establishing rapport and getting to know your host. This is considered rude.

▶ DON'T ask questions or make comments about an Arab man's wife or any female children over the age of twelve. This is a taboo.

▶ DON'T pose colloquial questions that might be misunderstood or wrongly interpreted by the Arab host.

▶ DON'T use swear words because they are considered to be in extremely bad taste. Likewise, avoid any inappropriate jokes.

▶ DON'T bring up subjects of either politics of religion.

Sources: Almaney, A.J., and A.J. Alwan. *Communicating with Arabs: A Handbook for the Business Executive.* Prospect Heights, Ill: Waveland, 1982.

Fernea, E.W., and R.A. Fernea. *The Arab World: Personal Encounters.* New York: Doubleday, 1985.

Minsep, F. *The Business Traveler's Handbook–How to Get Along with People in 100 Countries.* Englewood Cliffs, N.J.: Prentice Hall, 1983.

There are many dimensions to this concept of internal stakeholder culture. The values or ethics which people from different backgrounds accept, and to which they adhere, differ. Roles and relationships may also be influenced by cultural background. For example, Mohammed may consider the Western practice of backslapping as rude or, perhaps, even vulgar. The attitudes which each employee brings to the organization may differ significantly from one person to another.

Today's workers, more than ever before, encounter coworkers from diverse cultural backgrounds. The attitudes each employee brings to the organization may differ significantly from one person to another.

As a result, most organizations find it necessary to establish policies. A **policy** is a general guide to action. It may

▶ be specific or broad in its directive

▶ deal with one or many aspects of a problem

▶ place limits within which action is to be taken or specify the steps to take in making a decision.

policy-a general guide to action

A no smoking on the premises policy is a specific directive. It may deal with many aspects of the problem: danger of fire, second-hand smoke problems, and clean air, among others. Unless the policy indicates steps to be taken if the policy is abused, the third component of the definition is missing. If the policy states that violators will be suspended from work for three days, however, all components of the definition have been addressed.

The organization may also find it necessary to establish standards of employee behavior and job **norms,** which are set standards by which an employee's output must be measured. Some organizations rely on job descriptions to define what is to be done and also to specify in detail how

norms-set standards by which an employee's output must be measured

the work must be performed. While standards of behavior and job norms do not solve all coordination problems within an organization, they go a long way toward ensuring conformance among diverse members of an organization.

Myths are traditional or legendary stories about organizational heroes or events of exceptional character. The late Sam Walton's belief that involving employees in the organization as the way to make the business succeed is an important element within the organizational structure at Wal-Mart. The winning tradition of basketball teams at Kentucky, Indiana, and North Carolina promotes the exceptional character of each of these universities.

The organization's culture transmits in many ways the idea of "the way we do things around here." The values, expectations, standards, and procedures get ritualized and even celebrated. Special events such as retirement dinners, the hoopla that is used to mark special achievements, and organizational symbols add to the cohesiveness of any organization and unite its members into "one big family."

Figure 2.5 illustrates factors which are responsible for shaping internal organizational cultures. Organizations create culture which explains the pattern of assumptions and behavior formulated by members in response to their environment. Because each internal stakeholder brings to the organization a unique background (social, educational, and occupational), attitudes, biases, values and ethics, as well as other dimensions of human behavior, organizational members must be tolerant of such differences. They must maintain open minds and be sensitive to the necessity of avoiding tunnel vision. They must also be willing to compromise. Members who are unable or unwilling to display such characteristics will be viewed as militant organizational members lacking human relations skills.

myths-traditional or legendary stories about organizational heroes or events of exceptional character

Figure 2.5 **Factors Shaping Internal Organizational Culture**

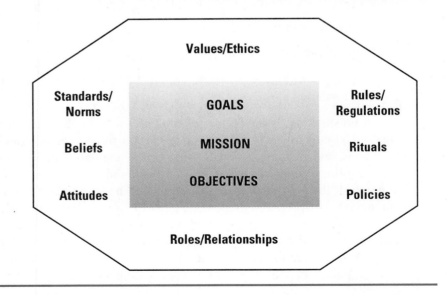

Values/Ethics

Standards/Norms

Beliefs

Attitudes

GOALS

MISSION

OBJECTIVES

Rules/Regulations

Rituals

Policies

Roles/Relationships

External Stakeholders. As indicated earlier, an organization may have multiple external stakeholders with varying interests. A financial institution which has provided loans to an organization is interested in seeing the organization succeed. Competitors, on the other hand, would not mind at all if the organization failed. People within an organization must be sensitive to the facts that external stakeholders are constantly changing, the preferences of external stakeholders change, and the values of society change over time.

When Disney Corporation executives decided to open theme parks in Europe, they acquired a new audience of customers, or stakeholders. If a new family moves to St. Louis and the family members shop at Schnucks Supermarket, they become new stakeholders. Business organizations are constantly acquiring new stakeholders and losing existing ones. New suppliers, a new advertising agency, a switch to a new long distance telephone service, and a new snow removal service represent examples of changes in stakeholders. It is important to recognize that each new stakeholder has a unique viewpoint of the organization's activities and a new set of preferences to satisfy. Sometimes the stakeholder's preferences are in opposition. Rather than placating the most vocal stakeholders, an organization should be honest in providing a rationale for its activities.

Stakeholders' preferences may change over time. Critics of Illinois Power's nuclear generating plant, for example, became strong advocates after viewing stringent safety precautions and after benefiting from taxes paid by the organization to support local schools.

Finally, the values of society change over time. Tobacco companies, for example, have experienced an increased number of critics as members of society associate smoking with health problems. Organizations providing riverboat gambling have become more acceptable to additional members of society, as revealed by legalization and popularity.

Just as human relations skills should be emphasized when coping with internal stakeholders, public relations become a key ingredient in coping with external stakeholders.

Organizational Cliques

Within many organizations, informal groups referred to as *cliques* spring up. A **clique** is an informal group that is unified by the members' desire to support some cause. The cause may simply be helping a popular supervisor or manager get promoted, or perhaps some rather strongly held belief about what the organization should or should not do. A clique may be loosely or tightly formed. A loosely knit clique may be little more than a group of people with common sympathies on an issue, who occasionally see one another for mutual support. Such a loosely knit clique lacks a central plan for dealing with the issue. On the other hand, a tightly knit clique is a well-defined faction that may hold clandestine meetings to pursue a central plan of action.

clique-an informal group that is united by members' desires to support some cause

Within an organization, a clique promotes its causes in many ways: by getting its members chosen for influential positions, by openly advocating its cause, by finding ways to reward organizational members who support the cause, and by proposing selected courses of action.

While a clique may be formed around a worthy cause, cliques within organizations are usually perceived to be undesirable. A strong clique can disrupt programs directed toward organizational objectives. Cliques may also be formed to promote selfish motives.

The local education association, made up of teachers in the Community Unit School District, has been working on a salary schedule to be presented during negotiations with the Board of Education. Teachers who have taught 15 years within the district reach the top of the salary schedule, and their salary increases are based upon whatever percentage of increase the Board of Education approves. A clique of senior teachers at the district has been formed for the purpose of obtaining additional salary increases for those at the top of the salary schedule. They reason that because they are not advancing to an upward increment on the salary schedule (as those with fewer than 15 years of experience), they are entitled to a larger percentage of new salary money.

Cliques have the potential for creating human relations problems within an organization. As in the scenario above, a clique may place workers in opposing camps and lead to internal organization conflict.

Organizational Development

Despite the importance of traditions, creeds, and goals, an organization must change. The speed of change is so great that organizations that fail to change and adapt cannot succeed. Interactive computers, fax machines, and other advances in communications technology have brought about an information explosion that is altering our world at an unprecedented rate. Almost all organizations, desiring to survive in today's competitive economic environment, must learn how to adapt and change.

Organizational development is a planned strategy designed to improve overall organizational effectiveness. To accomplish organizational development, emphasis is placed on collaborative change, involving participation by employees who will be affected.

Not too long ago, the managers at General Foods got their data from a central data processing department. Reports were slow in coming, and their format was inflexible. If an answer led to further questions, it often took weeks to get the desired information. The marketing people simply were not able to respond quickly enough to market conditions.

Two events changed all of this. One was the development of personal computers and software that could perform multiple functions. The second

organizational development-a planned strategy designed to improve overall organizational effectiveness

Unit 1·An Introduction to Human Relations

was the realization by General Foods management that they needed better decision-making tools. Now, survey results that once took five months to process, and cost $5,000, can be done in five minutes on a spreadsheet.[5]

Introducing change, such as that at General Foods, may be met with resistance and a desire to maintain the status quo. Employees are often worried about how they will be personally affected by changes. Organizational development consultants often criticize firms whose sole focus for change has been, "What's in it for the firm?" Instead, to discourage resistance, they recommend that firms also devote attention to the question, "What's in it for the individual?"

Interactive computers, fax machines, and other advances in communications technology have brought about an information explosion that is altering our world at an unprecedented rate.

[5]Virginia Dudek. "The Plugged-In Marketers at General Foods." *Marketing Communications.* March 1984, C9–C13.

- An organization is composed of people whose combined abilities make the accomplishment of goals possible. As the goals and work become more complex, additional people with more diverse talents are added.

- The study of organizations is important to the field of human relations because all work groups and most work activity exist within organizations.

- A line position is one which is involved in or contributes to the main activity of a firm, while staff positions are involved in specialized activities and are indirectly related to the main business activity.

- Four basic concepts which are inherent in the unification of individuals into an organization include common goals, division of labor, coordination of activities, and hierarchy of authority.

- Tall organizations are characterized by a narrow span of control; that is, few employees report to a supervisor or manager. In flat organizations, the span of control is much broader.

- Usually, at higher levels within an organization, the span of control is reduced.

- Tall organizations tend to experience more communication problems than flat organizations.

- Centralized organizations are characterized by decision-making reserved for a relatively few high-ranking officials, while decentralized organizations allow decision-making power to filter down to the lower ranks of the organization's hierarchy.

- Organizing workers into small groups tends to lead to greater social satisfactions, and—in some cases—greater pride by the group members in maintaining a low ratio of errors.

- Organizational isolation of workers leads to a reduction in social satisfaction.

- If social needs are to be satisfied, relationships with others must be reciprocal and a two-way exchange of information is essential.

- Self-perceived status is important in satisfying the need for self-actualization.

- Narrow, highly specialized jobs often lead to worker dissatisfaction.

- The higher the degree of freedom, the more satisfaction an employee can expect from asserting his or her ideas.

- Today the word *bureaucracy* has negative connotations and is associated with slow decision-making and inefficiency.

- Organizational effectiveness refers to human judgments about the desirability of the outcomes of organizational performance from the vantage point of various constituencies (stakeholders) directly and indirectly affected by the organization.

- The application of human relations skills becomes increasingly important when internal stakeholders find themselves to be in opposition.

- In an effective organization, exchanges of varying viewpoints are encouraged and accepted, while an ineffective organization is often characterized by intolerance to varying viewpoints.

- In today's organizational cultures, which are characterized by members with varying cultural backgrounds, members must develop coping skills and adaptive strategies in order to become successfully integrated into the group.

- A policy is a general guide which may be specific or broad in its directive, deal with one or many aspects of a problem, and place limits on action to be taken.

- Organizational cultures are manifested in values, attitudes, beliefs, myths, rituals, performance, and various other ways.

- External stakeholders are constantly changing; their preferences change over time; and sometimes the stakeholders' preferences are in opposition.

- A clique is an informal group whose members are unified by their desire to support some common cause.

- Organizational development is a planned strategy designed to improve overall effectiveness.

Key Terms

bureaucratic organization	organizational isolation
centralized control	partnership
chain of command	Peter Principle
clique	policy
coordination	proprietor
decentralization	span of control
flat organizations	staff position
line position	stakeholders
myths	tall organizations
norms	
organization	
organizational development	
organizational effectiveness	

1. What do you perceive to be the effects of both a tall organization and a flat organization? How are employees likely to be affected in either a tall or flat organization? Which type of organization would you prefer for employment and why?

2. The potential for human relations problems between staff employees and line employees is always present. Why is this statement true? What advice would you give to staff employees to reduce friction which may occur?

3. "When stakeholders—both internal or external—evaluate an organization, there will likely be considerable disagreement." Provide a rationale to support this statement.

4. Paris Community College, Paris, Texas, has established the following policy: "If an instructor elects not to administer a final examination during the time slot allocated for that exam, the instructor must be available for student consultation at the time the exam would have been administered." Does this policy statement contain the three components of a policy as outlined in this chapter? Explain.

5. Select an organization to which you belong or perhaps in which you have worked. Cite an example of a loosely knit clique in that organization. What was the "cause" which unified the clique? Cite an example of a tightly knit clique. What was the "cause" that unified this clique? Explain the central plan of action.

6. Why does centralized control seem to work better in small organizations than in large organizations? What effects have the computer and information retrieval systems had on the concepts of centralized and decentralized organizations?

Human Relations in Work Groups

Learning Objectives

Upon completing this chapter, you should be able to:

- Create a positive impression on coworkers and supervisors within a new work group.

- Cope with undesirable work assignments and respond to hazing incidents in a new work setting.

- Understand the differences between social versus formal work groups and temporary versus permanent work groups.

- Recall pointers for getting the best from a work group.

- Assume a role in a self-directed work group that is able to make decisions and accept ownership of work outcomes.

- Guard against groupthink and group polarization, thus avoiding infallible and cautious decisions.

- Employ group-building techniques that will enable participants to achieve goals by generating, evaluating, and choosing the most promising ideas for implementation.

Craig was excited about his new job at Circle City Motor Sales. Sandra Castillo, manager of the parts department and Craig's new supervisor, spent most of the morning showing Craig around and introducing him to other employees. She explained Craig's responsibilities at the sales and service counters, where both customers and Circle City technicians requested parts, including tires, batteries, and accessories. Craig learned that when parts were needed by the technicians in the service department and were not in stock at Circle City Motors, he would also need to assume the role of parts runner. That is, he should drive the firm's van to another parts vendor and pick up the needed items.

About 2 P.M. Craig noticed Troy Williams, a mechanic at Circle City, approach the service counter. Eager to be of help, Craig asked Troy what he needed. "Well," Troy said, "I'm working on a little Yamaha motorcycle out here and it needs a new radiator cap. Why don't you run down to Auto Vendors and pick up one for me." He then flashed a big smile and said, "I'm kinda in a rush." Craig walked over to Sandra and said, "I'm going to pick up a part for one of the mechanics; I'll be back shortly."

Craig noticed the salesperson smile and wink at one of the other employees at Auto Vendors when he asked for the radiator cap for a Yamaha bike. "I'll check and see if we have it," the salesperson said and disappeared into the rows of parts bins. Another employee walked over and said, "Hi, my name's Ben. You must be new over at Circle City." Craig said, "Yeah," and about that time, the salesperson reappeared. "We're out of those caps; I suggest you try Precision Auto Parts on West Market Street."

Upon entering the Precision parts store, a middle-aged man asked if he could help him. "I'm looking for a radiator cap for a Yamaha motorcycle," said Craig. "I'm sorry," the man replied. "We don't carry those in stock. You need to go to the Yamaha dealership out on Jefferson Parkway."

Craig tried to hurry, but the Yamaha dealership was way across town. There, Craig was greeted by a young man behind the parts counter. "I need a radiator cap for a Yamaha bike," Craig uttered. The man smiled and said, "I think you have been the victim of a practical joke." "What do you mean?" Craig demanded. "Well, to start with, Yamaha engines and all other bike engines for that matter are air-cooled. They do not have radiators and, as a result, they do not have radiator caps."

Suddenly, Craig understood the crafty smiles that he had encountered. As he drove back to Circle City Motors, he felt betrayed—the victim of unfair treachery. Upon entering the establishment, he was greeted by Troy Williams, who said, "Did you get my radiator cap?" "No, they had to order it," Craig replied. "It will be here in about three days." Troy grinned, slapped Craig on the back and said, "You'll be okay here."

Joining a Work Group

One of the problems of joining a group is learning to fit into the membership of that group. It really doesn't matter whether the new employee is 16 years old and busing tables at a fast-food restaurant or whether he is 45 and taking on the presidency of a Fortune 500 company; that employee is the new kid on the block and can expect to encounter new peers, new subordinates, and new supervisors.

Everyone wants to belong and to be liked, accepted, respected, and paid attention to as an important member of the group. Fitting in, however, isn't easy. In most situations, membership must be earned. An individual may encounter a new work group for a variety of reasons including the following:

► new job

► transfer to a new geographical location

► transfer to a new department or division

► promotion

► demotion

► reorganization

► assignment to a special project

► assignment as a substitute for another worker.

In approaching a new work group, different people may be apprehensive for different reasons. What will the other workers be like, and will I be able to get along with them? If I make mistakes, will my boss be understanding? A new manager or supervisor may wonder if needed information will be available so that correct decisions can be reached. The new manager or supervisor may also be concerned about subordinates and if they can

Unit 1 · An Introduction to Human Relations

be trusted. A woman returning to the workforce after raising a family may worry about the gaps in her resume and her need for retraining. Men and women near retirement age may worry about their lack of computer skills. Members of minority groups may fear possible discrimination. Almost all members of new work groups are anxious about fitting in, that is, being accepted as a member of the group.

A Letter to a Young Person Looking for a Job

Dear Lou,

Today you came into my office looking for a job. From your reaction as you left, I suspect this was not the first time you weren't hired. You may think kids do not have a chance to find a job! That's not true. Many companies are hiring young people every day.

I hired a seventeen-year-old person named Pat today. You saw the person; neatly dressed, polished shoes, just generally well-groomed. No special training or experience either, just a good positive attitude. You see, the attitude you present is more important than wearing your favorite old jeans. Pat was willing to take time to learn about our company and our product. Pat also did a good job acting like a mature person. There is plenty of time to wear the old jeans and relax after work!

It is true, managers who are responsible for hiring people may not be sympathetic to today's youth, but they do make the decisions about hiring and firing. Even though some young people may reject our ideals, I have not seen anyone reject the paychecks we sign.

Maybe you should take time to use your dictionary! Look up the word "empathy." Put yourself in my shoes. I'm sorry you feel no one understands you, but I do have a responsibility to my company and its success. I need employees who are enthusiastic and have a good attitude about work. You may have these qualities, but I failed to see them—I saw the bizarre clothes, the "chip" on your shoulder and a bit of rebellion! Wake up! These qualities don't make car payments . . .

Maybe you should take a look in the mirror and take time to examine your attitudes. Your school record indicates you have a lot of potential. You have some self-evaluating to do before your next job interview. Get your act together!

Employers are searching for young employees. Our country needs its youth. Many people leading our country and businesses in the next 25 years are entering the job market today just like you. For your sake I hope you change your attitude!

The Management

Source: You and Your Job. Division of Vocational Education, State Department of Education, Columbus, Ohio, 1982, 19.

Attitudes are important attributes which are of concern to most employers.

Acceptance versus Exclusion

Sometimes, newcomers feel unaccepted because of unintentional neglect. Other employees are busy with their daily routines and may forget to acknowledge or pay attention to a new employee. Many firms are under-staffed and the employees are overworked. When a new employee joins the work group, a heavy amount of work may be dumped on the unsuspecting new worker causing that person to feel hurt or angered. In some cases, the new employee may pout, withdraw, or become disagreeable, and human relations may be damaged beyond reconciliation.

To avoid exclusion, the new employee should observe others, watch for clues, and ask for help when needed. When a newcomer acknowledges the skill and knowledge of an experienced worker by asking questions or by asking for assistance, the experienced worker may be flattered that he or she was recognized as a competent worker. As a result, that individual may be willing to help the newcomer become familiar with other people, the physical layout of the work environment, work tasks, and other important factors.

In many firms, the **buddy system** or **peer mentoring** is relied upon; that is, one person is put in charge of the newcomer's integration into the group. In such cases, acceptance into the group usually occurs more rapidly.

buddy system or peer mentoring-one person is put in charge of the newcomer's integration

Creating a Positive Impression

It is impossible for the supervisor and coworkers to know what a new employee is really like from initial contacts. Yet, they will be studying the newcomer's appearance and mannerisms and will try to figure out what makes the person tick. Everything he or she says and does will play a part in the overall impression which the person creates.

Let's start with the most basic impression—appearance. Good grooming is very important. Selection of what to wear is also important. The right attire can help a person project a positive image and establish credibility and likeability.

A new employee should strive to make a good beginning by establishing himself or herself as a solid, capable worker who cooperates with others and follows through to get positive results. When arriving at a new job, it is a good idea for the newcomer to maintain a low profile until he or she understands the new work environment. Dale Carnegie, author of the best-selling book, *How to Win Friends and Influence People,* wrote, "Don't be afraid to give your best to what seemingly are small jobs. Every time you conquer one, it makes you that much stronger. If you do the little jobs well, the big ones will tend to take care of themselves."

A newcomer should create a good impression by being present at work unless the person is very ill. Absenteeism creates the impression of unreliability. The person should be quiet and unassuming and make his or her presence felt through work. In most jobs, there is a lot of routine work. The newcomer should be willing to work on all projects assigned to him or her,

Dale Carnegie believed that if a person gave the seemingly small jobs the best effort, the larger jobs would tend to take care of themselves.

even the ones he or she does not like. On a new job, the new employee can expect to make some mistakes. The way the person reacts to criticism about the mistakes determines what others will think of the individual as a person. When a mistake is made, it is far better to admit to being wrong than to rationalize one's performance.

Coping with Undesirable Assignments

New employees often face a major problem: they may be assigned to jobs no one else wants. The least interesting or rewarding jobs, the worst shifts, the most unpleasant clients or customers, the poorly maintained trucks, and the least powerful computers may be assigned to the newcomers. This phenomenon is known as "paying your dues." The new employee goes from outsider to lowest person on the totem pole. Newcomers frequently spend an unspecified time, ranging from a few days to a year or longer, at the bottom of the organization's hierarchy. Employees holding important positions are not immune to undesirable assignments. Supreme Court Justice Blackmun, as reported in an article appearing in *The New York Times Magazine,* garnered early assignments writing opinions in tax cases and other mundane fare that did little to raise his profile.

The newcomer gets labeled quickly. The new employee's reaction to an undesirable assignment may lead to an undesirable label.

Vicki Chonarzewski could not have been more elated. She had applied for a position at Americana Eye Clinic and was chosen to fill a position in the optical department. Mr. Rolinski, her new supervisor, had explained her duties by saying, "We will be training you to work with patients as they select frames for their glasses." Once a patient selected a frame, Vicki would be required to measure and determine the patient's pupil differential quotient (the distance between eyes) and the length of earpieces. She would also provide instructional training to new contact lens wearers, showing them the proper technique to use for inserting or removing a lens, using wetting and cleansing solutions, storing the lens, and other procedures.

After two weeks at Americana, Vicki had not met a patient. She had not even been trained to work with patients. Instead, she had spent her time sorting and organizing inventory—thousands of eyeglass frames, lens cleaners, contact lens wetting solutions, lens cases, and samples which had been sent to Americana by pharmaceutical firms.

During her break on Thursday afternoon, Vicki confided her feelings to Jim Morris, another employee in the optical department. "I was told I would be trained to work with clients," Vicki said. "Instead, I've been stuck back in the stockroom doing menial work that no one else wants to do."

Later, Jim told other employees in the optical department that Vicki Chonarzewski was arrogant, uncooperative, and not a team player.

A new employee should be cognizant of the need to appear to be trustworthy, cooperative, and a team player. Undesirable labels, even when they may be unfair, are difficult to overcome and may hamper the new employee's relationships with coworkers and supervisors.

A new employee who wishes to fit into the work group should consider the following pointers.

► Arrive at work on time and do not leave early. Employees who are tardy and who skip out early are viewed as less than trustworthy.

► Complete the work tasks assigned by your supervisor as well as you can. Supervisors and coworkers are dependent upon the performance of all employees, and so is a company's success.

► Overprepare for meetings and conferences with others. The new employee creates a positive image by appearing to be knowledgeable and competent.

► Meet deadlines. Be the kind of person who can always be counted on to do what you say you will do. Only a small percentage of people practice follow-through, and consequently, those who do are held in high esteem. It is particularly important for other employees to know that you are a person who possesses this rare quality and for them to view you as a totally reliable person.

▶ Do not make promises unless you can deliver. Recognize that someone else may be depending upon you to fulfill a commitment and failure to do so may disrupt the achievement of objectives.

▶ Keep your work area neat and clean. A neat, clean work area creates an image of organization and orderliness.

▶ Strive to achieve accuracy in all work assignments. A competent worker takes pride in his or her work, making it free from mistakes, and other workers can depend upon that accuracy.

▶ Project yourself as a team player. When people join work groups, it is essential that they strive to achieve common objectives. Each employee, in such settings, must cooperate and contribute to the cause.

Responding to Hazing Incidents

The opening scenario to this chapter depicted a hazing incident. The practice of hazing has been associated with college fraternities, military academies, and team sports. Yet many people encounter forms of hazing in the world of work. **Hazing** is defined as "to persecute or harass with meaningless, difficult, or humiliating tasks." Whether one agrees the practices are acceptable or not, anyone entering a new group should understand that hazing may occur, the reasons why it may occur, and how to respond to it.

hazing-to persecute or harass with meaningless, difficult, or humiliating tasks

Verna Terpstra was the first female worker ever hired as a sanitation officer in Springfield. Her job task required that she lift a heavy trash can to dump the contents into the back of the city's sanitation truck. As she raised the heavy can and started to tip it to pour out the contents, the driver observed her in the rearview mirror and sped off, leaving her off balance so that she spilled the contents in the street. Needless to say, Verna was upset and complained to her supervisor that she had been the victim of harassment.

Those who engage in hazing believe such practice socializes the newcomer in the ways of the group. Hazing is looked on as a test through which the newcomer can become a member of the group. According to some researchers, the unpleasantness and duration of hazing incidents depend upon three factors:

1. How different is the newcomer from other members of the group? The greater the perceived difference (gender, race, attitudes, education, and so forth), the more the person's competence, personality, and acceptance of the group's antics are tested.

2. How cohesive is the group? The tighter the group, the more difficult it is for newcomers to be accepted.

3. How well does the newcomer respond to attempts to integrate himself or herself into the group's culture?

While many individuals frown upon hazing practices, others view hazing as a way of gaining membership in a permanent work group. These proponents believe that such practices actually accomplish a set of goals for the group, including:

▶ Providing senior members of the group a way to establish their seniority and dominance;

▶ Forcing newcomers into letting go any former identity and loyalty to another group or organization;

▶ Ensuring that the organization's unwritten rules or norms will be followed;

▶ Making membership in the group something that will be valued.

Hazing incidents may become cruel and inhumane. In such cases, the perpetrators damage any possibilities of establishing a harmonious working relationship with a newcomer. Examples of such practices include:

▶ Placing the newcomer into situations of danger.

▶ Making the victim the object of cruel jokes or pranks.

▶ Making derogatory remarks about an employee's clothes, appearance, speech, mannerisms, or work habits.

▶ Making wisecracks that include obscene words, off-color jokes, or other inappropriate verbiage.

▶ Downgrading or disregarding the newcomer and causing that person to feel that his or her contributions are inappropriate.

Attaining Work Group Membership

A new person may be referred to by various labels: neophyte, beginner, apprentice, amateur, rookie, and/or novice. But at some point, the person is no longer new. The individual has learned how to perform his or her work, has successfully handled undesirable work assignments, and has passed the tests that the group has imposed on potential members. In short, the individual has finally become one of the team.

The length of time needed to move from an outsider to an insider varies from individual to individual and from one position to another. Table 3.1 contains a summary of the stages that new employees pass through as they attain membership in a work group. Acceptance into a work group is usually a subtle occurrence that is not marked by specific events. It simply occurs when the candidate for membership and existing members of the group recognize that inclusion is no longer questioned.

Table 3.1 Attaining Membership in a Work Group

Status	Stages	Description
Outsider	Acceptance vs. Exclusion	Orientation to Work/Group
▼	▼	▼
Probation	Creating an Impression	Winning Approval
▼	▼	▼
Probation	Undesirable Assignments	Paying Dues
▼	▼	▼
Probation	Hazing and/or Testing	Socialization
▼	▼	▼
Insider	Group Membership	Acceptance in Work/Group

Social versus Formal Work Groups

If the hottest business buzzwords of the day were ranked, *work groups, work teams, quality circles,* and other terms describing the pluralistic organization of workers would rank right up there with *empowerment, quality,* and *global strategies.* Yet, it is important to recognize that informal groups, or social groups, of workers exist as well as formal groups. Informal groups of workers spring up naturally whenever people work together.

Workers form informal groups in the workplace and often spend time together at lunch, during breaks, or while carpooling.

They are common in colleges, hospitals, governmental offices, and social organizations, as well as in business firms. Members of such groups see each other frequently at lunch, during breaks, or while carpooling home from work. Such groups are formed because members discover they have common interests. If one or two members tend to be leaders, their positions arise naturally out of the situation, rather than through formal selections.

Formal work groups, on the other hand, are simply given an assignment to be completed as a group. The work group may be permanent, such as a small group of laborers that specializes in the installation of drywall in new home construction. In such cases, the work group will be composed of members who collectively possess all of the skills necessary to complete an assigned task. In other cases, the work group is temporary. The group may be called a **project team, task force,** or **tiger team.** It is created to solve a specific problem, work on a special project, design a plan, or complete some activity. According to Jack Gordon, editor of *Training* magazine, 8 out of 10 United States organizations have assigned people to work groups.[1]

▼

project team, task force, or tiger team-created to solve a problem, work on a special project, or complete some activity

Permanent Groups

Members of permanent groups often derive day-to-day satisfaction from such groups. The workers are interested in the same occupation or profession, discovering new information or knowledge related to the occupation, and solving problems faced in the workplace. In a real sense, they may provide emotional support for each other. They strive to achieve objectives, encourage meaningful interactions, and maintain or strengthen the group. Those who deviate from the group's behavior may introduce conflict and disrupt group harmony.

Roberto Gomez was hired by Park Ridge Condominiums as a summer employee between his freshman and sophomore years in college. Roberto was assigned to the grounds crew, a closely knit group.

On his first day, Roberto rushed into the storage shed, started a new mower, and drove it onto the lawns where he started cutting the grass. At the end of the day, one of the crew members said, "Gomez, you used the wrong mower today. Tomorrow take this one." He pointed to an older model that appeared to be in poor condition. "Why?" Roberto asked. "Well, we have an informal policy around here. Part-timers and summer employees use the oldest equipment," the crew member replied. "That's totally unfair," Roberto responded. "I'm not going to work with cast-off junk day after day. The rest of you guys are already making more money because you have been here longer and gotten raises."

"Well, we see things differently, young man. This is the way we operate around here and this is the way we're going to continue to operate," asserted the crew member.

[1] Gordon, Jack. "Work Teams: How Far Have They Come?" *Training.* October, 1992, 59–65.

Obviously, Roberto introduced conflict by deviating from the group's behavior pattern.

Many researchers in the behavioral sciences have noted that people seem predisposed to congregate and act in groups.[2] Clearly, group membership has a significant impact on how people see themselves, feel about themselves, and act in the group. Groups can provide a comforting refuge for members in a hostile or threatening environment. The group's common goal provides a sense of purpose.

Temporary Groups

Characteristics of a temporary work group include (1) having one or more tasks to perform; (2) producing some outcome for which members have collective responsibility; and (3) operating in an organizational context. Establishing and maintaining a cooperative work environment is often critical for effective group performance. This may sometimes be difficult with temporary groups because

▶ team members do not work closely together in their regular organizational roles; instead they come together from different jobs specifically to perform the team task;

▶ the work of the team is nonroutine; the team task is a special one of a nonrepetitive nature;

▶ team members may not be committed to the task; as a result, they may show up late for meetings or not at all;

▶ team members may be uncomfortable with the makeup and structure of the group.

In United States organizations that have some type of work group, permanent work groups are established one and one half times more frequently than temporary project groups.[3] Nevertheless, temporary project groups have been acknowledged for accomplishing

▶ immediate increases in customer service satisfaction

▶ significant decreases in time lost to error

▶ measurable increases in work productivity

▶ dramatically reduced operating costs

▶ improved quality

▶ new employee "ownership" of products and services

▶ heightened employee morale and commitment

▶ improved interaction among diverse groups

▶ reduced levels of stress and conflict

▶ greater stability during organizational change.

[2] Kenneth Bettenhausen. "Five Years of Group Research: What Have We Learned and What Needs to Be Addressed." *Journal of Management.* vol. 17 , no. 2, 1991, 347.
[3] Jack Gordon. "Work Teams: How Far Have They Come?" *Training.* October 1992, 60.

Chapter 3·Human Relations in Work Groups

Ethics on the Loading Dock

Karen Walden, Editor-in-Chief of *New Woman* magazine, recently stated:

> The values of ethics, integrity, honesty, and a sense of justice are really important to both share with members of your organization and also to expect from them. If you are not in sync with these core values, you have a hard time working together, let alone loving and respecting one another. It's the foundation you start with. You can have everything else in common, but if these values are in conflict, it is impossible to make a situation work or an organization succeed.

Sometimes, workers whose values differ find themselves in the same work group. Consider the plight of Juwan Harris who worked in the shipping bay of a company that manufactured a liquid industrial cleansing fluid. The fluid easily cuts grease, grime, and oil spills and is sold primarily to automotive repair shops, service stations, and truck stops. Since industrial cleansing fluid in one-gallon cans is a product that can be sold easily—almost everyone needs a cleaner to remove oil spills from their driveways and garage floors—it is also an easy product to get out the factory door.

Groups that have been successful in achieving such accomplishments are classified as strong groups. A strong group, contrary to what might be expected, is one in which there are lots of conflicts and frequent arguments. Where arguments are welcomed, viewpoints are exposed and agreements are stronger. Weak groups are those in which the objectives are not very important to most members or in which a few aggressive individuals make all the decisions.

Size and Composition of Groups

group-*two or more people who are working toward some common purpose*

A **group** may be defined as two or more people who interact with each other, are aware of each other, are working toward some common purpose, and perceive themselves to be a group. The difference between a small group and a large group is primarily one of perception. Research has revealed, however, that as work groups increase in size, members are more likely to express dissatisfaction.[4]

[4]Kenneth Bettenhausen. "Five Years of Group Research: What Have We Learned and What Needs to be Addressed." *Journal of Management.* vol. 17, no. 2, 1991, 354.

It is such a big volume product that no one seems to keep track of the number of cans leaving the production lines, and sometimes workers would set aside a few cans. Then, when the supervisor was on break and the coast was clear, they would just carry out a couple of cans and stash them in the trunks of their cars. In fact, most of the workers did this a couple of times each week stating that "the company owed it to them."

Juwan didn't take any because he didn't feel right about it and, in addition, he didn't want to run the risk of getting caught and having it put on record. He didn't object when one of the workers gave him a can to use on his own garage floor, but Juwan continued to be uncomfortable about what was happening. Not only did he believe the workers lacked the virtues of integrity and honesty, he felt that by not telling his supervisor he, too, was being less than honest. On the other hand, if he told company officials, he would not only get members of his work group in trouble—he would jeopardize his own membership within the work group.

What advice would you have given to Juwan?

Sources: Hosmer, LaRue. Moral Leadership in Business. Burr Ridge, Ill.: Irwin, 1994, 1–15.

McFarland, Lynn Joy, Larry Senn, and John Childress. 21st Century Leadership: Dialogues with 100 Top Leaders, Los Angeles: Leadership, 1995, 125.

Group processes and outcomes are also affected by the degree to which members are similar or bring unique qualities to the group. Members of groups composed of both male and female workers, for example, report significantly more difficulty working together than all-male groups. In addition, members report higher levels of competition and tension, lower levels of work efficiency and cooperation, and a stronger desire to change groups.[5] Similarly, racial composition of a group may affect group process.

Cheryl Wollrab believes that members of her work group sabotage her. A recent graduate of Moberly Community College, Cheryl accepted a position as a manager of a St. Louis Copymat Printing Center. The owner, Louis McCain, owns six Copymat Printing Centers in the city and the other five have male managers. Once every week, Mr. McCain and his six managers meet to discuss mutual problems, formulate promotional plans, monitor sales activities, and examine other administrative concerns.

At a recent meeting, Mr. McCain asked the group to recommend strategies to prevent shoplifting, a persistent problem. Small items of merchan-

[5]Marilyn Gist, Edwin Locke, and M. Susan Taylor. "Organizational Behavior: Group Structure, Process and Effectiveness." Journal of Management. vol. 13, no. 2, 1987, 240.

Chapter 3·Human Relations in Work Groups

Body Language: An Important Consideration in Interpersonal Interactions

Imagine yourself in a meeting with a new coworker. As the newcomer tells you how pleased she is to join the firm and how she plans to work hard and earn the admiration of other employees, you sense that something is wrong. Her voice is high-pitched and rapid and her eyes avoid yours, focusing instead on a ring which she is nervously twisting on her finger. About a week later you meet her in the coffee lounge and she tells you that she plans to leave the firm. You are disappointed but not surprised, for you had understood some of the nonverbal messages from the earlier meeting.

According to authorities on nonverbal communications, many messages are communicated without words. We tell others what we feel through our facial expressions and eye, hand, and other body movements. We also communicate through the pitch, volume, and cadence of our voices, the physical distance we maintain between ourselves and others during conversations, and in other nonverbal ways. In fact, body language can tell us what others are saying without them uttering a single word. Here are a few ways in which nonverbal messages can be sent.

▶ By averting your gaze, that is, avoiding the eyes of another, you tell that person that he or she is not getting the message across. If, instead, you stare directly at someone, you will probably make that person extremely anxious. In the midst of an argument, the harder you stare, the more threatening you appear.

▶ Gestures, which include the movement of shoulders, arms, and hands, communicate a variety of nonverbal messages. You may have

dise—ballpoint pens, highlighters, liquid paper, markers, etc.—are constantly being lifted. The managers had suggested and discussed such measures as adding security personnel, displaying small items of merchandise in display cases, and installing surveillance mirrors. When Cheryl suggested the installation of surveillance cameras, the other managers scoffed at the idea.

It wasn't the first time. Just a week ago, Cheryl had suggested that advertisements for St. Louis Copymat Centers be placed in the student telephone directories of each local college. Again, her colleagues had pooh-poohed her idea.

Fortunately, Mr. McCain knew how to recognize a problem and how to take action to solve it. To promote harmony within the group and to estab-

detected unspoken messages from handshakes. A limp handshake, for example, is a sign of reserve and a lack of enthusiasm, while a firm grip communicates confidence and enthusiasm.

► When disagreeing or interacting with an individual whom you do not like, you may find your body turned away from that person. If, on the other hand, you admire your associate, you are more likely to face the person directly.

► As you speak, be aware that the pitch, tone, volume, and speed of your voice communicates sometimes as much as your words. Rapid voice patterns may signal excitement or nervousness. Hesitant speech is usually interpreted as expressing insecurity or doubt.

► Even the way you dress delivers an important message. If you are inappropriately dressed, expect negative reactions from your associates.

While nonverbal communication enables all of us to receive important messages, don't make the mistake of believing that such cues enable you to fully understand your associates. Nonverbal messages are extremely complex, varying with the situation and culture in which we find ourselves. A general understanding of body language, however, will prove valuable in interpersonal interactions.

For the next few days, observe several people and see if you can identify their nonverbal messages.

lish more effective working relationships, McCain sought out each member of the group, including Cheryl, and offered some sage advice. "Imagine that each manager has an invisible sign hanging around his or her neck saying, 'make me feel important!'"

A number of techniques may be used to make people feel important. Among the techniques are the following.

1. Achieve greater impact on others by listening instead of talking. It is crucial that coworkers know their suggestions and ideas are not only welcome, but are given careful consideration.

2. Call a person by his or her name and use it often in conversation. Nothing makes a person feel more important than hearing his or her name.

3. Encouragement for independent thinking is recognition of individual value. If an individual wants to inspire coworkers or subordinates to give their all, he or she should regularly ask for their input about improving working conditions and productivity, and for getting routine work done more efficiently.

4. Show respect and loyalty. Coworkers and subordinates work harder when they believe that other workers and supervisors respect them. Employees are loyal to supervisors and work harder for them when they believe their supervisor will represent their interests and points of view to others in the company.

5. A person with a positive attitude gives off friendly signals, which enables coworkers and supervisors to be more open. An individual's attitude is expressed before he or she even begins to speak. It shows in the way a person may look, stand, walk, and talk. When a person is cheerful and upbeat, his or her attitude acts like a magnet. The individual not only attracts others, but is more friendly because the person senses in advance that the individual already likes them.

Figure 3.0 illustrates strategies which may be used to make other members of a work group feel important.

Figure 3.0 **Strategies for Establishing Feelings of Importance in Coworkers and Supervisors**

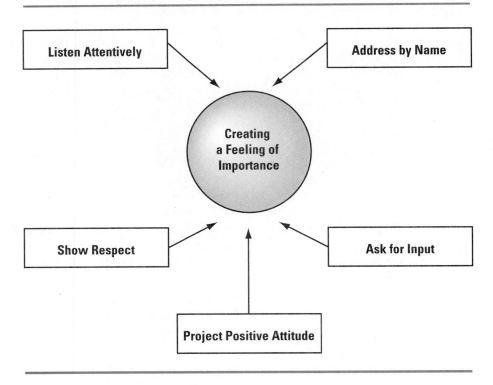

Work Group Conformity

Work groups exert pressures on members to conform to the group's norms. A norm is an unwritten expectation to which members of the group expect others to adhere. Such norms may specify working practices, the amount of work produced, responses to an employer's policies, style of dress, punctuality, and the number of hours one is willing to work. The idea that "everyone else is doing it" is indeed powerful pressure and the reason why many people are willing to conform to the work group's desires. Experi-mental research has demonstrated that social pressures may persuade people to do things they never viewed themselves capable of, such as committing acts of aggression against others.

Workers may conform for a number of reasons. In some situations, they conform because they do not wish to be singled out for criticism. Sometimes, they may feel there is safety in numbers. Perhaps they believe the work group exists to achieve a common goal and that nonconformity would signal dissension. Another reason for conformity is to send signals to others that we approve of them. Showing yourself to be similar to others around you confirms that you share interests and opinions.

Sharon Templeton announced that she would not join other employees at her Memphis-based company on an outing to Atlanta to see the Braves play the Astros. When pressed for reasons she would pass up the trip, Sharon admitted that members of her closely knit data management team had decided not to attend.

Some behavioral experts have suggested that people who feel insecure in a group and who have strong desires to fit in are more likely to conform. As a result, it is easier for groups to exert influence on low-status members, new recruits, and members who feel a strong need for approval and acceptance.

Deviants, strayers from accepted norms, and **scapegoats,** who bear the blame for others, help define a group identity and play an important role in the struggle between group identity and individual identity. People who wish to change the majority's view in a work group need to maintain a consistent position, to recognize the majority's arguments, and to be flexible in the way they argue their case. A member who desires to change a work group would probably be well advised to wait until he or she is a respected, established member of the group. Next, the member should seek support from other members so that others support the change and the dissenter is not dismissed as a resister or a troublemaker.

▼

deviant-strayers from accepted norms

▼

scapegoat-person who bears the blame for others

Sherri Ross achieved her goal. She found summer employment during her sophomore and junior years at a regional food wholesaler's warehouse on the southwest side of Chicago. The great thing about her job was the pay. Her union-scale wages, plus the time-and-a-half pay that she was receiving for overtime, would put her in much better financial position than other college students.

Yet, Sherri was faced with a problem. Because she was so well paid, Sherri believed that she should be as productive as possible. Perhaps it was her appreciation of the work ethic that she had heard her father speak about so often. Nevertheless, her coworkers were complaining. "Why don't you take breaks like the rest of us?" Sherri turned to face Ken Maurer who had posed the question. "After all, we have provisions for breaks in our union contract," Ken continued. "And, oh yes, you don't need to try to fill all the orders in an hour," remarked Todd Price, another order picker.

Later, Sherri received compliments from her supervisor, Joyce Watkins, who had noticed her diligent efforts. "I'll find a spot for you again next summer," the supervisor said.

Directed versus Self-directed Work Groups

Employers who organize work groups to achieve the firm's goals have two choices: to choose and assign a manager, supervisor, or project group leader to direct the work group or to permit the work group to be self-directed.

Directed Work Groups

In traditional organizational settings and indeed in many contemporary work environments, a leader—supervisor, manager, crew leader, boss—is assigned to mobilize others, that is, to make them share common goals, set the tasks, plan the work, delegate authority, communicate with work group members, enforce policies, motivate members of the work group, and evaluate performance. Being successful as a leader is rooted in having power of one sort or another. The power may be inherent in the perceptions of the position—the Dean of the Career Division at your school, the coach of the basketball team, or the boss or supervisor of the shipping department at a small plant that manufactures ceiling fans. Being effective as a leader, however, depends on a wide range of skills that include the ability to build cohesion within a group and to sustain morale under trying circumstances.

Hundreds of studies have been conducted to determine the traits and attributes of an effective leader. Most authorities in the human resources field tend to agree that an effective leader integrates motivation and human relations skills, management functions (planning, organizing, directing, and controlling), occupational knowledge and skills, and a good self-concept. Leadership behavior will again be examined in a later chapter.

Self-directed Work Groups

At the epicenter of all the national discussions about work groups lies the concept of self-directed or self-managed groups of workers. A **self-directed group** of workers, to a greater or lesser extent, performs roles and makes decisions traditionally reserved for management.[6] Self-directed work groups, at least by some authorities, are being hailed as "one of the most powerful strategies available to employers today."

Work teams perform various functions. As shown in Table 3.2, the results of *Training's* Industry Report Survey indicate that in half of all cases, self-directed work groups perform at least one of four roles: manage their own work schedules, deal directly with customers or clients in some way, set production quotas or performance targets, and train members of the group. Least common of the managerial functions that self-directed groups are allowed to perform on their own are hiring and firing. Thus it appears that employers are willing to allow work groups to make decisions about work activities but are less inclined to allow groups to make decisions concerning personnel.

> *self-directed group-performs roles and makes decisions traditionally reserved for managment*

Table 3.2 Functions Performed by Self-directed Work Groups

Function or Activity	Percentage of Work Groups
Set Work Schedules	69
Deal Directly with External Customers	59
Set Production Quotas, Performance Targets	57
Conduct Training	55
Purchase Equipment or Services	47
Deal with Vendors/Suppliers	46
Appraise Performance	37
Establish Budgets	35
Hire New Employees	29
Fire Employees	21

Source: Jack Gordon. "Work Teams: How Far Have They Come?" Training, October 1992, 63.

Self-directed work groups have been used by a number of companies, which have reported positive results. Goodyear, for example, reportedly doubled daily tire production without adding personnel. General Mills

---

[6]Jack Gordon. "Work Teams: How Far Have They Come?" *Training*. October 1992, 62.

South of the Border: Understanding the Culture

Mexico is just across the border. How different can the cultures be? Significantly different, say North American managers of a *maquiladora* (assembly plant owned by a United States corporation, but located south of the border).

"To get anything done here, the manager has to be more of an instructor, teacher, or father figure than a boss," says Robert Hoskins, who manages a *maquiladora* for Little Neck, New York-based Leviton Manufacturing Company, in the border city of Ciudad Juarez. Indeed, Ken Franklin, who manages assembly plants at Juarez's giant Bermudez Industrial Park, visits the production line every day at 6 A.M. to greet each worker individually. "In Mexico, everything is a personal matter," he says. "But a lot of managers don't get it." To emphasize the need for a good human relations program, one only has to look at the heavy turnover of both labor and management employees. The turnover of Mexican *maquiladora* workers is an eye-popping 12 percent a month. A less publicized problem has been the rapid burnout of North American managers along the border.

The Mexicans are a relaxed, hospitable, and warm people who may relate more to their Indian than Spanish heritage. They are proud, patriotic, and family oriented, and very hard working. Emotional, with a leisurely sense of time, Mexicans are generally comfortable with themselves and others. When dealing with Mexicans, it is wise for North Americans to take time for conversation and socialization. To avoid culture-based misunderstandings, it is also wise for Americans to remember:

▶   In conversations, Mexicans tend to maximize differences between persons due to sex, status, or age in contrast to North Americans who

attributed a 40 percent increase in productivity to self-directed work groups. Federal Express cited a 13 percent decrease in service errors. Advocates of self-directed work groups believe that when a group of workers are given the opportunity to make decisions, they accept "ownership" of work outcomes. Heightened employee morale and improved interaction among members of the work group are also cited as positive outcomes.

Table 3.3 compares operating procedures in traditionally managed group settings and in self-directed group environments. It should be noted, however, that not everyone embraces self-directed groups with enthusiasm. Some managers feel threatened and disenfranchised and in some situations have sabotaged the establishment of self-directed groups. In other cases, workers have heard a lot of work group talk from managers, but members of the work group have not been empowered to make decisions and, as a result, nothing really changes.

often minimize them (e.g., Mexicans defer to one of higher authority, and may say what they think the person wants to hear; reality for them is not just objective but interpersonal, so they may reply in a way that makes the receiver happy although it may not be fact).

▶ Mexicans take special occasions very, very seriously. A boss who gets into the spirit when a worker celebrates a birthday will show that he is *simpatico*, and that will keep productivity high and turnover low.

▶ *Pelado,* or "the plucked one," may express the essence of the national character (e.g., Mexicans often view themselves as being at the bottom of the pecking order, like a child before a parent or conquistador, so their cultural themes express self-doubt, frustration, and a tragic outlook on life). Many exhibit child-like behavior as a defense against feelings of inferiority.

▶ *Respeto,* or respect, in Mexico is an emotionally charged word bound up with values of equality, fair play, and democratic spirit and may involve in a relationship, pressures of power, possible threat, and love-hate affections.

As United States companies head south to Mexico in the pursuit of freer trade and the continued development of regional blocs, better understanding of each nation's culture is essential to the establishment of harmonious relationships.

Sources: Moffett, Matt. "Culture Shock." The Wall Street Journal Reports. September 24, 1992, R–13.

"How Different Is Mexico?" The Wall Street Journal Reports. September 24, 1992, R–14.

Harris Phillip, and Robert Moran. Managing Cultural Differences. Houston: Gulf, 1991, 376–37.

Federal Express had a 13 percent decrease in service errors resulting from use of self-directed work groups.

Table 3.3 A Comparison of Directed and Self-directed Groups

Traditional Work Group Problems	Self-directed Work Group Solutions
▶ Projects wait for supervisor approval	▶ Supervisors move from being watchdogs to expert advisors
▶ Focus is on getting the work done	▶ Focus is on getting the work done right
▶ Quality and costs are management's responsibility	▶ Goals for quality and cost are group-monitored
▶ Supervisors act as conflict referees	▶ Disputes are resolved by the group
▶ Supervisor sets and controls group goals	▶ Work group develops goals as a team
▶ Management promotes morale and motivation	▶ Performance standards are rewarded/remedied by the group
▶ Performance is evaluated by management	▶ Performance standards are rewarded/remedied by the group
▶ Employees and managers may be at odds	▶ Group members share in daily problem-solving and decision-making

task-oriented leadership-getting job done with greatest efficiency

people-oriented leadership-building a contented, cooperative work group

Considering all sizes and all types of organizations, however, self-directed work groups appear to have experienced more intrinsic job satisfaction than those directed by a manager. Experts in management science are quick to distinguish two major leadership types: **task-oriented leadership,** that is, getting the job done with maximum efficiency, and **people-oriented leadership,** that is, building a contented and cooperative work group. There is little doubt that employees working under people-oriented leadership are content with their manager or supervisor, while those working under task-oriented leadership favor self-direction.

*B*uilding the Work Group

Getting the best from a work group is dependent upon bringing the correct mix of people together. Group members who are too homogeneous tend to look inward, resist change, and oppose self-criticism and become inflexible. To get the best mix, the following pointers may be helpful.

▶ Think carefully about the size of the group. Choose just enough people so each person has a specified task or role to assume.

▶ Establish a heterogeneous group by choosing people with different skills, areas of expertise, and backgrounds.

► Emphasize that each member of the group can make suggestions and that each member's ideas merit a fair hearing.

► Allow an appropriate length of time in the decision-making process for reexamination of the merits of each idea. Hasty decisions and the reluctance to reexamine ideas that have been criticized may lead to faulty group outcomes.

► Encourage the work group to seek outside advice when they need it. A work group should act on the best information available, regardless of its source.

Efforts to create a work group should be characterized by attention devoted to improving communication, reducing conflict, generating cohesion, and nurturing commitment among work group members.

Communications

Horizontal communications, that is, communications among employees at the same level, should be the strongest flow of information in work groups. To accomplish work goals, members of work groups find it essential to communicate with other members who will help achieve the group's goal. The members of a group who are most valued for their abilities to contribute to the group's goals give the best information and advice; in short, the members who can communicate.

On occasion, communication within a group may be disrupted by a deliberately planted rumor. Experts in the behavioral sciences have concluded that people will initiate and spread rumors in two types of situations: when they are confused and unclear about what is happening and when they feel powerless to affect their own destinies.

▼
horizontal communications-communications among employees at the same level

Scott Greenspan believed that the new homeowner was being victimized. He had looked on in astonishment while members of his field crew, from the county assessor's office, overruled his recommendation for the appraised value of a newly constructed home. In Scott's opinion, the field crew had erred by placing an assessed value on the property which was substantially above homes of comparable value. When Scott protested, one of the crew members said, "We have to make sure homeowners pay a large amount of dough, so the tax-eaters can make more sandwiches." Without really thinking, Scott replied: "Well, I wonder how many of us will still have jobs after the joint review boards established by the County's Department of Revenue and the Taxpayer's Federation finish their review of our assessments." Some members of the field crew appeared nervous as a result of Scott's statement. Later, Scott tried to analyze his own uncharacteristic behavior, because the fact was: review boards did not really exist.

Members of a work group tend to direct their communications to those who can make them feel more secure and gratify their needs rather than to those who threaten them, make them feel anxious, and generally provide nonrewarding experiences. There is evidence that employees are reluctant to ask for help in some situations, because this might be interpreted as a threatening admission of inadequacy. Then, too, members of a work group may delete from their communications any references to their mistakes or errors in judgment.

Employees tend to communicate as if they are attempting to improve their positions. Workers may not be cognizant of their own behavior in this respect, but evidence indicates they want to increase their status, belong to a more prestigious group, gain more power to influence decisions, and expand their authority. Perhaps that is why Scott Greenspan reacted as described earlier. Persons attracted to membership in a particular group will be inclined to direct more communication in that direction than will those who do not want to belong.

Members of a work group should recognize that the effect of any particular communication depends largely upon the prior feelings and attitudes that workers have toward one another. While it is possible that feelings and attitudes may change, the attitudes and feelings of people often become polarized: those who were initially positive become more positive and those who began by being negative become even more negative.

The effect of any particular communication is also dependent upon the preexisting expectations and motives of the communicating persons. In a discussion about ways to accomplish a complex work task, for example, one party may believe the motive is to increase productivity, another party may believe the motive is to reduce labor costs, and yet another party sees the motive as finding an easier way to get the work completed.

Communications in human relations is so important that later chapters have been devoted to the topic. It should be clear to most people studying human relations that what is often called communications problems are often only symptoms of other difficulties which exist among members of a work group. Four problems which members of work groups must solve in order to facilitate communication include:

1. The problem of understanding and reaching common agreement about the social structure of the group, that is, questions concerning work, authority, prestige, and status.

2. The problem of creating interdependence among members: common goals and agreement about ways to achieve them.

3. The problem of trust or lack of trust among members of the group.

4. The problem of exacting credit for contributions by members of the group.

Conflict

Conflict among members of a group sometimes arises over leadership, power, and influence and sometimes because of perceptions of inequity. Some conflict is inevitable. **Interpersonal conflict** occurs between two or more persons when attitudes, motives, values, expectations, or activities are incompatible and if those people perceive themselves to be in disagreement.[7] There are times, strangely enough, when conflict may be beneficial. For example, conflict may

► generate different solutions to the problem

► bring arguments and areas of disagreement out into the open

► provide a means for the release of conflicting ideas

► define power relationships within the group.

On the other hand, conflict may prove to be destructive. Examples include:

► Reason becomes secondary to emotions.

► Splinter groups or factions are created.

► Goals become subverted.

► Defensive and offensive behavior becomes prevalent.

Much of the conflict that occurs within work groups is not confronted openly; instead, it is ignored. Sometimes, members of a group choose to deny the existence of conflict. If the issue is not critical, this may be an effective way to deal with the conflict. In other cases, members of the group may choose to suppress the conflict; that is, the conflict is smoothed over and group members simply agree that major differences do not exist. Another way to handle conflict is through compromise. Parties involved in the conflict modify their positions and views until agreement is reached. Finally, in conflicts where a dominant or prevailing position is accepted, the conflict may be resolved quickly. The disadvantage of dominance is that it divides the members of the group into winners and losers.

Conflicts can help build relationships, be a catalyst for change, and force members of a work group to face thorny issues. The following tips may prove helpful to members of work groups.

► Face disagreements before they turn into bigger conflicts. However, it may be acceptable to ignore an issue if it is minor, if parties could benefit from cooling-off time, or if the positions are irreconcilable.

► Try to resolve conflicts by influencing others, not forcing them.

---

[7] Jack Hart. *Managing People at Work*. London: McGraw-Hill, 1979, 64.

- ► Use your best listening skills. Don't interrupt. Demonstrate your interest with nonverbal cues (nodding, leaning forward). Summarize the other person's words. Ask questions.

- ► Clearly define what each person thinks is the problem. Each person may see it quite differently based on their values, beliefs, and experiences.

- ► Tell the other person that you believe he or she had good intentions.

- ► Let the other person vent emotions. Acknowledge them ("I can see you're angry"). This takes people off the defensive and encourages them to talk.

- ► Avoid conflicts by routinely exploring other people's expectations. Don't assume you understand what they mean. Ask clarifying questions.

- ► Work to prevent conflicts. Build positive relationships. Get to know your working colleagues.

Cohesion

Cohesion is the group's ability to stick together. Cohesion can enhance job satisfaction and work group productivity. Research has shown that cohesive groups experience less negative conflict. Members of cohesive groups assist each other. In general, cohesive groups tend to be more democratic, friendly, and orderly than noncohesive groups. Members appear to have more empathy for one another; they are more receptive to the ideas of others; and they seem to enjoy each other's companionship.

Numerous researchers in the behavioral sciences have attempted to determine why cohesion exists in some groups, yet is absent in others. While length of time the group members have been together may con-

Cohesion among group members can enhance job satisfaction and work group productivity.

tribute to cohesiveness, exceptions have been noted. A ten-day road trip, for example, may not foster cohesion among members of a college baseball team. Group-serving attributes have been found to be more important. When players blame themselves for failure and share responsibility for success, cohesion among group members is forming. Humor has been linked to cohesion by several researchers. Joking and laughing together creates better social relations among members. A common cause, which is accepted by all members of the work group, is a strong force in creating a cohesive group. In some cases, an outside threat to a group of workers may be sufficient to promote cohesiveness.

Faculty members teaching in the dance program at a large university in the southwest region of the country were constantly bickering. Housed in the Department of Physical Education and Recreation, some members of the group were pleased with the organizational structure; others wished to move the program to a department in the College of Fine Arts. Then, too, a number of disagreements had occurred about the curriculum. Morale was sagging and, in fact, some of the faculty members avoided others as much as possible.

As a result of financial constraints, the Board of Trustees announced that some programs would have to be eliminated, and the dance program was among those being considered. Almost overnight, the faculty associated with the dance program became a highly cohesive group striving for a common purpose.

Cohesiveness among members of work groups is desirable because it influences almost every facet of on-the-job behavior. Morale, productivity, order and discipline, interaction and communication, friendliness, willingness to accept the ideas of others, and cooperativeness are all trademarks of a cohesive work group.

Commitment

Commitment is defined as the state of being obligated or emotionally compelled. Commitment reflects an individual's willingness and desire to identify with and help achieve a group's goals or tasks. Commitment is associated with such variables as cohesion and an individual's satisfaction or dissatisfaction with the group's work tasks and goals.

It has long been proposed that participation by a work group's members in decision-making would increase their commitment and improve the group's performance. Perhaps this is one reason why the Japanese have experienced success with quality circles in manufacturing environments. Commitment is important to an employer as it indicates how much effort employees are willing to put into their work. In addition, there is an inverse relationship between employee turnover and employee commitment. Committed employees are less likely to leave; reduced turnover means reduced costs to an employer.

commitment-the state of being obligated or emotionally compelled

Determining Your Work Group Commitment

Read each of the statements below and choose the response that most closely corresponds to your reactions—"I strongly disagree," "I'm not quite sure," and so on. After responding to each statement, add the numbers together which represent your responses. In doing so, you will determine your work group commitment (WGC), that is, how committed you are to your work group. If you score 55 or above, your WGC is high, and it is likely, at least for the foreseeable future, that you will remain a member of your work group. If your score falls between 35 and 55, your WGC is average and your chances of leaving or remaining with your work group appear to be about even. If your score is below 35, your WGC is low and, given an acceptable opportunity, it is likely that you will leave your work group.

► I am pleased to be associated with the people whom I work with on a daily basis.

► Even if my work tasks proved to be less than challenging, I would be reluctant to leave my work group.

► I believe that members of my work group have accepted me as a valuable member.

► I believe that members of my work group provide mutual support for each other.

► The offer of more money either in another department or with a new employer would not seriously cause me to consider changing jobs.

Psychologists have been unable to explain fully why some people are so committed to their work that they become known as workaholics, yet others are content to loaf during work hours. There appear to be certain reasons, however, why individuals are committed to their work.

► Committed workers often come from families in which the work ethic is strongly emphasized.

► Committed workers tend to feel a need to achieve. Research has shown, for example, that successful entrepreneurs have a strong desire for accomplishment.

► Certain personality traits or characteristics appear to be present in individuals who are intensely competitive in their work.

► Some jobs simply mandate commitment. An individual pursuing a career as a doctor, for example, may hardly be able to escape from the job.

► To know that my coworkers value my opinions, respect me, and view me as a team player would please me.

Responses for each of the above statements:
1. No, I strongly disagree.
2. No, I disagree to a considerable extent.
3. No, I mildly disagree.
4. I am unsure.
5. Yes, I mildly agree.
6. Yes, I agree to a considerable extent.
7. Yes, I strongly agree.

► I sometimes consider leaving this work group.

► I am not willing to go out of my way to help my coworkers.

► I would not recommend a close friend to join my work group.

Responses for each of the above statements:
1 Yes, I strongly agree.
2. Yes, I agree to a considerable extent.
3. Yes, I mildly agree.
4. I am unsure.
5. No, I mildly disagree.
6. No, I disagree to a considerable extent.
7. No, I strongly disagree.

While commitment is considered to be a virtue, there may be side effects to overwork. Workaholics tend to neglect relationships both at home and at work. Family life may suffer. Researchers often subscribe to the Michigan Model, which in essence says that social isolation causes stress. Then, too, there is always the threat of burnout.

Members of work groups can be committed without placing themselves in potentially dangerous situations. Some suggestions for avoiding such situations include

► setting realistic goals

► varying the nature of skills used during a working day

► reducing anxiety by learning relaxation techniques

► engaging in strenuous exercise at least three times a week

► finding time for a stress recess at least once each week.

Work Group Participation

Many behavioral scientists believe that few techniques have been as successful in developing harmony and achieving goals as the development of participation by work groups. The simplicity of participation lies in its definition: to share in common with others. However, there is nothing simple about promoting and achieving work group participation, because members of the group often attempt to satisfy individual needs rather than group needs.

One or more of the following roles may be assumed by group members.

► The *initiator-contributor* suggests or proposes new ideas or different ways of approaching things.

► The *information seeker* wants clarification of comments, ideas, or suggestions.

► The *opinion seeker* wants clarification of the values pertinent to what the group is undertaking or clarification of the values involved in a suggestion.

► The *information giver* offers facts or generalizations that are "authoritative" or relate to his or her own experiences.

► The *opinion giver* states his or her values and beliefs.

► The *decision maker* brings the group discussion to closure by deciding what actions will be taken.

► The *elaborator* provides details (i.e., spells out suggestions in terms of examples, offers a rationale for suggestions made, or tries to deduce how an idea or suggestion would work).

► The *coordinator* tries to coordinate the activities of various members or subgroups and tries to pull various ideas and suggestions together.

► The *orienter* summarizes what has occurred, points to any departures from the course of action the group has agreed on, or raises questions about the direction the group is taking.

► The *evaluator-critic* questions the practicality, logic, facts, or procedure of some group discussions or group actions.

► The *energizer* prods the group to action or decision and attempts to stimulate the group to greater or higher-quality activity.[8]

Group participants often feel frustration and experience ineffectiveness in groups. Some people are reluctant to speak because they don't want to dominate the group. Others are all too willing to speak, but they have little to contribute. A lot of good discussion may occur, but no one records it,

[8]Gary D. Coleman, and Eileen M. VanAken, "Applying Small Group Dynamics to Improve Action Team Performance." *Employment Relations Today.* Autumn 1991, 348–49.

Unit 1·An Introduction to Human Relations

brings closure, or determines actions to be taken. No one is sure why this occurs. The question, however, has been posed: Are all groups that have no formal authority figure destined to lots of activity but little results?

If group participants are to achieve goals, that is, through the group process generate ideas, evaluate ideas, and choose the most promising ideas for implementation, the following group building and maintenance roles are essential.

▶ The *encourager* praises, agrees with, and accepts contributions of others.

▶ The *harmonizer* mediates the differences between other members, attempts to reconcile disagreements, and relieves tension in conflict situations.

▶ The *gatekeeper and expediter* attempts to keep communication channels open by encouraging or facilitating the participation of others or by proposing regulations on the flow of communication.

▶ The *standard setter* expresses standards for the group to attempt to achieve or applies standards in evaluating the quality of the group process.[9]

A group's problem-solving capacity is directly related to the interaction within the group. The more able the members, the more cooperative, and the more creative, the greater the odds are that the group will reach a good decision. Groups, however, are not infallible despite their collective wisdom and experience. Sometimes the phenomenon called groupthink occurs. **Groupthink** is a process of faulty decision-making that can sometimes occur when a group is particularly anxious to reach an unanimous decision. Groupthink is more likely to occur when statements such as the following are voiced.

▶ We all agree, so this has to be the best decision.

▶ This will, no doubt, benefit everyone.

▶ We know company executives will be pleased.

▶ We have examined all alternatives, and there is no reason to go over all the alternatives again.

▶ Since we have all agreed, let's go ahead.

It has also been suggested that group decision-making may be risky; that is, people may be unwilling to make risky decisions on their own, but when a group is involved, a tendency to pursue the risky option may be more acceptable. On the other hand, group decision-making may introduce greater caution. Discussion may lead a group that initially tended to be cautious to adopt an even more cautious approach. This phenomenon is known as **polarization.** Researchers continue to try to understand why group judgments tend to be more extreme than the judgments members would have made individually.

groupthink-a process of faulty decision-making that may occur when a group rushes to reach a unanimous decision

polarization-occurs when a group that tended to be cautious adopts an even more cautious approach

[9]Gary D. Coleman, and Eileen M. VanAken. "Applying Small Group Dynamics to Improve Action Team Performance." *Employment Relations Today.* Autumn 1991, 349.

Chapter 3 · Human Relations in Work Groups

Key Points Summary

- Fitting into a work group may be difficult because membership must be earned.

- To avoid exclusion, the new employee should observe others, watch for cues, and ask for help when needed.

- Appearance, mannerisms, cooperativeness, achievements, dependability, and showing up for work are among the attributes that help a worker create a good impression.

- New employees often encounter undesirable work assignments, and their positive reactions may earn them labels such as trustworthy, cooperative, and team player.

- Hazing incidents often are used as tests which a newcomer must pass before becoming accepted as a member of the group.

- Informal groups are formed because members discover they have common interests and they enjoy exchanging ideas, while formal work groups are composed of individuals who collectively possess all the skills necessary to complete the work assignment.

- A group's size and composition may be important variables in establishing effective working relationships.

- Conformity within work groups may come about because members desire to fit in; they do not wish to be singled out for criticism; they believe there is safety in numbers; and they believe nonconformity would signal dissension and conformity confirms shared interests and opinions.

- A self-directed work group performs roles and makes decisions traditionally reserved for management and, as a result, accepts "ownership" of work outcomes.

- Communications among employees at the same level should be the strongest flow of information in work groups.

- Interpersonal conflict is inevitable within groups; however, conflict often proves to be beneficial because different solutions to a problem are exposed, arguments and disagreements are brought out into the open, power relationships are defined, and conflicting ideas are released.

- Cohesiveness among members of work groups is desirable because it promotes better morale, higher productivity, order and discipline, interaction and communication, friendliness, cooperativeness, and willingness to accept the ideas of others.

- Commitment is considered a virtue; however, there may be negative side effects to overwork.

- Group building techniques should be employed to enable participants to achieve goals by generating ideas, evaluating ideas, and choosing the most promising ideas for implementation.

- Groupthink and group polarization may lead to infallible and cautious decisions and, therefore, should be guarded against.

Key Terms

buddy system	peer mentoring
cohesion	people-oriented leadership
commitment	polarization
deviant	project team
group	scapegoat
groupthink	self-directed group
hazing	task force
horizontal communications	task-oriented leadership
interpersonal conflict	tiger team

Discussion Questions

1. Why is work group participation an important element for making decisions in modern industry? Is it more important in some industries than in others? If so, identify some examples and provide a rationale for why you believe this is true.

2. Identify positive and negative outcomes of hazing incidents. Respond to the following: "Hazing is a sign of immaturity. It is usually practiced by delinquents and has no value in the workplace. Instead, it presents the potential for lasting damage."

3. What strategies would you recommend for a new worker who would like to demonstrate to other members of a work group that "we" should be emphasized instead of "I"?

4. Within this chapter, you were exposed to four C's—conformity, conflict, cohesion, and commitment. Cite examples how each C might be illuminated in each of the following groups.

    a. a university alumni association

    b. a club for singles

    c. an employee grievance committee

    d. dayshift workers at a fast-food restaurant

    e. chamber of commerce

5. Interview a representative of a work group of your choice. Ask the representative to identify an example of groupthink. Discuss.

6. Describe the following steps in attaining membership in a work group. What occurs during each of these steps: winning approval, paying dues, socialization, acceptance?

Chapter 4

Learning Objectives

Upon completing this chapter, you should be able to:

- Formulate strategies designed to groom employees to be good ambassadors for a firm.

- Identify the traits and characteristics of opinion leaders.

- Choose effective methods for providing interpersonal training for a group of employees.

- Identify both economic and noneconomic factors which may influence workers to join a labor union.

- Use terminology associated with labor unions.

- Understand the various roles of government and the interactions which occur between different levels of government and business organizations.

Human Relations and External Groups

My purpose in appearing before the Columbus Zoning Board is to protest the proposal by Tyler Construction Company to build multiple-housing units on the vacant lots at Washington Avenue and Jefferson Boulevard," the speaker explained. The speaker continued as he handed the petition to the chairperson of the Zoning Board, "I am serving as spokesperson for the Parkview Homeowner's Association, and you will note that all 167 homeowners have signed this petition opposing the request to rezone the proposed building site."

Jerry Burman, Operations Manager for Tyler Construction, listened intently as one homeowner after another from the Parkview subdivision made their way to the microphone to voice opposition to the proposed project. "Heavy construction trucks passing through a quiet residential area creating a hazard for children playing," "unacceptable levels of noise," "stirring of dust and dirt which will infiltrate our homes," "high-rise buildings which will block the scenic sunsets we have become accustomed to," and "increased traffic and possibly crime resulting from people residing in the units" were among the arguments presented by the dissenters.

Later, when Jerry provided a briefing for other officials at Tyler Construction, he said, "We simply failed to identify this group of homeowners who would be affected and we failed to address their concerns. As a result, we now have a problem."

External Groups

As discussed in Chapter 1, people within an organization also deal with people outside the organization—customers or clients, vendors, financial institutions, government agencies, the general public, and other constituencies. In Chapter 3, people outside the organization who have either a direct or indirect interest were referred to as external stakeholders. As illustrated in the above scenario, external groups should not be ignored. Influencing an organization's constituent publics through an open-system approach of interaction and communications is a complex task. Fortunately for the communicator, Americans have an unmatched penchant for organizing into common-interest groups. When this occurs, organizations such as Tyler Construction may address concerns, take precautions to allay fears, and exercise other strategies to satisfy the demands of the common-interest group.

The Community

An organization's relationships with its neighbors in a community are crucial because these neighbors supply the organization's workforce, provide loans to finance the organization's projects, set tax rates, and provide essential services, such as fire and police protection. They also buy the organization's products and services; sell the organization raw materials and supplies; design ads and record commercial messages for the organization; carry advertising messages to prospective clients and news releases to the general public; deliver raw materials and pick up outgoing orders; provide water, heat, and power; provide insurance to protect the organization's assets; and engage in various other transactions with the organization. The interdependence of an organization and its neighbors is clear. If transactions are to be conducted smoothly and successfully, relationships of a positive nature are of the utmost importance.

As mentioned earlier, it is essential to target messages and actions to common-interest groups. Such groups are illustrated in Figure 4.1. A word

Figure 4.1 **External Common-Interest Groups**

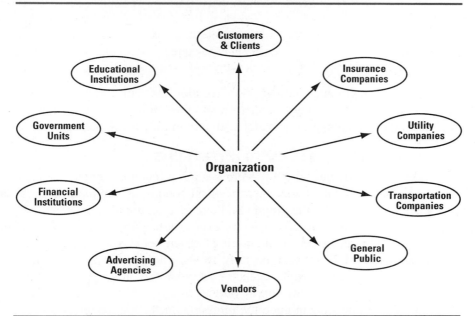

of caution should be noted: An organization, while addressing one specific common-interest group, must be consistent in what it says because the other common-interest groups may be eavesdropping. For example, an organization which tells its stockholders one thing but takes a different position with its employees will lose credibility. Then, too, there may be a question concerning an organization's ethics when one common-interest group is told something that is inconsistent with what another common-interest group is told.

The community, which is composed of various common-interest groups, is constantly changing. Most changes relate to the societal trends in the human environment. Some organizations are so sensitive to such changes that staff positions with responsibility for community relations or public relations may be established.

Community relations and public relations specialists study **demographic characteristics** of common-interest groups—population numbers and trends, ages, sex, family, households, incomes, education, and geographic location. They may also study **psychographic characteristics** of common-interest groups—lifestyles, personalities, and self-concepts. Demographic characteristics are useful in studying common-interest groups but do not reveal anything substantial about interests, likes and dislikes, and personality traits of individuals.

▼
demographic characteristics-refer to population numbers and trends, ages, sex, family, households, incomes, education, and geographic location

▼
psychographic characteristics-refer to lifestyles, personalities, and self-concepts

Derek Camby plays the trumpet for Twilight Sounds, a dance band in Culver City, California. The band is frequently booked in neighboring communities including Santa Monica, West Hollywood, Los Angeles, and Inglewood. When asked recently what types of information the band needed when booking an event, Derek replied: "Well, we need to know which songs are most popular among different audiences, whether a particular audience tolerates changes in popular songs or demands faithful renditions of them, and how hecklers, club owners, and groupies are best handled."

Psychographic characteristics are more difficult to obtain and measure, but Derek's band may find them worth the effort to understand the common-interest groups better with whom they must interact.

Community Change

Cities and villages, as well as organizations, cannot always anticipate events which will change their physical conditions and their destinies; and even if they could, they might be helpless to counter such events. The depletion of natural resources, for example, has impacted both communities and organizations. Gold mining created boom towns in the western regions of the country in the early 1800s. Many of those communities turned into ghost towns a decade later when the mines failed. Organizations, such as mining supply outlets, assayer offices, claims offices, and banks—all dependent upon the mining industry—were forced to cease operations.

Natural events, such as hurricanes, earthquakes, tornados, fires, and other disasters, sometimes change communities and organizations located in these communities.

In recent years, General Motors has closed plants, affecting the economic base of communities and, in some cases, other organizations that had supplied component parts and supplies to the plants. The United States government, too, has had a profound effect on many communities as military installations have been closed. Organizations located near such installations and dependent upon the bases have been affected in detrimental ways. Sometimes natural events, such as hurricanes, earthquakes, tornados, fires, and other disasters, may change communities and organizations located within these communities.

Common-interest groups change as communities change. Sometimes, members of the organization are able to anticipate change and, in some cases, may be able to devise strategies to cope with change. National boundaries are becoming less and less meaningful, for example. As **globalization**—the trend for businesses to operate throughout the world—continues, organizations will find that they must become involved. By 2030, the baby boom generation—the 76 million United States citizens born between 1946 and 1964—will be senior citizens. With fewer young workers to take their places, virtually every business organization will be affected. The workforce has recently undergone a major profile change as the surge of women joining it led to a dramatic growth in the number of

globalization-the trend for businesses to operate throughout the world

Chinese Protocol and Etiquette

One exciting avenue for the future is continued increases in imports and exports of products and services. Many business organizations are focusing their attention on Pacific Rim trade and the potentially huge China market. International airlines and hotel companies, for example, have their eyes on the potentially huge China tours and travel market. They see the potential for satisfying the needs and wants for flying, feeding, housing, and providing tours for huge numbers of people as China becomes the "in" place to visit and to conduct trade.

Success will be dependent upon how well Americans understand and adjust to Chinese protocol and etiquette. There are many cultural subtleties that must be appreciated and mastered. In China, for example, family names are given first. Chung Lin-Wu is addressed as Mr. Chung, not Chung or Lin-Wu. Chinese people dislike discourteous behavior and loss of self-control; visitors are well-advised to refrain from loud and boisterous actions.

If a visitor is invited for dinner, care should be taken to arrive on time or a little early. There may be many dishes, and it is polite, although not mandatory, to sample each one. When eating rice or soup, the visitor may hold the bowl close to his or her mouth. The chopsticks should be placed together on the table after finishing eating. The host may toast the visitor, and after a short time, the visitor should reciprocate by toasting the host. At a banquet, the guest may be expected to rise and make a brief speech responding to what the host says. People will leave soon after the meal, and the guest should make the first move to depart.

two-income families. In 1992, female workers, on average, earned about 72 percent of what male workers earned.[1] It is anticipated that the pay gap will narrow considerably in the future. It is these types of changes that members of organizations can predict and, subsequently, devise strategies for coping with their impacts.

Community Interactions

An organization's image is usually derived from the interactions which occur between the organization's representatives and representatives of common-interest groups within the community. While some business organizations spend large sums paying advertising agencies and public relations specialists to manufacture a desired image, a firm's reputation is determined by the satisfaction experienced by external individuals and groups as they interact with the business organization's representatives.

[1] Sharon Brownlee. "The Best of Times for American Women." *U.S. News and World Report.* January 13, 1992, 10.

At meetings, a person should be careful of using jargon, idioms, and humor that the Chinese do not understand. Expressions will be taken literally. In China red is considered a festive color, while white signifies death and mourning. Sensitive political or controversial issues should be avoided. The Chinese like to deal with quantitative data; advertisements filled with specifications are much better received in China than they are in the United States. Sports personalities and sporting events are also effective marketing vehicles in China.

The Chinese will provide a foreign visitor with an interpreter; therefore, it is not necessary to bring one's own or to understand the Chinese language. Negotiations may require lengthy communications and require months or even years to conclude. The Chinese negotiate as a team, and decisions are reached by a consensus of team members. Instead of interacting with a headstrong American entrepreneur, the Chinese would prefer to meet a team of experts at the negotiating table. The importance of careful preparation cannot be overstated because the Chinese team will be very astute and extremely well-prepared. The Chinese are tough negotiators, but it is possible to arrive at a fair deal in a smooth, nonconfrontational way.

Sources: Axtell, Roger E. Do's and Taboos Around the World. New York: Wiley, 1986, 183.

Horn, Mike Van. Pacific Rim Trade. New York: Amacom, 1989, 204–07.

Elizabeth Hendron reached a decision as to which community college she would attend. As a resident of Chenoa, Elizabeth's home was located halfway between Pontiac, Illinois, the home of Winston Churchill Community College, and Bloomington, Illinois, where Heartland Community College is located. Elizabeth visited both of the campuses to learn about their programs in floriculture. Unfortunately, at Winston Churchill she first met a rather surly parking attendant who shouted, "You can't park there. Why don't you read the signs?" Elizabeth then asked a student who was jogging if he could direct her to the admissions office. "There are campus maps at the visitors' center," the jogger uttered as he sped away. Even before Elizabeth reached the visitors' center, she could clearly see the sign on the door, "Closed." Finally, Elizabeth spotted the sign, "Admissions Office." In the office, she was greeted by a rather austere appearing lady who explained that she was an admissions counselor. When Elizabeth inquired about the college's floriculture program, she was told that she would need to make an appointment with the Dean of the Career Division, who was attending a meeting in Chicago. "It seems as if they were setting up unnecessary barriers instead of trying to help me," Elizabeth told her parents after returning home.

At Heartland Community College, Elizabeth encountered drastically different treatment. As she turned into the parking lot, she immediately noticed large signs with the marking, "Visitor Parking." As she left her car, she was greeted by a young woman on her way to class. After asking for directions to the admissions office, Elizabeth was surprised when the student went out of her way to accompany her to the destination. The middle-aged man who appeared after Elizabeth asked to speak with an admissions counselor had a nice smile. After carefully explaining the program in floriculture and the admission procedures, and providing other information, the counselor paged a guide to show Elizabeth some classrooms and labs, the library, and the greenhouses. The guide introduced Elizabeth to some faculty members they encountered during the tour. She also asked Elizabeth if she would like to talk with some of the students majoring in floriculture. Before Elizabeth left the campus, she was given toll-free Tele-Info telephone numbers which would enable her to listen to recorded information about 64 topics that new students frequently raise questions about. "It just seemed as if everyone I encountered was a good ambassador for Heartland," Elizabeth later told her parents.

All employers would like for their representatives to be perceived as good ambassadors by external individuals. As illustrated in Figure 4.2, the satisfaction or dissatisfaction derived from interactions between representa-

Figure 4.2 Satisfaction or Dissatisfaction Derived from Interaction

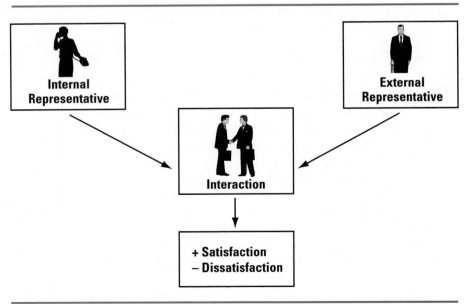

tives of the organization and external individuals is paramount in the firm's image and reputation as perceived by external individuals and groups. Ultimately, the firm's image or reputation may determine whether the firm prospers and survives or struggles and languishes.

Sometimes employees do not understand that their personal welfare is dependent upon the degree to which the employing organization succeeds. A prosperous business organization, for example, is better prepared to provide pay increases or additional employee benefits than one which is struggling to survive. Typically, firms experiencing success offer better job security for employees. Less successful organizations are characterized by downsizing and efforts to create a "leaner, meaner unit."

There may be other factors, however, that create problems for a firm's reputation and ultimately lead to the insecurity of employees' jobs.

Chicago-based Midway Connections pulled out of airports in Bloomington and Champaign, Illinois, and Kalamazoo, Michigan, in early 1994 as a result of financial problems. Dennis McLean, chief financial officer for Midway Connections, did not blame the airline's employees for the decrease in occupied seats. "Bad weather for winter flying had a big effect on the airline's revenues," McLean said. "For example, while normally an airline completes 97 percent of its flights, Midway Connections was able to complete only 80 percent in February," he said.[2]

While factors such as the weather may influence potential customers or clients to view a firm as being unreliable, employees who assume the role of good ambassadors have a tremendous impact on perceived images which potential customers or clients form.

Opinion Leaders

Identification of the influential leaders within the community is necessary for organizations seeking approval and support for specific issues. This may be a difficult task because opinion leaders may affiliate with different common-interest groups depending upon the issue. A prominent banker, whose opinions may influence others, may support a bond issue for a new high school. The banker, however, may oppose a bond issue for a new public library. Then, too, influential leaders may join in providing support for an issue, such as advocating a specific location for community tennis courts, but find themselves in opposition on another issue, such as promoting the community as a site for a new state prison.

The impact of opinion leaders is often quiet and behind the scenes. In other cases, opinion leaders—such as the press, radio, and TV, their editors and commentators—may be very loud and vocal. Opinion leaders may come from various members of the community, but frequently they represent

[2]Kathy McKinney. "Midway Leaves Area Creditors up in the Air." *The Pantagraph.* (Bloomington, Ill.), March 25, 1994, D–1.

The impact of opinion leaders in relation to issues is sometimes quiet and behind the scenes and at other times loud and vocal involving the press, radio, and TV and their editors and commentators.

► an employer and employees

► the press (newspapers, radio, TV)

► thought leaders (clergy, teachers, city officials, professional leaders, union officials, prominent citizens)

► leaders of fraternal, civic, and service groups

► crusaders, such as protest groups, petitioners, voice of the people, and representatives of such groups as the American Civil Liberties Union.

Opinion leaders may take an advocacy position or they may voice opposition. As a result of their position, either pro or con, others adopt the same stance. For this reason, it is essential that opinion leaders be identified.

Once opinion leaders have been identified, their support can be cultivated. If officials at Tyler Construction Company, discussed at the beginning of this chapter, had identified opinion leaders and addressed their concerns prior to the hearing scheduled before the Columbus Zoning Board, it might have been possible to avoid opposition to the proposal.

Almost any issue encounters the reactions of three groups. The three groups include advocates, independents, and dissidents. Advocates support the issue and will usually work to win its approval. Independents frequently don't care. They remain aloof and usually see no incentive for getting involved. Dissidents or resisters seldom can be won over. Their strength derives from being at odds, unconvertible, and uncontrollable. This group may include a segment that will stoutly resist change of almost any kind.

The key for most organizations is to win advocates for a proposal before they become dissidents.

Evansville, a southern Indiana city, has recently considered bringing riverboat gambling to the Ohio River, which flows along the city's southern boundaries. City officials could predict that some opinion leaders, such as the clergy, would certainly become dissidents. As a result, attention was focused upon providing information to taxpayers, civic leaders, and business owners and managers about how they could benefit from the proposal. A good starting point was an analysis of the benefits: jobs created as a result of the enterprise, a new source of tax revenues flowing into the city, increased tourism and additional visitors to the city who would patronize local business establishments, an additional recreation pursuit, and development of riverfront property.

While the advocacy of certain opinion leaders may be essential in winning approval, such advocacy should be won in an ethical manner. Overstating benefits or offering bribes are unacceptable strategies.

Building Goodwill

Goodwill describes the favor or prestige that an organization has acquired through relationships with external constituents. Goodwill is a valued intangible asset that every organization pursues. Employers expect every employee to make contributions directed toward earning goodwill for the organization; that is, through interactions with various constituents, employees should try to create a favorable impression for a firm, product, service, or organization.

goodwill-the favor or prestige that an organization has acquired

While actions which are taken to promote a favorable relationship with an external public or common-interest group are a public relations function, interpersonal relations between employees and external constituents occur constantly. The satisfaction or lack of satisfaction derived by the external constituents contributes in either a positive or negative way to goodwill. As a result, the organization must find ways of identifying special-interest publics or constituents and then find ways of appealing for the goodwill or support of those groups. Positive employee interactions are important as a strategy for winning goodwill.

The Human Factor

A fundamental and essential element of every business enterprise—either profit- or nonprofit-oriented—is people. People within the organization produce goods and services, and people outside the organization consume them. Often, the quality of goods or services is not enough; the public's perceptions of an enterprise's conduct also matters. A business enterprise may, as a result of the action of an employee, appear cold, greedy, and heedless of cherished social values.

In the early 1970s, the owner of a coffee shop in a small New Jersey community was enjoying a boom in business. Business flourished so much that an employee was added. Then, an ambitious young boy named Billy set up a stand just outside the coffee shop. Billy parked his small wagon containing a thermos of coffee and snacks near the entrance to the coffee shop. As customers approached the coffee shop, Billy sought their patronage by making derogatory remarks about the coffee shop's prices and the quality of the shop's food. The new employee chased Billy away and then a local health inspector, a friend of the employee, informed Billy that he could not sell without a license.

The national media picked up the story and depicted the coffee shop as a greedy, unethical firm that had taken unfair actions against an enterprising young man only 11 years old. Customers avoided the shop; phone callers denounced the owner; and business became so bad, the coffee shop closed. The message from this incident is clear. The action of a single employee can indeed be the catalyst which influences public opinion.

Consumerism

caveat emptor-let the buyer beware

The day when business could operate successfully using the Latin precept of *caveat emptor,* "Let the buyer beware," is long past. In today's society, sellers are expected to deliver goods and services of safe, acceptable quality on honest terms. Misleading claims and deceptive financial practices are considered to be misdemeanors. In fact, most organizations have subscribed to a marketing philosophy which in essence says, a company's total effort is guided by consumer demands for satisfaction. Each employee is expected to abide by this philosophy.

When thunderstorms knocked out electric service for a prolonged period during a July heat wave, the Baltimore Gas and Electric Company gave 7,000 customers free dry ice to preserve their perishable foods.

Representatives of the company who approved the action were sensitive to the marketing philosophy, and the result of their action sent a strong message to the public: "We are a company that cares about its customers."

Selling activities in past years were characterized by pushy salespeople trying to "fast talk" buyers into subscribing to magazines which they neither needed nor wanted or buying a used car which had undisclosed and hidden mechanical problems. In today's society, most salespeople are trained to use a consultation approach to selling, as depicted in Figure 4.3. The first step is an attempt to determine the customer's needs or wants. Salespeople ask questions to ascertain the customer's need for products and services, and they listen carefully. They then provide consultative assistance. Their demonstrations and sales presentations are designed to help the customer understand various features of the product or service and how such features meet his or her needs. After the customer reaches a purchas-

Figure 4.3 **Consultative Approach to Selling**

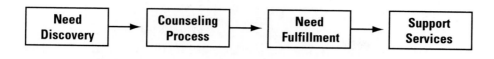

| Need Discovery | → | Counseling Process | → | Need Fulfillment | → | Support Services |

ing decision, the salesperson provides instruction on how to use and care for the new product. The salesperson also checks to see that delivery is made on time, contractual arrangements and promises are kept, and the customer is satisfied. When salespeople use the consultative approach, the interaction is likely to lead to a satisfied customer.

Press Relations

News about business organizations, whether the subject is a Marshall Field's department store in Chicago or Humana Hospital in Louisville, Kentucky, becomes known to the public through news media. Far too frequently, however, misunderstanding and suspicion between the business organization and the media result in stories that business representatives regard as inaccurate, incomplete, and biased against them. Editors and reporters, on the other hand, say that often they cannot publish or broadcast thorough, even-handed stories about business because many business representatives, uncooperative and wary, erect barriers against them. Then, too, they complain that some business representatives don't really understand the concept of objectivity and assume that any story involving unfavorable news about their company is intentionally biased.

Business representatives and media representatives function in a mutually dependent relationship. Business representatives are dependent upon the media to relay their communications to the public. Media representatives are dependent upon businesses for advertising dollars that support the media enterprise. Good relationships can be best achieved by the practice of a few basic principles: (1) be honest, (2) be cooperative, (3) avoid attempts at bribery, (4) exercise reason, and (5) know media personnel.

Be Honest. It is the job of the press to get the news, and they generally succeed one way or another. Anyone in the business organization who tries to thwart or block efforts to get the news will encounter tough opposition. A story candidly told, while perhaps embarrassing in its immediate impact, is less damaging than a cover-up version that generates rumors and suspicions much worse than reality. If a reactor in a nuclear power plant fails leading to a potentially disastrous meltdown, an employee at a savings and loan institution embezzles vast sums of money, or a toy manufacturer produces a product which is potentially dangerous for children, the best course is an honest, open communication policy.

Be Cooperative. A sure way to gain cooperation of media representatives is to provide them with facts, information, and pictures when they want them. Newspeople are appreciative of organizational representatives who respond promptly to their request for a biographical sketch of an employee who has just been selected to receive the Community Service Award.

Avoid Attempts at Bribery. Too often, attempts are made to influence the press by using advertising as a wedge. Most news reporters believe that advertising belongs in the advertising department and news belongs in news columns. Threats to withhold advertising as a means of keeping unfavorable stories out of the press will surely lead to conflicts and shattered relationships.

Marjorie Hendrix was livid as she read the Incognito Gourmet's appraisal of the food and service at the Aberdeen House, an upscale restaurant which she owned. She immediately grabbed the telephone and dialed the number of the local newspaper, the *Courier-Ledger*. Upon reaching the editor, Marjorie let her displeasure be known. "I want a retraction and an apology," she lamented. "And, furthermore, I want that incorrigible so-called connoisseur fired! After all, I've spent thousands of dollars for advertising space in your newspaper."

The primary service people in a service organization have direct and personal contact with customers.

While Marjorie felt betrayed—and perhaps she was treated unfairly—she should have recognized that the Incognito Gourmet was simply reporting a personal appraisal of the food and service encountered in her establishment. Perhaps she should reflect upon this statement contained in the book, *Service America*: "If you're not serving the customer, you'd better be serving someone who is."[3] In a service organization, people may be classified into three groups: (1) primary service people who have direct and personal contact with customers, (2) secondary service people who have only incidental contact with customers, and (3) service-support people who have no contact with customers. Marjorie would be well advised to analyze the activities of each group. Are the primary service people (waiters and waitresses) prompt and courteous when dealing with customers? Are the secondary service people (host, hostess, and cashier) polite, courteous, and helpful during their incidental contacts? Are the service support people (chefs, bakers, salad-makers) producing fresh, tasty, and nutritious food that appeals to customers? Such an analysis may not only produce more favorable results when the Incognito Gourmet calls again, it may lead to even greater numbers of satisfied customers.

Exercise Reason. When representatives of an organization expect or demand that the news media carry press releases which may be of little interest to readers and which may border on messages that should be presented in advertisements, relationships may become strained. In fact, it is not uncommon for media representatives to make comments such as, "We're constantly being bombarded by representatives of business organizations who try to convince us that they have a great idea for a news story about their firm, employees, products, or services. They're right. It is a great story idea for them, but not us. Our readers are simply not interested, and we resent being pressured to provide the free space." When members of an organization exercise reason in terms of the number of press releases and the content of the press releases, harmonious relationships can be cultivated with members of the press.

Know Media Personnel. Usually, employees in the upper echelons of an organization deal directly with representatives of the news media. This practice has the advantage of providing an authoritative spokesperson. There are, of course, exceptions to this practice. Regardless of who deals with the media, it is the responsibility of the employees to get to know media representatives. This requires continuous effort because press personnel tend to be transitory. The media representative is likely to be annoyed, however, when news releases are addressed to the person he or she has replaced. Facing the press is difficult for representatives of most firms. Such representatives will often admit that they are "scared" to be interviewed by news editors. Fears can be alleviated when the business representative knows the media representative and a trusting relationship can be established.

[3]Karl Albrecht, and Ron Zemke. *Service America.* Homewood, Ill.: Dow Jones/Irwin, 1985, 106.

Relationships with Other Firms

Most owners and professional managers recognize the importance of harmonious relationships between their employees and representatives of other firms. Business firms and other organizations are often dependent upon one another. For example, commercial airlines are dependent upon travel agencies; restaurants are dependent upon wholesale food distributors; contractors are dependent upon building supply centers; trucking companies are dependent upon manufacturers; and bookstores are dependent upon publishers. The reverse is also true; travel agencies are dependent upon commercial airlines; wholesale food distributors are dependent on restaurants; and so on. All firms may be dependent upon financial institutions, insurance companies, utility companies, among others. Likewise, financial institutions, insurance companies, utility companies, and others are dependent on the firms and organizations that depend upon them. When relationships between one or more dependent firms are disrupted, business activities are adversely affected.

The relationship between employees of dependent firms may lead to strained relationships between the two firms and possibly to a disruption of business activities.

A business executive, Kathy Marshall, got off the plane at Kansas City International Airport, collected her luggage, and moved to the bank of telephones under the sign, "Ground Transportation." She dialed the number of the hotel where she had reservations and was told that the hotel's van would pick her up in a few minutes. She waited just outside the terminal and soon the van arrived. A gum-chewing, wise-cracking teenager jumped out of the van, grabbed her luggage, threw it into the back of the van, climbed back into the driver's seat, and yelled, "Jump in!" Kathy climbed into the van, figured out how to close the door, and settled back into her seat for what turned out to be a wild ride.

The teenager drove as if the accelerator pedal was stuck on the floorboard. As he rounded curves and turned at intersections, Kathy was thrown from one side of the seat to the other. He puffed furiously on a cigarette as he drove, pausing often to swear at other drivers. He also treated his passenger to his taste in music, as the van's radio blared at maximum volume—almost shaking the van with the finest of acid rock fare. Upon arrival at the hotel, he dragged her luggage into the lobby and dumped it by the check-in desk.

Kathy headed straight to the concierge's desk to voice her displeasure. The concierge evidently wasn't having a good day because he suggested that in the future Kathy might wish to consider a taxicab. Upon checking in and arriving at her room, Kathy placed a long-distance call to her travel agency and voiced her complaint. The travel consultant from Kathy's agency immediately called the concierge, who reaffirmed his earlier suggestion to Kathy. The travel agency is now booking travelers into other

Unit 1 · An Introduction to Human Relations

Kansas City hotels and is recommending that clients avoid the hotel where Kathy stayed.

All business firms, as well as other business organizations, want to avoid curtailment of business activity caused by disagreements or misunderstandings between or among their employees. According to a study conducted by the Technical Assistance Research Programs for the U.S. Office of Consumer Affairs, the average customer who has had a problem with an organization tells nine or ten people about it. Thirteen percent of the people who have a problem with an organization recount the incident to more than 20 people. Thus when Kathy's travel consultant attends a conference with other travel agency personnel from across the country, the potential for relaying the experience to others is present and may lead to the curtailment of even more business activity.

Many managers or supervisors are so concerned about their employees' abilities to interact with others—both internal and external to the firm—that interpersonal skill training may be provided. **Interpersonal skill training** can be defined as programs designed to develop or improve skills which are used when dealing with others. Interpersonal skill training may be provided by academic institutions or in-company training programs. Frequently, companies contract with academic institutions to deliver interpersonal skill training to employees.

interpersonal skill training-programs designed to develop or improve skills which are used when dealing with others

The Need for Interpersonal Skill Training.

Before embarking upon any training program, it is important to identify the **developmental needs,** that is, the specific areas of improvement, which the program should address. Perhaps the employees are too abrasive, too blunt, too inconsiderate, or too self-centered. In other situations, employees might possess negative attitudes and personality traits which tend to clash with those of others. Employees may be intolerant of individuals who differ. Such differences may be based on gender, race, mental ability, physical condition, age, religion, ethnic heritage or culture, geographic origin, education, language or language usage, lifestyle, occupational position, or wealth. In other words, they have difficulty accepting people who are different. Some employees have difficulty showing respect to others; are unwilling to listen to coworkers, supervisors, or individuals external to the firm; dwell upon controversial topics and insist their viewpoints are the only acceptable solutions; use offensive language; and are unable to interact with others using diplomacy and tact. Employees may appear to be too aggressive, striving to accomplish personal goals regardless of the consequences to others. They may also appear to have inflated egos. Such employees may profit from interpersonal skill training.

developmental needs-the specific areas of improvement to be addressed by interpersonal skill training

Traditional Methods in Interpersonal Skill Training.

The very nature of human relations, involving the interactions between people, lends itself to a variety of useful methods of teaching. Most methods place the trainee in a participatory role and tend to be more effective than methods which place the trainee in a passive role.

Avoiding People Problems

Human relations has received much attention in supervisory training courses. "How to Get Along with People," "How to Motivate," "How to Handle Grievances," are common titles in such training programs, to say nothing of the shelves of books and stacks of magazine articles on the same subjects. Peter Drucker, a renowned management specialist, has stated, "The success and ultimately the survival of every business, large or small, depends in the last analysis on its ability to develop people. . . ." The responsibility for developing people belongs to every supervisor, manager, or executive. No individual is a good supervisor, manager, or executive unless that individual is also a good teacher.

The point to be emphasized here is that human relations training for employees is not a one-time undertaking. A company program in

▶ The *on-the-job training method* is sometimes selected, and, if this method is effective, the need for a good trainer is apparent. The trainer serves as a model, a coach, and an observer. Suggestions may be offered by the trainer, and good performance should be praised to build self-confidence.

▶ *Written materials* may be given to the trainee which explain the importance of good human relations skills. This method places the trainee in a passive learning situation and may be ineffective.

▶ *Lectures* are often chosen as a method of presenting material to large numbers of people. Unfortunately, lectures do not cater to individual needs and the learner is again placed in a passive learning mode. The trainer's ability to deliver a well-planned, interesting lecture can determine the effectiveness of the training. The lecture can be augmented with illustrative examples increasing the interest of the trainees.

▶ *Videotapes* depicting a variety of interpersonal interactions can be extremely valuable in providing human relations training. Discussions of strategies to improve interpersonal interactions can follow.

▶ *Role-playing* can also be useful as a method for depicting interpersonal interactions. Participants are given descriptions of the attitudes and behavior of the people they are to represent, and they then dramatize the characterization. Observers may provide feedback including recommendations about how role players might demonstrate better human relation skills.

human relations—regardless of how interesting and motivating—will not change the way people with different biases and interests react to one another over the long run. Human relations skills are based on attitudes. Attitude formation is based on a composite of experiences occurring at home, church, school, work, and in social settings. Because supervisors, managers, and executives cannot influence employees' experiences in these settings, they must continually assist employees in refining their human relations skills in the workplace. Many of the most costly, frustrating, and chronic dilemmas in the workplace have their roots in "people problems."

▶ *Simulation* is closely related to role-playing. Actual human relations problems may be simulated with the use of written materials and dramatization. For example, a trainee might be placed in a simulated setting where he or she would encounter an irate factory owner who had to shut down assembly lines because the trainee's firm had mislabeled component parts and shipped them to another state. Simulations allow trainees to refine human relations skills in a no-risk environment.

▶ *Case studies* provide a method of presenting a real or hypothetical situation or problem to a group. Group members analyze the problem, identify potential alternatives for resolving the problem, project probable consequences as a result of implementing each alternative, and then choose the most promising alternative as a solution for implementation. A hypothetical situation follows.

Devonshire Clinics are located within the southeastern region of the United States. The clinics operate in several large and medium-sized cities and are frequently selected as the health maintenance organization (HMO) by employees of organizations offering group health care plans. A large pharmaceuticals manufacturer and distributor recently introduced a new drug for the treatment of allergies. Samples were given to physicians at Devonshire, and two of the doctors gave patients the medication. Both patients suffered life-threatening side effects culminating in deep-seated mental depression. Both doctors were charged with malpractice in pending litigation. Needless to say, corporate executives at Devonshire are angry and, as a result, they are considering the suspension of business activities with the pharmaceuticals firm. Because Devonshire is such a valued customer, the pharmaceuticals firm is faced with a major problem. What strategy would be advisable for the pharmaceuticals firm? In what ways will human relations skills serve as elements of the strategy?

Most case problems affect individuals in organizations and cultivate group decision-making skills. They may also prove useful in cultivating trainees' abilities to engage in on-site decision making.

New Methods in Interpersonal Skill Training. Some newer techniques used in interpersonal skill training sessions include interactive media, programmed instruction, sensitivity training, and transactional analysis.

interactive media-a learning mode in which computer-assisted video hardware and interactive video software are used

► **Interactive media** places the trainee in a participatory learning mode in which computer-assisted video hardware and interactive video software are used. The software for the interactive video contains a variety of training scenarios involving interpersonal encounters. The trainee observes the scenario and selects an interactive alternative response. The selected response elicits a predetermined video response, and the interpersonal interaction continues. While interactive media is a newer, state-of-the-art training tool, its effectiveness is dependent upon the knowledge and creativity of the storyboard developer. The software requires time for development, and the training program may be costly. Once the

Interpersonal training is provided through use of computer-assisted hardware and interactive video software that place the trainee in a participatory mode.

program has been perfected, however, the cost may be lower than for other training alternatives.

▶ **Programmed instruction** is a self-teaching method which divides the material to be learned into small capsules of information called frames. The frames may be contained in an instructional booklet or presented by automated teaching machines, often a computer screen. The trainee can proceed at a self-determined rate and is given instant feedback.

programmed instruction-a self teaching method which divides the material into small capsules of information called frames

▶ **Sensitivity training** is a group process in which members learn to be more honest with each other, become more trusting of each other, and accept other points of view. Sensitivity training is concerned with one's feelings and the feelings of others. Within a sensitivity training group, participants are divested of status and authority. There are no problems to solve. Instead, the emphasis is placed upon understanding oneself and others. With no leadership or authority, group members gradually learn to be honest and open in their communication. They begin to trust one another and accept each other's points of view. In our society, people are conditioned culturally to shield their true feelings. The goal of sensitivity training is to provide an opportunity for emotions and feelings to be acknowledged, experienced, and shared. The hoped for result is change in behavior in individuals who tend to be intolerant and inflexible.

sensitivity training- group process where members learn to be more honest and trusting

▶ **Transactional analysis** is a method of studying communication by learning of the three ego states of child, adult, and parent. Proponents of transactional analysis believe that everyone's personality is made up of the three ego states. Muriel James and Dorothy Joneward, in their book, *Born to Win: Transactional Analysis with Gestalt Experiments,* demonstrate how transactional analysis can be applied to one's life.[4] In any of the three states—child, adult, or parent—an individual may hold very different attitudes toward himself or herself and coworkers. The feelings are defined in one of four possible classifications.

transactional analysis-a method of studying communication by learning the three ego states of child, adult, and parent

1. I'm OK—you're OK.
2. I'm OK—you're not OK.
3. I'm not OK—you're OK.
4. I'm not OK—you're not OK.

Table 4.1 contains the OK or not OK attitudes as associated with the three ego states. At one time or another, each person assumes each of the three ego states. It is not, however, uncommon for managers and supervisors to assume the parental ego state when dealing with employees. A study of transactional analysis may increase their ability, as well as that of other employees, to deal sensibly with others. Perhaps this in one reason why Sears, General Telephone Company, Pan American World Airline, and other corporations have experimented with such training.

⁴Muriel James, and Dorothy Joneward. *Born to Win: Transactional Analysis with Gestalt Experiments.* Reading, Mass.: Addison-Wesley, 1971.

Chapter 4 • Human Relations and External Groups

Table 4.1 Ego States and "OK-Not OK" Attitudes

Ego State	Child	Adult	Parent
OK	Negotiator Innovator	Communicator Offering Alternative	Supportive Informed Critic
NOT OK	Milquetoast Scatterbrain	Computer Always Testing	Dictator Do It My Way

Training in interpersonal skills represents a continuing responsibility for owners and managers of all types of organizations. New methods, training hardware and software, and individual abilities dictate that training not be considered finished after the worker assumes responsibility for a job. Human relations training programs should be provided for all employees, not merely for those who were recently hired.

Relations with Financial Institutions

For many organizations, harmonious relationships with individuals associated with financial institutions are crucial.

Paul Loomis was a successful athlete. After three years of playing in the National Basketball Association for pro teams, Paul suffered a career-ending injury. After looking around for other career options, Paul decided to purchase a "Use It Again" franchise, a sporting goods store that specializes in used sports equipment.

Paul's spirits sagged to a low ebb, however, when a financial counselor at the National Bank of Detroit informed him that his application for a long-term business loan was rejected. In checking Paul's background, bank officers discovered that Paul had had numerous altercations with the local police, most of which originated after fights they broke up in bars. The fact that Paul boycotted preseason practice sessions after team owners refused to renegotiate his contract was also a point of discussion during deliberations regarding his application. "I really question his stick-to-itiveness," said one loan officer.

A good relationship with financial institutions—commercial banks, venture capital firms, and small business investment companies—may be crucial for organizations faced with undercapitalization (not enough funds to start with), poor cash flow (cash in minus cash out), or inadequate expense control. At times, a firm may need financial assistance for daily operations, to manage accounts receivable, to finance the purchase of inventory, or to finance the purchases of major assets. The reputation of the firm and its record of harmonious interpersonal relationships may be important when a businessperson needs to borrow either short-term or long-term funds. Likewise, a firm that experiences good relationships with suppliers may be able to negotiate trade credit.

Good human relations with bankers, suppliers, and representatives of venture capital firms and business investment companies are necessary for most organizations. It is important for all members of the organization to be aware of the need to contribute to such relationships. Firms that maintain friendly and close relations with bankers may find it easier to negotiate unsecured loans, a line of credit, or a revolving credit agreement.

Relationships with Investors

As business firms grow, there usually comes a time when even more funds may be needed for a longer period of time. One way to obtain needed funds is to sell shares of the firm (stocks) or debt financing (bonds) to members of the public (investors). The reputation of the firm weighs heavily on investors' minds as they make investment decisions. If a firm enjoys a good reputation, it may find that its stocks and bonds are attractive to investors. In fact, if bonds are highly valued by investors, they may be classified as premium bonds (bonds that sell above their face value).

Good human relations with investors are important as well as publicity about human behavior within the firm. When employees are arrested for embezzling, managers are viewed as incompetent. When customers or clients charge the firm with unfair trade practices, the firm's ability to find investors willing to provide long-term financing may be impaired.

Relationships with Labor Unions

Unions are employee organizations whose main goal is to represent members in employee-management bargaining over job-related issues. Since unions are employee organizations, a question might legitimately be posed as to why relationships with unions are being examined in a chapter addressing human relations and external groups. Because labor unions are national and even international organizations, leadership is based outside the organization. Two types of labor unions exist in the United States: craft and industrial. A **craft union** consists of skilled workers in a specific craft or trade, such as carpenters, painters, machinists, and printers. An **industrial union,** on the other hand, is made up of all the workers in a given industry, regardless of their occupational skill level. Industrial unions include the United Steelworkers, the United Auto Workers, and the Amalgamated Clothing and Textile Workers Union.

labor unions-employee organizations that represent members in bargaining with management over job-related issues

craft union-skilled workers in a specific craft or trade

industrial union-made up of all workers in a given industry

The relationship between owners/managers and employees has never been smooth. Management has the responsibility to produce a profit through maximum productivity. Labor is interested in fair and competent managers, human dignity, and a reasonable share in the wealth their work produces. Because the goals are in opposition, workers united and formed unions which gave them more negotiating power and more political power.

History of Labor Unions. The first truly national union was the Knights of Labor, founded in 1869. By 1886, its membership swelled to 700,000 workers, but it later split into factions. The American Federation of Labor (AFL) was formed in 1886 and was made up of affiliated craft unions. In 1935, John L. Lewis, President of the United Mine Workers Union, broke with the AFL and formed the Congress of Industrial Organizations (CIO). The CIO grew rapidly in membership, and in 1955, under the leadership of George Meany, 16 million labor members merged to form the AFL-CIO. Today, over 100 labor unions are affiliated with the AFL-CIO, including the two largest labor unions: the Teamsters and the National Education Association.

During the 1980s, unions appeared to be losing appeal. This was attributed to a number of factors, including periods of high unemployment, a generation of new workers who grew up in the affluent and permissive 1960s and 1970s, the increasing popularity of Japanese styles of management where workers are treated as family and involved in decision-making, the shift of jobs from blue-collar to white-collar, and failure of unions—such as the Professional Air Traffic Controllers Organization—to protect the jobs of workers. (President Reagan dismissed air controllers when they went on strike in 1981.) The 1990s, however, appear to be characterized by a rekindled interest in labor unions. Some employees express an interest in unions because increased global competition and advanced technology have threatened their jobs. Some employees—especially female workers in the service industries—believe that their pay is below the standards of other industries. Since the early 1980s, the percentage of health care workers joining unions has risen. If unions are successful in attracting health care workers, can other service workers be far behind?

Employee-Management Issues for Today. A number of controversial employee-management issues appear to be growing. Among the issues are the following:

► Executive compensation, sometimes reaching $75 million annually, appears to be out of line.

► Golden parachutes, a hefty severance package for executives, seem unfair. Do executives deserve millions of dollars for losing their jobs?

► An equally pressing issue is that of pay equity for women. In 1992, women earned about 72 percent of what men earned.

► Early in the 1990s, sexual harassment became the third most critical employment issue, behind benefits and job security.

► With the increasing number of women in the workforce, child care issues are critical and will not go away.

► The spread of AIDS is a top national concern in the 1990s. AIDS testing, insurance, losses in productivity, absenteeism, and employee turnover are likely to become items of negotiation.

► Alcohol and drug abuse are also likely to be major concerns.

► Employee stock ownership plans (ESOPs) are becoming popular and are likely to continue into the 1990s.

► The movement of jobs to foreign developing countries, such as Taiwan and Mexico, where cheaper labor is available will continue to be an issue.

Sources of Dissension. Both unions (representing labor) and management (representing owners) possess a number of weapons which they may use to achieve their objectives. These weapons are tactics or strategies that when used have adverse effects on labor-management relationships.

Without doubt, the strike has historically been the most potent union tactic. A **strike** means that workers refuse to show up at work; in most cases, such actions cause operations to shut down. The strikers may **picket** the employing firm; that is, they walk around outside the employing organization's premises—often carrying signs—talking with media representatives and the public about injustices which they perceive to be occurring. In some cases, strikers have been known to engage in acts of violence when management countered by hiring **scabs,** that is, replacement workers who filled the jobs of strikers. Strikers may also attempt to disrupt any efforts to continue operations by stopping delivery trucks, blocking entrances, and using scare tactics to dissuade scabs from assuming their jobs.

Unions may also resort to boycotts in an attempt to achieve goals. A **primary boycott** occurs when union members, as well as the general public, are encouraged by the union to avoid conducting business transactions with the firm involved in the labor dispute. A **secondary boycott** is an attempt by the union to convince others to avoid conducting business transactions with a firm that is subjected to a primary boycott. While it is legal for union members to engage in primary boycotts, the Taft-Hartley Act appears to prohibit the use of secondary boycotts.

Members of the management team have sometimes resorted to **lock-outs,** that is, temporarily closing the business and denying employment to workers in an attempt to thwart labor demands. Members of the manage-

strike-a union tactic wherein workers refuse to show up at work

picket-strikers walk around the employer's premises, carrying signs and talking about perceived injustices

scabs-replacement workers who fill the jobs of strikers

primary boycott-union members and the public are encouraged to avoid business transactions with a firm involved in a labor dispute

secondary boycott-the union attempts to convince others to avoid conducting business with a firm that is the target of a primary boycott

lockouts-temporarily closing the business and denying employment to workers

The strike is the strongest weapon that union members possess in their quest to win concessions from management.

ment team may also seek an **injunction**—a court order which may order the workers to resume their work, limit the number of picketers that can be used during a strike, or otherwise deal with actions that may be detrimental to the welfare of the public. Historically, the owners and managers of some firms have used what was known as a **yellow-dog contract,** that is, potential employees had to agree not to join a union as a condition of employment. The Norris-LaGuardia Act, however, outlawed the use of yellow-dog contracts.

Government attitudes toward unionism, as expressed in acts passed by legislators, have varied considerably since workers initially sought to improve wages, job security, and working conditions. Table 4.2 contains highlights of the major provisions of labor legislation.

Table 4.2 **Labor Legislation**

Act	Year	Major Provisions
Norris-LaGuardia	1932	Outlawed yellow-dog contracts; restricted the issuance of court injunctions and guaranteed workers' rights to organize
Wagner (also known as the National Labor Relations Act)	1935	Encouraged collective bargaining and protected workers' rights to unionize. Created the National Labor Relations Board to investigate cases of alleged unfair labor practices
Fair Labor Standards Act	1938	Defined the 40-hour workweek; required time and a half for overtime; established a minimum wage
Taft-Hartley	1947	Prohibited a number of unfair labor union practices, such as coercing employees to join; discriminating against nonunion members; refusing to bargain with employers; and charging excessive initiation fees
Landrum-Griffin (also known as the Labor-Management Reporting and Disclosure Act)	1959	Protects individual union members from union corruption; guarantees each union member the right to vote in union elections and to sue the union for violation of rights

Operational Procedures. Today, labor tends to favor **union shops,** that is, a worker does not have to be a member to be hired, but must agree to join the union within a prescribed period of time (usually 30, 60, or 90 days) as a condition of continued employment. Prior to the Taft-Hartley Act in 1947, closed shops, in which workers had to be members of the union before they were hired, were common. The Act outlawed that practice, but did recognize the legality of union shops. The Act also gave states the power to pass **right-to-work laws,** and states enacting such legislation give the workers a right to determine whether or not to join the union.

Agency shops offer employment to all qualified workers, but nonunion workers have to pay a fee equal to union dues to the union. This arrangement is more acceptable to unions because it eliminates the "free riders" who might benefit from union negotiations without supporting the union financially, whereas in **open shops** membership is strictly voluntary and no fees are assessed nonmembers.

Unions engage in **collective bargaining,** a process of negotiating an employment contract with a firm's owners and/or managers, which specifies wages, fringe benefits, and conditions of employment. Union contracts, which typically cover a two- or three-year period, are often the result of days, weeks, and even months of discussion, disagreement, compromise, and eventual agreement. Upon agreement by the negotiating teams, union members must vote to accept or reject the contract. If it is rejected, the negotiating teams return to the bargaining table. If accepted, the contract is said to be **ratified.** On some occasions, however, negotiations break down. In such cases, the disagreement may be settled by **mediation,** the process of bringing in a third party (mediator) to make recommendations for the settlement of differences. If this process fails, **arbitration**—the process of bringing in an impartial third party (arbitrator) to render a binding, legally enforceable decision—may be instigated. **Voluntary arbitration** occurs when both union and owner/manager representatives decide to present their unresolved differences to an impartial third party. On rare occasions, the federal government has required both sides to submit to **compulsory arbitration.**

Even though the rights of union workers and owners/managers are specified in the contractual agreement, violations may occur. If a worker or workers believe that owners/managers are violating some provision of the contract, a **grievance,** or complaint may be filed. The grievance is first submitted to an immediate supervisor by the **shop steward,** a union member's representative in the organization. If the grievance is not resolved at this level, formal grievance procedures will follow with the complaint being addressed by higher level management representatives and union representatives. If no resolution is reached, an outside arbitrator may be mutually agreed upon and the arbitrator's decision becomes binding.

Establishing Cooperative Relationships. The owner/manager-union relationship may be parallel to the well-known Hatfield and McCoy feud. Historically, each side has viewed the other with suspicion and distrust. Each side has perceived the other as selfish and conniving. Owners/managers see the union as blocking the goals they wish to achieve, and union members view owners/managers as blindly ambitious in their pursuit of profit without regard for the welfare and needs of workers. Yet, labor (union members) and management (owners/managers) must find ways to cooperate, to work toward goals leading to mutual benefits, and to avoid conflicts if stable relationships are to exist.

Owners/managers should recognize that today's employees have more to offer. They are better educated than their predecessors and better prepared to engage in on-site decisions relating to their work. They want to be involved in shared decision-making. Moreover, they are likely to be more militant on issues which they are concerned about—environmental issues, for example. Owners/mangers should also be cognizant of the fact that while most workers are in situations where their basic needs have been satisfied, attention should not be wholly shifted to needs at other levels in the

collective bargaining- negotiating an employment contract which specifies wages, fringe benefits, and conditions of employment

ratified-union members vote to accept the contract

mediation-the process of bringing in a third party to make recommendations for settlement of differences

arbitration-the process of bringing in an impartial third party to render a binding, legally enforceable decision

voluntary arbitration-both union and owner/manager representatives decide to present unresolved differences to an impartial third party

compulsory arbitration- both sides are required by the federal government to submit their differences to a third party

grievance-a complaint filed by a worker who believes the contractual agreement has been violated

shop steward-a member of the organization who represents union members

hierarchy. The Plant Closing Notification Act of 1988, which required employers with more than 100 employees to give workers at least 60 days warning of a shutdown or massive layoff, was passed partially in response to workers' concerns relating to job security. In addition, it should be noted that organized labor supported the $1 billion Worker Readjustment Program which was created to assist workers displaced because of plant closings and/or massive layoffs.

All owners/managers, whether interacting with unionized or nonunionized workers, should demonstrate an appreciation for the contributions of employees.

Kay Nichols worked a routine eight-hour day as a secretary in an office of International Business Machines Corporation in Westchester County, New York. Then she went through a "career bend," as IBM calls it, and became a sales representative in New York City. Today, instead of pounding a typewriter, she sells IBM office equipment. Eager to advance—and to make her sales quota—she voluntarily puts in ten-hour days, or "whatever it takes," and loves it.

The 24-year-old Nichols does not go so far as to sing company songs at lunchtime, but her hard work and loyalty are typical of the benefits that IBM gets for offering near-total job security to its employees.[5]

Where unions and bargaining agreements are part of the relationship, a dual leadership is present, spurring divided loyalties. The owner/manager, by nature, tends to resent the intrusion and the loss of the right to deal directly with employees. Yet, if harmonious working relationships are to be established, representatives of the employer must treat employees with respect and demonstrate appreciation for the loyalty of employees.

While union members expect employers to fully accept collective-bargaining principles, employers have the right to expect union members to accept private ownership and operation of industry for a profit and of efficient productivity with the organization. Both parties should exhibit mutual trust in all dealings. Both parties should be willing to share information, keep communication lines open, and enter into consultation on matters of mutual concern. Communication must always be viewed as an indispensable tool for both parties. Both parties should also strive for prompt settlement of grievances.

Relationships with Legislators and Government

Good relationships with legislators and other government officials are becoming more important as governmental officials monitor both profit and nonprofit entities. In the area of human relations, for example, government

---

[5]Richard M. Hodgetts. *Management: Theory, Process and Practice.* Philadelphia: W.B. Saunders, 1979, 334–35.

over the past 20 years has instigated a number of initiatives under the umbrella term of *affirmative action programs.* **Affirmative action** means that employers aggressively seek a more equitable distribution of jobs among minorities in the communities in which they are located. The government has urged employers to do something affirmatively to compensate for past discrimination and to eliminate future restrictions on minority employees.

Pursuing affirmative action programs has led to some problems in the workplace. Nonminority employees have expressed negative comments at what they perceive to be preferential hiring treatment and arbitrary quotas of minority groups. The term **reverse discrimination** is used by nonminority workers to describe the problem of preferential treatment which may lead to fewer opportunities for other workers.

The Civil Rights Act of 1964 may have had more impact on relationships between employers and employees than any other legislative act. The Act was considered controversial and was amended a total of 97 times before final passage. Title VII of the Act prohibits discrimination in hiring, firing, compensation, apprenticeships, or training, as well as in terms, conditions, or privileges of employment based on race, religion, creed, sex, or national origin. Age was later added to the conditions set forth in the Act.

In 1972, the Equal Employment Opportunity Act (EEOA) was passed as an amendment to Title VII. This act strengthened the Equal Employment Opportunity Commission (EEOC), which was created by the Civil Rights Act. The Commission, for example, was permitted to set forth guidelines for acceptable employer conduct in administering equal employment opportunity. The Commission was granted the power of enforcement to ensure equal employment mandates are implemented.

In 1991, the Civil Rights Act again amended Title VII. Discrimination based on race, color, religion, sex, national origin, and disabilities was outlawed. Victims of such discrimination now have the right to a jury trial and punitive damages. Older employees (between 40 and 69) have also been guaranteed protection against discrimination in the workplace as a result of the Age Discrimination in Employment Act. This Act also prohibits mandatory retirement in most organizations before age 70.

Other important legislation includes the Equal Pay Act of 1963, which specifies that men and women who are performing equal jobs must be paid the same wage. The Occupational Safety and Health Act of 1970 (OSHA) regulated the degree to which employees can be exposed to hazardous substances and specified the safety equipment to be provided by the employer.

The government and its agencies look carefully into any improprieties concerning possible discrimination in hiring, firing, training, and so forth specifically related to race, sex, age, or disabilities.

During the early 1990s, two major controversies have been raised in federal legislative bodies. In 1991, the minimum wage was increased from $3.35 to $4.25 per hour. In 1994, Hillary Clinton's plan for national health

affirmative action-employers aggressively seek a more equitable distribution of jobs among minorities

reverse discrimination-preferential treatment which leads to fewer opportunities for other workers

Regulation May Take Time

The employees of Chicago's Metropolitan Water Reclamation District face difficulty if they want to socialize during their lunch breaks. One of their engineers, Kent Jones, a person with multiple sclerosis, is confined to a wheelchair and encounters difficulty entering a lot of restaurants. "In downtown Chicago, we're severely limited," he says. The problem is most restaurants have steps, leading upward or downward, which must be ascended or descended. Yet, according to the Americans with Disabilities Act (ADA), passed in 1990 and which required that businesses make "reasonable accommodations" to people with disabilities, Mr. Jones is entitled to rights such as access to public places.

Jones is among 43 million Americans with physical or mental disabilities. Within the group are large numbers of elderly people: 45 percent of people over 65 have physical disabilities to some degree.

insurance was released. Much of the controversy focused upon the effect of such legislation on business. While proponents of such legislation present strong arguments for increasing the minimum wage and providing health insurance for all workers, the question remains: Will the added expenditure cause business firms to lay off workers and increase prices?

Officials in employing organizations recognize that government at all levels—federal, state, and local—and business organizations interact in many ways. While the relationships may vary depending upon the level of government, business leaders want their organizations to be viewed as socially responsible entities which practice good citizenship. This is important because of the multiple interactions which may occur between units of government and business organizations. The government assumes many roles and interactions may take place as a result of any of these roles: consumer, employer, producer, regulator, allocator of resources, provider of services.

Consumer. As a consumer, government's appetite is exceeded only by the rest of the economy combined. Government purchases virtually every kind of item that is offered for sale. Furniture for government buildings; vehicles for the military, state police force, or local fire department; uniforms for conservation officers; food for the military, state prison, or local school are a few examples. Imagine how many light bulbs are replaced each day in the thousands of buildings operated by federal, state, and local units of government! To win the patronage of units of government, the practice of good human relations is essential. Sometimes an entire nation may be barred from doing business with a unit of government because of inhumane or unfair treatment of people.

(As age increases, so does the percentage—at age 70, the percentage goes up to 55 and by age 75, it jumps to 72 percent.)

Customers, including those with disabilities, can reach the food court, opened during summer 1993, by stairs or escalator in Chicago's Union Station. After the Illinois Alliance for Aging complained to local officials, plans for an elevator were formulated.

Robert Kilbury, executive director of the Coalition of Citizens with Disabilities in Illinois, points out that there is no policing of ADA. "Its enforcement is a complaint-driven process and it's going to take a lot of advocacy," he explains.

Adapted from: Leslie Whitaker, "Disability Laws Slow to Take Effect," (Commentary appearing in Modern Maturity) February-March, 1994, Regional.

Employer. Government is the biggest employer in the nation. Firms such as General Motors, IBM, Ford, Exxon, General Electric, and Westinghouse, which make people think big business, pale in comparison of the number of employees. Now think of the number of government employees interacting with employees of other firms. A number of these government employees have decision-making power; that is, they decide which firms will be monitored for adherence to strict air and water pollution standards, or if restaurants meet health and sanitation standards. Government interaction is a fact of everyday life. Harmonious relations with government employees are essential for all employees within a business firm.

Producer. While in most cases the government does not compete with private business organizations, the government nevertheless is an important producer. Much of this production is in the area of services, fire and police protection, military protection, garbage pick-up, and so forth. The government also produces public service projects as a contracting agency—streets and highways, bridges, dams, sewers, water lines, and other essential facilities. All business organizations use government services and facilities, and some contract with units of government to provide such services or construct such facilities.

Regulator. The opening scenario to this chapter illustrated one way in which government serves as a regulator. While government regulates private business and industry in areas in which the public interest, safety, or welfare is at stake, good relationships between government representatives and a business organization's representatives may be in the best interest of the business organization.

Sam Spade Would Be Proud

To keep their ranks clean of new Charles Keatings and Ivan Boeskys, companies say they are cracking down on potential troublemakers as they search for new employees. In an effort to screen out student cheaters, employers have become amateur detectives. Students who are caught cheating during their academic tenure have little hope of landing jobs with top companies, and for good reason. If students cheat in school, why wouldn't they cheat in the workplace where even more is at stake?

Only three years after graduation, David Bloom's star had risen. The art history major from Duke University had made a fortune in New York's financial markets by transforming a small investment service into a pecuniary gold mine. His love of art endeared him to the city's elite social set, and he was a regular at Manhattan's trendy nightspots and finest haberdasheries.

Was Bloom a financial genius? No, just a crook. The Securities and Exchange Commission charged Bloom with swindling 100 clients out of $10 million. Instead of investing clients' funds in stocks and securities, Bloom kept the money for himself. The once-cocky entrepreneur pled guilty to criminal fraud charges and was sentenced to an eight-year jail term.

David Bloom isn't the only college graduate who cheated to get ahead. Companies may be full of them, according to several recent studies of ethical behavior on college campuses and beyond. A comprehensive review of student attitudes by the Josephson Institute of Ethics in Los Angeles finds that 75 percent of all undergraduates say that they cheated at least once, and a survey of 300,000 college stu-

Allocator. Government assumes a role as allocator in determining how limited natural resources will be used. Examples of limited resources include oil, gas, water, forests, and some metals.

Provider. Some of the services provided by government, such as police and fire protection, have already been mentioned. The Social Security Administration also provides a service by collecting social security payments from employers and employees and disbursing financial benefits to millions of Americans—retired, disabled, or survivors of deceased workers.

Relationships with Special Groups

Business organizations may wish to cultivate harmonious working relationships with special groups, such as environmentalists, colleges and universi-

dents by the Higher Education Research Institute at UCLA revealed that 37 percent admitted to cheating on tests, while 57 percent said they had copied homework.

Acting on the premise, "If students cheat in school, why wouldn't they cheat on the job," employers are much more concerned today about making sure they hire honest people. Some employers require job candidates to take assessment tests designed to measure ethical behavior. Other are digging deeper into academic records and asking pointed interview questions.

A willingness among students to exaggerate past accomplishments in interviews—or even inflate their grade point average on a resume—is a sure sign of trouble, recruiters say. While GPAs are easily checked, some students feel pressured to appear smarter. According to a survey by Michigan State University, almost 90 percent of all campus recruiters say they check applicants for criminal convictions.

Wall Street scandals and the savings and loan crisis brought the focus of attention on deceitful actions within the workplace. To keep the ranks clean and to protect the interests of customers and clients, as well as those of coworkers, companies are increasing surveillance tactics as they examine potential employees' records of integrity.

Sources: Cole, Diane. "Companies Crack Down on Dishonesty." Managing Your Career. (College Edition of the National Business Employment Weekly) Spring, 1991, 8–11.

Hall, William D. Making the Right Decision. New York, Wiley, 1993, 1–9.

Hoffman, W. Michael, and Jennifer Mills Moore, eds. Business Ethics: Readings and Cases in Corporate Morality. New York: McGraw-Hill, 1990.

ties, sports enthusiasts, senior citizens, health conscious people, and almost any special group that can be identified. While their reasons may be varied, they can usually be traced to a simple question, "What's in it for me?" Perhaps the organization wishes to harvest timber, but an environmental group has voiced opposition. Maybe certain colleges or universities produce graduates who possess needed knowledge and skill, and the business organization hopes to recruit the graduates.

Interactions between employees of the business organization and representatives of the special groups often determine the extent to which the business organization is successful in accomplishing its goal. Effective human relations skills, when networked and practiced by all employees of the business organization, may be the most powerful approach that the organization has at its disposal.

*A*voiding Self-sabotaging Behavior

In all dealings with external groups, self-sabotaging behavior can create problems or cause others to react in negative ways. Here are some of the most blatant ways in which self-sabotaging behavior is exhibited.

► *Procrastinating.* Bankers, suppliers, coworkers, and others are not impressed by procrastinators. From time to time, we all put off what we don't want to do, but if you are chronically late with assignments and have to pull "all-nighters" to get the job done on time, you are engaging in self-sabotaging behavior.

► *Picking fights.* Some people appear to spring to life only when they are angry with someone—coworkers, bosses, spouses, other drivers, or someone with whom they disagree. No one likes to be around such people nor engage in business transactions with them.

► *Being a pessimist.* In almost every workplace, there are people who seem to thrive on finding reasons why something won't work. Instead of rolling up their sleeves and combatting the challenges, they enumerate reasons why the sales goals are too high, the new assembly methods won't work, or the weather is too hot or cold. A pessimist is always looking for barriers.

► *Being disorganized.* It is true that many of us seem to function well when surrounded by a certain amount of clutter. However, when we are so disorganized that we cannot function in a competent and efficient manner, we are sabotaging ourselves.

► *Lying.* Almost everyone stretches the truth at least a bit from time to time. If you are chronically dishonest, however, you will soon lose the respect of all the people with whom you interact. The old adage about "honesty is the best policy" is a wise resolution.

► *Stealing.* This can range from taking office supplies home or charging personal long-distance telephone calls to the company to more serious offenses such as stealing someone's wallet. Theft is a real problem in many workplaces today, and offenders may hold managerial and supervisory positions as well as rank-and-file operative positions.

► *Gossiping.* Most of us, from time to time, engage in a bit of gossiping. In almost every workplace, however, certain individuals become conduits for rumors, half-truths, and outright falsehoods about other people. Such individuals are self-sabotagers because no one trusts a gossip—neither members of internal nor external groups.

► *Lacking proper perspective.* We have all known people who blow up over the slightest incident. They imagine the worst at all times. Not only do they keep their own stress levels dangerously high, they affect the people around them. Their self-defeating behavior is obvious to everyone except themselves.

► *Projecting the wrong image.* People who fail to dress appropriately, who lack the good sense to practice basic hygiene, and who do not look, sound, or act like people holding similar positions may be their own worst enemies.

► *Expecting too much.* Some people expect too much from themselves and others. When this happens, they doom themselves and others to failure. Failure breeds a defeatist attitude. An individual possessing a self-perceived attitude of defeatism cannot expect others to be optimistic about his or her chances for success.

If we expect others to respond in an affirmative way, we must avoid or find ways to overcome self-sabotaging behavior.

*E*thics in Business

Perhaps nothing wins support from external groups as much as adherence to a strong code of ethics. We expect people in business, and even businesses themselves, to conduct their activities in an ethical manner. As discussed in Chapter 1, ethics is a code of conduct and values that is accepted by society as being right and proper. Employers and employees, for the most part, practice honesty, fairness, and adherence to the law. However, there is always the possibility of divergence from what is considered to be ethical and what is actually practiced.

*G*eneral Dynamics, the nation's largest defense contractor, allegedly billed the government improperly for entertainment and promotional costs. The Department of Defense held back on 1985 progress payments until the government had recovered $244 million that was inappropriately charged in the past.

The vast majority of Americans would probably agree with the adage, "Honesty is the best policy."

Business behavior impacts on others. As a result, business employers and employees must feel a sense of social responsibility to clients, customers, suppliers, other firms, financial institutions, investors, unions, government, the general public, and the community. Each of these groups has a vested interest in the firm and each deserves to be treated in an honest and fair manner.

- Because Americans have a penchant for organizing into common-interest groups, organizations may address concerns, take precautions to allay fears, and exercise other strategies to satisfy the demands of the common-interest group.

- Some organizations are so sensitive to external groups that staff positions with responsibility for external relations may be established. Specialists holding such positions study demographics—population, numbers and trends, ages, sex, family, households, incomes, education, and geographic location. They may also study psychographics—lifestyles, personalities, and self-concepts.

- Both common-interest groups and communities undergo change over a period of time.

- An organization's image is usually derived from the interactions which occur between the organization's representatives and representatives of common-interest groups.

- Identification of the influential leaders within the community is necessary for organizations seeking approval and support for specific issues.

- Goodwill describes the favor or prestige that an organization has acquired through relationships with external constituents and is a valued intangible asset that every organization pursues.

- The public's perceptions of an organization's conduct may be as important as the quality of goods or services produced.

- Today's salespeople use a consultative approach, that is, they help the customer understand how goods or services satisfy their needs.

- Business representatives and media representatives function in a mutually dependent relationship; thus, harmonious relationships based on honesty and cooperation are essential.

- Business firms are dependent upon one another. When human relations between employees of two dependent firms are strained, business activities may be disrupted.

- To improve employees' abilities to interact with others, interpersonal skill training may be provided.

- Methods of providing interpersonal skill training include on-the-job coaching, providing written materials, lectures, videotapes, role-playing, simulations, and case studies. Some newer techniques used in interpersonal skill training sessions include interactive media, programmed instruction, sensitivity training, and transactional analysis.

- Good human relations with bankers, suppliers, and representatives of venture capital firms and business investment companies are necessary for most organizations.

- Unions are employee organizations that have the main goal of representing members in employee-management bargaining over job-related issues.

- The 1990s appear to be characterized by a rekindled interest in labor unions. The rationale for renewed interests in unions is based on job insecurity, low pay in service industries, and controversial employee-management issues.

- Union tactics used to achieve goals include striking, picketing, engaging in primary boycotts, and—in the past—engaging in secondary boycotts.

- Management tactics used to achieve goals and combat union tactics include hiring scabs, seeking injunctions, resorting to lockouts, and—in the past—using yellow-dog contracts.

- Collective bargaining is a process which a union utilizes to negotiate an employment contract with a firm's owners and/or managers which specifies wages, fringe benefits, and conditions of employment.

- The government over the past 20 years has instigated a number of initiatives under the umbrella term, *affirmative action programs.* Affirmative action means that employers aggressively seek a more equitable distribution of jobs among minorities in the communities where they are located.

- Because the government assumes many roles—consumer, employer, producer, regulator, allocator of resources, and provider of services—business leaders seek harmonious relationships and strive to develop an image for their organizations which portrays socially responsible entities practicing good citizenship.

- Self-sabotaging behavior can create problems or cause others to react in negative ways. An individual engages in self-sabotaging behavior when procrastinating, picking fights, being a pessimist, being disorganized, lying, stealing, gossiping, demonstrating a lack of proper perspective, projecting the wrong image, and expecting too much.

- Perhaps nothing wins support from external groups as much as adherence to a strong code of ethics.

Key Terms

affirmative action	globalization
agency shops	goodwill
arbitration	grievance
caveat emptor	industrial union
collective bargaining	injunction
compulsory arbitration	interactive media
craft union	interpersonal skill training
demographic characteristics	lockouts
developmental needs	mediation

open shops	secondary boycott
picket	sensitivity training
primary boycott	shop steward
programmed instruction	strike
psychographic characteristics	transactional analysis
ratified	unions
reverse discrimination	union shops
right-to-work laws	voluntary arbitration
scabs	yellow-dog contract

Discussion Questions

1. What strategies would you recommend for an employer who would like all employees to serve as good ambassadors for the firm?

2. Identify the influential leaders within your community who would most likely be classified as opinion leaders. What common attributes or characteristics appear to be shared by the leaders you chose?

3. If you were asked to provide interpersonal training for a group of employees that was designed to help them overcome self-sabotaging behavior, what methods would you choose? Provide a rationale for your choices.

4. What conditions might influence a worker to join a labor union? Consider both economic and noneconomic factors.

5. Explain the difference between the following terms.

   arbitration/mediation

   craft unions/industrial unions

   discrimination/reverse discrimination

   primary boycott/secondary boycott

   strike/lockout

   compulsory arbitration/voluntary arbitration

6. Select a business organization within which you desire to hold a position. Which roles of government are of greatest benefit to the organization which you have selected? Devise some strategies for the business organization to follow in portraying responsible citizenship.

Unit 1

APPLICATIONS & CASES

Application 1

Addressing an Inefficient Employee

Donna Weiss operates a word processor for an insurance firm located in a suburb of Denver, Colorado. Donna has been with the firm for about six months, and her job usually consists of preparing reports. The reports are primarily manuscript copy prepared by using Word Perfect, version 6.0. Some of the reports contain graphics, and Donna has become very proficient in using Harvard Graphics software.

For the past month, Donna's work has been below par. She fails to catch errors even though her software program contains a spell-checker. Yesterday, you had to leave the office early and Donna was working on a report which you need for a meeting with other company executives today. When you arrived at work this morning, you found a note attached to the incomplete report stating that Donna did not have time to complete it and that she has a dental appointment this morning and will not be in until noon. As you peruse the incomplete report, you discover that it contains several errors.

Since you will be leaving for your meeting prior to Donna's arrival at the office, you decide to leave her a note stating your reaction to the incident.

Write the note from the stance which you believe a manager who adheres to Theory X would write. Write a second note from a manager who adheres to Theory Y. Finally, write a third note which depicts the position of a Theory Z manager.

Application 2

Fitting in at NCC

Maria McCloskey is a new faculty member at Northeastern Community College. After one semester in the position, she complained to one of her closest friends, "I don't think I'll ever fit in at NCC. I'm just a loner; the faculty members tend to go into their offices and close their doors. I guess I'm just being ignored, and I really haven't been able to establish an identity here."

This situation has not always existed at NCC. Until about two years ago, almost 90 percent of the faculty members would stop by the faculty lounge for coffee sometime each morning, depending upon their schedules. Then Dr. Lester Hill was hired as Dean of Faculty. Dr. Hill has never felt secure in his position. He finally concluded that members of the faculty were plotting his demise when they gathered in groups. Subsequently, he labeled the faculty lounge "the loser's room" and verbally assaulted those who congregated there. Soon, fewer and fewer faculty members stopped by for coffee; those who did, filled their cups and returned to their offices.

1. Provide Maria McCloskey with some pointers about how she might attain work group membership.
2. The chairperson of the faculty senate has asked Maria if she would be interested in serving on a committee to screen students and select a winner of the Estella Walters Scholarship. The committee is temporary and will be disbanded once a student is named winner. What difficulties might Maria encounter if she accepts the assignment?
3. Maria was selected to chair the committee. What suggestions can you offer her that would promote cohesion and commitment among committee members?

Application 3

Overcoming Bureaucracy

Describe an event in your life wherein you were frustrated by the rigid rules of bureaucracy. Then describe how practices might be changed to eliminate the bureaucracy which you encountered.

Application 4

Separating Social and Work Relationships

About six months ago, Steven Schwartz was promoted to a supervisory position at Extruded Alloys. Before the promotion, Steven had been close friends with Patrick Hart, a coworker and now his subordinate. In fact, both Steven's and Patrick's families socialized regularly, and both men played golf together and attended athletic events at the nearby university together.

Steven hoped the two could remain good friends after the promotion; however, he knew that he could not show favoritism. Steven commented to his wife, "There's nothing wrong with continuing to socialize with the Harts as long as I treat all people in my department fairly."

The last month, there has been a change in Patrick's habits. Twice he was late to work. Steven didn't say anything the first time, even though according to company policy a supervisor is supposed to give an oral warning after the first tardiness. A written notice is to be placed in the worker's file after the second offense. After the third offense, the worker is to be reprimanded by being suspended without pay for one-half of a day.

Unfortunately, Patrick was an hour late this morning. The dialogue between Steven and Patrick follows:

Steven: Pat, this is the third time you've been late this month. I don't really have a choice; I've got to put a written statement documenting your tardiness in your file.

Patrick: Oh, lighten up a little, Steve. I had car trouble. Give me a break this time and I'll make up the lost time.

Steven: I'd like to, Pat. But you know that if I did, I would be showing favoritism. I'm having trouble with Jerry Stoner getting to work on time. Evidently, he was at a bar again last night. He came in late and I suspended him until noon. If I overlook your tardiness, the other workers will complain.

Patrick: Well, I couldn't care less about Jerry's problems. I'm concerned about my own neck. You can overlook it this time. After all, doesn't my friendship mean anything to you?

1. Can an individual who holds a supervisory or managerial position maintain social friendships with the people he or she supervises? Provide a rationale to support your position.
2. How would you handle the situation if you were Steven?
3. Review Table 4.1, Ego States and "OK-Not OK" Attitudes. Which cell characterizes Patrick's behavior? Which cell characterizes Steven's behavior?

Application 5

Motivating a Subcontractor

You are the project coordinator for a contractor who is building a new $800,000 home for clients in Fox Chase Park, an upscale subdivision. The clients, husband and wife, are both surgeons and will be relocating to their new home in 90 days. Your orders are to have the home ready, complete with landscaping.

You have a problem centered around getting the electrical wiring installed. The electrical subcontractor is behind schedule and is causing other subcontractors to delay their work. The drywall installers, for example, cannot hang drywall until the wiring is in, and other tradespeople, such as plumbers, cannot install fixtures until the drywall is hung. You have contacted the electrical subcontractor several times and he replies, "You will just have to be patient. We have other jobs ahead of yours and we have experienced some labor difficulties."

Perplexed by the delays, you call your boss, who is the primary contractor. His reply is, "Find some way to motivate these electrical people to get the job done. With the demand for construction being what it is, it will be impossible to find another subcontractor. But make very sure the house is completed on time. Otherwise, I'll be paying a penalty for each day the job runs past the completion date."

1. How will you go about motivating the subcontractor?
2. What suggestions might you offer to your boss to prevent delays with subcontractors in the future?
3. What steps might you take to build mutual understanding and a stronger relationship with subcontractors?

Case 1

Women Need Not Apply

For more than a year now she has endured insults and intimidation. Her car has been egged and her parents' home has been spray-painted. She was even forced to move in with her attorney's family after receiving a death threat.

Meet Shannon Faulkner, an honors student from Powdersville, South Carolina. Her crime? Trying to attend The Citadel, a state-supported military college that for the past 151 years has barred women. Shannon strongly believes in equality for women and, as a child, she was taught to adhere to a family value, "Stand up for what you strongly believe in." "I don't think it's fair that taxpayers pay for a school that women can't go to," she says. The Citadel and Virginia Military Institute (VMI) are the only two publicly funded military colleges in the country that still refuse to admit women.

Forty years ago, the Supreme Court said in *Brown* v. *Board of Education* that states cannot maintain separate but equal schools for black and white students. The question now is whether that same principle bars single-sex institutions of higher education that are supported by public money.

The Citadel and VMI offer a unique educational experience. Both schools emphasize strict rules and discipline, along with a rigorous, military-style regimen that includes exhaustive physical exercise, spartan living quarters, and hazing by upperclassmen.

On her application, Faulkner omitted all references to her gender. The school accepted her in January 1993 and notified her six months later that she wouldn't be admitted because of her sex. In March 1993, Faulkner sued The Citadel and the state of South Carolina.

The state defendants argued that maintaining a single-sex college promotes diversity in educational opportunity. They argued that not all students want to attend coeducational institutions. In August 1993, a federal district court in South Carolina issued a preliminary injunction requiring The Citadel to admit Faulkner pending trial.

In January 1994, Faulkner began attending classes. After a trial during the summer of 1994, the court ruled The Citadel had violated Faulkner's right to equal protection of the laws. But the case isn't over yet. The defendants have appealed and obtained a stay of the lower court's August 1994 order. So Faulkner's status as a full-fledged member of the Corps of Cadets remains unsettled and she will continue as a day student until the appellate court renders its decision.*

1. In *Brown* v. *Board of Education,* the court ruled that separate but equal schools are unconstitutional if based on race. In your opinion, should separate but equal schools be constitutional if based on sex? Provide a rationale to support your response.
2. Since administrators at The Citadel obviously oppose the admission of Shannon Faulkner, do you think it is possible for harmonious relationships to exist between the administrators and Faulkner? between other students and Faulkner?
3. Which of the needs identified and arranged in Maslow's hierarchy would motivate Shannon Faulkner's behavior?
4. State defendants argued that maintaining a single-sex college promotes diversity. Prepare a position statement which counters the argument.
5. As a newcomer joining the group of Cadets at The Citadel, what advice would you offer Shannon Faulkner?

---

* Adapted from Michael D. Simpson, "Legal Times: Women Need Not Apply," NEA TODAY, Vol. 13, no. 5, December, 1994, 25.

Case 2

An Act of Civil Disobedience or a Remarkable Stand?

Tom Spiece is owner of R. I. Spiece Sales Company, Incorporated, a Wabash, Indiana-based chain of five northern Indiana stores that feature sports and athletic wear. The company opened a sixth store in Indianapolis in late fall, 1994. Industry experts say stores like Spiece are known as category killers because they cut into sales of jeans and footwear at mass merchants such as Target, or specialty retailers like The Finish Line.

Tom Spiece bought the business from his father in 1972 when gross sales totaled just over $1 million a year. In 1995, he expects to ring up over $30 million in sales.

Recently the 46-year-old Spiece spent most of August behind bars in the Huntington County Jail rather than obey a judge's order to turn over his company's employment records to state investigators. The investigators from the Indiana Department of Labor sought the records after it received an anonymous complaint that Spiece was employing 12- and 13-year olds and paying them under the table. Spiece demanded to know the source of the accusation. When state investigators wouldn't comply, he refused to turn over the records. The case ended up before a Wabash Circuit judge, who ordered Spiece to provide the records or go to jail. Spiece chose jail, saying the government had no right to rummage through his company's records based solely on an anonymous tip.

Spiece's refusal to comply with the judge's order might be characterized as an act of civil disobedience that solidified his folk hero image in his hometown and attracted national attention from the likes of *The Wall Street Journal* editors, who praised his "remarkable" stand against government intervention into business. It also exhibited the same intensity, competitiveness, showmanship, and downright pigheadedness that Spiece brings to whatever he does.

After three weeks of imprisonment, an angry Tom Spiece handed over the records which were examined by an investigator and the State Deputy Attorney General, who found no 12- and 13-year olds listed. "We're satisfied," the Deputy Attorney General told reporters gathered in the courthouse jury room. The retailer's employees, also present, applauded. They were wearing T-shirts, one with a picture of Uncle Sam saying, "I want you to free Tom Spiece" on the front and "It could be you!" on the back.

The case attracted the attention and support of several state legislators and businesspeople as well as local and national media. One state representative says he hopes to amend the law during the upcoming Indiana General Assembly to require the Labor Department to have probable cause before they demand a business's records.*

---

*Sources: Meyers Sharp, Jo Ellen . "Wabash Businessman Released from Jail." The Indianapolis Star. *August, 23 ,1994, F1–F2.*

———. I Don't Like to Be Told What to Do." The Indianapolis Star. *October 16, 1994, E-3 –E-11.*

1. What role was the Indiana Department of Labor assuming in Tom Spiece's business? For what reason?
2. Do you believe that Tom Spiece's refusal to turn over the records was justified? Why?
3. In your opinion, should Mr. Spiece be allowed to confront his accuser prior to being charged with an infraction of the law by employing underage workers?
4. If 12- and 13-year old youngsters had been allowed to work and had been paid less than the minimum wage, which act identified as labor legislation (see Table 4.2) would be the subject of violation?
5. Identify both the internal and external stakeholders likely to have a vested interest in the confrontation between Tom Spiece and the Indiana Department of Labor. Provide a rationale to support your identifications.
6. One might take the position that Mr. Spiece engaged in self-sabotaging behavior. In what ways did Mr. Spiece's behavior reveal such a tendency?

Case 3

Dual Careers: A New Phenomenon

Thad Sandler is a 34-year-old manager for a large city convention center. His wife, Carolyn, is a TV news reporter. They have one child, Alan, now six months old. Thad and Carolyn really hadn't planned ways to juggle their careers and family life. But when Alan arrived, career planning and family life suddenly became important. Thad and Carolyn are not in unique positions, however. Researchers have discovered that many dual-career couples, like the Sandlers, have not reached long-range career decisions regarding family lifestyle.

Dual-career families, however, face some real dilemmas. Relocations, child care, work versus family priorities, and a host of other problems may be encountered. If Carolyn is moving up in her career at the TV station, what happens if Thad gets a terrific job offer 600 miles away? What if the reverse occurs and Carolyn gets the terrific offer? What happens if the baby becomes ill? With a new baby, additional chores related to child care and housework become obvious. How will the chores be divided? As Alan gets older, PTA, recreational sports such as Little League or Scouts, and other time-consuming demands will need to be assumed.

Dual careers require planning. The plans should also be periodically reviewed. A couple with well-formulated plans in their mid-twenties may discover that their preferences have changed by the time they reach 30 years of age.

Employers, too, need to plan for employees with spouses also pursuing careers. This is a relatively new phenomenon in the workplace.

1. What are the issues faced by couples pursuing dual careers?
2. Has the phenomenon of dual careers influenced employers' policies as related to job sharing, flex time, paternity leave policies for men, transfer policies, and nepotism rules?

3. In your opinion, has the phenomenon of dual careers introduced more personal problems into the work environment? Explain.
4. How can dual-career couples minimize the problems of dual careers?
5. What are the advantages of dual careers? the disadvantages?

Case 4

Pyramid to Pancake: What It Really Means

If you still work for a large company, you may be fortunate. After all, one of every four jobs in Fortune 500 companies disappeared in the 1980s.

Middle managers have become an endangered species. During the 1980s, United States business—faced with a management structure that impeded creativity and productivity—slashed at least one million management jobs. And there are plenty of cuts to come. Most companies have middle managers on their hit lists.

According to William Bridges, a San Francisco consultant, "Until American companies find themselves in a better position, the pressure will be on to remove every bit of waste there is." By the year 2010, he predicts, the typical large business will have half as many management levels and one-third as many managerial positions.

While such cutbacks clearly take their toll on those who are fired, they won't be the only casualties. Surviving mangers will find that streamlined bureaucracies will force them to make traumatic adjustments in how they work. Workloads will increase while chances of promotion decrease. Lines of authority will get fuzzier and teamwork will become more crucial.

For workers accustomed to the excess baggage, the slimming down isn't easy. It changes the very nature of managerial jobs. "I tell my people I work for them. I am their servant," says Ted Sutyak, a general foreman who supervises 166 workers near Cleveland. The boss's job is to provide direction and guide group decision-making— to be a facilitator, a person who helps subordinates do their jobs.

Stephen Henson, a former marketing manager at Unisys Corporation, believes in streamlining management. "But when you flatten an organization, you must push decision-making down at the same time," he says. Management consultants say that, too often, companies seek to flatten their organization charts by simply eliminating jobs without analyzing business goals or what tasks are critical. Once jobs are cut, survivors are supposed to rebalance the workload among themselves.*

1. A close friend, presently enrolled in a community college and pursuing an Associate of Science Degree with a major in business administration, informed you that he or she plans to transfer to a university and major in production management. He or

---

*"From Pyramid to Pancake" by Thomas S. Boyle reprinted by permission of The Wall Street Journal Reports © 1990 Dow Jones & Company, Inc. All Rights Reserved.

she would like your opinion regarding the major which has been selected. What will you tell your friend?

2. If workloads assumed by managers continue to increase while chances for promotion decrease, what will motivate managers to remain at their jobs and continue the push toward higher levels of productivity?

3. In what ways will the roles of internal stakeholders of the organization change as a result of a flatter organizational structure?

4. In what ways will the roles/relationships between managers and subordinates change as a result of a flatter organizational structure?

5. Will flatter organizations eliminate isolated workers? Explain.

6. What rationale supports Ted Sutyak's statements, "I tell my people I work for them. I am their servant"?

Case 5

Workplace Diversity and Conflict

Larry Renaud, a janitor for the Central Okanagan School District in British Columbia and a member of the Seventh-Day Adventist Church, was fired by his school board for refusing to work on his sabbath. Renaud, whose Friday shift ended at 11 P.M., refused to work past sunset because his church forbids him to work on its sabbath from sundown Friday to sundown Saturday.

Renaud's union, Local 523 of the Canadian Union of Public Employees, failed to provide much help. Instead, the union took the position that "Minor interference or inconvenience is the price to be paid for religious freedom in a multicultural society." Further, the union argued that the integrity of its collective agreement was at stake. The school board, which had considered the possibility of creating a special shift for Renaud, beginning on Sunday and ending on Thursday, backed down in the face of a union grievance threat and dismissed the janitor.

As the case moved through Canadian courts, the union and the school district cited a 1977 case in which the U.S. Supreme Court said that granting an employee Saturdays off for religious reasons would lower the morale of other workers by giving one worker a privilege based on religion. The Supreme Court of Canada disagreed, saying accommodation in the Canadian context means providing "equal access to the workforce to people who would otherwise encounter serious barriers to entry."

The union and the school board were each ordered to pay about $6,000 in lost wages to Mr. Renaud and about $1,000 for emotional distress. In addition, the school board was ordered to offer Mr. Renaud its next available custodial position.*

1. Prepare a rationale to support the union's position that the integrity of its collective agreement was at stake if the school board switched Renaud's shift to Sunday through Thursday.

Scripps Howard News Service.

2. When an individual union member has a unique goal which differs from the common goals the union is working to achieve, should the union pursue the individual's goal? Give reasons.

3. In 1991, the U.S. Civil Rights Act was amended; discrimination based on race, color, religion, sex, national origin, and disabilities was outlawed. Why would the union and school board cite legal precedents which predated United States regulations?

4. Do you believe the Supreme Court of Canada should have ordered immediate reinstatement of Larry Renaud? Why?

Unit 2

The Essentials of Human Relations

Chapter 5
Interpersonal Communication

Chapter 6
Organizational Communication

Chapter 7
Human Needs and Motivation

Chapter 8
Job Satisfaction and Employee Morale

Applications & Cases

Interpersonal Communication

Antonio loved his job at the largest medical lab in the area. TechnoMed was a thriving business which provided services to several small-town hospitals and two regional hospitals. Antonio was director of client relations. He made sure all of TechnoMed's clientele, whether they were hospitals, doctors, small medical labs, or individuals, were kept informed. Tony sent regular communications to all the clients to tell them of new services or changes in services or to assist with solving client-lab differences.

One day Tony had a phone call from a doctor who was very perturbed. The doctor stated that she was not getting the same kinds of services that she was used to in the past—TechnoMed was not living up to her expectations. Tony checked his records and found that she was indeed receiving all the same services that other clients were receiving. Communications were being sent to her now just as they had been sent in the past. All of her lab work was being completed promptly, and results were being sent to her as soon as humanly possible.

Tony knew the lab had become extremely busy and there had been several new employees in the past few months. He felt that TechnoMed's services had not changed. He didn't want to lose a good client, and he wanted to make sure that there were no other complaints. But how could Tony make sure that communications and services were being completed as he thought? Did he have a communication problem of which he wasn't aware?

Learning Objectives

Upon completing this chapter, you should be able to:

- Explain the circular communication process for effective communication.

- Describe the characteristics of good verbal communication.

- Discuss the significance of nonverbal communication.

- Identify rules for effective written communication.

- Demonstrate listening skills appropriate for effective communication.

- Overcome challenges to effective communication.

communication-process of creating and sending a message to a receiver who will respond appropriately

A Communication Problem

Everyone, regardless of their job or personal situation, will at some time encounter a problem with communication. **Communication** is the process whereby a message is created and transmitted to a receiver who understands the message and responds accordingly. Tony wanted to make sure that he was doing his job. How could he determine what the problem was when he felt he was doing all he could do? Was there a problem with the postal service? Was the client receiving the reports but was not reading or filing them properly? Were there people in Tony's department who said they did tasks that never were performed? Was communication occurring?

Lack of communication is often at the root of problems that arise in an organization. All types of people make up our society, and those same people are found in the workplace. Workers often have different perceptions of what is communicated and may understand the same message differently. Some people don't listen very well and miss parts of the message; some people reach conclusions about the message before hearing it; and some people just aren't good at expressing themselves—their messages are incomplete or even incomprehensible.

Try the short exercise that follows. For each statement that is made, you have three choices: yes (Y) or no (N) or maybe (?). The correct responses can be found at the end of the chapter. This exercise helps illustrate that for communication to be complete and understandable, it is necessary to be specific in stating the message and the receiver of the message cannot make any questionable inferences or assumptions.

Figure 5.1 **The Cindy Snide Mystery**

Cindy Snide was found dead. Police officers have rounded up six suspects, all of whom are known criminals. All of them are known to have been near the scene of the death at the approximate time it occurred. All had substantial motives for wanting Cindy killed. However, Dangerous Darrin has been cleared of all guilt.

Answer the following statements yes or no or maybe based on the information presented above.

1. Dangerous Darrin is known to have been
   near the scene of the killing of Cindy Snide.   Y   N   ?
2. All six of the rounded-up gangsters were known
   to have been near the scene of the murder.   Y   N   ?
3. Only Dangerous Darrin has been cleared of guilt.   Y   N   ?
4. All six of the suspects were near the scene of
   Cindy's murder at the approximate time it took place. Y   N   ?
5. The police do not know who killed Cindy.   Y   N   ?
6. Cindy's murderer did not confess of his own
   free will.   Y   N   ?
7. Dangerous Darrin did not kill Cindy.   Y   N   ?
8. It is known that the six suspects were in the vicinity
   of the cold-blooded assassination.   Y   N   ?
9. Cindy Snide is dead.   Y   N   ?

A Communication Model

Several different communication models exist, but each defines the same general process. In other models different words might be used to explain communication, but understanding one general model is more important. Communication is a **circular process** which includes many steps as shown in Figure 5.2.

The following elements make up the circular pattern followed by good communicators.

Sender—Every message is sent by someone known as the **sender,** typically the **originator** of the message. Even though another person may have responsibility for the mechanics of getting the communication to the appropriate person and handling the response, the message originates with the sender: the person who has advice, a request, a greeting, or other purpose to convey the message.

Perceived Need—The sender of the message must feel the need for the communication before the process takes place. This need could be the result of a business transaction or a personal problem that needs attention.

Preparing the Message—If the message is to be understood by the recipient, it must be in a recognizable format. Computer programmers often say, "garbage in—garbage out," and this saying holds true for all communications. If the sender doesn't prepare a clear, concise message (garbage in), the receiver cannot interpret it and will not be able to respond appropriately (garbage out).

circular process-*complete cycle of a communication from sender to receiver, and continuing through the cycle*

sender-*person who sends a communication*

originator-*creator or sender of a communication*

Figure 5.2 Circular Pattern of Communication Flow

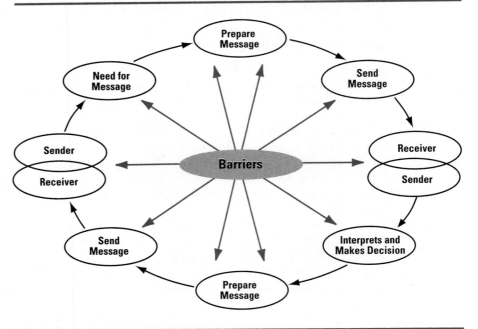

Sending the Message—The sender of the message is required to determine the **medium** of the message, or how the message should be sent. It could be a written statement such as a letter or memorandum, a telephone call, an electronic mail message via a computer, or a direct face-to-face verbal message, for example. The sender should choose the medium that is most effective and efficient for the message.

Receiver—All messages are meant to be received by someone, and this is true even if the correspondence isn't addressed to a specific person but to a general recipient such as Sir or Madam. The person who is the desired audience of the message is known as the **receiver.**

Interpretation and Decision—Upon receipt of the communication, the receiver must **interpret** the message and make a decision as to how to respond to the message and what the best medium is for the response.

Preparation and Transmission—Just as the original sender had to do, the receiver has to go through the same process to prepare a response to the communication and send it through the proper medium to the originator of the communication. This response is also known as **feedback** to the original sender of the message. At this point the original receiver becomes the sender of the return message. If the message sent by the receiver requires a response also, the cycle continues.

Barriers—Communication can be blocked by many different events or occurrences. The postal service might delay or lose a letter; a poor telephone connection may make hearing difficult; a speaker may have an accent and be difficult to understand; the listener may be thinking of something else. All of these examples are **barriers** to effective communication and can cause **interference** at any point in the communication process.

In the model shown in Figure 5.2, there are arrows to all points in the communication cycle to indicate that barriers continually exist. Because of

medium-*how a message should be sent*

receiver-*desired audience of a communication*

interpret-*determining what a communication means*

feedback-*response to a communication*

barriers-*events or occurrences that block communication*

interference-*events or blocks to communication*

Customs and Traditions: Watching for the Global Difference

Illiteracy: A Global Problem

The Wall Street Journal reported that global illiteracy is declining. This is encouraging since the ability to read and write is taken for granted in many countries. This is the first time that illiteracy has fallen. In a ten-year period between 1980 and 1990, the number of illiterate adults dropped from 945 million to 905 million. Although this seems small (4.2%), the impact is great.

The United Nations Education, Scientific and Cultural Organization (UNESCO) monitors these numbers and reported that illiteracy continued to rise in Africa. Education is badly needed in African countries, where starvation and disease are widespread. Educational efforts in the third world and the former Soviet bloc countries were made more difficult because of the wars in those areas.

CONTINUED

Developed countries like the United States, Canada, and European countries spend about 5.3 percent of their gross national product for education. Countries that are less developed and where education is needed even more spend 3.3 percent of their gross national product.

Source: The Wall Street Journal, *December 8, 1993, A10.*

Effective communication can be critical.

the barriers, it is critical that all communications be prepared very carefully and the appropriate medium for transmission be selected. Without careful planning and execution the process cannot be completed. It is much like a football coach who sends in a play to the quarterback. If the entire team does not hear the play that has been called or team members do not understand what their roles are, the play will fail. Many barriers can stand in the way of successful completion of the play.

*M*odes of Communication

Good human relations practices are influenced by using good communication skills, and there are many ways in which to communicate. Throughout the rest of this chapter and the next, many communication concepts will be discussed. You will be introduced to verbal, nonverbal, and written communication forms and concepts. The importance of effective communication cannot be overemphasized and is critical to all of the activities in which you are involved.

Verbal Communication

Verbal messages are voice messages used to convey different types of information. When the communication is long and detailed, it is usually best to verify the spoken words with written words. This will clarify anything the listener may not have heard or understood and emphasizes the importance of the voice message. When using verbal communication, the sender of the message should keep in mind that most people have a limited capability to remember and can recall no more than about 50 percent of what they hear after 48 hours. Besides, verbal messages are sometimes distorted beyond recognition when one person tells another person who tells another, and so on. The speaker (sender) has control over some of what happens, but the listener (receiver) is an important element in the process of verbal communication.

verbal messages-voice messages

Voice Quality. No doubt you have had an instructor or professor whose greatest attribute was lulling you to sleep. Listeners will quickly tune out someone who drones on without any change in voice qualities.

Tone of Voice. **Tone of voice** refers to the rising and falling of the voice, or the **inflection,** as the message is being stated. Inflection can indicate if the message is a question by rising at the end, or if it is a statement because the voice falls at the end. Tone can reveal if the speaker is angry, happy, self-confident, or doesn't care. Tone of voice is often a giveaway for someone who doesn't really mean what he or she says.

tone of voice-rising and falling of the voice

inflection-same as tone; rising and falling of the voice

Pitch. **Pitch** determines if the voice is deep or if the voice is high. Many people consider lower voices more pleasing and believe they convey self-confidence and authority. Pitch usually changes as a speaker's emotions change. Anger causes the pitch to get higher while relaxation causes the pitch to get lower, and an increase in volume almost always causes a speaker's pitch to rise. The implications are an important consideration for speakers with higher pitched voices; it may be necessary to use amplification or practice to help control the situation.

pitch-how deep or high a voice is

Volume. Quieter or louder is the best way to describe **volume.** Loud speakers have to be cautious so they do not overwhelm the listener, and speakers with soft voices must learn to raise their volume and to project so they can be heard. Volume and projection can often be aided by proper breathing.

volume-quieter or louder

Emphasis. Knowing when to emphasize certain words creates great impact in a verbal message. Meaning and context of a message can be changed by changing the **emphasis** given to words. For example, look at the three-word phrase "I love you."

emphasis-giving more impact to certain words

I love you. If the emphasis is on the word *I* the listener should realize it is the speaker and no one else. It could mean that the speaker is willing to argue with the listener that no one else has the same feelings.

I *love* you. The feeling or emotion is emphasized. The speaker wants the listener to know what feelings are being expressed and how strong they are.

I love *you.* The receiver is emphasized. The speaker loves only the listener, no one else.

Intonation Pattern. How something is said sometimes gives clues to the real meaning of the message. This is illustrated rather humorously in an article from *Reader's Digest,* which condensed parts of Michael Anania's book *In Plain Sight: Obsessions, Morals, and Domestic Laughter.* The article discusses "teen-speak," or how teen-agers often speak to others or parents. This language is often used beyond the teen years, as illustrated.

Most parents encounter the tonal dimension of teen language when dealing with the phrase "All right." In response to an ordinary request like "Take out the garbage," "All right" can mean: (a) Don't bother me; (b) Did somebody cut off your legs?; (c) I deeply resent the authority you have over me, but I acknowledge it and will take out your stupid garbage; (d) Out of affection for you and respect for your age, I will take out the garbage; or (e) Okay.[1]

Adults do the same thing, but perhaps in different ways. Jesse is employed as a busperson in a local restaurant. One day he dropped several water glasses and some of them broke. His supervisor said, "That is really great. Perhaps you should try to carry more next time. I love the sound of glass breaking." Sarcasm is one way of saying something that is not meant, but the way in which it is said has meaning. Jesse no doubt got the message.

Emphasis can also be used to convey a complete range of emotions. Bosses often use emphasis with employees when disciplinary action is being taken. Good use of emphasis along with the other voice qualities makes a speaker much more interesting and more likely to be heard.

Nonverbal Communication

The body often gives clues to what someone thinks. In the communication process, what someone is expressing in words is not always verified by the speaker's body. **Nonverbal communication,** the message communicated by one's body, including facial expressions, hand gestures, or eye contact, is an important part of any relationship. The following vignette illustrates this concept.

nonverbal communication-message communicated by one's body

[1] Michael Anania. "An Insider's Guide to Teen-Speak." Condensed in *Reader's Digest.* April 1992, 133–35.

Brock Barclay manages a catering division with 175 food service workers at the Hotel del Carlos on the West Coast. He makes sure all the scheduling is done properly and in a timely fashion for each of the banquets held in the hotel. There are often two or three large meal functions scheduled at the same time, and Brock is usually calm in spite of the chaos that is evident at these busy times. When he does get upset, he tries to keep it to himself. However, Brock has some characteristics that give away the feelings he is not expressing verbally. He always folds his arms across his chest while he talks to his employees. His eyes narrow and he has a slight twitch in his left eye. All of the employees who have direct contact with Brock know that this is a time to avoid him if possible until the problem has been resolved.

Brock Barclay's behavior (of which he is unaware) is an example of nonverbal signals that are communicated to others through **body language.**

Body Language.

The scientific name given the study of body movement and communication is **kinesics.** Body movement, or body language, has been the subject of numerous research studies in recent years. Some of the researchers believe that every movement of the body communicates something to others. **Nonverbal messages,** or body language, can be purposely planned, but very often the message is not intentional. For instance, nonverbal messages are transmitted when someone is happy, sad, upset, uncomfortable, or simply chooses to remain quiet. A parent learns quickly to read the nonverbal message of a baby who cannot speak. The parent can then respond to the needs of the child.

There are disagreements on the meaning of some of the signals communicated through body movements. This is important to consider when

body language-giving nonverbal messages

kinesics-study of body movement

nonverbal messages-messages communicated through body movement

Sometimes it is difficult to read another person's nonverbal communications and may take several clues and careful observation to interpret them correctly.

Chapter 5 • Interpersonal Communication

trying to interpret what the nonverbal message means. While general interpretations can be made, it is impossible to interpret every movement, especially if the sender is someone who is a new acquaintance or someone just met in a business or professional meeting. For that reason, a person should not rely on one clue that has been sent. It takes several clues and close observation to really understand what the nonverbal messages actually mean.

Eye Contact.

The spoken words "I only have eyes for you" might not mean exactly that if the speaker can't transmit that message with **eye contact,** the ability to look at someone to whom you are speaking. Some people have difficulty looking others in the eye when speaking. This may result from shyness, insecurity, or lack of self-confidence. One fraction of a minute of eye contact can send a message that has far more impact than many spoken words. The message might be joy and happiness, sadness and sympathy, or understanding and compassion. At other times the message might be one of indifference or untruthfulness. When someone is lying, it is difficult for the person to make and maintain eye contact while talking. Good eye contact is a sign of honesty in the American culture.

Eye movements also give clues to the speaker that indicate if the listener is still a part of the conversation. It is easy for the speaker who is aware of the messages given by the eyes to determine if the receiver is listening or if he or she has tuned out the message being sent. If the listener is gazing away from the speaker or is looking down, that is a clue that the listener is no longer engaged in the message. If the receiver has a blank look, the speaker has lost the person's attention.

Posture.

Careful observance of how others position their bodies will tell a great deal about them. The person who is rigid may be under stress. The person who walks stooped over seems to have heavy burdens to carry.

Body positions are considered to be either open or closed. An open body position conveys friendliness and self-confidence and is used naturally when speaking with someone who doesn't present a threat. Most casual conversations with friends are with an open body position: arms and legs uncrossed, leaning forward, and arms away from the body. Someone in an open body position may be more likely to listen and accept suggestions and new ideas. A closed body position projects unfriendliness, arrogance, or an untouchable attitude, and might include folded arms and crossed legs, leaning back and away from the other person, hands sometimes in pockets, or staying behind a barrier, such as a desk, to maintain distance. Someone in a closed body position presents a greater challenge, and barriers must be overcome for good communication to occur.

K irsten Schabacker summarizes gestures and their meanings in *Working Woman* magazine. She suggested to *lower your guard:* when confronted with a difficult question, men clasp their hands in front of them and women cross their arms over their chest. This is a signal that the question has caused stress. *Take up space:* filling your personal space by gesturing will make you seem more confident. *Don't speak hand to mouth:* if you put your hand near your mouth, your eyes, or scratch your cheek, these are sure signs that you aren't sure of what you are saying, or you may not be telling the truth. *Watch your eye contact:* women are more comfortable with face-to-face communication than men are . . . men may not be making eye contact but that doesn't mean they aren't listening.[2]

Posture can be confusing. Like eye contact and body language, posture can be interpreted differently by observers and is often misinterpreted. To truly understand the messages sent by someone else's posture, a person needs to know something about the communicator before making final judgments.

posture-body position

Touch. A touch can convey a powerful message. A hug and some consoling words for someone who has just suffered a major loss have a healing effect. A mother or father holding the hand of a frightened child and reassuring the child that he or she is safe makes a new adventure more tolerable. A shove along with some harsh words could mean that a fight is about to begin. A handshake and words of congratulations can make employees proud of where they work. It seems that words appropriate for the type of touch do reinforce the purpose of the touch. Close relationships can be established with appropriate touching, and touching often enhances communication.

Touch can be very effective in the communication process when it is used meaningfully. Inappropriate touching can be devastating. While it may be appropriate behavior to pat a child or a loved one on the buttocks, it is never acceptable behavior in the work environment. This type of touching in the workplace could, should, and often does result in charges of harassment. Inappropriate touching should be avoided in and out of the workplace.

Appearance. The ability to succeed in a job interview is often dependent upon how an applicant looks. Messages are sent through one's appearance. Good grooming and dress often create the first impression someone has of another person, and in many cases one's performance on the job is influenced by his or her appearance. A professional salesperson cannot gain the respect and confidence of others without appropriate dress and grooming.

In the workplace, professional appearance and grooming are important and transmit messages about the individual. Attractiveness conveys a message about people. It is perceived that physically attractive people are more likely to first get a position, but secondly, they advance to higher positions more rapidly. There seems to be charm or charisma associated with more physically attractive people.

---

[2]First appeared in *WORKING WOMAN* in April 1991. Written by Kirsten Schabacker. Reprinted with the permission of *WORKING WOMAN Magazine.* Copyright © 1991 by WORKING WOMAN, Inc.

It is critical for a job applicant to dress professionally to create a good first impression. Many employment decisions are influenced by the first impression created by an applicant.

Physical appearance is influenced by clothing, but is much more than how someone dresses. Other attributes of an individual which contribute to physical appearance include makeup or cosmetics, hair style, or eyewear. Appearance tells a great deal about an individual, including what the person thinks of himself or herself.

Space and Territory.
The distance a person allows between himself or herself and others is known as **personal space.** One of the early researchers dealing with personal space, or **proxemics,** was Edward Hall. He found that people allow different amounts of space depending upon the situation in which they are communicating. Hall used four classifications for space and distance:

personal space-*area allowed between you and others*

proxemics-*scientific name for personal space*

► intimate, which could include physical contact to a distance of about 18 inches;

► casual, from about 1 1/2 feet to 4 feet;

► social, an area from 4 to 12 feet; and

► public, from 12 feet to as far as one can see.[3]

Different situations dictate one's space and territory. A student would stand further away from a teacher while having questions answered than while talking to a close friend about where to go for the evening. The more

[3]E.T. Hall. *The Hidden Dimension.* New York: Doubleday, 1966.

Most people guard their personal space and territory. For instance, students often sit in the same place in a classroom from class to class.

emotionally intimate people are, the more spatially intimate they get when talking with each other. Social and professional circumstances dictate the comfort level a person has and the proximity to someone with whom he or she is interacting.

Territory plays an important role in the work environment. The best office space is ordinarily reserved for the highest ranking officials in the organization; "best" can mean location of the office or size of the office. The message transmitted by territorial occupation can be very obvious or subtle.

Most people guard their personal space and territory, and if someone invades that space, it can be very disturbing. Reserved seats at a sporting event assure that no one else can legally take that place. Students often sit in the same place in a classroom from class to class and semester to semester. Church members often have their favorite places; if someone takes their seat, it is quite distressing to them. In social gatherings like in the school cafeteria, students will ask friends to save their place while they get food or drinks.

Written Communication

When formality is needed, written communication is often the medium of choice. Written communication is typical within large organizations, especially in those with multiple locations, and is often required in small organizations. (The forms of written communication used in organizations are discussed in Chapter 6.) For example, if Jani James, who is the service manager of Key Automotive, is asked by a customer for an estimate to repair a chronic problem with brakes on his car, she will provide a written estimate. This type of communication is needed to ensure that both parties understand and agree on the estimate. The customer cannot later say that a much lower price was offered, nor can Ms. James say that the estimate was much higher.

Written communication can be very informal also. A letter to a long-time friend who lives in another state would typically be informal. A card to wish a coworker a happy birthday is a friendly and informal gesture. A congratulatory letter from a supervisor to an employee about a promotion can be informal, even though it may be sent on company letterhead.

Communication Rules. When preparing written communication, certain rules must be followed to increase the possibility of successful communication. Most of the same rules apply to preparing formal verbal communication. There are exceptions, though, because in verbal communication, the listener often has the opportunity to ask questions and respond immediately. That isn't always the situation with written communication.

Rule 1. *Be Thorough.* If the receiver of a communication is expected to respond or react, he or she must have all the information necessary to comply. That means that the message must be thorough. Thorough messages are more likely to get the desired response; they make more sense to the receiver, and they make the sender appear more professional. A thorough, or complete, message answers the questions *who, what, when, where, why,* and sometimes *how.*

A message, whether oral or written, must be complete to enable the receiver of the message to give the anticipated reponse. What might happen if the order as placed by a restaurant patron was not fully communicated to the cook?

Erin Reed was given the responsibility of contacting a group of 25 donors to the community food kitchen where she volunteered her services to prepare and serve food to the homeless. She was to invite the donors to a meeting at the Community Center to discuss the needs of the program. She composed a memo, the body of which read:

> Thank you for your desire to contribute to the community food kitchen. Your donations are needed and make the program a success. We would like to meet with several of our donors to discuss the changing needs of the program. Could you please attend a meeting on Thursday, March 18, at the Community Center? We look forward to seeing you then.

The day after the memos were sent, the food kitchen began receiving telephone calls from the donors. Erin thought she was thorough in her memo, but, she left out one critical piece of information . . . the time for the meeting. Erin had a couple of choices to correct the problem. She could either call each donor or send another message. She chose to send a second memo, which cost her time and cost the program money for additional postage, envelopes, and letterhead.

Being thorough means both providing all the information that is requested when responding to someone else's communication, and providing all the information needed so a receiver can make a decision or respond to a request.

Rule 2. *Be Brief.* Being brief means that the communication should be direct and to the point, in as few words as possible. The reader who receives the brief yet complete message will respond in a similar manner.

► *Don't be wordy.* Don't waste time with flowery phrases to describe something that can be said in a word. "In view of the fact that" could be more briefly stated as "Because" without losing meaning. The guideline to follow is to use one word rather than long phrases whenever possible, as long as the meaning doesn't change.

► *Don't be trite.* "Please find attached to this . . . " is an expression often used in written communications. Does this sound as though the writer is begging the reader to find something attached? The expression could be reduced to "Attached is" with equal results.

► *Don't overuse phrases.* Many writers begin sentences with overused phrases that are unnecessary in the communication. "However, there are several . . . " means the same as "There are several . . . " "It was assumed by Mr. Juarez . . . " should be "Mr. Juarez assumed . . . "

► *Get to the point.* Effective communication does not include a lot of unnecessary verbiage. It gets to the point and addresses the condition without hesitation. For example, "Please be informed that your corrected invitation to attend the donors meeting was received by me just yesterday, and I should be able to attend the meeting" could be stated "I plan to attend the food kitchen donors meeting."

▶ *Avoid repetition.* Saying the same thing over and over is repetition. Sometimes it is necessary to repeat a message to add emphasis. If a phrase like National Wildlife Federation is needed often in a communication, consider shortening it to NWF, Wildlife Federation, or the Federation. This can be done as long as the reader understands the reference.

Rule 3. *Use Empathy.* To be empathetic, or to use empathy, means the sender of the communication should think of the person who will receive it and visualize the reaction. When the sender of a message thinks of the receiver, a more appropriate communication can be prepared.

▶ *Focus on the recipient.* A positive "you" approach rather than an "I" or "we" approach directs focus on the recipient. When preparing the message, try to refer to the reader in the first paragraph and keep the reader in focus throughout the entire message. Starting a letter with "Your expertise in foreign matters is a valuable asset" is flattering and sounds better than saying, "I understand that you have experience with foreign matters which could be valuable to me."

A negative or accusatory communication in which the reader is placed on the defensive can have quite the opposite effect. Figure 5.3 illustrates this point. The letter was sent by a college to vendors, but note how many words were underlined for emphasis and the references to *I, my,* or *me.* Vendors who received this letter might be greatly offended by the director of accounting's lack of empathy. If this type of letter were sent by a privately owned company rather than by a public institution, the ill will that would result could mean lost business.

Figure 5.3 Accusatory Letter Sent to Vendor

Dear Vendor

College Purchase Orders will be <u>required</u> for all college purchases. The College <u>will not</u> be responsible for payment of any invoices for charges resulting from <u>unauthorized purchases</u>. Purchase Orders will be issued from my office <u>only</u> and authorized by my assistant, or myself. <u>No</u> payment will be made in excess of the amount of the purchase order.

Your cooperation in this matter is appreciated and will result in improved communications and timely payments between the College and your company.

If I can be of any assistance or answer any questions, please feel free to contact me at (telephone number).

Sincerely,

Director of Accounting

The positive "you" approach was used in Figure 5.4. The second letter doesn't place all the blame on the vendors and admits that the college has some deficiencies that need to be corrected. Vendors who receive the second letter will more likely respond more positively than will those who received the first letter.

Figure 5.4 **Revision of Accusatory Letter**

Dear Vendor:

You provide a valuable service to the College. To facilitate better processing of orders placed with your company, and more timely payment of bills, it is necessary that a purchase order authorized by the accounting department be used. If a purchase order is sent to you by a College employee without proper accounting authorization, please return it for authorization before filling the order.

If you receive a purchase order and the amounts are wrong, please return the order including correct information before filling the request. College policy allows only payment up to the amount shown on the authorized purchase order.

You should see improved services if we all follow the proper procedures. At your convenience, feel free to contact me with any questions you might have. Thank you for your cooperation.

Sincerely,

Director of Accounting

▶ *Create interest by showing benefits.* Rather than the attitude of "what's in it for me?" the attitude of "let me show you how you can benefit" is important in some kinds of communications. Not all communications can show benefits, but when the possibilities do exist, they should be evident. The nasty letter in Figure 5.3 doesn't show that there are benefits to the vendors. The second letter points out that improved services will result when everyone follows the correct procedure. The tone of a letter also helps create or detract from the recognition of benefits.

In many businesses it is at some time necessary to send collection letters to customers or clients who are not paying their bills. The most productive approach to use is to make sure the reader is aware of the benefits he or she will receive by paying the bill. A simple statement such as "Your credit rating can be enhanced by prompt payment of your bill" creates more interest than the statement: "Your charges of $500 are three months overdue. Prompt payment is requested." When the harsh communication is softened, the reader will respond in the same way.

Offensive Communication Practices

Writing can be offensive when inappropriate language and words are used. The people of minority races or ethnic groups are often the target of offensive efforts at communications. Much to the chagrin of some reporters with the *Los Angeles Times* newspaper, they have been instructed to avoid using the words *WASPs, Hispanics,* and *inner city*—at least when reporting news stories. Mr. Terry Schwadron, deputy managing editor, says, "If you write about Los Angeles and talk about a 'ghetto' area, I defy you to define where one starts and stops or where they are. Similarly, 'inner city,' denoting a poor black or Latino area, often is geographically inaccurate in sprawling cities. And 'WASP,' for white, Anglo-Saxon Protestant, is becoming pejorative."

▶ *Be ethical.* In work and in all business transactions, ethics are an important consideration. Ethics refers to what is right—what is appropriate and acceptable human behavior. Appropriate and acceptable can be interpreted to mean what is normal in society, the workplace being a part of society. There are often gray areas in which an individual must make a decision between partial truth and total honesty. In those cases a person's conscience is his or her guide.

ethical communication-honest communication

Ethical communications are honest and promise only what can be delivered. If a company is having difficulty meeting deadlines and a customer needs to have a product completed by a specific date, ethics dictate that the customer know the truth. While being honest and ethical can sometimes cost a business income that could have been assured by following unethical actions, over time ethical behavior is most profitable for an individual and for an organization.

Rule 4. *Be Specific.* A recipient of a message can deal with it more effectively and efficiently if it is to the point and understandable. When preparing the communication, don't "dance" around the meaning of the message, state it directly. Take for example two different advertisements for the same job. Which is more effective?

#1 – Wanted, experienced word processor who can prepare and send several business letters each day. Work full-time. Call xxx-xxxx.

#2 – Wanted, word processor with five years' experience. Must be able to transcribe documents on a computer at a rate of 80 words per minute. 45 hours per week. Call xxx-xxxx.

Being specific and stating facts directly leaves little room for interpretation. In the first advertisement, it is up to the reader to determine what *expe-*

The guidelines for good writing are significant for one of the nation's largest cities since Latinos, African-Americans, and Asian-Americans make up about half of the population of the city. While some minorities think that some of the rules in the new guidelines are a bit silly, they make sense and are supposed to make people think before writing—good advice for anyone who has a writing assignment.

Source: Wynter, Leon E. The Wall Street Journal. *January 19, 1994, B1.*

rienced, several, and *full-time* mean. In the second ad, those questions are given more specific answers and there has been little left for interpretation.

Classic Writing Tips.   Henry F. Beechhold gives these writing tips in the *Home-Office Computing* magazine.

► *Tips 1–2: Start with the foundation—your reader, your structure.* The two cornerstones for building a successful writing style are developing a sense of your audience and discovering the necessary structure for your documents.

► *Tip 3: Get to the point.* Say what you need to say with direct statements that are easy to understand.

► *Tips 4–5: Avoid fluff as you address your readers' needs.* Readers are more interested in what you can do for them, what the benefits are for them . . . not how great you or your products are.

► *Tip 6: Watch where you place words.* Misplacing one word in a sentence or phrase can change the meaning of what is said. Make sure words are selected carefully.

► *Tip 7: Attach adjectives to appropriate nouns.* Carelessness with modifying phrases often results in inadvertent humor—at the writer's expense.

► *Tip 8: Be careful with the little ones.* The little words often do us in: words like *only* can change the meaning of a sentence if used incorrectly.

► *Tip 9: Use plain English wherever possible.* You must ask yourself unceasingly: Will my words communicate what I want to say to the audience I'm trying to reach?[4]

'Reprinted by permission from *Home Office Computing Magazine* © 1990. For subscription information, call (800) 288–7812.

Listening

Effective communication is often the result of good **listening skills**. Many conversations consist of words that are not heard by the intended recipient. Children are masters at pretending to listen, but not hearing, what is said. Good communication requires effective listening habits. Listening requires involvement—listening is an active exercise, not a passive exercise.

listening skill-active exercise of hearing a communication

Women might argue that they are better listeners than men, or men might say they are better listeners than women. Patricia O'Brien wrote in *Working Woman* magazine that in and out of business, men don't listen. They smile and nod their way through conversations, but more often than not, they register little of what's being said.[5] Deborah Tannen, author of *You Just Don't Understand,* said both men and women are trapped by a cultural inability to hear each other. While gender may or may not cause a difference in listening, everyone can improve their skills.[6]

Improving Listening Skills. Several methods can be applied to improve listening wherever one might be—at work, at home, or in a social gathering. Being an **active listener** takes concentration and considerable effort. Much of a day is spent in communication, and listening constitutes about 45 percent of the communication time. If a listener hears a ten-minute presentation, it is likely that only about half of what was said will be understood, properly interpreted, and retained. If the same listener is quizzed 48 hours later, only about 25 percent of the presentation can be recalled. There are ways to improve listening skills, as illustrated next.

active listener-letting a speaker know you are listening and hearing

Don't Make Judgments. Stereotypes often stand in the way of effective communications. Don't make assumptions about the speaker based on the way he or she looks, sounds, or acts. If judgments are made, preconceived expectations will not allow full attention to the speaker. What the speaker has to say could easily cause a listener to make unfair judgments. Have an open mind as well as an open ear. Listen to everything the speaker has to say; then determine if there is agreement or disagreement.

Focus Attention. Interruptions and distractions are all around, causing interference to effective listening. Last night's argument, plans for lunch, a job that needs to be completed, the smell of the next-door bakery, a motor running, an ill spouse, and many other events compete for attention. A typical person speaks at a rate of between 125 to 150 words each minute. The average listener can comprehend words at a rate of about 500 words per minute. That difference allows the listener's mind to wander and daydream, getting in the way of effective listening.

To overcome distractions, concentrate on the speaker and what the speaker is saying. Make and keep good eye contact. Eye contact keeps the listener in the conversation and provides feedback to the speaker which reveals important information. It may be necessary to take notes, as well. Note-taking is another established practice that will improve listening

---

[5]Patricia O'Brien. "Why Men Don't Listen . . . And." *Working Woman.* February 1993, 56–60.
[6]Deborah Tannen. *You Just Don't Understand.* New York: Ballantine Books, 1990.

skills. Someone taking notes, preferably in outline format, will concentrate on the speaker while making eye contact and while writing the notes.

Different locations in the United States or in the world produce accents that are unusual to those not from the same locale. A speaker from the South addressing residents in Minnesota would sound differently. A speaker from New England, addressing an audience in Illinois would sound differently. These differences can cause the listener to have to focus more intently to understand. Sometimes the differences are amusing and make it easier to focus attention. Figure 5.5 contains some examples.

Figure 5.5 **Careful Listening Is Necessary**

Word/Phrase	Sounds like	Said by	Heard by
Tire	Tar	A Southerner	A Northerner
Creek	Crik	Midwesterner	Westerner
It's cool	Must be chilly	Teen	Adult
Car	Caw	New Englander	Illinoisan
Hit it	Slap it	American	European

Effective listeners maintain a focus on the speaker and the content of what the speaker is saying, not necessarily on how something is being said or who is saying it.

Active Participation. It is possible to be an active participant while listening without interrupting the speaker. Eye contact sends a nonverbal cue to the speaker that a listener is a part of the exchange. A nod of the head lets the speaker know that the listener is hearing what is said. A smile can show agreement; leaning toward the speaker shows interest; saying words like "I see" or "yes" shows involvement; and responding when asked questions is a critical form of feedback for a speaker.

Occasionally it may be necessary to interrupt a speaker, which of course wouldn't be done while a speaker is delivering an address to a large audience. Interruptions could occur in casual conversations, in group discussions, when receiving directions, or when appropriate in the work environment. Interruptions are appropriate when the listener does not understand something that is being said and knows the information is critical for understanding something later. Don't be blatant about the interruption; a small hand gesture such as a signal to the speaker may be all that is needed. Interruptions to make small talk, crack jokes, or criticize are not acceptable in formal communications.

Sometimes it is advisable to summarize or restate what a speaker has said. If a traffic officer gives directions to a lost motorist to find the expressway, it would be good for the motorist to restate what the officer said to verify understanding. This method of restating is effective for the speaker as well as the listener. This approach wouldn't work when listening

Chapter 5 • Interpersonal Communication

to a formal speaker at a large gathering unless there is an opportunity to meet with the speaker after the presentation. Restatement of the message provides valuable feedback for the speaker and helps the listener feel confident that he or she heard and fully understood the message.

Communication Challenges

Each time an effort is made to communicate, challenges must be overcome. Earlier it was pointed out that there are barriers to effective communications. Figure 5.2 illustrated that barriers threaten communications each step along the way. There are no exceptions; verbal and written communications are challenged in many ways.

Selectivity

Selectivity is a problem for message recipients and senders. Individuals often select the parts of the message they want to hear. Other parts of the message are filtered out. The same thing is done by message senders—information that appears to be useless or not necessary is left out or filtered out of the message. Selectivity causes difficulties because the complete message is not sent or received. As a result of not having complete information, the receiver of the message acts based on what he or she wants to do, or with the false assumption that the person has all the information to act successfully.

The mind is good at selectively filtering information that is perceived to be damaging or threatening. The information isn't always completely filtered out; sometimes it is interpreted as being less threatening.

Misinterpretation

Many miscommunicated messages are a direct result of the receiver not interpreting a message correctly. This may be a result of the receiver's own perceptions about a situation or the sender. At other times the result could be from incorrect information passed along to the receiver. Misinterpretation can occur when a message passes through several receivers/senders and is understood differently by each one. The final recipient may hear something totally different from the original message.

Distractions can cause misinterpretations; noise in a workplace, a TV or stereo system playing loudly, and busy streets are examples of distractions. When there are distractions, the receiver only hears parts of a message and must try to interpret the message based on partial details. The sender can also be distracted, and the message may not be as clear as intended. The receiver then has to make interpretations about the intentions and sometimes will be incorrect.

Feelings/Emotions

"I don't like you and I'm not going to go," were the words that came from the six-year-old girl's mouth. Anger caused by something, perhaps minor,

selectivity-selecting the parts of a message you want to hear

distractions-interruptions to the communication process

stands in the way of further effective communication. Unfortunately, this isn't a role played only by youngsters. Adults react the same way to events that are displeasing. The events could take place at work or elsewhere. When feelings or emotions reach a high level, communications suffer.

If workers are angry about being scheduled for a night shift, performance will suffer also. When people's feelings or emotions become too intense, it is difficult to communicate with them—they may not want to listen, at least not to the source, or about the source, of the problem. A conversation may be possible after some time has elapsed. Wait for the appropriate time to continue, or get an intermediary to resolve the conflict.

Unpredictable Behavior

Frustration levels rise and successful communication dwindles when the behavior of either the sender or receiver is unpredictable. Inconsistent actions cause others to withdraw from, or circumvent, the source of the difficulties. If a supervisor treats some employees in one way and others in a different way in response to actions that are the same, that is inconsistent and unpredictable behavior.

A supervisor or coworker who says one thing and does something different also causes difficulty. There are two or perhaps more different messages being sent. The receiver is confused and doesn't know which message to follow. The old adage which says "Do as I say, not as I do" does not result in good communications. The amount of confidence a receiver has in the sender, and in turn the sender's message, is directly related to consistent messages that are easily interpreted.

Key Points Summary

- Good communication is critical to everyone, including individuals and organizations, and to be a successful communicator requires understanding and following rules.

- Communication is a process that begins with a sender who has a need to communicate with someone and prepares the message, chooses the best medium for the message, and then transmits it to the intended receiver. The receiver of the message must interpret the message and make a decision regarding how to handle the communication. If the receiver determines that a response is needed, the receiver will follow the same process as the original sender to provide feedback to the original sender. Throughout the process there are barriers that make successful communication difficult.

- Many messages are verbal; they are spoken to the receiver using such media as the telephone or face-to-face contact. There are other media suitable for verbal messages, but they are typically used for specialized verbal communications.

- Verbal communications can be improved by enhancing voice quality. Voice quality includes tone, pitch, volume, emphasis, and intonation patterns. Each of these lends critical elements to successful verbal communications.

- The true meaning of a communication is often best reflected in the nonverbal communications of the sender. Several components constitute nonverbal communication, including body language, eye contact, posture, touch, appearance, and space/territory.

- Written communication can be the most formal method used in an organization to transmit a message. Written communications also can be informal and are often used to make sure that more detailed messages can be understood.

- Good communication rules to follow are (1) be thorough, (2) be brief, (3) use empathy, and (4) be specific.

- A thorough and complete message answers *who, what, when, where, why,* and sometimes *how* questions.

- Listening is also critical to effective communications. Many people are not good listeners but can improve their skills by being non-judgmental, focusing attention on the speaker, and participating actively without interrupting.

- Effective listening is challenged if feelings and emotions stand in the way. Additionally, if the speaker or the listener can't predict the reactions of the other person, effective communications will be challenged.

Key Terms

active listener	nonverbal communication
barriers	nonverbal messages
body language	originator
circular process	personal space
communication	pitch
distractions	posture
emphasis	proxemics
ethical communication	receiver
eye contact	selectivity
feedback	sender
inflection	tone of voice
interference	verbal messages
interpret	volume
kinesics	
listening skill	
medium	

1. You have been selected by your study group to prepare a complaint for your instructor regarding one person in your group. It seems that he seldom attends meetings and when he is at the meetings, he is a constant disruption. Discuss each of the following communication points.

   a. You have decided it would be best to prepare a written complaint. How will you get it to the instructor to make sure it is read?

   b. What can you say in the complaint that might prompt your instructor to respond to you so you know action is being taken?

   c. What are some of the barriers that might get in the way of your communication being complete and effective?

2. Explain what you think the ideal voice sounds like. What are the characteristics of the voice that have caused you to come to the conclusion that it is the ideal? How effective do you think this voice would be in communicating a well-prepared verbal message? Why?

3. Certain body movements and gestures have different meanings in different countries. Find an article in a current magazine or journal that discusses the meaning of body language in foreign cultures. Discuss your findings with your class or your colleagues.

4. There are several rules that should be followed in preparing written communications. Discuss each of the rules and give some examples of what each of the rules means. Be sure you have followed the rules of effective writing when completing question 1 above.

5. Discuss the differences, if there are any, in the listening skills and habits of men and women and various age groups. Who do you believe are the best listeners, and the poorest? Explain your reasoning.

Answers to The Cindy Snide Mystery, Figure 5.1

1. ? We can't assume that we know where D. Darrin was.
2. ? Don't assume they were gangsters.
3. ? We don't know if anyone else has been cleared.
4. ? We don't know that she was murdered.
5. ? We don't know what the police know.
6. ? We don't know if anyone confessed.
7. ? Just because he was cleared doesn't mean he didn't do it.
8. ? Was it a cold-blooded assassination?
9. Y The first sentence says Cindy was found dead; this we know for sure.

Organizational Communication

Carol Long owns and manages a medium-sized movie theater company in Idaho. Her company has theaters in several Idaho towns, and the business headquarters offices are located in Sun Valley. Carol is pretty good at communicating with all of the theater managers. She takes advantage of the latest communications technology but also uses traditional methods for communicating.

Carol runs her company efficiently. She has found that she doesn't need a lot of vice presidents, so she has only two. One vice president is responsible for finance and operations; the other is responsible for marketing and customer relations. Having few levels of managers in her organization, Carol feels she can communicate effectively with all the managers at each level. Carol has a reputation for being a good communicator. She feels her company runs much more smoothly because of her efforts to communicate frequently with employees.

Organizational Structure

Communication within an organization is influenced by the structure and intended flow, or channels, in an organization. Communication can be formal or informal. **Informal communication** results largely from the formation of informal groups within the organization, while **formal communication** is the result of organizational structure. Organizational structure is discussed in Chapter 2, but it is important to relate structure to the context of communication. **Organizational structure** is the order of relationships and responsibilities within the organization.

Almost every large organization and many small organizations have organizational charts. An **organizational chart** is a representation of the hierarchy of personnel within the organization. It shows who is responsible for the general tasks or duty areas and indicates who reports to whom. (See Figure 6.1.)

Informal communication takes place in an organization when employees get together in informal groups.

Besides showing relationships, the organizational chart shows the formal channels of communication within the company. For example, the president communicates with the vice presidents and the vice presidents communicate with the next in command.

Employees learn quickly that there is a correct procedure to follow in the formal communication process.

Figure 6.1 Organizational Chart

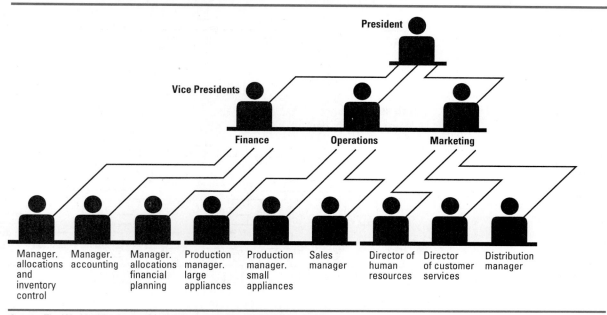

Source: The World of Business. *South-Western College Publishing, 1995, 274.*

had Donner supervises 12 workers in a medium-sized light bulb manufacturing plant. Recently he had a rather heated discussion with his boss, the director of the automotive lamp division, about the working conditions in the summertime. Some of the workers were complaining how they couldn't work effectively because it was too hot. Chad was assured that the concerns would be taken to the plant manager. Chad waited for about a month and nothing was happening, so he decided to talk to the plant manager himself. He tried to talk with the plant manager informally in the hallway, but the manager suggested he follow correct procedure and talk with his immediate supervisor. Chad was disappointed with the response, but he learned that there are proper procedures to follow in the organization.

One could argue that what Chad did was acceptable because his supervisor apparently didn't handle the problem. But did Chad know the circumstances? Should he have talked with his supervisor again? Did the plant manager handle the situation correctly?

Flat Organizations

As discussed in Chapter 2, a flat organization is one that has few managerial levels. (See Figure 6.2.) In a company with few managerial levels, each manager is responsible for more workers, or has a wider span of control. A flat organization makes it possible for more direct communication to take

Figure 6.2 **Flat and Tall Organizations**

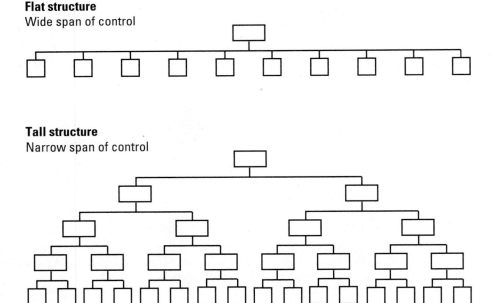

Flat structure
Wide span of control

Tall structure
Narrow span of control

Source: The World of Business. South-Western College Publishing, 1995, 279.

Unit 2 · Essentials of Human Relations

place from the bottom to the top or from the top to the bottom. More direct lines should result in more effective and efficient communications. There are fewer communications barriers to overcome in a flat organization and fewer people who must interpret the messages to pass along to lower levels.

Tall Organizations

A tall organization has several levels of managers, as shown in the bottom part of Figure 6.2. Each manager is typically responsible for fewer workers and has a narrow span of control. Communications flow through each of the levels from top to bottom or from bottom to top. In a tall organization, the possibilities are greater for interference and disruption of the communications, and more people have to interpret and handle the messages than in a flat organization. The taller the structure, the greater the possibility of flawed communication.

Formal Communication

Formal communication flows either downward or upward through an organization. The **channels of communication** follow the structure, represented by symbols in Figure 6.1, on the organization chart. These lines of communication are the official channels that employees are expected to follow when transmitting a message. Besides downward and upward communication, there is also horizontal communication, which occurs between workers at the same level. Horizontal communication is not shown on an organizational chart, nor are all the workers who might handle or have some responsibility for the communications.

channels of communication-follow the structure illustrated in an organizational chart

Vertical Communication

Vertical communication includes messages that are transmitted from the top of the organizational structure to lower levels and communications that originate at lower levels and are sent to higher levels of the organization. The origin of the communication has a significant effect on the content and the number of messages. More messages are sent downward from the higher levels of an organization than flow upward from the lower levels.

vertical communication-messages that flow downward or upward in an organization

Downward Communication. Any communication that flows from higher to lower levels in an organization is considered **downward communication.** The typical message is a directive, new information, or a request which originates somewhere at a higher level in the structure and is sent to a lower level. Downward communication travels rapidly through the organization because of its origin and the kind of messages that are sent. Based on face value of the message and the messenger, the communication is handled quickly. Downward communication can be written or verbal. **Verbal communication** might take the form of meetings or direct individual messages. Types of written communication will be discussed later in this chapter.

downward communication-flows from higher to lower levels in an organization

verbal communication-spoken messages in meetings or individual contact

There are problems with downward communications that cause difficulties for the organization. Managers often assume that subordinates have the same kind of information they have. The result is incomplete messages are sent based on false assumptions. Many workers at lower levels aren't interested in the same events that interest managers and supervisors, so they don't pay attention to what is happening. Managers who assume that workers are fully aware do not communicate effectively.

Downward communication is often filtered as it moves down the channels. Managers at each level pass along what they feel is most important for their workers. Messages can be misinterpreted by the managers and incorrect information is passed along. Verbal communication is more subject to filtering and misinterpretation than is written communication.

Some managers are too far removed from workers at lower levels to understand their positions, needs, and desires. As a result, communications are ill-prepared and don't reflect the concerns of the group to whom they are sent. This can cause distress and frustration, which often lead to unrest and dissatisfaction in the organization. Downward communication will be more effective when prepared at the lowest level possible.

Verbal or Written Communication. The decision regarding the choice of verbal or written communication should be based upon the nature and importance of the message and the intended recipient. Some subjects, such as extremely sensitive information, are best handled orally. If a company is being forced to reduce the number of employees, a meeting in which the reduction is announced would be more effective than letting the workers read about it in the newspapers or letting them know by letter. Personal contact and a verbal message will allow greater detail in explaining the problems and the reasons for the actions and will be quicker. Employees then have an opportunity to ask questions to reduce fear and anxiety.

Other situations are more appropriate for written communications. If an employee receives an award for service to the community, a congratulatory letter has more impact than verbal congratulations. The employee can show others the written letter or display it with the award. The impact upon the employee is greater with the written communication, which results in greater satisfaction with the company.

Written communication is often necessary when the message is complex, filled with facts or details, or must be remembered. Written communication can be referred to periodically while a situation is being resolved, and everyone involved has the same point of reference, the written message. Some written communications must be preserved and are used repeatedly. A company policy manual is a good example of complex information that must be written in order to be used for decision-making.

Upward Communication. Communication that flows from lower to higher levels in an organization is **upward communication.** It originates with a lower level employee, supervisor, or work group and is transmitted to someone higher up in the organizational structure. Upward

upward communication-
flows from lower to higher
levels in an organization

A service award can be accompanied by a congratulatory letter for even greater impact.

communication might occur for a variety of reasons: an employee requesting a transfer to a different division, a supervisor suggesting to a vice president that new procedures could be more effective, or a vice president recommending to the president that the company purchase a competing firm that is for sale are all examples of upward communications.

Communication from the bottom to the top of an organization is effective when management is open to receiving the communication.

Customs and Traditions: Watching for the Global Difference

Only English Spoken Here!

Many states in the United States have a large daily influx of non-English speaking immigrants from Asia, Eastern Europe, Latin America, and other regions. When the immigrants arrive in the United States, they seek employment. Some states have made English the official language of the state, which some employers have interpreted to mean that applicants cannot be hired unless they can speak English. Other employers feel that English is needed for some jobs—those where safety is important—and not for other jobs; therefore, if an applicant can speak enough English to ensure everyone's safety, he or she could be hired.

CONTINUED

The greatest controversy surrounding the state laws is not whether employees should be required to speak English, but whether they should be required to speak only English while on the job. Much of the discussion has come about because supervisors who have subordinates who speak a different language can't understand what the subordinates are saying, some of which the supervisors feel might be about them and their job as a supervisor.

The 1964 Civil Rights Act forbids discrimination on the basis of race or national origin. The guidelines of the Equal Employment Opportunities Commission (EEOC) clearly state that if an employer deprives a worker of the right to speak his national language, this may be presumed to be discrimination based on national origin. Lawyers don't generally feel that the law is so clear. No doubt the decisions will be made in courts.

Source: Sklarewitz, Norman. "English–Only on the Job," Across the Board. January/February , 1992, 18–22 .

Employees whose communication is ignored at higher levels will quit communicating and will be dissatisfied with the organization. Communication flowing upward is the most effective when it is attended to immediately. Some problems or requests can't be handled immediately; however, it is critical that the communicator or communicators hear from the recipient of the message. This is necessary even if the message is "We can't take care of that immediately, but will look into the situation when time permits." When employees feel that the organization is interested and cares about them, they will react with positive performance.

Alex Henderson was an inspector for a large private detective firm. He was interested in moving to a new office which was located closer to his home. He felt that if he could work closer to his home, he could spend more time with his family. He approached his supervisor and was told that he should prepare a formal request for the chief detective of the region. Alex prepared a letter requesting a transfer to an office closer to his home. The chief detective granted the request, and in his letter back to Alex, he commented on what an impressive letter he had written.

In this example, upward and downward communication occurred; however, Alex initiated the process with his upward flowing request for a transfer.

Upward communication takes on many of the same forms as downward communication. The manner in which the communication is transmitted is determined by the nature of the message, point of origin, urgency, and its formality. Messages that originate at the lowest levels of an organization are often verbal or in the form of brief written suggestions. The higher the originator is located in the structure of the organization, the more likely the message will be written. Higher level managers often deal with more complex situations which involve more detail.

Horizontal Communication

When individuals at the same level of the organization communicate with each other, they are involved with horizontal communication. Much of the horizontal communication that occurs is informal, thus verbal. However, there is need for horizontal communication to also be written. Written horizontal communication is often in the form of a memo, which is discussed in the next section.

Written Communication

Written communication is a more formal medium of communication which is used extensively by organizations where messages are usually prepared using a computer or word processor. It is important for workers at all levels and in all positions to know the forms of written communication used in an organization. Some forms are more appropriate for specific kinds of communications. In this section, letters, memorandums, reports, and proposals are discussed.

written communication-more formal messages that are prepared using a computer or word processor

Letters

A **letter** is the medium most often used for communications outside of the organization. A letter can have a great impact on the recipient, who judges it based on its appearance, content, and the way it is presented. In Chapter 5 there were two different versions of the same letter. The version in Figure 5.3 was sent to vendors, and the other version, in Figure 5.4, is one that could have been sent instead. The letters have the same appearance and content, but the manner of presentation is different. Many of the vendors who received the original letter were upset enough with the presentation style to take the time to write letters to the college accounting office in response. This could have been avoided if the sender had had empathy with the recipients.

letter-most often used medium for communication outside of an organization

Letters which come from an organization should be on letterhead. A stationery **letterhead** contains the name, address, and telephone number of the organization. If the organization has a logo, it is almost always included on the letterhead. Letterhead stationery makes the communication look more professional, and pertinent information is automatically included.

letterhead-stationery that contains the name, address, and telephone number of an organization

(Letterhead paper was not used in the sample letter to vendors in Chapter 5 to maintain anonymity.)

Letters should be prepared using a word processor or typewriter. Letters should be free of typographical errors, smudges, strikeovers, or noticeable erasures and should be neatly formatted on the letterhead paper. With the cost of technology being down substantially in recent years, most organizations should own a computer and printer or other word processing equipment which makes letter preparation easier. There are many references or short courses available to assist with proper format and style for business letters.

Memorandums

memorandum-more informal written communication used internally in an organization

The memorandum, or memo, is not intended to be sent outside of the organization. Communications which are used internally can be **memorandums** when informal written communication is warranted. A memo is sent from person to person, from department to department, from a person to a department, or from a department to a person. Some organizations have memo pads or packets for internal use. The memo forms follow the same format, may be on paper of a specific color so recipients know it is an internal memo, and may be multipage so copies can be sent to different people and easily filed.

The memo form contains the organization's name and a heading such as MEMORANDUM or INTEROFFICE MEMORANDUM. A standard format is used which includes:

TO:
FROM:
DATE:
SUBJECT:

The message follows the above information. Since a memorandum is a less formal internal document, it is sometimes acceptable to write the message by hand. People who have difficult-to-read handwriting should consider using a word processor or typewriter. The nature of the memo and the person to whom it is to be sent will influence whether the memo is handwritten or machine printed. In addition to prepared memo pads or packets, many organizations have preprinted envelopes to be used for interoffice communications.

Reports

report-presentation of facts which addresses a specific purpose

Employees, supervisors, managers, and other organizational representatives are often called upon to prepare written reports. Reports can take on many different forms and formats: some are long, others are short; some are formal, others are informal. A **report** is a presentation of facts to one or more people inside or outside of the organization which addresses a specific purpose. A report can be a very effective method to transmit the results of a significant event or the results of a year of events to clientele, constituency groups, employees, or other interested parties. Organizations use reports for many reasons when information must be presented accurately without reflecting biases or judgments. Reports should be factual and without opinions.

Reports can be organized in numerous ways. The best way to organize a specific report would be determined following analysis of the material to be included and identification of the report recipient. A report normally presents

▶ background information which may include the problem being addressed;

▶ an explanation of processes used in addressing the problem;

▶ alternative solutions to the problem;

▶ recommendations for solving the problem; and

▶ a rationale for the recommendations.

The extent to which each of the areas is covered, combined, or possibly eliminated will be determined by the length and type of report.

Using Graphics in Reports. Reports can often be enhanced through the use of tables, graphs, charts, or illustrations. Each of these can be prepared by using spreadsheet or word processing computer software.

Tables. **Tables** are effective when presenting large quantities of data that do not need elaboration. Figure 6.3 is a sample of a table. The data, employment information, do not require detailed explanation. Notice that the table has titles for rows and for columns. These should provide enough explanation to let the reader know what the data represent.

table-presenting large quantities of data in rows and columns

Figure 6.3 **Sample of a Table**

Locale	Labor force	Unemployed	Employed	Rate
United States	128,521.0	120,632.0	7,890.0	6.1
California	15,269.0	13,954.0	1,314.0	9.4
Illinois	6,124.5	5,782.8	341.7	5.6
Ohio	5,491.0	5,166.0	325.0	5.9
Texas	9,071.0	8,442.0	629.0	6.9

Graphs. A **bar graph** is another popular way to represent data. This graphic device is particularly effective when comparative data are being shown. The bars can be horizontal or vertical depending on which illus-

bar graph-horizontal or vertical lines (bars) used to illustrate data trates the data better. Figure 6.4 shows examples of a vertical and horizontal bar graph illustrating the same data.

Figure 6.4 **Samples of Bar Graphs**

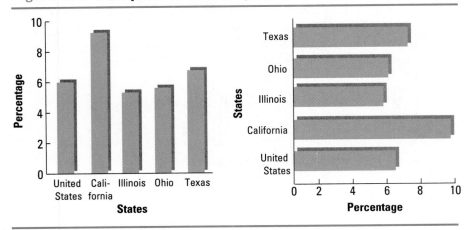

Charts. **Pie charts** are well suited for showing one part in comparison to a relative whole. If a report needs to illustrate how many employees an organization has in one of several age categories, a pie chart can be used to present the information. In Figure 6.5 the focus is on the number of employees over the age of 55 who will be retiring in the near future.

Figure 6.5 **Sample of a Pie Chart**

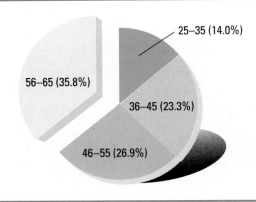

Illustrations. An **illustration** could be a picture with data included. This method of presenting information helps the reader visualize what is being reported and helps keep the focus on the subject. The illustration is there as a reminder. Examples of illustrations might be outlines of states or countries with information or data included within or nearby. Many different types of illustrations are available as a part of computer software, and the report writer can use the images and add data. This type of report enhancement is being used more widely as organizations gain the capability to produce the illustrations more economically.

Printing and Presentation. Reports can be further enhanced by selecting paper that reflects the quality to be projected in the report. First impressions are important with written documents. The quality of the printing and the illustrations also influence the reader. A report that is prepared using a low-priced printer with a ribbon that should be changed will have far less impact than the report printed on a laser printer that consistently produces high quality material. The choice to include a cover and have the report bound in some way also influences the reactions of the recipient. Most busy people would rather receive a well-prepared and well-presented report; it is easier to read and will get attention quicker.

Short Reports.
Concise and accurate information is what is expected in a **short report.** Decision makers want to have just enough detail so an informed decision can be made. A short report would normally contain a brief introduction, the discussion narrative, and the conclusions and/or recommendations. The data to support the conclusions and/or recommendations is included in the discussion narrative. A short report may or may not use graphs, charts, or tables. When included, their use is restricted to what is specifically needed to illustrate and support the conclusions/recommendations.

short report-presentation of concise and accurate information

Memorandum Reports. Short reports are sometimes presented in memorandum format. Reports like this are used if an employee is reporting on a meeting or conference. Sales people are often expected to present a report of their discussions with clients, especially if the product or service that is being sold is of high value. Organization of memorandum reports is topical. The employee completing the report is expected to provide information on each topic that is discussed.

Progress Reports. A progress report is another type of short report that is used to show progress on an assigned activity. If a committee at a college is assigned to investigate the possibilities of combining programs, the group would be asked or expected to complete periodic progress reports so top level administrators would know what is happening.

Letter Reports. Letter reports are another form of short report. This type of report is used to send information outside of the organization. The letter report follows the same format as a business letter. The body of the letter report is often longer and may follow the format used for other types of reports. It is usually necessary to introduce the topic, present the facts or data, and then draw some conclusions or make recommendations. While the letter report would certainly be longer than a typical business letter, it should be limited to no more than a few pages. If a longer report format is needed, it is better to prepare the document in a report format as though it were to be used internally, and then send it with a cover letter. This type of reporting to external audiences is readily used and allows enhancements that were described previously.

formal report-long report
that presents data in extensive detail

Formal Reports. Formal reports are similar to what has been discussed; however, we will give them additional attention because they are so widely used. A **formal report** is usually a long report that contains the same parts as shorter reports, but in more detail and further illustration. The formal report addresses more complete and critical issues.

The Wall Street Journal reported on discussions between cable-television and telephone industry leaders to open their systems for more competition. A group of executives called the Council on Competitiveness released a policy paper following six months of discussions. Their report was presented to lawmakers and administration officials as a "framework" for further deliberations. This formal report dealt with a critical issue in the communications industry, which provided needed information for further action and decision making.[1]

Long formal reports require that sections which are not used in a shorter or less formal report be added. There should be a cover on the report; inside should be a table of contents, a list of tables or illustrations, and an executive summary. The executive summary is used to give the reader a brief overview of the contents of the report. This summary should provide enough information so the recipients can determine if they want to read the entire document.

Formal reports often use footnotes, references, a bibliography, or explanatory notes at the end of the document. Providing notations like these allows the reader of the report to see the source of supporting information or data, and is a publication requirement.

proposal-written bid for
funds

Proposals. Many organizations are actively involved in writing and submitting proposals. A **proposal** is a bid for funds from another organization, such as a government agency, or a bid to complete work for another business. When a state highway department solicits proposals for road construction or repair, a formal process is used to announce the solicitation. In other cases a business or an individual may submit an unsolicited proposal to get funds for some type of project or activity.

A community service organization may need support to provide housing for the poor. In this situation the community service organization may submit proposals, which are really requests, for funding to be able to provide the service. The proposal may be written and submitted to a potential funding agency without that agency knowing it is coming (it is unsolicited). The agency would review the proposal and determine if it merits the requested funds.

A solicited (requested) proposal must often follow guidelines that are specified by the soliciting agency. In other situations the soliciting organization doesn't specify a format or present any guidelines. In that case good writing procedures must be followed, and the proposal should contain many of the same parts as any report. The typical proposal begins with an

[1]Daniel Pearl and Joe Davidson. "Telecommunications Companies Offer Framework for Widening Competition." *The Wall Street Journal.* December 17, 1993, B5.

introduction. In addition, the problem or need is presented; objectives are specified; procedures are outlined; and the capabilities of the proposer to complete the proposed activity are detailed. When a proposal is solicited, there is usually a deadline date for submission. If the deadline date is not met, the proposal will not be considered. Other solicitations are open, and there are no deadlines. Proposals are reviewed as they are received by the funding organization.

Informal Communication

Much of the communication that occurs in an organization is informal. This type of communication is controlled only by the communicators themselves. Their ethics and their customs influence what happens. Workers sitting around a table during a break or at lunch often discuss what is happening in their organization, and perhaps what they like or dislike about it. This is informal communication that has evolved from social interactions with coworkers. Some argue that informal communication is damaging to an organization, while others feel that it is healthy. Perhaps both are correct.

An Example of Informal Communication

Tamika Davis experienced a situation that made her understand informal communication quickly, but also made her feel uncomfortable.

Dr. Tamika Davis supervises several scientists in an agricultural genetic testing laboratory. She was recently selected by her colleagues for the position because they trusted her and knew she was a good scientist. She also exhibited the kind of leadership they felt was critical for the lab. Since Tamika had been a part of the group she now supervises, she was close friends with some of them. She had also previously developed a close friendship with some of the managers who were now her supervisors.

One day Tamika was asked by one of her superiors if she would like to go biking in the mountains over the weekend. Being an avid cyclist, she was delighted to be asked. When the manager who had asked her to go on the trip came to her house to pick her up, she was surprised to see the company president, one of her lab scientists, and a secretary along also. She didn't know that each of them had the same interest in biking.

The trip went quite well until lunchtime when the cyclists stopped to eat the food they had brought with them. The discussion during lunch revolved around one of Tamika's employees, who had caused some unrest in the organization in the past. He was one of the best scientists, however, and was critical of the current research in her division. Tamika was quite concerned about the criticism that was being voiced by the other cyclists.

She remained quiet throughout the lunch because she didn't agree with what was being said. She was not very happy with the discussion and remained quiet the rest of the day and on the return trip home. She didn't know if she should discuss the concerns with the employee, or if she should go to her manager and discuss the employee with him.

Dr. Davis was placed in a difficult situation because of the conversation and the people involved. She was surprised that the president and her manager would discuss the employee in a mixed group. She had to decide what to do. Should she talk to someone? If so, to whom? Should she just not worry about what was said and put the conversation to rest?

Grapevine Communication

grapevine-informal associations in an organization that don't follow traditional lines

The previous example illustrates the **grapevine.** Think of how a grapevine grows and how interwoven the branches can be. In an organization, the informal associations can be the same. The president is a friend of a lower level supervisor, so they communicate informally. The supervisor has an informal relationship with someone else at a different level in the organizational structure, so they talk. Someone may be a friend of someone else's spouse, so they talk, and the spouse passes the information along. Soon the grapevine has spread so much it encompasses all levels of the organization. In most organizations there is more than one grapevine because of the different relationships and associations that exist.

Information passed along the grapevine can include gossip as well as worthy company news. Often the grapevine works faster than the formal channels of communication and provides more detailed information. When information circulates through the grapevine, its accuracy must always be questioned. Rumor and gossip can be very damaging to individuals and to the organization. Sometimes the information that is being spread through the grapevine is meant to be malicious toward someone, so the source of the information must be considered. Some people love to spread rumors and gossip. The grapevine will always exist in an organization as a means for informal communication. There is no way this channel of communication can be eliminated as long as people talk to one another.

Electronic Communication

Electronic communication, or data communication, is growing rapidly and changing daily. This form of communication allows the use of electronic equipment such as computers and other technology to communicate from one point to another or from one point to several other locations. The subject is much too vast for coverage in this book; however, individuals are constantly exposed to some types of electronic communications in the workplace and perhaps in their personal lives. The intention here is not to create telecommunications experts, but to create an awareness of two very popular methods of electronic communication.

Electronic communication is growing and changing rapidly.

Voice Mail

The telephone has been in use for over a century. One of the disadvantages inherent in telephone communications is that when no one is around to answer the telephone, important messages may not be received. The development of voice mail has overcome this disadvantage. **Voice mail** is a system that allows callers to transmit a message which can be stored and listened to by the intended receiver at a later time. Voice mail is a flexible way to transmit a message to someone, even when the intended receiver is nowhere near the telephone.

In a voice mail system, when the sender leaves a message for someone who doesn't answer his or her telephone, the message is stored and is later forwarded to the receiver. The system is much like the mail service. When a large package is sent, it goes to the post office. If the postal service cannot deliver the package because the receiver is not available, a pick-up message is left and the package is stored at the post office until the receiver picks it up. Voice mail messages can be stored for varied lengths of time, depending on the system, and can be retrieved at the receiver's convenience.

voice mail-system of transmitting messages which can be stored and listened to at a later time

The Risks of Using E-Mail

Electronic mail has become widely used throughout business, government, educational institutions, and by individuals for personal use. Several large wide-area networks are available for users to make external connections. Dr. Karen Nantz, an Associate Professor at Eastern Illinois University and expert on electronic mail, conducted research related to the use of e-mail. In a personal interview, Dr. Nantz discussed the risks involved with using e-mail.

One risk is that most e-mail systems have lax security, so confidential messages often do not remain confidential. An employee who sends a negative e-mail message about his or her boss might discover that the message was read by the boss. Another risk is that there are no laws to protect users who send internal messages on an organization's e-mail system. The courts have maintained that if the organization owns the system, the organization also owns the messages sent on its system and has the right to monitor the e-mail messages on its system.

The third risk is that senders have no control over messages once they have been sent. Other people may forward the message, modify

Voice mail uses a touch-tone telephone, which allows the caller to record a message to be stored in the intended receiver's voice mailbox; the sender can listen to the message and can change it if desired before it is sent to the mail box. The message can then be sent to one or more recipients, or it can be sent to a predefined group such as a department or division in a business. The recipients check their voice mailboxes at their convenience to see if they have any messages. If there are messages, the receiver can scan to see who sent the messages and can choose the ones to listen to immediately and the ones to save and listen to later.

If the recipient is interrupted while listening to a message, the message can be stopped, replayed later, or skipped. The receiver can prepare a voice reply and send it to the person who sent the original voice mail message. It is the receiver's option to decide what to do with the message; one option might be to forward it to someone else, another might be to ignore the message and remove it from the mail box.

Voice mail systems differ and depend upon the service provider. Voice mail provides several advantages over standard telephone systems which have been used for over a century. With voice mail, a message can be left even if the recipient is not near a telephone, an important advantage when a company sends messages across time zones and around the world. One call

it, or simply take parts of it out of context. Technically, the person who wrote the message owns the copyright, and others must secure permission to use any part of the e-mail message. Still another risk is that most organizations do not have e-mail policies, so employees are left to interpret on their own what they can and cannot send via e-mail. Many people use it as a personal messaging system—often called e-chatting.

Employees should always determine if an organization has e-mail policies and find out whether users are being monitored and by whom. They should be very careful about what they say in e-mail messages. The rule of thumb is not to say anything that could embarrass the employee, cause the employee to be sued, or cause the employee to be reprimanded or terminated.

E-mail is a valuable communication tool that must be used wisely and ethically.

Source: Luft, Roger L. Based on a personal interview with Dr. Karen Nantz.

can be sent to several locations, thus eliminating the need to place several calls with the same message. Voice mail messages are easy to prepare and send since they do not have to be completed on a word processor or typewriter. Most messages can be ad-libbed by the sender. After a message is sent, there is no need to wait for a return call because the message can be sent to the voice mail address of the original sender who will check the mail box later. Voice mail is a solution for many companies and individuals; however, it is not the answer to every communication problem.

Electronic Mail (E-Mail)

Electronic mail, also called **e-mail,** is a medium of communication that requires a computer and keyboard or terminal where messages are transmitted through electronic networks. Communicating through electronic mail, or e-mail, is similar to voice mail with one major exception. The sender must key in the message, and the recipient will receive the message in a textual format. E-mail is important in the work environment, but anyone who has a portable terminal or a microcomputer with a modem can connect and send messages to an electronic mail network.

Many companies use electronic mail networks within their organization. Other companies and many educational institutions are connected

electronic mail, or e-mail-requires a computer and keyboard or terminal where messages are transmitted through electronic networks

through e-mail networks that have joined facilities around the world. Sending messages from Illinois to Ireland is as simple as sitting at a computer, preparing the message, and sending it to the recipient's e-mail address.

E-mail has the same characteristics as voice mail. Many people feel more comfortable with it because the sender can take time composing the message before it is sent. This could be critical when sending complex or very long messages that require precise wording and phrasing.

Electronic mail is used extensively in the corporate and educational worlds, which has influenced communication patterns. Communications occur from worker to worker, but e-mail allows executives to communicate with lower level supervisors and workers without face-to-face contact and with privacy. This is often critical because of the unwritten communications rules and expectations in businesses. E-mail messages are transmitted quickly, so it is a fast way to reach one or more people on the network with the same message and the confidence that they will receive the message in their mailbox even if they aren't at work when it is sent. One must assume that the e-mail messages will be read regularly and the needed actions will take place.

Organizational Groups and Communications

Groups are an integral part of every organization and are integral to the organizational communication process. Groups, or teams, are often formed for the purposes of completing a specific assignment. At other times, groups of workers unite for social purposes or to address a common cause such as world hunger. Almost everyone has been on a committee of some sort. A **committee** is a group that is given an assignment or a task. Understanding groups helps an individual to be a better group participant. Group performance depends upon how well each person completes his or her duties and how well the group is able to communicate.

committee-*group that is given an assignment or task*

Group Size

Groups can range in sizes from 2 to 20,000 or more, depending upon the purpose of the group. An established political party might have millions of registered members who have quite closely aligned interests but never all get together as one large body, and it would be impossible to get to know everyone within a group. A typical group in the workplace usually consists of from two to seven members, and generally averages three. Group size does have an impact upon the activities and performance of a group.

Relationships and communication processes that exist within a group are dependent upon the number of people in the group. If a group is made up of just two people, the possible relationship is between two people. If the group is made up of three people, then more possibilities for relation-

Some groups or teams form for social purposes or to attain a specific goal.

ships exist. If there are four, five, or more, then the opportunities for relationships within the group continue to grow and communication processes become more complex.

The larger the group size, the greater are the opportunities for groups to form within the group. This may occur naturally in a large group, or smaller groups might be appointed. Committees are often a branch of a larger group selected or appointed because the task is not conducive to being completed by a larger group. It appears that three to seven members are adequate for most activities. If the assigned task is too large for the group, it may be necessary for the group to solicit assistance from persons who are not group members.

Problems with Groups

Many people don't like to work in groups because they feel that it takes longer and is harder to accomplish something as a group. Some people feel that if a group has seven members, only two or three will do the work while the entire group gets credit. These are valid concerns for a group that is expected to work together.

Being a part of a group does call for some sacrifices. While group members might be happy with most of what the group does, not everyone will be pleased with everything. When one is unhappy, it is necessary to make compromises to remain a part of the group. Individual recognition is not typical for group activities when the group works as a team. If someone is used to or needs individual recognition, being a part of a work group may not be a stimulating experience.

Expectations are not always shared by every group member, and someone may decide not to follow the rules or norms which have been established. When some members want to change or completely disregard the rules of the group, there will be conflict. For example, group members may become incensed if someone is chronically late for meetings or even for work. The group may not be able to begin functioning, or may not function as effectively, until the tardy member arrives.

Norms are informal rules established by the group, sometimes out of tradition or ordinary, everyday operations. Most people attending a church would expect parents to keep their children quiet during the services. A gourmet dinner group may expect participants to dress formally for its dinners and would not be pleased to see a member arrive for dinner in casual denim work clothes. Students in a work group who expect all members to use a computer to word process their part of a report would be displeased with a member who comes to the final meeting with a handwritten section. Informal rules, or norms, are typically not written, which makes them more difficult to enforce, but they should be respected by all group members.

Committees and Meetings

The work environment cannot escape the sometimes dreaded committees and meetings. Many workers feel that committee assignments and meetings are a waste of time. Committees are a type of work group that can be very effective and a positive addition to an organization. Meetings are often nec-

Meetings are often necessary to resolve problems and are a practical means to communicate with workers.

Unit 2 • Essentials of Human Relations

essary to resolve problems and are a practical means to communicate with workers.

Sometimes individuals cannot make good decisions or don't want to have the burden of making a wrong decision. At times like these, a committee with a few people can use the collective intelligence and experience of all members to make better decisions. No one person is expected to know everything about all subjects. It is useful for a supervisor or executive to have the option of selecting a group of people to make decisions or suggestions so that better decisions might be made.

Heidi Winkler and Seth Samson were asked by their supervisor to represent the word processing department of Work Flow, Inc., on a committee of ten people, two from each department of the company. The two were told they were going to look at alternative methods of scheduling workers so that the company could go to a four-day workweek. Some of the departments worked two shifts each day and others worked only one. Heidi and Seth represented a department that worked two shifts, and workers weren't always happy about rotating shifts. Heidi had worked previously with a company that used flexible scheduling for its employees.

Heidi and Seth both attended the first meeting; in fact, they were the first ones to arrive at the boardroom where the meeting was scheduled. When the Vice President for Human Resources arrived, she was surprised to see them there about five minutes early. She knew Seth from previous committees but hadn't gotten to know Heidi very well since she was new to the company and was a little shy.

The Vice President called the meeting to order when all ten employees were present. She told them that she was only going to give them their charge and appoint someone to chair their committee; then she was going to let them begin their process. She knew that Heidi had worked with flexible scheduling in the past, so she asked her to chair the committee. Heidi did not want to chair the committee. Her shyness had kept her from speaking at meetings. The rest of the committee members happily endorsed the Vice President's selection, and Heidi felt she had to do the job or she wouldn't be accepted by the other members. She reluctantly accepted the responsibilities.

Heidi and Seth were selected for their knowledge, experience, and willingness to serve on a committee. Heidi's appointment as the chair of the committee was a surprise to her, but she was willing to accept the challenge with some hesitation. Committees are formed for numerous reasons and function in many ways. The same types of problems can occur with committees as with larger groups. What can Heidi expect when she conducts her first meeting of the committee? What are some of the unique characteristics of a committee? How does communication occur in a committee?

- Organizations of all types have a structure that can be shown on an organizational chart and which shows the flow of formal communications through the organization.

- Organizations can be tall, with more levels of structure, or flat, with fewer levels of structure. Taller organizations have more management levels, and managers/supervisors are responsible for fewer workers; that is, they have a narrow span of control. When the organization is flat, managers/supervisors are responsible for more workers, having a broader span of control. Communication is more direct when the structure is flat.

- Channels of communication follow the structure of an organization. Communication can flow downward, upward, or horizontally. Downward communication is from managers or supervisors to those who are at levels lower than the originator of the communication. Upward communication flows from lower levels of the structure to higher levels. Horizontal communications occur between people at the same level.

- Written communication is used when more formality is needed, when messages are complex, or when the information is long and detailed. Written communication includes letters, memorandums, reports, and proposals.

- Informal communication does not follow the organizational structure, but flows in all directions throughout the organization and creates a pattern that looks like a grapevine. Grapevine communications cannot be prevented in an organization and can be either healthy or harmful.

- Electronic communication is an important tool in an organization. The telephone is electronic, but more advanced methods of communicating expand the usage of the telephone and telephone transmission equipment. The most popular forms of electronic communications are voice mail and electronic mail (e-mail).

- Few organizations would survive without groups in the form of teams or committees. Group members typically have something in common, which might be a goal they are trying to achieve.

Key Terms

bar graph	electronic mail
channel of communication	formal communication
chart	formal report
committee	grapevine
downward communication	illustration
e-mail	informal communication

letter	short report
letterhead	table
memorandum	upward communication
organizational chart	verbal communication
organizational structure	vertical communication
pie chart	voice mail
proposal	written communication
report	

Discussion Questions

1. If you are employed, ask your supervisor for a copy of an organizational chart. Some companies may not have one, so this is your opportunity to create one for the organization. Once you have an organizational chart, analyze it to determine the following:

   a. Is the organization tall or flat?

   b. How many levels might a message have to go through to get from the top to the bottom of the structure?

   c. What are the communication barriers that are evident from the organizational chart?

2. If you are a supervisor and need to communicate with someone outside of the organization, what would be the best form of written communication to use? Why would you select this type over others? What are the advantages and disadvantages of each possible form of written communication?

3. How can the grapevine be a useful form of communication? How can the grapevine be a harmful form of communication?

4. Voice mail is used by many organizations to help ensure that the intended receiver of a message will receive it. How can voice mail be misused by an individual or an organization? Discuss your reactions to how organizations monitor voice mail messages.

5. Electronic mail (e-mail) is useful for someone who has the necessary equipment to send and receive messages. Should companies have access to e-mail messages sent or received by employees? Why or why not?

6. From your own experience describe some problems that groups might have. How did your experiences compare to those outlined in the chapter? What was different? Why do you think your group was different?

Chapter 7

Human Needs and Motivation

Learning Objectives

Upon completing this chapter, you should be able to:

- Profile the four elements that constitute the human self.

- Explain how a person's values are established.

- Summarize several different motivation theories.

- Discuss your personal meaning of success and evaluate how success might be achieved.

Ian Cantrell loved mornings, and when his alarm buzzed at 5:00 A.M., he was out of bed in an instant and hit the floor on the move. Most mornings he turned off his alarm before it sounded because he was wide awake and eager to start the new day. He was always full of cheer and was a delight to be around; his "fire" was contagious, and others caught his enthusiasm when they were around him.

Unlike Ian Cantrell, Nicole Allen liked to stay up late at night, and it was difficult for her to get herself out of bed at 7:00 A.M. when her alarm sounded. She liked to have fun at night and preferred to sleep late in the morning, but her job demanded that she be at work by 8:30 A.M. each day. She dragged herself around every morning because she had had only about five hours of sleep and she needed eight hours to feel rested and happy. She didn't like being around others in the morning and they didn't like being around her.

*I*ndividual Differences

All people have a unique set of characteristics that define who they are; what their needs, wants, and desires are; and what they expect of themselves and others. Because of individual differences a person may or may not like someone else; may find it difficult to work with other people because of their work habits; or might want to be with a particular group of people because of similar interests and goals. The question "What makes you tick?" is difficult to answer. Sometimes individuals themselves can't understand what it is that drives them and keeps them going. This chapter explores personal needs and motivation to develop an understanding of ourselves and others.

A Look at "Self"

The actions and reactions of individuals are closely linked to **personal needs,** an awareness of self in relationship to others. The human self is described as having four elements. The first is the body—a living, breathing entity that depends upon the automatic beating of the heart as its fundamental life-sustaining activity. The second is the ability to take in information about the outside world through the five basic senses: sight, touch, taste, smell, and hearing. These first two elements are considered to be the parts that are known as the passive self.

The third element constitutes the active self, the ability to respond to the environment. This is easily illustrated by the three-year-old child who runs into the arms of a parent whom she hasn't seen for a few days. The fourth element of the self is called the **reflexive self,** the part that causes individuals to be self-aware and reflective of their being. The reflexive self is an element that is lacking in other creatures. This is the one element that distinguishes humans from other animals. A normal person who is involved in a fight caused by anger is able to reflect on the activity and draw conclusions about the reasons and the results, while an animal that fights with another animal can't determine if the fight was right or wrong. It is the third and fourth elements that most people are concerned with in their relationships with others and in the work environment. The first two elements, being passive, have a way of almost always taking care of themselves.

Personal Values

Each one of us has a set of **values** that causes reflection and evaluation of thoughts and feelings and the resulting actions. This part of an individual's

personal needs-awareness of self in relation to others

reflexive self-part of self that causes reflection of one's being

values-beliefs that cause reflection and evaluation of thoughts and feelings and resulting actions

Figure 7.1 Passive and Active Elements

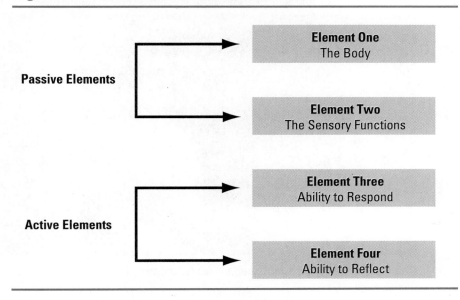

self is the values and **standards** which come from the culture, religion, and society around us as we grow up. Because there are such differences in people's environments, people's values differ. Societies, cultures, and religions reflect the expectations of their members by defining acceptable and unacceptable behaviors and standards. There are role models who are held up as the standards for acceptable behavior.

Standards and values vary from one culture, society, or religion to another. People have the freedom to choose or are born into their environment, and they later reflect the values they have learned. When there are disagreements with the values of a society, culture, or religion, the result is conflict. The conflict might be between external groups who have differences or within an individual who is having difficulty dealing with the values and standards of the group. Values can and do change in cultures, societies, and religions as time passes, just as values of an individual can change with maturity.

Coping with Personal Values

As we are involved in our social lives and in a work environment, values need to be measured and analyzed. A self-examination is critical to help determine personal values compared to the values of others and to standards expected by society. After self-examination, the individual needs to be honest and determine if his or her actions reflect what the person values.

An individual's values will not always be reflected in what that person does or says. If there is disparity between values and actions, then it is time

The values and the standards people set for themselves are often based on their needs.

to determine which values are most important to the individual and the people he or she wants to be around. Sometimes it is not only ourselves we must please, but also those around us. This applies to people in our immediate personal relationships and in the work environment.

Values are often a reflection of the needs of an individual. Considering the values and needs of others will determine the decisions a person makes or the actions he or she will take. Values will often determine how people perform in the workplace. If there is a difference in an individual's values and the values of others, it will be necessary to consider how to reconcile or negotiate the difference. Anyone who expects to have a good working relationship with others, or a close personal relationship with someone, should understand what makes him or her "tick." What are the values and needs that cause people to work like they do, or to manage others as they do?

Motivation

Motivation is a need, an absence of something, that drives a person to act or react, or to behave in a specific way. If this is the case, then it is the needs of other people that must be discovered to get them to act. The individual must provide the motive or the stimulation which will cause the internal tensions or needs to want to be satisfied. If a person can "push the right buttons," the actions of other people will be in response to how the person wants them to perform.

motivation-need or absence of something that causes a person to act or react

As an illustration, consider the affluent person who has just finished a rather large meal of his choice, and is stuffed; he couldn't eat another thing. If you offered him another large meal which had to be eaten right away, he wouldn't have any desire to eat so you couldn't provide the motive or stimulation for the person to respond. The person knows he could have the meal later or the next day. He would probably rather just walk away from the table and perhaps take a nap. There is no internal tension, need, or void which hasn't been taken care of by the first meal so there is no motivation to accept the second meal.

Now consider the man who hasn't eaten for days. How would he react to an offer for a second meal? Chances are he would feel the need for further fulfillment in anticipation of not having another meal for a few days. He may eat the meal even though he is on the verge of bursting. This is a person who has a need that must be satisfied, a lack of available food in the past and in the future.

Motivation seems simple, but it is a rather complex topic to understand. Many theorists have struggled for years to define exactly what it is that motivates people. Some experts believe that motivation is based on human needs while others say motivation is based on external or environmental elements. There is considerable agreement and disagreement among the experts. A discussion of some of the most popular theories follows.

Chapter 7 • Human Needs and Motivation

*M*aslow's Hierarchy of Needs

One of the earliest and most popular theories of motivation today is Maslow's need hierarchy. This theory was first introduced in the mid-1940s by Abraham Maslow. His theory has two basic premises, one being that humans are "wanting" animal beings motivated by a desire to satisfy certain needs. Second, Maslow says that the needs that individuals pursue are common across almost every population and that they are arranged in a logical and sequential hierarchy. In the hierarchy, there must be satisfaction of lower needs before the higher needs are satisfied.[1] It is this second premise that causes some experts to disagree with Maslow's theory because it is felt that individuals of different populations cannot be placed in the same classification. Maslow's hierarchy of needs looks like a pyramid and is discussed next.

Figure 7.2 **Maslow's Hierarchy of Needs**

Self-actualization needs

Self-esteem needs

Need for belonging and love

Safety and security needs

Physiological needs

Physiological Needs

At the lowest level of the hierarchy are the physiological needs, which include food, water, and shelter. To someone who is deprived of food or drink, nothing else really matters, and the need to eat or to have something to drink dominates the person's desires. Hungry people use all their capabilities to satisfy the need for food; there is an absence of conscious efforts to satisfy other needs.

---

[1]Abraham H. Maslow. "A Theory of Human Motivation." *Psychological Review.* vol. 50, no. 1, January 1943, 370–96.

When the physiological needs are satisfied, they no longer dominate the person's thoughts and other needs begin to emerge and become more important. Children and adults living in drought-stricken countries where there is widespread famine are good examples. With needs for food and drink, could they possibly think of their educational needs or about preparing for a job? The many homeless people around the world often resort to stealing to have food to eat or to provide food for their children; their shelter might be a cardboard box or an abandoned automobile. It is difficult for someone in this condition to think about satisfying needs beyond the basic physiological needs.

Safety and Security Needs

When most physiological needs are taken care of, a new set of needs will emerge, characterized as safety needs. The needs for safety are most important once food, shelter, and other physiological needs have been taken care of. Safety needs include protection from the natural elements, and from criminals, fire, and similar dangers. Safety and security also include having a job, perhaps a job with opportunities for long-term stability and growth and the capability of providing what is needed for a family.

There is security in having a savings account and being able to buy what is needed, to provide for the basics, without having to worry about from where the money will come. There is also security in being able to have insurance for medical and dental protection for oneself and one's family; this protection often comes from an employer. Once safety and security needs have been met, other needs begin to emerge and priorities for satisfaction shift to the new dominating needs.

Love and Belonging

After the physiological and safety needs have been pretty well gratified, the needs for love, affection, and belonging will emerge. After being satisfactorily fed, with a roof overhead, and having a job to go to regularly, the person who is without close associations will feel the absence of friends, a spouse, or children. This person will hunger for association with a group and acceptance by the group. The affiliation can be with a social group or with a group at work. This need for belonging and being loved dominates the individual's needs, and the needs for food and shelter will fade dimly into the past.

Affiliation needs have been studied more than any of the other needs and are perhaps better understood than all the other needs, with the exception of the physiological needs. Theorists of psychopathology have found that when love needs have been impeded, maladjustment typically results. Behaviorists are quick to point out that there is a difference between love needs and sex needs. Sex needs can be reduced to being purely physiological while the needs for love and belonging are far more complex and include both giving and receiving. When a person has found the affiliation that allows giving and receiving, the needs are largely satisfied and the next level of the hierarchy can be addressed.

Self-esteem Needs

Almost everyone in our society has a need to be stable with a firm foundation, to feel good about themselves, to have self-esteem or self-respect and the respect of others. This characterizes the fourth level on Maslow's hierarchy. These characteristics don't just happen without effort and achievement; it is necessary to earn respect from others and from one's own self.

Self-esteem needs can be classified into two categories. The first is the desire for strength, achievement, and competence, which can all contribute to the confidence needed to confront a variety of situations and to gain independence and freedom. The second category is the desire for a reputation or the prestige which can command the respect of others, for recognition, attention, or appreciation.

When the self-esteem need is satisfied, there are feelings of self-confidence, worth, capability, and adequacy, which all establish a sense of being needed in the world. If the self-esteem needs are not being met, the individual feels weak, inferior, helpless, and sometimes a burden to others. This level, and the feelings of self-worth are important in everyday life, including in the workplace. Managers and supervisors must be able to address these needs in order to make workers more productive, as will be discussed in the next chapter.

Self-actualization Needs

At the top of Maslow's hierarchy is the need for self-actualization, the need to be what you have the potential to be or do what you feel you must do. Even though satisfaction comes from meeting all of the needs below this level, a person may be discontent and have even greater needs. Consider the needs of Kyle Shoots, a highly respected teacher at a middle-sized high school.

Self-actualization, the need to be or do what you feel you must do, is the most difficult to achieve according to Abraham Maslow.

Kyle taught science courses, and the students liked him because he was sincerely interested in them and their success. He worked hard to keep himself current in his field and his lessons up-to-date. He usually spent 15 to 20 hours a week working on lesson preparation and developing materials after the regular teaching day. Kyle seemed to be happy, and others always commented on his success—he had earned the respect that teachers want from students, parents, and colleagues.

The principal of the school was surprised that after 20 years of teaching in the same school, Kyle submitted his resignation. No one wanted to see him leave his job, and in fact several of his colleagues and students tried to convince him to continue teaching. Kyle told them he felt a real need to do something he had always wanted to do and just didn't have time to pursue. He wanted to try his hand at writing and illustrating children's books, a very difficult profession in which to succeed. He felt he had to make the switch in order to be satisfied. His wife had a good job and their children were all through college and on their own. Kyle felt the need for self-actualization—he wanted to do something he knew he could do and for years had wanted to do.

Kyle was addressing his needs for self-actualization, the desire for self-fulfillment, or the desire to become what one is capable of being. Not everyone has the same needs for self-actualization. While society often looks at workplace accomplishments and promotions or wealth and riches as success, these may not be the measure of success that some people are concerned with. Self-actualization for one person may be completely different for another. Self-actualization may mean being the ideal mother and wife, or the ideal father and husband. For another person, self-actualization may mean being able to express thoughts and feelings through writing or illustrating, like Kyle; and to still another person, self-actualization may come from being able to repair any computer or software problem that could occur.

A Summary of Maslow

There has been much criticism of Maslow's theory because it is often viewed as being too simplistic; however, it is one of the most often mentioned and discussed theories in the literature today. It is widely known today that people don't have to meet the needs of one level completely before advancing to the next level. However, it is not known to what degree of satisfaction one need must be achieved before the next need is addressed.

What many experts feel is that once a person's need, for example the safety need, is met to a certain degree, the person will begin to work toward satisfying his or her self-esteem needs. Using arbitrary figures, if you are 40 percent satisfied in meeting your safety needs, for example, you may start working on esteem needs and be able to achieve 10 percent satisfaction. As the lower level need percentage increases, the higher level

Chapter 7 • Human Needs and Motivation

need could increase also. This means that technically an individual may never satisfy his or her needs 100 percent at the lower level and could be addressing higher level needs. It is believed that very few people achieve self-actualization, the level at which they are completely satisfied with who they are and what they are doing.

In spite of the criticisms leveled against Maslow's theories, they do provide a foundation for understanding ourselves and others. If the theories are applied in our individual situations and in the workplace, better relationships can be established and personal success is more likely. As other theories are discussed, you will see how closely related some behaviorists are to the thoughts of Abraham Maslow.

Figure 7.3 Self-actualization Survey

Answer each of the statements without a lot of thought—initial reactions are important. Circle either "a" or "b" to indicate the most correct statement. If you are uncertain, come back to it later. This is a survey of how you feel about yourself, not how you want others to think of you. There is no correct or incorrect answer, only your answer.

1. a My spare time is usually well spent.
   b I don't do much with my spare time.

2. a Life is lonely and means little.
   b My life is active and means a lot.

3. a I am concerned about what the future will bring.
   b I can't do much about the future.

4. a I like the work that I do.
   b My work is boring and I don't enjoy it.

5. a I am worried about failing.
   b My nature is not to worry about failure.

6. a I use good things right away.
   b I wait to use good things.

7. a I control most of my life.
   b Other people control my life.

8. a I give in easily.
   b I fight to the end.

9. a I will try to please others, even when I don't want to.
   b I am mostly concerned about pleasing myself.

10. a I often wonder about my worth.
    b I don't doubt my worth, even when others might.

11. a My moral standards are clearly defined.
    b Society's standards are what I use.

12. a My goals are critical.
    b I don't worry about personal goals.

13. a When I please myself, I feel guilty.
    b I feel good when I can please myself.

14. a I am often impulsive about what I do.
    b I am usually conservative in what I do.

15. a I am often concerned about the impressions I make on others.
    b Saying the wrong thing doesn't concern me.

16. a I usually do what I want to do.
    b I usually give in to others' wishes.

17. a I don't feel I have to justify what I do.
    b I often feel I must justify my actions to others.

18. a I don't count on intuition and feelings to guide what I do.
    b My feelings and intuition are used often for direction.

19. a I am often pessimistic.
    b I tend to be mostly optimistic.

20. a I am often overcome by the beauty of all that is around me.
    b Natural beauty doesn't do much for me.

21. a I don't have inferiority feelings.
    b I am bothered by feelings of inferiority.

22. a I get along with others regardless of their values and beliefs.
    b I can't relate to people with different values and beliefs.

23. a I feel like I belong.
    b I feel like I don't belong.

24. a I am able to love without reservations.
    b I find it hard to give myself completely in a loving relationship.

25. a I can't often show affection because I fear rejection.
    b It doesn't concern me at all to show affection.

26. a I know people to whom I would tell anything and everything.
    b I wouldn't divulge my innermost feelings to anyone.

27. a I don't feel as though I am needed.
    b I feel like I am needed by others.

28. a I am admired by several people.
    b I don't know of anyone who admires me as I am.

29. a I have difficulty admitting my mistakes.
    b It doesn't bother me to admit my mistakes.

30. a Most people do things for their own benefit.
    b People do things without expecting something in return.

31. a People should have freedom to do what they want as long as
        no one is hurt.
    b It is important that society has rules and people follow them.

32. a Political decision-making should include everyone.
    b Only those with political expertise should make political
        decisions.

33. a I am sometimes overwrought with happiness and wonderment.
    b I never feel overwrought with happiness and wonderment.

Chapter 7 • Human Needs and Motivation

Figure 7.3, continued

Scoring your Self-actualization Survey

After completing the survey, count one point for each of your answers that corresponds to these: 1a, 2b, 3b, 4a, 5b, 6a, 7a, 8b, 9b, 10b, 11a, 12a, 13b, 14a, 15b, 16a, 17a, 18b, 19b, 20a, 21a, 22a, 23a, 24a, 25b, 26a, 27b, 28a, 29b, 30b, 31a, 32a, 33a.

Low score = 0–11 You should review your relationships and see what can be done to improve them.

Medium score = 12–24 this is the normal range for most people. Look at each of your replies carefully in order to find which part of your life needs improvement.

High score = 25–33 If you are at the bottom of this range, you are heading toward self-actualization. If you scored at the top of this range, and marked "a" for questions 20 and 33, you are highly self-actualized. You are rare because few people meet these requirements.

Adapted from: Human Behavior: Your Personality and Potential. *Edited by Glen Wilson. vol. 5, New York: Marshall Cavendish Corporation, 1990, 534, 535.*

*H*erzberg's Motivation-Hygiene Theory

motivation-hygiene theory-*factors cause workers to be satisfied or dissatisfied on the job, which influences levels of performance*

job dissatisfiers-*factors such as company policy, interpersonal relationships, and working conditions that cause a worker to be dissatisfied*

motivational factors-*factors that cause worker satisfaction and growth*

hygiene factors-*factors that cause worker dissatisfaction and discontent*

Another popular theory of motivation that has stood the test of time, especially by managers in the workplace, was proposed by Frederick Herzberg in the 1950s. Herzberg's theory has also been called the two-factor theory and the dual-factor theory. This theory refers to what Herzberg called *job satisfiers* (motivational factors) and **job dissatisfiers** (hygiene factors). Herzberg is quick to point out that the opposite of job satisfaction is not job dissatisfaction, but lack of job satisfaction. Just like the opposite of job dissatisfaction is not job satisfaction, but lack of dissatisfaction.

Herzberg measured job factors that caused workers to be satisfied with their job, or dissatisfied with their job. The factors that caused growth, or for workers to be satisfied, were called the **motivational factors.** These included achievement, recognition, the work itself, responsibility, and advancement or growth. The dissatisfaction-avoidance, or **hygiene factors,** included company policy and administration, supervision, interpersonal relationships, working conditions, salary, status, and security. The motivators cause workers to be happy on the job while the hygiene factors are the primary cause of unhappiness on the job.

Herzberg's theory is similar in some respects to Maslow's hierarchy of needs theory. The main premise of motivation-hygiene theory is that environmental, extrinsic factors serve hygiene needs (which Maslow called lower order needs); whereas intrinsic, growth factors serve motivator needs (which Maslow called self-actualization needs). But unlike Maslow,

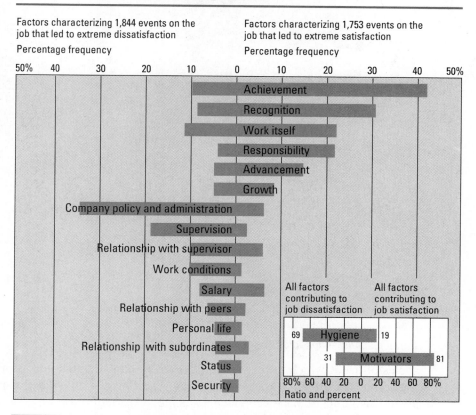

Figure 7.4 **Factors Affecting Job Attitudes, as Reported in Twelve Investigations**

Factors characterizing 1,844 events on the job that led to extreme dissatisfaction

Percentage frequency

Factors characterizing 1,753 events on the job that led to extreme satisfaction

Percentage frequency

50% 40 30 20 10 0 10 20 30 40 50%

Achievement
Recognition
Work itself
Responsibility
Advancement
Growth
Company policy and administration
Supervision
Relationship with supervisor
Work conditions
Salary
Relationship with peers
Personal life
Relationship with subordinates
Status
Security

All factors contributing to job dissatisfaction

All factors contributing to job satisfaction

69 Hygiene 19
31 Motivators 81

80% 60 40 20 0 20 40 60 80%
Ratio and percent

Herzberg holds that the relief of hygiene (lower order needs) can only be temporary and therefore cannot result in long-term satisfaction. For example, Herzberg's research found that good feelings over a salary increase seldom last more than six months. Although Herzberg's hygiene factors roughly parallel Maslow's lower order needs, Herzberg holds that the motivator factors tend to operate independently of hygiene. Workers are more or less satisfied with motivators and more or less dissatisfied with hygiene at the same time; therefore Herzberg disagrees that lower level needs must or can be satisfied before focusing on motivator achievement (quality production) and satisfaction. Giving the worker more training and responsibility which Herzberg called job enrichment has translated into the present trend toward worker empowerment.[2]

A few theorists would argue now that Herzberg and Maslow are outdated because the workplace has changed so much that their theories are not appropriate for a changing society. People and societies go through

[2]Herzberg, Frederick, Mausner, Bernard, and Snyderman, Barbara Bloch. *The Motivation to Work.* John Wiley & Sons, 1959. Reprinted as a Management Classic with a new introductory chapter. Transaction Publishers (Rutgers University) 1993.

Personal satisfaction in one's work comes from the nature of the work.

cycles of needs which influence their reactions to factors that may or may not stimulate normally expected reactions. The 1980s, a time when materialism was rampant, have been labeled as the "what's in it for me" era. The Yuppie generation earned high incomes and spent them just as readily. Money provided more satisfaction than at previous times. The dissatisfaction that came from money was not having enough to be able to buy everything needed to keep up with the neighbors or coworkers.

Even those who feel that Herzberg's motivation-hygiene theory is outdated attribute major changes in the workplace to him. Because Herzberg felt that much of a person's satisfaction and motivation comes from the intrinsic nature of the work, he also suggested that jobs could be redesigned in an effort to maximize job satisfaction. Job enrichment is a direct result of Herzberg's theory and is one of the topics of Chapter 8.

Achievement Motivation Theory

achievement motivation theory-*needs-based theory which assumes it is possible to predict performance based on personal needs to achieve*

The **achievement motivation theory** is another theory that is based on the concept of human needs, just as the theory of Maslow. According to this theory, it is possible to explain or predict much of an individual's performance based on how badly that person needs to achieve. This theory follows the concepts of motive or drive: when something is lacking in our life, we feel as though we must do something to fill the gap. An example might be the person who feels the need to score an A on a test to maintain a high average for a class. This person is going to study as much as is needed to get the desired grade while someone who doesn't care what he or she scores on the exam won't put much, if any, effort into preparing for the test.

David McClelland presented these views for motivated behavior by building upon the work of earlier researchers in the field. He said that if an individual spends time thinking about and doing a job better, accomplishing something that is important or advancing in a career, the person has a high need for achievement. This kind of a person can be difficult for low achievers to cope with. The high achiever is a good candidate to hold entrepreneurial positions, and this person will probably search for these opportunities in order to be satisfied. Someone with a strong need for achievement thinks about the achievement goals, and also about how the goals can be achieved, what the hurdles or roadblocks that might get in the way are, and what the result will be if there is success or failure.[3]

Understanding the Strong Need for Achievement

There are several reasons why some people have such a strong need to achieve. Do you know anyone who wants to achieve at all costs? Perhaps this will help you to understand them in personal relationships, or at work.

Need to Take Personal Responsibility. People who have high needs for achievement are the same ones who like to be in situations in which they can take personal responsibility for finding solutions to problems. The reasons for this behavior are obvious: if the person cannot be responsible for solving problems, there cannot be any satisfaction from achieving successful outcomes. The high achiever does not want to take great risks with outcomes that are left to chance but prefers to take risks that can be calculated and controlled.

Given the choice of winning a large amount of money by purchasing lottery tickets where the selection is made completely by chance, or making a large amount of money by making the correct decisions in a business situation, the high achiever will likely choose the business decision-making opportunity. In fact, the high achiever would probably choose this route even if the odds were the same in both situations. At least the business decisions can be controlled.

Setting Goals and Taking Risks. The individual who has a strong need to achieve will almost always set moderate goals and take calculated risks. This is understandable because with moderate goals, achievement and success will almost always occur and the planned route for achieving the goals is easier to define. When the high achiever takes on

---

[3]David McClelland. "The Business Drive and National Achievement." *Harvard Business Review.* vol. 40, no. 4, July-August 1962, 99–112.

Japanese Work Habits Can Lead to Death

On January 10, 1994, *The Wall Street Journal* reported that a study in Japan found that for the fiscal year prior to the study, one in every six men worked at least 3,100 hours per year. At this level, physicians said the result can be *karoshi,* death from overwork, something that is feared by 46 percent of the workers.

The number of health disorders among Japanese workers is on the rise as a result of the long number of hours of intensive work.

The Japanese work more hours on the job each year than do workers in other countries. Taking all Japanese workers into account, they work approximately 2,124 hours per year. United States and

a simple or routine goal, there is little satisfaction from the resulting success—there is no challenge, no opportunity to demonstrate ones ability, thus no satisfaction.

The middle ground, somewhere between responsibilities that are too easy to achieve and don't bring satisfaction and responsibilities that are almost impossible to achieve so satisfaction can't result, is where the high achiever is most comfortable and can achieve the greatest level of satisfaction. There is less chance for frustration and greater possibilities for controlled success.

Michael Jordan, perhaps one of the best basketball players ever to have played professional basketball, retired unexpectedly. What was left for Michael to achieve in basketball? He had been on NBA championship teams, a gold medal Olympic team, was earning millions of dollars with product endorsements and advertising. Perhaps he was no longer challenged with basketball. Shortly after his retirement from basketball, Michael Jordan announced he wanted to try professional baseball and did in fact sign a minor league baseball contract with the Chicago White Sox organization. He had not played baseball since his teen years. If you consider his decision, Michael chose baseball, a sport in which there are different levels of play and he could prove himself in the minor leagues—this is middle ground for professional baseball. He and the White Sox were taking less risk with him in the minors and, of course, he was a box office draw. There was personal satisfaction for Michael and monetary satisfaction for the Sox. He felt the need to achieve and was taking a calculated risk. For most people who don't have the athletic abilities of Michael Jordan, the risk would be immense, but Michael felt the chance of succeeding was great enough to give it a try. He had moderate success and gave up baseball to return to the Chicago Bulls to resume his basketball career.

British workers spend 200 hours less on the job than do the Japanese, and workers in France and Germany spend between 400 and 500 hours less on the job than the Japanese. The report also stated that the Japanese actually spend many more hours on the job than the government reports because most workers put in an average of 1.5 hours of service overtime—work that is not recorded and not paid. It is readily apparent that Japanese workers have considerable pressures to be high achievers.

"Japanese Work Habits Can Be Lethal." The Wall Street Journal. *January 10, 1994. A9.*

Figure 7.5 **Motivation**

Shoe

Need for Feedback.   The person who has a great need for achievement also has a need for concrete feedback on the progress that he or she is making to get satisfaction. Business people get feedback on a regular basis; a sales person who has a quota or goals for sales volume will know on a daily basis if he or she is achieving success; the production manager knows if a plant is producing at an established daily level. In a business chart, it is the lines that are moving upward that are usually positive indicators. Achievement is indicated by upward movement.

In some jobs there is little feedback to indicate successful achievement of goals. Many helping professions give little in the way of indicators that the workers are achieving what they want to achieve. People who have a need for concrete feedback to measure success would have to settle for less than desirable measures of performance and may satisfy their need for high achievement in other ways.

Ethical Dimensions to Human Relations

Why Bankers Become Criminals

Sometimes it is difficult to understand why people do what they do. What prompts them to take actions that might result in having to go to prison? This is a question to ask some citizens of the United States, but people in all countries of the world, as well. In 1983 there was a stock scandal in Israel that caused the collapse of the country's securities market and required that the Israeli government come to the rescue with a $7 billion bailout. Ten years after the debacle, former heads of Israel's top four banks were convicted of fraud for the parts they played in the financial collapse.

Perhaps out of the need for power and being driven by greed, the bankers allegedly manipulated their own banks' stock prices in order to offer investors higher returns. As the amount of money they could potentially lose increased, they had to continue to prop up prices for their own protection. Investors started selling the bank shares when

Understanding the Strong Need for Power

Leslie was the type of person who spent time thinking of ways to influence and control others. She didn't like to lose an argument and planned what she would say in order to win the argument. Leslie got great pleasure from changing the behavior of other people, and from being in authority and in a position with high status. Leslie had a strong need for power.

need for power-results in someone who tries to directly influence other people's behavior

People with a strong **need for power** will usually try to influence others' behavior directly by making suggestions, by offering opinions and evaluations, or by trying to talk them into something they personally feel strongly about. These people will usually seek control in a group situation, and the degree to which the control, or leadership, is accepted is determined by the personality and skill of the person who needs power. The person who needs power is often verbally fluent, talkative, and likes to argue. The power person is usually considered to be outspoken and forceful and often is described by others as demanding and aggressive.

The person with a strong need for power is likely to be a candidate for a position in which he or she will be able to exercise power and control. The power person enjoys positions in which there are opportunities to use persuasion to influence others, as does a politician, police officer, or teacher. This person usually strives to reach the higher levels of management in an organization. It is the need to achieve control to be in the power

other investments became more attractive and they feared prices of the bank shares would drop.

The Tel Aviv stock exchange had to shut down for two weeks while the government bailout was being negotiated. This shutdown prevented further calamity in the financial markets. Eventually the government took control of the banks and later began to sell them.

Because of the greed and the need for power and wealth that motivated a few executives in high positions, many people lost their life savings. These people had to start over, while the perpetrators of the crime were essentially free for the ten years that it took to complete a trial and reach a verdict. The question could again be asked, what is it that makes us tick? Why do we do what we do?

Source: Marcus, Amy Dockser. "Former Bankers Are Convicted in '83 Israel Case." The Wall Street Journal. February 17, 1994, A11.

position that distinguishes the need for power from the need for achievement. Someone with a need to achieve can be satisfied by merely achieving his or her goals and being recognized, but the person with a need for power needs to achieve control.

Understanding the Need for Affiliation

When people think about the warm, close relationships they have, or would like to have, they are said to have a need for affiliation. **Affiliation needs** cause people to want to restore relationships that might have gone by the wayside, to help or console someone who might be suffering from a loss, or just be with others at parties, friendly discussions, and activities. Rather than being concerned about themselves like the persons who need power, the people with high affiliation needs want to help and support others. They are willing to agree and give emotional support to avoid conflict.

affiliation needs-causes people to want to restore relationships, to help others, or be around others

People with the strong need for affiliation will be most satisfied in jobs where they can help and support others and where there are opportunities for friendly relationships. If people with a strong need for affiliation are placed in supervisory positions, they will work best in a position that requires excellent "people skills" rather than decision-making skills. It might be detrimental to place these people in management positions which require decisions that could cause dissension among workers. Counselors, nurses, and teachers often exhibit a strong need for affiliation and enter those professions to be able to help others without the need to make difficult decisions.

Equity Theory

equity theory-motivation
is influenced by an individual's perception of how
equitably he or she is
treated

The **equity theory,** based upon the research of J. Stacy Adams, proposes that motivation is influenced by an individual's perception of how equitably he or she is treated on the job. Individuals assess input—how much effort is going into the job—and outcomes and how much reward there is for the efforts. Often without even knowing what is happening, the worker calculates the ratio of output to input and compares it to what other workers are doing.[4]

The comparison to other workers allows people to determine if they are receiving equal outcomes for the amount of inputs. If they are not, then there is inequity and they will respond in a manner necessary to create equity. If there is equity and people are getting the same as the other workers, they will be content and the comparison results in continuation of what is currently occurring.

Consider Kirk Peterson, a hard-working college student who is employed part-time at a small auto parts store. He is paid minimum wage since he is employed part-time and works at times that are not wanted by the full-time workers. The full-time workers regularly leave him jobs that they don't want to do, like cleaning the restrooms and mopping the floors. Kirk needs the money to pay for his college expenses, but he feels he is having to work much harder than the full-time employees and is getting a lot less for his efforts. In other words, he feels that there is inequity in the workplace. His natural reaction is to want to reduce his amount of effort on the job; he is losing his motivation. Maybe he should get a different job, or should he talk to his manager? What would you recommend for Kirk?

This scenario illustrates the equity theory. Kirk feels as though he is doing as much as, or maybe more, since he gets a lot of the dirty jobs, than the full-time employees. Since he isn't treated equally to them, he feels and questions the inequity. His input will likely be reduced, since his rewards are not at the level he feels they should be, compared to the other workers.

The Expectancy-Valence Theory

expectancy-valence
theory-human behavior is
the result of the characteristics of the individual and
his or her perceived environment

The final theory that will be discussed is the **expectancy-valence theory,** also referred to by other names such as expectancy theory and path-goal theory. This theory suggests that human behavior, to a large extent, is the result of the characteristics of the individual, and what the individual perceives to be his or her environment. The most popular of the expectancy

---

[4]J. Stacy Adams. "Toward an Understanding of Inequity." *Journal of Abnormal and Social Psychology.* vol. 67, 1963. A22–36.

theories was developed by Victor Vroom. It was Vroom who defined **expectancy** as an action-outcome association. **Valence** relates to affective orientations, or the human/personal orientations, toward an outcome. Another way of explaining valence is what we think of an outcome, or what we perceive the outcome to be.

According to this theory, any action will lead to a number of possible outcomes, so the individual must compare the expected outcome with the performance needed to achieve the outcome and then determine if the result can be achieved. If the result of expectancy times valence (E × V) is zero, there will be no motivation to perform. For example, if a male worker is asked to move a pile of gravel using a wheelbarrow and shovel and is told he will be paid at a rate of twice his normal pay, here is what could occur.

The worker clearly understands that if he puts enough effort into the assignment, the result will be a gravel pile that has been moved to a different location, and he will be rewarded with more money than usual. However, if the worker thinks about the personal factors, such as possible back problems, or physical exhaustion, or maybe a heart attack, he probably would prefer not to do the work. If that is the case, valence is zero and

expectancy-action-outcome association

valence-human or personal orientations toward an outcome

Customs and Traditions: Watching for the Global Difference

Inequitable Wage Payments

Latin American countries have a long history of income inequity which has resulted in poverty because of the unfair income distribution. Between 1960 and 1980, Latin America was the only part of the world whose income distribution became more unequal. Between 1980 and 1990, the gap between the top 20 percent and the bottom 20 percent of wage earners widened even more.

In other countries around the world, workers are more satisfied because there is less disparity between the top and the bottom of the population. East Asian countries receive high marks for equity in wages. Malaysia, for example, is one of the leaders in closing the inequities between top tier wage earners and bottom tier wage earners.

One way in which governments can and do show support for the low-level wage earners is by providing basic education for the entire population. In the late 1980s Korea committed 78 percent of its education budget to primary education. Venezuela, on the other hand, committed only 20 percent. Although Latin American governments often subsidize education, it is done in higher education, which benefits the children of the wealthy rather than the children of low income earners.

Countries might choose different methods to distribute income in more equitable ways. Some countries have elected to redistribute land so the low wage earners can earn more income by farming. This is

CONTINUED

not the method that has been elected by Latin American countries. Many of the poor Indian peasants in Latin America have been forced to move to infertile highland that can't support them. The inequities continue and the discontent results in a fight for survival, fights that often lead to bloodshed and loss of life.

Source: Carrington, Tim. "Mexico's Rebel Uprising Is Symptom of Area's Long-Term Income Inequities." The Wall Street Journal. February 14, 1994, A9.

E × V results in zero, or no motivation to do the work even though there is an offer for higher wages.[5]

There are four points that further define the notions of expectancy theories.

1. When people have a choice of outcomes that are available to them, they will have preferences in selecting the outcomes.

2. People have clear expectations about the possibilities of their actions or efforts ever achieving the intended behavior or results.

3. People have expectations about certain selected actions or efforts on their part leading to the desired results.

4. Whatever the situation, when a person selects actions, they are based upon the expectancies or preferences that the person has at the time.

If the laborer in the previous example feels that he can't achieve the desired results, the chances of failure are great and the worker will not perform at the level needed to be successful. There will be low personal satisfaction from performing the job, so performance will reflect this perception. In this example, while the expectancy-action association is obvious (extra money for moving the gravel), the valence, or personal outcome (is it worth the effort if I might hurt my back?), will vary from one worker to the next.

*I*ndividual Needs and Drives

stimuli-needs that drive a person to do what he or she does

Each person responds to different **stimuli,** that means that each person has different needs which will drive him or her to do the things he or she does or chooses not to do. If someone is ambitious and has the drive or determination to succeed, that choice will drive the person to perform at a level that is needed for success. If the individual is ambivalent about success, he

[5]From *Work and Motivation* by Victor Vroom, © 1964 Fossey-Bass, Inc. Reprinted with permission.

Achievement helps people build self-esteem and is a universal need.

or she will likely not want to get too involved and will lack the drive and ambition to succeed.

Ambition, drive, and success are defined differently within various cultures and societies. What is considered to be great success in one culture, accomplished by someone with considerable drive and ambition, might be considered limited success in another culture or society. As was discussed earlier in the motivation theories, achievement is a universal need in most cultures, whatever differences there are in defining success. Achievement helps people to feel good about themselves and is the mainstay in building self-esteem.

What Is Success?

Success, to whatever degree of accomplishment, can be defined as achieving a goal. Hard work is necessary to achieve a goal that has been set by an individual. People who are ambitious and are willing to work hard will usually set more challenging goals than those with less drive or ambition.

Many societies measure the degree of success by the effort needed to succeed, which is an indication of the amount of ambition or drive, or the

success-achieving a goal

need for achievement in an individual. Reward for success doesn't have to be money or power; it can be personal satisfaction with what was accomplished. But what if goals can't be reached or success escapes a person, or the desire to succeed is so great the person is haunted by not performing as well as he or she would like?

For example, success in sports is often measured by the salary of the professional competitor, the number of points scored or tackles made, or the speed at which an athlete can move from the starting blocks to the finish line. United States speed skater Dan Jansen was considered to be the best in the world in the 500-meter sprint; however, in the 1994 Olympic competition a couple of slight slips on the ice prevented him from winning the gold medal, which he had been trying to do for a decade.

A couple of days later Jansen had another opportunity to earn a medal in the 1000-meter race. In spite of a couple of minor slips on the ice, he managed to set a new world record time and win his first gold medal ever in the Olympics. His determination, hard work, and commitment to himself, his family, and his sport led him to continue his pursuit until he achieved about all there was for him to achieve. In an interview after his successful gold medal race, he said he had accomplished all there was to accomplish in his sport and he didn't know what would be next.

Fear of Failure

The fear of failure often dictates the goals people set for themselves and the activities they choose to perform. Researchers who study motivation often use laboratory situations rather than workers in the workplace or family members in a home. The lab studies often show that people who have a need to succeed that is greater than their fear of failure will choose activities that are of intermediate difficulty. This increases the chances for success (more difficult activities could lead to failure), but eliminates the minimal satisfaction that results from accomplishing activities that are too simple (there is less reward for achieving simple goals).

In the lab studies, if the fear of failure exceeds the desire to succeed, the activities that are selected will be either very easy or very difficult. When the activity is easy, there is almost no possibility that failure will occur. When the activity is very difficult, it is easy to blame the failure on the difficulty of the activity.

In work situations, managers and supervisors are more effective if they know the success/failure tolerance of employees. Jobs and work activities can be assigned accordingly to assure success. In life situations when you select a career, if you value success more than you fear failure, you will probably choose a career that is more realistic. If you are success-oriented, you will likely choose a career of intermediate difficulty with regard to your abilities to perform. If you are failure-driven, you will pick the career path that is well below your talents and capabilities, or far beyond them.

Key Points Summary

- The human self has four elements: (1) human entity, (2) senses, (3) active self, and (4) reflexive self. The first two elements are passive and the last two are the ones that people are concerned with in their relationships with others.

- Everyone has his or her own set of values that are a reflection of the society, culture, or religion in which the person was raised. The choices we make throughout our lifetime are a result of our needs, which are determined by our values.

- Motivation is a need, a lack of something, that drives a person to act or react, or behave in a certain way, often guided by values. To get people to act in a specific way, it is necessary to provide the appropriate motive or stimulation to elicit a reaction.

- Abraham Maslow developed the hierarchy of needs, one of the earliest motivation theories, which says that there are basic needs that must be satisfied before higher level needs can be met. Maslow's needs hierarchy includes physiological needs, safety and security needs, love and belonging needs, self-esteem needs, and self-actualization needs, listed in the order of their hierarchy.

- Frederick Herzberg developed the motivation-hygiene theory which identified job satisfiers and job dissatisfiers. The job satisfiers include achievement, recognition, the work itself, responsibility, and advancement. Job dissatisfiers include company policy and administration, supervision, interpersonal relationships, working conditions, salary, status, and security.

- David McClelland gave us relevant research on the achievement motivation theory. Achievement motivation says it is possible to predict or explain much of what an individual's performance will be, based upon how badly that person wants to achieve. A person with a strong need for achievement has a requirement to take personal responsibility, will set goals and take risks, and needs feedback. People who are achievement motivated could also have a strong need for power and for affiliation.

- J. Stacy Adams offered the equity theory, which proposes that motivation is influenced by an individual's perception of how equitable he or she is treated on the job. If someone feels that others are treated better for doing the same work, inequities will result, and the desire to achieve will go down.

- Victor Vroom did considerable work with the expectancy-valence theory of motivation. This theory suggests that human behavior, to a large extent, is the result of the characteristics of the individual and what the individual perceives to be his or her environment.

- Each person is driven by different stimuli and is motivated to achieve to varying degrees of success. Success is defined differently in each culture or society. Some people are fearful of failing so they don't push themselves as hard as other people who might be willing to risk more for greater achievements.

achievement motivation theory

affiliation needs

equity theory

expectancy

expectancy-valence theory

hygiene factors

job dissatisfiers

motivation

motivational factors

motivation-hygiene theory

need for power

personal needs

reflexive self

self-esteem needs

standards

stimuli

success

valence

values

Discussion Questions

1. Discuss each of the elements that describe the human self and explain why some of the elements are passive and the others are active.

2. How do your personal values differ from those of others in your class? Pick about five of your classmates and talk to them to determine why they feel as they do about such things as getting to class on time, holding a good job, earning a degree, and family life. How do those values compare to your own?

3. Explain each of the motivation theories and give examples that describe the behaviors of people as they relate to what the theorists present in each theory.

   a. Maslow's hierarchy of needs

   b. Herzberg's motivation-hygiene theory

   c. McClelland's achievement motivation theory

   d. Adams' equity theory

   e. Vroom's expectancy-valence theory

   f. How would you apply what you have learned about the motivation theories to what you learned about individual needs and drives and one's desire to succeed? What influence does fear of failure have on motivating workers in the workplace?

8

Job Satisfaction and Employee Morale

Courtney Curtis was a new office assistant at General Radio and Electronics in Riverside, California. When she started working one week ago, her "training" consisted of being shown where her desk and computer were located, having the ladies lavatory pointed out, and getting instructions about when to take breaks and lunch. The rest of the job was hers to learn, create, or develop. She was the second in line in a two-person office. The office manager had been on the job for 33 years and assumed that everyone knew as much she did. Courtney was frantic trying to figure out what her job was without getting any assistance from the office manager. Courtney kept receiving more work each day but never was able to finish what was given to her the previous day. She was ready to quit after about two weeks on the job.

Learning Objectives

Upon completing this chapter, you should be able to:

- Describe job satisfaction and the elements of a job that are most likely to cause job satisfaction.

- Identify methods that are used to determine job satisfaction.

- Distinguish individual characteristics that influence job satisfaction.

- Explain how job satisfaction and job performance can be improved by changing the job environment.

- Itemize ways in which companies improve productivity.

- Outline facts relative to how employee compensation influences job satisfaction.

Job Satisfaction

Courtney Curtis found herself in a position similar to that of many workers. Without receiving proper training, considerate treatment by coworkers, and the respect of others, Courtney's job became very stressful. Many workers would have felt the same as Courtney: frustrated and unhappy. It is up to managers, supervisors, and coworkers to create the environment for job satisfaction.

Chapter 7 discussed theories of motivation—the how or what that makes people want to perform on the job. It pointed out that highly motivated people are usually those who are most satisfied with their jobs. But what about those who lack interest in their jobs and have no desire to perform at a level that is expected by the supervisor? Is it possible to get employees excited about their work and to perform in the time frame that is expected by supervisors and top-level management? What inducements can be used to get peak performance and create job satisfaction? Is it possible to get everyone excited about their jobs?

This chapter examines several methods that are used to create job satisfaction as defined below. Not all of the methods can make every worker happy. As you read, think about what would make you happiest on a job.

Understanding Job Satisfaction

job satisfaction-extent to which a person's needs are being met in the workplace

Job satisfaction generally refers to how happy someone is with a job. The problem with this general definition is that it is difficult to define *happy* or *happiness*. What makes one person happy, however, won't necessarily make another person happy. As the study of motivation revealed, people have different needs, so perhaps a better definition for **job satisfaction** might be the extent to which one's needs are being met at a place of employment. Individual needs include security, power, affiliation, equity, pay, promotion, recognition, among others.

When employers want to determine the job satisfaction of employees, they begin by measuring the factors of individual needs which are being met in the present job environment. Figure 8.1 illustrates some of the most typical job factors that measure, and ultimately help determine, job satisfaction. After the degree of satisfaction has been determined through employees' responses to a survey or interviews, management can begin to design programs that will increase job satisfaction and improve job performance.

Figure 8.1 Factors of Job Satisfaction

Factor	Explanation
Work	Variety, complexity, difficulty, appeal, potential for advancement, opportunity to learn new tasks, involvement in decision-making
Supervision	Human dimensions, style, trust, administrative ability, technical skill
Company/ Management	Policies, treatment of employees, pay practices
Coworkers	Working relationships, atmosphere, cooperation
Working Conditions	Work environment, schedules, location, difficulty of work
Pay	Methods, amount, equality
Promotion	Opportunities, requirements, equality
Benefits	Vacations, pension plans, leaves, insurance, child care, cafeteria
Recognition	Praise, credit for accomplishments, methods of criticism

Source: Locke, Edwin. "Nature and Causes of Job Satisfaction," in Marvin Dunnette, Handbook of Industrial and Organizational Psychology. *1976.*

Unit 2 · The Essentials of Human Relations

Cory Westin was a new employee at an architectural firm in Chicago that primarily designed and developed plans for high-rise office buildings. He had just graduated at the top of his class with a degree in architecture from a major university and had been interviewed by recruiters of several large companies. Cory had excellent skills, and his supervisors felt he was getting off to a terrific start with the firm. They immediately assigned him to work with one of the senior architects who was directing the design of a major office building for a leading oil company. Cory was excited that he was chosen to work with this senior employee, and he knew he would learn a great deal.

After Cory was on the job for about 18 months, something began to trouble him. He became less happy and unfulfilled with his work, even though he had received good pay raises and was getting what other newer employees felt were the best jobs. Cory talked with his former college classmate who was a management consultant at a large Chicago firm. After Cory expressed his feelings and explained what he was doing at work, his friend reminded him that it had been the housing development projects that really excited him in school. Cory had just loved to develop home plans for large housing developments.

Were all of Cory's needs being met on the job? Figure 8.1 shows what might have been missing in Cory's present job situation. What might happen with Cory's job performance if his job satisfaction continues to diminish?

The Importance of Job Satisfaction

The question "How important is it that I am happy with my job if I am paid well for what I do?" is difficult to answer because some people can be happy on a job if they are paid well while others require much more from a job than a high salary to be satisfied. It is also important to note that people who are not satisfied with their jobs can still be highly motivated workers, but for reasons different from the satisfied workers.

The average worker spends about one-half of his or her waking hours on the job. Since work dominates about one-third of people's lives from the time they begin employment until they retire, job satisfaction and job fulfillment are important considerations. For many people, work is the most important part of their lives. Many people work much more than eight hours each day, and many of them also work weekends. Some do this to keep up with their workloads, but others just can't seem to help themselves—work is what keeps them going.

Working Too Hard

Researchers have found that unemployed people are more likely to become ill, depressed, and lack self-esteem than people with jobs. On the other hand, retired people were found to have a greater degree of happi-

The amount of time a person spends on a job or how hard the person works depends on the needs of the individual.

workaholic-someone who is addicted to work

ness than working people. This is a direct result of having worked enough years to earn a rest and a chance to do other things without feeling guilty. Many people who are completely satisfied with their jobs look forward to retirement; others don't want to think about retirement because they don't know what they will do to occupy their time.

How hard does or should someone work on his or her job? The answer depends on the individual's needs. People who seem addicted to their work are labeled **workaholics.** These people spend long hours at the office, plant, store, or wherever they work, and when they finally go home, they take work with them. The worker rarely takes a vacation unless he or she is forced to because of failing health or a frustrated spouse.

Identifying the Workaholic. Given the choice, most people want to work and would continue to work even if they were financially independent. Work can be stimulating and provides a mental and physical challenge that is needed to keep the mind and body strong and healthy. Work also provides an outlet for social interaction. Work is good, up to a point, that is. After a certain point, which is different for each person, work can be detrimental to health, social life, and family situation.

There are relatively few workaholics in our society. Workaholics spend most of their daily life at work and appear to be addicted to it. They have an extremely limited life outside of the workplace. Workaholics find that vacations and social activities impose on what they must get done on the job. These people don't miss vacations, hobbies, or social interaction, and they tend to thrive on challenges presented by their work.

Workaholism is sometimes a way of hiding poor work efficiency or an attempt to live up to unrealistically high expectations. When designing job satisfaction programs, the individual's work habits must be considered. Figure 8.2 is a short exercise to determine if you might be a workaholic.

Figure 8.2 Identifying Workaholic Tendencies

Think about each of the following questions and answer them as honestly as you can. Draw a circle around the appropriate response—you must answer either yes or no.

While at Work:

Yes No Do you stay at work longer than normally expected work hours?

Yes No Do you work on a variety of projects at the same time?

Yes No Does being challenged with your work make you feel good?

Yes No Do you move forward regardless of the odds?

Yes No Are you often impatient?

Yes No Do you work better if you are faced with a close deadline?

Yes No Is it important that your work be completed to perfection?

Yes No Is it better to do work yourself rather than give assignments to others?

Yes No Do others take longer than necessary to complete projects?

Yes No Do you rush through one project so you can move on to other projects?

Yes No Are your decisions made quickly without much thought?

Away from Work:

Yes No Do you take work home to complete in the evenings?

Yes No Do you take work home to complete on weekends?

Yes No Did your work go with you when you last took a vacation?

Yes No Have leisure time activities been set aside in order to complete work?

Yes No Is it impossible to free your evenings for leisure activities or hobbies?

Yes No Do you think about your work when you are at home?

Yes No Do family requests sometimes come between you and your work?

Each question is worth one point. Count only the number of times you answered yes to a question. If you score between six and twelve points, you have some workaholic tendencies. If you score 13 or more points, watch out because you exhibit strong workaholic tendencies.

Adapted from Breakwell, Glynis, ed. Human Behavior: Shaping Your Life. vol. 17, New York: The Marshall Cavendish Corp., 1990, 2124.

Determining Job Satisfaction

There are several methods that are used to determine job satisfaction. Each method asks workers how they feel about the jobs or tasks they are performing and measures their attitude, whether positive or negative, about different elements of the job. Among the most popular methods of determining job satisfaction are (1) questionnaires, (2) interviews, (3) critical-incidents techniques, and (4) sentence-completion tests.

Questionnaires

questionnaire-most popular written method to determine job satisfaction

The **questionnaire** is the most popular method for determining job satisfaction. Some companies develop their own questionnaires, but most prefer to choose questionnaires that have already been developed, tested, and used successfully by other companies. Questionnaires are either distributed to workers at their place of employment or are sent to the workers' homes to be completed in privacy. Most often, answering a questionnaire is voluntary, and it is completed anonymously. Consequently, the administrators of the questionnaire are not able to determine who completed it. Anonymity is important if workers are expected to complete the questionnaire accurately and honestly.

Two popular questionnaires that have been developed for use in industry are the Job Descriptive Index and the Minnesota Satisfaction Questionnaire. The Job Descriptive Index measures the degree of satisfaction for five elements: pay, promotion, the work, supervision, and coworkers.[1] The questionnaire is short, which is critical for successful completion, and was first published in 1969.

The Minnesota Satisfaction Questionnaire is similar to the Job Descriptive Index in that it measures specific elements of the job. There is a long and a short form of this questionnaire. The long form measures 20 elements of the job and takes 30 minutes to complete. The elements measured include recognition, social status, independence, advancement, and working conditions. The short form takes 10 minutes to complete and measures general job satisfaction.[2] This questionnaire was published in 1967.

Interviews

Interviews are sometimes used in conjunction with questionnaires to obtain more in-depth information about workers' perceptions of job satisfaction. Interviews are costly because both workers and supervisors, or representatives from human resources departments, must commit time which would otherwise be spent on more productive activities.

---

[1] Patricia C. Smith, Lorne M. Kendall, and Charles L. Hulin. *The Measurement of Satisfaction in Work and Retirement.* Chicago: Rand McNally, 1969.

[2] David J. Weiss, Rene V. Davis, George W. England, and Lloyd H. Lofquist. *Manual for the Minnesota Satisfaction Questionnaire.* Minneapolis: University of Minnesota, 1967.

One negative aspect of interviews is that they can lack validity and reliability. **Validity** refers to the correctness of the information that is collected and **reliability** refers to the consistency of the information. Interviewers are not always trained to conduct interviews and may treat each person who is interviewed a little differently. Some interviews might be more in-depth than others, resulting in information that is not consistent.

validity-correctness of information

reliability-consistency of information

Stacey Andrews supervises a highway department survey crew in Montgomery County, Maryland. She has 17 employees in her department and knows that some of them aren't really happy with their jobs. She talked with her supervisor about measuring the job satisfaction of her employees. Stacey's supervisor recommended she work directly with the human resources department (HRD). Stacey's contact with the director of human resources resulted in arrangements for someone from HRD to interview all of her workers.

When the interviews were conducted, they took more time than Stacey had anticipated, but since she had agreed to the process, she didn't complain. When Stacey was presented with a written report and discussed the results with the interviewer, she was surprised at the wide range of perceptions and the big differences in job satisfaction among her employees. She felt she needed to give attention to the negative data but questioned the accuracy of some of the responses that were collected. In fact, some of the data seemed to be so far out of line that it seemed as though it hadn't been her employees who had been interviewed.

Stacey Andrews discovered through interviews what many supervisors learn about employees: there is great disparity in employees' perceptions of job satisfaction. She also learned that some data can't be interpreted easily and perhaps should not be used at all. Before taking corrective measures, Stacey needed further information about the interview techniques, the expertise of the interviewer, and the consistency of the interviewer's questions when soliciting responses from the workers. Stacey may also want her workers to complete a written questionnaire to see if the results are the same.

Critical-Incidents Technique

The **critical-incidents technique** involves collection of information through interviewing of employees. A trained interviewer asks employees to talk about incidents that occurred on the job that evoked very positive and very negative feelings. The interviewer then interprets the responses and relates them to the elements of job satisfaction.

critical-incidents technique-collecting information about job events by interviewing employees

This method can be effective because the employees are invited to talk about incidents in which they were directly, as well as indirectly, involved. Perhaps a worker has had positive feelings if one of his or her coworkers received recognition for an extraordinary performance. The worker certainly would have felt good about the incident if he or she was the person who had received the recognition.

Chapter 8 · Job Satisfaction and Employee Morale

The disadvantage of this technique is that the data collected is only useful if the person conducting the interviews and interpreting the responses is trained and has experience with this process. If the interpretations are not consistent, or if the interviewer allows personal biases to interfere, the data becomes invalid and unreliable.

Sentence-Completion Tests

sentence-completion test-
workers complete sen-
tences in order to express
their feelings

The **sentence-completion test** is another form of written test. This test requires workers to complete sentences, giving their feelings and reactions. The sentence beginnings might include: "My job is _____" or "My job allows me to _____" or "My job should _____" or "My job could be improved if _____." The workers' responses are then interpreted and analyzed.

This form of measuring job satisfaction works well with employees who can express themselves by writing statements. If employees do not like to write, or lack confidence in their writing abilities, they may be hesitant to complete this type of measurement. As with interviews, the interpretation and analysis can be subjective. It takes an expert to interpret the data correctly in order to recommend programs to increase job satisfaction.

The Individual and Job Satisfaction

Based on the discussions of motivation in the last chapter, and measuring elements of the job to determine job satisfaction, it might be assumed that it is the job alone that determines job satisfaction. This is a false assumption; the worker can also influence job satisfaction. An employee's satisfaction is affected by several characteristics which are unique to an individual. Although these characteristics cannot be changed by an employer, they provide clues to an employee's level of job satisfaction.

Gender

An individual's gender, male or female, is one characteristic that can help an employer understand job satisfaction. About one-half of the women in the United States between the ages of 18 and 64 are in the workforce. Although progress is slow, many women hold nontraditional positions that in the past were stereotypically classified as male positions, such as engineers, scientists, managers, draftspersons, computer operators, and others. However, a majority of women hold traditional positions such as secretaries, nurses, teachers, and cosmetologists. Many women do hold assembly line positions in factories and work beside their male counterparts, and a growing number of women are assuming leadership roles.

Women typically have different sources of job satisfaction, depending upon whether they choose to be in the workforce or whether they are

Many women in the United States hold jobs that were once classified as men's jobs.

forced to work because they must support families. Women who choose to be in the workforce find that the elements that satisfy them on the job are similar to those that satisfy men on the job. Women who work because they must support families get their greatest satisfaction from being with their families.

There are job elements which cause women to be less satisfied than the men whom they work beside. Chances are great that women doing the same jobs as men are being paid less. If opportunities for promotions arise, men will more likely be promoted than women, even if their qualifications are equal. When women are promoted to higher positions, they often perceive that they must work harder and perform at higher levels than men do to maintain the jobs and be rewarded equally.

Age

Younger workers are the least satisfied with their jobs; however, job satisfaction increases as workers get older. This relationship between age and job satisfaction is true for white-collar workers and blue-collar workers, as well as for women and men.[3] Young people often have high expectations from work and become disappointed because they aren't challenged and given enough responsibility.

It is difficult to speculate why older workers are more satisfied with their jobs than younger workers. One possibility is that older workers are less mobile. They know that similar jobs would be hard to find in other locations. Older workers are often unable to change positions because finan-

[3]Susan R. Rhodes. "Age-Related Differences in Work Attitudes and Behavior: A Review and Conceptual Analysis." *Psychological Bulletin.* vol. 93, 1983, 328–667.

Jurors' Responses to Age Discrimination Suits

There have been many claims of employment bias against older workers. Some people say they lost their jobs because of their age, or they were passed over for employment because they were too old, or perhaps they didn't receive the promotion they expected because they were too old. In the age of company restructuring, older workers are often the first to be let go when downsizing occurs. Many of these workers are midlevel managers and supervisors, some are executives, and others are skilled employees.

How ethical is it to let the older workers go first? Older workers typically have a more difficult time in securing a new position once they become unemployed. What do the courts say about discriminating against older workers? Most jurors are sympathetic to the older worker. Many jurors are themselves older and retired, but young jurors also have favored the employee in age discrimination cases.

Research conducted between 1988–1992 by Jury Verdict Research on age discrimination cases found that this form of employee discrim-

cial benefits such as company pensions could be lost. Additionally, family obligations, and obligations to creditors prevent older workers from changing jobs. Older workers who have restraints that prohibit them from relocating to different jobs are more appreciative of the positions they hold.

Younger workers who are dissatisfied with their jobs are mobile and will change jobs to find fulfillment. Many workers change jobs frequently or drop out of the workforce, so they may not be included in job satisfaction surveys. If this is the case, the job satisfaction studies include more older people, who have a higher degree of satisfaction with their jobs, which would affect the results.

Race

Forgionne and Peeters reported in "Differences in Job Motivation and Satisfaction among Female and Male Managers" that white employees in general report greater job satisfaction than nonwhite employees; however, the differences are not great enough to be statistically significant.[4] A far greater problem is the high unemployment rates of minority populations, especially the young minority. When young people belonging to minorities are employed, they often fill positions that are very low in pay and provide no opportunities for advancement and little job satisfaction.

---

[4]Guisseppi A. Forgionne and Vivian E. Peeters. "Differences in Job Motivation and Satisfaction among Female and Male Managers." *Human Relations*. vol. 35, 1982, 101–18.

ination is rewarded more than any other form of discrimination. The average awards for age discrimination suits during this time period was $302,914, compared to $255,734 for sex discrimination, and $176,578 for race bias. This information was based on 515 trial verdicts in wrongful-termination lawsuits.

There are possible reasons why age bias is rewarded more than other forms of discrimination. One reason is that the employees who typically file the lawsuits are higher paid employees and have greater financial loss from the termination. Because older workers have more difficulty in locating a new job, jurors will also award them prospective damages. Another factor for higher awards to older workers is that the Federal Age Discrimination Act of 1967 provides for double-back pay for plaintiffs in cases where wrongful conduct has occurred.

Source: Geyelin, Mike. "Age Bias Cases Found to Bring Big Jury Awards." The Wall Street Journal. December 17, 1993, B1, B8.

Experience

Job satisfaction increases after an employee has been a number of years on the job and steadily advances thereafter. Early in a worker's career, there is an initial period of satisfaction while new skills are being acquired. After this period, satisfaction decreases unless the worker is challenged and provided evidence of progress and growth. After several years of experience, satisfaction returns for the employee.

Job Challenges

Trained persons with high-level skills that are not being used do not feel challenged and will be less satisfied with their work situations than persons using their skills. The more opportunities workers have to use their skills, the greater their job satisfaction will be and the more highly motivated they will be, according to Forgionne and Peeters.[5] The use of workers' skills and abilities relates to Maslow's self-actualization level of motivation. If workers are not given an opportunity to excel by using their skills and abilities, they will most likely not be highly motivated and will not be satisfied with their jobs.

The earlier illustration of Cory Westin is a good example of an individual not using his skills and abilities in a way that will create job satisfaction. If Cory had been assigned duties to plan housing developments, the

[5]Guisseppi A. Forgionne and Vivian E. Peeters. "Differences in Job Motivation and Satisfaction among Female and Male Managers." Human Relations. vol. 35, 1982, 101–18.

chances are greater that he would have been satisfied with his job. Similarly, there is considerable dissatisfaction among students who are assigned to work for faculty or staff members at colleges. A student's typical assignment is to copy, collate, and staple papers, or perhaps to place labels on 20,000 envelopes and stuff them with an insert, organize them by zip code, and put them in boxes to be mailed. The work is neither exciting nor challenging, and it is difficult for the students to understand its importance. Tasks like these have caused many students to wonder why they are in school!

Intelligence and Education

In recent years many companies in the United States have reduced their workforces to become more efficient in operations. They have automated their operations, requiring fewer workers, or may have suffered economic problems. There are other reasons for downsizing, or rightsizing, companies, but the final result is that there are many highly qualified workers who are willing to take jobs that require less intellect and education.

Many employers are happy to hire overqualified workers because they think they will do a better job. This may be true at first, but it only lasts until the workers become dissatisfied with the fact that the work does not present the challenge they are used to. It is reasonable that a relationship exists between level of education and expectations from a job. The more education people have, the more challenge and fulfillment they expect from work.

Most jobs in the future will require education beyond high school, but relatively few will require four years of college. There are exceptions, of course, and there always will be. No one would want to be treated by a doctor who has not been properly educated, just as no one would want a poorly prepared lawyer to handle a court case for him or her.

In the future most jobs will require people to have education beyond high school. Some will require a four-year college degree.

Unit 2 · The Essentials of Human Relations

Figure 8.3 Individual Characteristics of Job Satisfaction

Characteristic	Definition
Gender	Approximately one-half of the workforce is women. Women have more challenges in the workplace than men.
Age	Older workers are more satisfied with their jobs than younger workers.
Race	White employees are more satisfied with their jobs than nonwhite employees.
Experience	Job satisfaction increases with job experience.
Job Challenges	Workers who have greater job challenges are more satisfied.
Intelligence and Education	Workers who are underemployed are less satisfied with their jobs than those in positions for which they are qualified.
Position	The higher the position in the company, the greater the job satisfaction.

Position

The position a worker holds influences satisfaction with the job. The higher the position in the organization, the greater the job satisfaction; therefore, executives are more satisfied with their jobs than supervisors, who in turn are more satisfied than their workers. This higher degree of satisfaction comes from the challenges of higher level positions, the degree of autonomy of the executive, and the kind of responsibility the executive has. There are greater opportunities for self-actualization and esteem at the higher levels of an organization, which results in greater job satisfaction.

Job Satisfaction and Job Performance

It seems logical that if people are satisfied with their work, their performance on the job will be better. That is one theory about the relationship of job satisfaction and **job performance** or how well someone does a particular job. If an employer wants employees to perform at higher levels, the employer needs to increase job satisfaction (this means morale must be increased) and an increase in job performance will follow. This theory was popularized by the Human Relations movement, which according to Victor Vroom stated that managers can improve production by raising morale of

job performance-how well someone does the job

workers.[6] This theory is sometimes, but not always, true. In other words, satisfied workers are not always more productive workers.

A second theory discussed in "Satisfaction and Performance: Casual Relationships and Moderating Effects" states that rewards which are based on job performance lead to satisfaction and increased performance.[7] In this case, it is the reward which is connected to job performance that leads to job satisfaction, which in turn leads to better performance and so on. You might consider the process to be cyclical, as illustrated in Figure 8.4. Researchers who have studied this theory find that it is easier to support than the theory which came from the Human Relations movement.

Figure 8.4 **Rewards Influence Job Performance**

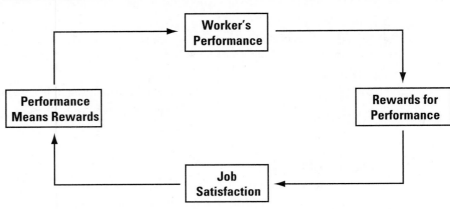

productivity-amount of output of an individual, group, or organization compared to the input

efficiency-how well workers perform

Increased employee job satisfaction and performance is an important consideration in increasing productivity for an organization. Companies are concerned with **productivity,** which is the output of an individual, group, or organization in relation to the input during the process of creating products or services. **Efficiency,** or how well workers perform, is closely related to productivity, that is, if people are efficient workers or belong to efficient work groups, their output will be greater.

American firms have been faced with declining productivity in the face of increasing productivity by many foreign companies. This topic has been of great concern in many corporate boardrooms and has resulted in streamlining of operations. Numerous companies have had to examine profitability and productivity and have discovered that they can do more with fewer workers.

Corporate downsizing in the 1980s changed the perspective of human resources departments from one of skepticism to one of welcoming laid-off job applicants. The 1980s was the merger era, and many executives, managers, professionals, and skilled workers lost their jobs as they watched

[6]Victor Vroom. *Work and Motivation*. New York: John Wiley, 1964.
[7]Jacob P. Siegel and Donald Bowen. "Satisfaction and Performance: Causal Relationships and Moderating Effects." *Journal of Vocational Behavior*, 1971, 1(3), 263–69.

Unit 2 · The Essentials of Human Relations

ownership of their companies change. Following the mergers, companies were forced to streamline, restructure, and downsize, which resulted in even more layoffs. One headline in *The Wall Street Journal* in February 1994 read "Decade of Downsizing Eases Stigma of Layoffs." This article discussed how the stigma of being laid off was not as great as it used to be years ago.[8]

*I*mproving the Job Environment

Companies have become more attuned to the needs of the worker, and the level of concern has been raised for improving the work environment. For several years, companies have used numerous methods to increase job satisfaction and improve the morale, the sense of common belonging, of workers. However, with the drastic changes taking place in the corporate world, workers are more concerned about job security, which causes companies to give more emphasis to improving job performance through changes in the work environment. Many companies have also discovered the need for greater involvement of employees in the organization. This is being done in a number of ways.

[8]Kevin G. Salwen. "Decade of Downsizing Eases Stigma of Layoffs." *The Wall Street Journal.* February 8, 1994, B1.

Of Human Interest

How We Will Work in the Year 2000

Our society has changed rapidly in recent years and will continue to change even more rapidly with gigantic leaps taking place in technology. Walter Kiechel III summarized six trends that will reshape the workplace.

► The average company will become smaller, employing fewer people.

► The traditional hierarchical organization will give way to a variety of organizational forms, with the network of specialists being foremost among these.

► Technicians, ranging from computer repairpeople to radiation therapists, will replace manufacturing operatives as the worker elite.

► The vertical division of labor will be replaced by a horizontal division.

► The paradigm of doing business will shift from making a product to providing a service.

CONTINUED

▶ Work itself will be redefined: constant learning, more higher order thinking, less nine-to-five.

Workers who are willing to change as the changes occur in the workplace will be more satisfied with their jobs. The jobs of the future will require workers to think more and make more decisions for themselves than at any point in the past.

Source: Kiechel, Walter III. "How We Will Work in the Year 2000." Time Inc., May 17, 1993, 39.

Quality of Work Life

One movement in corporate America is to decentralize operations of the company and to include workers in the decision-making process. This movement stems from the competition of foreign companies and the need to improve product and service quality and at the same time to improve the quality of work life for employees. Employers believe that if the quality of work life is improved for employees, there will be improved productivity and greater job satisfaction.

Quality of work life is increased when companies establish methods and processes to include workers in decisions about their jobs and the environment in which they work. Workers are active participants in an organizational climate that responds to their suggestions and criticisms and answers their questions in an effort to improve the company's environment. As active participants, workers are likely to offer suggestions that will lead to improved operational efficiency, greater job satisfaction, and improved productivity for the company.

Becky Morton supervised several women and one man at Forest Edge Community College. Becky was known as a supervisor who always had to have the final word in all decisions. In a college where most of the employees had at least a master's degree, there were many people with strong personalities and egos who had a difficult time coping with Becky's decision-making style. Educational program management jobs were hard to find, and several of the employees lacked mobility and could not leave the area. They were afraid to confront Becky because of how she treated employees with whom she was dissatisfied. The work situation was always tense, and several of the employees wanted to leave, if only they could find similar jobs. Their real dilemma was that even though the college president knew of the employees' dissatisfaction, she wouldn't confront Becky either. The workers knew they couldn't be happy unless something changed. This department was a good candidate for a program to improve quality of work life.

A company can improve quality of work life in many ways. Some programs which have been successful are discussed on the following pages. Many of these programs focus on the employee, but others emphasize changes in the work environment.

Worker Enhancement Programs

There are different kinds of worker enhancement programs. Some involve small groups of workers and are narrowly focused, while others involve broader participation of workers. Some programs are more popular than others and are used more frequently. Decisions about worker enhancement programs are based upon the size of the company, the type of business in which they are used, the educational level of the employees, and other considerations.

Quality Circles. Quality circles were instrumental in the rise to dominance of Japanese industrial firms. Quality circles rely on workers as the main source of input for solving company problems. The concept of quality circles is based on the belief that because workers are more directly related to problems, they are the best source to provide the input needed to correct the problem. Workers can more easily identify possible causes of a problem. (Quality circles are closely linked to total quality management, which will be discussed in Chapter 15.)

A quality circle consists of seven to ten employees from the same work group who meet regularly to discuss, define, analyze, and solve problems in their work area. Membership is voluntary. Quality circles typically meet one hour each week. The employees in these groups are initially trained in problem-solving techniques and then apply those techniques within their work area. Each group has a team leader, usually the first-line supervisor of the workers in the group. The leader is trained to serve as a **facilitator** and is the one who communicates the group's decisions to the appropriate people in the organizational structure. By having the supervisor as the group facilitator, communication should be increased and lines of authority within the organizational structure are observed.

facilitator-leader in a quality circle

Quality circles don't always provide solutions for company problems and productivity. There are times when quality circles don't work in an organization. One of the leading causes of failure of quality circles is lack of trust between workers and supervisors or managers. To be effective, the concept of quality circles relies on trust, open communications, managerial support, and workers' participation.

Empowerment. **Empowerment** means to select, develop, and share power with subordinates who are committed to the organization's goals. Decision-making and responsibility must be dispersed to accomplish

empowerment-management shares power with subordinates committed to organizational goals

current tasks and to prepare those who will be future corporate leaders.[9] Getting workers involved in the management of the company is empowerment, a process which has the potential to improve workers morale and job satisfaction, and, to improve productivity.

Louis Quast and Joy Fisher Hazucha define the elements of empowerment of group members by management.

▶ *Participation and Openness*
Group members have input and give and receive feedback.

▶ *Allow Latitude*
Group members are allowed leeway in making decisions and taking actions.

▶ *Deal with Difference*
The group handles conflict in healthy ways, allows opinions to be aired, and treats people fairly.

▶ *Share Power and Information*
Power and information are shared fairly in the group.

▶ *Reward Merit*
Good performance is encouraged and rewarded.[10]

Workers who have been empowered, given responsibility, and allowed to share in decision-making should feel an allegiance to the company that is usually not felt by workers who are not empowered. The result should be greater job satisfaction, and greater job satisfaction should lead to increased job performance and productivity.

Job Design Methods

Another approach to improving job satisfaction and productivity is oriented to changing the jobs in which workers are engaged and is called **job design.** This differs from worker enhancement programs in that the focus of change is on the job itself, not on the worker. Job design methods have been in use for several decades.

The Scientific Method. The **scientific method** of management and job design, which originated with Frederick Taylor, entails analyzing jobs to determine what the worker does and what the requirements for the job are. After analysis, the job is designed to ensure that employees will not perform work beyond their abilities. Another aspect of the scientific method is that jobs are divided into small segments which the worker performs. As with production work and piece-rates of pay, this method works well in determining expected levels of performance for workers. While not as popular as in the past, this method of job design is still used today.

job design-changing the jobs in which workers engage

scientific method-analyzing jobs to determine worker tasks and job requirements

[9]David Campbell. "The Leadership Characteristics of Leadership Researchers." *Impact of Leadership.* Edited by Kenneth Clark, Miriam Clark, and David Campbell. Greensboro, North Carolina: Center for Creative Leadership, 1992, 26.

[10]Louis N. Quast and Joy Fisher Hazucha. "The Relationship Between Leaders' Management Skills and Their Groups' Effectiveness." *Impact of Leadership.* Edited by Kenneth Clark, Miriam Clark, and David Campbell. Greensboro, North Carolina: Center for Creative Leadership, 1992, 205.

Contemporary Job Design Methods. A more contemporary method to design jobs is to include job rotation, job enlargement, and job enrichment.

Job Rotation. Job rotation increases the number of tasks a worker must perform because the worker is moved, or rotated, from one job to another. This method is used to increase the workers' importance to the company and to improve their self-esteem because they perform several different jobs and are therefore more valuable employees.

Hector Graza worked in a small manufacturing plant in Rocky Mount, North Carolina, that produced circuit boards used mostly for computers. He was first trained to assemble the board, then to solder the connections, and finally to perform quality control inspections for all the boards that were being produced. After he learned each of the jobs, he was placed on continuous rotation, four months on each job. He liked the role of the inspector the best and took pride in his accuracy. He was satisfied to complete the other jobs and did the work well, anticipating that he would soon rotate to the job he liked best. Hector was a believer in the job rotation system and knew that without it he would have to spend several years doing the other jobs before he could be permanently assigned to the inspector's job.

The worker who does a job from beginning to end will find its completion more meaningful.

Chapter 8 · Job Satisfaction and Employee Morale

Job Enlargement. Job enlargement may appear similar to job rotation, but it is different. Job enlargement adds job duties to those already being performed by the worker. While the scientific method tries to reduce jobs to the simplest task, job enlargement does just the opposite; it expands job responsibilities. Workers don't move from one job to another, instead they remain in their usual work location and receive additional job duties.

Job Enrichment. Job enrichment happens when a job is designed to be more appealing and enjoyable for the worker. This is accomplished by varying the duties that are to be performed, not in the sense of giving more to do as in job enlargement, but by creating opportunities to use different skills. Job enrichment can also be accomplished by making the work significant, creating value in what the worker is doing. If a worker is allowed to carry a job or project through from beginning to end, the completion of the job will be more significant. There may be opportunities to allow the worker to plan and schedule the job tasks to work more independently and as a result to feel better about the work.

Work Teams. Workers who are assigned to a small **work team,** a group of workers assigned to complete a job, often gain a sense of achievement when they are allowed to take a project from inception to completion. Not all work teams are granted an opportunity to complete entire projects, but when jobs are designed in this way, the team approach can be very successful. Workers are willing to contribute to the team because they can see progress. Work team members should all be involved in the decision-making process, and when their decisions result in greater output for the company, they all share in the rewards.

Workers who are assigned to a work team learn different job duties rather than completing just one job. A variety of tasks creates more interest in the project, and workers will feel they have contributed more. Some projects are too large for a work team to take from beginning to end, so each work team is assigned a smaller portion of the project. The smaller section of the project is then combined with what other work teams complete, and the result is the culmination of a larger project. A good example of working this way is the construction of a home where one team may frame the house, another team will do the electrical work, another the plumbing, still another the roofing and exterior finishing, and so on until the house is completed.

Environmental Concerns. Jobs can be designed around **environmental concerns,** often referred to as **ergonomics,** matching the worker to the environment in which the work will be done. There is greater concern now than at any time in the past to ensure that all workers are matched to their environment. Environmental, or ergonomic, concerns raise questions about the worker's needs and the changes that must occur so the worker can be physically compatible with the work environment. This first environmental concern gained importance because of the large

work team-group of workers assigned to complete a job

environmental concerns-matching workers to the environment in which they work (ergonomics)

number of women in the workplace; it gained even more importance as concern for the physically challenged grew. Studies report that workers who fit their work environment are more productive.

Company Options to Improve Productivity

We have looked at ways in which companies try to improve job satisfaction by improving the quality of work life. These programs focus on the worker or the job itself. There are other ways an organization can improve productivity that are more closely related to the company in general. Some of the company-oriented methods are not as "worker friendly" as other methods. If this appears to be uncaring, keep in mind that businesses must make a profit to continue operations. If the business does not operate, there are no opportunities for employment.

Restructuring

Many organizations are finding it necessary to restructure their operations completely to be able to compete with international firms located in Japan, Mexico, Germany, and other countries. As a result of the competition, organizations sometimes find it necessary to downsize.

Downsizing. **Downsizing,** sometimes called *rightsizing,* results in reducing the number of employees through permanent layoffs, temporary layoffs, termination, or normal attrition, that is, people leaving jobs or retiring. The outcome is that organizations are leaner but more efficient. The downsizing is not restricted to one specific level of worker, but affects all levels, including white-collar executives. The level most affected is the midlevel supervisor.

downsizing-reducing the number of employees in an organization

---

Customs and Traditions: Watching for the Global Difference

Changes Affect Productivity of Chinese Firms

The Wall Street Journal reported on the effects of the Chinese government's inattention to the Chinese worker, relating that economic slowdowns are a result of poor output. By the end of 1993, China began to realize the need to restructure many government-owned businesses to remain competitive and bolster operations, so the businesses could be listed on international stock exchanges. Many of the Chinese state-owned companies were also expected to be responsible for their own profits and losses, just as private companies are in a free enterprise system.

 CONTINUED

As a result of the Chinese government's efforts to restructure, many workers were expected to be laid off from their jobs. In 1994 about 30 million Chinese workers were to be idled because of government restructuring, which would make 160 million workers unemployed. The restructuring of Chinese companies has been extreme enough so that the predictions were that the economy would shrink before it even began to grow.

These statistics appeared early in 1994, but are representative of what could happen in any developing country. Look at what is happening in China today. Were the 1994 predictions correct? What has been the effect of restructuring on workers who lost their jobs? How does what happened in China relate to what has happened in other areas of the world?

Source: Brauchli, Marcus. "China's Much-Needed Effort to Improve Productivity Will Take Economic Toll." The Wall Street Journal. February 16, 1994, A13.

By eliminating the midlevel supervisor, companies are able to pass along decision-making and responsibilities to the lower level workers. In the process of decentralizing decision-making, the workers are encouraged to become entrepreneurs.

Entrepreneurship. The term *entrepreneur* is reserved for the person who takes the risks involved in operating his or her own business and may lose his or her investment. An **entrepreneur** is someone who takes risks and makes decisions, and then takes responsibility for these decisions. Within the structure of a large company, these people are often called **intrapreneurs**. This process has the potential to improve productivity and increase profits for an organization. Workers who are given opportunities to act as entrepreneurs are greatly satisfied because of the contributions they can make to the organization.

Not everyone fits the entrepreneurial mold. Many people are not willing to take the risks involved, even though there is less risk within the larger organizational structure. On the other hand, many people who are entrepreneurs are not satisfied on jobs that limit their entrepreneurial potential. The typical entrepreneur is someone who can set goals and work to achieve them because the person has a great appetite for accomplishment. The entrepreneur has a "fire inside" that must be satisfied. An entrepreneur competes against him or herself in accomplishing self-imposed standards. How would you function in an entrepreneurial position? Complete the exercise that follows to find out how you compare to others.

entrepreneur-someone willing to take risks, make decisions, and take responsibility for decisions in his or her business

intrapreneur-people given entrepreneurial freedoms within a larger company; they are not the business owners

Work Schedules

The traditional work schedule has been to report for work at a preset time, spend eight or nine hours on the job, and then leave for home. Many organizations are changing work schedules to accommodate the rising number of older workers, single-parent workers, commuters, and people wanting to spend more personal time with their families.

Telecommuting. One growing trend is **telecommuting,** requiring the worker no longer to go to a company office to work. The person works at home or in an office equipped either by the worker or a company. The home office, or "electronic cottage" as it is sometimes called, is connected to the company by a computer modem and telephone lines. Workers with this arrangement make periodic trips to the company office to receive new assignments or to return completed work.

Even though this arrangement may seem to be the ideal, it doesn't work for everyone. Some people need to have continual contact with other workers and cannot spend long hours at home away from the company workplace. A series of articles in The Wall Street Journal discussed "home work" and the difficulty some people have adjusting to what they think will be a great opportunity.[11] People who are unhappy working at home are those who need to interact with colleagues—workers found that pets don't provide the same opportunity for discussion and interaction, even though they might be good listeners! Reportedly at the end of 1993 some 7.6 mil-

telecommuting-corporate employees who work in their home, but maintain contact with the company through telecommunications

[11]Sue Shellenbarger. "Some Thrive, but Many Wilt Working at Home." *The Wall Street Journal.* December 14, 1993, B1.

Of Human Interest

Test Your Entrepreneurial Level

Answer each of the questions below in order to determine your potential to be an entrepreneur. Use the following scale to rate yourself:

1=never   2=rarely   3=sometimes   4=usually   5=always

_____ 1. Do you like things that are different?

_____ 2. Would you like to be wealthy?

_____ 3. Do you watch for opportunities to improve yourself?

_____ 4. Does it bother you to have to take directions from others?

_____ 5. Are you challenged to find new ways to solve problems?

_____ 6. Do you prefer to be alone?

_____ 7. Do you think the future looks bright?

CONTINUED

Chapter 8·Job Satisfaction and Employee Morale

_____ 8. Do rewards for what you do make you feel good?

_____ 9. Do you like to be independent in your activities?

_____ 10. Are you the one who usually takes charge of activities?

_____ 11. Do you rely on intuition to solve problems but later solve them using logic?

_____ 12. Are you happy when you can present new concepts to others?

_____ 13. Are you willing to suffer the consequences of your own decisions?

_____ 14. Do you have workaholic tendencies?

_____ 15. Do you like to make decisions based on systematically identified data?

_____ 16. Will you take risks in order to receive rewards in return?

_____ 17. Do you feel you are important?

_____ 18. Do you have confidence in yourself?

_____ 19. Do you do the best you can in what you try?

_____ 20. Is discipline and respect for authority important to you?

It is possible to score 100 points. Add all of your ratings together to arrive at a composite score. The higher your score, the greater the likelihood that you possess entrepreneurial skills.

Adapted from Breakwell, Glynis, ed. Human Behavior: Shaping Your Life. *vol. 17, New York: The Marshall Cavendish Corp., 1990, 2159.*

lion workers were telecommuters. Figure 8.5 summarizes what Joanne H. Pratt Associates of Dallas defines as the successful telecommuter, as reported in the same *Wall Street Journal.*

Flexible Scheduling.   Many companies have found that getting away from a traditional workweek of eight or nine hours a day, five days a week, increases employee morale and job satisfaction, reduces absenteeism, creates better labor-management relations, and allows employee decision-making. **Flex time** allows the employee to decide, within a certain band of time, when they will be at work. There is normally a specific core of time when the employee must be at work. The band of time during which employees can arrive at and leave from work varies from company to company. The purpose of flexible scheduling is to relieve workers of the stress associated with their jobs and to increase productivity. Workers who

flex time-employees decide within a band of time when they will go to and leave work

Figure 8.5 Defining the Successful Telecommuter

- ► Has little need for face-to-face contact with coworkers or customers.

- ► Can commute directly from home to customers.

- ► Has access to quiet office space at home free from interruptions

- ► Is a "self-starter" and able to work with little supervision.

- ► Performs tasks that can be done from home.

- ► Reports to supervisor who manages by results, not by surveillance or time clock.

- ► Works for someone who is trusting.

have less stress and are able to make their own decisions about when they will work will be more satisfied with their jobs.

Here is how flexible scheduling works. If you work for a company that allows a 12-hour band of time within which you will work eight hours, the company might require you to be on the job for the **core hours** of 9:00 A.M. until 11:00 A.M. and 1:00 P.M. until 2:00 P.M. This means you can choose to arrive at work at 9:00 A.M., take lunch from 11:00 A.M. until 12:00 noon, and then work until 6:00 P.M. You will have worked eight hours at the times, within limitations, that you selected. If you are an early riser and choose to go to work at 6:00 A.M., you could leave work at 3:00 P.M. and have worked the core hours and taken an hour for lunch.

core hours-specific hours that flextime workers must be on the job

In the article "More Companies Experiment with Workers' Schedules," *The Wall Street Journal* offered the following suggestions that make flexible scheduling work.

- ► Work goals and criteria for success must be made clear.

- ► Responsibility for performance and team effort must be shifted to employees.

- ► There can be no taboos on talking about personal or family needs in the workplace, since these roles play a big role in employees' ability to pitch in when flexible scheduling situations demand it.

compressed workweek-longer workdays but only working four days during the week

The same *Journal* article reported on the results of an alternative scheduling policy at Harris Bank. Requests for flexible scheduling included 64 percent wanting **compressed workweeks** (longer workdays but working four days a week), 24 percent wanting flex time, 7 percent wanting **flexplace** (the opportunity to work at home), and 5 percent wanting to be scheduled part time.[12]

flexplace-opportunity to work at home

[12]Sue Shellenbarger. "More Companies Experiment with Workers' Schedules." *The Wall Street Journal.* January 13, 1994, B1.

Part Time and Job Sharing. Some workers don't want to work full time in jobs, but would rather be available to attend to family needs or other situations. Companies are responding to these needs by assigning some workers to part-time positions permanently. In the past, the part-time worker was typically a fill-in when needed, but now the part-timer can be a permanent employee.

A similar option is job sharing, a situation where two people fill the duties of one full-time person. The workers determine how the job will be divided—they could split the time in half or one worker might take more of the time than the other worker. Employees who share jobs or are permanent part-time employees have more loyalty to the company than do temporary workers. Workers in these positions are granted benefits that temporary employees do not receive, but not necessarily the same benefits as full-time employees. Job sharing and permanent part-time employees receive benefits that are prorated or are in proportion to the time they spend working.

Automation

▼
automation-using machines
to do the work often done
by humans

Company downsizing has been accompanied by a revolution in **automation,** the use of machines to do work that used to be done by humans. This revolution has occurred in manufacturing and in the office. It is automation that has allowed the opportunity for some employees to work at home. In

As companies are downsizing, they are using machines to do many of the jobs that were once done by people.

manufacturing robots are being used extensively, which requires fewer assembly-line employees but operates with more efficiency. Robots don't tire, don't need lunch, and are consistent in performance. The number of workers who have been displaced by automation is about 4 percent. Many of the workers who are replaced by machines will be retrained for other jobs such as servicing the automated equipment.

Office automation has increased productivity for managers and professionals as well as for secretarial and clerical workers. Office automation takes the form of word processors, computers, electronic calendars, electronic retrieval systems, cellular telephones, electronic mail, and voice mailboxes. As technology changes and computer software developments continue, it is difficult to know just what the future will be for workers who spend most of their time in an office or take their office with them in their vehicles.

Pay and Job Satisfaction

There are many different ways in which employees are paid for the work they do. The method selected by the company is sometimes determined by the position. Payment methods fall in one of two categories: **payment for time** or **payment for production;** the two can be used in combination as well. The most common method of payment is based on increments of time in which the work is performed.

Payment for Time

Payment based on time includes payment by the hour, day, week, month, or year. Blue-collar workers are usually paid wages based on hourly or daily time periods. Professional, managerial, and office workers are typically salaried; they are paid for a set time period such as a week, month, or year. Anyone paid by the hour who works 40 hours would receive a different amount than someone who works 30 hours; the basic amount, such as $10.00 per hour, would stay the same. The difference in pay would be due to the number of hours worked. If the payment schedule is based on work for a month, an employee would be expected to be on the job for a predetermined amount of time to receive the monthly amount.

In the previous chapter, we learned that Frederick Herzberg called money a dissatisfier, rather than something that motivates workers or something that creates satisfaction on the job. One might argue with Herzberg about his conclusions; anyone who works expects to be paid. Payment for time doesn't provide the same kind of satisfaction as other payment methods. If a salaried employee has to work 60 or more hours each week just to keep up with the assigned workload but is paid the same as those who are working 40 hours each week, the employee might be dissatisfied. It is reasonable then to agree with Herzberg that money can cause dissatisfaction.

payment for time-workers are paid by the hour, day, week, month, or year

payment for production-workers are paid based on what they produce

On the other hand, assume an employee is being paid a high monthly salary and is only required to work 30 hours each week to complete the job. Based on the equity theory of motivation, the employee would feel that his or her input to the job should match the rewards received and would feel that he or she had to do more. With this notion, the worker who is paid for a time period will be motivated to do more to feel satisfied on the job.

Payment for Performance

Payment plans that tie a worker's earnings to performance on the job are widely used but are perhaps not as popular as time payment plans. Assembly line workers, sales professionals, managers, and others could receive some form of compensation based upon performance. **Performance-based payment plans** can be based completely upon performance or can be used in conjunction with time payment plans.

▼
performance-based pay-ment plans-workers are paid based on performance, like payment for production

Piecework. **Piecework** is the oldest type of performance-based payment plan, having its roots in the early assembly line plants. With this plan a worker is paid for each piece he or she is able to produce as an individual. For example, suppose a worker is responsible for installing windows in a prefabricated window frame and is paid $1.00 for each installed window. If the worker installed 100 windows each day, the person would earn $100 for the day. If on a good day the person installed 125 windows, he or she would earn $125. The opposite would be the case if the worker had a bad day.

▼
piecework-workers are paid for the number of pieces they produce

Tom Hanson was a crop duster in a farming area around Havre, Montana. He spent several hours calculating his expenses and determining what he would have to charge farmers for his services. Of course he wanted to cover his expenses, pay himself and his helpers, and make a nice profit. He determined that the best method for him would be similar to a piecework plan—he would charge by the acre but would vary the amount per acre depending on whether he was dusting for weeds, insects, or both. His income from crop dusting depended upon how many acres he could dust each day and for the season and what he would dust for.

▼
group incentive payment plans-workers are compen-sated based on the perfor-mance of the group

Group Incentive Payment Plans. Group incentive payment plans are also popular. With a **group incentive plan,** each person is compensated based upon the performance of the entire group. This method causes workers in the group to provide encouragement to group members who might not perform at expected levels. One of the disadvantages to this method of payment is that people who perform at high levels are rewarded the same as poor workers. This could be a disincentive for more productive workers, especially if they felt that some slower workers could be doing

Combination Payment Plans. Sometimes combination payment plans are used. A person might be paid a set amount for a time period and receive additional payment based on performance. Sales people who work on a salary plus commission fall into this category, and a manager who receives a salary for the year and a year-end bonus based upon the company profits is also under a combination plan. The incentive with this plan is to produce at higher levels to increase commission or bonuses.

Payment plans based upon performance provide more incentive for workers to do their jobs better and can create greater job satisfaction. Achievement based upon performance which is rewarded provides recognition and is a job satisfier, according to Herzberg.

Performance-based payment plans must be carefully developed to be effective. Some of the difficulties with these plans lie in determining what the acceptable level of performance should be. Once the performance level has been set, it is important to establish a credible reward system—one that provides incentive and creates job satisfaction. It is important that the employees understand how the performance-based payment system works, otherwise they will not trust management or the company and performance will suffer. When developed with the worker in mind, a pay-for-performance reward system can be very effective.

Key Points Summary

- Job satisfaction refers to the extent to which an individual's needs are being met in the workplace. What makes one worker satisfied may have no effect on another worker.

- Job satisfaction is important for workers to be happy in the workplace. Some workers can be productive even though they are not happy with their jobs. Some people are considered workaholics; their work is their life. Working too hard can cause many personal problems for employees, and a supervisor must be prepared to deal with the person who works too hard.

- Methods to determine how satisfied employees are with their jobs include questionnaires, interviews, critical-incidents, and sentence-completion tests. Each method has advantages and disadvantages that must be understood before use. Sometimes more than one method is used to collect data from workers.

- Individual characteristics influence job satisfaction as much as job characteristics do. The individual characteristics include gender, age, race, experience, intelligence and educational attainment, the need for challenges, and the position held by the worker.

- There are different thoughts about the relationship between job satisfaction and job performance. One thought is that if you are satisfied with your job, you will perform better. The other thought is that it is the rewards that come from good job performance that provide greater job satisfaction.

- Another method to increase job performance is to improve the job environment. Improving the quality of work life for employees by involving them in decision-making is successful for some companies. Quality circles are used to get employees more involved with the company. Another method to improve job performance is to empower workers by involving them in decisions typically made by the management of the company.

- Job satisfaction and productivity can be increased by changing the job design. One method is a scientific method in which the job a worker does is broken into small parts to ensure the worker can successfully perform the tasks. Other methods used are job rotation, job enlargement, job enrichment, changing the work environment, and creating work teams.

- The company can take steps to improve productivity in addition to giving attention to worker characteristics and the job design. The ways in which companies can change include downsizing, encouraging entrepreneurship, altering work schedules, or automating.

- Employee compensation influences job satisfaction. Some payment methods are more effective than others and some employees prefer one type of payment plan over others. Payment is usually for a period of time at work, for performance on the job, or a combination of both plans.

Key Terms

automation

compressed workweek

core hours

critical-incidents technique

downsizing

efficiency

empowerment

entrepreneur

environmental concerns

ergonomics

facilitator

flexplace

flextime

group incentive payment plan

intrapreneur

job design

job performance

job satisfaction

payment for production

payment for time

performance-based payment plans

piecework

productivity

questionnaire

reliability

scientific method

sentence-completion test

telecommuting

validity

work team

workaholic

Discussion Questions

1. Explain in your own words what job satisfaction means to you. What do you think it would take to make you happy on a job? If your answer is money, how long do you think you would be satisfied before you would want even more money?

2. Why is it important for companies to create job satisfaction for their workers? Should the company be concerned for all workers or just a majority? If you think it is not possible to satisfy all workers, which ones do you think the company should work hardest to satisfy?

3. Discuss each of the ways that a company could use to determine job satisfaction. Which of the methods do you think would be most effective and why?

4. Which of the individual characteristics do you feel would have the greatest influence on your level of job satisfaction? Why do you feel the way you do?

5. Define the ideal company at which your dream job awaits you. What has the company done to make it the place you would like to work? What worker enhancement programs does the company have in place? What is the job environment like that makes the company the ideal place to work? What has the company done in general for all employees to make it the best place to work?

APPLICATIONS & CASES

Application 1

Responding to a Memo

You have just received the following memo from your supervisor. The memo has correctly made allegations about the behavior of one of your employees, and now you must explain what actions you will take. Your response must be a well-phrased business letter. Additionally, rewrite this memo using more appropriate language and a better writing style.

To: Your Name, Supervisor
From: Jennifer Walkman, Division Head
Subject: Barry Jacobson Performance
Date: June 15, 19xx

It has come to my attention that Mr. Barry Jacobson has become a disruptive force within your unit. He constantly arrives late for work, takes extended breaks, and often leaves early at the end of the day. Why hasn't this situation been dealt with prior to this time?

Without hesitation, please inform me in writing how you plan to remedy this situation. What disciplinary procedures will you follow? I also want to know why you have not dealt with this problem prior to this time. Failure to handle the problem in the most expedient manner may affect your evaluation as well.

Application 2

The Difference in Motivators

Arrange for an interview with three to five different workers in a business, government agency, or manufacturing plant in your area to determine what they feel motivates them to perform to greater levels on the job. When you select your individuals, try to talk to people who are at different levels within the organization. Talk to a manager, a supervisor, and a line worker, for example.

After you have completed your interviews, prepare a summary of the responses you were given. What are the differences between the employees at the different levels? What do you think is the primary cause for the differences between these individuals? If you were the supervisor of each of the people you talked to, what would you have to do to keep them on task and performing at peak productivity? What would happen if you treated each of them the same way? What motivates you to perform better? How do you like to be treated by supervisors? How does this differ from those people you interviewed? Be prepared to discuss your results with your colleagues, or prepare a written summary as directed by your instructor.

Application 3

Determining Communication Flow in an Organization

You learned that some organizations are tall and some are flat. Visit a business in your area to find out how communication flows through the organization. Ask to see the organizational chart if there is one, and discuss with the manager, or a supervisor, how the communication flows. You might find that in very small organizations there is no defined pattern of communication. Does that mean that all of the communication is through the grapevine? How does formal communication get passed from one level to the next? How about communication that flows horizontally; is it usually formal or informal? After you have visited with the manager or supervisor, write a short report about your findings. Share it with the rest of the class.

Application 4

Completing a Business Report

Business reports are completed every day in the business world. Not everyone who writes a business report is happy with the assignment, but the task must be done. Some reports are very long while others are very short. Practice your business report writing skills by completing a short report of five pages on the topic "The Effects of Rapidly Changing Technology on Careers in (insert your career area here)." The report should follow good report writing techniques and should use several references which will be cited at the end of the report. Complete your report in a format that would be acceptable to a business supervisor, which means it must be keyboarded and printed on a quality printer. Use graphs, tables, and charts to illustrate your narrative. You can get a lot of help with your writing from South–Western Educational Publishing's *Reference Manual for the Office* by Clifford House and Kathie Sigler.

Application 5

Understanding Personal Values

Every individual has different values based upon his or her background and personal needs. Discuss values with some of your classmates. How do they feel about work, school, the welfare system, health care, families, children, and parents? How do the feelings differ from one person to the next? What do you think has caused some of the feelings or values that were expressed by some of your classmates? Discuss your own feelings and what you found from others with the rest of the class and your instructor.

Case 1

The Garbled FAX

Final arrangements were being made for a three-day summer sales conference that was about to take place in Jackson, Wyoming. It was expected that about 500 people would attend the meeting. This was to be the largest meeting of this group in years because everyone wanted to go to Jackson in the summer. Trevor Wrigley was making the final adjustments for the important meeting, but he needed one piece of information from Sharon Haggerty to finalize the program. Since Trevor lived in Jackson, and Sharon lived in Andover, Massachusetts, the fastest way to deliver the information was via facsimile (fax).

Sharon had a fax/modem in her computer which occasionally experienced problems with transmission to common fax machines. She transmitted the program, and Trevor received part of the fax before the last several pages turned into a garbled mess. Trevor called Sharon on the telephone and asked her to send the information again. He could tell that she was a little perturbed because she knew as well as he did that the information was needed immediately. She sent the fax a second time and the same problem occurred once more. Trevor called Sharon again and after she angrily scolded him for having such a poor quality fax machine, she agreed to try a third time; however, it wouldn't be until the next day even though time was getting short in order to meet the printer's deadline.

The third time always works, right? Not this time—three strikes and still no program! Trevor was almost afraid to call Sharon again. He wanted to maintain his friendship, but he absolutely needed the program and knew that Sharon would have to be the one to get it to him. He gingerly called Sharon and her response was, "Can't you ever get anything right? I'll send it to you by next day air mail. They do have airplanes in Wyoming, don't they?" Trevor ignored her comments because he knew Sharon was frustrated and he had to have the information so the programs could be printed.

Was Sharon right in acting the way she did? Whose fault was it that the message was garbled? Did Trevor handle the situation correctly? What do you expect the first face-to-face meeting of Trevor and Sharon will be like following this incident? What kind of communication was taking place? What motivations did Trevor have for completing the job? Do you think Trevor will want to host a similar meeting again? If you were Trevor, what would you have done?

Case 2

The Plant Cheerleader

Maureen Carter was known as the plant cheerleader at the Longhorn Bread Company in Plano, Texas. She was a supervisor whose philosophy was to keep moving around the plant offering encouragement and giving motivational speeches to keep workers happy and on task. She hardly ever had anything negative to say and seldom disciplined workers. She just kept cheering them on.

There was a group of workers in the plant who felt she should be more direct and should take disciplinary actions when workers were not performing up to expectations. They didn't like her constant cheering. A little was OK, but they had had about enough. Sara Hernandez was the leader of this group.

Sara came from a background where everyone worked hard and completed their jobs without questions and did not interfere with other peoples' work. One Friday morning, Carrie Stark was late as usual and was slowing production for Sara's work group. When she arrived, Maureen merely approached her and told her how happy she was that she was finally able to make it, how important she was to the rest of the group, and what wonderful work she did. Sara and others just couldn't take it anymore; they decided that they would ignore Carrie and not include her in anything they did. They told her she better start getting to work on time and not slow down their production or she would be sorry later.

Was Maureen Carter a good supervisor in her philosophy and approach? What type of supervisor was she? How would you classify her leadership style? Should she have taken stronger actions with Carrie and all workers who ignore company policy? What about Sara and her group? Were they justified in their actions and threats? What could they have done differently? What are the possible implications of their threats?

Case 3

The "I'll get to it" Repair Company

Bill and Nancy Dugan were the owners of Dugan Appliance Repair in Shelbyville, Illinois. Theirs was a small business operated out of their home. Bill did most of the repair work, but Nancy also helped. They had a good reputation for being excellent repair people, but didn't always get the work done when they said it would be done. In fact, they much preferred being out in their boat and fishing in Lake Shelbyville. They fished year round. Because they specialized in furnace repair and were the best in town, the amount of time they spent fishing caused potential customers problems in the winter months.

Tammy Lane had been having problems with her furnace, and she knew she needed to have it fixed before the cold winter winds and the snow began. Bill Dugan had been to Tammy's house to check the furnace and told her that it needed a new relay for it to work properly. When Bill left Tammy's house, he said he would order a relay and return with it in a couple of days. A month had passed and Bill still hadn't gotten back to Tammy.

Tammy called the Dugan's home and talked with Nancy. Nancy assured her that Bill would call back as soon as he could. This went on for a couple of weeks and each time Tammy called the Dugans they had a reason why Bill hadn't called back—there had been two funerals; they were extremely busy because of the approaching winter; the children had been sick; Bill had been sick. Tammy wanted her furnace fixed and wanted it done by the best person in town. She knew that Bill and Nancy had been spending quite a bit of time on the lake because fishing had been reportedly pretty good. She also knew that it was near enough to colder weather that if she called someone else, she would have to wait a long time before they would look at the furnace.

Aside from Tammy's frustrations and difficulties, the Dugans have a problem. Is their problem one to do with lack of motivation? What are the implications for long-term business operations if they continue to operate this way? Will all customers accept the fact that if they want the best, they'll have to wait until the Dugans are ready? What suggestions do you have for the Dugans and their business?

Case 4

A Child's Safety

Monica Murphy owned and operated a child care center about 50 miles from Indianapolis, Indiana. She started accepting children as early as 6:00 A.M. because most of her clientele commuted into the city to work. Her community was primarily blue collar with a strong work ethic. Her policy was that children had to be picked up no later than 8:30 P.M., since some of the workers ended their shift at 7:00 P.M. Monica was lenient with the clientele if they would notify her that they would be late, or if they needed to drop children off a little earlier.

Tim Mason was a single father who really depended on the services provided by Monica, and sometimes he took advantage of her extended evening hours to stop on the way home from work for a few beers. This concerned Monica because she worried that sometimes Tim drank too much and still drove the car. She saw him on a few occasions when he shouldn't have been driving. Monica wanted to approach the subject with Tim, but she wasn't sure how to do it.

Monica knew she would have to use her best communications skills and she didn't want to make Tim angry. She was more concerned about the child than with losing a client. How should Monica approach Tim and what should she say?

Case 5

Choosing a Compensation Plan

Turnkey Display Systems is an established business in Bakersfield, California. It specializes in retail store design and layout and also installs all the display equipment for business owners. This makes it possible for the owners to stock the shelves and racks and open the doors for business much sooner. Turnkey has several salespeople who travel a large area. The company has a good reputation in southern California and is beginning to gain a foothold in Nevada and Arizona.

Turnkey's salespeople have been paid a straight monthly salary for years. Now that the company is growing more rapidly and sales are brisk, the salespeople are beginning to feel that some kind of commission arrangement might be best for them. The salespeople were being paid as much in salary alone as competitors were paying their salespeople in salary and commission combined. Turnkey's company management is hesitant to switch pay systems because there could be problems. They aren't certain if sales would go up or go down if the switch were made.

What suggestions would you make to the Turnkey's management? What effect will a change have on employee performance and job satisfaction? Will sales go up or down with a change? What will the effect on sales performance be if a change isn't made?

Unit 3

Problems in Human Relations

Chapter 9
Counseling, Rewarding, and Disciplining Workers

Chapter 10
Coping with Employees' Personal Problems

Chapter 11
Stress in the Workplace

Chapter 12
Managing Time

Chapter 13
A Workplace of Mutual Respect

Chapter 14
A Rapidly Changing World of Work

Applications & Cases

Chapter 9

Counseling, Rewarding, and Disciplining Workers

Learning Objectives

Upon completing this chapter, you should be able to:

- Explain how attitudes affect a worker's performance.

- Determine the differences in employee counseling, coaching, and discipline.

- Identify types and processes used for employee discipline.

- Discuss the reasons for employee performance appraisals and how appraisals are completed.

- Profile the methods used by companies to reward employee behavior.

Alex Stouffer, a long-time employee of the Wheeling Tire Company in Wheeling, West Virginia, was heard telling one of his coworkers that he was planning to be gone for three days next week. Stephanie, his coworker at the plant, knew that Alex had already used all his vacation days and asked him about his plans. Alex replied, "I am just not going to show up for work and if someone calls, I'll say I am sick. They wouldn't fire me; I've been here too long and they need me." Stephanie knew that Alex was partly right; his expertise was needed, but she wasn't too sure about him not being fired.

The Substance of Worker Attitudes

The example of Alex Stouffer is typical in many businesses if employees are not happy with or committed to their jobs. Many workers don't care if they miss work or report late; some workers call in sick so they can do other things. These problems must be addressed in the workplace specifically but are also common occurrences among people in volunteer organizations.

What is the best way to deal with a worker like Alex, someone who is so sure of his value to the organization that he thinks he can do what he chooses? Many companies have special programs for counseling and assisting employees. Additionally, they have established reward and disciplinary systems to address situations that occur in the company. The situation with Alex at the tire company would probably be addressed through an established system. When there are too many violations of the system, the final result is often termination of the employee from the company.

Attitude is a difficult concept to define and to explain. Attitudes relate to what an individual believes and the way he or she acts relative to a specific person, event, or thing. The definition of attitude becomes more complex since each person may act differently in different situations. For example, when under stress, a worker may do or say things that he or she wouldn't say at other times. A manager must be concerned about the attitude of a worker because attitude helps define work behavior. A parent must be concerned about the attitude of a child because attitude helps define behavior in school. You might be concerned about the attitude of a friend because of the possible actions that he or she might take.

Attitudes That Affect Work Performance

At the beginning of this chapter, we looked at a situation with Alex Stouffer, a long-time employee of the same company. What do you think was the attitude of this employee? There is no doubt that his attitude is affecting his own work performance and raising concern among other employees. If he does miss work without first letting someone know, other workers might be affected, which in turn affects the company.

Involvement

Some workers are more involved with their jobs than others. In fact, some people are more involved with everything they do than are others. **Involvement** is the degree to which a worker becomes involved with his or her job. For some workers, jobs are a lifetime commitment and the most important

involvement-the degree to which a worker becomes involved in his or her job

Teacher tutoring after school hours is an example of commitment.

Chapter 9 • Counseling, Rewarding, and Disciplining Workers

Customs and Traditions: Watching for the Global Difference

Women as International Managers

The number of women who hold management positions in most countries is limited, causing many organizations to question if women can succeed in international positions. Dr. Nancy Adler outlines several myths that are held by organizations regarding women in international managerial positions.

Adler's first myth states that women do not want to be international managers. Adler's second myth states that companies refuse to send women abroad. Many companies are hesitant to send women abroad for a number of reasons. An article in *The Wall Street Journal* discussed Japanese career women for whom the situation is somewhat different. Women who aspire to managerial positions often have to leave Japan because men hold the power positions in the country. It would be unlikely that the aspiring Japanese managerial women could get positions without leaving the country.[1]

Adler's third myth states that foreigners are prejudiced against women expatriate managers. She found that women expatriate man-

part of their lives, placed ahead of family, and the things they do away from work. As discussed in a previous chapter, some workers, classified as workaholics, are so involved in their work that their health is often adversely affected. Other workers don't want to be highly involved in their work and would rather devote time to hobbies or other pursuits.

Commitment

As was previously pointed out, the Japanese culture expects a commitment from workers to the company that employs them. Commitment to a company is similar to loyalty. Many workers who are committed to their companies will stick with them through all kinds of difficulties.

Not all employees who are committed to their jobs make good employees. Commitment can be a disadvantage to the company if the worker is committed but not a good employee. If the commitment is too strong, the employee may not want to leave and other actions will have to be taken. This can be determined through the employee appraisal process and the subsequent follow-up activities, which will be discussed later in this chapter.

Satisfaction

Employee satisfaction with specific job duties and the job in general is critical to effective work performance. Job satisfaction is the degree to which a person is happy with the work he or she does and with the place of employment. Job satisfaction is important to the health of an organization. When employees are not satisfied with their jobs, the health of the organi-

agers are more successful than male expatriate managers.[2]

Stephanie Derderian pointed out that because more and more companies have international offices, it is becoming more critical to conduct cross-cultural training for expatriates and others who travel internationally for their work. Her suggestions for companies include adding cross-cultural training to other ongoing training in the company, expanding company libraries to include materials for cross-cultural training, offering activities and discussion on international topics, and conducting better assessment and appraisal to select the international candidates.[3]

---

[1] Nancy J. Adler. "Women Managers in a Global Economy." HRMagazine. September 1993, 52–55.

[2] Jennifer Cody. "To Forge Ahead, Career Women Are Venturing Out of Japan." The Wall Street Journal. August 29, 1994, B1, B5.

[3] Stephanie Derderian. "International Success Lies in Cross-Cultural Training." HRfocus. April 1993, 9.

zation suffers. Dissatisfied employees are more likely to be absent from work, much like Mr. Stouffer in the opening vignette. His lack of concern about missing work is a sign of dissatisfaction with his job and the company. (Job satisfaction was extensively discussed in Chapter 8, and you may want to review what you read in that chapter.)

The Importance of Attitudes

A basic understanding of attitude, and the effects of attitude on an organization, is critical in order to understand the role an individual plays in a work or personal environment. What a worker does on and off the job is a reflection of his or her attitude. Managers and supervisors need to be concerned with a variety of behaviors that are reflective of employees' attitudes.

Work behaviors are continually evaluated, either formally or informally. Evaluations may take the form of a written rating instrument that is completed by a supervisor and then discussed with employees. When evaluations are completed, the behaviors that are reviewed are reflective of the employees' attitudes.

Many behaviors are judged informally; attendance, tardiness, cooperation, and other actions are monitored regularly by supervisors and managers. No written evaluation instrument is used, just the perception of others. Again, these behaviors are a reflection of an individual's attitude. Informal observations can be documented and may be the cause for follow-up actions, just as with formal evaluations.

Managers and workers are in situations in which they will be responsible either for acting upon the behaviors of others or receiving further actions themselves. In either case, it is important to understand the critical role that counseling, reward systems, and disciplinary actions play within an organization, whether the organization is a profit-oriented company, a volunteer group, a government agency, a school, or a personal environment.

Kelly Attebury directed a volunteer organization in Jerome, Arizona. The major purpose of the organization was to provide services to tourists visiting the area. Kelly was employed by the Tourist and Convention Bureau and was its only paid employee. Kelly worked hard to recruit local volunteers who were friendly, loved the area, and knew the history of the town.

Edgar Cravens, a volunteer who was a retired auto dealer and had been in the area for over 60 years, knew the history, and met all the qualifications that Kelly sought in volunteers. He started out as one of Kelly's best volunteers. Tourists loved Edgar's stories and his personality. But as time went on, Edgar started missing some of his scheduled tours and someone else had to be called in to pinch-hit at the last minute. Kelly was quite concerned about how to handle the situation. Edgar was a likable person and did an excellent job when he showed up. He always seemed to have legitimate excuses for his absences.

In a volunteer organization, Kelly couldn't actually fire someone and needed all the help she could get. Perhaps you have some suggestions for Kelly. See how your suggestions compare with what you read in the remainder of this chapter.

*E*mployee Counseling and Coaching

▼

counseling-formal communication process used to assist someone through problems or to increase personal effectiveness

▼

coaching-assisting others to improve performance by giving suggestions and support

▼

employee counseling-a means to develop an employee

In a work situation, employees who have problems or shortcomings are often provided with counseling or coaching or both. There is a difference in counseling and coaching. As the word *counseling* implies, the person who is being counseled is being assisted through a problem. **Counseling** can be defined as the process of formal communication used to assist someone through problems or to increase personal effectiveness. On the other hand, *coaching* implies giving direction and assistance. **Coaching** is assisting others to improve performance by giving suggestions and support.

Counseling

Counseling is a long-term process which deals with employee behavior and changes of behavior over a period of time. The purpose of **employee counseling** is to develop the employee. Counseling is provided prior to taking disciplinary actions. Initial counseling may be done by supervisory or managerial personnel, possibly with the result of correcting the problems or potential problems. More difficult situations should be left in the hands of qualified personnel who have been trained for the task.

D. Cameron, in *Managing People: The Art and Science of Business Management,* suggests that counseling can be a simple process, and just merely suggesting to an employee that he or she is violating a work rule could correct the actions. If this semipassive approach doesn't work, then more direct counseling methods must be used. The suggested steps are as follows.

1. Meet with the employee in private.

2. Point out the work rule violation or wrong behavior.

3. Listen to the employee's explanations.

4. Outline the behavior that needs to occur and explain why.

5. Set a future date for a performance review.[1]

These steps should not be interpreted as being disciplinary at this time, and the supervisor should not make threats of future disciplinary action. The employee should realize from the session that his or her performance needs to change and what changes are expected. Following the counseling session, the supervisor records in writing what recommendations were made and what the expectations are for the employee.

Types of Counseling. Employee counseling can be used to correct actions that are potential causes for problems within the employee. The **corrective counseling** might need to occur as a result of something the employee does or to alter the attitude that appears to be at the root of the potential problem. Another type of counseling is **restorative counseling,** an opportunity to prescribe an "elixir" that will cure the difficulties that are the cause of further problems. Restorative counseling might be nothing more than a change in work habits to reduce stress, or perhaps a recommendation to see a medical doctor so prescriptive medications can be administered.

Some counseling is instructive, a method to provide information needed by the employee to solve problems. **Instructive counseling** can be and often is used as a means to prevent problems rather than to solve them after they have begun.

Developmental counseling helps employees grow and fully realize their potential. This process is used to help the employee become more effective and more efficient in the workplace. This is beneficial for the employer and could result in the employee being more satisfied with his or her job performance. If you are already a highly motivated worker and are working to the best of your abilities, you would not be a candidate for this type of counseling.

corrective counseling-correcting actions that are potential causes for problems within the employee

restorative counseling-a means to prescribe a cure for difficulties that may cause further problems

instructive counseling-a means to prevent problems rather than to solve them after they have begun

developmental counseling-helps employees grow and fully realize their potential in the workplace

---

[1]Dan Cameron, and A. Dale Timpe, editors. *Managing People: The Art and Science of Business Management.* New York: KEND Publishing, 1988.

Figure 9.1 Four Types of Employee Counseling That Lead to Employee Performance Improvement

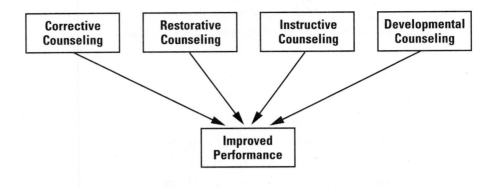

Approaches to Performance Counseling. Michael Armstrong identifies three approaches to performance counseling which can be used in development programs. Keep in mind that as a supervisor you must use an approach that is best for you or the employee being counseled.

1. *Tell and sell counseling* is a method in which the supervisor tells the employee how he or she is doing. Acceptance of the evaluation is gained; finally an improvement plan is "sold" to the employee.

A supervisor may counsel employees by discussing the tasks and problems on the job.

2. *Tell and listen counseling* first details the performance evaluation to the employee, then allows the employee to respond. The employee determines what must be done to improve job performance.

3. *Problem-solving* allows the supervisor to be a helper rather than a judge. The evaluation is not communicated to the employee, rather a discussion takes place in which the employee is encouraged to discuss his or her problems on the job.[2]

Carlos de Varela, the line supervisor for the evening shift at the new Border Cheese factory in Beloit, Wisconsin, had just completed his first evaluation of the workers on his shift. All but Karen Jackson were performing equally well and meeting production quotas set for a new plant. Karen seemed to have her mind elsewhere. She didn't cause problems and kept to herself most of the time. Carlos knew he had to bring about a change in Karen's job performance or the other workers would notice that she was getting away with doing much less. Carlos was aware that Karen was a moody person and could not deal with criticism, so he knew he would have to handle her situation very delicately or be accused of picking on her. From the approaches just discussed, which one might be best to use with Karen? She really hasn't done anything wrong. It's just that her performance is not on par with the rest of the workers. Carlos would be talking to each of the workers so Karen wouldn't feel as though she were being singled out.

Employee Coaching

Coaching may appear to be the same as counseling, but there are differences. **Employee coaching** is a personalized on-the-job method which is used to develop job skills, knowledge, and attitudes. Coaching is a job training technique which will improve performance and therefore enhance the company's probability of increasing profits. Coaching is usually a function of management or supervisory personnel and can be informal but should be planned.[3]

Coaching sessions are designed to overcome deficiencies that are discovered in the evaluation process. Used in conjunction with counseling, coaching is the follow-up activity after the employee is aware of deficiencies. Coaching must be planned and cannot occur incidentally. It is not appropriate for the supervisor to just "pop" in on the employee and tell him or her what should be done differently to improve performance. Employees shouldn't be lectured on what they have done wrong; instead they need to be trained or retrained to enable them to do the job at the expected level of performance.

*employee coaching-
a personalized on-the-job method which is used to develop job skills, knowledge, and attitudes*

[2]Michael Armstrong. *A Handbook of Personnel Management Practice*. New York: Nichols Publishing, 1988.
[3]Ibid.

*E*mployee Discipline

If counseling and coaching efforts fail to change behavior and work performance, a systematic process to discipline the employee should be followed. Disciplinary actions are usually taken when the employee breaks rules of the organization. Because discipline can be a critical step, it is important for organizations to have an established disciplinary system in place.

Establish Rules

The first step in the disciplinary process is to establish work rules that are in line with the organization's goals or objectives. These work rules should become the basis for disciplinary actions when the rules are broken. The rules should not be established by management only. Employees should have an opportunity for input to ensure that rules are fair and can be followed by the workers. Work rules are directly related to work behavior and productivity. For example, one rule might state that employees can take a 20-minute break in the morning and in the afternoon. If employees constantly take 30-minute breaks, productivity will be hindered, and the disciplinary process can be initiated. Another rule might be to keep a work area free from clutter, an important rule especially where safety is a concern. Employees who continually violate the rule are candidates for the disciplinary process.

Communicate the Rules

Employees must know the rules that have been established for the organization. Even though employees might have input in the development of the rules, it is the employer who will create the final version. It is critical, then, that the rules be in a printed format and that each employee is given a copy. This is usually accomplished in the form of an employee handbook. The handbook may have other information, but a critical part of the handbook is the rules.

In some companies the rules are discussed at meetings, seminars, or training sessions. This can also easily be done when new employees begin their jobs and are being trained. It is essential that employees with long tenure in the company review the rules periodically. Rules should be

Figure 9.2 **Process Leading to Employee Discipline**

- ► Establish work rules in line with the organizational objectives.

- ► Communicate the rules to all employees and make sure they are understood.

- ► Evaluate employee's performance on a regular schedule.

- ► Take disciplinary action if the employee evaluation (performance appraisal) indicates there is a necessity.

reviewed from time to time and, if necessary, revised. You might wonder, why do rules change? It is possible that if a company makes major changes in the way it operates because of new equipment, expansion or contraction, new ownership, or numerous other reasons, it will need to revise its rules accordingly.

Small companies with only a few employees also need to have rules. Such companies may not have an employee handbook; even so, it is still wise for the rules to be written and presented to each employee. In addition, the rules could also be posted in a spot where all employees can easily read them.

Employee Evaluation

The employee evaluation process, whether formal or informal, will often reveal behaviors requiring disciplinary actions. Informal evaluation might be occurring at all times as supervisors monitor employees. Formal evaluations of each employee should be completed regularly so deficiencies can be discovered and discussed with the employee. When employees violate rules, a change of behavior must occur. Small companies with only a few employees may not use a formal written evaluation, but they should nevertheless evaluate employees regularly. Small companies may find it easier to take corrective actions than large companies because of the closeness of the supervisor to each of the work situations. In contrast, a supervisor in a large organization might be responsible for 50, 100, or more workers.

Changing Behavior

When an employee is breaking the rules of the organization, assistance is needed to change behavior and get the worker to operate within the established parameters. Counseling and coaching could be a part of this process, but they usually take place prior to disciplinary actions. If the employee changes behavior as a result of the disciplinary actions and conforms to the company rules, there is no need for further discipline. If a change in behavior does not take place, harsher actions should follow.

Disciplinary Actions

Most organizations use **progressive discipline,** a process that helps to ensure that the minimum penalty which matches the violation of the rule will be imposed. If that action does not correct the behavior, a more severe penalty is imposed. Again, if the more severe penalty does not correct the behavior, an even more severe penalty is imposed, ultimately leading to the employee's dismissal from the job. This process is called progressive discipline because the penalty gets progressively more severe.

Progressive discipline is administered in different ways within different organizations. In one organization the first minor infraction of a rule could result in an oral warning, whereas in another organization the rule violation might result in a written reprimand. In the case where an oral warning was given, the second violation would probably result in a written warning, per-

progressive discipline-a process that helps ensure that the minimum penalty which matches the violation of the rule will be imposed

Chapter 9 • Counseling, Rewarding, and Disciplining Workers

haps signed by the employee to verify that the person has read the warning. If the employee refuses to sign, another supervisor should sign as a witness to the fact that the employee received and read the warning. A further violation of the rules could result in a third warning, again signed by the employee and witnessed by another supervisor. This third warning could state that termination is imminent if the employee does not change his or her behaviors.

This is just one example of a progressive disciplinary system and how it functions. Some employee actions are justification for immediate dismissal, without a progressive process. For example, if an employee threatens a coworker or supervisor with bodily injury or actually hits someone, that employee's actions could be grounds for immediate dismissal without progressive discipline.

Joyce Kaplan was a supervisor at Johnny Bell's Catering, a well-known catering company in Minneapolis. The company had a fleet of specially equipped trucks that could be driven to an industrial plant during lunchtime and could be opened like a cafeteria. The trucks were loaded with sandwiches, assorted chips, salads, pastries, hot coffee, cold drinks, and other tasty items. With the exception of the chips and some other processed foods, the items were made fresh each day. Joyce noticed that when she and Angela Lane counted the unsold fresh products at the end of the day, Angela was never able to balance her account. She never had sandwiches left over, but neither did she have enough money to match what she sold.

Joyce questioned Angela about the discrepancy. At first she said she didn't know what the problem was, yet she appeared to be uneasy about being questioned. Angela had just had her route changed and said that maybe there was a discrepancy because she hadn't gotten used to the new route. After a couple more discrepancies, Joyce again asked Angela what was going on. By now she should have made the adjustments to the new route. Angela became very uncomfortable, but she confessed that she had been giving "just a small number of sandwiches" to some homeless children along her route. This was the first time Angela had done anything against the rules, and Joyce knew that Angela was a very caring person and had a big heart. Joyce didn't want Angela to quit her job, but she knew that the company had to enforce rules that required the drivers' accounts to balance.

Performance Appraisal

Performance appraisal has been mentioned in relation to employee counseling, coaching, and discipline. The appraisal process is a critical one and most larger organizations have a system to follow to assure that employees are evaluated regularly. Performance appraisal in small businesses may be more informal, but does take place continually. In a small business with only a few employees, the management knows each person on a more personal level and communicates with the employees regularly and in the communication process is able to provide performance feedback.

The main purpose of a **performance appraisal** is to determine how well individuals perform on their jobs. The appraisal process is a measure of what they can do and are doing so steps can be taken to improve performance and productivity. Other reasons for conducting performance appraisals include measuring how employees impact the operation, image, or profitability of the organization. These secondary reasons could be related to employee theft, unethical practices, and drug or alcohol abuse, all of which affect company profitability. Keep in mind that companies must operate profitably or they can't continue to exist.

Performance appraisals are used to make decisions about an individual's readiness for promotion, or to accept greater job responsibilities. Performance is evaluated to determine if a pay raise is in order, or if an employee should be demoted or terminated. When performance appraisals are used in this way, they are evaluative.

Other performance appraisals are used to determine what kind of training or retraining is needed for an employee. Appraisals of managers, or potential managers, can be made which will identify the need for management development programs. In some cases the appraisal process might

*performance appraisal-
a means to determine how
well individuals perform on
their jobs*

Ethical Dimensions to Human Relations

Equality in the Workplace

One of the key functions of management is to ensure that employees are treated equally and are respected individually for what they do. In reality, there is often disparity in the treatment of employees in different ranks of companies. W. Steven Brown, president of the Fortune Group based in Atlanta, cited examples of how an investment firm traditionally gave secretaries a rose on Secretaries Day. The secretaries were referred to as staff, and the other employees were called professionals. One Secretaries Day a chain reaction occurred when a secretary threw her rose in the wastebasket. Secretaries wanted to be known and treated as professionals, just as everyone else at the firm. Brown said that management functions at the highest level when it helps employees reach their objectives.

Equal treatment of all employees carries over to the appraisal system used by a company. While the appraisal instruments might be somewhat different, the process can be the same regardless who is being evaluated. An example of an appraisal process for all employees is

1. Schedule an appointment with the employee regardless of his or her position.
2. Allow time for the employee to read the appraisal before leaving the appointment.

3. Explain the performance categories so the employee understands the importance of different aspects of the job.
4. Focus on employee behavior; don't attack the employee's personality.
5. Use examples which illustrate the employee's performance rating.
6. Mix areas of concern with positive performance characteristics to prevent the employee from becoming defensive.
7. Listen to what the employee has to say.
8. Think about the future, help the employee set goals for improved performance.

All employees should be treated equally and evaluated fairly. If one type of employee isn't considered important to the operation of the company, perhaps there isn't a need for the person. The appraisal process is an opportunity to show all employees that they will be treated fairly.

reveal that additional employees are needed to maximize productivity in the firm. This type of performance appraisal is developmental.

The Process of Performance Appraisal

Performance appraisal must be based upon valid criteria and standards. There have been court cases which have challenged performance evaluation procedures and the basis for the evaluations. One such case challenged the basis upon which an evaluation instrument was founded. In the case of *Kirkland* v. *New York Department of Correctional Services,* it was found that if a formal job analysis has not been completed to establish the validity of the performance appraisal form and the job appropriateness of the selection process, courts may deny all claims of the validity of the form. This means that for the performance appraisal form to be valid, it must be related to the job an individual is doing and appropriate to the tasks the person was hired to complete.[4]

After the performance criteria or the tasks that should be performed on the job have been identified, it is necessary to determine and establish the levels of performance at which the job should be performed. Some examples are "completes 30 units per hour," "sells 25 cars per month," or

---

[4] EEOC, 1979, 2319.

Figure 9.3 Sample of Subjective Performance Appraisal Items

► What are the strengths of the employee?

► What are the weaknesses of the employee?

► What recommendations can you make for additional training or retraining?

► What considerations should be given for professional advancement?

"arrives for work on time." These standards become the level of performance that is expected and are based upon the job analysis.

The performance appraisal form can be objective, subjective, or both. When the rater is expected to evaluate (evaluation implies judgment) an employee's level of performance, the evaluation is subjective. Figure 9.3 illustrates a **subjective evaluation.** Subjectivity is most often present when affective, or attitudinal, characteristics are being evaluated.

When possible, it is best to make performance appraisals objective. An **objective evaluation** is one in which the criteria are easily interpreted without having to make judgment. It is similar to counting beans: when you are all done you will have a number. There is no argument unless, of course, someone obviously miscounted. A sample of objective performance appraisal items is illustrated in Figure 9.4.

It is important that employees know what tasks and behaviors are being appraised and what standards of performance are expected of them. Communication of the process and the product (criteria and standards) to the employees is critical. You might think that employees will emphasize the tasks on which they know they are being evaluated to get higher

subjective evaluation-a rater must judge the level of performance of an employee

objective evaluation-criteria are easily interpreted without having to make judgments

Figure 9.4 Graphical Rating Scale Example

	High				Low
Dependability Employee reliable in performing tasks accurately as assigned.	❏ Exceptional. Works on own and meets deadlines.	❏ Very dependable. Little supervision needed to complete assigned jobs.	❏ Mostly dependable. Usual supervision required, but a good worker.	❏ Requires frequent supervision and must constantly be prodded to complete work.	❏ Always procrastinates. Never completes job without help from others.
Work Quality Compare the amount of work output to standards for the job.	❏ Standards are always exceeded. Work completed rapidly. Excellent output on job.	❏ Consistent, high rate of production. Usually exceeds standards. Effort is better than average.	❏ Normal output. Meets standards regularly. Average worker.	❏ Usually produces less than average. Low producer seldom meeting standards.	❏ Consistently lags in production. Very slow worker with unacceptable output.
Cooperation What is the employee's attitude toward _____ ?	❏	❏	❏	❏	❏

Chapter 9 • Counseling, Rewarding, and Disciplining Workers

Figure 9.5 **Numerical Rating Scale Example**

	Low				**High**
Dependability Employee reliable in performing tasks accurately, as assigned	1	2	3	4	5
Work Quality Compare the amount of work output to standards for the job.	1	2	3	4	5
Cooperation What is the employee's attitude toward _____?	1	2	3	4	5

marks. This is OK if the form is developed based on a job analysis and the items on the form include what is critical to the job. The attitudinal items should be a part of every person's behavior.

Forms of Performance Appraisal

There are several forms of performance appraisal which include subjective and objective methods. One form of evaluation is to use items that are rated. These could appear in several different ways, as will be shown and briefly discussed on the following pages. Another form of evaluation, which is much more subjective, is done by using essay questions.

Graphical and Numerical Scales.

The most conventional format for performance appraisals is to have stated criteria that are evaluated using descriptors which define different levels of behavior. Figure 9.4 illustrates this format, which is called a **graphical scale.** Each of the stated behaviors describes a level of performance. This type of rating scale is difficult to develop but easy for the rater to use. This format can be altered so that numbers are used to rate the criteria; however, the rater has to make more judgments of the employees' levels of performance based on the set of numbers such as is shown in Figure 9.5. This type of rating format is known as a **numerical rating scale.** The tendency is for raters to evaluate using numbers at the center or higher.

Forced Choice Format.

Some performance appraisals use a **forced choice** format. Raters are given pairs of descriptors which represent employee behavior. The raters are then asked to select the best descriptor for the employee. This form helps eliminate biases the evaluator might have and avoids rating at a safe central point. The evaluators might be

graphical scale-descriptors define different levels of behavior

numerical rating scale-numbers are used to rate the criteria requiring the rater to make more judgments

forced choice-raters select the best descriptor from a pair to describe performance levels

Figure 9.6 Sample of Forced-Choice Appraisal Items

1. ❑ Prepares interview summaries accurately.
   ❑ Treats interviewees with respect.

2. ❑ Works well with other employees.
   ❑ Follows through when given directions.

3. ❑ Self-starter who realizes work to be done.
   ❑ Has potential for supervisory work.

asked to either pick the statement from the pairs that is most descriptive of the workers' behavior, or perhaps the least descriptive of behaviors. This format is not very popular in industry because of the difficulty in validating the behaviors. A short sample is included in Figure 9.6.

Employee Objectives. Some forms of evaluation are based on employee objectives. These objectives are often derived through the management-by-objectives process. MBO, as the process is called, occurs in two major steps. The process is long and sometimes tedious, but here is a simple explanation.

The first major step in the MBO process is for the employee to establish goals or objectives. Employees meet with supervisors to discuss goals and objectives which are in line with the company's objectives. Each employee will have objectives that he or she wants to achieve in a predetermined time period, usually in one year. After the meetings are held during which objectives are established, the employee and the supervisor both know what is expected of the employee.

The second major step in using MBO in the evaluation process is to conduct the evaluations. The employee meets with the supervisor and both evaluate progress toward achieving the employee's objectives. This is a mutual process in which both the supervisor and the employee participate to complete the evaluation. The results of the evaluation are based on the employee's actual performance in meeting the established objectives.

We don't want to leave the impression that management by objectives is a simple process; it is not. It takes time to implement the process and to get total commitment to using objectives. One great advantage of using MBO in the appraisal process is that employees are evaluated based on their objectives. They know what they need to do to be judged satisfactory or higher in their work performance.

There are other methods that are used to evaluate the performance of employees; however, space does not permit us to discuss all of them. Managers may be appraised differently than other employees. Supervisors may be appraised differently than managers. Some companies use different forms of appraisal and follow their own performance appraisal systems. It is important that employees and supervisors know what system and what forms are used in their organization.

Kristy Thomas was the newest employee at Central Water Resources, an environmental firm in Springfield, Illinois, that consults with and provides recommendations to cities and municipalities that have problems with their water supplies. Kristy was hired because of her expertise with environmental issues; she has an environmental science degree.

Ms. Thomas was given her first major assignment in her fourth month on the job. Up to that time she had been working with her supervisor to learn more about the company. When she was given the assignment, her supervisor told her that it was expected to be a two-month job, and she would have her probationary evaluation when it was done. Kristy asked her supervisor what criteria would be used to complete the evaluation. The response was, "Well, with consulting you just have to do what needs to be done and we'll evaluate that." Kristy didn't have any concerns with being evaluated for attitudinal behaviors, but she was uneasy with the answer she was given.

What Kristy faced is not unusual. In some types of work it is more difficult to identify criteria for evaluation, other than the affective, or attitudinal, behaviors. What recommendations would you make for Kristy? What should the company do to make the appraisal process more fair for employees?

Rewarding Employee Behavior

Reward systems are closely related to evaluation and motivation. You can review the motivation theories in Chapter 7. When reward systems are developed, they are prepared to provide incentives, or inducements, which will get employees to work more efficiently and productively.

As children, some people may have received an allowance, except for weeks in which they didn't complete their chores. Or, perhaps they were given money, an edible treat, or an afternoon at the movies when they did extra chores. Maybe they didn't receive any reward for the extra work; they may have done it because it was expected of them. Those same reward systems are in effect today in many businesses and in our personal lives.

In the work world, rewards for good performance come in many different ways. Some companies might reward an employee's outstanding performance with paid time off. Another company might recognize outstanding employees at a recognition gathering. Still another company might have a designated parking spot for the outstanding employee.

Rewards for work performance are either extrinsic or intrinsic. **Extrinsic rewards** are external to the worker and are concrete. Employee benefits such as health insurance, vacation days, promotions, and pay are all examples of extrinsic rewards. Intrinsic rewards are internal to the employee. Examples of **intrinsic rewards** might be job satisfaction, pride, accomplishment, or job autonomy. Each person responds differently to

reward systems-ways to provide incentives, or inducements, which will get employees to work more efficiently and productively

extrinsic reward-external to the worker such as pay and vacations

intrinsic reward-internal to the worker such as satisfaction and pride

Extrinsic rewards for work performance are paid time off and vacation days.

both the extrinsic and intrinsic rewards depending on his or her own needs, level of education, social status, job level, and other factors.

There are many ways to reward employee performance. One of the common extrinsic ways is through compensation plans tied directly to performance. These compensation plans are intended to stimulate employee performance, to be a motivator for employees, and in turn to improve the productivity of the organization.

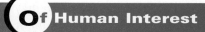

Human Interest

Employees Provide Input to Appraisal Systems

There are many changes taking place in the corporate world. Many companies are right-sizing to become more efficient and productive. In the process, internal company procedures are also being handled differently. Pressures are being applied to companies that don't want to listen to employees. Team approaches to decision-making are being used. Sue Shellenbarger reported one example in *The Wall Street Journal* about a growing number of employees who value having a job that does not interfere with their personal lives. They don't want to have to spend numerous hours outside the regular workday doing company business.[1] Employee involvement in the operation of companies is critical to the changing corporation. When employers don't listen, workers take action.

Ron Sorensen and Geralyn McCluse Franklin told of a positive process to develop an appraisal system which included a team approach. The Forests Division of Temple-Inland Forest Products Corporation developed an appraisal system that handled typical problems using a representative committee of employees, even though

CONTINUED

most of the employees had no experience in developing a formalized appraisal system. The resource team of divisional personnel were allowed three months to develop the workable system.

The resource team used a very basic problem-solving approach to attack the goals. They defined desired goals or outcomes, generated alternatives to achieve the goals, and selected the best alternative. In the end, the resource team had a much different plan than what they envisioned at the start of the process. The important factor is that they worked as a team, the employer listened, and the end result was a workable system taking into consideration the needs of the workers in the division.[2]

---

[1] *Shellenbarger, Sue. "Work and Family." The Wall Street Journal. August 31, 1994, B1.*

[2] *Ron Sorensen, and Geralyn M. Franklin. "Teamwork Developed a Successful Appraisal System." HRfocus. August, 1992, 3–4.*

Merit Pay Systems

merit pay increase-pay increase based on how well an employee performs

Some companies choose to reward employees for meritorious performance. This practice is especially predominant among managerial and professional employees. Employees are evaluated, and the level of their performance, identified on a rating scale, will determine the **merit pay increase** they receive. The higher the performance rating, the higher will be the merit pay increase. Not everyone in the organization will receive the merit pay increases; the poorest performers may not receive any increase at all. In some organizations, merit pay increases are given in addition to a standard pay increase that is received by everyone.

merit award-one-time award based on employee performance

Several employers have elected to use merit awards. **Merit awards** differ from merit pay increases. The merit pay increase is a pay raise that improves the employee's salary base. A merit award does not increase the base rate of pay; it is an award based on job performance. The award might be made once each year or in some cases more often. Merit awards are beneficial to the company also, since they don't have to be awarded and the financial expenditures can be reduced. It might be argued that such plans could be misused by employers. That could be true; however, merit plans are tied to performance; and good performance leads to greater potential for company earnings to grow.

Lump Sum Payments

lump sum payment-employee can take a portion of earnings in a lump sum

Lump sum payment allows the employee to take a portion of annual earnings as one lump sum. For example, if an employee is being paid a merit award each time he or she meets a certain level of performance, the employee might ask to receive the award in one payment at the end of the calendar year. The employee can plan for the lump sum payment and may be able to defer some expenditures until the sum is received. In that way, the employee does not have to borrow money for the down payment of a new car, for example, and the purchase can be made using the lump sum payment.

Performance-Based Incentive Plans for Individuals

Several individual incentive plans are used to stimulate production and reward employees for performance. You will be familiar with some of the plans, and perhaps you are familiar with companies that use these incentive plans.

Piecework Plan. When a **piecework plan** is used, employees are guaranteed a base hourly rate of pay, normally minimum wage, for producing at an expected rate. An employee who works in a factory sewing seams in backpacks, for example, may receive minimum wage and be expected to sew 12 backpacks per hour. The incentive for greater production comes from payment for the number of backpacks sewn over the piece rate of 12. If the worker can sew 18 backpacks per hour, the person would receive more than if he or she could sew 15 pieces.

> *piecework plan*-employee receives a base rate of pay and is rewarded for producing over a quota

Commissions. **Commissions** are popular in selling jobs and are payment for performance when production occurs or when production quotas are exceeded. Straight commissions are paid in several types of sales jobs, such as real estate, investments, and automobiles. If the salesperson doesn't sell, the individual doesn't get paid. It is easy to see what the incentive is that causes a person to produce in a job like this.

> *commission*-payment for performance when production occurs or when quotas are exceeded

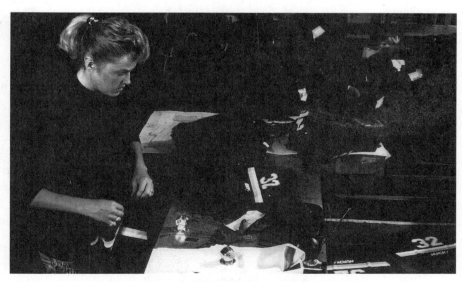

One advantage of doing piecework is that the more an employee produces over the predetermined rate, the more she gets paid.

A variation to the straight commission is to pay workers a base salary and then a commission on top of the salary once predetermined quotas of production are met. This method takes off some pressures from the worker but may not provide the inducements that come from straight commission plans.

Standard Time Plan. The **standard time plan** is similar to the piecework plan, except the process is changed. Rather than determining that an employee can complete final assembly of 10 computers per hour, for example, the time to complete each computer would be measured and that becomes the **standard time.** Employees are then rewarded based on the number of units they complete. The measurement is time per unit, rather than units per time period.

Managerial Incentive Plans. **Managerial incentive plans** often take the form of cash bonuses for suitable performance by a department or division. The bonuses are paid at the end of a year, usually the company's fiscal year. Additional managerial incentive plans could be stock options, where the manager is given the opportunity to purchase stock in the company at a later date, but at an agreed-upon price. Other plans devised by and unique to companies are also used.

Suggestion Plans. Companies often have **suggestion plans** which allow employees to give suggestions which will improve operations of the company. The suggestion may be a way to simplify one procedure which might save the company thousands of dollars each year. Or, the suggestion might be a way to get employees to work more cooperatively. When suggestions such as these are made, employees often receive rewards for their money-saving ideas. Most often the reward is a small monetary incentive, but sometimes it could be a percentage, for example 30 percent of the first year's savings. If the reward is too small, there is little or no incentive for the workers to offer suggestions.

Group Incentive Plans

Some employers have group incentive plans and pay incentives to groups of employees. The growing complexity and interdependence of work group members necessitates rewarding more than the individual worker. It is often difficult to determine an individual worker's level of performance because what the worker does is masked by the groups' performance. For group incentive systems to work, an organization must have an objective way to measure the performance of the group. It must encourage group performance and cohesiveness for these plans to be useful. The basic approach to group incentive plans is to share the gains with employees.

Gainsharing. **Gainsharing** is a group incentive plan that represents a managerial philosophy or approach. This plan works best in small companies where production and costs are under the control of employees, where a trusting and open relationship exists between managers and

standard time plan-a payment plan based upon time needed to complete task

standard time-the time needed to complete a task

managerial incentive plan-bonuses or other forms of incentives paid to managers for good performance

suggestion plans-an opportunity for employees to suggest ways to improve company operations

gainsharing-a group incentive plan such as payment, or incentives, for suggestions that help the company gain profits

employees, and when the workers are technically competent. Gainsharing can be designed to meet the needs of each different work situation.

One of the best-known gainsharing plans is the Scanlon Plan, which was developed in the 1930s by a steel industry union leader, Joseph Scanlon. This plan includes a participatory management philosophy and uses pay incentives and a suggestion system. A production committee made up of supervisors and employees represents each unit. This committee screens the improvement suggestions that come from the employees and managers. If the suggestions are accepted and the result is a gain or cost saving, the gain is shared with the work group. Individuals are not rewarded since it is a team effort, even though the suggestion may have come from one individual.[5, 6]

All gainsharing plans use pay as a reward for tying individuals' goals with the goals of the organization. This is accomplished by sharing gains that result from the increases in productivity and profitability, which come from improvements suggested by employees.

Profit Sharing. **Profit sharing** could be considered gainsharing, but profit sharing plans are not usually connected to an employee suggestion system. With profit sharing plans, employees receive a regular share of company profits to supplement their normal compensation. The company usually establishes a set amount of the net profits that will be shared with employees. If 25 percent of the net profits is the amount determined for sharing, then all participating employees will receive a reward. The profit sharing amount can be paid quarterly, annually, or in some cases is held for the employee until retirement.

profit sharing-employees receive a portion of company profits to supplement normal compensation

Not every year will be profitable for businesses. In unprofitable years, a company cannot share with employees because the profit sharing is based on net profits, or what the company earns. If the company is not making money, there is nothing to share. Reduced profits may not be related to employee performance but to a downturn in the economy resulting in less sales for the company. Regardless of the reason, there would be no profits to share.

Reinforcing Positive Performance

What we have been discussing are ways to reinforce positive performance. It is important to recall from the previous discussion of motivation that not everyone responds in the same way. That is why it is critical that counseling, coaching, disciplinary actions, and reward systems be suited to individuals or groups of individuals. United States companies spend billions of dollars each year for programs to motivate employees to work toward

[5]Linda Tyler, and Bob Fisher. "The Scanlon Concept: A Philosophy as Much as a System." *Personnel Administrator.* July 1983, 33–37.

[6]Fred Lesieur, and Elbridge Puckett. "The Scanlon Plan Has Proved Itself." *Harvard Business Review.* September-October 1969, 109–11.

company objectives. Some programs are more positive than others, but the employee who is undergoing disciplinary actions may feel that the process isn't positive.

Positive performance should be recognized and rewarded, even if only a pat on the back is given for a job well done. It is necessary to get beyond the barriers that might preclude positive reinforcement. The following tips for positive reinforcement should be kept in mind.

1. *Focus on others.* If you are too focused on yourself, you will overlook the needs of others. Think of others as well as your concerns for your own needs.

2. *Make time for others.* Closely related to thinking about others is to make time for others. For positive reinforcement to be effective it must be sincere, which includes giving of your own time to others.

3. *Choose your words carefully.* Many attempts at positive reinforcement are diminished because the words used are not sincere or are inappropriate to the situation. Think about what should be said to make the other person feel good and be sincere in your message.

4. *Be a good role model.* Modeling behavior that is expected of others will reinforce their positive actions. Don't subscribe to the "Do as I say, not as I do" philosophy.

Positive reinforcement will make employees more satisfied in their work and with their company. It is important for anyone in a management or supervisory position to recognize the importance of positive reinforcement. If you are not a manager, you know how good positive reinforcement feels when you do something that you know should be rewarded.

Key Points Summary

- Work performance is greatly affected by the worker's attitudes toward the job. Some of the key attitudes related to job performance include: involvement with the job, commitment to the job, and satisfaction with the job.

- Employee counseling is a long-term process which approaches employee behavior and changes in behavior over time. Employee counseling is one way to improve the performance of an employee to meet company objectives. This process precedes disciplinary actions. Employee counseling can be corrective, restorative, instructive, or developmental.

- Employee coaching is a personalized on-the-job method used to develop job skills, knowledge, and attitudes. This process is a job training technique to improve performance and increase the potential of achieving the company's objectives. Coaching is usually done by management or supervisory personnel.

- Employee discipline is a systematic process which is followed when employees break the rules of the organization. To implement

an effective disciplinary policy, the organization must first establish
and communicate the rules.

- Violations of rules are often discovered during evaluation. If an
employee breaks rules, the behavior needs to be changed. If it
doesn't change, disciplinary action is necessary.

- A process called *progressive discipline* is used by most organizations. Progressive discipline means that the disciplinary action
becomes more severe with each violation of the rules and could
lead to termination of the employee's employment.

- Employee performance appraisals are the means to determine what
the employee is doing on the job. The results of the performance
appraisal might be used to determine if training is needed, if the
employee is eligible for promotions or greater job responsibilities,
if a pay raise is in order, or if an employee should be demoted or
terminated.

- Performance appraisals are typically done using a written form.
Appraisals can be subjective where the rater's opinion is greatly
reflected, or objective where the rater has little opportunity to let
his or her own opinions sway the process. Common types of performance appraisals are graphical scales, numerical rating scales,
forced choice, and achievement of objectives.

- Companies use different methods to reward employee behavior.
Employee rewards are tied closely to employee motivation.
Employee rewards could include time off from work, special recog-
nition in front of a group, or perhaps a special parking spot.
Rewards are either intrinsic, internal to the employee, or extrinsic,
external to the worker.

- Extrinsic rewards include compensation plans such as merit pay,
lump-sum payments, or performance-based incentives which are
tied to production of the individual or to a group.

- While not all employee behaviors are positive, those that are
should be rewarded and reinforced. If positive behaviors are reinforced, they are likely to continue.

Key Terms

coaching	forced choice
commission	gainsharing
corrective counseling	graphical scale
counseling	instructive counseling
developmental counseling	intrinsic reward
employee coaching	involvement
employee counseling	lump sum payment
extrinsic reward	managerial incentive plan

Chapter 9 · Counseling, Rewarding, and Disciplining Workers

merit award

merit pay increase

numerical rating scale

objective evaluation

performance appraisal

piecework plan

profit sharing

progressive discipline

restorative counseling

reward systems

standard time

standard time plan

subjective evaluation

suggestion plan

Discussion Questions

1. Attitudes appear to be important in the workplace. You may have been told you had a good or bad attitude about something. Why do you think someone would label you as having a bad attitude or a good attitude?

2. What are the worker traits that you might associate with attitudes? Why are each of these so critical to an organization?

3. Discuss the difference between employee counseling and coaching. Which of the two would likely be used with an employee who is judged to have an attitude problem? Which of the two would be used with an employee who is slow to learn new skills, like possibly using a computer?

4. Discuss each of the types of counseling that were described in the chapter. Give examples of how each type would be applied in a real work situation.

5. Design a plan that uses progressive discipline for a work situation. The situation could be for the place you work if you are employed. If you are not employed, use a hypothetical situation.

6. Employee evaluation, or performance appraisal, is a constant in organizations. There are different types of formal performance appraisal forms. Discuss different ways performance criteria such as "arrives for work on time" or "meets production quotas" might be written for the appraisal form using subjective and objective methods.

7. Describe reward systems which might be used to provide incentives for workers. What are the differences between intrinsic and extrinsic rewards? For each of the rewards you describe, identify if it is intrinsic or extrinsic.

8. Discuss why it is important for positive behavior to be reinforced.

Chapter 10

Learning Objectives

Upon completing this chapter, you should be able to:

- Describe how drugs and alcohol impact the workplace.

- Understand how family responsibilities impact job performance.

- List and utilize counseling techniques.

- Develop plans for reducing employee turnover and absenteeism.

Coping with Employees' Personal Problems

Lucy Ramirez was an excellent employee. She was well liked by her coworkers and her supervisors. Lucy was always one of the first people at the office in the morning. She took great pride in her work. It was accurate, well done, and completed on time. The future was bright for Lucy. She would be promoted up the corporate ladder quickly. Then something happened. Things changed; everyone at work noticed a difference in Lucy . . . the changes happened slowly.

Both Lucy's attendance at work and performance changed. She was reporting to work late with some regularity. When she seldom used sick leave before, she suddenly was calling in sick often. Supervisors and coworkers noticed she seemed frazzled and tired. She was not getting her work completed on time. Something was wrong with Lucy or her life.

Personal Problems at Work

People thrive on things they do well and often it is their work. A healthy, happy worker is likely to be a productive one. However, personal problems can hamper an employee's performance, just like Lucy's. Sometimes these problems are short term and can be alleviated quickly. Often, however, the problems extend over long periods of time, and the necessary action is one of developing coping mechanisms in lieu of problem resolution. Some personal problems just cannot be "fixed." These problems can originate from within the individual or can be caused by external forces. The impact on the employee will vary, but there will usually be a noticeable change in behavior and attitude. Personal problems are significant hurdles that every person living in today's complex society will confront in one fashion or another. Lucy's problem could be any one of a hundred tough issues.

Employee personal problems can have many sources. Most can be categorized into one of the following categories:

▶ substance abuse

▶ health related

▶ family related

▶ financial

Almost every adult will deal with one or more of these problems at one time or another. It is how the individual deals with the problems, and the level of support they receive in addressing the issue from family, friends, employer, and coworkers, that will determine the intensity of the problem's impact on the job.

This chapter will explore some of the more common problems that employees face. While the problems may be typical, each individual's own issues will seem unique and solitary. Each person's problems are indeed his or her own. This chapter will look at some universally accepted ways of extending a helping hand to an employee with problems. Later chapters will explore in depth some specialized ways to help reduce job-related problems. Practices that businesses have initiated to assist employees through their personal problems will also be identified. These chapters will examine employee assistance programs and specific measures that the workplace environment can take to reduce the impact of stress originating from the job itself.

Life in today's society is complicated. Those complexities can cause people to feel tension, anxiety, and guilt. These responses can cause major distractions in completing even routine work. The distractions can manifest themselves physically, emotionally, and mentally.

Substance Abuse— Alcoholism and Drug Concerns

alcoholism-a problem with alcohol that has medical, social, and economic ramifications

Although **alcoholism** is a problem with medical, social, and economic ramifications, experts view it as a disease with identifiable causes and a variety of treatments. The disease generally progresses from a mild social or psychological dependence, to a physiological dependence, and finally to a true addictive state. The entire process can take as little as a few months to 20 years or more to develop. Consequently, most middle-stage alcoholics in business are middle-aged.

It could be that Lucy was suffering from problems with alcohol. Perhaps she had progressed from a social drinker to a problem drinker, and the disease was now intensifying. Perhaps she was genetically prone to alcohol abuse and concealed a family history of substance abuse. The condition was now impacting her work performance. Perhaps Lucy was not the

Alcoholism progresses from a psychological dependence, to a physiological dependence, and finally to a true addictive state.

alcoholic but was married to an alcoholic or was the parent or child of one.

One of the effects of alcohol is that it blunts some human emotions on a short-term basis. But excessive consumption can impair work performance. It can cause inefficiency and dull sensitivity and common sense, all of which are important for a quality job performance. Predictable behavior is critical to working well; excessive alcohol consumption can cause an employee to lose his or her predictability.

Relatively few fully developed late-stage alcoholics remain employed for extended periods. The symptoms at this stage are completely insupportable in a work environment.

The workplace is not necessarily concerned with the heavy drinker until the heavy drinker becomes a problem drinker and work performance is adversely affected. Alcoholism costs American business billions of dollars each year. Paying for absenteeism, medical services, wasted time, and ruined materials is costly for employers.

Identifying the Alcoholic

Supervisors typically keep records of absenteeism and investigate causes of on-the-job accidents. They must determine if there is a decline in the quality of work produced by a typically competent individual. The alcoholic employee can remain on the job unnoticed for years after the onset of alcoholism. This is accomplished by some very inventive ways of camouflaging excessive drinking and poor work habits. Some signs of alcoholism include:

Chapter 10 · Coping with Employees' Personal Problems

Figure 10.1 **How Serious Is Substance Abuse?**

More than 53 percent of the executives surveyed do not believe substance abuse is a serious problem in their companies. Over 28 percent believe it is a serious problem.

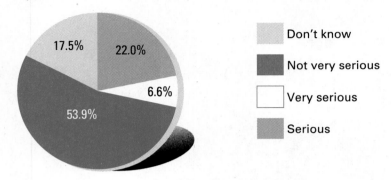

	Don't know
	Not very serious
	Very serious
	Serious

Source: "Waging War." Human Resource Executive. *October 1993, 39.*

► avoiding supervisors

► excuses for deficient work

► sloppy appearance

► increased nervousness

► frequent use of breath fresheners

► increased trips to the break room.

Alcoholism and Absenteeism

Absenteeism among known alcoholics was estimated some years ago at 22 days per year by Dr. Seldon Bacon, the Director of the Yale Center of Alcohol Studies. It has subsequently increased. Yet managers have frequently failed to heed the telltale signs of Monday absences, Tuesday hangovers, the evidence of below average work, and the damage that is done by alcoholics to themselves and their families. Up to now, there is no dependable way of measuring the losses incurred while friends, fellow workers, and even supervisors cover up for the alcoholic worker before the problem is recognized as one that needs medical attention. It is also impossible to assess the inconvenience and irritation resulting from the disruption of production or office schedules.

The effect of alcoholism on absence records is difficult to determine when absentees are not full-blown alcoholics. The employee who occasionally drinks to excess also impacts productivity. This **half employee** may be known to fellow employees and supervisors, who cover the lapses in productivity and occasional absenteeism. When these lapses become chronic, however, a cover-up can no longer work. The half employee needs to come out of hiding in order to become whole again. Here the role of the supervisor is to understand and implement a supportive organizational policy that can speed the rehabilitation of the alcoholic.

half employee-the employee who occasionally drinks to excess

Programs to Reduce Alcoholism

In a survey conducted by *Human Resource Executive Magazine* in 1993, 94 percent of the polled organizations had an alcohol and drug abuse policy that applied to all workers. Supervisors need to be trained in working with their policy and knowing when to refer an employee for professional help. Employees should know their job may be in jeopardy if the situation is not corrected. Once an employee has been identified as having a drinking problem, the person will probably be sent to the employer's medical office or the human resources office for further referral. Many organizations' health care insurance covers some or all of the cost for residential or outpatient treatment.

*D*rug Abuse

People take drugs at work not to induce pleasure but to avoid unpleasant situations. Problems may come from the home or may be caused by the workplace. Regardless of the cause, effective companies realize that many drug problems can be successfully treated, provided the problem is identified early and treatment is available and convenient. As with alcohol, drug use can lead to inefficient work habits and excessive absenteeism. Signs of **drug abuse** include:

drug abuse-the harmful use of legal and illegal substances

► slurred speech
► dilated eyes
► uncontrolled emotions
► unsteadiness
► lack of dexterity.

Figure 10.2 **Change in Substance Abuse**

A survey of work supervisors showed that 14 percent believe that over the last five years substance abuse has increased. Forty-five percent reported they did not know.

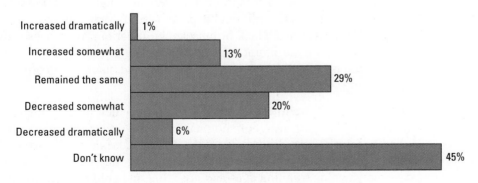

Increased dramatically	1%
Increased somewhat	13%
Remained the same	29%
Decreased somewhat	20%
Decreased dramatically	6%
Don't know	45%

Source: "Waging War." Human Resource Executive. *October 1993, 39.*

Drug-Testing Policies

Many employers have instituted worker drug-testing programs to address the multimillion-dollar problem of employee drug and alcohol abuse. However, employers can run into problems with employee lawsuits claiming intrusion if their policies are not sound. A sound testing policy should be based on employer objectives such as health and safety, protecting trade secrets, or maintaining product quality. Once the objectives have been determined, the policy should be tailored to fit these objectives.

Other factors to consider when formulating a drug policy include:

▶ The policy should outline whether testing will be administered for preemployment, for just cause, or randomly.

Drugs Used by Workers

It is possible for supervisors to receive enough information at a workshop to be knowledgeable enough to identify employees with drug problems. The first things covered in such workshops are the four major categories of drugs and behaviors associated with them.

Stimulants. **Stimulants** act on the central nervous system and are often used to keep people awake. The most used is caffeine. The most misused are amphetamines. Cocaine is a stimulant that is similar to amphetamines. It can be sniffed or injected and produces increased activity, nervousness, dilated eyes, and the ability to go for long periods without sleep.

Depressants. **Depressants,** many of which are barbiturates, also affect the central nervous system but are used for their sedating effects. They are prescribed by doctors to treat anxiety and high blood pressure. Barbiturates often create a physical dependence, and when usage stops, a person may experience a lack of muscle coordination. A supervisor may be able to identify a barbiturate abuser by such signs as staggering, falling asleep on the job, appearing disoriented, and having difficulty concentrating.

Narcotics. **Narcotics** are a family of drugs which induce sleep and relieve pain. The four most common narcotics are opium, morphine, heroin, and codeine. These drugs depress the central nervous system to produce reduction in sensitivity to pain. A narcotics abuser may have symptoms of excessive yawning, running eyes and nose, hot and cold flashes, vomiting, loss of appetite for normal meals, and a preference for sweets and snacks.

stimulants-drugs that act on the central nervous system and are used to keep people awake

depressants-drugs that affect the central nervous system that are used as a sedative

narcotics-drugs that are intended to induce sleep and relieve pain

- Cutoff levels for personnel subject to the policy should be determined. For example, will the policy cover applicants or employees in certain positions? Will it cover part-time employees?

- Once the parameters of a policy are determined, all employees must be informed about the program. Include the policy in employee orientation sessions, and train supervisors to interpret and enforce the policy.

- While the Americans with Disabilities Act does not protect those engaged in current drug use, employers cannot exclude individuals who have used drugs in the past.

Hallucinogens. **Hallucinogens** are so named because they produce hallucinations or mental illusions. When experiencing a hallucination, a person's ability to perceive is based upon a distorted reality. A user has difficulty distinguishing between fact and fantasy. The user's judgment of direction, distance, and objectivity are out of proportion. A hallucinogen abuser has such symptoms as dilated pupils, sensitivity to light, chills, sweating, and trembling.

hallucinogens-drugs that produce mental illusions and impact a person's ability to perceive reality

Drug Testing and Alcohol

It is difficult to pick up a newspaper or turn on the TV set without reading or hearing about drug testing. Most large companies are either testing applicants and employees for drugs or are considering doing so. Drug testing through urinalysis is a fast-growing business. The United States government has not only endorsed testing in general but in fact ordered it for private companies regulated by the Department of Transportation.

In its new program to detect and deter alcohol abuse, the Department of Transportation will subject workers to five tests.

- preemployment testing
- testing after an accident
- random testing
- testing when a supervisor suspects abuse
- testing before and after returning to work after treatment.

Contractors who do business with the United States government by providing goods or services are now required to provide a substance-free work environment. Employees are usually required to sign a statement

Figure 10.3 **Results of Drug Testing**

When asked what percentage of applicants test positive during their drug screening, 56 percent said under 3 percent.

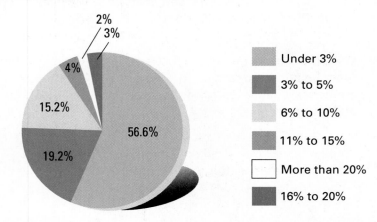

Legend:
- Under 3%
- 3% to 5%
- 6% to 10%
- 11% to 15%
- More than 20%
- 16% to 20%

Pie chart values: 2%, 3%, 4%, 15.2%, 56.6%, 19.2%

Source: "Waging War." Human Resource Executive. October 1993, 42.

which says they have read and will abide by the employer's requirement of a substance-free workplace. These signed agreements must be provided in case of a federal government audit of the workplace. The organization may lose government contract work if the policy is not followed and enforced.

Health-Related Personal Problems

In the chapter-opening scenario, Lucy's behavior change while on the job could be attributed to a health problem that she is experiencing. Perhaps Lucy's job is being impacted by health problems of one of her family or a close friend. It is not unusual for an employee to withhold medical problems from coworkers and supervisors. Medical problems are personal and many are highly confidential. Nonetheless, these problems can influence the worker's performance on the job.

Gary was a very intense but sincere worker. He worked hard to perform beyond the expected norm. When Gary's behavior changed quickly, many people noticed. He had a difficult time focusing upon his work. He was tired and became frustrated easily. It was evident that Gary was not physically ill. But something was wrong. He told no one at work that his only sister, to whom he was very close, had developed AIDS and was months from dying.

Gary was having a very difficult time dealing with his sister's health problem. He felt compelled to drive 90 miles one way to visit her almost daily after work. He would return home from his sister's bedside about midnight, night after night. He became physically exhausted. These daily round trips physically and mentally drained Gary of energy. Typical home chores were delayed or ignored. Clothes did not get laundered. He forgot to pay bills, and subsequently, utilities were terminated; his life became highly complex because his regular routine was completely disrupted. His concern for his sister, combined with his concern for his deteriorating job performance and the decline of completing regular household duties, developed into a serious problem of clinical depression. One medical problem was now two. Gary was bright enough to seek professional psychiatric help.

Neither problem was the kind that Gary could comfortably discuss with his employer. It was not a matter of pride or fear of his employer misunderstanding. It was Gary's staunch, self-sustaining upbringing that told him to "keep these kinds of things to yourself." Gary carried a big burden to work daily and his job suffered.

Gary's employer noticed that there were problems. The employer wanted to retain Gary and hoped that his behaviors would return to their previous predictable quality. Without prying, Gary's supervisor counseled him and offered to let Gary adjust his work hours. Gary also asked if some telecommuting could be substituted for at-the-office work. Telecommuting allowed Gary to do certain job functions at home on his home computer and then transfer the work to the office computer system via modem. These accommodations along with good professional care allowed Gary to regain his composure and his physical condition. He was able to cope with, but not solve, both his and his sister's problems.

During the cold and flu season, employees commonly take more leave to care for sick children than for themselves. In dual income families and in single parent households, care-giving duties are a priority that cannot be ignored. Increasingly, employers are addressing the need for helping employees care for ill children. According to a Bureau of National Affairs study completed in 1993 ("Expecting the Unexpected: Sick and Emergency Child Care"), employers stand to save thousands of dollars by making special arrangements for employees' mildly ill children.

While sick-child care centers/facilities at employee worksites tend to be very expensive and require specialized licensing, employers are finding ways to help. A growing number of employers are contracting with local child care centers with get-well facilities for mildly ill children. Another alternative is to provide a subsidy to provide in-the-home care giving. As still another alternative, many employers find it cost effective to join a **child care consortium.** The consortium may contract to retain a certain number of child care slots from a child care center or with an in-home care agency offering corporate rates.

child care consortium-a group of employers that forms an organization to provide child care for their workers

Scitor Corporation, based in Sunnyvale, California, decided to explore special child care arrangements after an informal study showed that 200 hours were lost in one year because employees stayed home to care for their sick children. The 200 hours translated into a direct revenue loss of

Chapter 10 · Coping with Employees' Personal Problems

between $10,000 and $16,000. The cost to care for the children at a nearby sick-child care center came to about $800. Over an 18-month period, Scitor saved over $15,000 by paying for 240 hours of sick-child care. The company also introduced the use of flex time to meet family commitments, which allows employees to adjust their work schedules.

Family Problems

The American family is changing. The following are just a few of the changes that have taken place during the last ten years with the family.

- ▶ Dual income families, with both partners having demanding careers
- ▶ Increase in teenage pregnancies
- ▶ Women opting for later childbirth
- ▶ Care for aging parents
- ▶ Increase in single parent families

Each of these factors can create problems or at least stress for selected workers.

Today's Family Issues

The dual income family must juggle the social and work demands of the two earners. Budgeting time for household chores, child care, relationship maintenance, and social obligations can mean problems spilling over to the worksite. Added to this are the demands of job-related travel.

A parent of a pregnant teenager and a teenage father will need time and energy, often taken at the expense of their jobs. Obviously a pregnant teen worker may have unique problems.

One of the family problems that is growing ever larger is dependent care. Finding quality child care and elder care are identified by a growing number of workers as a significant problem. **Caregivers,** workers who must provide child or elder care, report extreme anxiety and guilt which can reduce productivity at work. This stress accompanies workplace consequences such as absenteeism, unscheduled time off, arriving late or leaving early, and personal phone use.

caregiver-someone who must provide child care or elder care

Elder Care: A Special Issue

Elder caregiving is becoming more of a pervasive problem. Every day more than 5600 people in the United States celebrate their 65th birthday. Parent care, like child care, is increasingly becoming a business issue. According to the American Association of Retired Persons, 14 percent of elder caregivers have switched from full-time to part-time jobs; 12 percent have left work entirely; and another 28 percent are searching for alternatives from the present position due to caregiving. Most employed caregivers are in their 40s and many are likely to still have responsibility for dependent children.

elder care-having the responsibility for an older person

Elder care is becoming a business issue since significant numbers of caregivers have switched from full-time to part-time jobs or have left work entirely.

Elder caregiving is not a short-term process. Employees spend an average of five years in the elder care process. About 30 percent of the people who care for an elderly relative live a significant distance from the person. According to Connecticut Community Care Inc., distant care giving is often more stressful and time consuming than in-the-home care provisions.

Customs and Traditions: Watching for the Global Difference

Assisting Employees Avoid Culture Shock

As business is becoming more global, employers are scrambling to learn new ways of recruiting employees for overseas positions and motivating and compensating employees working at distant divisions. They are also looking for ways to help employees and their families adjust to their new environments.

Cultural and language training programs for both employee and family members help smooth the transition, but it is also important that people get a chance to explore their potential new homes beforehand. Nearly every company sends an employee to the new location

CONTINUED

before an assignment—two days of discussion of Saudi Arabia is not the same as being there.

A trip to another country can be expensive, especially if family members are included in the trip. However, it can be cost effective if it prevents the expense and disruption that occurs when an employee is dissatisfied and leaves an overseas assignment prematurely.

Studies of failure rates vary, but between 16 and 40 percent of transplanted personnel return early. Some reasons cited for returning early include:

▶ responsibility for aging parents

▶ learning disabilities of a child

▶ behavior problems of teenagers

▶ school-related issues

▶ inability to adjust to the new environment.

Compensation is also a tricky issue because a company must consider currency fluctuations and tax equalizations. The employee may be required to pay host country taxes and continue to file the domestic income tax return.

Source: "Avoid Expatriate Culture Shock." Human Resources Magazine *July 1993, 58-60.*

Business and Health Magazine reported that in May 1991 about 5500 companies offered some sort of child care programs for employees. At the same time, about 300 programs for elder care existed. But elder care programs are increasing.

Lucy's problem may be finding the safe, appropriate, and affordable caregivers for her children, parents, or both. If the search for the correct care becomes prolonged, Lucy's job may suffer and her performance may deteriorate. In a later section we will examine how various employers have established programs to assist workers with child care and elder care problems. These programs include efforts from flexible work schedules to direct services at the work site.

Elder care can be a more complicated issue emotionally than child care. Employees may wrestle with guilt or fear at the thought of asking their parents to go into an adult day-care facility or nursing home. In contrast to child care, which one can plan for, the time when an older adult will need care often cannot be anticipated. Many employees who are taking some responsibility for their parents do not see themselves as caregivers and may not recognize that they need assistance.

Family Stress

If our friend Lucy is going through a divorce, it is highly predictable that financial, emotional, and physical or energy resources or both that would have been directed toward her work would be shifted to her personal life. Persons who separate from a spouse will pass through a variety of emotions from grief to rage to denial to frustration to acceptance. In the process of terminating a relationship, the job performance will be impacted. Lucy's many feelings will reduce her productivity and her ability to perform. Most times the problems are short lived and the employee is able to recover and get on with his or her life. Many employers have assistance for the employee who is going through family stress.

Figure 10.4 **Tipping the Balance**

A survey of 1,000 workers found that employers can help balance work and family responsibilities by providing the following:

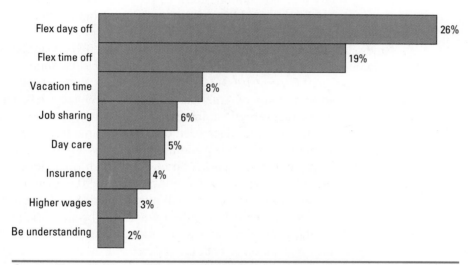

Source: "Facts and Figures." Human Resource Executive. December 1993, 62.

Financial Problems

Lucy may be experiencing some sort of financial stress that is impacting her ability to meet her work responsibilities. Perhaps Lucy, who was recently divorced, has not received her child support payment for several months. She is confronting serious financial problems in sustaining her household. Perhaps Lucy had to take on an additional job to help her family make it through the next few months. Perhaps Lucy has a gambling problem, and her earnings are quickly becoming someone else's winnings.

According to a random survey of 559 New England workers conducted by the Work/Life Group of Boston, 23 percent of the employees feel a

Chapter 10 • Coping with Employees' Personal Problems

"great deal of pressure" caused by their financial condition. Only "lack of time for family" was reported as causing more personal stress (29 percent).

Insufficient income to the household is a great source of stress. Money problems—who doesn't have them? But when almost a quarter of the employed persons report stress due to financial problems, employers must take notice. Providing a pay raise might seem the obvious solution—but one that is not available from most employers if they hope to remain competitive in their selected marketplace. Increasingly, finding that second job to help make ends meet means that personal energy and attention that were once focused on one position are now distributed across two or more jobs. Working two jobs oftentimes places additional stress on relationships with family members and additional time constraints on the worker and both employers.

In the past ten years, there has been a significant increase in the use of part-time employees and "temps." **Temporary employees** work for an agency or broker, who in turn places them in either full-time or part-time positions. Usually there are no long-term employment commitments with temp placements. Many second incomes are derived from temporary employment arrangements.

Americans are working more hours than they did 20 years ago. A study by the Economic Policy Institute (*The Great American Time Squeeze: Trends in Work and Leisure 1969–1989*, Public Interest Publications) reviewed the working hours of Americans between 1969 and 1989. The work time of the average American increased by 140 hours per year; paid time off for nonwork activities decreased during this same time period.

One societal reason for working additional hours or holding more than one job is the increase in single parent families in which financial child support is not provided on a regular basis. About 85 to 90 percent of noncustodial parents are male. Employers with many female employees may see the stress of economic hardship in their workforce because mothers are more likely to have custodial responsibility for children.

However, new legislation at both the federal and state levels has created additional financial stress for the noncustodial parent who fails to provide court-ordered child support. The Family Support Act of 1988 includes a provision that went into effect January 1, 1994. This law allows for the *immediate* withholding of a portion of earnings for child care support payments. Many states have established regulations requiring all present employees, and all new hires, to complete registration forms. This information is entered into a data base to match employees with a list of noncustodial parents with outstanding child support obligations. If a match is made, the employer is then mandated to withhold a portion of earnings for the custodial support payments.

The changes in Lucy's job performance may be due to financial stress. As a result, she may be working additional hours; she may be holding a second job; or she may be feeling tense because of her financial problems.

temporary employees-employees who work for an agency or broker who in turn places them in full- or part-time positions.

Gambling

Nancy has a personal problem that she does not recognize. She works as a registered nurse and provides excellent care to her patients on most days. But about two days each week, Nancy quietly leaves work "just a little early" and drives to a nearby casino. She spends three hours playing slot machines and blackjack, waiting to "hit it big." She knows that day will come.

In the meantime, Nancy may lose between $50 and $250 per trip to the casino. Nancy's income as a nurse is good but she is experiencing some problems at work. Creditors are calling her while she is working and asking for payment. Nancy's gambling has created both direct and indirect problems for her, yet she cannot or will not recognize her gambling as a problem.

Like many other addictions, gambling can become all consuming. **Gambling** addiction is a growing problem for employees and employers alike. States with legalized gaming have provided specialized resources to assist those with gambling problems.

gambling-putting resources at risk

Credit Problems

Another financial problem that many workers confront is **excessive purchasing on credit.** Many workers find themselves wanting more things than their paycheck allows them to buy. Credit cards and bank loans that enable workers to buy these things can cause problems.

excessive purchasing on credit-abusing credit privileges for nonessential purchases

Credit cards and bank loans enable workers to buy more things than their paychecks allow, causing credit problems.

Chapter 10 · Coping with Employees' Personal Problems

Jim is a human resources coordinator in a small firm. He is a compulsive buyer. As a result of having charged his credit cards to the limit, he has reverted to a series of schemes to keep his creditors at bay. But these schemes are having an effect on Jim at work. He has a hard time focusing on his job duties and makes mistakes. Creditors call him at work asking for payment. He is considering a second job or a better paying job even though he likes his current position. He cannot get ahead financially.

Jim has heard of credit counselors and has considered getting some help. He has considered filing for bankruptcy but feels that is too drastic. Yet he worries about what to do. He worries at work and as a result performs with less accuracy. When questioned about his job performance, Jim becomes more stressed. He finds release from his problems by shopping, starting the cycle all over again.

Counseling

No matter what the personal problems are, you, your coworkers, or your subordinates may need counseling. Supervisors and coworkers may be called upon to provide some form of counseling for a coworker or to refer this employee to a professional. Formal and informal counseling sessions are useful. There are three major types of counseling: directive, nondirective, and cooperative counseling.

Directive Method

The traditional method of counseling is called **directive** because the counselor directs and controls the form, flow, and content of the exchange between himself or herself and the employee.

Even though it may be impossible for one person to understand exactly the situation of another, there may be times when a person in a troubled state wants concrete advice. Asking questions, making a diagnosis, and giving advice are characteristics of the direct counseling approach. Counseling is often expected in an organization with a strong chain of command. The direct counseling technique tries to establish what the employee is thinking to clarify facts and set the chain of events into logical order. Directive methods usually appeal to novice supervisors because they seem the easiest paths to follow in difficult situations. They are fast and require little skill. Providing advice and reassurance are examples of directive counseling.

When Lucy Ramirez was having problems she discussed them with her best friend. Her best friend might tell her exactly what she would do if she were in the same situation. That would be directive counseling. In fact, Lucy might seek such suggestions from her friend, a coworker, her supervisor, and her minister. Securing suggestions from several sources might help Lucy chart her course of action.

directive method-the traditional method of counseling because the counselor directs and controls the counseling session

Nondirective Method

Nondirective counseling, also known as client-centered therapy, lends itself to current human relations practices in industry. This type of counseling is the way in which professionally trained people practice active listening as a counseling technique. Nondirective counseling is so called because the counselor does not direct the client with advice at any stage. The client determines what will be discussed.

The basic theory of nondirective counseling holds that through the skill of **active listening** a counselor can help a client release pent up emotions. The process of obtaining relief from tensions by talking about deeply felt emotions is called **catharsis.** Only after the client experiences catharsis can he or she admit to, identify, and solve personal problems in a rational frame of mind. Minimum advice from the counselor is needed according to this counseling technique.

The ultimate goal of nondirective counseling is to stimulate the growth of self-knowledge. The theory and the goal are based on the belief that people are responsible for themselves. The counselor must remain neutral and accept all statements and actions without judgment. With this method the individual is considered capable of solving his or her own problems if given the opportunity. It is assumed that every person wants to do the right thing.

Nondirective counselors follow four basic practices when conducting interviews.

1. *Readiness* The counselors learn as much as they can about the person in need.

2. *Active Listening* The counselors listen to all feelings. They repeat what they do not understand until both (client and counselor) understand the intended meaning.

3. *No Advice* They answer questions but do not tell clients what to do. The counselors believe that if the clients express everything they feel about the problem, they will eventually come up with self-generated advice.

4. *Clarification* When the person in need begins to arrive at a solution, the counselors encourage the exploration of the ideas through to their logical consequences. They may offer questions and suggestions at this stage.

If Lucy went to a coworker with her problem and the coworker listened and asked probing questions but did not offer suggestions on how to solve the problem, the coworker would be using nondirective counseling.

Cooperative Counseling

Somewhere between directive and nondirective counseling lies the style called **cooperative counseling.** It is a blend of the direct guidance and authority typical of directive counseling and the nonjudgmental, active listening behavior typical of nondirective techniques. This form of counseling

nondirective counseling-
a counseling approach in
which a professionally
trained counselor does not
direct the client with any
advice

active listening-the coun-
selor listens to feelings and
repeats what is not under-
stood until both client and
counselor understand the
intended meaning

catharsis-the process of
obtaining relief from ten-
sions by talking about
deeply felt emotions

cooperative counseling-an
approach to counseling
that blends direct guidance
with active listening

Chapter 10 · Coping with Employees' Personal Problems

is especially effective during job-related performance reviews. It is also useful in counseling employees with personal problems. When using this method, the counselor's role is neither that of judge nor sympathetic listener, but a mixture of the two.

In cooperative counseling, the counselor tries to stimulate the client's thinking by asking specific questions. These questions are directive in that they determine the subject of the interview, but are also nondirective in that the client is encouraged to express emotions as well as thoughts and attitudes.

This style also uses the nondirective device called **mirroring,** that is, restating the client's own words not only to reflect and clarify the client's feelings but also as material from which to form nonthreatening questions. Silences and pauses for thought are customary in cooperative counseling, but they are not as long or as frequent as in the nondirective approach. Because of its combination of directive and nondirective features, cooperative counseling is particularly effective in dealing with some alcoholics and drug addicts. Its nondirective aspects encourage and stimulate honest communication quickly; its directive features allow the counselor to set realistic behavior limits for employees who need help.

The Counseling Session

The objective of counseling is to change behavior and develop the worker into a productive member of the organization.

Present the Facts.   The first step for a supervisor is to assemble the facts before confronting the worker. When the supervisor has reviewed the facts surrounding a problem, they must be presented to the worker in specific detail. There is a big difference between "you seem to be drunk while at work" and "you have shown signs of being intoxicated seven times this month." The second statement shows that the supervisor has facts concerning the employee's on-the-job performance. The supervisor is prepared to talk about the specifics of the behavior. The subordinate in this case should have no questions about the counseling session.

Follow with Direction.   After the initial statement, the supervisor should follow up with effective direction. The logical follow-up to the discussion is to tell the subordinate how you want them to change their behavior. "Our worksite is alcohol-free and consumption of alcohol will not be tolerated." The supervisor has clearly communicated not only the problem but also the behavior that is expected in the future.

Explain the Penalties.   The last step in the process is to explain to the worker the penalties for further violations. It is rare that a person in trouble will accept full responsibility when they are in trouble. The classic response is for the employee to try and deflect the blame or shift the focus to someone else. That deflection may be as simple as "I'm not the only one drinking here." It is easy to fall into the trap of talking about someone else instead of the person being confronted. One should try to direct the conversation to the subject at hand. The supervisor must control the conversation's flow. However, that does not mean the supervisor dominates the conversation.

Choose an Appropriate Time and Place.
The time and place chosen for a counseling session creates an advantage for the supervisor. If an employee is caught in the act, some supervisors may let the employee think about the event for a short while before calling them into the office. That does not mean the supervisor waits days, or even hours before a discussion takes place. Good management practice dictates that a problem be addressed quickly, but a little time for the employee to reflect can be therapeutic. This time also is good for the supervisor. The time can be used to gather thoughts and cool down if necessary and formulate a strategy for addressing the problem. This technique is especially effective for supervisors who are subject to losing their tempers. The location of a counseling session may also impact the session's effectiveness.

The above illustrates a situation where a supervisor must take a corrective action with an employee for a violation of workplace policy. The same counseling process could be used without the authority figure influence that a supervisor might pose.

Keep Written Records.
Today, more than ever, a written record of the counseling is necessary when it involves a supervisor/subordinate situation. Properly written counseling notes ensure that a supervisor has strong grounds if it becomes necessary to fend off a grievance or court case. For such notes to be effective, a supervisor must accurately describe the situation, record what he or she expects the employee to do in the future, and verify that the employee has understood these requirements. A written record is also valuable when counseling repeat rules violators. During face-to-face counseling sessions, the supervisor must address the issue at hand and not the employee's total performance.

Use Proper Techniques.
Every supervisor has a different counseling approach. However, it is important to formulate a plan of approach when counseling is necessary.

Voice modulation also tells a lot about the moment. Supervisors should emphasize words when making a point. The voice tells the worker how the supervisor feels at the time. Humor should be avoided during the counseling session. Humor dilutes the effectiveness of counseling, and the employee may walk away not understanding the seriousness of the event.

Employees should not be cross-examined during counseling. The supervisor should tell the known facts and proceed. The supervisor must not allow the dialogue to become argumentative. The session should also be summarized by the supervisor before the employee leaves.

Offer Peer Assistance.
Talking to a coworker about a personal problem is easier for most people than discussing it with a supervisor. **Peer assistance** programs train employees to help coworkers and emphasize

peer assistance-a program that trains employees to help coworkers and emphasizes prevention rather than intervention

prevention rather than intervention. Using coworkers as counselors deemphasizes disciplinary measures and encourages employees to come forward with their problems. This form of assistance with personal problems has the distinct advantage of being available on the job site and eliminates or reduces the need for outside assistance that may require time away from work and increase attendance costs. Formalized peer assistance programs are relatively new to businesses but appear to be a highly effective way of helping some employees through their personal problems.

Time Away from Work

Regardless of the personal problem, time away from work is almost a certainty. Various kinds of absences affect group efficiency and stability in different ways and may be significant indicators of individuals' attitudes toward their jobs. Excessive absences can negatively impact self-directed work teams; the work of one absent worker must be completed by the other members of the team.

Different Kinds of Absenteeism

Occasional and excused absences, arranged in advance with the supervisor, result in minimum disturbance of group activity and may be justified by unusual demands outside of work. Absence that cannot be prearranged may be caused by an emergency. It therefore becomes an excused absence if the person promptly notifies the supervisor. Such notification indicates a responsible attitude on the part of the absent person. The term **absenteeism** has acquired a moral connotation. For this reason, it should be used with care. Indiscriminate blasts by management against all absences as absenteeism are detrimental to employee morale, because they lump

absenteeism-time away from work

Sometimes absence that cannot be prearranged may be caused by an emergency.

together people whose behavior, attitudes, and circumstances may be significantly different from one another.

An absence of which the supervisor is not immediately informed interferes with workplace efficiency. Sometimes it is impossible to know at the start of the day whether a missing person is absent or merely late. However, the fact that no notification has been received does not necessarily indicate a willful disregard of company rules. Sometimes the absence is unavoidable, and for some valid reason notice did not reach the supervisor. Among such reasons are ignorance of company rules, fear of a supervisor, lack of a telephone, and forgetfulness on the part of someone who was entrusted with a message. The danger of jumping to conclusions is that an absence from work due to the death of a parent can be classified the same as an absence due to a hangover.

Any employee who regularly misses work is very disturbing to work efficiency and morale. It makes such individuals less acceptable on a work team, no matter how much they have to offer when they do come to work. More than any other form of absenteeism, chronic **unexcused absences** indicates lack of team spirit. If counseling and informal warnings fail to reduce this type of absenteeism, disciplinary penalties are warranted.

unexcused absences-time away from work not approved by one's employer

Creating an Attendance Policy

Absenteeism costs employers a staggering amount of money each year. Many employers think of absenteeism as an unavoidable cost of doing business. However, if a strong stand is taken on attendance that encourages employees to come to work, attendance can be greatly improved. The most important element of an effective absenteeism control program is communication. Employees must have a clear understanding of how the company will deal with chronic and excessive absenteeism.

The **attendance policy** should state the types and number of absences that are acceptable, and whether or not employees will be compensated for **excused absences.** The number of allowable absences within a given period of time must be specified. For example, employees may be allowed ten sick days a year. It is also important to spell out the procedures employees are expected to follow: How much advance notice must be given for a pre-arranged absence? To whom should the employee report an absence? Under what conditions is a doctor's verification of illness or injury required? How are absences recorded and who will monitor them?

attendance policy-guidelines that state the types and numbers of absences that are acceptable and whether or not employees will be compensated

excused absences-time away from work approved by one's employer

The policy should also describe any reward or disciplinary measures related to attendance. Punishment for poor attendance is the most commonly used method of controlling absenteeism. Surveys show that 80 percent of companies use discipline to control absenteeism, while only 20 percent offer cash or other types of rewards to encourage attendance. If a rewards approach is taken, the type of reward should be clearly stated. For example, a $200 bonus will be given to all employees who have perfect attendance for one year. If discipline will be used, employers must explain what will be considered an infraction and what subsequent steps will be taken.

Controlling Absenteeism

Management gets the attendance it expects and the absenteeism it accepts. It might also be said that management gets the attendance it demonstrates. Employee attitudes toward attendance generally mirror management's attitude towards attendance. If managers come to work on time and every day, it sets a positive tone for the corporate attendance culture. If managers are late, absent, and exempt from discipline, a negative corporate attendance culture will result.

Management tardiness also tends to have a domino effect on subordinates. For example, if a production supervisor is consistently 20 minutes late for work, it is likely that at least some of the production workers will soon follow suit. Before long, this can amount to a significant reduction in productivity. Then, if only the workers are disciplined for excessive tardiness—and not the supervisor—the department may suffer a drop in morale.

Of course, some absences are justified. People get sick. Cars break down. Personal matters sometimes warrant a day off. A certain level of absenteeism is excusable. But when absences become chronic or excessive, the company and the coworkers who carry the extra load for absent employees pay the price.

Two primary factors motivate employees to come to work: job satisfaction and attendance inducements. When employees enjoy their work, they attend regularly. Conversely, when workers are not satisfied, they will miss work unless they are persuaded not to, through rewards. Texas Instruments is a major world-wide manufacturer of semiconductors and other electronic products. It annually provides a recognition dinner, by department, for employees who have superior attendance records. Employees and a guest are treated to an elegant dinner, a certificate, and a small token gift as positive reinforcement to encourage good work habits.

Inducements can take several forms:

▶ positive inducements, such as incentive or reward systems tied to attendance

▶ negative inducements, such as threat of punishment for unsatisfactory attendance

▶ personal inducements, such as appealing to one's strong work ethic or commitment to the company

▶ external economic inducements, such as heavy personal financial commitments including holding compensation increases.

To choose the appropriate method for controlling absenteeism, several factors must be determined. Are employees generally satisfied with their compensation and responsibilities? Is teamwork and attendance stressed as an important part of the corporate culture? Is the work environment safe and comfortable? Depending on the factors that influence absenteeism in a company, a reward approach or a disciplinary approach may give better results. There are advantages and disadvantages to both methods.

A small manufacturer with 65 employees found that not only were disciplinary measures too cumbersome to administer, but they also failed to curb absenteeism. The company nipped its absenteeism problem in the bud with a profit-sharing program based on the number of hours worked, coupled with a quarterly bonus system for perfect attendance.

Another manufacturer with 290 employees, on the other hand, switched to a discipline system when its pay program caused serious morale problems for hourly production workers not covered by the program. This company found that a disciplinary system of three warnings with appropriate disciplinary actions attached to them did more for controlling excessive absenteeism than did the inequitable pay program.

Rewarding Good Attendance

In recent years, there has been much debate regarding the merits of taking a positive approach to reducing absenteeism. Critics of the reward system claim that employees should not receive an extra incentive for doing what they are already being paid to do—show up for work. Those in favor of the reward system argue that discipline adversely affects the productivity and morale of all employees, and in some cases, increases absenteeism. They claim that punishment undermines supervisors' efforts to maintain open, cooperative, and productive relationships with subordinates. Also in their favor is that the use of reward systems continue to grow. Some examples of reward programs include:

- ▶ **Continuous reinforcement.** Employees with perfect attendance records can be paid small bonuses. This constant reinforcement encourages good attendance.

continuous reinforcement-employees with perfect attendance records are paid small bonuses

- ▶ Monthly lottery. Employees with good attendance records qualify for monthly drawings for a small prize or bonus. For example, on the last working day of the month, one winner is selected at random from the eligible list of employees.

- ▶ Sick leave bonus. Employers can discourage sick leave abuse by paying employees a bonus at the end of the year for each unused sick day.

- ▶ Poker plan. Employees who arrive on time receive a card from a deck of playing cards. At the end of the week, those with perfect attendance and punctuality will have five cards. The best hand wins a bonus.

- ▶ Profit sharing. Tying absenteeism costs to profit sharing can be a powerful attendance incentive, with peer pressure encouraging employees to attend work. When absenteeism costs go up, share profits are reduced; when absenteeism goes down, profits are increased. This method is most effective when absenteeism costs are posted regularly. Many employees are not aware of the costs associated with absences.

well pay-employees receive an extra day's pay for each month in which attendance and punctuality are perfect

- ▶ **Well pay.** Employees receive no pay when absent, but receive an extra day's pay for each month in which attendance and punctuality are perfect. Thus, each day of absence means loss of wages and bonus.

▶ Minilottery. With a minilottery, the company can give a cash prize to all employees when absenteeism is held under a certain percentage. For each additional one percent drop, additional prizes are awarded. This plan fosters teamwork because it rewards the entire workforce, not just individuals.

▶ Time off plan. Some companies have found that granting time off for good attendance is an effective way to discourage absenteeism. Plans are usually structured to discourage taking extra days off on Mondays and Fridays or near holidays.

The rewards approach can be an effective attendance motivator for most employees. But rewards systems alone are generally not enough to motivate chronic abusers to correct their behavior. For these individuals, it may be necessary to use the discipline approach to encourage better attendance. Many companies apply a combined approach with incentives and punishment. The combined approach affects the behavior of employees who respond to positive incentive as well as those who respond to discipline.

Using Discipline to Control Absenteeism

In most cases, attendance abuse is limited to a small group of employees. Even so, the discipline policy should take into account the behavior of the majority of employees, not just the offending few. A blanket discipline policy that punishes all absences lowers morale. A policy designed to discipline primary offenders in certain absence categories tends to have a ripple effect, improving attendance throughout the company.

The disciplinary program should be designed to change behavior rather than get rid of employees with attendance problems. This can be done through a progressive disciplinary system, with penalties becoming increasingly more severe with each unwarranted absence. Progressive discipline usually includes the following measures:

Oral reprimand. When an employee's absences exceed a specified limit, the worker is warned verbally. The supervisor should meet with the individual, compare company records for missed time with the employee's own records, and discuss the employee's attitude toward attendance. At this time, the supervisor should make sure the employee understands the attendance policy.

Written warning. If the employee's attendance continues to be unsatisfactory, a second reprimand in the form of a written warning is given. The supervisor should once again meet with the employee, discuss the reasons for poor attendance, offer assistance in correcting the problem, and explain the comments contained in the warning. The supervisor should stress the importance of the written warning.

Suspension. Should absenteeism continue, suspension from work without pay may motivate most employees to improve attendance. The

oral reprimand-when employees violate a company policy, they are verbally warned

written warning-a tool for documenting an employee's unsatisfactory behavior

suspension-barring an employee from his or her job without pay

length of the suspension is best left to the supervisor's discretion, but must be consistent with company policy. When the supervisor informs the employee of the suspension, it must be made clear that there will be no further warnings, and that this is the last chance to change the behavior before being terminated from employment.

Discharge. An employee who continues to violate attendance policies after being suspended is discharged. At the termination conference, the supervisor explains the reasons for the discharge, reviews the employee's attendance patterns, and emphasizes the company's efforts to correct the problem. The supervisor should thoroughly document this and other meetings with the worker. Legal counsel should be consulted before dismissing a worker for excessive absences. Firing an employee who suffers from chronic illness, injury, or handicap may be illegal.

discharge-releasing an employee who continues to violate attendance policies after being suspended

All disciplinary action should be documented and placed in an employee's personnel file. The original copy is signed and retained by the employee, and the copy is filed. This is good protection in the event the employee is later terminated and files a claim or wrongful discharge.

Most employers agree that absenteeism is one of their most difficult, expensive, and pervasive employee problems, yet many feel powerless to control it. Employers can do much to curb absenteeism by creating a corporate attendance culture in which good attendance is valued and poor attendance is dealt with in a firm and consistent manner.

Lynne Jackson is the owner and operator of a small machine shop in Portland, Oregon. On most days, Lynne is on the floor with her employees producing specialty parts on contract for a large international defense contractor. For the past eight months, Lynne and her staff have worked extensive overtime hours averaging 55 hours a week. While her workers generally enjoy the extra income that accompanies overtime, lately Lynne has heard negative comments about the excessive hours. Besides the comments, she has noticed that employees who always had been highly reliable were calling in sick. Scheduled Saturdays and Mondays were the most common sick days.

Lynne considered several alternatives to the ongoing overtime. Hiring additional workers was a possibility, but it would mean a big investment in another work station. And although her contracts were good right then, the defense industry being undependable, she didn't want to take the chance. She also considered adding a second shift of three or four workers, but she didn't have a good supervisor for the shift and she wasn't able to take on the second shift herself. The best alternative was to ask her small staff to continue working overtime.

But Lynne also realized that the growing use of sick time had to be addressed. Lynne consulted with an employment specialist from a local university who specialized in small business management. After careful analysis, Lynne and her consultant agreed the sick leave situation was a natural outgrowth of the long hours her staff was working. Her workers were in some cases actually getting ill; in some cases they were just tired.

Lynne decided to put her employees on a modified schedule. Each week, a different employee would be scheduled with a Saturday/Sunday or Sunday/Monday off. Every two months, each employee could plan on having a two-day weekend. Employees could trade time schedules with one another as long as Lynne approved the trade at least one week in advance.

Lynne also initiated a quality bonus plan. Each quarter, a portion of the organization profits would be disbursed among the employees based upon the total hours they worked during that quarter. After the first quarter, Lynne examined several factors of her operation. Production was actually up, as was quality. Sick leave was back to the preovertime level; and overall morale was up. She also noticed that several workers were putting in more time under the new arrangement and several were putting in less. But foremost, Lynne was able to predict her production capacity and could keep promises she'd made about product delivery.

Employee Turnover

Mobility of employees among organizations, and between subunits within a given organization, confronts managers with many interrelated problems. Employees leave jobs for the following reasons:

► **Accessions.** Hiring new employees or rehiring former employees.

► **Separations.** Terminations of employment, usually subdivided between those who voluntarily quit and those who are laid off because of a lack of work. Such separation is presumably without prejudice to the employee.

► **Disciplinary layoff.** This is turnover due to dissatisfaction with an employee's performance or conduct. Therefore, a disciplinary layoff and a discharge would be prejudicial to an employee's record.

► Retirement or death.

Cost-minded managers are always on the lookout for ways to cut unwarranted expenditures. But before attempting to reduce the waste incurred by excessive mobility, they need to examine current figures for causes. Because many of these causes are more difficult to identify than the costs, an analysis of underlying causes can help reduce excessive mobility. Naturally, the means to this end are as varied as the causes themselves.

Gaining Control of Turnover

Employment **attrition,** or turnover, is the permanent departure (voluntary or involuntary) of individuals from an organization. It is usually undesirable but can be desirable if ineffective employees are leaving or if an organization needs to reduce its workforce. Turnover is generally considered to be the best measure of morale. Poor morale can result from many things. Two of the most important of these are poor supervision and having the wrong person in the wrong job. The wrong person in the wrong job can mean poor hiring procedures or poor placement.

accessions-*hiring new employees or rehiring former employees*

separations-*termination of employment usually subdivided between those who are laid off because of lack of work and those who voluntarily quit*

disciplinary layoff-*unpaid time off due to unsatisfactory behavior*

attrition-*the permanent departure of individuals from an organization*

The Cost of Employee Turnover

Although recent technological advances are having a profound impact on the workplace, employees continue to be an organization's most important asset, and unplanned turnover is costly. Costly recruiting efforts are mounted to attract the best and the brightest workers. Training and development add further to this investment, and employees do not "pay for themselves" immediately upon hire. Often an extended nurturing period is required before new employees become productive employees.

Unplanned attrition prevents organizations from recouping this investment, lowers morale, and increases stress levels. While it is natural and even beneficial to have some employee turnover, most employers cannot afford high rates of turnover. The cost of employee replacement is significant in terms of out-of-pocket costs as well as time and effort. Often unplanned turnover occurs at inopportune times, resulting in scheduling problems and poor utilization of staff.

The financial success of a business depends in part on its ability to manage employee turnover. Successful management of turnover must be a continuing activity, directed by a plan that addresses the relationship of the employee with the firm and the job.

Minimizing Turnover Through Good Hiring Practices

One important way of minimizing unplanned turnover is to hire the right person. Competition for the best personnel is intense. To succeed, businesses must be willing to expend the necessary effort to attract outstanding employees. The recruiting effort should be taken seriously, and interviewers should be trained and knowledgeable of each position opening. Recruiting should not be viewed as a means of filling a slot. Employers should look for the requisite social skills and attitude necessary to be successful in the position, as well as for the appropriate technical skills. It is easier to define technical skills than to predict how an individual will adapt to a firm's culture.

Management of Turnover

Successful management of turnover can be accomplished only if unplanned terminations are minimized. An organized management effort is needed to lessen unplanned turnover. The key is to understand and respond to the needs of employees. This effort must be ongoing. The result will be a satisfied, productive, and stable staff.

When devising ways to reduce excessive mobility, managers need to take an overall view. This entails seeing all elements and activities within the organization and factors in the surrounding environment as interactive parts of an integrated whole. Implicit in all the means adopted by personnel-minded managers to regulate turnover is to attract, develop, and retain superior employees. Human nature being what it is, this goal can probably never be reached for all employees.

Conclusion

Even the best employees, like Lucy Ramirez, will experience personal problems during their careers. It is unlikely that people who live in today's complex society can avoid issues that will have a profound impact on their personal and professional lives. Absenteeism is usually one result of these problems.

Often it is through the support and understanding of coworkers and employers that employees are able to devise solutions or coping mechanisms that mitigate these life problems. Personal problems can range from health-related difficulties to family and financial concerns.

Employers realize that the investment they have in productive workers must be protected with assistance and job flexibility during time of personal problems. Providing caring response and support for a valued employee like Lucy Ramirez is good business. Most personal problems can be dealt with when appropriate assistance is matched with employees in need.

Many times formal or informal counseling is a necessary step in helping employees back to their productive best. Supervisors and coworkers can be a source of guidance. Directive, nondirective, and cooperative counseling techniques are the typical measures used to assist individuals with their personal problems. Any one of these methods may be appropriate depending upon the person in need and his or her situation. Listening and caring are powerful tools in assisting with personal problems. Organizations can impact work attendance by establishing rewards and punishments for work attendance behaviors.

Sources: Employment Guide. *Bureau of National Affairs, January, 1993.*
"Facts and Figures." Human Resources Executive. *December, 1993, 62.*
"Facts and Figures." Human Resources Executive. *July, 1993, 58.*
Lefkovich, Jeff. Business Responds to Elder-Care Needs." Human Resources Magazine, *June, 1992,* 103–108.
Michaelis, Jessica. "Waging War." Human Resources Executive. *October, 1993, 39–42.*

Key Points Summary

- People thrive on what they do well, but at times an employee's performance is hampered by personal problems.
- The intensity of an employee's problems will depend on the support he or she receives from family, friends, and employer and coworkers.
- Alcoholism is a disease with medical, social, and economic ramifications.
- Predictable behavior is critical to working well; excessive alcohol consumption can cause employees to lose their predictability.
- Alcoholics become experts at hiding excessive drinking and poor work habits.
- Signs of drug abuse include slurred speech, dilated eyes, uncontrolled emotions, unsteadiness, and lack of dexterity.

- Many companies are either testing applicants for drugs or are considering doing so.
- During the cold and flu season, employees commonly take more leave to care for sick children than for themselves.
- One growing family problem is the ability to find dependent care for children and elders.
- Second jobs, gambling, and credit problems can also negatively impact an employee's performance.
- The directive method of counseling is one in which the counselor controls the exchange between the employee and counselor.
- The nondirective method of counseling is one in which the counselor does not direct the client with advice at any stage.
- Cooperative counseling is a blend of direct guidance and active listening typical of nondirective counseling.
- Various kinds of absence affect group efficiency and stability in different ways.
- Chronic, unexcused absenteeism is most disturbing to work efficiency and morale.
- Employees must have a clear understanding of how their company will deal with absenteeism.
- A variety of inducements can be used to improve attendance.
- Measures to curb absenteeism include oral reprimands, written warnings, suspensions, and discharges.
- Unplanned turnover prevents organizations from recouping training investments, lowers morale, and increases stress.

Key Terms

absenteeism	directive method
accessions	discharge
active listening	disciplinary layoff
alcoholism	drug abuse
attendance policy	elder care
attrition	excessive purchasing on credit
caregiver	excused absences
catharsis	gambling
child care consortium	half employee
cooperative counseling	hallucinogens
continuous reinforcement	inducements
depressants	management tardiness

Chapter 10 · Coping with Employees' Personal Problems

mirroring

narcotics

nondirective counseling

oral reprimand

peer assistance

separations

stimulants

suspension

temporary employees

unexcused absences

well pay

written warning

Discussion Questions

1. Why is it a good idea to assist employees with personal problems? Identify some methods that might be used.

2. In what specific ways do personal problems impact productivity on the job?

3. There are three typical approaches to counseling. Identify the conditions under which one method would be more appropriate than another.

4. Describe a program that you believe would increase work attendance.

5. Describe what is meant by the statement, "Attrition can be positive and negative."

6. Compare the following statement to an employer's policy of not hiring smokers. "What I do on my own time is my own business."

7. Reflect on an employment situation of your own or a friend. Identify the potential impact of employee absenteeism on this situation.

8. Explain the statement, "Management gets the attendance it expects and the absenteeism it accepts."

Chapter

Chapter 11

Learning Objectives

Upon completing this chapter, you should be able to:

- Understand the impact of stress on workers.

- List sources of stress and ways to deal with them.

- Develop strategies for combating stress.

- Distinguish between broad-brush and single-issue employee assistance programs.

- Develop strategies for dealing with workplace violence.

Stress in the Workplace

He came home elated. After 16 years of service to Sadler and Associates of Council Bluffs, Iowa, Senior Accountant Cecil Mounds was being promoted to office manager of the new Sioux Falls, South Dakota, office. Cecil was an accountant's accountant—a perfectionist. He checked his work and calculations two, sometimes three times to make sure they were correct. He added detail after detail to reports to increase the chances that his projects would survive the most critical review. But now, he was management. He had no formal training to be a manager, but he had paid his dues and now the opportunity was his.

He explained to his wife Karen that they would need to move. She would have to find another job— but the company would assist with both of these issues. The move was not easy. Finding a new home with the right school for their children was time-consuming and nerve-wracking. Karen's job hunting seemed to produce little in the way of results. Starting the new office for Cecil was harder than he expected. He had never interviewed potential employees, so he asked for help from the home office. The human resources office sent a 60-page booklet on questions and issues that the interviewer can and cannot raise at interviews.

Each step of office management seemed to have roadblocks and barriers. Now, in addition to accounting and tax work, he was expected to go out and call on strangers to gain more work. Cecil was a large, athletic man who could tell stories and entertain friends and coworkers. But this was different; this was business and it was *his* business. He was expected to produce.

He was argumentative or completely passive. His blood pressure was up; he was regularly having self-doubts. He would go home in the early afternoon and just lie in bed, unable to move. He called his boss one day after not returning phone calls to anyone for two weeks. His supervisor asked what was wrong, and Cecil broke down into tears on the phone. His boss told him to go see his family physician and ask for a referral to a mental health specialist. Immediately! Cecil's attempts to achieve perfection, to succeed in his dream, and to be a hero to his children were now a shambles. Cecil was clinically depressed. Within a few months, after some medication, therapy sessions, help from Karen, and discussion with his manager, Cecil gave up his manager's job but stayed with the firm to continue doing what he did best—be an excellent accountant.

What Is Stress?

Cecil's story is repeated hundreds of times daily by workers. Stress from the job and from home do impact people. Some stress is beneficial for people: it causes them to work hard, explore new things, and stretch their abilities. For example, when Cecil started his new assignment, the challenge created positive stress and caused him to learn a significant amount of management-related material. But excessive stress or stress that is ill-managed or poorly mitigated can be destructive and debilitating.

Hans Selye, widely considered the father of modern stress management, defines **stress** as the "rate of wear and tear on the body." Any change may elicit a bodily response referred to as stress response. This grows out of a prehistoric person's response to a life threatening situation. Confronted with the prospect of being eaten for breakfast by a saber-tooth tiger, a cave dweller's alarm triggered a survival mechanism. Scientists agree that modern **physiological responses** to stress are similar to prehistoric reactions.

stress-the rate of wear and tear on the body

physiological response-the way one's body reacts to certain situations

Sources of Stress

When placed in a life threatening situation, human physiology reacts with fight or flight decisions meant to ensure survival. Today's society seldom involves intermittent life threatening events. The "wild animals" staved off today more often include relationship troubles, job insecurity, economic worries, and communication clashes. These stress factors are more chronic, more unremitting, and many times outside of a person's control.

In today's highly technical world, the fight or flight response can be triggered many times during the day. While it may not always involve a response to danger, the result is the same. The caveman fought or fled, resolving the situation and shutting off the alarm. The nature of contemporary stress, however, often prohibits releasing this tension, and stress continues to build.

Following a bombardment of stress, the body begins to accept an alarmed reaction as the normal state of affairs. It then enters the resist-or-adapt stage of stress response. In this stage, no opportunity exists for fight or flight and stress continues to mount. Maintaining this stage becomes a problem when the body tires and enters the third stage: exhaustion. Resources for combating the effects of stress are depleted. Exhaustion may contribute to stress-related diseases, such as hypertension, heart disease, and oftentimes diabetes.

Positive Stress. When managed effectively, stress can boost productivity, enhance creativity, and maximize a person's potential. Winning the lottery, receiving a promotion, going on vacation, getting married, having children, and excelling on an exam ordinarily represent examples of **positive stress.** The body does not know the difference between positive and negative stress, however, and reacts the same physiologically. Although positive stress is more enjoyable psychologically, managing good stress is as important as managing negative stress. Wellness is attained more by harnessing stress, managing it better, and avoiding debilitating stress than by eliminating it altogether.

To do their best work, individuals need to generate some tension, some stress. They need to get the adrenaline flowing to do a good job. There is no way that anyone could, or would want to, eliminate all the excitement and its accompanying stress from the workplace. There is a thrill about a new project or client or procedure.

Work Induced Stress. Many causes of stress originate away from the job and only disrupt it. This stress results in reduced productivity, lower morale, inadequate concentration, tardiness, and strained relationships. For Cecil, the stress of a family move, new schools for his children, and building new friendships were difficult. As mentioned in earlier chapters, good managers deal with employee problems regardless of their cause.

Having children is an example of positive stress.

▼
positive stress-examples include going on vacation, excelling on an exam, and receiving a promotion

Figure 11.1 **How to Calm Angry Coworkers**

Try these techniques to calm angry or unreasonable coworkers:

► **Agreeing.** Disarm them by agreeing whenever possible with whatever truth or generalization they present. Keep in mind that some part of what they're saying, even though greatly exaggerated, is probably true.

► **Repeating.** Echoing what they say lets them know you're not about to fight with them over it. If you refuse to take part in a conflict, you'll control the situation better.

► **Disarming.** Give them a chance to reconsider any rash statements by saying, "Excuse me, I didn't quite catch what you said." They probably won't repeat their statements and may calm down.

► **Privacy.** Suggest talking to them in private. An audience may inspire these people, and they may calm down once they're in private.

► **Getting out.** Sometimes, this is the only way to let irate people know they've gone too far. Tell them, "I'm finding it very difficult to talk to you right now. And I can't help you if we aren't able to work together on this situation. If you feel we can't do that, perhaps you'd like someone else to help you or to address this at another time."

As with Cecil, an inappropriate promotion frequently will create added stress that can ruin a person's work and spill over into his or her home life. Some persons welcome and thrive on heavy stress and pressure at work. We have all heard of people who work better under pressure. Some recognize when they have had enough (like Cecil) and give up the promotion.

Stress is more than a matter of emotional problems and personality conflicts; it is a problem affecting the corporate balance sheet. Stress-related diseases such as stroke, heart attack, alcoholism, and drug addiction can lead to lower productivity, absenteeism, hospitalization, and premature death.

Role of Supervisors. A nationwide survey of 28,000 workers by a United States insurance company found troublesome supervisors cited as the most common cause of stress in the workplace. What does this mean for employers? At the least it signals that effective relations between supervisors and their employees are worth addressing. Stress in extreme doses can be physically unhealthy to the sufferer, whether it simply causes a tension headache or upset stomach, or more critically, elevates blood pressure levels or leads to depression. Either way, the cost is high to both individuals and to employers, who inevitably find that the productivity of an overstressed employee suffers.

While work induced stress is not always the fault of the supervisor, little prevents a bad employee from blaming a good supervisor for it. For example, employers need to be sensitive to signals from their workers that a supervisor may be generating unwarranted stress. When a particular department's productivity falls or its attrition rate increases, or when complaints against a supervisor become more frequent, the supervisor's relationship with his or her employee should not be overlooked as a possible source of the problem.

If the supervisor is found to be the source of unwarranted stress in the workplace, corrective measures have to be taken. If professional advice from a senior manager is not effective, the supervisor could be enrolled in a training program that focuses on employee relations. Employers also should be prepared to offer employees suffering from acute stress a means for relieving it. Often just listening is very helpful. Perhaps professional counseling will be needed. The rewards of improved productivity may more than pay for the cost of treatment.

Managers can zap employee morale in different ways. A short list includes criticizing employees in front of others, being dishonest, taking credit for work of others, being inaccessible, and showing favoritism. These are all things managers can and should control so that employee morale and productivity are not lowered.

Solutions to Workplace Stress

When stress invades the workplace, both employers and employees pay dearly. For employers, the costs include high turnover, stress-related health

Figure 11.2 **Stress Relievers**

Today's world produces plenty of stress.

At times when the pressure seems to be too much and you can't concentrate anymore, don't just reach for the aspirin bottle. Try one of these stress relievers.

► **Visit the beach** or any other pleasant scene from your past. Imagine it! Stimulate your other senses too. Smell the salt air. Feel the warm sun on your skin. Hear the waves crashing on the shore.

► **Take deep breaths.** Breathe in through your nose, out through your mouth. Take the time to notice how your abdomen expands as you fill your lungs with air.

► **Stretch.** Stand up. Raise your arms above your head. Stretch left and hold 1-2-3-4. Stretch right and hold 1-2-3-4.

► **Hug someone.** Four hugs every day will do a lot to calm you down. Hug the kids. The dog. Your spouse.

► **Change the scene.** Walk to your window and watch the birds. Take a stroll around the shop floor or the office.

► **Find a friend.** Choose a patient soul, one who won't butt in or give advice, to listen to your complaints.

► **Take an exercise break.** Take a brisk walk at lunch. Climb the stairs instead of riding the elevator. When your mind is cluttered, move your body. Exercise will improve your frame of mind.

► **Have a good laugh.** Pull a joke book out of your drawer and read it. Visit with a coworker who is known for a fine sense of humor. Your spirits will rise immediately.

► **Finish something.** Bogged down by lengthy and complex projects? Give yourself a quick sense of accomplishment. Pick a task you can easily finish in the next ten minutes. Then do it.

► **Play.** A few minutes spent playing brings renewed energy and concentration to the job. Use your break time to work a crossword puzzle.

► **Change your focus.** Put your job concerns aside for five minutes, and concentrate on your life away from work. Plan how you will spend this evening or the weekend. Think of those friends you've been meaning to call and decide when you'll do it.

claims, and reduced productivity. For employees, workplace stress can take its toll on health and well-being, work performance, morale, and stability at home. Employee workers' compensation stress claims have become so controversial and at times fraudulent that some states have passed strict legislation to limit them. Still, workers' compensation awards continue to be made for nervous breakdowns, depression, and even workplace suicides brought on by alleged stressful working conditions.

According to a survey of 1,299 employees by Northwestern National Life Insurance Company, 4 in 10 American workers say their jobs are very or extremely stressful, while 39 percent say they often think about quitting their jobs. Half of the surveyed employees say job stress reduces their productivity, and a third say they experience stress-related illnesses. Of the employees who say they have high-stress jobs, 65 percent suffer from exhaustion and 44 percent report headaches or migraines. Also, employees in high-stress jobs are nearly three times as likely to experience anxiety, ulcers, anger, or depression as those in low-stress jobs.

Based on the survey findings, Northwestern National Life Insurance researchers suggest the follow steps to reduce tension and stress in the workplace.

► *Allow employees to talk freely with one another.* Employees thrive in an atmosphere where they can consult with colleagues about work issues. Moreover, in organizations where employees are allowed to talk freely with one another, productivity and problem-solving are enhanced.

► *Reduce personal conflicts on the job.* Employers can reduce stress by training managers and employees how to resolve conflicts through open communication, negotiation, and mutual respect. Managers can minimize conflicts by treating employees fairly and clearly defining job expectations.

► *Give employees adequate control over how they do their work.* Employees take greater pride in their work, are more productive, and are better able to deal with stress if they have some control over how they perform their work. Managers who let employees make decisions create an atmosphere that reduces stress and increases job satisfaction.

► *Ensure adequate staffing and expense budgets.* Staff reductions and budget cuts usually increase stress in the long run. Overburdened employees frequently suffer high stress levels that cause lower productivity, illness, turnover, and accidents.

► *Talk openly with employees.* Open communication between management and employees can reduce job stress and helps employees cope better with the challenges of the workplace.

► *Support employees' efforts.* When employers show their support of employees' contributions to the organization, stress levels are significantly lower. Managers can show support by regularly asking employees how their work is going, listening to them, and addressing issues that are raised.

► *Provide competitive personal leave and vacation benefits.* Workers who have time to relax and recharge after working hard are less likely to develop stress-related illnesses.

- *Maintain current levels of employee benefits.* Workers' stress levels increase when their benefits are reduced. Employers should determine whether the savings from reduced benefits are worth the risk of employee burnout.

- *Reduce the amount of "red tape" for employees.* When employees must deal with too much bureaucracy, they become discouraged and demoralized. Employers should ensure that employees' time is not wasted on unnecessary procedures.

- *Recognize employees for their accomplishments and contributions.* A pat on the back, public praise, or a bonus or raise can result in significant increases in employee morale and productivity.[1]

Burnout

When I first became a pediatric nurse," says Eileen, "I loved going to work every day. But here I am ten years down the road and I just can't bear it anymore. I'm exhausted before I even do anything. And every time I see a new kid with leukemia, I feel he can read the defeat on my face. What depresses me the most is the feeling that I spend the better part of my workday feeling like a failure, and when I get home, I look at my own healthy children and feel even more guilty. And sometimes I'm so irritable that I worry they get the brunt of it."

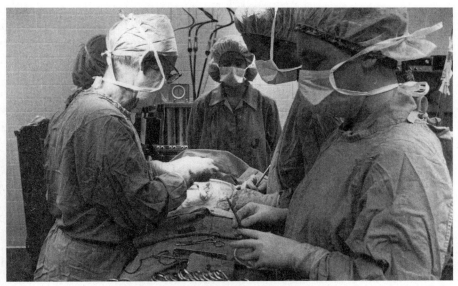

Nurses and other dedicated workers experience exhaustion and feelings of defeat, guilt, and hopelessness because of burnout on their jobs.

[1]"Reducing Violence in the Workplace." *Employment Guide.* The Bureau of National Affairs. March 18, 1994.

Customs and Traditions: Watching for the Global Difference

A Country's Culture Can Add to International Workers' Stress

Companies harvesting the benefits of diversity in the United States naturally consider exporting diversity initiatives to their operations abroad. But it is risky to assume that policies and practices which work well in the United States will also work well in other countries. One manager recently returned to the United States after 15 years of work in Japan. There, Sam saw highly capable women, some with MBAs, typing, filing, answering phones, and serving tea.

He said it doesn't make sense to let this potential to go to waste. If Sam had seen women's talents unused in an American office, he could have exercised his decision-making power to bring about change, confident that his efforts would enjoy wide acceptance because the values motivating him would be widely accepted. This is not necessarily the case overseas, where other widely honored sets of values lead people to have different perspectives.

burnout-occurs when someone is putting in much more than he or she is getting back from a certain situation or activity

Eileen is suffering from burnout, a syndrome that affects hundreds of thousands of people each year. The term **burnout** usually applies to the workplace, although full-time homemakers and retired persons can suffer from it as well since it generally occurs when someone is putting in much more than he or she is getting back. Ironically, the people most affected by burnout are those who begin their career with a high degree of dedication and idealism. In other words, to suffer from burnout you must first be on fire.

The symptoms that herald the onset of burnout are very much like the ones Eileen experienced. There is a sense of malaise; emotional, physical, and psychological fatigue; and a general lack of enthusiasm about work and life. There are also feelings of helplessness and hopelessness. Unfortunately, these symptoms are often difficult to notice because they develop over an extended period.

Road to Recovery

What can be done when people reach the burnout stage? First, they have to be aware that there is a problem and think about it as a function of work and not a personal failure. Second, they must assume responsibility for resolution and take some kind of action. That alone will make them feel better. Third, they need to look realistically at which aspects of the problem they can change and concentrate their efforts where they will make a difference. Last, they need to develop coping skills to combat future burnout.

As difficult as it may be to recognize the symptoms of burnout, the truth is that many people who recognize their symptoms respond by denying them. Their denial usually comes through by simply saying "That's life."

"One woman in my department was especially bright," continued Sam. "I decided to see if I could get her promoted. I spoke to a senior executive about this idea. He did not seem enthusiastic about a promotion for this woman. He finally revealed the reason for his lack of enthusiasm: In Japan, men do not report to women."

This Japanese executive provides a good example of someone assuming that people's birth-given or ascribed traits (gender, for example) are a proper basis for assigning an economic role and social status. Although Americans believe it is critically important to evaluate people on the basis of their achievements, people abroad are not as enamored of achievement as we are. Does that mean Sam, who had been diversity minded, will give up? Fortunately, he did not. His experience is instructive.

Jane, a lawyer specializing in poverty law is a case in point. "If I hadn't cared deeply about injustice, I would have joined a corporate law firm when I got out of school and made a lot of money," Jane says. "But after eight years of working for very little money and watching my classmates enjoy the good life, I'm tired, I don't enjoy my work, and I'm not very effective. I've got to face the fact that injustice is a part of life, and I might as well start thinking about how to take care of myself a little better."

The "that's life" attitude leads to cynicism, and cynicism usually increases burnout. Jane's resolution is no resolution at all. She will take her bitterness and feelings of helplessness with her into a new job, and even if she makes a great deal of money, those negative feelings will remain powerful.

Getting Support. Psychologists generally agree that strong support systems are critical in preventing or remedying burnout. Parents who are at home full time and isolated from their peers are more likely candidates for burnout than those parents who make it a point to connect with others. Dentists, who work alone on patients whose mouths are stuffed with gauze, and psychiatrists, who not only work alone but also are expected to keep the events of their day strictly confidential, have a high incidence of burnout. Firefighters, on the other hand, who have a strong sense of camaraderie on the job and are universally regarded as heroes, suffer very little from burnout.

We all need people to appreciate our efforts and offer emotional support. Beyond that, we need people with whom we can share our burdens. The key to burnout is to understand that we cannot expect one person or one setting to meet all of our needs. The richer and more varied our lives are, the more opportunity we'll have to find the kind of support we need.

*E*mployee Assistance Programs

The term **employee assistance program (EAP)** refers to programs that provide business and industry with the means to identify employees whose job performance is negatively affected by personal or job-related problems. The EAP arranges for structured assistance to solve those problems, with the goal of reestablishing the employee's effective job performance. The services of an EAP may be contracted, or the program may be an employer's own creation, designed to fit the unique needs of a company. EAPs provide professional, confidential no- or low-cost assistance for employees with personal problems.

EAPs help employers by identifying the troubled worker. This may be done by supervisory referrals or self-motivated referrals. Each employee is assessed, and a plan of action is designed to suit his or her needs. This requires the ability to uncover the employee's primary problem. This course of action should make it possible for the employee to again work at peak levels. An effective EAP requires a knowledge of resources available in the community. Depending on the EAP, it may be a one-change-only situation.

History

No one knows when the first employer offered counseling and social work services to its employees. But in 1917 Macy's Department Store in New York City opened an office specifically devoted to helping employees deal with personal problems. Metropolitan Life Insurance Company and Western Electric were also pioneers in the field, but it was not until the years immediately following World War II that a limited form of EAP became relatively common.

In those days, Alcoholics Anonymous was a new organization gaining widespread attention. For the first time, alcohol abuse was perceived by business to be a problem in the workplace. Many companies started alcoholism programs for their workers. Usually, those programs were staffed by recovering alcoholics who trained supervisors to spot alcoholics with symptoms such as shaking hands, bloodshot eyes, and alcohol on the breath. These early programs produced gratifying results. But they were severely limited because they only identified late-stage problems. Alcoholics in the early stage whose hands did not shake and who did not drink on the job were passed over. It was not until the 1950s that a new method of identification was pioneered at the Chino Mines Division of Kennecott Copper.

Figure 11.3 **Monitor Your EAPs**

As mental health costs climb and claims of job-related mental injury multiply, some employers may be tempted to tighten up monitoring of their employee assistance programs' (EAP) performance—and possibly jeopardize confidentiality. Here are some suggestions to balance the two apparently conflicting needs.

▶ **Quiz** EAP providers on their procedures to maintain confidentiality: policies, communications, training, management systems.

▶ **Establish** your own confidentiality procedures, especially if your programs are managed by full-time or on-site personnel.

▶ **Track** costs to pinpoint potential problems before they lead to claims; use aggregate statistics, without employee names.

▶ **Combine** findings from EAP and managed mental health programs into overall safety education programs.

▶ **Include** mandatory referral to the EAP as part of progressive discipline programs geared toward giving employees a last chance to rehabilitate themselves and keep their jobs.

Today, EAPs must pay close attention to the specific needs of clients. For example, until recently, few EAPs dealt with gambling-related issues. But now counselors are being trained to deal with gambling addiction and related problems. A number of companies also have EAPs that offer financial and legal referrals to employees with consumer credit or bankruptcy problems and legal concerns. These services are in addition to assistance offered for emotional, family, work, and substance abuse problems.

EAPs often help workers deal with natural disasters such as floods.

Another area that EAPs frequently deal with is critical incident intervention—helping workers handle deaths, suicides, hostage situations, major accidents, and natural disasters. In recent years, companies have faced an onslaught of natural disasters, including fires, earthquakes, and mud slides on the West Coast, floods in the Midwest, and hurricanes in the Southeast.

Modern Employee Assistance Programs

Let's assume when Cecil was in need of assistance, Sadler and Associates had an employee assistance program and Cecil would have had access to help for his troubles. He would have been made aware of the services that were a part of the program. He may have learned about the services by attending a staff meeting where the process and possibilities were explained. A contact person in the EAP Service Center office was identified as the first connection. Once this contact person and Cecil had an opportunity to discuss the situation, he or she could assess the problem and direct Cecil to a counselor outside of the company. (Company resource representatives must be trained so they know what kinds of assistance employees need and what is available.)

Organizational development, managed care, workers' compensation, child care, and catastrophic disasters are just a few of the issues that are expanding the scope of today's EAPs. The changes going on in corporate America are tremendous. As a result, the role and scope of the company's employee assistance program has evolved with the times. Some EAPs offer workers professional organizational counseling. This service runs the gamut from counseling work group members who are having problems getting along with one another to counseling survivors of downsizing on how to handle stress. Some EAPs employ as many as 40 professional counselors.

Managers today are also having to terminate both good employees and difficult ones. Besides the emotional effects, there is also a practical side to letting workers go. There is documentation and a procedure to follow. Human resources staff members are stretched to the limit in some cases.

A new trend for EAPs seems to be moving into the realm of disability management. Companies today want to complement the traditional disability arrangement with a whole-person approach. In many cases workers' self-esteem is tied to their jobs. As workers sit at home recuperating from injuries or disabilities, they become bored and depressed. In other cases their disabilities may put financial strains on their families. Therefore, there is a need to supplement the medical care a person is receiving with counseling on issues he or she is facing. The goal is to keep the worker connected to the workplace.

Today's EAPs have grown in both size and sophistication. In some places EAPs are operated through employee associations. Sometimes professional groups or similar businesses and small industries unite to form a consortium. Although all EAPs aim to help management and employees, there are differences in how they do it. Boiled down to the essentials, these differences come under two headings: who is helped and how that help is provided.

Single-Issue Programs.
Single-issue programs aim to help only employees impaired by drugs and alcohol. Their focus is clear, and they are generally small enough to cost the employer relatively little. A disadvantage of single-issue programs is that they may become stigmatized because of the negative connotations addiction and alcoholism bear. Some people may tend to be afraid to use the program for fear of being labeled drunks or addicts. Since the per-person cost of an EAP decreases with the number of people who use it, this stigmatization is an important issue to consider. Furthermore, supervisors tend to look only for symptoms of abuse instead of concentrating on declining job performance.

The greatest weakness of single-issue programs is their lack of preventive power. Late-stage alcoholics and addicts have the highest relapse rate and the least chance for permanent recovery. Single-issue programs tend to find these late-stagers but are not even recognizing those in the early stages for whom help can be most effective.

Broad-brush EAPs.
Broad-brush EAPs offer help to employees suffering from all kinds of problems as well as chemical dependency. For example, a broad-brush program may provide crisis management services for those whose problems can be dealt with over a short term. Sometimes all that is needed is a chance to talk a problem through with a sympathetic listener. The great advantage of broad-brush programs is their ability to uncover drug and alcohol problems in their early stages. Early-stagers come to their EAP presenting problems that make no mention of alcohol or drugs. At first clients complain about financial woes, a troubled marriage, abuse, or problem children. It is only after working with a skilled counselor that the truth reveals itself: cocaine is bankrupting an executive; a marriage is in trouble because the wife drinks and the husband enables her; children act out because they cannot get the nurturing they need from addicted parents.

One disadvantage to the broad-brush programs is the fact that they are usually more expensive than single-issue programs. There are ways to minimize costs by designing a program suited to the workplace or in conjunction with other businesses. In the long run, EAPs can save businesses money by making them more efficient and productive, by reducing accidents, by raising employee morale and decreasing grievances, and by cutting back the number of unnecessary insurance claims.

Modes of Service
A major difference among today's EAPs is the mode of service they deliver. It would be impossible to describe all the variations that exist, but a short description of several of the most common varieties will provide some insight.

► Some EAPs are just a **hotline.** Employees are encouraged to call a particular number and ask for help. The person on the other end provides
the names and numbers of local public service agencies that may be able
to address employees' personal problems. Alone, this just barely quali-
fies as employee assistance. However, a hotline in combination with
other services may prove helpful in drawing out fearful employees for
whom anonymity is essential. And hotlines can be extremely beneficial
during the holiday season when depression is a serious problem.

► Other EAPs amount to no more than a single individual in the personnel
department or the medical office who can direct an employee off site on
the basis of his or her problem. This is not much better than the hotline,
and employees may not go near the office for fear of being labeled.
Employees required to report there because of poor job performance
evaluations and the fear of losing their livelihoods will complain loudly
about the lack of confidentiality. Furthermore, the help they get may
prove useless in the long run, since individuals in such superficial programs rarely have the expertise needed to assess the full range of problems that may be presented.

► A few very large companies have elaborate on-site EAP divisions with
full staffs including doctors and nurses.

► Companies with like concerns, products, or geography (all situated in
the same industrial complex, for example) may join together to form a
consortium that makes a single contract with a consulting EAP organization to provide services to employees from each site.

Most EAP providers emphasize the confidential nature of their services
and will give employer numerical information only, without divulging
names of EAP-assisted employees. Otherwise, many employees would be
hesitant, if not totally unwilling, to admit a personal problem for fear that it
would jeopardize their job status or chances for promotion.

However, there may be situations in which an employer may need to
know certain types of information. For example, when an employee is
engaged in dangerous duties (operating heavy equipment, driving a school
bus, fighting forest fires, and so on), supervisory personnel may need to
know general information about the employee's condition for safety conditions. Therefore, the employer's promise of confidentiality and privacy to
employees is extremely important. Whatever level of confidentiality the
employer establishes must be maintained; notice must be given to employees and consent obtained for variances. Also, it is important that an
employer give employees clear warnings that such disclosures are permitted. Further, specific state privacy laws may affect the availability of
information.

Some EAP programs provide services to groups of employees during a
crisis. For example, a team of counselors from an EAP may work with an
entire department affected by a violent workplace incident.

Violence in the Workplace

An executive at a high-tech firm who helped plan layoffs at several plants started receiving threats through untraceable electronic mail messages. In the notes the harasser indicated he or she was watching the woman at home, where she lived alone. She spent Sunday working in her garden. The next day her e-mail read: "Watch out for the flower you didn't pick." The terrified woman left her home and job. A year and a half later she has not returned to work.

Stress at home or on the job, burnout, personal problems, and relationships that have soured when taken to an extreme can be manifested in violent acts at work. Experts estimate that more than 100,000 incidents of workplace violence occur annually in the United States. The typical workplace killer is a middle-aged man, most likely a loner frustrated by problems on the job with few personal contacts outside the workplace. One study showed men were responsible for 98 percent of all violence committed at a workplace. The average age was 36, and firearms were used 81 percent of the time. Following workplace homicides, one-fourth of the murderers killed themselves. Faced with an uncertain world, many men have difficulty adjusting. American women possess better outlets to circumvent such outrage.

Workplace violence, whether it involves harassment, threats, or a physical attack, is a serious and growing problem for employers. The lack of attention to the issue means lost lives, discontent, and fear among employees, as well as tremendous cost to companies involved. "Only in the last couple of years have people begun to realize this is an issue they needed to worry about," said Mary Pigatti, a consultant, who through United HealthCare Corporation helps companies assess and reduce their risks. "No one is safe, whether you are a bank teller or a supervisor in corporate America."

workplace violence-harassment, threats, or physical attacks on the job

Indeed U.S. Labor Department research shows violence is now the number one cause of death on the job for women and second for men, behind transportation accidents. For corporate America, violence has meant a hard punch in its most vulnerable spot—the bottom line. On-the-job violence cost American companies about $4.2 billion in 1993, said Ira Lipman, president of the national security enterprise Guardsmark and an authority on the issue.

Corporations without preventive measures are particularly subject to lawsuits and higher costs. Among precautions companies can take toward preventing violence are establishing clear guidelines on appropriate behavior, screening applicants carefully, training employees to identify warning signs, and setting up procedures for managers to respond to cries for help. Companies also should look closely at the procedures they use when they

Workplace violence is a serious and growing problem for employers and employees.

terminate employees. Perhaps most important is maintaining a healthy work environment. It really boils down to one person's relationship with another and whether or not the environment fosters mutual respect.

In 1986, Patrick Sherrill, a part-time letter carrier about to be dismissed, shot and killed 14 people at a postal service facility in Edmond, Oklahoma, and then took his own life. Within the last 10 years, 10 disgruntled workers have killed 34 supervisors and coworkers at postoffice installations throughout the United States.

Prevention, postal officials knew, was the first step of the cure. One approach to the problem was simple but effective. A 24-hour hotline was established in November 1991, following another tragedy, this time at the Royal Oak, Michigan, post office. The hotline allows employees to report threats or other concerns about safety to the U.S. Postal Inspection Service.

All threats are taken seriously. "If you are threatening others, or if you are exhibiting threatening behavior, it's going to be followed up on right away," explains Paul Griffo, national spokesman for the U.S. Postal Inspection Service in Washington. The plan put into place by the Postal Service to combat violence includes a partnership between a professionally trained intervention team that includes medical people and the employee assistance program.

Additional steps included fingerprinting, which allowed a database check for any FBI criminal records. Additional support came from labor unions. One key to improving the relationship between labor and management is reducing stress in the workplace.

Difficult Employees Need Special Attention

There is one particular group of employees who feels the stress of what is happening to corporate America perhaps more than others. These people may have been hired during the 1960s when it was easier to find a job with minimum skills. They have been with the organization 15 or 20 years, but now they are looked on as "dead weight." They are people who never quite made the grade, but got along in spite of their below-par performance. Only, it is not possible now to justify keeping them on the payroll unless they become more productive. When companies are terminating valuable employees with high skill levels, they cannot carry nonperformers. These people need to be handled with sensitivity.

For example, Durand Electric managed to salvage a less than ideal situation that followed this pattern.

John had been getting adequate reviews for years because his supervisor did not want to deal with his unsatisfactory performance. After a merger, the company culture changed and employees were expected to perform more. John was given a performance appraisal that threw him into an absolute panic. The review was so potentially sensitive that the supervisor's boss and the human resource manager both decided to attend the meeting.

John was very controlled but totally devastated by the criticism. He was told the people he worked with found him intimidating. "Perhaps they know I've been trained to kill," he said. Then he began to attack the supervisor verbally. He was told by the manager to take the review and think about it and that he would be placed on an improvement program. No dates were set and no threats were made.

On Monday John called the office sobbing and hysterical. He told a secretary they had taken away his manhood. On Tuesday he was in a local hospital in the psychiatric unit. John had severe anxiety; he could not face the people who he perceived as having insulted him so badly. Later he called and told the human resources manager that he would not back down from anybody.

The human resources manager, worried about workplace safety, called the employee assistance program for advice. The counselor told her to take practical security measures, such as locking doors that had been propped open, and suggested she set up a network of people who knew John. If he came to work, his coworkers were instructed to be understanding and pleasant, and then to contact the police immediately.

Being prepared to deal with situations such as John's can avoid possible disaster. Layoffs, terminations, mergers, and acquisitions are all causes of employee stress. Management sometimes is so involved with the restructuring that they forget to look at the human consequences. Companies that ignore feelings and provide no mechanisms for support for their employees may pay for years to come. It is one reason employee assistance programs are full of referrals.

Reducing Violence in the Workplace

An employer's commitment to reducing workplace violence can make a difference in the extent of human and financial costs involved or whether such incidents occur at all. Employees whose companies had effective grievance, harassment, and security programs reported significantly lower levels of violence and harassment. An employer plan to minimize the risk of violence is more realistic than a plan to eliminate violence completely.

The goals of a violence risk reduction are to reduce the frequency, severity, and long-term effects of violence. A company workplace violence plan should include:

► Involvement of an interdisciplinary incident management team, to include security, human relations, and employee assistance staff, as well as legal and psychological personnel.

► Preemployment screening, particularly a review of an applicant's criminal record.

► Drug and alcohol testing. While substance abuse is not a predictor of violence, most people think it is, and employers should perform testing as a legal defense in case they are faced with a drug-related incident later.

► Preemployment interviews and reference checks. Interviewers should be trained to ask probing questions and talk to people not listed in the résumé. Interviewers should also ask applicants about any gaps in employment history.

In many workplaces, employees may hesitate to report incidents of violence because of a lack of understanding of the value of reporting, fear of reprisal, fear of being blamed, embarrassment, or guilt. Employers should develop methods of learning everything possible about all incidents, even minor ones. Reports should go to a person who has been properly trained to respond to such situations. Employers should not list the kinds of misconduct employees should report, but instead have employees report any behavior that causes suffering or discomfort.

Confidentiality and Worker Privacy

Arkban Aradah in Portland, Oregon, is an administrative assistant for an international holding company. Arkban's family is large and by tradition a close group. Arkban works extra hours and is a diligent employee. He was astonished one day when his supervisor "wrote him up" for spending an excessive amount of time on the phone for personal calls. The supervisor indicated that the new phone switching equipment was capable of tracking incoming and outgoing calls by phone number and of measuring the amount of time spent on each call.

According to Arkban's supervisor, many of the phone numbers electronically recorded on Arkban's extension were not business-related phone numbers and were traced to his home or that of others with the same last name—all local calls.

During the conference with his supervisor, Arkban was told that he was misappropriating the company's time and equipment and was monopolizing external phone lines that customers or other business callers might need. Arkban explained that both his small son and parents had been seriously ill and that he phoned them regularly to check up on them. He was very surprised to learn that the organization was monitoring his calls without his knowledge and asked if his phone conversations were being recorded by the voice mail system. His supervisor just explained that they had hard evidence about phone abuse and he had to correct his behavior.

The right to privacy, including the right to **workplace privacy,** has long been controversial. In the last several years, as the result of advances in technology, rising health care costs, and additional legislative scrutiny, workplace privacy issues have become a focal point of employer-employee rights debates. The boundaries of employee privacy in the private sector have been subject to a hodgepodge of legislation, case law, and accepted employment practices.

> ▼
> *workplace privacy-freedom of unauthorized intrusion from the job site*

Workplace privacy issues can typically be divided into **on-the-job** and **off-the-job employee behavior.** On-the-job privacy issues range from property issues and testing—drug testing, psychological testing, medical testing, and so forth—to use of video cameras and other forms of monitoring such as tracking by computer, listening in on phone calls, or reading electronic mail. While employees have challenged many of these practices, arguing that they are invasive, employers have countered that they are necessary to ensure safety or job performance.

> ▼
> *on-the-job employee behavior-issues that range from drug testing and the use of electronic equipment to track employee's activities while at work*

Off-the-job privacy issues cover much broader terrain and range from an employee's political activities, medical treatment, and recreational activities to whether an employee smokes and whom she or he may date. Employees have argued that on-the-job performance, as opposed to off-the-job behavior, should be the basis of employment decisions.

> ▼
> *off-the-job employee behavior-a broad range of employee activities from an employee's political activities to whether or not he or she smokes*

Advances in technology have spawned new variations on old privacy themes. Federal law for example, prohibits tampering with employee mail. Yet some employers regularly open and read electronic mail. The question becomes: Is e-mail fundamentally like or unlike other kinds of mail? Is monitoring computer work fundamentally like or unlike other accepted means of employee assessment?

Rising health-care costs have also created new privacy issues, particularly in the area of off-the-job privacy. Some employers, for example, do not hire employees who smoke on the grounds that smokers present the

Workplace privacy issues have become a focal point of employer-employee rights debates.

not hire employees who smoke on the grounds that smokers present the risk of higher health care usage, and controlling costs is a legitimate concern. Over the next several years, we will likely see more effort to enact or expand workplace privacy laws, because today's workers are less likely than their predecessors to agree with the presumption that employing someone for 40 hours a week entitles the employer to determine what the employee may or may not do in the other 128 hours.

Personal Questions

People are for the most part comfortable with job-related inquiries from employers, but draw the line at questions regarding their personal lives, according to a 1994 study by the American Civil Liberties Union. The study was based on 933 in-person interviews of adults, representing a cross-section of the population nationwide. An overwhelming majority of the participants in the study said it is appropriate for an employer to ask prospective employees questions about previous employment and educational background. Moreover, 60 percent of the participants agreed that employers must maintain some control over whom they hire to maintain quality in the workplace.

People's demand for privacy increased even more when it came to employer questions on matters of personal conduct. For example, just 27 percent of the study participants agreed that an employer should be entitled to know whether someone smokes off the job. Support was even less when it came to employers asking about off-the-job drinking (17 percent), psychological counseling (23 percent), and sexual orientation (23 percent).

Opinions about electronic monitoring of employees hinge on whether or not the employees are aware of the monitoring. Even for a phone-intensive job such as airline ticket agent, more than half of the participants said employees have the right to know when their calls are being monitored. Outside of telephone intensive jobs, 65 percent of the respondents said an employer has no right to eavesdrop on workers' conversations.

The Legality of Workplace Monitoring

Workplace monitoring can be a useful tool to help employers maintain quality control, product security, and customer protection. The proliferation of electronic technology, while making it easier for unscrupulous employees to get into unauthorized computer systems, also has enabled many employers to check up on their workers more effectively. However, new worker privacy legislation may severely restrict employers' ability to monitor their workers.

workplace monitoring-a tool to help employers maintain quality control, product security, and customer protection

Monitoring employees for security purposes can save employers a significant amount of money. According to the United States Chamber of Commerce, theft and equipment vandalism cost employers more than $3 billion annually. In addition, the theft of data such as trade secrets tops $2 billion a year and crimes involving computers (such as electronic transfer of funds) exceed $1 billion a year. Used for security purposes, electronic monitoring can help employers spot such crimes as employee theft, misuse of personnel records, and unauthorized access to telephone voice mail effectively and without disruption.

Monitoring also can help employees improve their job performance and productivity. For example, some telemarketing firms may discover that

Ethical Dimensions to Human Relations

Woman Fired for Wearing Political Button

Recently, a woman was fired by her employer for wearing a political button to work. A federal judge said the company's requirement that a Phoenix, Arizona, woman cover the button to avoid offending other employees was reasonable. The judge said the woman was fired because of her political beliefs—that she should wear the button—but that U.S. West had given her a reasonable alternative to losing her job.

The woman could have continued to wear the button covered in some way. This compromise would have allowed her to wear the button in the workplace and would have avoided turmoil with her coworkers. A self-described "devout political fanatic," she vowed to always wear the button.

CONTINUED

The woman, who worked for her employer from 1969 to 1995, contended that the company violated the 1964 Civil Rights Acts and her right to equal employment. The attorney for U.S. West said the case was not about politics but about disrupting the workplace. Several coworkers had complained about the button. The attorney also said the case really never had anything to do with free speech or politics. It was simply a case about whether U.S. West reasonably accommodated the plaintiff in her political beliefs.

employees who have trouble carrying out their tasks can have these troubles pinpointed through monitoring, then corrected through training. For new employees, monitoring can provide some security against making mistakes.

Conclusion

Stress is part of everyone's life. The critical issue is how we deal with stress. Cecil Mounds was unable to manage the level of stress in his life, and he was subjecting himself to burnout. This condition requires self-help and help from others if it is to be overcome.

An employee assistance program can be a way for businesses to help their employees work through some of their problems. Cecil's situation may have been very different if his employer had had such a program. Many companies also offer wellness programs to help their employees counteract the effects of stress. Many provide incentives to employees to stay healthy.

Some stress in life is beneficial and helps keep a person motivated. The goal, therefore, is to learn how to identify it and then manage it. People can take great strides in managing stress in their lives by controlling their goals, watching their diet, exercising, and taking time for rest and relaxation.

Stress sometimes leads to violence. Workplace violence is a serious and growing problem for employers. Preventive measures can help employers control lawsuits and costs. Among precautions companies can take toward preventing violence are establishing clear guidelines for appropriate behavior, careful screening, and setting up procedures for managers to respond to cries for help.

Sources: Darrell Browning. "Stamping Out Violence." Human Resources Executive. *April, 1994, 22–25.*

Levine, Karen. "Burnout!" Parents. *October, 1992, 52–59.*

"Privacy Issues in the Workplace." HR Magazine. *August 1992, 93–94.*

"Reducing Violence in the Workplace." Employment Guide, *The Bureau of National Affairs. March 28, 1994.*

Key Points Summary

- Scientists agree that modern physiological responses are similar to prehistoric reactions.

- When managed effectively, stress can boost productivity, enahance creativity, and maximize a person's potential.

- Many causes of stress originate off the job and disrupt work.

- Supervisors are often cited as a source of stress.

- There are several things managers can and should do to raise morale and productivity.

- Burnout occurs when someone is putting in much more than he or she is getting out.

- Strong support systems are critical in preventing or remedying burnout.

- The employee assistance program (EAP) refers to programs that provide employers with the means to identify employees whose job performance is negatively affected by problems.

- In 1917 Macy's Department Store opened an office specifically devoted to assisting employees with personal problems.

- The role and scope of employee assistance programs has evolved with the times.

- Single-issue programs aim to help only employees impaired by drugs and alcohol.

- Broad-brush EAPs offer help to employees suffering from all kinds of personal problems.

- Workplace violence, whether it involves harassment or physical attacks, is a growing problem for employers.

- Corporations without preventive measures are particularly subject to lawsuits and higher costs.

- The goals of a violence risk-reduction plan are reducing the frequency, severity, and long-term effects of violence.

- In the last several years, as a result of advances in technology, rising health care costs, and additional legislative scrutiny, workplace privacy issues have become a focal point of employer-employee rights debates.

- Monitoring employees can save employers money, but state and federal legislation may restrict an employer's ability to do that.

Key Terms

broad-brush EAPs

burnout

employee assistance program

hotline

off-the-job employee behavior

on-the-job employee behavior

physiological response

positive stress

single-issue programs

stress

workplace monitoring

workplace privacy

workplace violence

Discussion Questions

1. In what ways is today's stress similar to prehistoric stress?

2. Define *positive stress* and provide several examples.

3. In what ways can supervisors contribute to workplace stress?

4. What can an employer do to reduce tension and stress on the job?

5. What jobs are more likely to lead to burnout than others? Why?

6. Describe the characteristics of an effective employee assistance program.

7. What constitutes violence in the workplace?

8. What is meant by the "costs" of workplace violence?

9. Why is workplace privacy more of an issue today than it was 30 years ago?

Chapter 12

Learning Objectives

Upon completing this chapter, you should be able to:

- Discuss the importance of time management in personal and work situations.

- List ways in which a person can manage himself or herself to become a better time manager.

- Record time usage and determine ways in which time is being wasted.

- Explain the relationship between setting goals and managing time.

- Cite examples of intrusions that make it difficult to manage time.

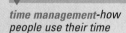

time management-how people use their time

Managing Time

Terri Middleton is a student at a community college in Wyoming. She is involved in so many activities in addition to her courses that she is always in a frazzle, trying to meet her commitments on time and running from place to place with hardly enough time to catch her breath. Terri doesn't know what to do because she has just accepted another responsibility—working part time in a child care lab at the college. How can she possibly squeeze in one more thing? She just couldn't say no because she needs the experience. Does Terri remind you of anyone you know? Is Terri really that busy, or does she have a time management problem?

*T*ime Management

How often have you said, "I just don't have enough time!" or, "There aren't enough hours in the day!" or, "Time goes by too fast"? Think about these statements. Doesn't everyone have 24 hours in the day, 60 minutes in an hour, and 60 seconds in a minute? Since everyone has the same time frame in which to work, perhaps it isn't time that is the problem but how people use their time.

Statements such as "There isn't enough time" are myths. Everyone has the same amount of time; some people just manage their time better than others. Terri is a good example of someone who needs to manage her time better. **Time management** refers to how people use their time. Good time management includes being able to say no to some requests and being able to prioritize one's responsibilities.

*A*nalyzing Your Time

The best place to start time management is with a self-evaluation of how you manage yourself. Don't be worried at this point if you think someone else may have more control over your time than you do. We'll deal with that situation later. Right now, think about the many things you spend time on. You probably are thinking about school, work, and perhaps

Some people manage their time better than others; everyone has the same amount of time.

family responsibilities, and you are wondering how you can get everything done. A question many people might ask themselves is "When am I going to have time to do something I want to do for myself?"

We live in an age of instant this and instant that and five-minute microwave meals; we wear headphones while doing chores so we can catch the news and not miss a beat while doing other activities that must be completed; some women have become quite adept at applying makeup while driving and some men shave in the car on the way to work; we take our automobiles to places where we can get an oil change in 12 minutes or less, guaranteed! We are thankful there are take-out meals or home delivery for almost any kind of food. How did we let ourselves get into such a situation?

Didn't our parents and grandparents have lots of free time to do what they wanted to do? They seemed happy, and more than likely only one of them was working. Today both people in a marriage are probably working, and they still have a difficult time making ends meet. One or the other parent often works late; and kids are busier than ever with school activities and sports. There is hardly time to sit down together for a family meal. Where does time go? Figure 12.1 will help you understand.

If you completed the quiz to determine your relationship with time, you may or may not have had some surprises. How you act upon any new-found areas of need will affect you, your work, and your leisure activities.

Figure 12.1 **Influences of Time Pressures**

To assess the degree to which time pressures influence your life, answer all questions by circling the number of the best alternative, even if no single answer feels exactly right. Scoring instructions are at the end of the quiz.

1. In a typical week, how often do you wear or carry a watch?
   (1) regularly   (2) part of the time
   (3) occasionally (4) almost never

2. How many hours do you sleep in an average week night?
   (1) five or less (2) six
   (3) seven   (4) eight or more

3. When driving, how often do you exceed the speed limit?
   (1) regularly   (2) often   (3) seldom   (4) almost never

4. As you approach a stoplight while driving, if a green light turns to yellow, are you most likely to
   (1) speed up to get through before it turns to red
   (4) slow down and wait for the next green light

Which statement best describes your attitudes?

5. (1) When I have a train or plane to catch, I like to arrive as close as possible to the scheduled departure time so I won't have to waste time sitting around.

   (4) I always try to leave extra time to get to an airport or train station so I won't have to worry about missing a train or flight.

6. (1) At a restaurant, I like my food to arrive as soon as possible after I've ordered.

   (4) I don't mind waiting a few minutes for the food I've ordered at a restaurant

7. (1) What I like about microwave ovens is that they cut way down on the amount of time it takes to prepare meals.

   (4) I'd rather spend extra time preparing meals than use a microwave oven on a regular basis.

8. (1) I often use a remote control device to scan a lot of television channels so I can see what's on.

   (4) To me a remote control device is a convenient tool for turning the television on and off from a distance, adjusting the volume, and occasionally changing channels.

9. (1) I like the lively pace of today's television programs.

   (4) I have trouble keeping up with the pace of today's television programs.

Figure 12.1, continued

10. (1) With so many other demands on my time, I find it hard to keep up with friendships.

(4) I try to make time to see my friends on a regular basis.

11. Compared to your life ten years ago, would you say you have more or less leisure time?

(1) less   (2) about the same

(3) a bit more   (4) a lot more

12. How would you compare the amount of time you spend running errands today with the amount you spent ten years ago?

(1) more   (2) about the same

(3) somewhat less (4) a lot less

13. During the past year, how many books would you estimate you've read from beginning to end?

(1) 0–2   (2) 3–5   (3) 6–10   (4) 11 or more

14. How good are you at glancing at your watch or a clock without anyone else noticing?

(1) very good   (2) good   (3) fair   (4) not good at all

15. How would you rate your ability to conduct a conversation and appear to be paying attention while thinking about something else at the same time?

(1) excellent   (2) good   (3) fair   (4) poor

16. How often do you find yourself interrupting the person with whom you're talking?

(1) regularly   (2) often

(3) occasionally (4) rarely

17. When talking on the telephone, are you most likely to

(1) do paperwork, wash dishes, or do some other chore

(2) straighten up the surrounding area

(3) do small personal tasks (e.g., file nails, reset watch)

(4) do nothing else

18. In an average week, how many evening or weekend hours do you spend working overtime or on work you've brought home?

(1) 16 or more   (2) 11–15   (3) 6–10   (4) 0–5

19. During a typical weekend, do you engage primarily in:

(1) work for income

(2) household chores and errands

(3) leisure activities

(4) catching up on sleep and relaxing

20. In a typical year, how many weeks of paid vacation do you take?

    (1) 1 or less   (2) 2   (3) 3   (4) 4 or more

21. On the whole, do you find vacations

    (1) frustrating   (2) tedious

    (3) relaxing   (4) rejuvenating

22. How often do you find yourself wishing you had more time to spend with family members or friends?

    (1) constantly   (2) often

    (3) occasionally   (4) almost never

23. During a typical day, how often do you feel rushed?

    (1) constantly   (2) often

    (3) occasionally   (4) almost never

24. Which statement best describes your usual daily schedule?

    (1) There aren't enough hours in the day to do everything I have to do.

    (2) On the whole I have just about enough time to do what I have to do.

    (3) I can usually do the things I have to do with time left over.

    (4) The day seems to have more hours than I am able to fill.

25. During the past year, would you say that your life has grown

    (1) busier

    (2) about the same

    (3) somewhat less busy

    (4) a lot less busy

Scoring: Add up the total of all circled numbers. A score of 25–40 indicates you have time problems; 41–55, pressed for time; 56–71, in balance; 72–86, time on hands.

Gaining Control of Your Time

If you feel the need to gain better control of your time, you could keep a time log of your activities for all hours of the day. A **time log** is a method to record what you do so you can see how your time is spent. If you were to keep a log for about a week and then were to complete a critical self-analysis, you might be surprised by what the log reveals. It is difficult to be honest with yourself because you may perform differently while under the microscope of your own watchful eye than would ordinarily be the

time log-a method to record what you do in order to see how time is spent

case. An even better way to keep track of your time is to have one or more other persons log your activities. This is difficult and often impractical because one or more persons have to spend a substantial amount of time in your company to observe you and record how you spend your time. The advantage of this method is that the other people may be more precise than you are. Figure 12.2 is a sample part of a form that could be used to log activities.

Figure 12.2 **A Sample Time Log**

Activity	Begin Time	End Time	Total Time Used	Observations about Time Usage	Quality

Tracking Your Habits

Let's look at time logs in more depth since they are the most-used method of determining how people spend their time. We can then identify your work habits. If you always feel rushed or that you don't have enough hours in the day, you need to find out what is happening to your waking hours. Keeping a time log may seem like an inconvenience and a time waster itself; however, the benefits far outweigh the drawbacks. During a typical day you are probably interrupted often with small intrusions that singly don't take much time, perhaps 12 minutes here and 12 minutes there. If you keep track of all those 12-minute periods, however, you will find that by day's end you have lost an hour or more of on-task time.

Keeping a Time Log. To get an accurate picture of how you spend your time, it is critical that you keep a precise time log for several days (at least three but preferably five). Figure 12.3 shows a partially completed time log for a typical day for a fictitious person. Note the hourly breakdown in time and information shown on the log. Alec Mackenzie, a time management expert, suggested that several important elements be recorded on the time log, among them the following.

► *The date the log is being kept.* It is also beneficial to note the day of the week. When you look back later, you will be able to compare the log for a certain day of the week with other logs for the same day of the week. You may find that Mondays are bad days for getting work done compared to Thursdays.

► *Short written goals for the day.* The time log should identify goals to be completed during the day. They should be simple and should be used as reminders.

► *Each activity of the day with beginning times* and length of time used for the activity. Rate the quality of the time that was spent on the activity using a rating such as this one.

1 —Activity was critical.

2 —Activity was important.

3 —Activity could have been given to someone else.

4 —Activity was wasted time.

► *Written comments about the use of the time*—what could have been done differently, who could have done the work, how the time could have been used better, and so on.[1]

Figure 12.3 A Partially Completed Time Log

Activity	Begin Time	End Time	Total Time Used	Observations about Time Usage	Quality
Started Lansing Project	8:00	8:40	40 min	Good start—Interrupted	1
Fred had questions—took coffee break	8:40	9:15	35 min	Fred just wanted to visit	4
Lansing Project	9:15	10:00	45 min	Good progress	1

What should be recorded on the time log? The answer is, everything you do! Each time you switch activities or direct your attention to something else, record the time of the new activity on the log. You may miss a few details when you begin, but you will soon remember that you should be logging everything. Don't try to go back and remember when you started something and when your activities were diverted to something else; record as you go along. If you are like most busy people, you probably won't remember what you did, let alone what time you started each activity.

Analyzing Your Time Usage. One of the primary benefits of completing a time log is being able to ascertain where the time goes. To do that requires a critical analysis of what you have recorded on the time log. You can't be kind to yourself, or your intentions of gaining control of your time won't be met.

[1]Adapted, with permission of the publisher, from *THE TIME TRAP* by Alec Mackenzie, © 1990 Alec Mackenzie. Published by AMACOM, a division of the American Management Association. All rights reserved.

In your analysis, look at your goals for the day to see if each of these goals was completed. What was the quality of the time assigned for each of the goals? You may find that your goals only took a short time to complete and you spent most of your time dealing with interruptions or unplanned tasks. You might also learn that you wasted too much of the day and didn't meet some of your goals. You could also discover that you were doing too many tasks that could have easily been delegated to someone else.

From your time log, can you determine when you are most productive? Is it first thing in the morning, or does it take you a while to get on track? Maybe the last hours of the day are most productive for you. After you have logged your times for five days, you should begin to see patterns forming. If there are times when you are more productive than others, try to determine why and then take advantage of those opportunities.

You should also analyze the quality of your work and your performance. Were you rushed to get through an assignment? If so, what was the effect on the quality of your output? Were there jobs that had to be redone because the final result was unsatisfactory? If you had to redo jobs, how much time was wasted? There is a saying that rings true for most people: "If you don't have time to do the job right the first time, when are you going to find time to do it over?"

Does your analysis indicate that you need to be more organized? Perhaps you are spending too much time shuffling through stacks looking for lost papers. Perhaps you don't know where to begin because you are working on too many different projects at the same time. How can you sequence your duties better to take advantage of the time needed for each task?

Determining Your Goals

▼
goals-statements telling what you want to accomplish

Goal setting is a critical element in gaining control of your time. **Goals** are statements telling what you want to accomplish. After you have analyzed how you spent your time, identify your goals in life. You could identify your goals before you analyze your time, but however you do it, think about what is most important for you and what you want most in your life. You should think about your family, job, hobbies or leisure time, money, friends, or whatever consumes your time.

Your goals should be prioritized in order of importance to you. What do you want most, or what do you want to complete first? After you have prioritized your life goals, compare them with the analysis of your time. What do you spend most of your time doing? Are your top priority goals given the most amount of time each day? If they aren't, you are not alone. Most people spend the most amount of time on goals that have lower priority. We'll discuss priorities in more detail in a few pages.

Writing Your Goals

It is one thing to have goals, but it is another to write them down in a form that will cause you to think about them. If you don't keep your goals visible, they are too easy to set aside and not pursue. Goals are end results that you can work toward. The question is, "If you don't know where you are going, how will you know when you arrive?" Setting and writing out goals will let you know when you arrive and should give an indication of how long the journey will take.

When writing out goals, you should follow some general rules.

► *Place demands upon yourself.* If you do not make demanding goals, they won't provide the stimulus that motivates you to achieve them.

► *Be realistic.* If you set your goals too high, you will become frustrated and will give up on them. If they are too easy, you won't find the motivation. Your goals should push you to, and sometimes beyond, what you think your limits are. Winning $40 million in a lottery may be something you would like, but is it a realistic goal? What are your odds of winning that much money?

► *Identify the end result.* You should be able to tell when you have reached your goal. The goal should have a **specific and measurable outcome,** or result, so you will readily know when you have achieved it. If there is no ending result, you might not be able to determine when you have reached your goal.

► *Establish time lines.* If your goal is long-term, it is best to set **time lines** for completing smaller steps along the way. For example, if the goal is to be completed at the end of five years, determine what should be accomplished by the end of the first year, the second year, and so on. When you do this, the goal will seem more achievable and the time frame will be more realistic.

► *Revise the goal if needed.* No goal should be so rigid that it can't be revised if failure is certain. If uncontrollable circumstances arise and the goal cannot be achieved, make adjustments to something that is reasonable within the time frame, and reestablish the goals for a longer time span.

► *Evaluate your results.* It is not enough to say, "Wow, I reached my goal, I'm great!" Evaluate how you got there. Could you have done more? What is the next step? Does this goal logically lead to establishing another?

Types of Goals

When you looked at your life goals, you probably realized in an instant that some of them are controlled by basic needs and some are controlled by others.

Externally Enacted Goals.

Unless you are independently wealthy or dependent upon someone else for support, you probably have goals that relate to employment. You must be at work at a certain time and can't leave until a certain time. Goals such as this are **externally enacted goals,** and you have little control over them. Externally enacted goals are imposed by someone else and you may not be very interested in them. An

Goal setting is a critical part of gaining control of one's time.

▼

specific and measurable outcome-identifiable results which can be observed

▼

time lines-specific periods to accomplish steps toward a goal

▼

externally enacted goals-goals imposed by someone else

Multicultural Management Requires Different Ways to Manage Time

Today's global economy has caused many changes in the way managers and supervisors direct what once were routine activities. These changes also have impacted the way human resource personnel work with managers within a company. In a study of global changes in roles and responsibilities for HR and line managers, it was learned that by the year 2000 shared responsibilities will be expected for strategy, policy development, administration, communications, and management.[1] This means there will be a closer working relationship between the human resource personnel and managers for duties that are closely related to the use of employees's time and to managing the productivity of others.

If communication and management responsibilities are shared by HR managers and line managers, it is imperative that cultural differences be considered. According to the study noted above, Japanese managers were skeptical about HR managers taking the leadership for some of the roles. Alvin Hill and James Scott noted that there are differences in the way managers function in a multicultural environment. One notable difference is that managers must recognize that there is no one solution to all problems.[2] Allowances may have to be made that concern the employees' use of time, including holidays. People from

example might be your spouse wants you to dress in a costume for a masquerade dance that you aren't very interested in attending in the first place. This is an externally enacted goal that affects your life, but you have an obligation to follow through.

Internally Enacted Goals. Other goals are **internally enacted goals;** these are goals that you set for yourself and want to accomplish; they are the goals that will in all likelihood give you the most personal satisfaction. Internally enacted goals get you motivated and keep you going. They sometimes get you past the drudgery of what must be done to meet the goals enacted by external sources. Internal goals may be difficult to identify, but they are there driving you to achieve, perhaps to be the fastest swimmer on the team, or the most respected outdoor cook in the housing subdivision.

Layering Goals for Maximum Effectiveness. Goals can best be achieved if they are layered. For example, at any given time you should have some **short-term goals,** pursuits that you want to accomplish in a very short time. You should also establish **intermediate goals,** perhaps up to a year or two ahead. Then determine your **long-term goals,**

internally enacted goals-goals you set for yourself

short-term goals-goals which can be achieved in one year or less

intermediate goals-goals to be achieved in one to two years

long-term goals-goals to be achieved in three or more years

different cultures will want to be able to observe the holidays that are meaningful for them and will want time away from work to observe those holidays.

Rosalie Tung states that management policies and practices that once worked for organizations staffed by white males at the professional and managerial levels are virtually inoperative. Tung goes on to relate how the average American employee only expends about 25 percent of his or her potential on the job.[3] This means there is considerable room for improvement in usage of time and work performance. Now that the workforce is no longer made up of only the "average" American, managers are challenged even further to improve employees' usage of time and increase productivity for the firm.

---

[1] Staff. "Global Study Reveals New Roles and Responsibilities." HRfocus. May 1992, 19.

[2] Alvin. C. Hill, and James Scott. "Ten Strategies for Managers in a Multicultural Workforce." HRfocus. August, 1992, 6.

[3] Rosalie Tung. "Managing Cross-National and Intra-National Diversity." Human Resource Management. 32(4), 461–77.

what do you want to have happen three or more years later. If you layer your goals in this manner, you will always have purposes and will find satisfaction in your successes.

Enrique Oliveira was the sales manager for First Flight, a limousine service in St. Louis. He booked the limo for individuals and groups, but made most of his money from businesses that needed the limo services for transporting visiting international business executives. He found that the business was growing very rapidly as St. Louis became more of a convention city. In fact, the demands on his time were becoming so excessive that he was finding less and less time to spend with his family and had little time for the activity he loved most—sailing. He felt he was losing control of his time.

Enrique discussed the situation with his general manager, but the manager wasn't sympathetic, although she was thrilled with the growth of the company and was enjoying its success. Enrique had to make some decisions before he became more unhappy. He realized he didn't really enjoy the job like he once did and decided he wanted to get back to a lifestyle that allowed him to spend more time with his family and sailing.

Enrique's situation probably sounds familiar because much of our American lifestyle is closely related to our work. Our time as well is controlled by our work rather than by us. Perhaps Enrique needs to begin by analyzing his time, setting goals, and determining priorities.

Setting Priorities

Goals are of little value if you don't take the time to prioritize your activities. Some of the goals you want to achieve are more important than others. The activities required to accomplish the less important goals should not cannibalize your time; they should be given less priority. There are three important considerations when setting your priorities. Each of them is discussed next and is outlined in Figure 12.4.

Identify Your Most Important Goals

It is critical that you identify your most important goals first. These are the goals on which you should concentrate most of your time and activities. In the process of identifying your most important goals, you will also determine which of the goals are less important. These goals should not be forgotten or set aside; they will become secondary to the most important goals and will be achieved at a different rate.

Setting goals and prioritizing them are difficult tasks and require you to make tough decisions. Consider the adult student who has children and a spouse. The student knows how important it is to study and get good grades, but the parent also knows how important it is to spend quality time with his or her children. The choice is obviously left to the student/parent who must determine which goals have the most priority, or whether the goals can be treated equally.

Setting goals and determining priorities are difficult tasks that require making tough decisions.

Figure 12.4 **Steps in Setting Priorities**

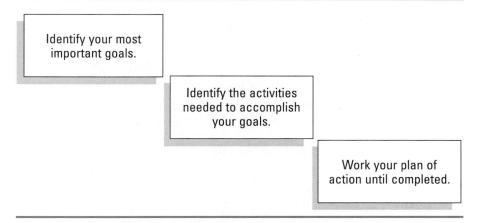

Identify your most important goals.

Identify the activities needed to accomplish your goals.

Work your plan of action until completed.

Your goals should be written down regardless of whether they are short term, intermediate, or long term. Written goals can be kept where they are visible, and you can refer to them often. If you write your goals on small note cards, you can arrange them easily in order of priority. You can be in control of the situation, rather than having to rely on recall as you progress through your goals. You could establish a color-coding system, with one color note card for the top priority goals, another for lower priority goals, and still another for the lowest priority goals.

Identify Activities to Accomplish Goals

Your goals won't be achieved unless you take action. Sometimes you might find it difficult to imagine what has to be done to achieve some of your goals. Even so, it is critical that you develop a **work list** of activities to help you accomplish the goals. This list may change as you work toward the goal, but that shouldn't deter you; keep moving toward the end.

Many activities on your work list could take a long time to complete. To prevent this from becoming overwhelming or discouraging, complete a **to-do list** each day of just what you must accomplish during that day. Your list might include several activities related to more than one of your goals. After you have completed the list, you need to prioritize these items by importance or urgency, beginning at the top of the list. It is always best if you complete one activity before you go on to the next. By doing this, you will steadily accomplish small steps toward achieving your bigger goal. When developing a to-do list, it is good to

▶ prepare a new list each day.

▶ be realistic within the time frame available to you.

▶ think of the demands that will be placed upon you by others and by your schedule that is already in place.

work list-a list of tasks which must be completed to achieve a goal

to-do list-a daily list of activities to be completed

► schedule in a little free time for possible interruptions or getting sidelined.

► carry items over to the next day if you can't complete them and they are still important.

► consider whether the activity must be done by you or whether someone else could just as easily do it.

► stay with the activity until it is done. If you can't complete it on the specified day, you may have tried to do too much.

Work Your Plan

Successful time managers work consciously to complete the tasks that are important to make progress toward achieving the larger goal. You must deliberately weigh the importance of the demands of others and their impact upon you and your goals. If you set aside your plans for the day to accommodate someone else, when will you be able to complete what you have on your list? Did you build in time for such interruptions knowing that they are likely occurrences? After working with to-do lists and work plans, you will be able to determine how much flexible time must be included.

Persistence is important, especially if you are just beginning to think about managing your time by using goals, priorities, and work lists. Beginners often become frustrated because they set goals that are too lofty or try to do too much in one day. Goals and lists must be realistic within the capability and time constraints of the individual.

To aid the completion of tasks and duties, set schedules for times during the day you would like to begin and end your tasks, making sure the tasks relate to your goals. For example, you might determine that you could have six pages of a 20-page paper entered in the computer and saved to a disk if you begin at 9:30 A.M. and finish at 10:15 A.M., and then you will have time for a short break before a 10:30 A.M. class. You will finish the paper after class and will then move on to another activity on your to-do list. Your highest priority goals must be achieved first.

When scheduling time, you must realize you have time that only you control and you also have time that others control. The time that you control is your time and no one else can tell you what you must do. You can make your own decisions about how you will use this time. You may be influenced, however, by your own feelings about what you think you should be doing and your guilt if you are not doing what you think should be done.

Time controlled by others is the time taken up by activities given to you by others; you have little control over the time needed to complete the activities. There are ways to control this time, such as quitting your job, but that may not be realistic. So, you must include the time that is controlled by others into your schedule. Your job, or whatever you do that is influenced by others, will determine how you schedule to allow for time that is controlled by others.

G ina Rowan was an office worker at Hickory Pointe Convalescent Center in Cambridge, Massachusetts. She had held this job for about four years. She was getting more frustrated with her work as her new supervisor of two months started giving her more tasks to perform in a week than she felt she could complete in a month. Gina didn't know how she could meet the deadlines that were imposed upon her. Besides, she really wanted to learn the new piece of data base software her office had just received, because she could use it to simplify all the mailing she had to complete. She wasn't allowed to work overtime and was told she shouldn't take work home.

Gina didn't know how to approach her supervisor to let her know she was being overloaded, but she did know that if she approached her, the supervisor would reward her with more work. The supervisor had quickly developed a reputation for unfair treatment of employees who questioned her or suggested better methods for completing the work. What Gina did know was that she had to get better control of her time; but where should she begin?

Time Intrusions

You have learned that some of the difficulties with time management are caused by external factors while others are self-induced. The self-induced factors are those that only you can control, such as **procrastination,** never saying no, and others.

procrastination-delaying what needs to be done

Procrastination

"Never do today what you can put off until tomorrow" is the motto for the chronic procrastinator. And, it seems that tomorrow never comes, or there is always another tomorrow. Why do people delay tasks until another time?

One reason for procrastination is the fear of failure. Most people don't want to fail and when confronted with a new or difficult task, they would rather delay it than get started on it so it will be over. There is often considerable risk involved in completing new and difficult tasks, and many people are not willing to risk the unknown. It takes them time to get the courage to get started.

Some people are afraid of success. Success breeds success, meaning that if a person is successful at one thing, he or she might be given greater responsibilities the next time. All this leads to more duties, more responsibility, and more stress.

Some people dislike their jobs intensely or don't want to complete certain responsibilities related to their work. Disdain for jobs and tasks causes people to delay beginning or completing what must be done. Not many people like cleaning bathrooms, but someone must do the task or the consequences could be unpleasant. It is the kind of task that is easy to put off until later, or perhaps not do at all in hopes that someone else will get the job done.

Persons who procrastinate usually inflict more pressures and problems on themselves than others do on them. They rush around at the last minute to get jobs done. They are often late for meetings, class, church, and other activities. When given responsibilities, the procrastinators will usually rush to complete them after they finally get started and their work is often less than adequate because they didn't take the time necessary to do a good job. They won't have time to correct mistakes or improve their work because of a late start.

If you are a procrastinator, you need to set deadlines. If the project is long term, break it down into smaller units. Set intermediate deadlines and stick to them even if the entire project doesn't need to be completed for some time. Set starting times for the next unit of the project so that there is less tendency to delay beginning. Stick to the deadlines and reward yourself for meeting your deadlines.

The cure for procrastination is in your own hands. You need to recognize that only you can cause change and that you must want to correct the problem. When you have a task to complete, you must decide to tackle it right away. There will be tasks and projects that will take a long time to complete and sometimes you will get tired of them; however, persistence is necessary to get started and follow through to completion. There is great satisfaction in completing an activity with time to spare and knowing that you have done a superior job and have had time to correct any deficiencies.

Inability to Say NO

Many people have difficulty saying no when asked to do something. They may be told that a task just takes a couple of hours a week and that their help is really needed, or that it will only take a few minutes a day and that it is really important they are involved. This seems to go on forever until the point is reached where the person has said yes so many times to these small demands that his or her day is filled with work for others and the person has no time for his or her own work.

The main reason some people are asked to do so much by others is because of the talent or capability they possess. If you have a skill that is in high demand, others will want to use it, and you will have to learn to say no. If you have the skill coupled with the desire to please others, it becomes worse because they know you won't turn them down when you are asked.

A person's desire to please others, the need to feel wanted, and the satisfaction of feeling needed all lead to the inability to say no and to become overloaded to the point of not being able to manage one's own time. Perhaps there are better ways to feel needed and it isn't necessary to take on so many different tasks. Stop to think about why you are about to say yes to someone's request. If you say no, could you do a better job with what you already have in progress, or is it possible that you might have a little time for something you want to do for yourself? Don't be timid, learn to say no to others' requests.

I Can Do That

"I'm terrific," you may think, "just give me more to do. I can get the work done, and it will be just as good as someone else's work." Never mind that you already have enough going on to last for a lifetime. Some people think they can do everything and anything that comes along. They are filled with confidence in their abilities and often feel that no one else can do a job as well as they can. They take on so many responsibilities that they are too busy to take the time to plan and get organized.

For the person who wants to take on everything, there are so many pressures to meet deadlines that tasks are finished late and many projects are done poorly.

Sara Rawlings is an overly confident sales manager for Buttercup Supplies in Little Rock, Arkansas. In addition to being a sales manager and spending at least two or three days on the road arriving home late in the evening, Sara has three children and a husband and takes care of many of the homemaking chores. She is also an active scout leader and a member of her church board of directors and teaches ballet on Saturdays. Sara is a prime candidate for physical and mental health problems if she doesn't change her lifestyle. She is trying to do too much and should cut back on some of her activities.

If you are one of these people who attempt to do too much, you need to learn to budget your time and realize that others can also do a good job. Even if someone else doesn't carry through with an assignment, is it your duty to pick it up and do it? The answer is no, unless you are the person who has the responsibility for seeing the assignment is done and the person who didn't carry through is someone to whom you delegated the job. Self-confidence should be used to do an outstanding job on fewer activities, not to grab everything that comes along.

Telephone Interruptions

How many times when you were interrupted by telephone calls have you mumbled something under your breath that shouldn't be heard by others? How many times can you let the telephone ring before you have to answer it or it will drive you crazy? And, how many times did you receive a call that you didn't really care to receive, perhaps from someone selling something that you can live without and will pay far too much for if you say yes?

With telephone answering machines and voice mail, it is possible to screen calls that you don't want or that aren't urgent. You can listen to the incoming call and if it is someone you must talk to immediately, pick up the telephone and answer it. If it is someone you don't need to talk to, you can continue with your work. If the caller leaves a message, you can make a decision to return the call at a time that is convenient for you. You may find that many of the calls you receive will be eliminated because the caller will not leave a message. Keep in mind that the caller doesn't know if you are there or what you are doing.

If you do answer the call because it is important, or because you can't get over the compulsion to answer before the end of the first ring, be efficient on the telephone. Keep your calls to the business at hand; when the discussion is done, terminate the phone call. Try to limit each call; most phone calls can be completed in no more than three minutes. Anything over three minutes is probably social conversation.

When you are the one placing the telephone call, get to the point immediately. There is no need to chat about the weather when that isn't the purpose of the call. If you have a question about supplies that have been ordered, ask the question. The person on the other end will know right away why you are calling and that you have a purpose. He or she will be less likely to want to socialize. The call might sound like this: "Hello, this is Kenton Kershaw in Altus, Oklahoma. I ordered four dozen boxes of file folders three weeks ago and haven't received them. Would you tell me the status of my order?" The person on the other end knows that Kenton has a purpose—he wants to find out where his file folders are—and he probably doesn't care if it is 40 or 112 degrees in Altus. It is not rude to get to the point and to get your business done.

Suppose someone calls you and the caller's first question is, "How is your weather? I hear there is a lot of rain in Missouri right now." You could easily answer with a statement such as "Yes, we are having a lot of rain. How can I help you out?" It is not rude to direct the caller to the purpose of the call, and you will be sending a message that you don't have time for idle chatter. If the caller persists in pursuing social conversation, you may have to let him or her know that you are in the middle of a project and must meet your deadlines. There are always exceptions: for example, if a coworker calls and you want to maintain good rapport, you might have to visit a short time before the coworker gets to the point of the call. Don't let the social chatter go on too long.

Chatty Coworkers

Imagine yourself sitting in your office or at your work area when you hear that unwanted question, "Hey, how are things going with you? Do you have a second?" Before you can think of anything else to say, you respond, "It's going well, come on in." Did you really mean that, or would you have preferred to say, "I'm great, but I am really busy right now. Could we visit later when I have more time?"

One of the biggest time wasters includes uninvited visitors, people who may mean well but don't understand or care that you are busy. They may stop by for brief but frequent visits, or they may stop for longer visits.

Either way, they take up much of your time and are an intrusion. These intruders are our friends, perhaps people we commute with or socialize with on weekends. How can we turn them away without offending them?

When someone interrupts you, find out what the person has on his or her mind. If it is something that can wait, schedule a time when it is more convenient for you to meet with the person. If the visit is purely social, let the individual know that you need to meet deadlines and you would like to visit at another time. Some problems can probably be handled by the intruder or by someone else. You should suggest that the intruder spend more time solving the problem or you can refer the intruder to a more appropriate person. Is that passing the buck? Not if the other person is better able and more qualified to handle the situation. If the question is brief and can be solved quickly, take care of it so that you can get on with your own project.

Following an intrusion, it takes a short period to get back on track with your own work. Alec Mackenzie suggests that after an intrusion, it could take as long as three times the length of the intrusion to regain focus and concentration for the project that was interrupted.[2]

One possible solution to interruptions by coworkers and others is to close your door. It is more difficult for people to intrude if they must knock and be invited into an office. If you share a work area or cubical with others, you will not have the luxury of shutting out intruders. Try to handle these intruders by placing a note on your cubicle asking not to be disturbed, block the entrance with a chair, or think of some other friendly method to let the intruders know that you are busy. You must gain control of your time, so don't let others intrude because they have less to do than you or they may not care if they get their work done. And most important, don't you be an intruder either. If you intrude, you are extending an invitation to others to reciprocate.

The Meeting Syndrome

How could our society exist without meetings? Probably much better! We have meetings at work; we have meetings for volunteer organizations; we have meetings for children's activities. Sometimes we spend more time at meetings than we do in productive work. The feeling that many people have is that most meetings take much longer than required, and much of the meeting time is wasted. Many reports that are given or read could have been distributed without a meeting. Too much time is spent on topics that are unimportant or irrelevant. There are several tips that can make a meeting more productive.

► When planning or conducting a meeting, start on time, have an agenda that specifies times for each topic, and stick to the topics and the time.

► If people are late, start without them and don't take time to fill them in on what has happened. If they want to participate in a discussion, they will know that they must arrive on time.

---

[2]Adapted, with permission of the publisher, from *THE TIME TRAP* by Alec Mackenzie, © 1990 Alec Mackenzie. Published by AMACOM, a division of the American Management Association. All rights reserved.

- If some topics aren't of importance to everyone, organize the agenda so the topics that concern everyone are handled first. Don't ask people who are not concerned with the topics to stay for the meeting. If they are dismissed, they can return to their work area and be productive.

- Don't attend meetings that aren't of importance to you or don't have any impact on what you are doing. You can rationalize this to your supervisor by saying that since none of the agenda items concern your work, it would be better to remain productive than to sit and listen to others.

Being Disorganized

Disorganization can be the cause of many stressful situations. Papers and folders stacked all over a desk or the floor are not necessarily the sign of a busy person. More likely they are the sign of a disorganized person. If you can imagine someone like this, and perhaps you do know someone who is disorganized, think about how often the person has to search for something that is needed to complete a project. A person may go through the same stacks of papers several times a day searching for missing pages that are needed to start, continue, or end different projects.

This same disorganized person is the one who will probably come to a meeting late, forget an appointment with the boss, or never finish a job because the details that need to be completed were on the tablet that soaked up spilled coffee and are now illegible. People who live and work like this appear to be in constant chaos. They never seem to get a good grip on a situation, and many opportunities pass before them because they are in such a state of disarray.

Figure 12.5 **A Personal Time Schedule**

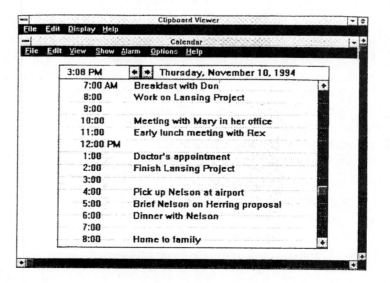

Keeping things shelved and filed and focusing on just the task at hand can be critical to time management.

The disorganized person needs to begin by taking the time to get organized. This will seem like an insurmountable task, but it is essential. The desk must be cleaned and papers must be filed. It will be necessary to create files for incomplete tasks and they must be organized by priority. The desk should contain only current projects that are being worked on. Other projects that need to be done should be kept in files until they are ready to be addressed.

To avoid disorganization, use a schedule to guide you through the day and be sure to prioritize what you want to get done. A systematic approach to staying organized will make you efficient and keep you on task. There are many commercially produced planning systems available. You may be able to use one of these, or you may want to develop your own system that is unique to your situation. Regardless of the system you select, you should be able to gain control of your time and not let disorganization control you.

Too Much Paperwork

Paperwork includes letters, memos, reports, forms, and other forms of communication that could easily control your time. A discussion of the mechanics of writing good communications is not included here since it was included in previous chapters; but as Roy Alexander suggests, when communicating you must use clear, simple words and statements that everyone can understand. The goal of completing communications or any type of paperwork is to say what must be said without excessive verbiage.[3]

---

[3] Roy Alexander. *Commonsense Time Management.* New York: AMACOM (American Management Association), 1992.

Concerns with Time

There are many situations in life that can cause frustration when a person's time is impacted and infringed upon by others. One of those moments often comes when you are a patient having to wait for a late physician. Waiting 15 or 30 minutes or even longer can often wreck a planned schedule for the rest of the day. The American Medical Association reports that the average length of time patients spend in the waiting room is 20.6 minutes, and the wait for specialists is usually longer.[1] There is concern about the ethics of keeping patients waiting—especially those who might be just as busy as the doctor. Solutions to this kind of infringement upon your time may have to be as drastic as switching to another doctor.

Another situation that can cause frustration and stress for individuals is a company that is not flexible enough to accommodate employees' needs. Waiting in a doctor's waiting room may seem like a small problem to a working mother or father compared to handling their children's emergencies. It used to be that mothers were the ones primarily concerned with having flexibility to be able to take care of children in need; however, today men are also expressing more need to have flexible hours to take care of family needs. A survey found

Businesses seem to be inundated with paperwork that must in some way be managed before it manages the workers in the business. One records management director of a large international corporation spoke of moving 75,000 boxes of records when the records facility was being moved, and the need to move without other workers in other divisions knowing it was occurring. If others in the corporation knew that all the records were in that many boxes, they would panic for fear of not being able to retrieve the records they needed on short notice. The move was successful!

While you personally might not have 75,000 boxes of papers to manage, it is critical that you create a system that will allow you to manage your own paperwork in an efficient manner. Neither you nor others should have to sort through files and stacks of materials to find what is needed. Papers should be handled as quickly as possible, and when people are finished with one activity file, they should put it away and move on to the next activity. A system of priorities as discussed earlier will help determine what needs to be done first.

This point is illustrated very well in a discussion by B. J. Hateley in which she calls herself "the clutter queen." She usually kept her work in disarray on her desk, with stacks of files and papers all around her. She feared that being organized would drain her of her creativity. She wouldn't

that 79 percent of the working fathers at Johnson and Johnson who have used the child care center provided by the company say the facility is the major reason they want to stay with the company.[2] The center allows flexibility in scheduling because it is on-site. To what extent should companies accommodate working parents to allow them to have more time to spend with their families?

Another company that recognizes the need for flexible scheduling for its employees is the publisher of the Official Airline Guides in Oak Brook, Illinois. This small company has established a core set of operational hours and allows its employees to determine their start and stop times, and in some cases their lunch breaks, around these core hours. This flexible scheduling allows the employees to attend to the needs of their children and other family matters, such as waiting in doctors' offices, and still work a full schedule.[3]

[1] Marilyn Chase. "Whose Time Is Worth More: Yours or the Doctor's?" The Wall Street Journal. October 24, 1994, B1.

[2] Staff. "Men Need Family Time Too." Working Mother. October, 1993, 24.

[3] Sarah Hutter. "Flexibility at Work." Working Mother. March, 1994, 26, 28.

make plans or commitments because she might not have felt like doing anything on the day for which she committed herself. After receiving some training on time management, she discovered the importance of planning, assigning priorities, and making lists of ideas and goals. She was surprised that she was able to continue the good practices of managing her time more effectively for an extended period of time.[4]

Key Points Summary

- Time seems to be an elusive creature which is never available when we need it the most. At least that is a myth that has been perpetuated for years, when in reality everyone has the same amount of time available to them. Some people manage and use their time more effectively than others.

- To manage time effectively, you first need to understand how you manage yourself. Determine the pressures you have on your day, each and every day.

[4] B. J. Hateley, "The Clutter Queen Loses Her Crown." Training. June, 1993, 96.

- To gain control of your time rather than be controlled by time, start by tracking your habits. The best method is to keep a time log of a typical day. The time log should be quite detailed to be revealing and therefore more useful. A critical analysis of your time usage is the important next step.

- After you have determined that better organization will help you gain control of your time, you must establish some goals that you want to achieve. The goals must be in writing. Goals can relate to personal needs, work activities, or anything that is occurring in your life.

- After you have written your goals, prioritize them in order of importance, that is, in the order in which you want to achieve them. Identify activities which you can follow to accomplish your goals. From the activities, complete a to-do list for one day at a time. Complete the items on the list before moving to other activities. Stick to your plan to achieve your goals.

- Having too many intrusions makes it difficult for people to follow plans to stay on task and accomplish goals. Some examples of the intruders in our day include procrastination, never saying no, attempting too much, telephone interruptions, talkative coworkers, too many meetings, disorganization, and paperwork.

Key Terms

externally enacted goals

goals

intermediate goals

internally enacted goals

long-term goals

procrastination

short-term goals

specific and measurable outcome

time lines

time log

time management

to-do list

work list

Discussion Questions

1. Talk with your classmates and create a list of all the reasons why your jobs or tasks go uncompleted. When you have compiled your list, examine the reasons to see if they are excuses or if they are legitimate. How can better time management help you improve your completion ratio and speed on your activities?

2. Keep a time log for one week. Create your log using the example provided in this chapter as a model. After you have completed the log, analyze it to see how you actually spent your time. Be sure to go about your daily activities just as though you were not keeping

a log. Be honest with the information you record and when you have analyzed it discuss the results with your class. What kinds of similarities or differences are there with your colleagues?

3. Why is it important to have goals for different lengths of time? Why not just set a goal for a project and go for it? What are the benefits of having goals for each day?

4. Once you have set your goals, you should identify the activities that need to be completed to reach your goals. The activities might fall into the category of a "to-do list" for each day. Discuss some of the considerations when developing this list.

5. What are the benefits of setting schedules that allocate beginning and ending times for your activities?

6. Identify several intruders upon your time. For each of them, list the methods you could follow to overcome the intrusion and to make your time more useful.

Chapter *13*

Learning Objectives

Upon completing this chapter, you should be able to:

● Describe diversity in the American workplace.

● Understand what constitutes harassment and its legal implications.

● Describe the economic and psychological factors of prejudice.

● Develop a harassment audit to be implemented in the workplace.

● Understand the implications of the Americans with Disabilities Act.

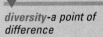

diversity-a point of difference

A Workplace of Mutual Respect

In 1980, the Howard R. Green Company, a small consulting engineering firm located in Cedar Rapids, Iowa, was a very typical professional services organization. Engineering has traditionally been a male-dominated profession. Even today less than eight percent of graduate engineers are women, although this percentage is up considerably from 1980. Typically, in 1980 the racial makeup of this firm's employees was 100 percent white; all managers and supervisors were male; and all engineers and technical staff were male. There were three female workers—all in clerical positions.

Today the firm is considerably larger than it was in 1980. In order to grow, the Howard R. Green Company hired talent instead of tradition. Eight engineering positions and four other upper level positions are held by women. Four engineers are from India, including one of the firm's principals. Several clerical positions are held by males. An African-American engineering designer is taking educational leave to return to school to become an electrical engineer at the age of 42.

*D*iversity

Diversity in the workplace is a reality for the Howard R. Green Company. According to Dennis Schrag, Manager of Human Resources, "Our business is based exclusively on the talents and capabilities of employees. Even with its midwest location in a community with less than three percent minority, we hire the best people we can. We just don't accept any other factor except talent."

Managing diversity is an idea whose time has come. More and more, employers of all kinds are awakening to the fact that a diverse workforce is not a burden, but a potential strength. One of the reasons for this awakening is the increasing diverse marketplace. Today, as you call United Airlines to make flight reservations, the automated attendant asks if you would feel more comfortable talking to a

Spanish-speaking customer service representative. Who can best understand and serve this changing market? It takes a diverse workforce at all levels.

Take the test given in Figure 13.1 to check your understanding of the changing market. The answers are provided at the end of the chapter.

Figure 13.1 **What's Your Diversity IQ?**

1. Among 31 million African-American consumers, the percentage who feels that most commercials and print ads are designed for white people is

   a. 20%   **b.** 30%   **c.** 50%   **d.** 60%

   Source: Timm, Paul. "50 Ways to Win New Customers." Careers Press, 1993.

2. In the 1990–91 recession, a net job loss was experienced only by
   a. Hispanics   **b.** women
   c. African Americans   **d.** none of these

   Source: "A Guide to the U.S. Census." U.S. Department of Commerce, June 1993.

3. When women communicate with a man in the workplace, most women prefer to stand
   a. closer to the man than he would prefer to stand from them.
   b. further from the man than he would prefer to stand from them.
   c. the same distance from the man that he would prefer to stand from them.

   Source: Tannen, Deborah. You Just Don't Understand. Morrow, 1990.

4. One of every four businesses is owned by a woman.

   a. true   **b.** false

   Source: "The New Economics Force." Nine-to-Five Business Women's Union, 1992.

5. According to the 1991 "Glass Ceiling Report" by the U.S. Department of Labor, the few women and minorities who were in upper management positions were almost always in
   a. line positions such as operation and production.
   b. line positions such as sales.
   c. staff positions such as human resources and public relations.
   d. temporary positions.

   Source: "Glass Ceiling Report." U.S. Dept. of Labor, 1991.

6. Corporate managers from diverse Asian-American backgrounds have consistently observed that

   a. they have benefited from positive assumptions about their work ethic and skills in being given fair opportunities for advancement.

Figure 13.1 continued

   b. they have been discriminated against in all areas of organizational advancement.

   c. they have been stereotyped as being good at technical tasks but weak in people management.

   d. they have been promoted to positions of managerial responsibility but have been excluded from areas of technical expertise.

   _____

   Source: "Japan in the Mind of America." Time. *Feb. 10, 1992.*

7. Recent surveys of corporate managers, university professors, doctors, lawyers, and first-line supervisors have revealed that in a comparable job, women earn
   a. 1 dollar for every dollar that a man earns.
   b. 80 cents for every dollar that a man earns.
   c. 40 cents for every dollar that a man earns.
   d. 70 cents for every dollar that a man earns.

   _____

   Source: "A Guide to the U.S. Census." U.S. Department of Commerce, *June 1993.*

8. Among Americans with assets of $500,000 or more, the percentage of women is approximately

   a. 10%   **b.** 25%   **c.** 40%   **d.** 65%

   _____

   Source: Foster, Kent. "Estate Planning." The Business Exchange. *vol. 2, April 1993.*

9. According to the U.S. Census Report, the percentage of households in which no adult speaks English fluently is about

   a. 42%   **b.** 23%   **c.** 36%   **d.** 43%

   _____

   Source: "A Guide to the U.S. Census." U.S. Department of Commerce, *June 1993.*

10. According to the study released in December 1993 by the National School Boards Association, the region with the most integrated schools was the
   a. Northeast   **b.** Northwest
   c. South   **d.** Midwest
   e. Southwest   **f.** Far West

   _____

   Source: Arbogast, Ted. "Preparing Expert Teachers." Educational Horizons. *April 1994.*

11. From 1980 to 1992, the percentage of women in the top 20 jobs in Fortune 500 companies increased from
   a. 10% to 35.5%   **b.** 1% to 7.5%
   c. 20% to 41%   **d.** 10% to 16.5%

   _____

   Source: Adler-Yates Survey. Pepperdine University, 1993.

12. In 1967 women represented 2.6 percent of the MBA graduates. In 1992 women made up approximately

    a. 10%   **b.** 50%   **c.** 30%

Source: Adler-Yates Survey. Pepperdine University, 1993.

13. Among the so-called Hispanic groups in the United States, the largest group is

    a. Puerto Rican   **b.** Cuban

    c. Mexican   **d.** other

Source: "A Guide to the U.S. Census." U.S. Department of Commerce, June 1993.

14. According to U.S. Census Bureau estimates, the largest minority group in the United States in the year 2000 will be

    a. African Americans   **b.** Hispanic Americans

    c. Asian Americans   **d.** European Americans

Source: "A Guide to the U.S. Census." U.S. Department of Commerce, June 1993.

15. As of November 1993, minorities constituted 44% of the total United States workforce. The percentage of minorities in top-level executive jobs, however, was

    a. 12%   **b.** 9%   **c.** 5%   **d.**   2%

Source: "A Guide to the U.S. Census." U.S. Department of Commerce, June 1993.

A second and even more urgent reason for the increased interest in managing diversity in the workplace is the stark facts of demographics. The growth in the United States labor force and its customer base will in the foreseeable future be largely composed of women, minorities, and immigrants. They will constitute about 85 percent of the new entrants into the workforce, according to the landmark Hudson Institute Study. In an article entitled "Tough Customers" published in the May 1994 *Human Resource Executive,* customer service is discussed. "With more diversity comes different expectations of service, as well as possible language barriers." Customer service training consultants are adding diversity to their curriculum because customers are varied and expect personalized service. Employers realize they must attract, retain, and promote a full spectrum of people to be successful. So great is their need that advice on the management of diversity has suddenly become a growth industry.

Some employers have developed special programs to deal with the workforce diversity issue. Some of these programs, known as **valuing differences programs,** are geared to individual and interpersonal levels. The objective is to enhance interpersonal relationships among employees and to minimize blatant expressions of racism and sexism. Often valuing

valuing differences programs-intended to enhance interpersonal relationships among employees and minimize blatant racism and sexism differences initiates focus on the ways that men and women or people of different races reflect differences in values, attitudes, behavior styles, ways of thinking, and cultural backgrounds. These educational sessions can vary in length from one day to several days or can occur on an ongoing basis. They usually concentrate on one or several of these general objectives.

► Fostering awareness and acceptance of differences.

► Fostering a greater understanding of the nature and dynamics of individual differences.

► Helping participants understand their own feelings and attitudes about people who are different.

► Exploring how differences might be tapped as assets in the workplace.

U.S. West Telecommunications based in Denver, Colorado, has implemented such a human relations training program for many of its employees. It includes heightened awareness of minority groups. Figure 13.2 shows the increase in human relations training programs among 55 corporations.

Figure 13.2 **Steps to Sensitivity**

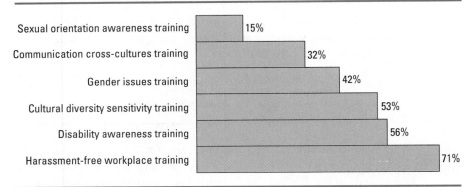

Sexual orientation awareness training	15%
Communication cross-cultures training	32%
Gender issues training	42%
Cultural diversity sensitivity training	53%
Disability awareness training	56%
Harassment-free workplace training	71%

*E*mployer Responsibilities

Providing a workplace free from **harassment** is one of the basic responsibilities of an employer. Although sexual harassment has received most of the public attention, harassment takes many forms. As employers add staff from a variety of ethnic, religious, age, and cultural backgrounds, maintaining a harmonious workplace is critical. Given our increasingly litigious society, it is inevitable that court decisions related to other forms of harassment will increase.

Seniors, immigrants, and employees with disabilities are taking an increasing role in the workplace and might suffer from a hostile environment. To avoid future litigation, prudent managers curb such an environment. To reduce the likelihood of harassment charges, several proactive approaches have been employed.

Employees need to accomodate seniors, immigrants, and employees with disabilities in the workplace.

Employee Handbook

An employer is obligated to take all necessary steps to see that harassment does not occur. A good way of doing this is to incorporate a policy on all forms of harassment into an employee handbook and then see that managers clearly communicate the information to employees. Managers are expected to enforce the no-harassment policy.

The handbook policy should express strong disapproval of harassment and not only provide guidelines, but also outline specific complaint procedures and the actions management will follow once a complaint is received. Top management needs to clearly indicate to all managers that the organization is serious about eliminating harassment and that no form of harassment will be tolerated under any conditions.

The Equal Employment Opportunity Commission offers the following guidelines for preventing harassment.

► Affirmatively raise the subject.

► Express strong disapproval of harassment.

► Develop appropriate sanctions for offenders.

► Inform employees of their rights.

► Develop methods to sensitize employees about harassment.

While at work an employee made a crude remark to a coworker. The coworker said he felt humiliated by the comment, which referred to his religion in a demeaning way. The employee who made the remark had been warned repeatedly in the past for inappropriate speech and behavior, and on one occasion had received a three-day suspension for using profanity.

Chapter 13 • A Workplace of Mutual Respect

After a thorough investigation of the incident, including a testimony by a supervisor who overheard the remark, the employer discharged the employee for violating its policy against harassment. The written policy specifically prohibited derogatory words concerning an employee's religion and imposed disciplinary action up to, and including, termination for infractions of the rule.

The employee protested the severity of the penalty, claiming that he was "just joking around." He also said he did not know the employee was taking it seriously.

The employer argued that the serious nature of the offense and the employee's past record of harassment justified the decision to discharge him. In addition, the employer claimed that it had a legal obligation to enforce its policy in view of the fact that a local ordinance also prohibited harassment related to religion. The discharge was upheld.

Getting All Employees Involved

A major challenge for all employers is to assimilate a variety of employees into the mainstream of corporate life. Women and minorities are sometimes excluded from social activities or left out of informal (yet important) communication networks. The result appears to be a sense of isolation, lower organizational commitment, and ultimately a decision to seek employment in a more hospitable environment. For example, a woman feeling left out may think that "a lot of emphasis is placed on getting along with others in senior management. As a woman, I do not fit into the group of males who go to lunch together and play golf together. These are the guys who get the promotions."

As workforce diversity increases, perhaps exclusion and isolation will disappear. In the meantime, a few organizations are encouraging women's support groups, black caucuses, and other ways to help subgroups tie into social and communications networks. More importantly, organizations are becoming more sensitive to sponsoring social activities that will allow full participation by all employees. Organizations that continue to exclude segments of their workforce risk sending the subtle message that some employees are less valued, less important, and less welcomed.

Discrimination

Making a **prejudgment** is normal, for we cannot handle every event freshly in its own right. If we did, what good would past experience be? Although prejudgments help give order to our daily living, our minds have a habit of assimilating as much as they can into categories, which can cause irrational judgments. A person acts with prejudice because of his or her personality, which has been formed by family, school, and community environments.

prejudgment-an assessment of a person or situation without the requisite information

Prejudice has been defined as an attitude, not an act; an opinion based partly on observation and partly on ignorance, fear, and cultural patterns, none of which has a rational basis. A prejudiced person tends to think of members of a group of people as being all the same, without consideration of individual differences. This kind of thinking gives rise to stereotypes. **Stereotypes,** like prejudices, are based partly on observation and partly on ignorance and tradition. For example, a person who assumes all women are overly emotional is subscribing to a widely held but false stereotype of women.

Stereotypes are difficult to overcome because they have developed over long periods of time and because so many people share them, giving them an illusion of rationality. However, many people today are trying to rid themselves of stereotyped thinking about other people. This effort shows a growing consciousness that people are individuals and can and should be treated as such.

Economic and Psychological Basis of Prejudice

"The Koreans came into this neighborhood and took any job that was offered to them. They don't care about the pay or conditions. They took jobs away from us and now they are buying up our houses. They just don't think or act like us. They are different and I don't want my kids involved with them," explained Melissa Cartwright, a 29-year-old Caucasian single mother of two.

As in the case of Melissa Cartwright's prejudice, the basis of prejudice toward a subgroup of society is often found in economic or psychological factors. In most free market countries, a diversity of social groups is typical. The **social mobility concept** says that as one subgroup moves up in economic terms, it is replaced by a less fortunate subgroup who is seeking a better way of life.

Since the mid-1800s, various ethnic groups immigrated to the United States in waves.

Social distress, economic hardships, and lack of opportunity forced August Masterpole to leave Fasalto, Italy, when he was 22 years old and move to New York City with his wife and four-month-old daughter. To earn passage from Italy in 1910, he worked three years in the coal mines of South America performing hard manual labor that was dangerous and dirty. He saved enough money to move his family to America. He was one of hundreds of thousands of Italians immigrating to the United States.

When he reached Ellis Island, he was quickly processed and sent to an Italian neighborhood in the Bronx, New York. The neighborhood had been home for many years to a Romanian group, but after one generation in the United States, some of the Romanians had acquired enough wealth to move to better housing and better jobs. The Italians, hungry for a new

prejudice-an attitude based partially on ignorance, fear, and cultural patterns

stereotypes-thinking of members of a group as all the same without consideration of individual differences

social mobility concept-says that as one subgroup moves up in economic terms, it is replaced by a less fortunate subgroup who is seeking a better way of life

Chapter 13 · A Workplace of Mutual Respect

start, would quickly take whatever the Romanians vacated—in terms of jobs, housing, and material goods. The new life offered opportunity not dreamed possible in Italy.

But the Italians and Romanians were very different from one another. They had different religions, different languages, different social values, different art and music, and different appearances. As more and more Italians like August Masterpole moved to the Bronx, those Romanians who remained felt threatened. Their homes, jobs, and social structures were being impacted by the new immigrants. There were fights. There were work conflicts. There were threats. Why would an employer hire a Romanian for a job when an Italian would work for 25 percent less? In one generation, the Italians would face a repeat of this replacement when the next wave of immigrant groups landed at Ellis Island.

In more recent times, the United States has seen similar social waves of immigrants from Latin-American countries, Korea, Southeast Asia, and the Caribbean.

Many ethnic groups that immigrated to the United States since the 1800s have faced prejudice.

Unit 3 · Problems in Human Relations

Tension between subgroups is often a result of economic competition for jobs, shelter, and social status. When physical differences and religious beliefs, ethical values, and traditions differ, subgroups can feel threatened and sometimes take inappropriate actions.

Unfortunately, there is a macroeconomic gain for employers in aiding and abetting discrimination in the workforce. Competition for jobs among workers can help employers lower wages and neglect working conditions. Employers often threaten striking workers with the prospect of being replaced since there are usually members of minority groups, having previously little or no chance at jobs, who are willing to take jobs that pay lower wages. This situation is ripe for social unrest. Until we have an economy that can assure jobs and a living wage for everyone, competition for survival will tend to express itself in prejudices and discrimination.

As the United States is becoming more involved in the international markets, business managers are increasingly becoming aware that discrimination can make a disastrous impression on the potential buyers and sellers abroad. When we preach democracy but practice discrimination, our credibility is lost. Establishing oil trade with Nigeria, for example, becomes more complex when Nigerians see the United States establishment discriminating against African Americans.

Racial Prejudice. From its beginning, the United States was divided by racial tensions. White settlers drove out Native Americans and set up a system of labor based on black slavery. These two types of racism are still with us today. The Native Americans were decimated so that statistically relations are not as complex as with African Americans, who are the largest ethnic minority.

Customs and Traditions: Watching for the Global Difference

The Legality of English-Only Rules

Requiring employees to speak only English at work is unnecessary in most cases and infringes on basic individual rights, opponents of such policies insist. Some employers, however, have English-only policies, claiming that they increase harmony and safety, and despite the EEOC's opposition, some courts have upheld these rules.

No federal law prohibits English-only policies in the workplace as long as they do not create a disparate impact on a race or nationality. But once an employee is off company property, then the legality of enforcing an English-only policy would be questionable. One argument in favor of English-only rules is that they allow employers to know if their workers are breaking any rules and/or harassing coworkers, something a foreign language could mask.

CONTINUED

With employees speaking foreign languages, it would be impossible to know if they are following company policies. For example, an employer cannot prevent a sexually hostile work environment if the employees are making sexual comments in a language a supervisor does not understand. Moreover, if company policies only are enforced against English-speaking workers, a disparate impact case could result.

Immigrants' rights advocates argue that an employee can be harassed in any language, but a manager will not know it until it is brought to his or her attention. They also concede there may be some jobs that are safety-sensitive, but such jobs are the exception and not the rule.

Reprinted with permission from Employment Guide, *vol, 9, No. 3, p. 18 (Jan. 31, 1994). Copyright 1994 by the Bureau of National Affairs, Inc. (800-372-1033)*

Racial differences have a complex and constantly changing impact on relationships in the workplace. With regard to organization stress, minority groups have two important effects. First, certain stressors are unique to particular minority groups. Second, several cultural and social factors magnify the impact of the stressors. Blatant racial prejudice is the most obvious stress for ethnic individuals. The impact of racist attitudes and behaviors can be magnified by a sense of inadequacy or low self-esteem.

Minority groups represent subcultures which often establish their own norms and values. These are not always understood by the majority group. For example, African Americans' social relations are sometimes characterized by an outlook which they describe as **ecosystem distrust.** Ecosystem distrust subsumes such phenomena as lower interpersonal trust and suspicion of authority figures. When this type of outlook is brought into a traditional white middle-class work environment, there can be misunderstandings and mistrust. Lack of awareness of these phenomena can easily lead to false assumptions by management about the worker. Due to cultural differences, cross-cultural training of both majority and minority groups is being conducted by many employers.

Gender Issues.   For many years, most women have felt discrimination in the workplace. This is true especially as it relates to advancement into management positions. However, more and more women are not only entering the workforce but also taking on management positions. As this happens, a new style of leadership is emerging, according to Stanley Smits of Georgia State University and Patricia Smith of Berry College.

Based on a study of the leadership roles of male and female small

ecosystem distrust-such phenomena as lower interpersonal trust and suspicion of authority figures

business owners, Smits and Smith find that female leaders influence the workplace differently from male leaders primarily because of a difference in leadership styles. The researchers observe that, in general, women exercise leadership through strong interpersonal and communication skills, and this **feminine style of leadership** tends to produce positive results. Male leadership generally is more direct, impersonal, and results focused.

For instance, the study shows that male and female small business owners instituted similar personnel policies and practices, but employees in female-owned businesses appeared to understand the policies and practices more clearly than employees in male-owned companies. Employees working for female owners were happier in their jobs, and employees of both sexes at female-owned businesses reported similar levels of job satisfaction. Because of the individual strengths of both men and women, a diverse leadership team incorporating feminine and masculine strengths will do more to help employers succeed in today's marketplace.

Another area of discrimination for women has been pay. Although the wage gap continues to narrow, women's groups urge action to achieve true pay equity as the 30th anniversary of the Equal Pay Act approaches. The Act prohibits bias on the basis of sex in payment of wages for equal work on jobs that require equal skill, effort, and responsibility.

The weekly salary of women reached a record 76 percent of men's median pay in the fourth quarter of 1992, according to data from the Labor Department Bureau of Labor Statistics. Women who usually worked full time had median earnings of $386 a week, or 76 percent of the $508 median for men. The 76 percent reading is 1.8 percentage points higher than one year earlier. The pay gap has narrowed by 13 percentage points since the fourth quarter of 1979.

Although the wage gap is narrowing, the reason may not be because women are earning more. In recent economic downturns, many high-paying manufacturing jobs have disappeared, forcing many men into jobs in service industries. These service jobs typically pay approximately minimum wage. Another study by the National Association of Female Executives concluded that men employed in predominately female fields tend to earn more than their female counterparts and are disproportionately represented in the upper ranks of those fields. For example, the nursing workforce is 93 percent female, as is bookkeeping, yet male nurses earn an average of 10 percent more than female nurses and male bookkeepers earn 16 percent more than women in that field.

The Glass Ceiling. In a survey of chief executive officers and human resource professionals, 79 percent said that there are barriers to women advancing to top levels of management. In response to a survey by Catalyst, a not-for-profit research organization that works with business to effect change for women, 81 percent cited stereotyping and preconceptions as a barrier, and 49 percent cited management's being averse to taking risks with women in management roles. Forty-seven percent cited lack of careful career development and planned job assignments for women.

feminine style of leadership-
exercising leadership through strong interpersonal and communication skills

Companies have begun to address the **glass ceiling** issue. The glass ceiling is defined as a limitation of women's ability to advance to upper level management positions. Some companies have implemented training programs to meet the professional needs of women. Corning Inc., Avon Products Inc., and Xerox Corporation are just three examples.

Some companies have awareness training seminars to meet the professional needs of women.

Corning Inc. provides racial and gender awareness training for workers. Employee coaches help female workers develop their potential. Avon Products Inc. has a workforce that is 75 percent female. Of its 40 corporate officers, 16 are women. Diversity training is a part of employee development. Xerox has a Balanced Work Force strategy that sets specific goals for women at every level. Some companies are trying to create a culture in which women can be successful.

*H*arassment in the Workplace

The **Equal Employment Opportunity Commission** is the federal government agency responsible for enforcing antidiscrimination efforts. In *Guidelines on Harassment Based on Race, Color, Religion, Gender, National Origin, Age or Disability,* the EEOC has identified what constitutes unlawful harassment. It is verbal or physical conduct that denigrates or shows hostility or aversion toward an individual because of his or her race, color, religion, gender, national origin, age, or disability; or that of his or her friends, relatives, or associates. It must also

1. Have the purpose or effect of creating an intimidating, hostile, or offensive working environment.
2. Have the purpose or effect of unreasonably interfering with an individual's work performance.
3. Otherwise adversely affect an individual's employment opportunities.

Figure 13.3 illustrates the types and number of charges that have been brought against employers.

Figure 13.3 **Types of EEOC Charges**

Issue	1993	1992	Change (%)
Race	31,695	29,648	+7.6
Sex	23,919	21,517	+11.2
Age	19,884	19,271	+3.2
Disability	15,274	1,077	+1318.1
National origin	7,454	7,179	+3.8
Religion	1,449	1,386	+4.5
Equal pay	1,334	1,288	+3.6

Source: "Data Summary Reports," Equal Employment Opportunity Commission. July 1993.

Examples of unlawful harassment include epithets, slurs, negative stereotyping, or threatening or hostile acts related to race, color, religion, gender, national origin, age, or disability. Other examples include written or graphic material placed on walls, bulletin boards, or elsewhere on the employer's premises that denigrates or shows hostility or aversion toward an individual or group. Included in this definition are acts that purport to be pranks but in reality are hostile or demeaning.

To be illegal, harassment must be sufficiently severe or pervasive to alter the conditions of employment and create an intimidating or abusive work environment. Although courts do not usually hold employers liable for violations based on isolated derogatory remarks in the workplace, many recognize that in the right context one slur can effectively destroy a working relationship and can create a hostile environment, particularly if the comment is made by a supervisor. For example, a direct supervisor's use of patently offensive and denigrating racial or ethnic slurs, even once, can rise to the level of civil rights violation.

The EEOC takes the position that an employer is under the affirmative obligation to maintain a work environment free of harassment. Conse-quently, this liability extends beyond the conduct of the supervisors, agents, and

Chapter 13 · A Workplace of Mutual Respect

coworkers to acts of nonemployees, such as independent contractors or even clients and customers.

Claiming that the employee harassed her during his off-duty hours over a ten-month period by threatening bodily harm as well as damage to her personal property, a woman filed a complaint with her employer as well as criminal charges with the local sheriff's department. On one occasion, she recorded a phone conversation in which the employee said, "I'm going to hurt you like you hurt me," and said she had "dug her own grave." The woman took his threats seriously, and she became fearful of being harmed or even killed.

The employer then launched an internal investigation of the woman's complaint, and placed the employee on administrative leave after it was learned that he had been arrested for failing to attend a court hearing on the matter. Subsequently, the employee was indicted by a grand jury for engaging in terroristic behavior. The employer asserted that letting the employee return to work would be detrimental to the order and morale of the employee's department and its relations with the victim's department.

"I swear she made that stuff up about me stalking her," insisted Harry. "We used to go out, and I would never do anything to hurt her. And even if I did, what does that have to do with my job? You can't fire me for something I did or didn't do on my own time!"

"Come on, Harry, you've been indicted by a grand jury for your threats and you didn't even bother to show up in court," replied personnel department head Arnie Goodwynn. "Now the people over in her department are understandably upset. I'm afraid there's just no way we can allow you to work for us anymore." Was the discharge for just cause?

The employee protested the discharge denying that he engaged in any misconduct. He claimed that his ex-girlfriend misinterpreted his behavior and that he never intended to harm her. The termination was ruled as legal.

Sex Discrimination

Sexual harassment in the workplace is the most noteworthy form of harassment. Female employees upset by their employer's depiction of women in a beer commercial sued their employer. In California, a man received a $1 million jury verdict against his female boss. A nominee to the United States Supreme Court faced televised allegations of graphically inappropriate sexual conduct.

Sex discrimination in employment has been illegal under state and federal law for 30 years. Nonetheless, until the mid-1980s it was not clear that a sexually charged atmosphere at work necessarily amounted to sex discrimination. Under federal law **sexual harassment** occurs when unwelcome conduct affects a person's job. Specifically, the Equal Employment Opportunity Commission defines sexual harassment as unwelcome sexual

▼
sex discrimination- bias based on gender

▼
sexual harassment- unwanted attention of a sexual nature

advances, requests for sexual favors, and other verbal or physical conduct of a sexual nature when

- ▶ lewd jokes are made
- ▶ obscene photographs are posted
- ▶ submission to such conduct is made either explicitly or implicitly a term or condition of an individual's employment, or
- ▶ submission to or rejection of such conduct by an individual is used as a basis for employment decisions affecting the individual, or
- ▶ such conduct unreasonably interferes with an individual's work performance or creates an intimidating, hostile, or offensive environment.

Nearly all of the legal debate arises in **hostile environment** cases. People disagree about hostile environment claims because touching, adult comments or jokes, and pin-ups constitute illegal sexual harassment only if unwelcome and offensive to a reasonable individual.

hostile environment-the atmosphere created by unwelcome and offensive comments, jokes, and touching

A woman claiming that she had to work harder because her male supervisor was preoccupied by an affair with a female coworker failed to establish a hostile work environment in the *Herman* v. *Western Financial Corporation* case.

The employee claimed that initially her supervisor had made sexual advances toward her. After she rejected his advances, he began an affair with another employee. The affair, coupled with the supervisor's heavy drinking, created a hostile environment, the employee charged. Many people became aware of the affair, and the situation was embarrassing for other employees, she asserted. The employee further claimed the affair unfairly resulted in increasing her workload.

In dismissing the employee's sexual harassment lawsuit, the court found no evidence that female employees were more affected by the alleged affair than male employees. The employees may have felt burdened by their supervisor's shortcomings, but the only sexual activity in the charges involved the supervisor's alleged affair. At one time the supervisor allegedly made an unwanted advance to the employee but her claim was not based on that.

Courts generally recognize that employers must be given disciplinary discretion if they are to eliminate sexual harassment. However, employers still should follow certain procedures to ensure that their actions are just. Such procedures include informing employees of the rules; notifying employees of charges against them and giving them an opportunity to respond; applying the rules equitably; and imposing penalties in proportion to the offense.

Obviously, society and the community shape what is or is not offensive to a reasonable person. Men and women may have different views on what is appropriate in a work setting. In a 1993 survey of 250 Cedar Rapids,

Testifying on Harassment: The Implications

The following letter appeared in the March 16, 1994, Dear Abby column.

Dear Abby:

My employer is being sued for sexual harassment. I and at least a dozen other employees must give a deposition very soon. We have discussed whether or not to tell what we have seen for fear of losing our jobs. Many of us would like to see the company atmosphere improve, but we are afraid to come forward.

The executives, from the top on down (including the head of personnel), have harassed some of the women and created a hostile environment here. The woman who is suing was terminated for refusing to have relations with some of the male executives.

I have recently heard there is a law in Florida called the "whistle-blower's law," which supposedly protects an

Iowa businesswomen, 75 percent reported they had observed or experienced sexual harassment in their work and nearly 50 percent had personally experienced sexual harassment.

The following preventive actions have been widely accepted as both legally defensible and effective to reduce sexual harassment in the workplace.

► Review the policy prohibiting sexual harassment.

► Review the grievance procedure.

► Investigate complaints quickly and comprehensively.

► If charges are valid, the guilty party should be punished.

► Make sure employees are familiar with the company policy.

Harassment Audits

harassment audit-designed to measure the extent to which employees understand harassment policies

To determine whether harassment exists within the organization and also to protect the organization from potential litigation, employers may conduct a confidential **harassment audit.** Although selected interviews or direct observation can be used, one or more questionnaires are more appropriate.

The questions in an audit measure the extent to which employees believe that they understand the organization's harassment policies and procedures. These questions measure how confident employees are that they really know this information. An organization can conduct follow-up interviews to confirm the employee perceptions revealed by the questionnaire.

employee who has reported an employer for sexual harassment. Can you tell me if there really is such a law?

—Fearful in Florida

Here was Abby's response.

Dear Fearful:
I had never heard of the "whistle-blower's law," but my staff called the Florida Department of Labor and Employment Security Office in Tallahassee, and were told there is indeed such a law. However, I suggest that you talk with a lawyer before you blow any more whistles.

Another questionnaire can measure employees' awareness of behaviors that have the potential to create a hostile environment. This information could offer management insights on the overall level of harassment in the organization and may point to specific behaviors (See Figure 13.4). The results of this questionnaire may suggest the need for a more specific audit which asks employees about very specific behaviors that create a hostile work environment.

Each organization must determine its own list, based on answers to the general questionnaire, interviews, and the personal experience of man-

Figure 13.4 **Sample Harassment Audit**

STAR, Inc.

Please indicate by checking yes or no if you are aware of any of the following behaviors within this organization.

1. sexually related printed materials	___ yes	___ no
2. derogatory slurs	___ yes	___ no
3. religious intolerance	___ yes	___ no
4. sexually charged comments	___ yes	___ no
5. ageism	___ yes	___ no

agers. The answers to this specific questionnaire will help to pinpoint behaviors that require immediate corrective action. If state law goes beyond the federal protections, the questionnaire may need to be modified. The questionnaires should be pretested to identify ambiguous questions and develop a more reliable and accurate instrument. The resulting final questionnaires can be administered to either a select group or all employees. Since the purpose is not scientific data gathering, this decision is not especially critical.

Depending on the survey results, various corrective actions may be warranted. If many of those polled do not understand what constitutes harassment or the organization's harassment policy, instituting new training programs or modifying current ones may be necessary. Alternatives include requiring supervisors to attend harassment training programs; distributing special newsletters, brochures, or memos that clarify misunderstandings; and making this information part of new employee orientation. In addition, meetings between the firm's EEOC compliance officers and selected departments may be appropriate. In the event the questionnaires reveal potential harassment within the firm, top management needs to take immediate action to stop the behavior and correct whatever precipitated it.

In some states, workers who report harassment, or **whistle blowers,** are protected from any action from the employer. This is to ensure that workers can feel safe reporting such harassment.

whistle blowers-people who call attention to the real or imagined misdeeds and unscrupulous behavior of their colleagues or sometimes their supervisors

The Disabled Worker and the ADA

The **Americans with Disabilities Act (ADA)** was signed into law in July 1990. The ADA is a major federal civil rights law which makes it illegal to discriminate against individuals with disabilities in employment, public accommodations, public services, transportation, and telecommunications. The ADA defines an individual with a disability as a person who has a physical or mental impairment that substantially limits one or more major life activities.

Americans with Disabilities Act-a federal civil rights law that makes it illegal to discriminate against individuals with disabilities

The first part of the definition makes it clear that the ADA applies to persons who have substantial, as distinct from minor, impairments, and that these must be impairments that limit major life activities such as seeing, hearing, speaking, walking, breathing, performing manual tasks, caring for oneself, and working. An individual with epilepsy, paralysis, substantial hearing or visual impairment, mental retardation, or a learning disability is covered. But an individual with a minor, nonchronic condition that is short in duration, such as a sprain or infection, generally is not covered.

The second part of the definition includes persons with a history of cancer that is currently in remission or persons with a history of mental illness. The third part of the definition protects individuals who are regarded and treated as though they have a substantially limiting disability, even

A person with physical or mental impairment is protected by the ADA against discrimination in employment.

though they may not have the impairment. For example, this provision would protect a severely disfigured qualified worker from being denied employment because an employer feared the negative reaction of others.

The law prohibits discrimination against qualified individuals who may have a disability. If the individual is qualified to perform essential job functions except for limitations caused by a disability, the employer must consider whether the individual could perform this function with some **reasonable accommodations.**

reasonable accommodations-assistance provided to workers with limitations so they may perform work tasks

Shirley Rasmussen is a 54-year-old woman with over 20 years' experience as a professional secretary. While Shirley suffers from a chronic back problem, her mobility and skills as a secretary cannot be questioned. To accommodate her back problem, Shirley's work station needs a few minor adjustments. Using a telephone headset instead of a traditional handset reduced the amount of reaching and stretching necessary to answer the phone. In addition, Shirley needs a secretarial chair that can be adjusted upwards to better fit her comfort level with her desk.

Under the ADA regulations, Shirley's back problem could not be identified until after she was offered a position. Since the accommodations she needs to perform her work successfully are reasonable (a headset and an adjustable chair), her employer could not discriminate against her for her back problem and would be required to provide the headset and chair.

Consider the following case. A 305-pound female, 5' 4" tall, applied for one of three job openings at a health food store. When she was not hired, the woman sued, charging that she was discriminated against because she was perceived to be physically handicapped by her weight.

She did not contend that her obesity was caused by some physiological condition or disorder. In testimony presented on behalf of the employer, a safety engineer said working in the store would be hazardous for the woman because of the store's narrow aisles and the danger that step stools and ladder might not support her. The trial court instructed the woman to show that her weight was the determining cause in the company's refusal to hire her. The jury ruled for the store.

Complaints Against Employers

Obesity sufficient to "make a significant impact on major life activities" can constitute a disability under federal law, the Equal Opportunity Commission maintains, as does alcoholism, diabetes, emphysema, and heart disease. Through a legal brief filed by the EEOC, recent court rulings and most state fair employment practice laws, discrimination suits based on obesity are taking on new significance in the area of disability rights litigation.

An applicant lawfully was rejected for a flight attendant's position for being over the employer's maximum weight limit. The reason was because the applicant's weight was the result of body building and he was not substantially limited in any major life activity.

Here is another case related to a different disability.

Ever since I hurt my arm, you've treated me differently," said Milly Jones. "Now you're using my job performance as an excuse to get rid of me."

"We've tried everything possible to help you," responded Dan Slocum, supervisor of the hospital food service center. "Unfortunately, nothing seems to work, and we can't just keep giving everyone else your work. I'm afraid we're going to have to let you go." Was the discharge justified?

Milly developed carpal tunnel syndrome after sustaining an injury to her right arm and shoulder when she fell in the employer's parking lot. Although she returned to work, her medical condition seriously impaired her job performance, and on three occasions over the following two years, she required surgery to alleviate the pain.

In view of her disability, the employer gave her light duty assignments in keeping with her physical limitations. An agent from the state division of rehabilitation was hired to conduct a worksite survey of how the employee could be accommodated, and then her job duties were restructured in accordance with the survey. To accommodate the disability, the employee was offered a voice-activated tape recorder so she would not be required to perform any writing with her hands and a reassignment to a different position.

Despite the employer's efforts to accommodate her, the employee either would not or could not perform the essential duties of her position. Moreover, she was not willing to suggest ways that her condition might be accommodated so that she could perform her duties. When her supervisor asked her to review other employees' work and to conduct business over the telephone (both activities authorized by her physician), the employee refused to complete the assignments. As a result of her inability or unwillingness to work, other employees had to do her work in addition to their own, causing worker morale to deteriorate within the organization. Faced with declining efficiency in the department, the employer decided to terminate the employee. Over the two years, she had complained about being treated in a disparate manner by her supervisors and had even filed a complaint with the EEOC. That complaint was dismissed.

Her termination was upheld because the evidence clearly showed the employer made a good faith effort to accommodate the employee's physical limitations. The employee refused to fully cooperate with these efforts.

Many employers do not fully understand their rights and obligations in relation to the Americans with Disabilities Act. Figure 13.5 lists the requirements. The ADA does not mean all individuals with disabilities are automatically entitled to a job. Most disabled persons do not want to be patronized—they want to be treated as equals. The EEOC received 7129 ADA-related charges in the first eight months of the law. Forty seven percent were discharge cases, 21 percent involved reasonable accommodations, 14 percent alleged discrimination, and 9 percent concerned harassment.

Figure 13.5 **Americans with Disabilities Act Requirements**

Employment Fact Sheet

► Employers may not discriminate against an individual with a disability in hiring or promotion if the person is otherwise qualified for the job.

► Employers can ask about one's ability to perform a job, but cannot inquire if someone has a disability or subject a person to tests that tend to screen out people with disabilities.

► Employers will need to provide reasonable accommodation to individuals with disabilities. This includes steps such as job restructuring and modification of equipment.

► Employers do not need to provide accommodations that impose an undue hardship on business operations.

Who needs to comply:

► All employers with 15–24 employees must comply effective July 1994.

Many employers thought ADA would involve mainly job applicants, but they are finding ADA is about their own employees. Many workers become disabled over the course of their employment. Back problems are cited as the number one disability.

What Employees with Disabilities Need

Some supervisors may hesitate to give a disabled person sufficient feedback, reasoning that they are doing the best they can. But like all employees, disabled people can't do their best without the right guidance. When working with disabled employees, supervisors should keep standards high. Don't accommodate workers with disabilities by lowering standards. Supervisors should also get used to communicating with the employee in the manner the employee prefers. The best way to show compassion as a supervisor is by giving all people the opportunity to do their best. Some workers with disabilities need more attention; others may be the most self-reliant workers in a department. But however employees with disabilities fit into the department, they are just like any other worker in their need for support and guidance.

Figure 13.6 contains a list of appropriate words and phrases that can be used in referring to a disabled person and a list of words and phrases that show lack of sensitivity and should not be used.

Figure 13.6 **Use Words with Dignity**

The following words have strong negative connotations.	The following words are more affirmative and reflect a more positive attitude.
Do not use:	**Words with dignity:**
handicap	disability
the handicapped	person who is differently abled
crippled with	person who has multiple sclerosis
victim	Paraplegic (person with limited or no use of lower limbs.
cripple	
spastic	person who has cerebral palsy
the brain damaged	person with a brain injury
the head injured	person with a head injury
patient (except in hospital)	person with AIDS
invalid	person who has tested HIV positive
paralytic	person who has polio
stricken with	person who is blind
AIDS victim	person who is visually impaired
quad	person who has a speech impairment
para	person with a learning disability
blind guys	person who is mentally challenged
mentally ill	person with a psychological disability
crazy	
birth defect	
inflicted with	
afflicted/afflicted by	
deformed/deformed by	
incapacitated	
poor	
unfortunate	

Age Discrimination

At the age of 56, Nancy Swanstrom of Durant, Oklahoma, had been awarded her organization's 30-year service pin. Nancy was a veteran in the small electrical appliance manufacturing organization. Nancy had started her job on the assembly line, working the graveyard shift. She had worked her way up into an office position in which she processed accounts receivables for the firm. She was a highly reliable, neat, and dedicated worker. She worked overtime whenever her supervisor asked her to do so. Her job performance as verified by her evaluations was glowing. Nancy had earned the maximum company benefits package, which included four weeks' vacation per year, a maximum sick leave account balance, profit sharing, and stock options. While her hourly rate of pay was not superlative, she was in the highest rank of her salary classification. Nancy was a model employee. Shortly after the firm was bought out by a conglomerate from out of state, Nancy noticed a shift in upper management's orientation toward the more tenured workers. Many of the upper level executives and senior supervisors were being encouraged to retire early or were being forcibly transferred to other corporate locations. Nancy rationalized that these were management level changes due to the buyout and that the lower level workers like her would be safe. After all, she had considerable tenure and her pay rate while reasonable was nowhere near an executive salary.

Suddenly one day Nancy's supervisor informed her that she was being transferred back to the production line. Her compensation would not change, but she would be required to work the second shift. Her supervisor was deeply apologetic about this transfer but said that a number of employees were being moved—all more tenured employees. Nancy was crushed. After 30 years, she was being forced to vacate her office job and return to her production line duties. A less expensive person would be taking her position. Could it be that Nancy was the victim of age discrimination?

Employees and prospective employees who are over the age of 40 are protected by several federal laws from arbitrary actions of discrimination. The Age Discrimination in Employment Act (ADEA) and the Older Workers Protection Act, both administered by the EEOC, are designed to safeguard the opportunities of older persons in the workforce.

Many times older workers who have significant tenure (and hence higher total compensation packages) within an organization can be the target of efforts to reduce or replace staff. In 1994, the EEOC filed a class action suit against Texas Instruments of Dallas, Texas, that alleged layoffs targeted supervisors who were above 50 years of age.

Seven manufacturing supervisors above that age had been dismissed. Texas Instruments noted that 35 of the 45 persons who held the supervisors' positions that needed reduction in the force were over 40 years old.

The EEOC in its accusations presented statistical evidence that Texas Instruments' actions showed a conscious effort to reduce the older, more expensive employees. The case was settled out of court and a financial settlement was provided the workers.

Many European countries have passed laws that protect older workers' jobs. In Germany, employers and employees over the age of 45 are required to provide six months' notice if the employment situation is to be terminated or significantly altered. Employees over the age of 55 cannot be terminated from their employment except for gross misconduct or negligence.

While not as liberal as Germany's older worker protection laws, United States EEOC regulations do provide some protection to older workers. Like other protected classes of workers, persons over the age of 40 are afforded some protection under EEOC regulations against arbitrary and unilateral employment discrimination.

On a more positive note, employers are finding a new wealth of potential employees in the ranks of the retired. More and more organizations are recruiting older, often-retired Americans for positions that have been traditionally entry level jobs. According to the Society for Human Resource Management, these older workers are seeking additional income and the opportunity to be productive contributors. They enjoy the opportunity to socialize and feel needed. Most attractive to these older workers are those jobs that allow flexible hours and schedules. Employers report that these older workers have an excellent work ethic, are dependable, work well with others, and perform their jobs with quality. Employers also note that many older workers will take positions that younger entry level students and new graduates would not consider.

Conclusion

In a survey conducted in 1994 by Olsten Corporation, a nationwide temporary employment agency based in Westbury, New York, 49 percent of the 510 major United States employers polled indicated that the root of the understaffing problem they had identified was a shortage of skilled workers. Given the need for qualified workers, employers recognize that their business performance depends upon employing the best-qualified person for the job, regardless of race, age, gender, sexual orientation, or disability. To further the productivity of this diverse workforce, the workplace must be one that supports, in fact demands, mutual respect among all workers. The roots of discrimination are based in psychological and learned responses toward people who are different from one's own heritage and background. With training and personal knowledge, prejudice can be reduced and eliminated at the personal level.

At the organizational level, employers must be sensitive to a wide array of both state and federal regulations that address all types of discrimination in employment, promotion, and termination. Enforced by the Equal

Employment Opportunity Commission of the U.S. Department of Justice, these regulations are influencing how workers are treated by their supervisors and coworkers. Federal and state regulations banning discrimination have been the springboard that regulates on-the-job harassment. Harassment is one of the most sensitive issues employers are confronting today. It is an emotional and psychological issue. The goal, however, is to increase the chances of equal opportunity for all workers and mutual respect in the workplace.

Sources: Drake, Samantha. "Tough Customers." Human Resources Executive. May 1994, 28–31.

Champagne, Paul, Bruce McAfee, and Phillip Moberg. "A Workplace of Mutual Respect." HR Magazine. October 1992, 78–81.

"How to Make Work More Appealing." Practical Supervision. January 15, 1992, 1.

Rosen, Benson, and Kay Lovelace. "Fitting Square Pegs into Round Holes." HR Magazine. January 1994, 86–88.

Smith, Vernita. "Glass Ceiling: Take Two." Human Resources Executive. October 1993, 30–33.

Key Points Summary

- Diversity in the workplace is a reality, and diversity must be managed.

- The growth in the United States labor force and customer base will be composed of women and minorities.

- Providing a workplace free from harassment is one of the basic responsibilities of an employer.

- An employee handbook should clearly communicate an employer's harassment policy.

- A prejudiced person tends to think of members of a group of people the same, without consideration of individual differences.

- The basis of prejudice toward a subgroup of society is often found in economic or psychological factors.

- As the United States becomes more involved in the international market, business managers are becoming aware that discrimination can make disastrous impressions on potential buyers.

- Women historically have been discriminated against in terms of advancement to management positions and pay.

- The Equal Employment Opportunity Commission is the federal government agency responsible for enforcing antidiscrimination efforts.

- Examples of unlawful harassment include epithets, slurs, negative stereotyping, or threatening or hostile acts related to race, color, religion, gender, national origin, age, or disability.

- To determine whether harassment exists within an organization, employers may conduct a harassment audit.

- The Americans with Disabilities Act makes it illegal to discriminate against individuals with disabilities in employment, public accommodations, public services, transportation, and telecommunications.

- Employees who are over the age of 40 are protected from arbitrary actions of discrimination by federal laws, including the Age Discrimination in Employment Act.

Key Terms

Americans with Disabilities Act	prejudgment
diversity	prejudice
ecosystem distrust	reasonable accommodations
Equal Employment Opportunity Commission	sex discrimination
feminine style of leadership	sexual harassment
glass ceiling	social mobility concept
harassment	stereotypes
harassment audit	valuing differences programs
hostile environment	whistle blowers

Discussion Questions

1. Discuss the meaning of managing diversity and the implications for those employers who do not manage diversity.

2. What kinds of activities should be included in a valuing differences program?

3. Discuss the difference between sex discrimination and sexual harassment.

4. As the United States becomes more involved in international trade, why are the issues of harassment and discrimination even more critical?

5. Describe the difference between male and female managers according to the Smits and Smith study.

6. The wage gap between men and women is narrowing but it may not be because women are earning more. Discuss.

7. Describe a situation of illegal harassment. What specifically makes it illegal?

8. What kinds of information should be obtained in a harassment audit?

9. Provide some examples of reasonable accommodations and whom they would assist.

Answers to What's Your Diversity I.Q.?

1. d	9. c
2. c	10. a
3. b	11. b
4. a	12. c
5. c	13. c
6. c	14. b
7. d	15. d
8. c	

Chapter *14*

Learning Objectives

Upon completing this chapter, you should be able to:

- Complete a cost/benefit analysis for a change effort.

- Understand why human beings resist change.

- Develop a plan for dealing with driving and restraining forces.

- Implement change using the team approach, with the necessary team members.

- Distinguish between redesigning and reengineering.

A Rapidly Changing World of Work

Nowhere. That is where she felt she was going. She had drive and more ability than her present position demanded. Maryanne Peters knew she needed to do something. As a single mother with two small children, she had to find a better-paying job. She had been thinking about going to her area community college to upgrade her skills and make her resume more attractive. Maryanne thought about her current job as an administrative assistant and wondered, "Is this what I will be doing fifteen years from now?"

That was motivation for personal change. But Maryanne needed guidance. She needed a broader vision of the future than her background and position provided, so she started her homework. Maryanne decided to "work her contacts" and find out what others saw in the future. If Maryanne was going to retrain for the future, she needed to know what the future might be like.

One Friday afternoon, she was wrapping up some statistics for her boss, and things were more relaxed than usual in her fast-paced office. The time was right. "Jerry, you see things, business in general, as well as this company, from a broader point of view. Where is it all going? If you were preparing for the next 10 to 15 years, what would you get ready for?" she asked her boss.

Without hesitation, Jerry Turner responded, "Globalization. The world is getting smaller. With better telecommunications, less expensive travel, and fewer trade restrictions, international trade and marketing is where future opportunities lie. If we are going to compete as a company and as a country, we'll have to be competitive world-wide. There are lots of opportunities for small organizations like ours, Maryanne."

On her way to work on Monday morning, Maryanne tuned in to public radio. Charles Handy was being interviewed about organizational change. She turned up the volume. Handy's book, *The Age of Unreason,* was being discussed. Maryanne heard Handy say that successful organizations are those that do outrageous things, those which stretch the traditions. He talked about the **"shamrock organization."** That organization of the future will be structured to have fewer full- and part-time employees, more consultants, and more temporary employees.

shamrock organization-
a new structure for
employees with the three
major components being:
fewer full-time employees,
more consultants, and
expanded use of temporary
employees.

On Monday afternoon, a salesperson for a local computer supplier stopped by to provide some information on a digital scanner. Steve Bocker announced with some glee that the prices had dropped by 23 percent within the last six months on the model Maryanne's office was considering. Since she was on a roll, Maryanne thought that Steve might be another person with a sense of the future. After all, he was in the computer business.

"Steve, what do you see in the future? You deal with new equipment all the time. I am doing a little personal research," Maryanne said.

Steve responded, "The problem with the future is that it keeps getting closer and closer. We will continue to see fast-paced technological change. I was talking to a fellow in our office who has been there a long time. He was talking about the introduction of the Correcting Selectric IBM typewriter, about twenty years ago. Then came those huge monster single-purpose word processors that used magnetic cards as a storage media. Expensive and slow by today's standards. The personal computer has really changed the office environment. Almost everyone has a PC on their desk now. They used to be a luxury: now, in just a few short years, they are a necessity. You know, Maryanne, I think that trend will continue."

Steve continued without any prompt from Maryanne, "We are going to see more and more technology everywhere. I was in a fast-food restaurant the other day and saw a machine that loaded frozen French fries into a basket, dropped the basket into the fryer, timed the cooking process, monitored the temperature of the oil, lifted the fries out, and dropped them on a holding pad where a light shower of salt came out. That machine replaced someone's job. That same kind of technology will be everywhere." Bocker was very sincere, very believable.

Maryanne expected Steve's anticipation of technology, but she had no idea he would be so intense about it.

The Speed of Change

The mathematician and philosopher Alfred North Whitehead once observed that "the major advances in civilization are processes which all but wreck the society in which they occur." We live in times that reflect such turmoil. Never before has there been so much change so fast and with such dramatic implications for the entire world. From the nuclear family to nuclear arms treaties, our way of life is transforming.

At a personal level, change is intensifying for everyone. People face an unsettling amount of individual adjustment as evidenced by the alarming frequency of marriages, pregnancies, divorces, promotions, career shifts, relocations, health problems, drug abuse, retirements, and family strife in society today. People juggle marriage, children, and careers; they try to be sensitive parents after skirmishing on the corporate battlefield. In the workplace, people are also confronted with massive change—ever-changing technologies, mergers, acquisitions, rightsizing, new policies, reorganizations, shifting duties, and reengineering.

Besides changes at the individual and organizational levels, there are profound national and global transitions that are altering our lives as well as shaping those of our children and grandchildren. For example,

▶ The primary mode of communication has shifted from written to electronic, thus changing the way people think, converse, and educate themselves.

▶ Advanced media technology means that a significant shift in one part of the world is almost instantaneously known in all areas of the globe.

▶ The growth of information is occurring fast, and that has implications for everyone.

▶ The planet's fragile ecosystem will no longer sustain humankind's demands for natural resources or generation of waste.

▶ Nations bordering the North Atlantic Ocean are not the only dominant economic forces in the international arena.

▶ Advances in health care and genetic engineering promise new ways of fighting disease, but they also pose a myriad of ethical questions.

▶ Faster modes of transportation are becoming available, creating greater economic opportunities, but with potential psychological and environmental costs.

▶ The redefinition of traditional male and female, ethnic, and racial roles is reshaping the structure of our society.

*I*mplementing Change

change-making something different in a particular way

Change is defined as making something different in some way. Its synonyms are *alter, vary,* and *modify.* It has often been said that change is the only constant. Two things related to change seem evident: first, leaders play a key role in change and should play a key role in managing it; second, change does not always occur in the manner in which it is foreseen. Intellectually, it is easy to acknowledge the need for change, but emotionally it is far more difficult. There is a tendency on the part of some to resist change by extolling the merits of the past and to cling to ways of doing things that are no longer adequate.

Wrong Reasons for Change

Some people have been accused of doing the right thing for the wrong reason. Ego trips, imitation, overkill, and tinkering can all be cited as examples of change for the wrong reason. When a change effort is initiated for

Unit 3 · Problems in Human Relations

Change takes place continuously, but not always in predictable ways.

the wrong reason, things may quickly deteriorate, making the situation less desirable than it was before the change. Worker morale can also be adversely affected.

Ego Trips.   Near the end of her tenure, the CEO of a large corporation pushed through the construction of a new corporate headquarters, one that went far beyond the current needs of the organization. When asked why such a building was needed, an employee replied, "It was her parting shot." This remark may be snide but it does highlight the fact that those with power sometimes make changes on the basis of personal preference. When leaders act in this fashion, they leave their followers unmotivated to make the change succeed.

ego trip-an act that enhances and satisfies one's ego

Imitation.   There is a natural proclivity to keep up with the Joneses in businesses as in neighborhoods. A medium-sized firm may try to imitate the way a successful, large firm does business, oftentimes without getting the success it sought. Procedures that work well for a large business might not work well for a medium-sized business. Prudent people learn from the experience of others, but they must be sensitive to the difference between

imitation-to pattern, follow, or copy

Chapter 14 • A Rapidly Changing World of Work

an "o" and an "a": Nothing can be adopted because it has worked well for others. It must be adapted to the realities of a given situation.

overkill-changing too much too soon

Overkill. The inexperienced often try to change too much too soon. This is commonplace in government programs that start out dramatically and end up failing. The itch to change things also affects some newly appointed managers who are so insecure they attempt to wipe the slate clean instead of building on the strengths and accomplishments of a department.

tinkering-changing this or that aspect of a system without realizing the change may not be an improvement

Tinkering. Some managers find it almost impossible to leave well enough alone. They are forever tinkering with this or that aspect of a system without realizing that rearrangement is not a synonym for improvement. The Ford Mustang was a brilliant recovery from the disaster of the Edsel. Within two years, 1.2 million were built. Ford gradually added 600 pounds to its weight. Sales eventually slowed, but the people who recommended and approved the changes in the Mustang's design probably thought their ideas were good. If change is desirable, stability is no less necessary.

Return on Investment

Any change, even a minor one, brings with it a variety of costs. It disrupts familiar ways of doing business; it reduces efficiency at the outset; it may offend the status quo of some; it may create a certain amount of resistance; and it takes time and energy to implement. Accordingly, no change should be introduced until a costs/benefit analysis has been completed. If the returns do not considerably outweigh the costs, then putting the change on the back burner may be the thing to do. Figure 14.1 illustrates the steps in making any substantial change in current operations. Each box represents a place where the situation can be evaluated. If the realities associated with each step are not favorable, the planned change will not be as successful as it might be.

Figure 14.1 **Implementing Change**

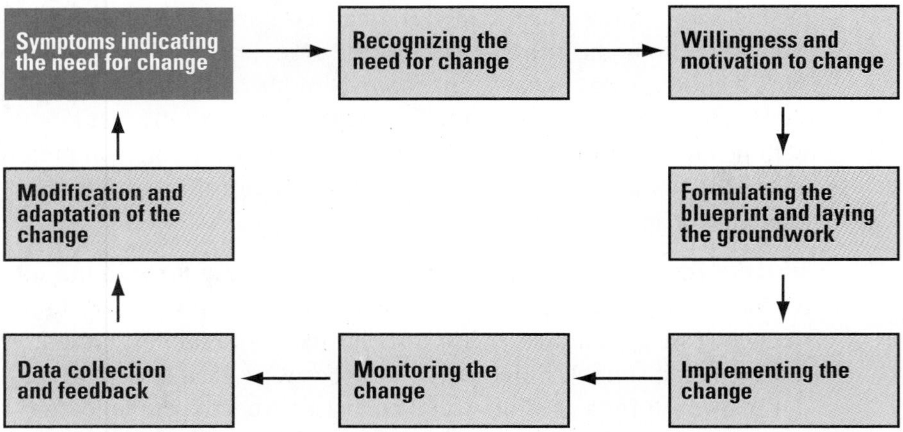

Need for Change

The stimulants to change may be positive, negative, or some mix of the two. Negative influences are such factors as loss of competitive position; new legislation or regulations; a system that is buckling under the load; falling productivity; escalating costs and waste; and unacceptable morale, absenteeism, friction between workers, and poor quality of the workforce.

Positive reasons for change include the need to implement strategic plans and policies; a desire to capitalize on new opportunities; a plan to introduce old products into new markets or new products into old markets; a determination to capitalize on surplus or underutilized talent; a decision to upgrade the technology of production; the introduction of a data management system; and the startup of an organizational development program.

The opening up of fast-food hamburger places in Germany is an example of introducing old products into new markets.

The symptoms indicating the need for change are usually clear and identifiable, but they are usually ignored by those in power. Organizational and personal inertia are very difficult to overcome. Here the problem is psychological rather than intellectual. The paralyzing effect of habit and the secure feeling of the familiar blind people to the need to change. If self-deception is not to take over, the leader must frankly admit that the matters requiring attention will not cure themselves.

The Palmer Company is an old, established Mountain States service organization. Back in the 1950s the best way to provide secretarial and support services for the organization was through a centralized secretarial pool. In fact, when the Palmer Company moved into its new headquarters, all dictation and documents that needed to be typed or copied went to a single central location, the secretarial pool. Trudy Freet assigned each work task to one of the secretaries in the pool for completion. One secretary spe-

Ethical Dimensions to Human Relations

The Ethical Ploy

In the future, the world you consider now to be disorganized, irregular, and convoluted will appear by comparison relatively stable. Whether the time horizon you envision is five years or ten generations from now, change-related crises will be more frequent and more complex than today. History tells us that regardless of the intensity of these challenges, some people will emerge as winners while others will lose ground.

The people and organizations who survive and prosper during times of change learn to take advantage of the mechanisms that foster resilience. The opportunities in store for those who are resilient are abundant, but along with these opportunities come definite responsibilities.

We all know that deception is bad. Fraudulent snares confirm our worst fears about people who try to manipulate others covertly to achieve their own selfish desires. Nevertheless, there are certain ways in which we attempt to influence one another that involve an honorable form of masquerade. These efforts are called *ethical ploys.*

cialized in proposals and another in specifications. They shared the load among them. There was little turnover in the secretarial positions.

As the organization began to grow, technology was introduced, and Trudy was not excited about giving up those trusty correcting typewriters. But reluctantly she and her staff made the shift to personal computers. Word processing software was selected because it was the least expensive. It was not easy to learn and required an entirely new way of thinking about document preparation. Each person who generated work had his or her own disks. It seemed like a logical way of keeping things straight.

The firm continued to grow. People started to work more in teams, and the support services staff had to do more specialized work such as spreadsheets and calculations. The files of disks continued to grow larger and larger. There were now unique disk boxes of proposals, specifications, vendors, and special reports. The members of the secretarial pool had a hard time finding things. If one member of the pool was ill, the others were lost if a document was needed.

There were more documents coming to the pool with shorter deadlines, and it seemed there was always a temporary secretary using a typewriter. Just as everyone finally became comfortable with the unique coding system of the software, a major client mandated that all work be delivered to them on a disk using different software. Trudy and her staff revolted. It was too much to demand from them.

An ethical ploy is at work when one person grants another's request to do something but fulfills the obligation in such a way that the recipient not only gets what was promised (the ethical part) but also has an opportunity to gain a great deal more than was requested (the ploy). These honorable deceptions are used to lead people into seeing a point of view which they otherwise would not have been able or willing to relate.

Take the example of Jerry, a secretary in a power company. He needed to upgrade his skills using a spreadsheet program. He also had expressed some interest in providing some training to the rest of the staff. His supervisor then told him that once he learned the spreadsheet program, he would be providing training to the rest of the staff. She used his desire to become involved with staff training to get him to learn the spreadsheet. She used an ethical ploy.

Do you agree? Describe some situations in which ethical ploys are used.

A study was initiated to see if the pool concept was the best and most efficient way of providing support services. The results were clear: things had to change. Each department needed its own secretary. One coordinator would set internal standards for formats, fonts, and filing systems. The coordinator would also approve the secretarial vacation days and arrange for a floater to cover if someone was absent. All documents would be stored centrally on the computer network.

Trudy was no longer in charge. She became one of the departmental secretaries. The changes were happening too fast. They were too bold. The old system worked—it was just a little slow. After years of trying the new system, Trudy decided to retire. She liked her job and liked the people she worked with and they liked her, but the demands of the changes were too great. She said it was just too much for her old ways of doing things.

Diagnosing Problems

With respect to change, there are four types of leaders: those who give lip service to the need to change; those who acknowledge the need but procrastinate; those who adopt half-hearted measures that tranquilize the situation temporarily without resolving it; and those who analyze the situation and then cope with it. It is essential to distinguish between root causes, minor causes, results, and symptoms. Unless this is done, the change will most likely fail.

Chapter 14 • A Rapidly Changing World of Work

International Trade—Toward Increased Globalization

CalPacific exports disposable wooden chopsticks to Japan. Since the Japanese do not have a readily available supply of lumber, they import some 130,000,000 chopsticks—every day.

If someone told you that an American firm sold oil to the Middle East, would you believe the person? STP buys oil from the Middle East region, processes and packages it in the United States, and exports it back to the Middle East in STP-branded containers—an unusual but profitable export endeavor.

For high quality leather shoes, Italy immediately comes to mind as the country of origin. But some of the most popular leather shoes in Italy have a Made in the USA label in them. Timberland Shoes adopted the attitude, "Let's give it a chance and see if it works," and it has.

International trade and the globalization of organizations of every size is a trend that is sure to continue. In 1960 the sum of all Direct Foreign Investment (financial investments in manufacturing and non-stock/bond business investments abroad) among nations was estimated to be $105 billion. In 1989 the value was estimated at over $1,263 billion—a ten-fold increase in just over 20 years.

What has fueled this exponential change in international trade? Experts attribute the globalization of nations' economies to a number of technological and personal changes.

Communications devices like the fax, modem, and inexpensive long-distance phone service has made international business significantly easier and less risky. With these devices, one can usually easily overcome time zone changes and many language barriers. A fax sent

Driving and Restraining Forces

force field analysis-a way to look at a change effort without getting emotionally involved

driving forces-supporters of change such as new legislation or changes in competition

Once convinced that a change is necessary, there is a temptation to become emotionally involved with the idea. **Force field analysis** is a method for preventing emotional entanglement with one's own views. It requires critical analysis of the driving and restraining forces that the change must take into account. **Driving forces** are supportive of the change. They may be external, such as legislation or a competitor gaining a larger share of the market. They may be internal, such as the active interest of key authority figures, or the need to make changes to carry out a new strategic plan. Similarly, the restraining forces may also be either external or internal.

The manager must calculate the driving forces in order to capitalize on them. What is to be done with the restraining forces that are internal to the organization? The quick answer—overcome them—is often wrong. Only a manager who possesses sufficient power can achieve this. However, people who feel they have been forced to submit may try to sabotage the change.

from the Midwest at 6:00 P.M. will arrive the next business day at 9:00 A.M. in Japan—almost instantaneously.

One of the biggest barriers and risks to international trade is knowing and having trust in one's foreign trading partner. The other barrier is time. In business, TIME is MONEY. Through technology like the fax and modem and inexpensive air travel, people-to-people trust can be established and maintained over thousands of miles with minimal time or cost investment. Likewise, with increased speed of document movement, overnight communication is almost a certainty. Knowing one's trading partner through frequent and immediate communications establishes trust and reduces risks.

In the same time span, countries have made efforts to reduce barriers and to increase international trade. GATT (General Agreement on Tariffs and Trade) and NAFTA (North American Free Trade Agreement) have been adopted to phase out cumbersome tariffs and other import restrictions, thus making international commerce faster, less complicated, and less expensive for consumers and businesses. In 1993 Mexico imposed a 100 percent duty on vehicles imported into the country. A $15,000 United States-made auto cost over $30,000 in Mexico. The transaction could take months to complete. Today, with NAFTA, that same vehicle can enter the country duty-free.

The future of international trade is bright and optimistic as individuals, governments, and technology work together to reduce barriers.

It is better if the leader can win over or at least neutralize the opposition. Often people are reacting to their own fears, rather than to the proposed change. Pointing out the benefits, letting them ventilate their feelings and doubts, and seeking out their suggestions frequently undermine the resistance to change.

Although it is helpful to write down the various driving and restraining forces, both internal and external, it is important to concentrate not on their number but rather on the importance and impact. The active support of one key person may be more significant than the disagreement of several people.

Determining the Extent of the Change

Radical surgery? Minor change? Small modification? Fine tuning? Which is most appropriate to the situation? The answer probably is: the one that changes as little as possible to attain the change. Another criterion has to do with the benefits that the change will produce in relation to the costs that it will require. Finally, it is necessary to be sensitive to unanticipated consequences. The economic return on the change may be substantial, but if the hidden costs of future conflict will be excessive, the change may not be worth it.

Two myths still live on: it is necessary to get all the facts, and the leaders must choose the best solution. No one can ever get all the facts. As many computer printouts prove, excessive data often serves to blur the meaning of the facts. Managers should make sure they have examined the critical facts, the vital few rather than the trivial many. The best solution may never be found; the preferred alternative may be the better option from a field in which all have shortcomings. The change should be the most realistic and practical the circumstances allow. If it resolves a problem or capitalizes on an unexploited opportunity while avoiding long-term costs, it should be implemented.

Total Quality Management and Change

"We just cannot continue business as usual!" How many American workers have heard that phrase at staff meetings or read it as the introductory paragraph of an office memo? An entire new vocabulary is being used that describes changes in workplace organization: downsizing, rightsizing, corporate acquisition, megamerger, continuous process improvement, reengineering. Organizational change is like R. Buckminster Fuller when he said, "I am not a noun, I am a verb—actively evolving."

Total Quality Management (TQM) is one of the organizational change concepts that permeates American businesses and institutions. One of the critical concepts of TQM is that change is a continuous process that occurs in spite of us. People may either plan for the change or react to it. TQM suggests that planning for change, in fact leading change, is the preferred action for the progressive organization.

Total Quality Management is a management method that aligns the activities of all employees with the common focus of customer satisfaction through continuous improvement in the quality of all activities, goods, and services.

The TQM philosophy views work as a system of interlocking needs. Organizational needs, such as updating products or reducing the amount of time necessary to deliver a work product, make up one component. Technical issues are the second related need. Technical issues include adjusting to new types and amounts of data or the introduction of new software or hardware or production equipment. Finally, there are individual needs. Organizations depend on people to prepare and produce their products and services. All three of the work system components will have change issues that must be addressed.

Total Quality Management—an organizational change concept that suggests planning for change is the preferred action

People must work together to make improvements in the workplace. Technology will be provided and often adjusted in the workplace to increase efficiencies and to meet the changing demands of the marketplace. Workers will find new ways of producing more and better products, and their training will determine the success of the other organizational shifts necessary in today's highly competitive environment.

Myths About Change

From day care through college and the working life beyond, organizations have an immeasurable impact on how people view themselves in relation to change. From their experiences in school, church, the military, and many other organizations that touch their lives, most people have come to accept assumptions about change. Although firmly held, these assumptions are based mostly on fears and prejudice rather than fact. Here are some of the more popular myths about change.

► It is impossible to understand why people accept or resist change.

► Bureaucracies cannot be changed.

► What leaders say about change should never by confused with reality.

► Change will always be mismanaged.

► Organizational efficiency and effectiveness decrease when change is attempted.

► Those who help implement change are the heroes, those who resist are villains.

► Management is inherently insensitive to problems caused during the implementation of change.

► Employees are prone to resist any change that is good for the organization.

This kind of unconscious indoctrination is so widespread that most people think it is natural for change to be poorly handled and fail. To the contrary, research indicates that badly handled organizational change is merely the result of deeply ingrained habits, and these habits can be modified.

People can be redirected to see successful change as a real possibility. The victimization lessons most people learn from their change experience can be replaced with a real sense of empowerment, which stems from the application of certain guidelines that foster resilience.

The amount of time people spend at work and the impact their jobs have on their lives make the workplace an ideal location for the development of resilience skills. One of the most effective ways to help people develop the necessary resilience for prospering during major change is to provide guidelines that can be used in the office. An employee's place of employment can become a classroom for learning the basics of resilience, which can then be applied not only to work but other aspects of life as well.

Resistance to Change

Resistance to change is too often viewed as a dimension of personality, rather than as a logical consequence of proposals for change. Some people are described as open to change; these, of course, are the good people. Others are described as closed to change; these are the bad people. In truth, however, human beings resist change for good and logical reasons. The changer needs to discover those reasons and deal with them. In other words, resistance is the problem of the changer, not the changee.

Sources of Resistance

Every organization, like every family, is different. There is no single set of descriptors that will work for all organizations. Nevertheless, a list of the most common sources of resistance follows. Catalysts of change need to analyze each source of resistance to see the degree to which each source is operating in a setting.

Lack of Ownership.
Changees will resist efforts to change they see as alien. If they lack a feeling of ownership in the change, they will in all likelihood refuse to go along with it. The best predictor of ownership is participation, whether that participation relates to defining the change or only to its implementation. Involvement at both levels—the what and the how—maximizes the chances of achieving change.

People often receive change demands from others, both above and around them. In these cases, they have limited room to define the what of change, but they can still define the how. In either case, it is important to make change user friendly and not alien to give changees some opportunity for self-determination. Participation is defining how change is to be implemented. It is a key to overcoming resistance.

resistance to change-
to withstand the implementation or the effects of an effort to make a situation different

Without a long-term perspective on rewards, resistance to change is likely among employees. The long-term reward would be the ease of finding data on a computer.

Lack of Benefits. Perhaps the most common source of resistance to change is the lack of a payoff. Employees, spouses, friends, and even the most committed individuals will resist doing something new if they see no benefits or advantages in it for themselves. Far too many change proposals are ripe with advantages for the changers but without any benefits for the changee. *Payoff* is not a negative term. It simply reflects human nature. People perform those acts best that give them rewards, whether they be money, satisfaction, image, affection, or power. As long as they maintain a long-term perspective on rewards, payoff is a desirable component to change.

Increased Burdens. Related to payoffs is the issue of burdens. All people have limited time, money, and energy; anything that robs them of these they strongly resist. This is a problem. Virtually every change takes time, money, and energy. Of these, energy and money are elastic and expandable, whereas time is not; therefore, the most precious and closely guarded of the three is time.

All people have the same amount of time; they can gain no more. If someone's change effort will reduce people's burdens—save them money, replenish their energy, or reduce wasted time—then they will eagerly pursue it. But if the change effort consumes these resources, their only sane response is to resist. Thus, even though change consumes time, money, and energy, its net effect must be to reduce people's burdens.

Lack of Support from Management. Most employees will not implement change unless they believe that those vested with responsibility for the organizational management also support the change. This runs counter to the notion that much change is grassroots—that it swells up from the lowest levels of the organization. Occasionally grassroots change does occur, but typically the commitment of managers at upper levels is crucial to the commitment of managers throughout the organization. Top brass support is important to a successful change effort.

Insecurity. Personal and psychic security is a prominent issue in almost every theory of motivation. Researchers from Maslow to Herzberg have argued the importance of security. If you propose a change that threatens an individual's security, even one that is merely perceived as threatening, he or she will resist. The drive for survival is more powerful than almost any other drive. One must keep in mind that the changer's perception of the threat to security is irrelevant; the key lies in how the changee sees the threat. If someone feels threatened, then they will resist and fight back. In industry, for example, robotics represents a real threat to worker security. In education, where computers are not real threats to job security, they are nevertheless often seen as such. In both cases, employees may resist. They will foresee the loss of their jobs, and the resistance will be overcome only by a demonstration that their jobs are secure. Change that enhances security holds a much better chance for success.

"We don't do it that way around here" or "We've always done it this way." These words can tell people that their change effort has run headlong into the norms of the organization and that they are in trouble. Norms are powerful and tend to overwhelm individual preference. The norms and culture in the organization are customs and practices that have been built up over years. They serve the members' individual needs and also represent a source of identity for the organization. They are functional and necessary. Change that runs counter to these norms will be resisted by all but a few. If individuals find themselves in a situation like this, they must work on changing the norms—a huge undertaking. An alternative may be to recraft the change to fit in more easily into the established culture.

▼

chaos-uncomfortable situations where people are not in control

Chaos. Control is closely connected to security. Terms like *out of control* or *uncontrollable* can be used to undercut change. For most people, the issue of control and security is prominent. When change is occurring, this issue manifests itself as a need to maintain order. When a change proposal offers the real possibility of fostering chaos, individuals tend to resist. They imagine uncomfortable situations where they are not in control and then reject anything that increases the probability of actualizing those images. Figure 14.2 gives the potential resistance factors. Conversely, if the change

Figure 14.2 **Potential Resistance Factors**

In this change effort, to what extent do you find:	**+ Driving ——→ Change ←—— Restraining –**				
	Not at all				Very much so
Lack of ownership	1	2	3	4	5
Lack of benefits	1	2	3	4	5
Lack of burdens	1	2	3	4	5
Lack of top management support	1	2	3	4	5
Loneliness	1	2	3	4	5
Insecurity	1	2	3	4	5
Extremes of organizational structure	1	2	3	4	5
Chaos	1	2	3	4	5
Superiority	1	2	3	4	5
Differential knowledge	1	2	3	4	5
Lack of recognition	1	2	3	4	5
Sudden wholesale change	1	2	3	4	5
Failure	1	2	3	4	5

Any factors rated 4 for 5 are resistance factors needing attention.

proposal suggests they will have more control and security, they are likely to embrace it. Change must be gradual. Workers will resist large, major, wholesale changes. Change that creates the perception of more control inspires allegiance. Perception is the critical issue.

Superiority. Some change efforts are really morality plays posing good against evil. "I'm for innovation and goodness and you're for the status quo and evil." This simplistic notion of morality tends to dominate people's approach to change. They are likely to resist change instigated by others who tell them—directly or indirectly—they are superior. Most people avoid using words such as *superior,* but they communicate their sense of superiority through comments like these: "As you become more experienced, you'll see what I mean" and "You need to learn how to take risks."

Managers should present new ideas as options that will work to solve a problem or satisfy a need. They should try to understand the changees' needs and drives to sense the acceptance or rejection of the change. The situation should not pit good against evil.

Differential Knowledge. Information is power, and unequal information means unequal power. Unequal power leads to resistance and competition. Even though people don't always rely on information and data to make decisions, they want to be kept informed and knowledgeable about the environment in which they work. People want to feel part of the organization. The "trust me, I know more about this than you" approach signals a differential in information. If change is to occur, the changees must have adequate and equal information about the change. Information means inclusion, and without it there will be resistance to change.

▼
differential knowledge-
when some have access to
information and others do
not, causing unequal power

Lack of Recognition. Every workplace has professional resisters, people who receive organizational recognition by opposing things. "That will never work here. We've already tried that." They have never met a change they found irresistible. The often-used strategy of isolation seldom works with these resisters. It only increases their recognition and sometimes arouses sympathy. The real issue for them is not change—it is recognition.

To overcome professional resisters, managers must give them recognition by publicly acknowledging their worth and including them in the change process. By making them a part of the solution, a person can convert these opponents into proponents of the change. New ideas, differences of opinion, cautions, and conflict are all proactive elements of the change process.

To most people, change is a fascinating subject, partly because they are interested in creating it, but also because they are sometimes its victim. Most people are bombarded by change efforts. Frustrated by the array of demands placed upon them, they long for more control. Sometimes it is the speed of change that creates confusion. Faced with repeated fast-paced change, they feel like a car out of control and struggle to bring it under control. Sometimes it is a case of having their expectations violated. People plan on things working out in certain ways and then things change.

Chapter 14 · A Rapidly Changing World of Work

For most, this is a disconcerting attack on their hopes and expectations. They have a belief that things will turn out as planned.

Sometimes it is the loss of control that terrifies people. They work in organizations because they believe in coordination and cooperation. Change that attacks their sense of control also attacks their faith in the organizations. The increased burdens may also frustrate them. Almost all change entails more time, effort, and money—three scarce resources. The more someone takes from them, the more frustrated and resistant they become.

For these reasons and many more, people often feel like victims of change. And victims fight back sooner or later.

Teams and Change

Some of the most effective change endeavors are team efforts. Decision theory states that multiple input and multiple decision makers improve the quality of decisions. No one person can know it all—all of us are smarter than one of us. In addition, a team approach broadens the range of investment in the outcome, and investment is critical to change. A team approach also expands available resources—time and energy.

Some would argue that every change effort should be pursued through a collaborative team process, and that this sense of collaboration should expand beyond the team members to include all those who will be affected by the change effort. In some cases, these teams may be already established groups or standing committees. Most change teams are ad hoc bodies that are formed for a particular reason and exist solely to plan and implement the change effort.

Sometimes it is difficult to let these ad hoc groups die a natural death. Colleagues who have worked well and hard together resist giving up those associations and successes, but they must. Once the change is implemented, it is time for the team to move on.

Having many student decision makers work on this student government project will improve the quality of the decisions regarding the project.

Forming the Team

A frequent dilemma in team formation is the **Noah's Ark syndrome**— having every group represented on the team. Team formation requires more focused planning. Change teams should have five to ten members (Peters and Waterman, 1982). They should have at least five to get a variety of ideas and disagreements. Five are also needed in case of attrition. Research on group dynamics indicates that groups larger than ten tend to split into subgroups and become unmanageable. Since cohesion and communication are very important in this process, teams of five to ten members are optimal.

Composition

The worst thing to do is select people because they represent various constituencies. The best is to select those who represent key decision-making categories. One or two people who fit into each of the following categories should be involved in the team.

▶ **Decision Maker.** This is someone who has the authority and responsibility to make a decision related to the proposed change, or someone who has the ear of the decision maker. The more important the problem or change effort, the greater the involvement required of senior staff.

▶ **Stakeholder.** This is someone who has a vested interest in how the change occurs; this person will likely be called upon to carry out the decision made or at least will be directly affected.

▶ **Expert.** This is someone who has considerable knowledge about this issue, the organization, or the change process.

▶ **Supporter.** This is someone who has already committed to seeing the change occur and has some ideas about potential changes.

▶ **Resister.** This is someone who likes the status quo and is dubious about proposed changes, the questioner for the team. It is useful if the resister is politically important to the organization.

▶ **Facilitator.** This is someone who has no vested interest in the change but is eager to make the process work. This person should be both task oriented and people centered; skills in collaboration management and meeting facilitation are important here.

In a group that has been formed, one person may represent more than one category, but the entire team should include all categories: decision makers, stakeholders, experts, supporters, resisters, and a facilitator. The individual forming these teams should seek voluntary participation. Forced participation cannot be effective, nor can people be justly compensated for participating in a group. Released time, when people are free of the regular duties, is often productive; but most change efforts succeed as a result of the passionate belief of willing volunteers, rather than any rewards that are offered.

Noah's Ark syndrome-having every group represented on a team

decision maker-someone who has the authority and responsibility to make a decision related to change

stakeholder-someone who has a vested interest in how change occurs and who will likely be called upon to carry out the decision made

expert-someone who has considerable knowledge about an issue, the organization, or the change process

supporter-someone who has committed to seeing change occur and has some ideas about potential changes

resister-someone who likes the status quo and is dubious about the proposed changes

facilitator-someone who does not have a vested interest in the change but is eager to make the process work

Initiating the Team

The first meeting of the team should have no task involvement, but should focus solely on team building. Alan Filley (1985) proposes three very productive steps to be taken before any problem solving begins.

Review and Adjustment of Relative Conditions. At this point, people should introduce themselves and begin to establish mutual trust. Activities that encourage interpersonal sharing and communication should be used.

Review and Adjustment of Perceptions. This is the time for people to discuss their hidden agendas, their hopes, and despairs for the change effort. They should also discuss their private grievances and pitfalls. This is a time for reality checks and disclosure.

Review and Adjustment of Norms and Beliefs. The team should review its beliefs and add any others it feels are important. The team should also establish norms for how it wishes to operate. For example:

► We will keep all team discussion confidential.

► We will operate by consensus.

► We will meet all timelines.

Both beliefs and the norms should be written on large charts and posted during meetings. This posting may seem hokey, but it acts as a constant reminder of the group's beliefs and how it wants to operate. This process, as well as alternatives to it, emphasizes two critical elements within the team process: rational and orderly discussion of ideas and the exploration of feelings and values. Both are important to successful change.

Knowledge About Change

One problem that interferes with team effectiveness is lack of knowledge about how to create change. Creating change is like coaching—most people think they know how to do it, but few actually can. All jobs entail more complexities and complications than most casual observers detect. The change process, too, is more complex than most people realize. The person forming a team must be familiar with the research and literature about effecting change and must make early efforts to discuss effective change. The team needs to operate from a base of real knowledge.

Providing Resources

A team working to create change must have the necessary resources, including time, leadership, funds, freedom, energy, recognition, a chance to network, and empowerment.

Time. Change agents need to have realistic, reasonable time lines. An eager board may want results in a couple of months, but change generally takes longer than that. A year is a long enough time to accomplish some things but a short enough period to sustain interest and commitment. If the change is major, it may ultimately require three to five years for full implementation. The team may get to that point through a series of one-year plans. Undue haste in planning may only lengthen the time needed for implementation.

Leadership. Every team needs a natural leader. He or she may emerge from within the group or may be supported, but there must be leadership if change is to occur. James Kouzes and Barry Posner (1987) found five fundamental practices that enabled leaders to get extraordinary things done.

- ► Challenging the process
- ► Inspiring a shared vision
- ► Enabling others to act
- ► Modeling the way
- ► Encouraging the heart

Gloria Steinem emerged as a natural leader in the feminist movement.

   Successful change advocates need to be attentive to these leadership practices. As a change team is formed, it is necessary to provide a leader who will take up these practices.

Funds. The power of budgets lies not in their overall size, but in the amount of discretionary funds available. If a change agent has a $40 million budget but only $10,000 in discretionary money, he or she has little power. Conversely, if the change agent has a budget of $1 million, but $100,000 in discretionary funds, the person has significantly more power. Effective change groups need discretionary money to fuel their decisions and reward their ideas. The team should be provided a budget and the discretion to decide on its use. If the CEO must approve every expenditure, the change team will not feel it controls the money. Change agents should be given both money and the freedom to use it.

Freedom. Not all change efforts fall neatly within rules. Most change efforts in fact violate some established procedures or policies. To empower a team or pursue change, the changer must be prepared to modify standard procedures. This does not mean giving the team carte blanche in all that matters. As change evolves, it will likely batter and bruise some of the longtime routines.

   Change teams need the freedom to bend rules but also the freedom to fail. Effective change occurs in an environment that promotes experimentation and supports those who dare to go beyond the easily attainable. If there is an environment in which failure is not accepted, no one will dare to risk.

Energy. Change calls for celebration and excitement. If the change effort is vested with sparks of energy, the team will achieve more. Energetic, interested people are needed to join the change team. Not much will happen unless individuals have the drive to succeed and the will to

Chapter 14 · A Rapidly Changing World of Work

overcome resistance. Tired, burnt-out people rarely achieve greatness or create change. Moreover, if team members are to feel energetic, the leadership of the organization must have this quality.

Recognition. Another important resource is recognition—a prime motivator. It fuels action and inspires effort. Change attempts should be recognized at the beginning, at the end, and periodically during the process. This recognition may occur in a variety of ways: at meetings, through written communications, in speeches, and so on. The important thing is to recognize the effort. Too much recognition may be a problem. It may send a message to others that they are not as important. This dilemma has no simple solution. Managers must be sensitive to the fine line between reasonable recognition and apparent favoritism. The best bet is to spread recognition widely throughout the organization.

Networking. A rich source for change is the experience of others. It is important to give a change team the opportunity to visit other sites, talk to other people, and observe the operations at different agencies. Many new ideas evolve from the opportunities to network. At the very least, the team may return with a renewed faith in their manager's ideas and approaches.

Networking within the organization is also important. Changers need a support base and encouragement from colleagues to dare to try their ideas. The insights of people who are not directly involved are an invaluable resource to change teams. Networking both within and outside of the organization provides this perspective.

Empowerment. The last resource may be the most important. Empowerment occurs when people feel their survival is in their own hands and when they feel they have important work to do, sense a clear purpose, and are committed to achieving that purpose. If people are given unimportant work, they feel unimportant. Lacking a sense of control over their own survival, they do not seek new possibilities. If they have no purpose, direction, or commitment, they simply react or even come to a dead stop.

Managers who form change teams must empower their teams to move forward. If team members suspect they are merely a dumping ground for a bad idea, they will fail. Managers who want to achieve vital change need to examine these factors of empowerment and make sure their teams have the resource power to get the job done.

Reengineering with Technology

The driving forces are diverse worldwide: expense pressures, questions about staff functions, changes in customer base, and competition in a changing marketplace. All require organizations to examine their current way of conducting business. This examination may result in the reengineering of operating procedures.

The words *redesign* and *reengineer* are often used interchangeably. While the desired results of these two efforts are similar—productivity, gains, cost savings, quality, service improvements, cycle time reductions—the two differ dramatically. Process **redesign** is a systematic method that seeks to simplify and streamline existing operating procedures. Process **reengineering** creates new operating procedures, making radical and innovative changes to business methods to achieve improvements. The differences between the two processes are outlined in Figure 14.3.

redesign-a change that seeks to simplify and streamline existing operating procedures

reengineering-creates new operating procedures, making radical and innovative changes to business methods

Figure 14.3 **What Are the Differences?**

Process Redesign	Process Reengineering
▶ Incremental enhancements	▶ Involve radical and dramatic change
▶ May include modified work design	▶ Work is fundamentally restructured
▶ Usually leaves structure and hierarchy intact	▶ Radically changes structure and hierarchy
▶ Modifies the rules	▶ Breaks the rules
▶ Streamlines and simplifies existing process	▶ Creates new process
▶ May not include technology	▶ Usually depends on new technology or use of technology
▶ Typically results in modest gains	▶ Typically results in dramatic gains
▶ Risk is low to moderate	▶ Risk is high
▶ Costs are low to moderate	▶ Costs are high

Experts say process redesign occurs when approximately 10 to 20 percent of the workflow is changed to improve results. Reengineering occurs when 70 to 100 percent of the work processes are altered.

People often confuse the word *reengineering* with *restructuring,* even though the two functions are quite different. Generally, when reengineering takes place, more work is accomplished with fewer people; productivity improves and profits increase or both. Restructuring reduces the workforce or modifies the organizational structure to meet the same or lower demand, or to cut costs.

With reengineering, automation is often used to reduce workloads and increase efficiency and quality. Technology is usually the enabler of the effort. Some attributes that help organizations use technology to reengineer include:

▶ *Commitment to innovation.* Despite uncertainty about the future, reengineering efforts must embrace the notion of discontinuous thinking—identifying and abandoning the outdated rules and fundamental assumptions that underlie current business operations. The ability to see a different future and to take risks underlies every reengineering effort.

▶ *Shift in focus*. Departments should give up long-standing controls in favor of manager and employee controls. The reengineering effort is directed at a solution: not the forms, the people, or the technology. Efforts are centered on the needs of the customer and business, rather than on the internal processes.

▶ *Willingness to commit resources*. Reengineering teams will take on projects that are complex and demand a new set of skills. Significant staff resources have to be totally committed to the effort; and in most cases, outside expertise is needed to supplement in-house experience. Companies look to outside resources to deal with the methodology for reengineering and for an understanding of how technology can enable the process.

Conclusion

The answer is: the answer changes.

Change is the only constant in today's fast-paced society. Personally and professionally, people will confront situations in which they must lead the effort for change or resist it with vigor and fervor. Whether it is organizational change through Total Quality Management principles or implementation of new software, what was is likely to be challenged, adjusted, enhanced, merged, or eliminated.

The change process can be controlled and can be directed. Both personally and professionally, individuals recognize that training, acquisition of new skills, and embracing knowledge make coping with change not only bearable, but fun. Maryanne, dissatisfied with the prospect of being in a rut, initiated her personal change by seeking a vision of the future. She sought the advice and counsel of others to broaden her perspective and orientation. She was motivated to alter her life: she just needed the right direction. Maryanne could not predict with certainty each sequential step necessary to reach her goals. But she was seeking the resources to formulate a broad sense of her future.

Organizations also recognize they must change or fall behind. They too seek ways to capture a vision of the future. More than ever, they are mustering the energy of their human resource talent and are providing the resources and time to invest in the future. Change is the only predictable component of the future. And you cannot have a future if you do not plan for it.

Sources: *Filley, Alan C.* The Complete Manager: What Works When. *(1995).*

Kouzes, James, and Barry Posner. Organization and Management. *1987.*

Peters, Tom, and Robert Waterman. In Search of Excellence. *1982.*

- People face an incredible amount of individual change in both their personal and work lives.
- Some people do the right thing for the wrong reason.
- Any change brings with it a variety of costs.
- The stimulants to change may be positive, negative, or some mix of the two.
- No change should be introduced until a cost/benefit analysis has been completed.
- Human beings resist change for good and logical reasons.
- Changers need to analyze each source of resistance to see the degree to which each source is operating in its setting.
- Almost all change entails more time, effort, and money—three scarce resources.
- Some of the most effective change endeavors are team efforts.
- The technology that is available today can be a facilitator of change.
- The TQM philosophy is one of the organizational change concepts that permeate American business.

Key Terms

change

chaos

decision maker

differential knowledge

driving forces

ego trip

expert

facilitator

force field analysis

imitation

Noah's Ark syndrome

overkill

redesign

reengineering

resistance to change

resister

shamrock organization

stakeholder

supporter

tinkering

Total Quality Management

Discussion Questions

1. Compare and contrast how change impacts one's personal and professional lives.

2. Provide some examples of people making changes for the wrong reasons.

3. *Stimulants to change may be positive or negative or some mix of the two.* What is meant by this statement?

4. Give some examples of driving and restraining forces.

5. Why do some employees resist change?

6. How can the Noah's Ark syndrome prevent a team from accomplishing its mission?

7. Discuss the considerations of forming a team to work on a change activity.

8. How can technology impact the change process?

9. Compare and contrast the TQM approach and the more traditional approach to managing change.

10. Discuss the differences among reengineering, redesigning, and restructuring.

Unit 3

APPLICATIONS & CASES

Application 1

Stress in Your Life

Write down the events, situations, people, and other things at work that are or could be most stressful for you. Then list the emotional and physiological indicators of stress for you. Next, note some action steps you might take to cope with either the sources of stress for you and their effects on you.

Application 2

The Effects of Substance Abuse

Locate a local substance abuse counselor and interview him or her. Ask the person to describe the implications of substance abuse on family life, work performance, the abuser's health, finances, and other things. Compare the information you gained through the interview with that of other class members. Compare the results of your interviews. What conclusions can you draw from the interviews?

Application 3

Harassment Policies That Work

Obtain harassment policies from local employers. Compare them and discuss what most employers are doing to prevent harassment on the job. Then write a harassment policy you think adequately addresses this critical issue.

Application 4

Components of an EAP

You are responsible for setting up an employee assistance program for a large employer. Describe the critical components and explain how such a program would be implemented.

Application 5

Workplace Violence in the News

Read your local newspaper for two weeks. Clip the articles that report violence related to the workplace. Can you find any similarities in the reports? What kinds of things might have prevented these incidents?

Application 6
Making Change Fun

Change efforts are more likely to succeed if excitement is associated with the change. Too often people assume that change calls for a somber atmosphere. Many believe that changers should establish a tone of excitement and joy. If you were responsible for implementing a new office procedure, what kinds of things would you do to establish a tone of excitement?

Application 7
Personal Views of Discrimination

Assemble a panel of local community members to discuss discrimination. Ask them about issues relating to diversity in the workplace, about the impact of discrimination, and how discrimination can be dealt with effectively in the world of work.

Case 1
A Supervisor Who Reveals Problems

As business manager for a large school district, Jerry Scott feels intense pressure daily. Confronted with increasing demands for more resources to deal with students who have more needs than ever before, he is also pressured by taxpayers who need relief from increasing taxes.

Jerry has held his position for over 15 years and is respected as an innovative and creative financial officer. He is also an alcoholic. Daily, after his intense schedule of executive committee meetings, budget balancing, and problem-solving, Jerry goes home and consumes at least a 12-pack of beer. He drinks at home, often alone. He seldom discusses his professional problems at home.

At a state conference for school district financial officers, Jerry and his first assistant, Marge Schnoeblen, were honored for their work in preparing a summary report on school finances for a legislative committee. Marge has worked with Jerry for many years, but did not discover Jerry's drinking problem until this meeting. After the first evening banquet, Marge and Jerry went to the hotel lounge for a nightcap. Jerry consumed several beers quickly—very quickly—and began to confide in Marge. He talked about the pressures he felt and the obligations he had to the school district. He continued to drink. His speech was not blurred, nor were his thoughts. But Marge realized that Jerry had a problem and perhaps was asking for some help.

Marge had never seen any indication that Jerry's drinking was a barrier to his work. She had the utmost respect for his professional and personal integrity.

The next day, Marge wondered, "How should I handle this situation? How should I react toward Jerry now? Should I bring up the subject again? Should I let it slide? Should I offer to help Jerry find a counselor?"

If you were Marge, how would you process the information you had? Would you seek help for Jerry? Ignore his comments? Wait until the condition worsened?

Case 2

Preemployment Drug Testing

It was her big opportunity. After years of training and taking night school classes, Maria Sanchez was offered a middle level management position with a conservative and highly respected public accounting firm. The firm had a reputation as a no-nonsense, image-is-everything, highly professional national organization. Its employment processes were tough. Everyone in accounting circles recognized that Barnes, Fritch, and Frederick (BF & F) were sticklers about their reputations and the reputation of their employees. Rumors about the firm's personal appearance policy and the code of conduct for employees were common among CPAs in the region. BF & F was the upper crust of the accounting business. The firm had the most sought-after clients, offered the best cutting-edge technology for its clients, and performed better than anyone else in the business.

Now Maria, a young woman from the poor part of town, was about to step into a position of prominence in this firm. She was not only a woman but was also Hispanic. She would be a role model for others.

Maria had passed BF & F's standards. Now all she had to do was pass the firm's mandatory drug testing program. Maria was not concerned about marijuana or cocaine. Those drugs were not an issue for her. She was concerned that the Prozac she had been taking for the past three years to treat her depression would be discovered during the drug test.

She knew that BF & F would have problems with someone on drugs designed to control emotional problems. Maria's dilemma was simple: She could either tell her future boss of her physical/mental condition before the drug test or she could remain silent?

If she did not tell BF & F in advance, and the test results indicated her prescribed medication, might her future employer disqualify her for the position for lying on the application form? She had answered no to the question: Do you have any medical condition that might prevent you from performing the duties of this position, or do you need any accommodation to equip you for this position?

If you were Maria, would you discuss this medical condition with the potential employer? Would you refuse to take the required preemployment drug test? How would you resolve this problem?

Case 3

The Wellness Program

"But stress isn't all bad; this is a high-pressure business. If our people can't take it, they should look for some other kind of work," said Dennis O'Hara, project manager. He was talking to the president of Johnson Engineering, Dana Slocum, about general well-being of some of the managers in the company. One had back trouble, another had had a mild heart attack, and a third was being treated for high blood pressure. Moreover, data on medical treatment needs showed that the company spent more money than similar companies. This year alone costs had increased 30 percent.

One of Dana's concerns was that the company's way of doing things was causing health problems for its employees. He had read about burnout and wondered if it were happening at Johnson Engineering. There had been complaints about overloads, tight deadlines, and confusion in assignments, but he thought that was just how business was done. But if too much stress was leading to burnout, ill health, and poor performance, it might be cost effective to do something about the problem.

Johnson Engineering hired a consultant, Sharon Foley, to provide information on dealing with quality of work life and productivity. Sharon started the meeting by outlining the purpose of wellness programs from the corporate point of view. According to Sharon, wellness programs should

► promote mutual respect and trust

► get workers to see that company goals and personal goals are not mutually exclusive

► improve recognition

► improve morale

► promote stress management

Sharon said, "We want to be more sensitive to people's needs at work. We want to provide challenging jobs but we also want to ensure that people have control over their own work and are involved in the decisions that affect them." She went on to explain how a wellness program focuses on a healthy lifestyle. Sharon emphasized that people take health risks daily when they combine stress, physical inactivity, and poor diets. A wellness program is designed to reduce these risks and prevent disability and premature death.

Physically fit workers have more endurance, fewer stress-related disorders, and fewer absences than workers physically inactive workers. They also have more confidence and self-esteem. The pressures of work life sometimes cause people to eat too fast or skip meals. An unbalanced diet has a negative effect on health and job performance.

The average American's style of working involves competition, challenges, negotiations, deadlines, and endless demands. Wellness programs deal with all of these issues, according to Sharon.

Dana was interested in taking the next step. However, before he committed to any program, he asked for input from employees. One employee responded, "This all sounds good, but we don't really have time to spend on helping people stay healthy."Another said, "We have work that has to be done by next week. We can't relax."Others seemed mildly interested. Given the mixed reaction, Dana was unsure about what to do next.

What is the connection between stress, health, and performance? How much responsibility do companies like Johnson Engineering have for the well-being of their employees? What do you think about the comment, "If they have the right staff, they will thrive in this environment"? If you were Dana Slocum, would you be worried about the situation in this company? What would you tell Dana to do?

Case 4

Sick Leave Abuse

"I've had it! We just cannot afford all of these employees calling in sick on Mondays and Fridays. It's not fair to the other employees who show up to do their jobs, only to be frustrated by a few people who habitually want a long weekend. We work as a team here. When one person is out, it impacts many. I'm going to push for a much more conservative sick leave policy. No pay for the first two days of illness, and sick leave benefits won't kick in until the third consecutive day of absence due to illness. If employees have to pay for their absences instead of me, they will think twice about staying home with a sniffle."

Joe Roman was a good employer. He was fair and was recognized by his employees and others in the community for his sincere concern for his employees. His 76-person light manufacturing operation had struggled in the 1980s but became profitable due to Joe's hard work and ingenuity. He worked on the floor with his production staff. He knew that efficient production was the key to profitability in his contract tool shop.

But absenteeism, especially among young workers, was a growing problem. Joe described it this way: "When I grew up, I wanted a career. Work was the major focus of my life. I'd never think of missing a day of work to go shopping, or even to take one of my kids to the dentist. I made other arrangements so I could keep my job. Today's workers see work differently. They are the X-generation. They don't value a career—just a paycheck. They want all kinds of benefits and then exploit them with reckless abandon. OK, our values are different but I cannot afford this cavalier attitude toward work. Sick leave is like an insurance policy. Use it only when you really need it. I've got to change the policy."

How do you feel about Joe's problem with employees who seem to abuse sick leave? Should employees come to work when they are sick? What are the implications of such a policy?

Case 5

An Unstable Coworker: What Should You Do?

When Rich was hired as a first-year accountant, he was identified as a bright self-starter. He was also considered self-reliant and strong-willed. Rich was a detail-oriented accountant who had a real concern for the environment.

He was assigned to share an office with Caroline, also a bright, self-reliant accountant. These two young professionals became a solid work team. They worked long, hard hours to meet the needs of their clients. During the second year of working together, Rich began to show severe changes in his behavior. He lost 30 pounds; his hair was unkempt and his dress became progressively less professional. He kept unusual work hours, approved by his supervisor. He would start late in the morning and stay until 11:00 P.M. He said he could get more done when the office was quiet and empty. People at work bothered him.

There also were other changes. His eyes were often dilated, and he was moody. Many coworkers thought it was a reaction to the divorce he was going through. There was speculation about whether he and his office mate were having an affair. There was talk in the office about possible substance abuse. But the work Rich produced was quality. The firm was busy and his supervisor was nonconfrontational. "I don't care what he's doing, just as long as his accounting work is what the client needs."

Rich began to have run-ins with other employees. An office coordinator who was managing an office redecoration project found threatening notes on her e-mail shortly after Rich's and Caroline's offices were changed. Simple rules became major issues. For example, a rule that no items could be posted on the exterior of cubicle walls was received by Rich as a threat to his free speech. He threw a tirade using harsh language and tossed some chairs in the office.

Rich became more outspoken with time and more unkempt. He had problems with people at work regularly. One of his coworkers reported that someone turned on his car lights during the day so his car battery was run down. It happened frequently but anonymously, and Rich was suspected. .

Other employees expressed concern about Rich's working relationships. One business office employee filed a formal concern about Rich's behavior—she said she corrected one of his time sheets and he "went crazy." She was concerned about her safety.

Rich's immediate supervisor did nothing except explain there was too much work and too few accountants to get it done. "I need him," the supervisor kept saying.

More and more workers reported changed behaviors or expressed concern about working with Rich. Several said his profile was the same as that of persons who had exhibited workplace violence at several post office locations. He was a loner—strong-willed, and had recent dramatic changes in behavior, was suspected of substance abuse, and exhibited violent behavior at work.

If you were Rich's supervisor, how would you proceed? If you were the firm's human resources manager, what would you do?

Case 6

Separation of Work Life and Personal Life

It was 3:30 A.M when the phone rang. Mark Kelly, half asleep, answered thinking the worst. "Where's my husband,"asked Rebecca Jordan, the wife of one of Mark's senior employees, John Jordan. "He's in Forest City on a job, Rebecca. You know that."

"That's what I mean. I just got a call from Steve Sanders. He said his wife was supposed to be in the home office for training, but when he called the hotel just now, no one answered. Steve thinks his wife is having an affair with John. What do you know about this, Mark?"

Mark was still half asleep. Deb Sanders was a bright 30-year-old secretary in the office that Mark managed. She was at least 25 years younger than John Jordan. John had a reputation for an active social life, but Mark never saw any evidence at work that the two employees were involved.

"Rebecca, I don't know what you are talking about. Your husband is in Forest City on a job and Deb is at the home office. That doesn't mean that there's anything going on. Why would Steve call you and say such a thing? This is crazy! Go back to bed."

"Mark, those two are involved and we both know it. What are you going to do about it?"said Rebecca. "Nothing, except go back to bed,"explained Mark.

The next day Mark called the human resources manager at the home office. He asked if Deb Sanders had arrived for her training. "She got in late for the meeting. She must have driven in this morning because she looks tired—but she's here,"explained the human resources manager. Mark Kelly then told of his early morning phone call.

Could it be that Deb Sanders and John Jordan were having an affair? The human resources manager told Mark to stay out of it unless there was evidence their work was affected.

Two days later, Rebecca Jordan called Mark again. "I want a copy of all of his cellular phone records for the last three months,"said Rebecca. "I know those two are up to something, and I'm going to get to the bottom of it."

"I'm sorry, Rebecca, those records belong to the firm and I have no intention of letting you see them. I'm really sorry you are so distressed over this, but I will not get in the middle of this real or imagined situation. It's just none of my business,"said Mark.

"You mean to tell me that when two of your employees are having an affair and there are kids and spouses being hurt, your position is hands off? That's really cruel, Mark,"Rebecca screamed.

If you were Mark, what would you do? Is it possible to separate a personal life from a professional life?

Case 7

Change: What's in It for Me?

What's in it for the changee? What will she or he gain from the change effort? This may be the most important question asked while implementing a change effort. Look at payoff as positive and necessary in motivating workers. Unless they perceive a payoff, workers may not willingly change. Change without payoff makes no sense.

The Iowa City Community School District wanted to create a teacher advisory program. According to the proposed program, teachers would spend their free periods counseling small groups of students. When asked what was in the program for the teachers (changees), the response was, "It'll ease up the registration process and give counselors more time."

Great, but what's in it for the teachers? "It will be really good for the students,"was the reply once again. Somehow school officials failed to grasp the importance of payoff for the changees. They focused only on benefits for everyone else. While the teacher advisory program may be an incredibly good idea, what is likely to happen in this case? What intervention could be done to assure a successful change effort?

Case 8

Another Award

Osamu Sato managed the Flower Pot, a garden center and greenhouse in Davis, California. He had 12 employees in addition to four family members who worked in the business. He thought it was a great idea to give an award when an employee did something that he felt exceeded his expectations. Since he had good employees, he gave out several awards each week, and sometimes an employee would get an award a day. The award was always the same—a small certificate that read "You are the Greatest." The employees laughed each time they received the award because they liked their jobs and would have done the work even if no awards had been given.

What could Osamu do differently that might be more meaningful in recognizing employees? Think of a reward system for a small business that could serve effectively as a motivational tool. Explain your reward system in writing or discuss it with your classmates.

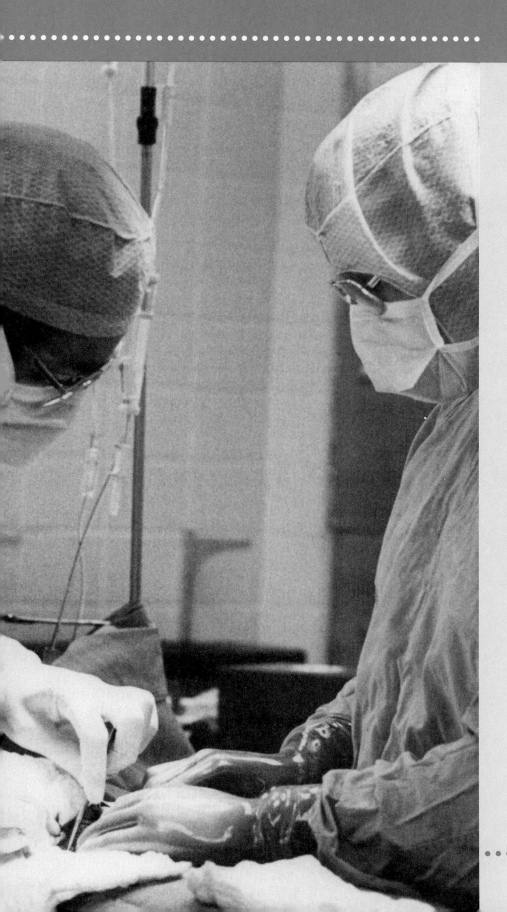

Unit 4

Improving Practices in Human Relations

Chapter 15
*Developing a
Leadership Lifestyle*

Chapter 16
*Understanding
Power and Politics*

Chapter 17
*Applying Personal
Values, Business
Ethics, and Social
Responsibility*

Chapter 18
*Professionalism—
the Key to Human
Relations*

Applications & Cases

15

Learning Objectives

Upon completing this chapter, you should be able to:

- Define leadership.

- Identify styles of leadership used to influence others.

- Explain several different theories of leadership.

- Articulate the benefits of Total Quality Management.

- Profile the changes needed for leadership in a multicultural environment.

Developing a Leadership Lifestyle

Jacques Delacroix was about to begin a new job as the managing director of the Harbourfront Plaza, one of the finest hotels in Toronto, Canada. Jacques had worked in several positions in smaller hotels in the United States, but moving to Canada was going to be a new experience. He was told in the interview process that Canadians would respond to his leadership much like the United States workers he was used to, but he was still quite nervous about the position. Would his employees respond to him as they did in previous jobs? What would he have to change to be an effective leader in a different culture? He knew French, but did he know it well enough to gain the respect of the people he would be leading? Jacques had legitimate concerns which are no different than concerns anyone moving to a new leadership role would have, especially in a different culture.

If people can develop good leadership skills for their work and personal lives, they can learn to adapt them to different cultures and work styles.

What Is Leadership?

In order to have a leader, there must be followers! Not everyone wants to be a manager or leader in the sense that he or she will make all the decisions and be accountable for those decisions. Many people are comfortable to let someone else decide what to do, and they will do what is expected of them. They want to be followers. Other people thrive on the opportunities that are presented in a leadership role. Some people are willing to take leadership responsibilities in their personal affairs but would rather someone else be the leader at work. Or, perhaps the opposite is true. They might be willing to be the leader at work, but in their personal lives, they would rather someone else lead. What exactly is leadership?

Douglas McGregor concluded through his extensive research that leadership involves at least four major variables. He suggests that leadership includes

1. the characteristics of the leader;
2. the attitudes, needs, and other personal characteristics of the followers;
3. the characteristics of the organization, such as its purpose, its structure, the nature of the tasks to be performed; and
4. the social, economic, and political milieu.[1]

According to McGregor, **leadership** is not a property of the individual, but a complex relationship among several variables. Even the personal characteristics of an individual differ depending on other influential factors.

A **leader** is the person who can influence followers to accomplish goals. Not all managers or supervisors are leaders. Leaders are those who can cause change to occur, usually through the influence they have upon others. Leaders inspire their followers to believe, to the point where they will expend extra effort to accomplish tasks that would ordinarily not be done. Not all managers or supervisors can inspire and cause change, nor can they accomplish goals. In the management process, the reward system is most prevalent, while leadership is inspiration. In personal situations, you might look to someone whom you would follow, or perhaps you are the person who is able to influence others to follow you to accomplish what you or a group would like to accomplish.

Leaders are also expected to be followers. A good leader can offer leadership or influence by following when the situation changes. Organizations and personal lives are not static; change is occurring constantly and therefore requires new leadership. A good leader recognizes when it is important to let someone else lead, sometimes permanently. A good analogy is geese flying in the form of a "V." One goose is at the front providing leadership and doesn't get the benefits of an updraft created by the other birds, so it will eventually need to be replaced. When that leader moves back into the ranks, a different goose takes over and provides new leadership.

> **leadership**-a complex relationship among several variables such as leader and follower characteristics, and the social, economic, and political milieu

> **leader**-a person who can influence followers to accomplish goals

When geese fly in a V formation, they change leaders often to allow for rest periods and new leadership.

[1] Douglas McGregor. *The Human Side of Enterprise.* New York: McGraw Hill, 1985, 25th Anniversary Printing.

Chapter 15 · Developing a Leadership Lifestyle

Leadership Characteristics

Researchers use many different descriptors to define the characteristics of a leader. There is general agreement among the researchers; however, some differences occur due to the process used to arrive at the terms. Dr. David Campbell is one of the researchers who has conducted several studies to determine **leadership characteristics,** which resulted in the development of the Campbell Leadership Index (CLI). In his research, Campbell determined that leadership is most often defined with traits rather than tasks which are performed by the leader.[2] The trait and the descriptive adjectives for the traits are shown in Figure 15.1

leadership characteristics- traits such as leadership, energy, affability, dependability, and resilience

Figure 15.1 **Campbell Leadership Index**

Trait	Descriptors	Psychological Interpretation
Leadership		
Ambitious	Competitive, forceful	Determined to make progress, likes to compete
Daring	Adventuresome, risk-taking	Risk oriented, willing to try new experiences
Dynamic	Enthusiastic, a leader	Takes charge, inspires others, seen as a leader
Enterprising	Impressive, resourceful	Works well with the complexities of change
Experienced	Savvy, well-connected	Has a good background, well-informed
Farsighted	Insightful, forward looking	Looks ahead, plans, a visionary
Original	Creative, imaginative,	Sees the world differently, has many new ideas
Persuasive	Convincing, fluent	Articulate and persuasive in influencing others
Energy	Active, healthy	Physically fit, energetic
Affability		
Affectionate	Emotional	Acts close, warm, and nurturing
Considerate	Cooperative, helpful	Thoughtful, willing to work with others
Empowering	Encouraging, supportive	Motivates and helps others to achieve
Entertaining	Extroverted, humorous	Clever and amusing; enjoys people
Friendly	Cheerful, likeable	Pleasant to be around, smiles easily
Dependability		
Credible	Candid, trustworthy	Open and honest; inspires trust
Organized	Orderly, methodical	Sets up systems and follows through
Productive	Dependable, effective	Uses time and resources well
Thrifty	Frugal, not extravagant	Uses and manages money wisely
Resilience		
Calm	Easy-going, serene	Has an unhurried, unruffled manner
Flexible	Adaptable, not stubborn	Easily adjusts to changes
Optimistic	Resilient, well-adjusted	Positive; handles challenges well
Trusting	Trusting, not cynical	Trusts and believes in others

[2]Kenneth E. Clark, Miriam B. Clark, and David P. Campbell, eds. "The Leadership Characteristics of Leadership Researchers." *Impact of Leadership.* Greensboro, North Carolina: Center for Creative Leadership, 1992.

In various resources, words such as *charisma* (leading by charm or magnetism), *personality, education, assertiveness,* and many others are used to describe the characteristics or traits of a leader. No matter what words are used, most of the meanings describe the same qualities of a person who will most likely influence others to accomplish personal, group, or organizational goals.

Leadership Styles

Every person, because of personal traits, might handle others differently when placed in a leadership role. Even though leaders may act differently in certain situations, their response or approach to influencing others can be placed into a category called a leadership style.

Marti Bartelmai is a single mother living in Topeka, Kansas. She has two teen-age children—a son and a daughter. Marti's daughter, Maria, is an honors student who studies without being told to get her homework done. Her son, Brian, on the other hand, is quite the opposite. He has to be coerced, cajoled, and practically threatened before he will do his homework. Marti feels she has to be very strict, or autocratic, telling Brian exactly what he needs to do. Both children will have to rely on scholarships to attend college. Maria has a very different work style from Brian's, and Marti knows she can let Maria make many of her own decisions because she will be fully responsible for her decisions.

Marti's children are no different from people in the workplace. Some people need close supervision and others respond better to less supervision. It is up to the leader to determine what styles are best suited to work groups or personal relationships. We will first look at leadership styles that have been identified over the years, and then we will review the current trends in the workplace. We have a rapidly changing workforce, and workers respond to leadership differently than they did in the "You'll do as I say or you'll be fired" industrial age.

Classifications of Leadership Decision-Making Styles

Management and *leadership* are terms that are often used synonymously, although they shouldn't be. They mean different things. Managers plan, organize, direct, and control; leaders influence. Hopefully, a manager who is expected to manage people can also function as a leader. A leader uses different methods to influence followers to perform as desired. The approach used by the leader to influence the performance of others is called the **leadership style.**

Leadership includes decision-making, a process which can be done by the leader or shared with others. The process depends upon the decision-making style of the leader. Decision-making styles fit into a broad spectrum of participation, varying from none to extensive.

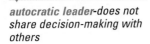

autocratic leader-does not share decision-making with others

participative leader-shares the authority to make decisions with others

free-rein-empowers employees to function on their own

Autocratic Decision-Making. An **autocratic leader** does not share decision-making with others. The leader makes a decision and announces it to the employees who are expected to follow it. The leader may ask others for opinions, but they are usually ignored unless something critical was overlooked which could be harmful to someone or the organization.

Participative Decision-Making. The **participative leader** shares the authority to make decisions with others. The amount of participation depends on the people involved, the situation, and the time available. Participative decision-making could involve the workers completely in the process, or the participative leader could make a tentative decision to be presented to the employees for feedback and possible suggestions to change the decision. This is a very popular leadership style today while companies are rightsizing (adjusting the number of employees to improve financial efficiency) and creating work teams. The growing importance of participative decision-making will be examined later in this chapter.

Free-Rein Decision-Making. The **free-rein** style empowers employees to function on their own without managers being directly involved. When this style is used, managers set parameters within which employees must function, and then they let the employees make decisions. This style of leadership is especially effective with highly educated professionals. It relies on delegation of authority and works best when employees are proficient in their jobs.

Theories of Leadership

Several theories have been developed to help explain how leaders influence others. They apply to the workplace as well as in personal situations. Some of the highlights of the most popular theories are presented here. Be sure to observe how closely leadership style fits with the leadership theories. Watch for similarities and differences in the theories that are discussed.

Theory X and Theory Y Leadership

Douglas McGregor presented his ideas in 1957 and later published his leadership theory in a book called the *Human Side of Enterprise.* McGregor theorized that behind every managerial decision or action lies assumptions about human nature and behavior. What he determined was that people react to leadership in opposing ways. One classification of human behavior is based upon assumptions of the Theory X leader; the other is based upon the assumptions of the Theory Y leader.

Theory X leader-has little confidence in workers to think and act independently

The Theory X Leader. The person who shares the beliefs of the **Theory X leader** doesn't have a lot of confidence in a worker's ability to think and act independently. The Theory X leader believes:

- The average human being has an inherent dislike of work and will avoid it if possible.

- Because of this human characteristic of disliking work, most people must be coerced, controlled, directed, or threatened with punishment before they put forth adequate effort toward the achievement of organizational objectives.

- The average human being prefers to be directed, wishes to avoid responsibility, has relatively little ambition, and wants security above all.

According to the beliefs of the Theory X leader, the man is giving the child directions because he lacks confidence in her and thinks she does not want to take responsibility for herself.

Perhaps as you read the previously mentioned characteristics, you thought to yourself, "I know people who fit those descriptors." Everyone knows people who are lazy and don't really want to work, but the X leader, as he or she is called, places all people in the same category.

Interestingly, McGregor believed that Theory X explained the consequences of a particular management or leadership style but doesn't explain human nature. The X leaders are so limited because of narrow beliefs about human performance, they overlook the possible outcomes of other leadership styles. McGregor relates this style to raising a child. As the child grows and matures into adulthood, control strategies must change as the child changes. Many managers or leaders feel that adults have stopped growing and remain in their early stages of adolescence, hence the need to act as X leaders.

Theory X leaders are said to be autocratic. Autocratic leaders are in charge, much like drill sergeants; they are the persons who will direct others and make the decisions. Autocratic leaders use their power, gained pri-

Chapter 15 · Developing a Leadership Lifestyle

marily from the positions they are in, to accomplish the objectives of the organization. Their style is called "hard" leadership because they expect others to respond obediently to their commands. Under the direction of autocrats, there is little to no opportunity for others to make decisions.

The Theory Y Leader.

The opposite of the Theory X leader is the **Theory Y leader** who places considerable confidence in humans to function as independent individuals. The assumptions of the Theory Y leader are as follows.

► The physical and mental effort used in work is natural and workers will respond positively.

► Humans will respond with self-direction and self-control to accomplish the objectives to which they are committed.

► Commitment to objectives results from the rewards associated with the accomplishment.

► In a proper environment, most human beings learn to accept and to seek responsibility.

► Most people will use a relatively high degree of imagination, ingenuity, and creativity to solve problems.

► Most people are not being challenged in the workplace and their potential is not being utilized.

Theory Y assumptions elicit a different type of leadership. The Y leader realizes that humans grow and develop; the environment is not static and constantly changing; different people respond to different forms of leadership; and individuals are a resource with potential. You will see later in this chapter how the assumptions of Theory Y relate closely to some of the changes that have taken place in corporations in recent years.

The Theory Y leader follows a participative, or democratic, style of leadership. The Y leader involves others in the decision-making process, sometimes by asking for suggestions and recommendations, and then makes the final decision. This person is known as a consultative leader. A democratic leader involves others in the decision-making process and does what the majority wants to have done.[3]

The Leadership Continuum

Another popular theory of leadership is illustrated in the Leadership Continuum. The **Leadership Continuum** (Figure 15.2) shows that managers allow subordinates a varied amount of freedom to participate in organizational decisions. With some of the leadership tactics, the boss makes all the decisions and announces them to the employees. This is the most autocratic approach to leading employees. This approach is fast but excludes workers from involvement. This can lead to resentment and lack of cooperation from the subordinates.

[3] Douglas McGregor. *The Human Side of Enterprise.* New York: McGraw Hill, 1985, 25th Anniversary Printing.

Figure 15.2 Leadership Continuum

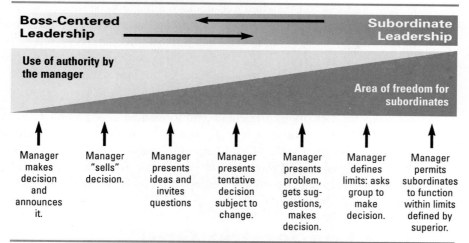

Boss-Centered Leadership ← → **Subordinate Leadership**

Use of authority by the manager

Area of freedom for subordinates

| Manager makes decision and announces it. | Manager "sells" decision. | Manager presents ideas and invites questions | Manager presents tentative decision subject to change. | Manager presents problem, gets suggestions, makes decision. | Manager defines limits: asks group to make decision. | Manager permits subordinates to function within limits defined by superior. |

Reprinted by permission of the Harvard Business Review. *An exhibit from "How to Choose a Leadership Pattern" by Robert Tannenbaum and Warren H. Schmidt (May/June 1973). Copyright © 1973 by the President and Fellows of Harvard College; all rights reserved.*

At the opposite end of the continuum is the leader who gives subordinates considerable freedom to operate within preestablished guidelines. This approach is participative and is similar to that of the Y manager discussed previously. Most managers find that employees appreciate being involved in the decision-making process and favor this end of the continuum.

The difficulty for people in leadership positions is to find a balance for most of the workers. Some need a more autocratic leader, while others function better when they are given more freedom and involvement in organizational decisions. Robert Tannenbaum and Warren Schmidt emphasized that a manager should give careful thought to three factors before selecting a leadership style.

► *Characteristics of the manager:* education, background, experience, values, goals, and expectations

► *Characteristics of employees:* education, background, experience, values, goals, and expectations

► *Situational requirements:* size, structure, organizational complexity and climate, technology, time pressures, and the work itself[4]

ae-Soo Lee was studying business management and science, with a specialization in horticulture, at a community college in Cincinnati, Ohio. He wanted to manage a nursery that used at least some hydroponics. He had the scientific skills to tackle most situations that would arise but was concerned about his leadership skills. He knew he wasn't a very good

----

[4]Robert Tannenbaum, and Warren Schmidt. "How to Choose a Leadership Pattern." *Harvard Business Review.* May–June 1973.

Chapter 15·Developing a Leadership Lifestyle

group worker and preferred to do jobs himself so they would be done right. He also knew that if he wanted to manage a nursery, he needed to rely on others and would have to provide leadership that would encourage workers to respond positively. Because he had a lot of uncertainty, he felt he needed to have more information about leadership before he could make a career decision. Mr. Lee decided to study more about leadership to see if he could develop leadership skills.

Like Mr. Lee, many students begin to wonder about being good managers and leaders. Sometimes it all seems so complex and too much of a challenge. Questions like "Can I help employees become satisfied with their jobs?" "How do I motivate workers?" and "What kind of a leader am I?" are all legitimate questions. Perhaps Tae-Soo Lee knew further information would be helpful.

The Leadership Grid®

Leadership Grid®-shows leadership style based on concern for people or production

The **Leadership Grid**® is a recent development by Blake and McCanse based on earlier research by Blake and Mouton in 1964.[5] The leadership style classifications are based upon the amount of concern for people versus the amount of concern for production. (Refer to Figure 15.3.) Concern for production is the 1 through 9 scale on the horizontal axis of the grid. Production concerns are for keeping employees on task and generating profit through high productivity. The 1 through 9 vertical axis measures concern for people. Concern for people relates to trust and respect for employees, employee involvement in decisions, and job security for employees.

The grid has seven areas which describe different styles of leadership. Leadership styles for each of the areas of the grid are discussed here, but the explanations on Figure 15.3 should also be noted.

Leadership Grid® Style Overview

9,1 Authority Compliance management — Managers in this position have great concern for production and little concern for people. People are seen as 'tools' for production. They demand tight, unilateral control in order to complete tasks efficiently. They consider creativity and human relations to be much less important.

1,9 Country Club management — Managers in this position demonstrate high concern for people and low concern for production. They exert strong effort to create a friendly work environment, even at the expense of production. Production is less important than friendly interpersonal relations. Their goal is to keep people happy.

Robert Blake, and Jane Mouton. *The Managerial Grid.* Houston: Gulf Publishing Co., 1964.

Figure 15.3 **The Leadership Grid® Figure**

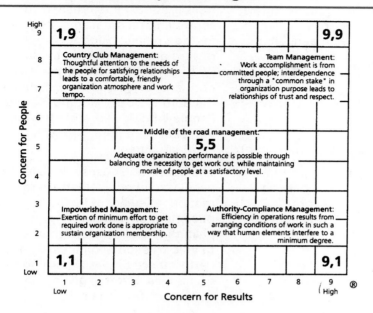

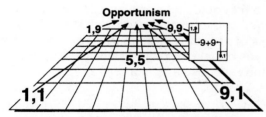

In Opportunistic Management, people adapt and shift to any Grid style needed to gain the maximum advantage. Performance occurs according to a system of selfish gain. Effort is given only for an advantage for personal gain.

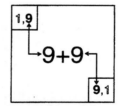

9+9: Paternalism/Maternalism
Reward and approval are bestowed to people in return for loyalty and obedience; failure to comply leads to punishment.

Source: The Leadership Grid® Reproduced by permission of the owners.

1,1	Impoverished management	This style is often referred to as laissez-faire. Leaders in this position have little concern for people or productivity. To maintain low involvement, they avoid taking sides and stay out of conflicts. They do enough to maintain group membership.
5,5	Middle of the road management	Leaders in this position have medium concern for both people and production. They rely on proven techniques and precedents and avoid taking untested risks. The goal is to maintain membership and excel within 'safe' boundaries. Conflict is dealt with by diverting polarized views by seeking compromise. Compromise is encouraged even if it diminishes a sound resolution.

9+9	Paternalistic "father knows best" management	This leader takes the high 9 level of concern from 9,1 and 1,9 to create a combined style of controlling paternalism. The paternalist strives for high results (High 9 from 9,1) and uses reward and punishment to gain compliance (High 9 from 1,9). Loyalty is rewarded with support, encouragement, opportunity, and more freedom to "carry out the Paternalist's ways." People who deviate from the Paternalist's guidelines are punished with more monitoring and restrictions.
Opp	Opportunistic "what's in it for me" management	The opportunist uses whatever Grid style is needed to obtain selfish interest and self-promotion. They adapt to situations to gain the maximum advantage. They may use 9,1 to push their own goals with one person, and 1,9 to gain trust and confidence with another. Performance occurs according to a system of exchanges. Effort is given only for an equivalent measure of the same.
9,9	Team management	These managers demonstrate high concern for both people and production. They work to motivate employees to reach their highest levels of accomplishment. They explore alternatives openly and aggressively. They are flexible and responsive to change.[6]

Developing a Leadership Style

A leader tends to have one style that is more dominant than the others. This style will be used most often, regardless of the leadership situation. If the results are not satisfactory, the leader, or manager, may switch to a backup style which will usually facilitate the needed response. For example, if a leader tried a middle of the road approach (5,5) because he or she was new in a leadership role and was not getting the expected response, the leader might have to switch to a 9,1 style to meet production requirements.

Which style is best? The answer may depend on the situation in which a person is providing leadership. For example, if someone manages workers in an assembly plant, the person may not get the same response he or she could as with the style the person would use managing or leading a group of lawyers. When Blake and Mouton developed the original grid, they supported the 9,9 managerial style. The team approach usually results in greater job satisfaction, less absenteeism, and lower turnover of employees. The teamwork concept coincides with some of the contemporary

---

[6]Robert Blake, and Anne A. McCanse. *Leadership Dilemmas—Grid Solutions.* Houston: Gulf Publishing Co., 1991. Reproduced by permission of the owners.

Unit 4 · Improving Practices in Human Relations

thinking in the corporate world. The article "Trends in Leadership Practices" is an illustration of current trends.

Contingency Model of Leadership

Fred Fiedler developed one of the more controversial theories of leadership, the **Contingency Model,** which describes how the situation influences the relationship between leadership traits and effectiveness. Fiedler attempted to predict leadership effectiveness based on a trait measurement labeled as the **least preferred coworker** score (LPC). The leader is asked to rate the past or present coworker with whom he or she would least like to work. The rating scale consists of a bipolar set of adjectives like that shown in Figure 15.4.

Contingency Model- describes how the situation influences the relationship between leadership traits and effectiveness

least preferred coworker- score based on rating of past or present coworker with whom the leader would least like to work

Figure 15.4 **Example of Fiedler's LPC Rating Scale**

friendly : ___ : ___ : ___ : ___ : ___ : ___ : ___ : ___ : unfriendly
            8   7   6   5   4   3   2   1

cold : ___ : ___ : ___ : ___ : ___ : ___ : ___ : ___ : warm
        1   2   3   4   5   6   7   8

Of Human Interest

Trends in Leadership Practices

John Huey started a *Fortune* magazine article dated February 21, 1994, with this Chinese proverb: "Of the best leader, when he is gone, they will say: We did it ourselves."[1] This proverb reflects the contemporary thinking of many corporate leaders. They are realizing that their style of leadership must change to keep pace with the rapidly changing demographics of the workforce. Much of the workforce is no longer white, middle-class, and male; instead it includes workers of many races, languages, and both sexes.

Because of the changes in the workforce, pressures are growing to change the way organizations are being led. Present thinking reflects that information is critical to leadership. Walter Kiechel III, quoting Michael J. Driver, wrote that as we move into the information age, managers will have to develop adaptive, multifocus thinking because change is everywhere.[2] Managing will require an integrative style. Managers need process skills such as team leadership, team membership, and the ability to communicate.

Huey, in the *Fortune* article, stated that leadership involves getting things started and facilitating change. A good example of current management trends is W. L. Gore & Associates, the company that makes Gore-Tex. It considers itself an unmanaged company. The late

CONTINUED

Wilbert L. Gore founded his company based on McGregor's Theory Y and never wavered from his style. This style is now termed *empowerment*. All of the production at Gore is done by work teams, or cells, who select their own leaders by consensus through discussion, not by voting.

At Levi-Straus the philosophy has changed to creating leadership opportunities for everyone. Levi began changing plant operations to a team management approach after decades of operation. Teams of workers are cross-trained for 36 tasks instead of one or two, and they take part in running the plant, including organizing supplies, setting production goals, and making personnel policy. The Levi team managers get much of their direction from the workers rather than from someone higher in the organization.

Organizations are becoming flatter as a result of downsizing or delayering (removing layers of management).[3] This creation of what is known as a horizontal corporation should result in empowered employees. Not all corporations are ready for this kind of change and may not be able to make the shift. They continue to function as vertical organizations, just as they have in the past, even though they have removed layers. Corporations that want to act as horizontal corporations have to maintain a few executives at the top and should have everyone else work together as multidisciplinary teams. The result is less bureaucracy between the lowest and highest levels in the organization. This appears to be what has happened at Levi and at Gore. The company has the type of leadership that theorists like McGregor, Blake and Mouton, and others have said is most suitable for companies.

---

[1]John Huey. "The New Post-Heroic Leadership." Fortune. *February 21, 1994, 42, 44, 48, 50.*

[2]Walter Kiechel III . "A Manager's Career in the New Economy." Fortune. *April 4, 1994, 68–72.*

[3]John A. Byrne. "The Horizontal Corporation." Business Week. *December 20, 1993, 76–81.*

If the leader is critical in rating the coworker, the LPC score will be lower. If the rating is generally positive, the LPC score will be high. The low LPC leader is more task oriented, while the high LPC leader is more people oriented. The low LPC leader is primarily motivated to achieve tasks, and the secondary motive of this leader is to establish good relations with subordinates. The high LPC leader is primarily motivated to have close working relationships with others, while achievement of task objectives is secondary.

The relationship between the leader's LPC score and effectiveness depends on complex situational variables called *situational favorability.*

Favorability is defined by Fiedler as the extent to which the situation gives the leader control over subordinates. There are three characteristics which leaders might change to make a situation more favorable.

1. *Leader-member relations,* the degree of support and loyalty the leader has from subordinates which will cause subordinates to trust and follow the leader's wishes.

2. *Task structure,* the degree to which there are standard operating procedures established to accomplish the task, step-by-step processes which can be followed, and measures which show progress toward completion of the task.

3. *Position power,* the degree to which the leader has authority to measure subordinates' performance and to offer rewards or administer punishment.

Fiedler uses a weighted system and combines the three characteristics to determine favorability. He divides the classifications into eight octants. According to the model, the situation is most favorable when relations with subordinates are good, the leader has substantial power, and the task is highly structured. This situation is illustrated in Figure 15.5 as octant 1. This situation promotes cooperation and, because the leader has high position power and the tasks are structured, is easier to influence and instruct subordinates.

Ethical Dimensions to Human Relations

Questionable Workplace Practices

There are many elements in the corporate world that can cause concern among workers at all levels of an organization. Many companies, after considering their size and structure, determine that they have too many workers and some must be laid off. This can be very traumatic to employees, especially in situations in which generations of family members have worked in the same place.

Some employees react vindictively and unethically. *The Wall Street Journal* reported that an unknown employee of a bank created, that is, forged a memo relating to travel policies and sent it to sources inside and outside the company. The memo stated a tongue-in-cheek set of policies which reflected the aggravations of one employee.

Many companies are reporting that violence in the workplace is increasing. The American Management Association surveyed 311 companies. It found that 25 percent of the companies had had at least one of their workers attacked or killed on the job since 1990, and an additional 31 percent reported threats against their workers. In 1992, 1,004 Americans were murdered on the job, mostly during robberies and miscellaneous crimes.

CONTINUED

Managers are also experiencing difficulties in the job market. Some are accepting jobs, only to find later that the job they thought they were starting was eliminated. In the meantime, they may have quit another job and, as a result, find themselves unemployed. Written employment agreements are recommended for the protection of employees. The written agreement should provide a description of all the benefits and the terms of employment.

Because the workplace is a constantly changing environment, managers and leaders must be willing and able to adapt to the changes that are occurring. Flexibility, understanding, and ethical practices are important characteristics of an effective leader.

Sources: Ryan, Suzanne A. "When Management Gets Tough, the Tough Forge Internal Memos." The Wall Street Journal. April 19, 1994, B1.

Rigdon, Joan E. "Companies See More Workplace Violence." The Wall Street Journal. April 18, 1994, B1.

Lublin, Joann S. "Before You Take That Great Job, Get It in Writing." The Wall Street Journal. February 9, 1994, B1.

The least desirable position for the leader is when relations with subordinates are poor, the task is unstructured, and position power is low. This is octant 8 as described by Fiedler. In this situation, it would be difficult for the leader to accomplish anything, task achievement or personal relationships.[7]

Fiedler's work has been disputed by many researchers but did cause others to look more closely at contingency leadership. His notion that leaders should be matched to the situation to gain more control is an important contribution to other research on leadership.

Figure 15.5 **Fiedler's LPC Contingency Model Relationship**

Octant	Labor-Member Relations	Task Structure	Position Power	Effective Leader
1	Good	Structured	Strong	Low LPC
2	Good	Structured	Weak	Low LPC
3	Good	Unstructured	Strong	Low LPC
4	Good	Unstructured	Weak	High LPC
5	Poor	Structured	Strong	High LPC
6	Poor	Structured	Weak	High LPC
7	Poor	Unstructured	Strong	High LPC
8	Poor	Unstructured	Weak	Low LPC

[9]Fred E. Fiedler. "A Contingency Model fo Leadership Effectiveness." *Advances in Experimental Social Psychology,* edited by Leonard Berkowitz. New York: Academic Press, 1964.

Tyler Green managed a small department at O'Brien's Furniture Warehouse in Jacksonville, Florida. He had five workers in his department, and their main duty was to set up the floor displays whenever new furniture arrived or floor displays needed to be changed. His workers were usually cooperative, that is, except Troy who seemed to march to a different drummer. He always wanted to do his own thing. Tyler would have liked to get rid of him, but he didn't have any authority to hire or fire employees.

Tyler had about all he could take with Troy's antics, so he went to his boss, Laura, to discuss the situation. After hearing about the problems Troy was causing, Laura knew she had to make some changes to allow Tyler to be an effective leader. Laura decided that Tyler should be able to make decisions about firing employees who didn't meet the requirements for the job. By doing so, Laura gave Tyler more power, which would affect the performance of his workers.

This situation illustrates how contingency management is applied in a real situation. After evaluating the state of affairs in Tyler's department, Laura, the manager, determined that the situation required contingency actions to be applied. Tyler was given more power so he could use different methods to lead his workers.

Leadership and Quality Management

Today's organizations are changing, workers are changing, and leadership within organizations is changing. The trend in the workplace is worker empowerment, which requires the leader to be responsible for teamwork. Total Quality Management (TQM), sometimes called *Quality Management,* is a way to continuously improve performance at every level of operation and in every functional area of an organization, using all available human and capital resources.[8] Quality management relies on people and involves everyone. It is a philosophy and a set of guiding principles which are used to improve the organization continuously, the processes used by the organization, and the manner in which the needs of the customer are met.

Quality Management has been discussed in detail by Bruce Brocka and Suzanne Brocka in *Quality Management: Implementing the Best Ideas of the Masters,* from which their suggestions for implementation have been adapted for the discussion below. There have been many extensive books written on the subject of TQM, and our discussion here is only an orientation so you can see the importance of worker empowerment and teamwork.

---

[8]Bruce Brocka, and Suzanne M. Brocka. *Quality Management: Implementing the Best Ideas of the Masters.* Homewood, Illinois: Business One Irwin, 1992.

1. *A process-orientation rather than a results-orientation should be adopted.* It is important to view processes with an eye for change. What can be done better, and what does it take to improve the processes? An early analysis of the processes will allow for changes that will result in improved quality from the beginning.

2. *Everyone from the top down should be involved.* Quality Management begins with the top executives in the organization and flows down to the lowest levels and eventually to suppliers as well. To implement TQM successfully, leaders must understand, demonstrate, and teach its principles to workers.

3. *Top leaders must be committed.* If continuous improvement is to occur, it is necessary for top leaders to be committed. Leaders will show their commitment by acting upon the suggestions and recommendations that come from worker involvement.

4. *Communications must flow in all directions.* All efforts must be made to remove blocks to communications. Communication must be able to

A successful business always puts the customers' needs first.

flow in all directions, so leaders can communicate with subordinates and subordinates feel free to communicate with leaders. Communication should flow freely from worker to worker, as well, while team efforts grow and continuous improvement is a focus.

5. *Internal and external continuous improvement is necessary.* Every aspect of an individual's work should be continuously improved. With TQM, problem identification and problem-solving tools are introduced to prevent defects.

6. *Share vision and consistency of purpose.* There must be a common purpose or set of principles that guides the organization. This purpose or vision must be known throughout the organization. Consistency is critical to success. If goals are conflicting, there will be frustration.

7. *The customer rules.* The adage of the customer being king has been pervasive throughout the sales world for years. This philosophy must be the guiding principle for all workers. Each person has a customer. It may be the next person in the process or someone external to the organization. Without the customer, a business cannot exist.

8. *Invest in human resources.* The largest and most critical investment an organization makes is in its people. People are the vital link in the process of continuous improvement. Training, team building, and quality of work life are all important to an environment where workers can grow and develop to increasingly contribute to the organization.

9. *Training is fundamental to TQM.* All staff must be constantly trained and their training should be used immediately. Training could be done to improve work skills or to help employees to better communicate or write. Training should result in measurable or observable outcomes.

10. *Accentuate positives and reward success.* Positive reinforcement provides better motivation than negative reinforcement. A reward system should be achievable by everyone, and everyone should know what is needed to receive the rewards.

11. *Teamwork is critical.* It takes teamwork and complete team involvement to be successful with Total Quality Management. Teams work together as a single unit, rather than as a committee in which there is minimal participation and maximum direction. Team activities build communication and cooperation, and the result will be continuous improvement.

12. *Everyone is involved in goal setting, and goals are communicated.* Before employees can be expected to be a part of the team, they must be allowed to participate in the goal setting process. Goals should be communicated to others so each person is aware of the impact of the goals upon them.[9]

---

[9]Bruce Brocka, and Suzanne M. Brocka. *Quality Management: Implementing the Best Ideas of the Masters.* Homewood, Illinois: Business One Irwin, 1992.

Customs and Traditions: Watching for the Global Difference

Managing Cultural Differences

Immigrants play an important role in the economy of the United States, and managing these workers from other cultures is becoming increasingly important. States with large numbers of immigrants have experienced the biggest impact. California is one state in which immigrants have been in the forefront of economic recovery. Some of the most common names of home buyers are Lee, Martinez, Rodriguez, Garcia, Nguyen, and Wong.

The California immigrant entrepreneurs have focused on industries such as food processing, textiles, and medical equipment. In Orange County, six of the nine top manufacturing firms have CEOs who were born outside of the United States. Other parts of the state have also felt the impact of immigrant workers. In the Silicon Valley, one in three engineers is an immigrant, and throughout the state a large proportion of the workforce is from other countries.

Companies doing business outside of the United States must also deal with cultural differences, and knowledge of the culture is the key

This concept revolves around the notion that for an organization to improve and become more competitive, the changes and improvement must be continuous and take place in small increments. For this improvement to occur, employees must be included as team members. The result of involving team members is a flatter organization. John Byrne discussed the horizontal corporation in a *Business Week* article. The key elements of a horizontal corporation directly mirror the TQM process. They include:

1. organize around process, not task;
2. flatten hierarchy;
3. use teams to manage everything;
4. let customers drive performance;
5. reward team performance;
6. maximize supplier and customer contact; and
7. inform and train all employees.[10]

Many companies are moving toward flatter organizations, such as Eastman Chemical's Kodak unit which eliminated several senior vice presidents in favor of self-directed teams. At Xerox new products are being developed with multidisciplinary teams that work in a single process rather

....
[10]John A. Byrne. "The Horizontal Corporation." *Business Week*. December 20, 1993, 76–81.

to success. One Minneapolis company, H. B. Fuller, makes adhesives in China. It employed William E. O'Brien to manage its China operations. Mr. O'Brien studied in China, married a Chinese woman, and is very fluent in the Chinese language. He knows and understands the culture and is able to provide empathetic leadership to workers who were previously employed by a state-owned enterprise. He knows the fine art of negotiating with the Chinese, which can be an ongoing process. The company started earning a profit two years before it expected, primarily because of a manager who understood a different culture and adapted his leadership style to the culture.

Sources: Kotkin, Joel. "Immigrants Lead a Recovery." The Wall Street Journal. April 22, 1994, A10.

Brauchli, Marcus. "When in Huangpu..." The Wall Street Journal. December 10, 1993, R3.

Lubman, Sarah. "Round and Round." The Wall Street Journal. December 10, 1993, R3.

than being departmentalized. These examples require drastic organizational changes. When the TQM process is used, leadership comes from groups rather than from individuals in a hierarchical structure. Even though worker empowerment is a key element, workers must be willing to be leaders within work teams.

Multicultural Leadership

It is becoming more important for leaders to have the necessary skills to function in multicultural settings, since women, minorities, and immigrants are expected to make up 80 percent of the workforce in the year 2000. People of other cultures are used to being treated in a way that might be foreign to managers in the United States. The Japanese, for example, have been involved with quality circles and quality management for years.

If workers originally from other countries are to respond positively to a United States work environment under American managers, different managerial styles will have to be implemented. This is realistic considering the number of immigrants who come yearly to the United States. What are the effects on American workers when an international company takes over manufacturing plants on American soil and then imports managers? They often have to adjust to leadership styles of managers from other countries.

Effective multicultural leaders are innovative and are able intercultural communicators and negotiators. They are as comfortable operating in

Successful leaders adapt and work well with people from many different cultures.

China as they are in the United States or Greece. Multicultural leaders typically

► think beyond local perceptions and transform stereotypes into positive views of people;

► prepare for new mindshifts while eliminating old mindsets;

► re-create cultural assumptions, norms, and practices based on new insights and experiences;

► reprogram their mental maps and constructs;

► adapt readily to new and unusual circumstances and lifestyles;

► welcome and facilitate transitional experiences;

► acquire multicultural competencies and skills, including foreign language skills;

► create cultural synergy whenever and wherever feasible;

► operate effectively in multinational/multicultural environments;

► envision transnational opportunities and enterprises; and

► create optimistic and doable scenarios for the future.[11]

[11]Farid Elashmawi and Phillip Harris. *Multicultural Management: New Skills for Global Success.* Houston: Gulf Publishig Co., 1993.

Anyone who wants to be an effective leader in a multicultural environment, abroad or at home, must be diverse in global thinking and talents. The person must be flexible and willing to adapt to different situations while always thinking about future opportunities for his or her workers and organization. There are many challenges in providing effective leadership in a multicultural situation. The individual who wants to survive in a multicultural leadership role must learn as much as possible about cultures and must remain flexible in dealing with diversity in people.

Key Points Summary

- A leader is someone who can influence followers to accomplish goals. In that regard, before someone can be a leader, there must be followers. A leader can cause change to occur, usually through the influence he or she has upon others.

- Leadership is most often defined by traits rather than by the tasks that a leader performs. Traits or characteristics that describe leaders include charisma, personality, education, and assertiveness.

- Leaders use different styles to influence others to accomplish goals that have been established and determine the decision-making styles that are used. Leadership decision-making styles include autocratic, participative, and free-rein.

- Several theories have been developed to help explain how leaders influence others. There are many similarities and differences among the leadership style theories. Popular leadership theories include:

    —*Theory X and Theory Y,* developed by Douglas McGregor. The Theory X leader is a task master who believes that workers must be directed. The Theory Y leader believes workers will work because they want to, and that they don't need close direction.

    —*Leadership Continuum,* developed by Tannenbaum and Schmidt. Two opposite beliefs about leadership are illustrated by the continuum. The leader at one end feels tight control is needed and the leader at the other end feels that subordinates should have freedom to operate within preestablished guidelines.

    —*The Leadership Grid®,* developed by Blake and McCanse. Leadership styles are placed in seven different areas of the grid depending upon the leader's concern for people or for production. The more people-oriented the leader, the more freedom the workers have; and the more task-oriented the leader, the more tightly the leader will control.

    —*Contingency Model of Leadership,* developed by Fred Fiedler. This leadership theory describes how situations influence the relationship between leadership traits and effectiveness. To predict leadership effectiveness in different situations, Fiedler established a trait measurement, called the Least Preferred Coworker (LPC) score.

- Total Quality Management is being adopted by several organizations in the United States. TQM, sometimes called Quality Management, is a way to improve performance, hence quality, continuously at every level in the organization using all the human and capital resources that are available. The Quality Management process empowers workers and causes the formation of work teams to improve performance and quality. Leadership must be handled differently to get all workers to function as team members. Teams should establish their goals, rather than the top leaders telling the teams what must be done.

- The workplace is rapidly changing into a multicultural environment. Effective leaders must have a multicultural orientation if they want to have their workers respond positively. In a multicultural environment, leaders must think globally and must be flexible enough to accept and adapt to cultural differences.

Key Terms

autocratic leader	leadership style
charisma	least preferred coworker
Contingency Model	participative leader
free-rein	quality management
leader	Theory X leader
leadership	Theory Y leader
leadership characteristics	
Leadership Continuum	
Leadership Grid®	

Discussion Questions

1. Describe the person you feel is the best leader you know. Perhaps it is you. What are this person's traits or characteristics that cause people to want to follow? How does this person compare with someone who you think is a poor leader? What are the traits of the poor leader?

2. What do you think are the pros and cons of each of these leadership decision-making styles: autocratic, participative, and free-rein? To which style do you think you would respond best as a follower? If you were in a leadership position, which style would you mostly use?

3. Explain each of the following leadership theories. What are the similarities and differences of the leadership theories? You may answer the question by summarizing the information in chart form.

   a. Theory X and Theory Y

   b. Leadership Continuum

   c. Leadership Grid®

   d. Contingency Model

4. Total Quality Management involves everyone at all levels of an organization. How cooperative will workers at the lowest level of an organization be when TQM is being implemented? What would cause workers to want, or not want, to cooperate in the process? What effect might organized labor have on implementing TQM?

5. Assume you are a supervisor in a multicultural business in the United States. You have workers from at least five different countries, some of whom speak little English. You have both male and female workers. What would you have to do differently to lead this work group than you would if you only had white, middle-class Americans working for you?

Chapter *16*

Learning Objectives

Upon completing this chapter, you should be able to:

● Explain the various kinds of power that people in organizations may possess and identify its sources.

● Select and implement tactics or strategies designed to acquire power.

● Recognize tactics or strategies for acquiring power which involve devious behavior and are considered unethical.

● Understand that today's general trend is toward wider use of participative practices which require relationship or people power.

● Identify the integral ingredients involved in the initiation of an empowered workforce.

● Determine when participative styles of leadership may not work in organizational settings.

● List factors which contribute to perceptions and impressions of power.

politics-tactics or strategies used to achieve one's objectives

Understanding Power and Politics

Gary Iverson is a bitter young man. Gary earned a bachelor of science degree with a major in insurance at a large midwestern university. All during school, Gary was a diligent student and his academic transcript revealed nearly all "A" grades. Upon graduation, he quickly found a job with a major insurance company based in Minneapolis. Now, just five years later, Gary has returned to school as an MBA candidate.

Gary was the only member of his work team who received no promotion during these five years at the insurance company. However, he had earned merit recognition and numerous awards for his prolific work. In relaying his story, Gary complained that he came to work early and stayed at his desk long after office hours were officially over (often while his colleagues and boss went out for an after-work drink). He usually worked through lunch, while the same crowd was out socializing over salads and burgers. He even came in on Saturday mornings when, yes, you guessed right, the others were on the golf course.

The often-cited statement that many deals are made on the golf course has a ring of truthfulness. Likewise, there is a degree of significance to one's choice of lunch partners. Some individuals, such as Gary, believe that if you demonstrate dedication to your organization's goals and work hard, you will eventually achieve personal goals. Such beliefs, while admirable, may be only partly right. Reality dictates that you also engage in what many define as **politics,** keeping yourself in the information flow, making sure people know who you are, understanding how power is wielded, aligning yourself in power plays, and, yes, going to lunch with the right people. In short, organizational politics, sometimes referred to as OP for office politics, refers to tactics or strategies used to achieve one's objectives through any means other than merit or just plain luck. In any organization—church, class, or place of work—people are jockeying for positions and are trying a variety of subtle maneuvers to achieve that position or win approval for their ideas.

Organizational Power

Organizational power and politics are so closely related they require simultaneous discussion. **Power** can be defined as the ability to control anything of value, while, as noted in the previous paragraph, the concept of politics refers to tactics or strategies used to acquire power. In pyramid-shaped organizations, people holding positions in the upper echelons have more power than those below. To simplify the concepts of power and politics, consider the following scenario.

▼
power-the ability to control anything of value

Sarah Mintzberg has just purchased the Loaf and Ladle Restaurant in Brookville. At the present time, Sarah holds the power. She can make all the decisions: which items will appear on the menu, what hours the restaurant will be open, who will be hired and how much they will be paid, what policies will be adhered to within the establishment, and a variety of other concerns.

Sarah would like to relinquish much of her power to devote her attention to other interests. She has hired two individuals, Bonnie Britton and Kenneth Eskey, in an effort to find a professional manager. During the next couple of months, Ms. Mintzberg will observe both Bonnie and Ken and assess their managerial skills. One will be chosen as Ms. Mintzberg's replacement and will wield the power, that is, hold the influential position.

Bonnie and Ken are both aware that they are competing for the leadership position. Each will employ both offensive and defensive strategies in their quest to secure the position. In short, they will engage in organizational politics.

The power that people in organizations possess takes different forms. It is important to understand what kind of power they wield as well as its source. Psychologists have identified and described four main kinds of power.

Legitimate Power

People hold **legitimate power,** sometimes referred to as position power, when they occupy a higher level position within an organization. This is the kind of power that both Bonnie and Ken are seeking. If the host or hostess in a restaurant reports to work late or if a waitperson is rude to a customer, the manager has the right to reprimand that employee. Likewise, the manager has the right to sponsor a Little League baseball team. Usually, however, a person may place limits on someone's power. If after assuming the professional manager's position, either Bonnie or Ken decide to donate some of the firm's profits to a subversive group, Ms. Mintzberg might override the decision. If she is displeased with the way power is wielded, she may dismiss the manager.

▼
legitimate power-
the power held by people occupying higher level positions

coercive power-used by managers and supervisors to reward or punish workers for compliance or noncompliance

personal power-influential power an individual possesses because of knowledge or expertise and/or charisma

referent power-is possessed by individuals who capture the admiration of others to the extent that they try to emulate traits and behaviors

A person acknowledged to possess personal power is Maya Angelou.

Politicians hold legitimate power as a result of being elected to office. If they abuse such power, they may be reprimanded or may even be removed from office. If voters are unhappy with the way power is wielded, they may elect another candidate in the next election.

Coercive Power

Bonnie or Ken, depending upon who is chosen as the manager, will probably make use of **coercive power.** Coercive power is used by managers and supervisors to reward or punish workers for compliance or noncompliance. If a sales manager can reward sales representatives with cash bonuses for good performance, the manager exerts considerable power. Outstanding performance awards may be viewed by individuals with esteem or self-actualization needs as significant rewards. Obviously, leaders who use reward power effectively are more popular among workers than those who attempt to coerce workers by threatening or using punishment.

Some leaders, however, experience good results with the threat of punishment, at least in the short run. A liquor control board, for example, may suspend an establishment's operating license if it finds that underage drinkers have been served. Professional athletes may be fined for missing practice sessions and for initiating or becoming involved in brawls.

Personal Power

An individual may possess **personal power** because of knowledge or expertise and/or charisma. Highly knowledgeable people have power even when their organizational rank is low or when they are self-employed. From time to time, we have all heard remarks such as, "The boss will take care of Matt because she needs him." The remark in essence means that Matt is so respected for knowledge or expertise that he has more influential power than the boss. When the boss (supervisor or manager) is perceived to possess expert knowledge, that individual can exert considerable power over others. College basketball coaches Dean Smith, Bob Knight, and Mike Krzyzewski are able to sway the opinions of many people when offensive or defensive strategies are being discussed. The basis of their power is expert knowledge, not their formal positions.

Some people have charisma, that is, the power to influence people, because of their magnetic personality traits and characteristic behaviors. People with charisma are somewhat rare; however, some lawyers, politicians, and sales representatives, among others, have experienced success primarily as a result of positive subjective reactions to personal characteristics. Occasionally, an individual has so much charisma that other people admire and try to emulate his or her personality traits and behaviors. This is known as **referent power.** If Bonnie or Ken is able to capture the admiration of workers at the Loaf and Ladle Restaurant to the extent that workers strive to please their manager, he or she will have succeeded in acquiring yet another kind of power and influence, that is, referent power.

National advertisers sometimes attempt to use referent power to sell products and services. When a celebrity—actress, actor, or athlete—is paid to endorse a product or service, the advertiser is using referent power.

Subordinate Power

The power based on expertise of an individual and subordinate power are related. An individual with a relatively low rank or status, but with unusual talents, may be able to force his or her demands on upper level supervisors or managers. A university seeking to hire a specific individual because of her remarkable talents for writing grant proposals that attract external funding may be receptive to the demands of that individual. She may, for example, require a private secretary, additional computer equipment, and a research assistant, privileges which no other researchers or faculty members are granted.

When power is exerted from lower levels within an organization, such as in the previous example, **subordinate power** is being exerted. It should also be noted that employees are willing to accept orders that lie within a certain range of behaviors. When the orders appear to be outside that range, they may refuse to carry out the directive. If an employee, for example, is asked to dispose of hazardous waste materials by dumping them into a stream, the employee may refuse. If the leader persists in attempting to gain compliance, the leader will lose power. Other employees will sympathize with their colleague, and the leader will become ineffective.

subordinate power—is exhibited when an individual of low rank is able to force demands on upper level managers or supervisors

Ethical Dimensions to Human Relations

Moral Questions

Who will be hurt and how badly? An answer to this moral question focuses on the outcomes or consequences of decisions and actions. The question also requires one to think about what is right, what is just, and what is fair.

The New York Times reported that a group of church members from Harlem in New York City engaged in applying whitewash over billboards containing advertising messages for cigarettes and alcoholic beverages. Armed with ladders, long-handled paint rollers, and buckets of white paint, the brigade set out to combat efforts to market unhealthy products in neighborhoods already struggling with poverty, disease, and despair. It is, of course, illegal to deface private property. In your opinion, is it right, just, and fair to deface private property when the messages contained on the private property promote products that will be harmful to those who buy them? Should advertisers be hurt and consumers be protected, or should consumers be hurt and advertisers be protected?

CONTINUED

A second moral question is related to the fact that over the past several years attention has been focused on what some refer to as an ethical crisis, a breakdown in behavior deemed to be in accord with accepted ethical norms. The accepted ethical norm in this country, for example, has always guided hiring decisions insomuch as the best-qualified candidate was expected to win approval of those in decision-making capacities.

LaJune Smith explained why she voted for an African-American female to fill a position as department chairperson at Concordia College. "I realized," she stated, "that Joseph Renard (also a finalist for the position) was better qualified as a result of his experience and educational background. I just think women—particularly African-American women—have far fewer administrative jobs than white men. If we are an equal opportunity employer, then women should have priority simply because white men have dominated such positions for so long. In addition, women—particularly African-American women at this institution—expected the vote which I cast."

In your opinion, is reverse discrimination right, just, and fair? Should accepted ethical norms that have guided hiring decisions in the past be discarded? Has Joseph Renard been hurt as a result of LaJune Smith's rationale?

Strategies for Acquiring Power

Bonnie and Ken may employ a number of tactics or strategies in their quest to acquire power. The tactics or strategies are usually classified into three categories: personal political action, political action involving others, and political action directed at the opponent.

Personal Political Action

There is little doubt that both Bonnie and Ken will attempt to create favorable impressions on Ms. Mintzberg. They may devote attention to dress and appearance. An employer may believe strongly that managerial employees should project the proper image. They may also make sure Ms. Mintzberg becomes aware of their accomplishments. They may attempt to appear industrious at all times, may also try to develop the expertise which the job requires. We have already learned that a person who controls the vital resource of information becomes more powerful by virtue of acquiring expert power. Each of the two candidates may volunteer for assignments to show willingness to become involved. Each may find ways to display loyalty. Most employers value loyal workers, however traditional the idea. Many aspiring managers have found that knowing when and how to praise people is a valuable skill that enhances one's reputation within an organization. Finally, it is often recommended that a person attempting to achieve power laugh at his or her boss's jokes. Demonstrating an appreciation for a boss's sense of humor may help establish good rapport.

Political Action Involving Others

An individual cannot be effective politically without the support of other people. Bonnie and Ken will learn quickly that contacts with superiors, peers, and subordinates are needed to establish coalitions that support the courses of action one takes. Most people resent being approached solely for political reasons; therefore, it is best to establish connections without making the political purpose explicit.[1] Establishing an influential ally may enhance a person's political activities. If Bonnie, for example, can establish good rapport with Martin Lopez, the banker who provided the financial resources to purchase the Loaf and Ladle and a long-time personal friend of Ms. Mintzberg, and Mr. Lopez expresses favorable comments concerning Bonnie's managerial skills—Bonnie may have established a political ally who will help her cause.

Some agreements or endorsements that take place in work organizations are based on the idea of exchanging favors or, in colloquial terms, are based on "mutual back-scratching." Behavioral scientists suggest that it is best to exchange favors with people who hold higher rank. The result may be increased power or simply the granting of an important favor when it is needed.[2]

When Ken Eskey was a student at the University of Rhode Island, one of his professors—who taught small business management—was chairing a search committee for a new dean of the business college. Due to conflicting appointments, the professor asked Ken if he could drive one of the visiting dean candidates from campus to the airport. Ken not only complied, he also drove the candidate through a new residential area which the candidate expressed a desire to see. Later, Ken's professor told him that if he ever needed help in the job market to give him a call. Ken had hardly hung up the phone before the professor called Ms. Mintzberg and gave Ken a very favorable recommendation.

---

[1]David Brass. "Men and Women's Networks: A Story of Interaction Patterns and Influence in an Organization." *Academy of Management Journal.* vol.28, 1985, 327–43.

[2]Andrew Dubrin. *Human Relations: A Job-Oriented Approach.* Reston, Virginia: Reston Publishing Co., 1984, 173.

Closely related to mutual back-scratching is the tactic of helping your supervisor succeed. Unless your supervisor is emotionally insecure, i.e., fearful of capable subordinates, he or she may become so indebted to you that you gain favor within the organization.

Political Action Directed at Opponents

Most of the following tactics or strategies are political ploys which involve devious behavior and are viewed as unethical. In some organizations, politics becomes so vicious that unethical patterns of behavior have been observed. It should be emphasized that an individual attempting to gain an unfair advantage runs the risk of being caught and fired. Unethical behavior is unacceptable in reputable organizations.

False Blame. Employees have on occasion attempted to gain favor, or at least escape blame, by making a rival look bad in the eyes of influential organizational members. Falsely attacking or blaming others is a form of character assassination.

Roger Roseman and Cal Lyons, two college students working part-time at the Cedar Valley Par 3 Golf Course, were left in charge of the enterprise on a Friday afternoon. Troy Johnson, the owner and pro, had personal business to transact, but he planned to be back to open the course at 7:00 A.M. on Saturday—the week's heaviest business day at Cedar Valley Par 3. When he arrived on Saturday morning, Troy discovered that the sprinklers had been left on all night and the ground was saturated with water. The course had to be closed until noon to allow the ground to dry out. Numerous customers had to be turned away, many of whom were angry and intolerant. When confronted by Mr. Johnson, Cal said that Roger was responsible for turning the water off. The truth was, Cal had told Roger that he would shut the sprinklers off and he simply forgot to do so.

In more serious situations, character assassination may lead to litigation.

Undue Credit. Another devious tactic is to receive undue credit. Sometimes an employee may be in a position to claim credit for work performed by another person.

Michael Reszka enlisted the help of Patti Emerick as he worked on a proposal to provide consulting services for Allied Chemical Corporation. The fact was, Patti contributed substantially to the contents of the proposal and to the wording and organization of the document. Upon review by the vice president in charge of new accounts, Cheryl Ginsberg, Michael was singled out for praise and recognition. Michael failed to mention that his colleague, Patti, had made significant contributions to the proposal, and her name was conspicuously missing from the cover page.

The Setup. The setup, as a political tactic, places a rival in a position where he or she looks ineffective.

Phil O'Rourke, an account executive at Behrman's Advertising Agency, was insecure in his position. Brad Shearer, manager of the agency, had hired Jennifer Chasteen as an additional account executive. Jennifer, a recent college graduate, was a bright young woman whose enthusiasm had captured the interests of several new clients. Phil was fearful that Jennifer would soon be handling his accounts. He knew that Thompson's Dairy, one of the firm's most lucrative accounts, was ready to switch agencies. Others in the firm were not aware of this development. Phil suggested that the Thompson's Dairy account be transferred from his group of clients to Jennifer's. A month later when Thompson's chose a new advertising agency, Phil suggested to Mr. Shearer that Jennifer's talents had been overrated.

Blackmail. Perhaps one of the most unethical tactics sometimes used to gain power is blackmail. An individual engaging in such devious behavior should recognize that the person being blackmailed also practices deviant behavior and cannot be trusted.

Kyle Bradford, a young, aggressive consultant at Innovative Business Development Center, discovered that his supervisor Amy Hudson was padding her expense vouchers. After gathering incriminating evidence, Kyle confronted Amy. She agreed that if Kyle would not disclose the evidence, she would help him advance in his career. Kyle received an enviable evaluation and an accompanying pay increase. Then, Amy was fired for misleading a client and, before leaving, she blew the whistle on Kyle. Kyle is now unemployed and looking for a new position.

Customs and Traditions: Watching for the Global Difference

The Golden Rule

All religions have their own golden rules which are said to have come from their Supreme Being. While interpretations differ—even within the same religious group—do the rules really differ in governing compassion for others?

Buddhism: "Harm not others with that which pains yourself."

Christianity: "All things whatsoever you would that others should do unto you, do ye even so unto them."

Confucianism: "Loving kindness is the one maxim which ought to be acted upon throughout one's life."

CONTINUED

Hinduism:	"This is the sum of duty; do naught to others which if done to thee would cause thee pain."
Islamic:	"No one of you is a believer until you wish for everyone what you love for yourself."
Jainism:	"In happiness and suffering, in joy and grief, we should regard all creatures as we regard our own self."
Judaism:	"What is hurtful to yourself do not do to others."
Sikhism:	"As thou deemest thyself, so deem others."
Taoism:	"Regard your neighbor's gain as your gain, and regard your neighbor's loss as your loss."

It should be obvious that political tactics or strategies directed at opponents can have an adverse effect on people and the entire organization. In some cases, people who do not experience success attribute their plots to organizational politics. They perceive that favoritism has worked against them in some way and cannot accept responsibility for their lack of success. While this may be true on occasion, it is more likely that the individuals were simply inept in selecting and implementing tactics or strategies to acquire power.

Table 16.1 contains a summary of popular forms of organizational politics.

Table 16.1 Strategies and Tactics for Acquiring Power

Personal Action	► Enhancing personal image ► Becoming knowledgeable and informative ► Demonstrating loyalty ► Volunteering for assignments
Action Involving Others	► Winning support of influentials ► Establishing coalitions with allies ► Engaging in mutual back-scratching ► Helping the boss succeed
Action Against Others	► Blaming a rival ► Receiving undue credit ► Creating a setup ► Using blackmail

*T*he Trend Toward Empowerment

Chapters 1 and 15 introduced McGregor's Theory X, an authoritative approach that called for leaders to hold all the power and make all the decisions. Employees were expected to do what they were told. Then, McGregor came up with Theory Y, based on the assumption that workers would respond well in a free-rein environment; that is, the power would be vested in workers who would make decisions and assume self-direction while performing work activities. Ouchi was then credited for Theory Z, an approach which retains management staffs and which delegates some power to workers and allows them to participate in decision-making and problem-solving. Figure 16.1 depicts the sources of power for each theory.

Figure 16.1 **Different Sources of Power in Organizations**

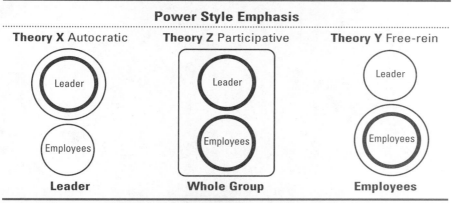

Davis and Newstrom,. HUMAN BEHAVIOR AT WORK, *8E. © 1989 McGraw-Hill, Inc. Reprinted with permission.*

Today's general trend is toward wider use of participative practices, and most leaders agree that rigid hierarchy is dying because it runs on position power instead of relationship power or people power.[3] Many human resources specialists believe that participative power or team power is superior to even the best managerial excellence. Participative approaches involve the people who know the most about the work to be done.

Participative power styles are not readily accepted by all supervisors, managers, and executives. In some cases, bosses want to be bosses because they want to run things. Bosses want to see things done and are convinced they can get it done. Some want power; most like having it and exercising it. Many bosses frankly say so. Albert Casey, American Airlines chairman, was quoted as saying, "I enjoy power, no question about it."[4] Many human resources specialists, however, believe that participative power or team

[3]Lynn J. McFarland, L. Senn, and J. R. Childress. *21st Century Leadership.* New York: The Leadership Press, 1993, 51.

[4]Robert J. Schoenberg. *The Art of Being a Boss.* Philadelphia: J. B. Lippincott, 1978, 254.

power is superior to even the best managerial excellence. Participative approaches involve the people who are closest to work activities and know most about the work to be done. Barbara Levy Kipper, chairman of Charles Levy Company, voiced this position well when she said, "There can no longer be rigid hierarchy of leadership. The people closest to any given situation know how to handle it best. The more voices that are heard, the stronger the organization."[5]

To establish participative cultures in the workplace, empowerment—that is, the sharing of power at every level with everyone—becomes the catalyst. Empowerment is increased involvement and participation, shared knowledge and decision-making, plus encouragement for everyone to contribute his or her maximum.

Empowerment does not mean that the leader (supervisor, manager, or executive) abdicates responsibility and just counts votes. The leader,

Chances of attaining the objective are helped when everyone's knowledge and involvement counts.

[5]Lynne Joy McFarland, Larry Senn, and Childress, 64.

instead, becomes a coach, one who facilitates the decision process, reaching closure, and creating alignment. To illustrate the concept of empowerment, consider the following scenario.

Cindy Warner finally had the opportunity that she had been anticipating for a long time. Cindy received word that she had been selected as the new manager of the Decorating Nook, a shop that specializes in custom draperies, blinds, bedspreads, wallcoverings, and upholstery. The shop, located on Chicago's Southside, provides interior decorating consultation either in its showroom or during prearranged home appointments.

Upon arrival at the Decorating Nook, Cindy noticed some things that would have to be changed. Housekeeping left much to be desired; the interior of the store was simply messy. The outside didn't look much better; the windows were streaked with dirt and grime and the sidewalk looked as if it hadn't been swept in months. The displays inside the store were unappealing; the shelves were not stocked; and the stockroom was piled high with incoming orders that had not been unpackaged, checked in, and prepared for the sales floor. Swatches of drapery material and upholstery material, as well as carpet samples, were unorganized and contained discontinued remnants while missing materials newly introduced to the market.

Cindy was faced with a decision. She could grab a clipboard, make a list of everything that needed to be done, and order the employees to make the needed changes. Fortunately, Cindy was sensitive to the esteem and self-actualization needs of her employees. She knew that if she could make them feel as though they were part of a team, that they were consulted and participated in decisions that resulted in changes, they would be better satisfied with their jobs.

Cindy was prepared for her first staff meeting. She told the employees that she wanted the Decorating Nook on Chicago's Southside to be the best outlet in the chain. She explained that "best" meant being sensitive to customers' needs; knowledgeable of innovative and contemporary decorating ideas; an efficient, profitable operation; and structured as a harmonious working force that was well rewarded. Cindy emphasized that to achieve this goal, everyone would have to contribute. Everyone would need to contribute to the on-site decision-making process that would propel the firm toward achieving its goals. Then, Cindy introduced a nominal group technique that allowed the employees to brainstorm and prioritize needed changes. All of the things that Cindy noticed that needed to be changed appeared on the prioritized list, along with some other great ideas that Cindy had overlooked. In addition, the employees volunteered to make the changes and Cindy was relieved from making work assignments.

Similar meetings followed, with employees empowered to make decisions about groups of customers to be targeted, lines of decorative products to be added and dropped, ways to improve efficiency, and other operative concerns.

Initiating an Empowered Workforce

Executives or leaders at the top level of an organization must be committed to the concept of empowerment if it is to become reality. Organizations are often referred to as "shadows of their leaders." This suggests that the top tier of leaders need to model empowerment if it is to become a practice and if the organization is to adopt a collaborative management style to replace a directive management style. Leaders who have wielded all the power and control must recognize the value of employees and their ideas. Further, they must recognize that new ideas are seldom perfect; instead, they must be nurtured and perfected. When leaders are willing to help employees nurture and perfect ideas that will lead to improved practices, greater efficiency, or better quality, collaborative management styles and empowered employees emerge. Empowerment is power-sharing, that is, inviting, urging, and coaching leadership in every employee.

Spreading Leadership Among the Workforce

In firms operating as autocratic, boss-dominated entities, rigid rules and policies are enforced. This often hinders operations and customer service. At the American Airlines counter, for example, customers were told that a myriad of rules had to be followed when they needed to change their flights. "No, I'm sorry, but our policy forbids us from doing that," was a statement often repeated to customers. In some cases, customers may have thought their request was reasonable and deserved attention. Perhaps for future flights, they chose a different airline. American Airlines then empowered its employees, giving them decision-making powers to handle individual customers' requests, using common sense and good reasoning. This made customers feel that the airline was concerned about their well-being. When leadership is disbursed among employees, no one is left out, not even the janitor.

In recent years, employers have recognized the importance of on-site decision-making. An empowered workforce has the authority to make on-site decisions. To exercise this authority, workers must have information and knowledge. In firms operating with autocratic power structures, information is dispensed on a need-to-know basis. Leaders in organizations adhering to the empowerment concept recognize that sound decisions are based on current information. As a result, employees have access to complete, up-to-date information.

Accountability Is an Integral Ingredient

Power, freedom, and rights come at a price. The price of empowerment is personal accountability which becomes an essential ingredient if empower-

American Airlines workers now are empowered to make decisions no matter what their job title.

ment is to work. In organizations characterized by position power, leaders often seek to protect themselves by blaming others and making excuses.

When Carol Miller, Vice President of Customer Services at Midland Airlines, received numerous complaints about lost luggage, she turned to Harold Cougar, supervisor of baggage handlers, for an answer. "The people that I am able to hire for the wages we pay are simply incompetent," Mr. Cougar replied.

After interviewing several baggage handlers, Carol discovered that employees had a different perception. The employees believed they were never properly trained; they perceived Mr. Cougar as lacking organizational skills; and they indicated that Mr. Cougar was seldom on the tarmac supervising their work.

If Midland Airlines were to adopt an empowerment model, Mr. Cougar would no longer be able to protect himself by blaming others and making excuses. Baggage handlers, likewise, could no longer point the finger at Mr. Cougar as being responsible for the lost luggage. Instead, training and coaching would occur at all levels within the organization, eliminating the victim syndrome and focusing upon the desired results. Personal accountability must be present if employee empowerment is to succeed. It was also evident in the last scenario that respect and trust between the leader and the employees left much to be desired. People are more likely to accept leadership and accountability for their actions when respect and trust are built into their relationships. Such relationships can only be fostered by discarding some old beliefs that have become self-limiting for leaders. These old beliefs, as set forth in the book, *21st Century Leadership,* include:

"If I'm the boss, I'm supposed to have all the answers."

"If I'm the boss, I'm not supposed to make any mistakes."

"I'm in charge; no one should question my authority."

"If you want the job done right, you have to do it yourself."

"If we create new things around here, they should be my ideas."[6]

The above beliefs are inconsistent with the concept of empowering employees. Instead, they should be replaced with beliefs such as the following.

"As the leader, my role is to solicit the best ideas and increase participation and involvement from other employees."

"As the leader, my role is to recognize that ideas are never perfect at first; however, ideas which have been tested and refined may lead to real breakthroughs."

"As the leader, my commitment is to lead in a participative way, improve communications, personalize relationships, and encourage teamwork."

"As the leader, I respect and trust the employees and their abilities. I am willing to share power and place decision-making authority in the hands of front-line people."

"As the leader, I recognize, acknowledge, and reward quality, initiative, and innovation."

Figure 16.2 depicts the traditional organizational structure built on position power and today's contemporary organization built on the concept of empowerment.

Other Key Ingredients

Other key ingredients of a successful empowered workforce may be highly correlated with the characteristics of a winning athletic team. Coaches of most winning teams emphasize these ingredients and constantly remind team members, as well as themselves, of the importance of each of the

....
[6]McFarland, Senn, and Childress, 184.

Figure 16.2 Traditional Hierarchical Organization and Contemporary Flat, Flexible Organizations

Traditional

Top-down formal structure

Bureaucratic culture
(compliance with policies, procedures)

Position-power leadership

Contemporary

Collaborative teams

Participative culture

Power-sharing leadership

---

ingredients if the team is to continue to be a winner. Leaders and members of the workforce, likewise, must recognize the importance of the following ingredients: cohesion, teamwork, high morale, and esprit de corps.

Cohesion. **Cohesion** means sticking together or putting the interests of the group over personal interests. Obviously, a football player who is committed to helping the team gain necessary yardage to score a touchdown is more valuable than a football player who is committed to setting a personal record and winning personal recognition. The workforce which sticks together and works toward a common goal is more successful than the workforce in which members place personal goals above common goals. A cohesive workforce is created when the leader cultivates pride within the group. The workforce believes that it is the best; that is, that it has the hardest workers who tackle the toughest assignments; that its members work the longest hours and perform their work the fastest; and, in addition, that the workforce is the most courteous, demonstrating the greatest amount of creativity, and is the most productive. In some organizations in which leadership is weak, members of the workforce may foster pride and become a cohesive group. Often, however, organizations are "shadows of their leaders," and if cohesive workforces are to exist, the leader will encourage workers to take pride in their work group.

cohesion-sticking together or putting the interests of the group before personal interests

Teamwork. **Teamwork** can be defined as working together to maximize the strengths of individual group members and minimize their weaknesses. Winning teams recognize the importance of capitalizing upon strengths. A fund-raising group may send its most persuasive solicitor to talk to a philanthropist about donating funds for humanitarian purposes. To foster teamwork, the leader should again cultivate pride in group membership. History and tradition may be valuable in attempts to instill pride among team members. A business organization may also cultivate teamwork as a result of its history or tradition. Organizational slogans or mottoes, such as "Quality constructed homes by Pen," "Like a good neighbor, State Farm is there," and "Virginia's premier personal injury law firm,"

teamwork-working together to maximize the strengths of individual group members and minimize their weaknesses

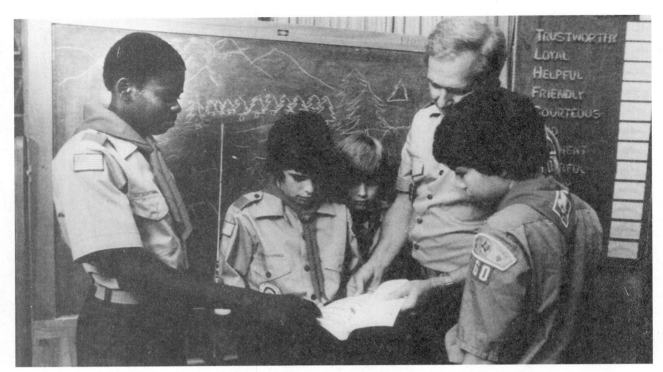

Often it's best for people to work together in a group to maximize their strengths.

may be as helpful in promoting teamwork among employees to achieve the firm's mission as they are in conveying the firm's image to potential customers or clients. If the motto or slogan is simply a shallow, superficial ploy, however, it may not result in an increased level of teamwork. Employees are as quick to spot a con job as are customers. Then, too, if employees are a close-knit group in which the people enjoy each other's company outside work, teamwork on the job is more likely to occur.

Morale.   Morale may be loosely defined as a combination of employee attitudes toward work. Such attitudes include how workers think and feel about their jobs, wages, supervisors, coworkers, employers, working conditions, and other aspects of employment. Obviously, high morale is a positive inner feeling, while low morale connotes negative inner feelings.

Morale involves attitudes which are a response or feeling that a person has for objects, situations, ideas, or people. Most behavioral scientists suggest that attitudes are learned and can be adopted, modified, replaced, or dropped. Morale has a major impact on productivity. During the past decade as comparisons between productivity levels in America and Japan have been cited, the level of morale between workers in the two countries has not escaped scrutiny. Suggestions have been made that the major difference between the two groups is that American workers look forward to weekends whereas Japanese workers look forward to the workweek.

The leader should recognize that enthusiasm is contagious. An enthusiastic leader can have a positive influence on workers. Unfortunately, some

Many difficult tasks are more easily accomplished when people work together.

leaders do not recognize the impact of enthusiasm nor do they recognize that they should demonstrate an upbeat, optimistic viewpoint. Instead, they are sometimes credited with statements such as: "It's difficult to soar with the eagles when I have to work with a bunch of turkeys." When a discontented, frustrated leader expresses pessimistic and negative attitudes, the morale of workers will be adversely affected.

The leader can also improve the morale of a work group by letting the group in on the action. John Sculley, chief executive officer of Apple Computer, Inc., advocates putting critical thinking and decision-making into the hands of a fully educated workforce. He cites Volvo in Sweden as an example, where workers have been given the tools that allow them to make decisions right on the front line where the products are being built, that is, where the autos are being assembled.[7] In other words, it is essential to improve the morale of workers by giving them ownership in the decision-making process.

Esprit de Corps. **Esprit de corps** is the common spirit existing among the members of a work group that inspires enthusiasm, devotion, and strong regard for the honor of the group. Esprit de corps is established when members of the work group do the following.

esprit de corps-the common spirit existing among members of a work group that inspires enthusiasm, devotion, and strong regard for the honor of the group

[7]McFarland, Senn, and Childress, 67.

- demonstrate personal integrity;
- build mutual confidence by showing real concern for the welfare of others;
- focus upon contribution, not personal gain.

Personal integrity is demonstrated in a story that has often been repeated about Babe Zaharias, a professional golfer in the 1930s, who penalized herself two strokes after the round she was playing was over. The penalty strokes cost her first place in the tournament. Why did she do it? It turns out that she accidently played the wrong ball. Later, a friend asked her why she penalized herself. "After all, Babe," said the friend, "no one saw you. No one would have known the difference." "I would have known," replied Zaharias. Personal integrity is a characteristic that wins respect, admiration, and trust. Astute leaders and employees recognize the importance of demonstrating concern for the welfare of others.

Mickey Monoski, a postal employee at the Woodbridge Station in Homewood, Illinois, inadvertently discovered that Steve Blevins, a custodian at Woodbridge, had been sued as a result of an accident and was facing financial ruin. When Mickey told Steve that she was genuinely sorry about his misfortune and that if he needed someone to talk with she was available, a special bond of mutual confidence was established.

Just listening to others, being sensitive to their needs, and engaging in acts of humane behavior contribute to the creation of esprit de corps. Finally, those individuals who are able to focus upon contributions as opposed to personal gain contribute to esprit de corps.

A successful, well-known college football coach decided to enter the season with a dual quarterback system. One of the quarterbacks, a senior, would start and the sophomore quarterback was to rotate in as the flow of the game dictated. Both quarterbacks were considered to be outstanding.
"I don't know how you can play two quarterbacks," said the senior. "This is my last year and if I'm to have a shot at the pros, the huddle belongs to me." The sophomore said, "I like the quarterback plan. I'm a young guy who just wants to play and help the team by being as productive as I can."
By the end of the season, the sophomore quarterback was handling virtually every snap of the ball. "The team is just more cohesive when he is in there," the coach said.

Obviously, the attitudes of the two players may have influenced the outcome. One wanted to look good so he could be drafted by the pros. The other simply wanted to help his team win.
Figure 16.3 illustrates the interconnecting ingredients of an empowered workforce.

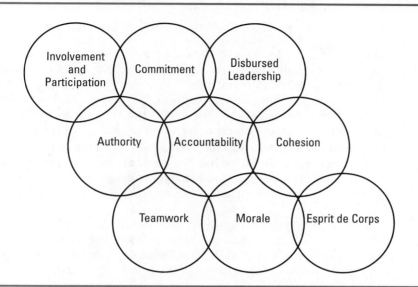

Figure 16.3 Interconnecting Elements of an Empowered Workforce

Exceptions to an Empowered Workforce

While today's contemporary business leaders may visualize empowerment as a way of life in workplace settings, they acknowledge that a great deal of controversy still surrounds the notion of empowerment in business and other organizational settings. Certainly, there is a danger in concluding that the best style of leadership is always participative. Employees must be willing to participate actively in decision-making processes if participative styles of leadership are to succeed. If workers' attitudes are negative toward employers and the workplace, it may be impossible to adopt participative leadership styles until the negative attitudes are modified. Some people are very uncomfortable when they are faced with decision-making chores. They may achieve more in a very structured work environment where the decisions are made for them by a supervisor or manager.

Perceptions and Impressions of Power

Why are some people perceived as being powerful and effective? What do they do that creates an impression they are powerful? On the other hand, why are others perceived to be relatively powerless and ineffective?

Singapore: A Good Place to Do Business

Which of the Pacific Rim nations aspires to become a more powerful, industrialized nation and has the fewest restrictions on American businesses and American expatriates? Hint: Its Chinese culture is compatible with the way Americans like to do business. English is the language of education and business, and the languages of high technology and Western-style management are dominant in business. If you answered Singapore, you are right. In fact, Singapore is trying to become a Silicon Valley of the Far East. Singapore, along with Korea, Taiwan, and Hong Kong, has been referred to as one of the "four dragons." The four dragons are the awakening economic powers of Asia.

While Singapore has been noted as an Asian nation with a hard-working labor force, it has many labor shortages. Except for Japan, it has the highest labor cost in Asia. Even so, Singapore does not have enough technical people to meet the needs of industry. This has led to two problems: (1) wages are bid up to higher levels and (2) some workers have developed and display an "I don't have to work for you" attitude. These problems are being somewhat alleviated by guest workers from Malaysia and China. Still, Singapore has moved from an economy that turned out cheap copies of pirated cassette tapes and low-cost assembly work to high-tech and engineering.

Because Singapore is predominantly an overseas Chinese culture, some business and industrial leaders express concern about the appropriateness and permanency of its economical base. There is an old Chinese strategy that proposes that one "trade a brick for a piece

An impression of power may be created by clothing. Wearing a suit and tie may convey a powerful image; whereas a T-shirt is associated with lower status. Closely related to how one looks is how an individual acts. When an individual appears to be nervous or ill at ease, he or she projects an image that may be perceived as lacking confidence and control. A firm handshake also projects the image of power, while a limp handshake may convey the image of a weak-willed or indecisive individual. Lack of eye contact and slow or hesitant speech patterns may also create impressions of weakness and ineffectiveness.

One of the simplest things that powerful people do is to talk more than others. A person who talks a lot is likely to give the impression of leadership. He or she may appear to be more influential and authoritative than a reserved counterpart. The style of speech also affects impressions of power. The choice of words and accent, as well as pronunciation, suggest high or low power to listeners. Some researchers have examined how **vocabulary**

of jade." To compel another to become a willing partner in such a one-sided exchange, the rationale must convince the party that the brick is of greater value than the jade. Certainly, even a casual observer must be impressed with Singapore. Singapore is one of the world's busiest ports; the efficiency of shipping facilities is unsurpassed. Its airport is one of the world's most modern, and new subway cars are equipped with cellular telephones for business commuters. The country is clean, efficient, and virtually free of corruption. It is almost up to Japan's standard of living, and issues of race, language, religion, and culture appear to be defused. In fact, Singapore is sometimes described as "the Switzerland of Southeast Asia."

Some business leaders, however, remain suspicious. They emphasize that occasional shifts in governmental policy direction can create problems. Of greater concern is the challenge of political maturation and a tight labor market, which represent barriers to Singapore's continued prosperity.

Anyone interested in doing business in Singapore needs to be sensitive to environmental concerns. A motorbike without a muffler will likely be impounded; smoking is discouraged; and garbage tossed from a car may result in a severe penalty.

Sources: Axtell, Roger E. Do's and Taboos Around the World. *New York: John Wiley, 1986, 183.*

Van Horn, Mike. Pacific Rim Trade. *New York: American Management Assoc., 1989, 318–22.*

richness, the quality and diversity of one's choice of words, influences impressions formed by others. Not surprising, it has been found that use of a rich vocabulary is associated with impressions of high status and a great deal of competence. On the other hand, the use of a limited vocabulary with frequent repetition is likely to portray negative impressions. Then, too, assertiveness of words and phrases suggest high or low power. Qualified statements such as, "I sort of like the idea," or "it was a pretty good class" are less assertive than "I like the idea," and "it was a good class." Another feature of speech linked to impressions of power is the rate of speed at which one speaks. An individual who speaks at a high rate of speed may convey the impression of low trustworthiness. An individual who speaks very slowly may not appear to be as competent as others. A moderate rate of speech is usually recommended. Researchers have also examined the effects of visual communication. If you stare at another person, for example, you may be perceived to be dominant. A word of caution

vocabulary richness-the quality and diversity of one's choice of words should be noted, however, since increased dominance may be associated with impressions of decreased friendliness and politeness.

Figure 16.4 summarizes the factors which contribute to a powerful image.

Figure 16.4 Factors That Contribute to Impressions of Power

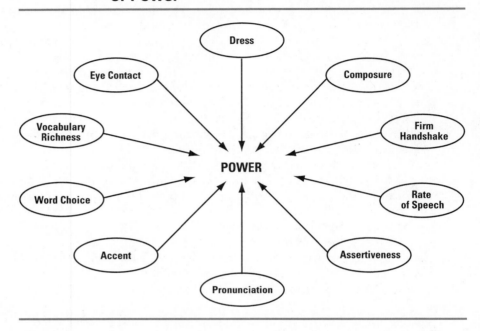

Summary

- Organizational politics may be defined as keeping oneself in the information flow, making sure people know you, understanding how power is wielded, and aligning oneself in power plays.

- Power may be defined as the ability to control anything of value.

- Legitimate power, or position power, is held by individuals occupying a higher level position in an organization than the people below them.

- Coercive power is used by managers or supervisors to reward or punish workers for compliance or noncompliance.

- Personal power is held by individuals who are respected for their knowledge and expertise.

- *Charisma* is a term used to identify magnetic personality traits which are possessed by few individuals.

- A person has referent power when other people admire and try to emulate that individual's personality traits and behaviors.

- Subordinate power is exerted when an individual occupying a position at lower levels within an organization is able to force his or her demands on upper level supervisors or managers.

- Tactics or strategies used in acquiring power may be classified into three categories: personal political action, political action involving others, and political action directed at the opponent.

- Personal political action is exercised when one develops expertise, becomes knowledgeable, demonstrates loyalty, appears to be industrious, and projects a professional image.

- Political action involving others occurs when coalitions or alliances are established to support a course of action.

- Political action directed at opponents may take different forms, such as blaming or falsely attacking a rival, accepting undue credit, designing a setup, and blackmail.

- Today's general trend is toward wider use of participative practices in flatter, more flexible organizations.

- Empowerment occurs when power is shared at every level with all employees, and they are given authority to make on-site decisions.

- The price of empowerment is personal accountability.

- Other key ingredients to a successful empowered workforce include cohesion, teamwork, high morale, and esprit de corps.

- There is danger in concluding that the "best" style of leadership is always participative; there are situations where it may not work.

- Perceptions and impressions of power may be created by dress, how one acts, a firm handshake, eye contact, speech patterns, and assertiveness.

Key Terms

coercive power

cohesion

esprit de corps

legitimate power

personal power

politics

power

referent power

subordinate power

teamwork

vocabulary richness

1. What is the relationship between power and politics?

2. One of the premises developed in this chapter focuses upon the necessity of engaging in organizational politics, that is, using a variety of tactics or strategies to achieve positions of power or to win approval for ideas. Yet, an overwhelming number of workers voice statements such as "I'm sick and tired of organizational politics or office politics." Devise a rationale which explains the dichotomy between the premise and workers' reactions.

3. Explain the differences between the following kinds of power.

   legitimate

   coercive power

   referent power

   subordinate power

4. Sanford McDonnell, Chairman Emeritus of McDonnell Douglas Corporation, stated: "One of the most important ways to empower people is to help them build their self-esteem." Describe ways to accomplish this.

5. Describe examples of empowered employees whom you have observed within an organization where you have worked or transacted business.

6. A friend needs advice on how to create an impression of powerfulness and effectiveness in an organization. What suggestions will you offer?

17

Applying Personal Values, Business Ethics, and Social Responsibility

Well, I sure had my eyes opened," commented Roberto Lopez to fellow student, Carol Stirtz, referring to his experiences as an intern at a Big Six accounting firm in Chicago. He continued, "The attitude of the employees was 'anything goes.' People waited until they got to work to place their private long-distance calls. The phone lines were always tied up. The words *lunch hour* certainly didn't describe the length of time people spent away from their jobs at noon. Some of the guys would go to a fitness center, work out for an hour, shower, and then spend another hour at a trendy deli. Expense accounts were a joke. Receipts for expenses under $25 were not required, and employees took advantage of that situation. Most of the employees just plain cheated on their expense vouchers. Note pads, pens, pencils, magic markers, and boxes of new computer disks disappeared continually. All of this concern about declining personal values must be true. The behavior of the employees was counter to everything I have always been taught. I didn't participate in any of this, but I never said anything to the senior partners either. I felt uncomfortable, and I didn't know what to do. I sure hope it will be different at my new company."

Understanding Attitudes and Personal Values

It is not uncommon for new employees to be shocked when they discover that their personal values differ from those adhered to by others. The personal values of people vary, depending upon cultural, religious, social, and economic experiences to which an individual is exposed. Often when people encounter individuals whose personal values differ, they may immediately reject their values and recognize that they have conflicts. At other times, people may reexamine their personal values and modify them somewhat.

Attitudes and values are related inasmuch as both represent affective behaviors. As noted in Chapter 1, an *attitude* is a mental position one possesses about a fact, issue, or belief. A *value,* on the other hand, is a deep preference that motivates an individual. A value can also be defined as a pervasive standard that influences an individual's moral judgments, responses to others, and commitments to personal and organizational goals. Values give direction to the hundreds of decisions made within organizations every day. Both attitudes and values are intangibles; both are made tangible to others through one's personal, affective behavior.

A manager might hold the attitude that loyalty combined with hard work will lead to greater rewards. Perhaps the manager started at a low-level position and as a result of hard work and loyalty received promotions and pay increases, advancing into the managerial position. Based on this experience, a belief or mental position served as the rudiments for the formation of the attitude that loyalty and hard work will be rewarded. Assume that within the manager's span of control, that is, the number of employees who report to the manager, three employees are viewed as exemplary. Their work ethics are strong, and they have exhibited loyalty in every instance. The manager views each of the employees as candidates for promotions and pay increases. The board of directors and corporate executives, however, have reached a decision to downsize the organization, and the three exemplary employees' positions are scheduled for elimination. The manager regrets very much that the three employees feel betrayed; but wanting the organization to survive and knowing that to do so it must undergo changes to remain competitive motivates the manager to sever employment ties with the three exemplary employees. Thus, values are the means by which goals are accomplished. They give direction to (both popular and unpopular) decisions and constitute our personal "bottom line."

Because the manager encountered a new experience in which loyalty and hard work were not rewarded, the manager's attitude may be modified. Although people do not readily adopt new attitudes or discard old ones, they do change them as a result of new information or new experiences. The manager, for example, may modify his or her original attitude to one that views loyalty and hard work as desirable, which are not necessarily always rewarded.

While attitudes and values are related, they may, indeed, be in conflict with one another. Referring back to the manager's decision to sever employment of the three exemplary employees, one could easily take the position that the manager should have valued their loyalty and hard work and, consequently, should have protested the downsizing strategy by refusing to fire the employees. Whichever value proves to be the strongest at the time the decision is made will determine the course of action. In the previous scenario, the preference for the company's survival was greater than the desire to protect the three employees.

Irwin Federman, president and chief executive officer of Monolithic Memories, has been quoted as saying, "Your job gives you authority. Your behavior earns you respect."[1] Values give direction to people's decisions and behavior. While a value itself is intangible, the decisions people reach and how they behave are observed by others. People in leadership positions, coworkers, and employees holding subordinate positions appraise everyone through their observations. People's values reveal to others exactly what they stand for.

Development of Personal Values

Values are influenced by culture and social class, family, peer groups, educational experiences, work experiences, and countless other elements. Values are more dominant than attitudes and consequently change more slowly. Collectively, an individual's values make up his or her **value system;** that is, what a person places value on or believes is important. Studies of values, traditionally, have focused upon broad areas such as economic, social, or religious values.

value system-what an individual places value on or believes is important

Culture and Social Class Influence

The customary beliefs, social forms, and material traits of a racial, religious, or social group influence what a person values. Business practitioners in South and Central America and large parts of Africa and Asia, for example, believe that it is perfectly acceptable to make small payments to government officials to facilitate needed documents and permits. An individual growing up in a society in which members took pride in manipulating government officials would learn to value such behavior. In the United States, such behavior would be labeled bribery and would be viewed as unacceptable.

The social class to which an individual belongs also influences what the individual values. A classical study conducted 50 years ago yielded results which emphasized the differences of perceptions and values among social classes.[2] The researchers found that while individuals in American culture do not tend to perceive people in higher social classes as their superiors, they do perceive people in lower classes as their inferiors. People in middle-class categories tended to label lower class people as a "no-account lot." People in the upper-lower class perceived themselves as "poor but honest"; however, they labeled the lower-lower class of people as "shiftless." People in the lower-lower class perceived themselves as "people just as good as anybody." While there are many exceptions to social class mem-

---

[1]James M. Kouzes and Barry Z. Posner. *The Leadership Challenge.* San Francisco: Jossey-Bass, 1987, 11.
[2]A. Davis. "American Status Systems and Socialization of the Child." *Social Review.* 1941, 6: 345–56.

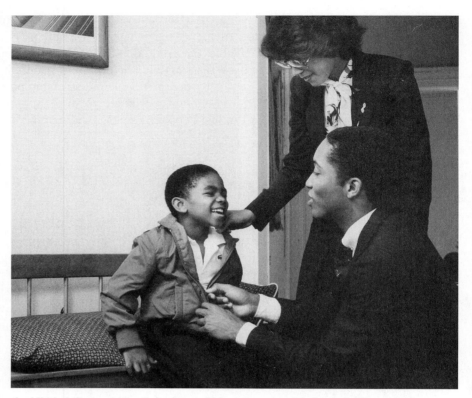

A child is influenced by the values of his or her own family, as well as of other groups, in developing his or her own values.

bership and values held by individuals, correlations between values for education, grades, respect for property, respect for authority, cleanliness, ambition, and nonhostile behavior appear to follow the continuum of social classes. People in the upper echelons of the social class structure collectively tend to place greater value on such factors than people in the lower echelons.

Family Influence

Families influence values acquired by their children either in a positive or negative manner. Traditionally, parents have, through their own behaviors, illustrated what they stood for and what was important. In short, they transmitted values to their children. In today's contemporary society, however, parental and family influence on the formation of values has been weakened. In many homes both parents work and as a result have little time or energy to influence the values of their children. Other homes are headed by a single parent resulting from unwed parents or a broken marriage. The single parent may be coping with a career, raising a child or children, and getting his or her own life back on track. The degree of stability necessary for the parent to serve as a role model may simply be lacking. As a result, the influence of parents and families upon the development of values has been diminished.

When parents work, grandparents or bigger brothers or sisters can help children develop positive values.

Peer Group Influence

Young people, especially teen-agers, are strongly influenced by their peers. Psychologists have suggested that teen-agers often care more about what their friends or clique thinks than about what their parents or teachers think. Many people believe that our society has entered an era wherein a "value crisis" exists. They point to increased gang violence, drive-by shootings, guns in schools, a lack of respect for the rights and property of others, cheating, dishonesty, and a general drift away from norms, that is, societal expectations for behavior. It should be recognized, however, that peer group influence may be positive in nature and sometimes that is the case.

Matt Williams doesn't have a father. His mother was so concerned about the lack of a male role model that she enrolled him in a Little Brother/Big Brother program. Matt was quickly matched with Steve McNaire, a sophomore at the local college. Matt developed a deep admiration for Steve and soon was exhibiting some of the behaviors that represented values to which Steve adhered: integrity, honesty, best effort, fair treatment of everyone, respect for rules and the authority who made the rules, and a genuine concern for others.

If a preference that motivates behavior is to become a value, it must last. If the behavior is of short duration, it is more correctly classified a fad.

Influence of Educational Experiences

There is some controversy about the role of schools in transmitting values to students. Some people believe that the family has broken down as an institution that traditionally influenced values. The church as an institution that in the past provided instruction relating to moral values has for many youngsters also lost its ability to influence. As a result, some people believe schools should assume this role. Other segments of society are fearful that values different from their own may be imposed upon their children. Teachers, caught in the middle of such debates, are aware of past accusations of indoctrination and the risk of being accused of presenting religious beliefs. Then, too, some teachers resent being asked to assume responsibility for society's problems. Nevertheless, most schools do address issues relating to "right" and "wrong" and integrate value clarification concepts in their curricula.

Influence of Work Experiences

People may encounter experiences at work which influence their values.

Julie Koman expressed the following value judgment: "No one expects you to tell the truth all the time in business, and you have to be willing to lie occasionally to get ahead quickly." That was before Randy Eskew was hired as a buyer at the large supermarket which she managed. Secretly, Randy instigated stocking fees or shelving costs which he demanded from vendors before agreeing to stock new items. The substantial cash payments greatly augmented the lucrative compensation which Randy was already receiving. After Julie inadvertently discovered Randy's source of income, which she labeled as "theft and bribery," Randy offered the following rationale: "My performance is partly evaluated on stocking items which customers want. Since I don't know if a new item will be successful, I believe that I am entitled to a reward for taking the risk." As a result of this experience, Julie no longer adheres to her former value judgment.

While past workplace experiences have influenced values, the workplace also provides a setting in which workers experience value conflicts. A **value conflict** is where one or more workers' values are in conflict with those of other workers. As the United States moves toward a more diverse workforce, the potential for value conflicts is heightened. Perhaps this is one reason why more and more business organizations are emphasizing the concept of shared values.

value conflict-occurs when one or more workers' values are in conflict with those of other workers

Influence of Television

It has been estimated that the average United States home contains 1.8 television sets and that a television set is usually on 52 hours a week. While often no one is in the room or watching a program, children between the ages of 2 and 17 watch over 20 hours a week. Some estimates have led to conclusions that by age 18, children will have spent almost one and one-half as much time in front of a television set than in classrooms. By age 18, the typical child has seen 13,000 killings and 100,000 other assorted acts of violence, including rapes, beatings, assaults, explosions, fires, street robberies, home entries, gang confrontations, car crashes, and police brutality.[3] Many of the killings or other acts of violence may have been committed by an actor who has become a role model for the viewer. The question, which has often been strongly debated, is whether this continual exposure to acts of violence and other behaviors which are counter to societal norms influences values and behavior. Certainly some of television's role models who capture the admiration of young people depict behavior and associated values which if emulated create hostile relationships with others. On the other hand, some televised shows transmit positive values and influences.

Relationship of Attitudes, Beliefs, and Values

Values, attitudes, and beliefs may be viewed, depending upon the occasion, as distinct, interrelated, or synonymous entities.[4] Each of the following scenarios and the illustration in Figure 17.1 describe such relationships.

Figure 17.1 Relationships of Beliefs, Attitudes, and Values

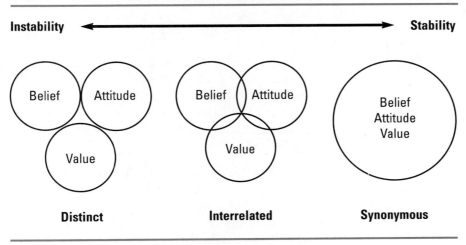

[3]Larue Tone Hosmer. *Moral Leadership in Business,* © 1994, Richard D. Irwin, Inc., p. 45. Reprinted with permission.

[4]Andrew F. Sikula. *Personnel Administration and Human Resources Management.* New York: John Wiley, 1976, 83–84.

Rob Cappas believes that punctuality is a desirable trait. Unfortunately, he has developed an attitude of self-importance. Because of this attitude, Rob has been late for several appointments while he was engaged in an activity that took longer than planned. Although Rob has been careless about keeping appointments, he has not been consistent in his behavior. Rob values personal gain. If he believes that keeping an appointment will be personally beneficial, he will disrupt any activity in which he is engaged and keep the appointment. Rob's belief, attitude, and value may be viewed as being almost totally distinct in this situation. At some point, he will likely reexamine the three entities and modify one or more until they show greater relationship or synonymy.

An illustration of interrelated beliefs, attitudes, and values may be characterized by Laura Walsh.

Laura believes that an individual should be rewarded for his or her contributions. Laura's attitude toward work is, "I'll do what I'm required to do on the job, but no more." Her behavior is motivated by a personal value that is characterized by the question: "What's in it for me?" The editor of the newspaper for which Laura works asked that in addition to her regular weekly column, "The Business Agenda in Hamilton County," she prepare a story dealing with international protocol for a special edition of the business section. Laura certainly wasn't happy, and she was overheard complaining to a coworker that she should receive additional compensation. An examination of Laura's beliefs, attitudes, and values reveals an interrelated connection.

When beliefs, attitudes, and values are synonymous, the intensity or strength of the values is magnified.

Nathan Vencel firmly believes "Honesty is the best policy." His attitude reflects the premise that "one's word is one's badge of honor." When Nathan is placed in situations where a harmless lie might resolve a dilemma, he always adheres to a value that triggers the decision to reveal the truth. When beliefs, attitudes, and values are synonymous, the values are less likely to undergo modification.

Beliefs, attitudes, and values, as depicted in Figure 17.1, may be viewed on a continuum of intensity. Distinct beliefs, attitudes, and values are unstable and subject to clarification and modification. Interrelated beliefs, attitudes, and values are more stable, and change or modification does not quickly occur. Synonymous beliefs, attitudes, and values represent the highest degree of stability, and intensity and modification is least likely.

Modification of Values

Changing values is not a new phenomenon. Every generation has tended to believe that the values of society's younger generation have deteriorated from its own. Perhaps values which change from one generation to another contribute to the "generation gap." Nevertheless, astute observers will recognize that values change as a result of other changes. The people who run an organization change; the organization grows and adopts new technology; and the social, political, and economic settings in which an organization operates are in constant flux.

Job security and loyalty to an employer, for example, are values shared by many older workers. These values may not be as intense for people just entering the workforce and are likely to undergo future modification. Change is the cause. Downsizing, increasing reliance on temporary employment contracts, employee leasing and **outsourcing**—where a whole department may be suddenly taken over by a specialized contractor—are contemporary changes which are altering the relationships between employers and employees.

> *outsourcing-an entire department may be taken over by a specialized contractor*

Take Steven Bitterman as an example of an individual who has become the victim of change. A former employee of Chase Manhattan Bank, he still sits at his same desk at the bank's downtown Brooklyn operations center, surrounded by many of the same coworkers, doing the same work he did before as a controller for the telecommunications department. But now he works for American Telephone and Telegraph. Over a weekend in spring 1994, Bitterman's department was outsourced to AT&T, which now handles the bank's communications operations. "On Friday we went home Chase people and on Monday we came in AT&T people," Bitterman remarked.

Bitterman, who is 50 years old, said that after 16 years inside one company, quickly adapting to another company's culture was, indeed, stressful.[5]

No doubt Mr. Bitterman preferred this stressful change to unemployment. Yet, his beliefs, attitudes, and values will likely be modified as a result of this experience. This is especially true if his salary, retirement plan, or fringe benefits package was altered when his department was outsourced. Rhonda L. Miller, a human resources consultant, believes that loyalty to a company as a value is being changed to loyalty to a profession.[6] The American Management Association surveyed 713 major United States companies with an estimated 2.6 million workers and found that 47.3 percent of the companies eliminated positions as a result of downsizing from mid-1993 through mid-1994.[7] As firms continue cutbacks and American

---

[5] Kirk Johnson. "Downsizing Launches a Rise in Offices with Leased Workers." (New York Times News Service), *The* (Louisville, Kentucky) *Courier Journal.* October 9, 1994, E–4.

[6] Ibid.

[7] Stuart Silverstein. "Corporate America Escalates Downsizing." (Los Angeles Times), *The Indianapolis Star.* October 9, 1994, E–1.

Bitte (sehr) or You Are Welcome in Germany!

The United States is the largest importer in the world. Occasionally, Germany claims the title of leading exporting nation, as it did in 1990 when German exports totaled over $421 billion worth of products and services. Is it any wonder that business representatives from the two countries meet in the international marketplace?

Germans value business protocol, and United States importers and exporters, as well as others involved in international business negotiations, would be well advised to become familiar with the country's customs and protocols.

The following suggestions may be useful:

1. Try to contact an executive at the highest possible level. In small- to medium-sized firms, which account for about three-fourths of all businesses, contact the head of the firm, the *Geschäftsführer.*

2. Germans are conservative in dress and expect their counterparts to be conservative as well. Anything that is flashy or overly fashionable should be avoided, as Germans adhere to the belief that seriousness of purpose and serious dress go hand in hand.

3. Business meetings are traditionally started with a handshake of all parties involved. Women should be first to extend their hand for a handshake.

4. A visitor to Germany should be aware of the protocol of the left and right side. For example, when a junior executive is walking with his senior manager, the junior executive walks on the left side, the side of deference. With a woman, the man should walk and sit to her left.

5. Executive status in Germany is indicated by the number of doors one must pass through before reaching the executive's office.

6. Titles are important. They are used liberally as a signal of respect.
   Geschäftsführer—top executive
   Generaldirektor—general manager
   Direktor—top-level manager
   Abteilungsleiter—department head

7. Germans are very punctual and expect others to be on time. If unavoidable delays occur, telephone to explain lateness as soon as possible.

8. At the onset of meetings, last names only will be used, preceded by titles. The most common titles are "Herr" (Mr.) and "Frau" (Mrs.). The title "Fraulein" (Miss) is considered obsolete, but it is polite to use "Frau" to address all women except the very young.

9. Business cards may be exchanged during a first meeting, with the visitor taking the initiative. If your firm has been in business a long time, print the founding date on your card. Add any academic degrees you may have. Germans value business longevity and formal higher education.

10. If your German host does not understand English, it is up to you to provide an interpreter. When communicating through an interpreter, look at the party who is addressed, not at the interpreter. The same applies when listening to an interpreter.
11. In negotiations, be direct, factual, and concrete. Germans value such attributes. Be careful not to overemphasize the superiority of your product or service, since Germans are proud of their own achievements.
12. Price will be an important factor in your proposal and it must be highly competitive. Presentations should not take a gimmicky approach. Germans do not value "tricks" of advertising or marketing. Technical data should conform to German standards by using the metric system and referring to the Deutsche Mark.
13. Business lunches are common in Germany, but an invitation to a business associate's home is rare. Gifts are not appropriate at initial meetings, and even modest souvenirs may make your German counterpart nervous.
14. The Germans shy away from using their intuition in trusting their negotiating counterparts. They concentrate on the past performance of the individual or company. Trust is not as important in Germany as it is in most other countries; yet once trust has been lost, it is difficult to regain.
15. Germans are embarrassed by direct compliments and they dislike it when people are too ebullient, too friendly, too nonchalant, or too pushy.

Stereotypes applied to Germany over the years, particularly those evolving as a result of World War II, do not accurately portray today's business person in Germany. Achievements by the German people deserve admiration. Although the country was politically partitioned into two entities for more than 40 years, West Germany has managed to forge one of the strongest economies on earth. After absorbing its eastern sister in 1990, the country continues to exhibit creative and innovative traits. Germany is considered by many to be the country most likely to emerge as the leader of the European Economic Community.

Sources: *"Germany Ousts U.S. as Leader in World Trade."* St. Louis *(Missouri)* Dispatch. *March 26, 1991, 58.*

Moran, Robert T., and William G. Stripp. Successful International Business Negotiations. *Houston: Gulf Publishing, 1991, 174–80.*

workers become increasingly insecure about their jobs, modification of values related to job security and loyalty to an employer will continue to be modified. This is simply one example of how change influences values. The global revolution, information-driven organizations, increase in the number of older Americans, restructuring, and other changes will have profound influences on values in the foreseeable future.

Organizational Values

Just as personal values direct decisions which each of us face daily, an **organizational value system** provides direction for the numerous decisions reached in the workplace as well as in other organizations. The values of employers—owners or professional managers—influence the organization's values. Such values are usually swayed in terms of "what is good for the organization." Owners or professional managers, for example, may place value on customer service; they may believe that customer service is the key to everything else. Perhaps this is one reason service-oriented owners and managers are proponents of the time-worn slogan, "The frontline people are really the ones who make us or break us."[8] It must be recognized, however, that personal values and organizational values are not always compatible.

Wal-Mart is an example of a company having success by allowing its employees to feel ownership.

Some organizations are taking note of disparity in value systems, and if an applicant's value system is obviously inconsistent with that of the organization, the applicant may not be chosen. In cases in which individuals are already employees, they may find their futures in jeopardy. An announcement by Jack Welch, chairman at General Electric, indicated that executives who did not live up to GE's values—even if they produced positive results—would not have a future in the company. He elaborated by saying:

[8]Karl Albrecht and Ron Zemke. *Service America.* Homewood, Illinois. Dow Jones-Irwin, 1985, 96.

Unit 4•Improving Practices in Human Relations

For years we looked the other way while executives drove an organization, intimidated our people, and beat the results out of them to make the numbers. Today we do not believe this person will make it. We don't believe this behavior is sustainable. You need to live by our values, to energize every mind and get everybody involved to win in this globally competitive environment. You simply can't have that old leadership style.[9]

It is obvious that at least the executive officers at GE are expected to share organizational values.

Current literature is filled with articles that identify organizational values which business leaders repeatedly mention as important. Among the listings of contemporary organizational values are the following:

► Conducting business affairs honestly and with integrity.
► Creating an atmosphere of openness and trust.
► Establishing a caring organizational attitude.
► Providing quality, service, and a customer focus.
► Fostering respect for the individual and for diversity.
► Nurturing innovation.
► Striving to become the best.
► Exhibiting a "can-do" spirit.
► Accepting organizational and personal accountability.
► Demonstrating teamwork and mutual support.
► Stimulating and becoming open to change.
► Exhibiting community involvement.
► Accepting social responsibility.

While the above list of values which business leaders advocate to guide decisions and behavior may appear to be "pie-in-the-sky" standards, shared values serve as unifying forces that galvanize the energy of everyone in the organization.

Shared Values in Organizations

A clear vision establishes an organization's direction. Vision is to an organization what purpose is to an individual. An individual who has a compelling purpose becomes motivated and exerts efforts toward achieving the purpose. Within an organization, vision establishes the direction and perhaps gets organizational members excited about moving in a certain direction; however, it does not guide people's decisions and actions. According to Burt Nanus, professor of management at the University of Southern

[9]Lynne Joy Farland, Larry Senn, and John R. Childress. *21st Century Leadership: Dialogues with 100 Top Leaders.* New York: Leadership Press, 1995, 117.

California, values are the principles or standards that help people decide what is worthwhile and desirable.[10] When an individual exerts efforts toward the achievement of a purpose, personal values serve as signposts to guide the individual's decisions and behavior. Likewise, when an organization pursues a vision, it is important that shared values guide the decisions and behaviors of the organizational workforce.

Having shared values means there is a consensus among organizational members; that is, they understand and agree with the organizational values. Organizational values are clarified. When employees within an organization share values, the following outcomes may be achieved:

► strong feelings of personal effectiveness, as well as group effectiveness, among workers

► higher levels of loyalty among employees

► greater consensus in establishing goals, strategies, and control mechanisms

► more adherence to codes of ethical behavior

► reduced levels of job stress and tensions.

Although shared values among organizational members exist in varying degrees in most organizations, one would have to be naive to believe that all organizations are characterized by members who share all values. Conflicts do occur as a result of varying values.

Conflicting Values in Organizations

Each worker or member of an organization may adhere to personal values which are counter to the organization's values. When this occurs, value clashes or value conflicts arise. They may arise between workers of differing ages (generation gap), races, cultures, ethnic backgrounds, and religions. They may occur between men and women, supervisors and workers, or top executives and middle managers. Often, however, clashes occur as a result of differing philosophies, priorities, and interpretations which influence values.

I'm really supportive of the bank's emphasis on appropriate business appearance by all employees," Jack Locke commented to other members of his work group. "It's just that I have difficulty conforming to a dress code that specifies that every guy employed here must wear a blue or gray suit or blazer and slacks. After all, the world has changed and casual dress on the job is more acceptable today than ever before. Some of the other banks in town have even set one day aside for casual dress each week."

[10]Burt Nanus. *Visionary Leadership.* San Francisco: Jossey-Bass, 1992, 51.

While the objection to the dress code may appear to be trivial, it is not, because conflicting values have the potential for reducing cooperation and teamwork and for introducing hostility into the workplace.

When one or more members of a group adhere to a value or values which are not synchronized with values held by other members, it may be useful to examine barriers which make it difficult for everyone to share the value or values in question. Figure 17.2 illustrates some common barriers to selected values.

Figure 17.2 **Barriers to Shared Values in Groups**

Barriers	Values
▶ Turf building and Pyramid structures	Empowered work teams
▶ Opportunistic and Lack of principles	Ethics and integrity
▶ Hidden agendas Dishonesty Lack of openness	Open, honest communication network
▶ Dishonesty and Inconsistent behavior	Trust
▶ Emphasis on short-term profits	High quality service
▶ Placing blame and Making excuses	Personal responsibility and accountability
▶ Prejudices and Biases	Diversity and respect for differences
▶ Resistance to change	Innovations
▶ Strict rules and Rigid policies	Flexibility and responsiveness
▶ Isolationist Strictly bottom-line driven	Social and community responsibility

Overcoming Barriers to Shared Values

When employees and their leaders do not share the same values, the organization flounders. It can be compared to an automobile whose tires are unbalanced and whose wheels are misaligned; it cannot run at maximum performance levels and its full potential is never realized. Just as an auto needs corrective adjustments, values must be synchronized if organizational behavior is to be consistent and goal-oriented.

Since values are manifested in affective behaviors that are not quickly or easily changed, everyone within the organization must work to overcome barriers to shared values. The process includes the following stages:

1. Reviewing the organization's current values.
2. Modifying the list of values by making changes or adding new values.
3. Establishing role models among leaders within the organization.
4. Training all organizational members to adhere to the adopted values.
5. Monitoring the display of values by organizational members and providing reinforcement.

What Are the Current Values? Values provide the direction for decisions at all levels within the organization; that is, decisions reflect what is considered to be important. Some organizations place value on high quality and reasonably priced products or services. Other organizations place value on the highest quality and expensive products or services. While some organizations value centralized decision-making, others value decentralized decision-making. Some organizations place value on low operating costs; others value a compensation plan that yields above-average rewards for employees and drives up operating costs. Everyone in the organization needs to understand what is considered to be important in all areas of decision-making, including operations, treatment of customers, treatment of employees, and quantity/quality issues.

With more mothers being in the workforce, the importance of day care has grown over the last few years.

What Modifications Should Be Made in Current Values?
Values shift over time. It is therefore important to review the values identified in the first stage for needed modifications. Perhaps an organization valued a permanent workforce in the past. Needing now a more flexible workforce whose size can be expanded or contracted quickly, the organization needs to modify the earlier value. Social, economical, environmental, and governmental developments sometimes dictate the need to modify values. Today's emphasis on equal opportunity for minorities, for example, may signal the need for organizations to establish a value that guides decisions relating to minority personnel.

What Role Should Leaders Serve?
A **role** is behavior oriented to the general expectations of others: managers, coworkers, subordinates, customers and clients, among others. It arises as a result of occupying a position in an organizational structure. Leaders cast shadows of behavior which others in the organization emulate. Stated another way, if the leaders in an organization do not live by the organization's values, no one else will either. It is absolutely critical that leaders accept and adhere to the organization's values. They must interact and communicate in ways that serve as a role model for all members of the organization.

role-behavior oriented to the general expectations of others

How Can Others Become Acclimated to the Organization's Values?
Use of training sessions can be an effective and efficient method to communicate the organization's values to work teams. The training programs should be vertically integrated and consistent. One value-shaping seminar is not sufficient, since it is likely to be organized as an informational session. The training can be enhanced by follow-up sessions involving problems in which the values guide decision-making. Organizational leaders must recognize the importance of this stage in overcoming barriers to shared values.

How Can the Adherence to Organizational Values Be Strengthened?
Affective behaviors can be assessed over a period. Some behavioral scientists suggest that it may take as long as three years before attitudes, beliefs, and values become accepted as a way of life within an organization. A tracking system can identify the disparities between a value that guided a decision and the organizational value that should have guided the decision. It is important that everyone understands that values do indeed count and are crucial to the organization. The tracking system will enable organizational leaders to monitor the display of values and to provide reinforcement or additional training as needed.

Business Ethics Defined
The word *ethics* is derived from the Greek word *ethos,* meaning character or custom. **Business ethics** refers to what is right or wrong, or good or bad, human behavior. Peter Drucker summarizes the concept of business ethics as "being able to look at your face in the mirror in the morning."

business ethics-refers to what is right or wrong, or good or bad, human behavior

Joyce Lain Kennedy, who prepares a syndicated column dealing with careers, received the following note.

I have a small business and recently filled a position, asking applicants to fax their résumés to me. One young woman knocked herself out of consideration before she even got out of the gate because she used the cover sheet of her current employer and her employer's fax machine.

I decided she is either a cheat or that her employer encouraged her to do whatever it took to get her out of his hair.

Either way, she comes out a loser.[11]

Ms. Kennedy responded by admonishing readers to refrain from stealing office supplies. She further warned workers to take personal time for job interviews. She suggested that when asked during an interview where your current employer thinks you are, if it's during working hours, you should be able to honestly say you're taking personal time. If you say, "At the dentist," the prospective employer may think that if you lie to one employer, you'll lie to all employers. While philosophers, from time to time, distinguish ethics from morality, most people interchange the words *ethical* and *moral* in everyday application to describe actions they believe to be right and good. Conversely, they interchange the words *unethical* and *immoral* to describe actions they believe to be wrong and bad.

As noted earlier, personal values sometimes conflict with organizational values. Personal ethics, likewise, cannot be neatly divorced from organizational ethics. In recent years, Wall Street corruptions, corporate refusals to confront occupational hazards such as asbestos, bribes and kickbacks, deceptions in labeling and packaging products, and other wrongful practices have kindled a sensitivity to ethical behavior in business. The American Assembly of Collegiate Schools of Business (AACSB) has suggested that business ethics represent an important area of study in business administration programs. As a result, the study of ethics has become common in college classrooms. Today's organizational executives are also placing heavy emphasis on building reputations based on integrity, leading to widespread workshops and seminars dealing with ethical behavior designed for corporate employees.

*E*thical Dilemmas

Business organizations, as well as members of society in general, are plagued by the fact that there are liars, cheats, and thieves among us. Liars, cheats, and thieves are not new nor are they likely to disappear. In the daily scramble to get ahead, earn a profit, and outwit competitors, some people don't play by the rules. Sometimes, the culprits are respected and ordinari-

---

[11]Joyce Lain Kennedy. "Be Ethical on Old Job While Looking for New One." *The* (Louisville, Kentucky) *Courier Journal*. October 9, 1994, F–G 1.

ly well-behaved persons. Some coaches of college athletic teams, for example, bend recruiting rules and attempt to gain unfair advantages. While on occasion the offending coach may have found an inappropriate excuse to convince himself or herself that no wrong was being committed, the excuse was found because the coach was looking for one. Actions are unethical if they won't stand scrutiny by others. Consider the following situation:

Maria Garcia is the business manager for the Green Valley Metropolitan School District. When the cost of new equipment being purchased exceeds $5,000, Green Valley solicits bids from vendors, and as business manager, Ms. Garcia reviews the bids and offers a recommended course of action to the board of education.

Recently, the District placed an advertisement in local newspapers soliciting bids for 90 personal computers (486 SX), with color monitors, keyboards, and printers. Kris Giordano, a sales rep from Computer Solutions, immediately made an appointment with Ms. Garcia to review the specifications and offer information about the service her firm would provide. A couple of days later, a new 486 personal computer—complete with color monitor, keyboard, mouse, and laser-jet printer—was delivered to Ms. Garcia's home. The accompanying card contained the following message: "As a token of my appreciation for your time and interest, I would like for you to discover, firsthand, the advantages offered by Computer Solutions. I am sure you will want to recommend that the Green Valley Metropolitan School District choose this equipment for their students."

Dilemmas of this nature are not uncommon in the world of work. One might take the position that Maria Garcia would be stupid to return this expensive gift. After all, the gift was thrust upon her; she did not make promises, so why should she return the equipment? Accepting the gift would be wrongful behavior and a breach of ethics. Such behavior cannot stand scrutiny of others for the following reasons.

1. If Ms. Garcia recommends that the board of education accept the bid from Computer Solutions, she has, in fact, accepted a bribe. Others may suffer as a result of her action, including competing vendors and taxpayers.

2. If Ms. Garcia keeps the gift but fails to recommend that the bid from Computer Solutions be accepted, she has accepted a gift under false pretense. Ms. Giordano's letter clearly implies the action expected from Ms. Garcia.

3. If some party or agent is to benefit from a gift as the result of a potential sales transaction, the Green Valley Metropolitan School District should be the beneficiary, not its agent, Maria Garcia.

While one may convincingly argue that Ms. Giordano and her employer, Computer Solutions, acted in an unethical manner by sending the gift to Maria Garcia, it is Maria's actions which will be judged by her employer, taxpayers, and other vendors.

The Scrutiny of Others

Increasingly, those interested in stopping the country's perceived slide into an ethical morass are discovering that some members of society have become adept at assigning blame away from themselves; that is, if they exercise poor judgment, they blame someone else. Take Robert Bowen, for example, who said, "I realized I had made a big mistake," while complaining to the Better Business Bureau.

Like most doting parents, Robert Bowen believed his petite, photogenic, preschool-aged daughter, Jenny, was destined for stardom. His belief was intensified after he responded to a newspaper ad seeking models. The promoters said Jenny was pretty, articulate, and had star potential which could yield as much as $1,500 a day, no experience necessary. That proved to be strong enough motivation for forking over $300 for slides and photos which the promoters said were necessary to show agencies. Thousands of parents are attracted to ads each year promising fame and fortune through child modeling, only to find themselves duped. The Better Business Bureau says modeling and talent agencies ranked in the top third in consumer complaints in 1993, and the ranking would have probably been higher had many parents been less reluctant to complain.

Sometimes when a firm receives a complaint, the remedy which it offers may be viewed as less than desirable. An independent, nonregulated payphone company sent a customer an exorbitant bill for col-

Unfair and unscrupulous actions hinder the development of harmonious relationships between workers and workers, and between workers and supervisors. A person who cannot be trusted to do the right thing fails to win the respect of others. It should be recognized, however, that ethical dilemmas are faced by people at all levels within an organization. Unfortunately, executives and members of managerial staffs sometimes fail to adhere to ethical behavior. Consider the following event which occurred at Beech-Nut Nutrition Corporation.

The director of research at Beech-Nut sent senior executives a memorandum stating that he suspected a supplier was selling Beech-Nut a fake apple juice formula. The formula was the major component used to make apple juice for infants. The executives tended to ignore the memorandum until a private investigator reached the same conclusion. Instead of pulling the product off shelves and issuing an apology, they attempted to sell the remaining inventory by using price-cutting tactics. Two executives were sentenced to prison but were later freed on a technicality.

It is apparent from the above incident—which is not an isolated event because other firms have experienced similar breaches of ethics—that

lect calls. After the customer protested, the company offered a calling card with 100 minutes of "free" long distance calls. The customer, who believes the company acted in an unethical manner, responded by saying, "I will definitely not be taking advantage of their offer."

Even when a company follows "do-good" business policies, it may face doubters. Ben & Jerry's (ice cream) locates its plants in areas of high unemployment. It supports efforts to save the Brazilian rain forest. It created a blueberry ice cream so it could buy blueberries exclusively from a group of Maine Native Americans to help support their economy. It quit selling a handmade brownie-and-ice-cream sandwich because its workers' hands were developing repetitive stain injuries. Ben & Jerry's donates 7.5 percent of its pretax profits to charities each year—more than $500,000 in 1993. Ben Cohen, a chief executive officer and cofounder of Ben & Jerry's Homemade Incorporated, encountered an accuser, who said: "You're just doing this to sell ice cream."

Sources: Gallagher, Jim. "Children's Modeling Poses Risks." The (St. Louis, Missouri) Post-Dispatch. October 30, 1994, E–1.

Manor, Robert. "Ben and Jerry Say Social Goodness Is Good Business." (St. Louis Post-Dispatch), The (Bloomington, Indiana) Herald-Times. July 2, 1994, B–10.

Shapiro, Esther. "Customers Have the Right to Complain." (Knight-Ridder Newspaper) The Indianapolis (Indiana) Star. October 11, 1994, D–1.

respected business firms suffer damage to their reputations when questions concerning ethical behavior arise. Perhaps this is one reason formal codes of ethics, developed by many business organizations and trade associations, are popular today.

Codes of Ethics

A **code of ethics** is simply a compilation of the rules that are meant to govern the conduct of members of a particular organization or profession. Figure 17.3 contains the code of ethics compiled by the American Marketing Association. A recent survey found that 94 percent of the *Fortune* 500 service and industrial companies have a written code of ethics.[12] Companies and trade associations expect their members to abide by such rules as a condition of their engaging in the profession.

There are at least two noteworthy limitations to codes of ethics. First, the written rules are sometimes so vague and general they prove to be of

> *code of ethics-a compilation of the rules meant to govern the conduct of members of a particular organization or profession*

[12]W. Michael Hoffman and Edward S. Petry, Jr. "Abusing Business Ethics." *Phi Kappa Phi Journal.* Winter 1992, 10–11.

Figure 17.3 The Code of Ethics Adopted by the American Marketing Association

Members of the American Marketing Association (AMA) are committed to ethical professional conduct. They have joined together in subscribing to this Code of Ethics embracing the following topics:

Responsibilities of the Marketer

Marketers must accept responsibility for the consequences of their activities and make every effort to ensure that their decisions, recommendations, and actions function to identify, serve, and satisfy all relevant publics: consumers, organizations and society. Marketers' professional conduct must be guided by:

1. The basic rule of professional ethics: not knowingly to do harm;
2. The adherence to all applicable laws and regulations;
3. The accurate representation of their education, training and experience; and
4. The active support, practice and promotion of this Code of Ethics.

Honesty and Fairness

Marketers shall uphold and advance the integrity, honor, and dignity of the marketing profession by:

1. Being honest in serving consumers, clients, employees, suppliers, distributors and the public;
2. Not knowingly participating in conflict of interest without prior notice to all parties involved; and
3. Establishing equitable fee schedules including the payment or receipt of usual, customary and/or legal compensation for marketing exchanges

Rights and Duties of Parties

Participants in the marketing exchange process should be able to expect that:

1. Products and services offered are safe and fit for their intended uses;
2. Communications about offered products and services are not deceptive;
3. All parties intend to discharge their obligations, financial and otherwise, in good faith; and
4. Appropriate internal methods exist for equitable adjustment and/or redress of grievances concerning purchases.

It is understood that the above would include, *but is not limited to,* the following responsibilities of the marketer:

In the area of product development and management:

▶ Disclosure of all substantial risks associated with product or service usage
▶ Identification of any product component substitution that might materially change the product or impact on the buyer's purchase decision
▶ Identification of extra-cost added features

In the area of promotions:

► Avoidance of false and misleading advertising
► Rejection of high pressure manipulations, or misleading sales tactics
► Avoidance of sales promotions that use deception or manipulation

In the area of distribution:

► Not manipulating the availability of a product for purpose of exploitation
► Not using coercion in the marketing channel
► Not exerting undue influence over the resellers' choice to handle a product

In the area of pricing:

► Not engaging in price fixing
► Not practicing predatory pricing
► Disclosing the full price associated with any purchase

In the area of marketing research:

► Prohibiting selling or fund-raising under the guise of conducting research
► Maintaining research integrity by avoiding misrepresentation and omission of pertinent research data
► Treating outside clients and suppliers fairly

Organizational Relationships

Marketers should be aware of how their behavior may influence or impact on the behavior of others in organizational relationships. They should not encourage or apply coercion to obtain unethical behavior in their relationships with others, such as employees, suppliers or customers.

1. Apply confidentiality and anonymity in professional relationships with regard to privileged information.
2. Meet their obligations and responsibilities in contracts and mutual agreements in a timely manner.
3. Avoid taking the work of others, in whole, or in part, and represent this work as their own or directly benefit from it without compensation or consent of the originator or owner.
4. Avoid manipulation to take advantage of situations to maximize personal welfare in a way that unfairly deprives or damages the organization or others.

Any AMA members found to be in violation of any provision of this Code of Ethics may have his or her Association membership suspended or revoked.

Source: Reprinted by permission of the American Marketing Association.

little value. Second, codes of ethics are neither a complete nor a completely reliable guide to one's moral obligations. It is impossible for the drafters of such codes to anticipate all of the moral dilemmas which may be encountered and impossible for them to draft rules to govern all behavior.

Whistle Blowers

Whistle blowers are the people who call attention to the real or imagined misdeeds and unscrupulous behavior of their colleagues, or sometimes their supervisors. A whistle blower informs management, a union, the press, or a government agency that some behavior within the organization is not consistent with ethical standards. Some organizations encourage employees to report breaches of ethical behavior. In other cases, the whistle blower may be treated as a traitor, ostracized, and subtly induced to leave the organization.

Some observers believe that whistle-blowing is essential. They point to the need for whistle blowers to keep others honest. In a recent book, Gellerman wrote, "Whistle blowers serve as a kind of auxiliary conscience for the rest of us, and like our own consciences, they achieve their purposes primarily by making us uncomfortable."[13]

Whistle-blowing may lead to conflicts and disharmony and should, therefore, not be undertaken lightly. The activity being reported should be serious in nature with the potential to harm other people, be contrary to the public purpose and legitimate goals of an organization, or violate human rights. The whistle blower should make attempts to resolve the problem within the organization before going public.

Fostering Ethical Behavior

What can a company do to foster ethical behavior by its executives, managers, and workers, that is, what can a company do to change or prevent behaviors that are subject to whistle-blowing? Most authorities would probably agree that the best solution would be to try to change the nature of organizations so as to diminish the need for whistle-blowing.

Raised Risk of Exposure

To foster ethical behavior, the risk of exposure should be increased. The idea is not to catch more nonconformers, but to dissuade honest people from yielding to temptation. Every organization should consider the merits of establishing internal channels for reporting wrongdoing. Employees at all levels could be rewarded for using such channels. Senior executives and board members could be appointed to committees to investigate and elimi-

---

[13]Saul W. Gellerman. *Motivation in the Real World.* New York: Dutton, 1992, 276.

nate wrongdoing. Committees may wish to draft policy statements that, if violated, lead to severe punishment. Thus, rewards and punishments may serve as effective tools in encouraging ethical behaviors.

Steps can also be taken to eliminate or minimize conditions in which unethical acts are likely to occur. Temptation, in the path of even the most honorable people, should be avoided. Another technique for encouraging ethical behavior focuses upon keeping each individual's conscience alert. Training sessions should be conducted periodically to review and update codes of ethics. Individuals faced with ethical dilemmas should be taught to ask themselves questions such as these.

► Is it legal? Is it right? Is it beneficial?

► How would I feel if my decision were printed in the local newspaper or aired on a local news broadcast?

► How would my bosses, coworkers, and family members react to my decision?

Social Audit

Another technique sometimes used, especially by larger organizations, is the **social audit.** A social audit monitors the ethical behavior of executives, managers, supervisors, and employees and attempts to discover how well the organization's ethical policies are being followed. The social audit may be conducted by an ombudsman or perhaps an ethics committee similar to the one recommended earlier.

social audit-monitors the ethical behavior of executives, managers, supervisors, and employees

Organizations and Social Responsibility

The concept of **social responsibility** refers to an organization's consideration of the social as well as economic effects of its decisions. It may, for example, be more profitable to dump toxic wastes in a stream than to adhere to regulations designed to protect the environment. Milton Friedman, the author of *Capitalism and Freedom,* forcefully argued that business has no social responsibilities other than to maximize profits.[14] Others, however, have advocated obligations in addition to pursuing profits. They believe that social responsibility implies that business organizations, while pursuing profit interests, are obligated to take actions that protect societal interests.

Business today is confronted with five major areas of social issues: the economy, human relations, ecology and environmental protection, consumerism, and the scarcity of natural resources. Members of managerial staffs, as well as all other employees, must exercise sensitivity to social issues which concern most citizens.

social responsibility-refers to an organization's consideration of the social effects of its decisions

[14]Milton Friedman. *Capitalism and Freedom.* Chicago: The University of Chicago Press, 1962, 133.

Ben and Jerry (at a mike) operate a socially and environmentally aware organization.

The Economy

Decisions made in business organizations play an important role in the health of the United States economy. Decisions to retrain workers, offer employees transfers, and provide severance pay are examples of socially responsible actions. Business often joins organized labor to advocate protection against foreign products that threaten the jobs of United States workers. In other cases, business organizations have moved production lines to Mexico or other countries where labor is cheaper, arguing that unless they took such actions they could no longer be competitive and the firm would eventually fail.

Human Relations

Insensitivity to human needs looms as a critical issue for all organizations. Minorities, older workers, former criminals, individuals with life-threatening diseases, the physically handicapped, and other groups pose special problems in employing organizations. Conflicts with other employees, harassment, increased absenteeism, higher insurance costs, and a host of other potential problems are prevalent. Yet, if business organizations fail in their social responsibility to employ people who often face discrimination and safeguard these people, society faces insurmountable problems.

Ecology and Environmental Protection

Ecology, the relationship between people and other living things in the environment, is a significant social issue. We are constantly being reminded of the dangers of water and air pollution. Automobile emissions, smoke-belching factories, toxic spills, and soft-drink and beer bottles and cans which are not biodegradable, are among the problems created by business organizations for which the organizations must accept social responsibility. Organizations failing to accept accountability for environmental violations are likely to encounter adverse public relations. As employees become aware of such violations, human relations among members of the organization may become strained.

ecology-the relationship between people and other living things in the environment

Consumerism

Consumerism, the demand that business organizations give proper consideration to consumer wants and needs, has become a significant social concern in recent years. In 1962, President Kennedy outlined the rights of consumers in a speech to Congress: the right to be informed, the right to safety, the right to choose, and the right to be heard. Ralph Nader and other consumer protection advocates have continued to contribute to the movement. Today, most business organizations exert considerable efforts to assure consumer protection and to give full hearings to consumer complaints.

consumerism-the demand that business organizations give proper consideration to consumer wants and needs

Scarcity of Natural Resources

In recent years, we have become painfully aware that certain natural resources face depletion. The vast petroleum resources in the United States which provided the American domestic market with energy have been greatly diminished. In parts of the country, having an adequate supply of clean, uncontaminated water is a major concern. In addition, concern is often voiced about the rapid depletion of forests in this country and the rain forests in tropical areas. Clearly, the decisions reached by business organizations in regard to the use of natural resources affect everyone. It is no surprise, therefore, that business has been asked to assume social responsibility by conserving such resources and finding alternatives.

Other Social Responsibilities

In Chapter 2, we discussed business organizations' responsibilities to both internal and external stakeholders. Many business organizations also feel a strong commitment to the communities in which they are located. They may, for example, donate an executive's time and company funds to run a United Way campaign. In many cases, they engage in **philanthropy,** that is, giving funds to charities and financially supporting social causes or both.

philanthropy-giving funds to charities and financially supporting social causes

- The personal values of people vary, depending upon cultural, religious, social, and economic experiences to which an individual is exposed.

- A value is a deep preference that motivates an individual and serves as a pervasive standard influencing moral judgments, responses to others, and commitments to personal and organizational goals.

- Values give direction to decisions (both popular and unpopular).

- Even though attitudes and values are related, they may on occasion be in conflict with one another.

- Whichever value proves to be the strongest at the time a decision is made will determine the course of action.

- Collectively, a person's values make up that person's value system, that is, what the person believes is important.

- An individual's social class, family, peer group, educational and work experiences, as well as television, influence values acquired by the individual.

- Norms represent societal expectations for behavior.

- Value conflicts occur when one or more workers' values are in conflict with those of other workers.

- Values, attitudes, and beliefs may be viewed, depending upon the occasion, as distinct, interrelated, or synonymous entities.

- Distinct beliefs, attitudes, and values are unstable and subject to clarification and modification. Interrelated beliefs, attitudes, and values are more stable, and change or modification does not occur quickly. Synonymous beliefs, attitudes, and values represent the highest degree of stability and intensity, and modification is least likely.

- Values may change over time as a result of other changes.

- An organizational value system provides direction for the numerous decisions reached within the organization.

- Business leaders cultivate shared organizational values. Shared values serve as unifying forces that galvanize the energy of everyone in the organization.

- Since values are manifested in affective behaviors that are not quickly or easily changed, everyone within the organization must work to overcome barriers to shared values.

- A role is behavior-oriented to the general expectations of others: managers, coworkers, subordinates, customers and clients, and a variety of other individuals.

- Training sessions may prove to be an effective and efficient method of communicating the organization's values to various work teams.

- Business ethics refers to what is right or wrong, or good or bad, human behavior.

- Personal ethics cannot be divorced from organizational ethics.
- Actions are considered to be unethical if they cannot stand scrutiny by others.
- Unfair and unscrupulous actions hinder the development of harmonious relationships between workers and workers, and between workers and supervisors.
- A code of ethics is simply a compilation of the rules that are supposed to govern the conduct of members of a particular organization or profession.
- Whistle blowers are the people who call attention to the real or imagined misdeeds and unscrupulous behavior of a colleague or superior.
- Every organization should consider the merits of establishing internal channels for reporting wrongdoings.
- A social audit monitors the ethical behavior of executives, managers, supervisors, and employees to ascertain how well the organization's ethical policies are followed.
- The concept of social responsibility refers to an organization's consideration of the social as well as economic effects of its decisions.
- Business today is confronted with five major areas of social issues: the economy, human relations, ecology and environmental protection, consumerism, and the scarcity of natural resources.

Key Terms

business ethics

code of ethics

consumerism

ecology

organizational value system

outsourcing

philanthropy

role

social audit

social responsibility

value conflict

value system

1. Socially responsible behavior is good business. Develop a rationale to support this sentence.

2. How should a supervisor treat an employee who constantly violates ethical norms by making racial, ethnic, and/or religious slurs?

3. How do values differ from attitudes? beliefs? ethics?

4. What is an ethical dilemma? Provide some examples of ethical dilemmas.

5. A professor recently described whistle blowers as grudge-holding fault-finders. Was such a description justified? Explain.

6. You have been retained as a consultant for International Multifoods Incorporated, a frozen foods processor. Your role will be to work with executives to familiarize them as to how to go about fostering ethical behavior among all company employees. What will you recommend?

18

Professionalism— The Key to Human Relations

Learning Objectives

Upon completing this chapter, you should be able to:

- Explain the characteristics of a profession.

- List the marks of a professional.

- Understand that character encompasses a person's honor, integrity, constancy, and moral fiber.

- Recall the equation for professional behavior.

- Learn to cope with problems rather than attempting to pass them on to others.

- Develop a plan for acquiring the qualities, characteristics, or attributes which mark the identity of a professional.

▼

business etiquette-refers to courteous behavior in business settings

Jon Dahlinghaus was standing in the middle of the office doing his favorite impression of Mr. Osburn, owner and general manager of the firm. Several employees were snickering until they saw Mr. Osburn coming down the hall. Jon had his back to the door and didn't see his boss enter the office and quietly observe the impressions. As Mr. Osburn started clapping, Jon turned to face his boss and suddenly felt very uncomfortable.

Jon's behavior always seemed to attract the attention he craved. Perhaps this time, he had gone too far. He had never been popular in the office, primarily because he didn't practice good human relations techniques. He was neither friendly toward his coworkers nor overly helpful. His work, when he wasn't clowning around, was satisfactory; however, Jon's immediate supervisor, Nina Kaslow, commented on his semiannual evaluation report: "Jon has never practiced business etiquette."

*P*rofessionalism Defined

Business etiquette refers to courteous behavior in business settings. In our society, individuals who command the respect of others observe the so-called rules of etiquette. They refrain from using obscene language in public and say "please" when requesting and "thank you" when receiving. In business, too, there are certain rules for accepted behavior. Bankers, for example, are expected to keep financial information about a private firm or an individual confidential. It is accepted business etiquette to return telephone calls, dress appropriately, and treat employees or coworkers in a fair and impartial manner. When members of a business organization, such as Jon Dahlinghaus, violate the rules of business etiquette, they are considered ill-mannered, impolite, and unprofessional.

To fully understand the concept of professionalism, a person must examine the characteristics of a profession.

Training

A profession is marked by the need for special training. Doctors, lawyers, teachers, engineers, accountants, and professionals in other specialized fields require four or more years of college. Other professions, such as real estate brokers, cosmetologists, auto service technicians, morticians, and management information specialists, may complete specialized study in a two-year college program or at a technical trade school. While many of the jobs available today and projected for the future do not require four-year college degrees, they do require some type of specialized training which involves study beyond high school.

Permanence

A second characteristic of a true profession is permanence of the occupation. While some individuals who enter law, medicine, and engineering, for example, eventually change occupations, they do not prepare for these occupations with the intention of using them as stepping-stones to other occupations. When people look upon an occupation as a temporary job or as a mere stepping-stone to another occupation, they lack the professional pride noticeable in doctors, lawyers, engineers, and other professionals who stay in their professions permanently.

Architecture is one example of a well-paid profession that can hold personal satisfaction.

As requirements to enter an occupation continue to be refined and often raised, the permanence of individuals filling that occupation will be noted. The easier it is to enter an occupation, the more likely it is that those who enter will leave it.

Professional Rewards

A third characteristic by which a profession is judged consists of rewards. These rewards take two forms—monetary compensation and satisfaction from rendering service to others. Some professionals earn more money than others. Doctors, for example, earn higher salaries than accountants. The extent to which an individual derives personal satisfaction, likewise, varies. A firefighter may experience as much satisfaction from saving a child from a burning building as a physician does when curing a person with a life-threatening illness. A cosmetologist may experience satisfaction when a client is pleased with a new hair style, while a travel consultant may feel elated when a client reacts enthusiastically to a planned vacation trip. Professional workers in all occupations derive satisfaction from fulfilling the needs of others.

Professional Ethics

Chapter 17 presented the Code of Ethics adopted by the American Marketing Association in Figure 17.3. Other professions, likewise, have adopted formal codes of ethics so that the members of the professions

Ethical Dimensions to Human Relations

The Good, the Bad, and the Ugly

Professional codes of ethics are the rules that are supposed to govern the conduct of a given profession. Generally speaking, members of a profession agree to abide by the rules as a condition of engaging in that profession. But when they don't or when the actions of a few begin to tarnish the image and reputations of others in the profession, an attempt may be initiated to help the public distinguish the good from the bad and ugly. That is what happened in the law profession when the International Society of Primerus Law Firms was launched in 1992.

A recent American Bar Association study shows the public thinks highly of lawyers who advertise in positive ways. But most of us, from time to time, encounter billboards with messages such as "Call 1-800 SUE THEM" or "INJURED? 555-HURT, NO FEES UNTIL YOU ARE PAID." TV ads have featured ladies slipping on storefront sidewalks and unsuspecting men tumbling down rickety ladders. Newspaper stories have highlighted events such as an 80-year-old woman winning multimillions as a result of burning her legs with hot coffee. Indeed,

CONTINUED

some lawyers are noted for their money-grabbing, ambulance-chasing antics. The International Society of Primerus Law Firms, with members in 23 cities in Michigan, Indiana, Wisconsin, Oklahoma, South Dakota, Texas, and California, is committed to the adherence to lofty principles in marketing legal services.

The organization thus far has made information available to the public by providing tips for finding a good lawyer. The search, according to the Society, should begin with a review of lawyers' ratings published in the *Martindale Hubbell Directory of Lawyers and Law Firms.* The ratings, based primarily on the opinions of other lawyers, rank lawyers on legal ability, experience, ethics, reliability, and other qualifications.

Other professional groups also make efforts to self-regulate and self-police the activities of members. The American Association of Advertising Agencies, for example, has adopted the AAAA Creative Code, which points out what is considered objectionable by advertising agencies. Member agencies agree to stop advertising that is in violation of the Code.

Sources: Holeway, Lisa. "Group Tries to Overhaul Lawyers' Image." The Indianapolis Star. *December 18, 1994, E–2.*

Shaw, William H. and Vincent Barry. Moral Issues in Business. *Belmont, California: Wadsworth. 7–8.*

Wray, Ralph D.. Advertising Services. *New York: McGraw-Hill, 1990, 109.*

know what unethical practices to avoid. The oldest code of ethics is that of the medical profession—dating back to the famous Oath of Hippocrates, the great physician of the 4th century B.C. The present-day code, adopted by the American Medical Association, is based on the Hippocratic Oath. The American Bar Association has a code based on a set of resolutions adopted in 1836. The National Education Association approved an official code of ethics for teachers in 1941. Other professional groups have also adopted codes of ethics.

Professional Criteria

In addition to the foregoing characteristics of a profession, there are a couple of minor criteria by which we judge whether a particular occupation may be classed as a profession. One of these minor criteria is the availability of adequate professional literature; another is the association of the members of the occupation in professional organizations.

In summary, a profession is characterized by special training for practitioners, permanence of the occupation, and professional rewards, ethics, literature, and associations.

It is somewhat trite and not always correct to label an individual who fills a position in a profession as a professional. A **professional** has met the requirements to practice the profession, usually as the result of special training and—in some cases—licensing. A professional exhibits loyalty to the profession, experiences professional rewards, adheres to the profession's code of ethics, engages in activities designed to keep himself or herself current in the occupation, and participates in professional associations. Not everyone who fills a professional position meets the criteria and, consequently, should not be labeled a professional. In addition to professionals, there are specially trained individuals who work along with professionals, but in a subsidiary or supportive role; they are known as **paraprofessionals.** Later, we will look at other marks of a professional.

The conduct, character, and qualities that mark the behavior expected of a person who engages in the pursuit of a professional career is called **professionalism.** The expectations in behavior are usually determined by others in the profession; however, in some cases, customers, clients, and members of society may influence the expectations. Professional behavior (professionalism) is the key to human relations. Professionalism may be practiced not only by professionals but also by paraprofessionals and other workers.

professional-an individual who has met the requirements to practice a profession, exhibits loyalty, experiences professional rewards, adheres to ethics, keeps current in the occupation, and participates in professional associations

paraprofessionals-specially trained individuals who work with professionals in a subsidiary role

professionalism-the conduct, character; and qualities that mark the behavior expected of a professional

The Marks of a Professional

Almost everyone aspires to become a professional. Most college basketball players hope to play for a franchise team in the National Basketball Association; country music singers strive to record a best-selling song; medical researchers laboriously pursue a preventive measure for the common cold; and homebuilders in suburban subdivisions try to create the best-constructed, most appealing homes. The sources of motivation to become a professional may vary; some people are motivated to become professionals because they can earn more money, achieve a national identity, become famous, capture the respect of their peers, or simply overcome challenges which they set for themselves. The source of motivation may not seem important. What is important is that people be the best they can be. If they do less, they shortchange themselves and all other members of society.

What qualities, characteristics, or attributes mark the identity of a professional? The answer to this question is of interest to both employers and employees. Employers are interested in professional employees because their judgments are accepted by supervisors, without much direct supervision. Employers are interested in learning what measures are used to achieve professional status. Behavioral psychologists have identified a number of traits, characteristics, and attributes which are associated with individuals who have achieved professional status and who practice professionalism. These may be classified into three categories: personal qualities, social behavior, and personal behavior.

Personal Qualities

maturity-a state of becoming the best that an individual can be

Maturity is one of many criteria that separates those who are going somewhere from those who are not. When referring to **maturity** as a personal quality, according to most dictionaries, it means having completed natural growth and development and attaining a final, desired state of being. Most behavioral scientists, however, argue that maturity is not a state of being but is instead more of a state of becoming. Abraham Maslow pointed out, "The mature person wants to be the best he or she can be." Most people, at some point in their lives, have been made aware of the old adage, "There is always room for improvement." Thus, maturity is somewhat elusive; we constantly strive to achieve excellence, but there is always room for improvement. Even though the quality itself is somewhat elusive, maturity is demonstrated by the way workers resolve their conflicts and cope with problems. Important decisions are based on slow, careful consideration of all aspects of the problem. People with maturity work effectively by themselves or with others while under pressure. In the face of unexpected problems, the mature worker does not fall apart, panic, or make rash decisions. Instead, maturity enables a worker to deal with things as they are, not as they might have been or as he or she wishes them to be.

Filled with unexpected, dangerous problems, firefighting requires mature persons who can tolerate the pressures of life and death situations and who have the ability to make deliberate decisions.

Individuals exhibiting professionalism model highly principled behavior, that is, behavior which is determined by one's personal standards or character. **Character** encompasses an individual's honor, integrity, constancy, and moral fiber.[1] Stated another way, professional behavior is guided by the motto "Honesty is the best policy." The people who truly adhere to pro-

character-encompasses one's honor, integrity, constancy, and moral fiber

---

[1]David Francis and Mike Woodcock. *Unblocking Organizational Values.* Glenview, Illinois: Scott Foresman, 1990.

fessionalism will never be guilty of deception, schemes, or corrupt practices. Such people are deserving of trust and can be counted upon to exercise ethical behavior. Professional behavior is exhibited by those with a strong sense of values and an underlying philosophy which guides their behavior. They are not wishy-washy; instead, they are willing to commit themselves to ideas, causes, or principles.

A final personal quality is openness. Professional behavior demands consideration for others. This means being able to speak openly of problems and conflicts and, sometimes, unpopular messages. In doing so, professionals are able to listen to others and respect them whether they agree or disagree. True professionals have learned to be forthright without being caustic, impassioned without being abrasive, and firm without being cutting.

Figure 18.1 summarizes the personal qualities associated with individuals who practice professionalism.

Figure 18.1 **Personal Qualities of Professionals**

► **Maturity**

► **Highly Principled Behavior**
Character
Trust
Honesty
Ethical
Convictions and Values

► **Openness**

Social Behavior

Professionalism is revealed through social behavior. Every time we interact with another person, whether at work or in a social setting, our social behavior causes the other person to form an initial impression or reinforce or modify past impressions.

Mindy Greenbaum from Designscape followed Alan Hoffman from Nature's Garden in presenting her firm's proposals for landscaping work at the new Twin Lakes Park to the city council of Hampton. Mindy had accidentally discovered that Alan's firm, Nature's Garden, was being sued by the city council in Columbia for failure to fulfill contractual obligations. Mindy was also aware that Nature's Garden had violated a state mandate which required quarantine of flowering dogwood trees and prohibited their planting. Mindy refrained from mentioning these facts even though it would have ensured that Designscape would surely win the contract.

"I just have great respect for her," Alan Hoffman revealed to his associates. "She's a real professional and a straight-shooter." While Mindy's firm was awarded the contract, her professionalism won the admiration of the Hampton city council but also of her competitors and other observers.

Unfortunately, there are times when professionalism is not practiced.

I simply do not want my advertising account serviced by Bruce O'Malley," Evelyn Burkle, owner of Exercise Incorporated, told Clark Surman, publisher and editor-in-chief of the *Commercial Times*. "Imagine how I felt when, one day before our new sales promotion was announced, our competitor, the Fitness Health Center, duplicated and announced the promotion. I have learned from a completely reliable source that Bruce O'Malley revealed our planned promotion to Don Scofield, manager of the Health Fitness Center."

When confidential information is revealed, professional behavior is breached. Such information may give others an unfair advantage. The injured party would be justified in looking for a new firm to transact business. Evelyn Burkle's conversation with Clark Surman might have taken the following stance:

I've decided to let the local radio station, WTCU, carry all of my advertising messages from now on. Your representative, Bruce O'Malley, cannot be trusted to maintain confidentiality. His unprofessional behavior has cost my firm an anticipated $3,500 in lost profits."

Confidential information is not confined to external customers and clients; certain internal information about the firm, its operations, and its employees may also be confidential.

As illustrated in Figure 18.2, desired social behavior requires acceptance of others, a sense of humor, and adherence to fairness.

Figure 18.2 **Keys to Desired Social Behavior**

- ▶ **Acceptance of others**
- ▶ **Sense of humor**
- ▶ **Fairness**

Acceptance of Others. Most workers must function within the framework of other people's strengths, weaknesses, abilities, and deficiencies. Acceptance of others means acknowledging one's dependency on people—dependency that is realistic and reciprocal. One of the major problems in human relations is being mature enough to respect the differences in others. A well-coached basketball team, for example, will be creative in capitalizing upon the strengths and abilities of each player. Any weaknesses and deficiencies that exist are simply accepted and deemphasized. A professional is able to work with diverse individuals and groups in achieving goals, regardless of their race, cultural background, political beliefs, lifestyle, and other diverse characteristics.

Administrators and faculty members in professional schools at major universities throughout the world have recognized the difficulty in nurturing future professionals to accept others. Perhaps this is one reason why multicultural and diversity studies are so popular today. As people continue to move closer to being part of a global society, the need to accept diversity becomes more pronounced. A member of a work group does not become a giant solely because of his or her own abilities; he or she must depend on others for support. When a patient is wheeled into the operating room to undergo open-heart bypass surgery, each member of the professional medical team recognizes the importance of accepting the other team members and depends on each member's contributions. The anesthesiologist, the heart surgeon and associates, the cardiologist, nurses, nurse's aides, and other attendants are dependent upon the contributions of one another. Skin color, national origin, political viewpoints, religious beliefs, and other diverse differences are cast aside—acceptance of one another is not an issue.

Sense of Humor.   A person's sense of humor reveals his or her attitude toward other people. Jon Dahlinghaus, referred to at the beginning of this chapter, garnered laughs at the expense of his boss. Ethnic jokes fall into the same category as ridiculing someone's mannerisms. George Bernard Shaw once said, "Some people would rather have their joke than their friend."

A professional should recognize that humor should be good-natured rather than demeaning or hostile. It is all right to make ourselves the object of a joke, but it is in poor taste to poke fun at others to make them look silly or inferior or to hurt their feelings.

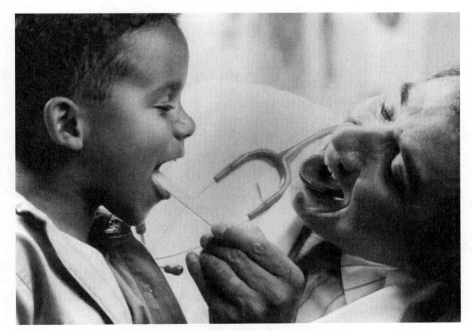

Having a sense of humor is important to success in most jobs.

Humor serves important functions in the workplace. Among them are

► the reduction of tension

► relief from boredom

► the diffusion of hostility

The test of a professional's sense of humor is whether the individual has the ability to laugh at himself or herself. A story is sometimes repeated about an irate politician who stormed into President Lincoln's office and accused him of being two-faced. Lincoln, aware of his own homeliness, said, "I assure you, sir, that if I had another face I would be wearing it."

Adherence to Fairness. The term *fair*, or *fairness*, has multiple but related meanings. **Fairness** implies impartiality and honesty, conformance with established rules, and freedom from self-interest, prejudice, or favoritism. Other words, such as *just, equitable, unbiased, dispassionate,* and *objective,* are also associated with the term. When an individual is treated unfairly in the workplace, the individual may have been made to suffer some burden that he or she had a right to avoid, or some benefit has been denied that he or she had a right to possess. Consider the plight of Brenda Zimmerman.

B renda Zimmerman had completed three years of service as an attorney in the Morgan County Prosecutor's Office. She is one of seven attorneys (including Ted Montague—the elected county prosecutor). One of the operating policies within the office governs vacation time. The policy states that each employee is to designate a two-week vacation period and that if two persons request the same time period, only one attorney may be on vacation at a time. The attorney who first requests a time period will be given priority.

Brenda started planning her vacation months ago. She requested the first two weeks in June and discovered that no one else had requested that period of time. She purchased cheap, nonrefundable airline tickets to Hawaii and was excited about spending time on the beach.

Three days before Brenda's scheduled departure, she learned that she would be unable to go. Ted Montague informed her that he would be away on vacation and according to operating policy, only one attorney could be absent at a time. Brenda's protest that she had requested the time period first was to no avail. She was told the policy applied to employees and not to the elected official.

Injustice, a form of unfairness, occurs when similar cases are not treated in the same manner. If a number of employees violate an operating procedure but only one is singled out and reprimanded, it is obvious that fair treatment did not occur. The principle of impartiality and consistency in justice requires nonarbitrary treatment, that is, all employees guilty of the infraction would be reprimanded in the same manner. Yet, there may be

fairness-implies impartiality and honesty and freedom from self-interest, prejudice, or favoritism

injustice-occurs when like cases are not treated in the same manner

extenuating circumstances which make differences in treatment consistent with equality. If one of the employees is new and is unfamiliar with operating procedures, should that employee be subject to the same reprisals as longer-term employees who are knowledgeable of the procedures?

As previously alluded to, today's workplace calls for professionals who are bold enough to build their reputations on integrity. Certainly, adherence to fairness is a key ingredient of integrity and a practice which wins the respect of others.

Personal Behavior

Personal behavior may be observed to determine how an individual thinks and acts. Behavioral scientists have identified a number of essential elements of professional personal behavior.

Self-acceptance. Most employees, regardless of their status, find it easier to admit their strengths than to concede their weaknesses. Professionals recognize their deficiencies and either formulate plans for overcoming deficiencies or learn to accept themselves with such deficiencies. Self-acceptance does not mean self-satisfaction. If professionals can overcome deficiencies, they will do so. Professionals, however, have to learn to be realistic and accept what cannot be changed. Individuals who accept themselves grow in self-confidence and self-esteem, are comfortable with others, and refrain from wallowing in self-despair or self-pity. People who can accept themselves are able to put things into proper focus.

Self-acceptance is crucial to the acceptance of others. It is a prerequisite for building relationships with others. People cannot be comfortable with others until they are comfortable with themselves.

Self-confidence. Self-confidence is a trait that often spells success or disaster. The employee who is confident that he or she has the knowledge and ability to succeed usually does. That individual does not perceive others to be a threat. As a result, the self-confident employee is comfortable working with other employees who generate ideas, confront challenges, and earn the label, "accomplishers."

Leah Schlesinger is an interior design consultant at Rainbow Furnishings and Import Gallery. Leah lacks self-confidence and appears to be somewhat indecisive. Her supervisor, Gene Whitlock, has suggested that Leah work with Doris Crumley, an experienced consultant whose clients always express satisfaction. Leah hasn't been very receptive to the idea, preferring instead to work with Nichola Kritz, a yes person who never reminds her of her shortcomings or weaknesses.

Employees like Leah who exhibit low levels of confidence are likely to exhibit other undesirable characteristics, including negative thinking, blaming others for failures, fear of taking action, and fear of asking for help.

The International Résumé

Today, American students are pursuing international studies, learning about business practices and cultural diversities prevalent in various countries. Indeed, it is not uncommon for them to enroll in exchange programs or sign up for studies abroad. Many of these students aspire to work in another country—either in a foreign branch of an American-owned corporation or for a foreign-owned enterprise. Applicants often don't know what is right and what is wrong when seeking employment in uncharted territory.

Among the differences that job seekers should remember when applying for a position with a foreign-owned entity are (1) they will not be protected by the Equal Employment Opportunity laws, (2) their sex, race, or religion may prevent them from being hired, and (3) foreign employers generally seek longer and more detailed résumés than American employers. Specialized books about résumé writing in specific countries can be found in most libraries, and the job seeker would be well-advised to review them.

Career consultants often remind job aspirants that a good résumé won't get them a job; however, a bad one will lose plenty of them. A résumé should be an accurate presentation of what an individual has accomplished as it relates to employment. Employers outside the United States tend to prefer detailed résumés, often six to eight pages long or even longer. A shorter résumé may cause foreign recruiters to believe that the applicant is hiding something. Of course, there is always a tendency by some people to include so much trivia in their résumés that they go on for pages and obviously are too long.

When a job aspirant's experience and accomplishments have occurred in another country, prospective employers may be reluctant to interview the applicant because they may not believe the applicant knows their country's procedures and ways of doing business; they may worry about a language deficiency; and they may be concerned that the status of citizenship will be a problem for them. Knowing these concerns in advance will enable a job aspirant to address them in the résumé and accompanying cover letter.

Employers in some countries may insist on knowing such personal details as race, sex, age, and the occupations of parents. Personal data that employers ask for can include relevant facts such as foreign language fluency, previous overseas experience, foreign travel experience, single or dual citizenship, passport number and date of expiration, security clearance, student temporary work permits, and personal hobbies and interests. The status of one's health may also be requested.

The chronological order of listing major educational and employment experiences, starting with the earliest experience and ending with the present, tends to be preferred in European countries. Non-European international recruiters, including many in the United States, often advocate a format in reverse chronological order, beginning with the most current information and working backward to the earliest. Tips concerning preferred résumé formats by employers in various countries can be found in reference books.

When preparing a résumé, a job aspirant may wish to begin with personal information, followed by information relating to his or her education. Listing computer competence (such as spreadsheet, data base, and word processing) and foreign language fluencies in a résumé is a way to set an individual apart from other 20th century workers.

Work histories should contain the major accomplishments that an applicant achieved for his or her employer. Here's why. Joe prepared budgets for 19 years. It could be argued that he had one year of experience 19 times, because his job function remained basically the same for all these years. But from year to year, Joe streamlined the budget process, saving his employer several thousand dollars as a result of his work. If Joe were looking for a job, he should include this information in his résumé because focusing upon accomplishments strengthens an individual's credentials.

Some career consultants recommend that when applying for a job in a non-English speaking country, the applicant should have his or her résumé translated into that country's language.

Cover letters often suffer from an overabundance of words. Recognizing that initial screeners only have time to scan the letters for highlights, it is necessary for applicants to state facts succinctly. In some European countries, including Italy, Germany, France, and Spain, handwritten cover letters are preferred because they sometimes are scrutinized by graphologists. Graphologists are experts who study handwriting as a basis for character analyses.

"Ignoring cultural differences isn't innovative or clever. It's arrogant," warns Mary Murray Bosrock, author of a four-volume set of books covering Russia, Europe, Mexico/Canada, and Asia. It is important to respect cultural diversities in all areas dealing with work and play.

Sources: Lasky, Jane. "Respect Cultural Differences Wherever You Work and Play." The Dallas (Texas) Morning News. December 11, 1994, 7–G. The "Business Travel Report" column by Jane Lasky is used by permission of Chronicle Features, San Francisco, California.

Pawlak, Jim. "Research, Resources, and Résumé—The Three Rs to Landing A New Job." The Indianapolis Star. October 16, 1994, F–5.

People with high levels of confidence, on the other hand, are able to cope with problems and disappointments. Even though they experience all the dimensions of emotions, emotions do not affect their behavior in negative ways. They are able to help others and are not afraid to accept help themselves. They can accept criticism without feeling threatened and are able to express their opinions even when they differ from those of their managers. In short, self-confident people are well-adjusted employees who set and achieve goals.

Self-knowledge. A few years ago, manual workers were responsible for turning the wheels of industry. They worked with their hands and used brawn to perform manual tasks. Today, the focal point in human resources has shifted to knowledge workers. They are a growing army of people who perform work requiring a high degree of mental effort. Knowledge workers include the traditional professionals: doctors, lawyers, accountants, teachers, nurses, dentists, architects, and others. In addition, they include librarians, statisticians, data processing designers, computer programmers, systems analysts, editors, economists, market analysts, graphic designers, and a host of other occupations. Automation has hit hard at repetitive, strong-back jobs that require no thinking. Computers have descended on almost every conceivable business activity. The result has been an increase in the numbers of knowledge workers.

A **knowledge worker** is a person who applies specialized knowledge or information, usually acquired through extended study and considerable experience, to an occupation that requires a high degree of mental effort such as analysis, reasoning, interpretation, and creativity.[2] According to futurists, about one-half of all service workers will be involved in collecting, analyzing, synthesizing, structuring, storing, or retrieving information as a basis of knowledge within the foreseeable future.[3] In fact, some forecasters believe that employees will work a 32-hour workweek and prepare for their next job in the remaining hours. In the future most employees—including service workers—will be engaged in decision-making and critical thinking. As a result, employees will need to be better prepared, that is, better educated than ever before.

In addition to job-related knowledge, today's career aspirant must also have a keen sense of self-knowledge. One of the prime tenets of Greek philosophy can be summarized in two words, "Know thyself." Without in-depth knowledge of one's self, an individual is handicapped in dealing with job demands and interpersonal relationships. An individual who knows his or her strengths and weaknesses can avoid the frustrations of trying to assume roles that are too ambitious. The individual who possesses self-knowledge will not turn away from opportunities which can realistically lead to success. The importance of self-identity and self-knowledge must be instilled in future workers and reinforced through positive educational

*knowledge worker-
a person who applies specialized knowledge or information to an occupation that requires a high degree of mental effort*

[2]Lester R. Bittel. *What Every Supervisor Should Know.* New York: McGraw-Hill, 1985, 580.
[3]Marvin J. Cetron, Wanda Rocha, and Rebecca Luckins. "Long-Term Trends Affecting the United States." *The Futurist.* July/August 1988, 30.

experiences so workers understand their interests, abilities, and aptitudes and how they relate to the future pursuit of a career.

Individualism.
Today's workers who believe in themselves and know what they can deliver carve their own paths. They have learned how to accept authority and organizational constraints without being conformists.

Some behavioral scientists believe that such individualism is becoming a rare quality among young Americans. They point to the fact that as the 20th century winds down, more young Americans are enrolled in colleges, but fewer are graduating. Students are taking longer to get their degrees and are also taking longer to establish careers and to marry. Unable or unwilling to pay for housing, many return to the nest or are slow to leave it. They are postponing making choices and spurn long-term commitments. Life's on hold; adulthood can wait.[4]

Indeed, some employers worry about the younger generation viewing work as an opportunity for immediate gratification, rather than for long-term growth and commitment. Twenty years ago, sociologist James S. Coleman warned that the young were becoming expert consumers long before they were learning how to produce.

Unfortunately, there is no SAT score to measure how a student handles frustration, resolves conflicting choices, or develops intellectual interests in people, events, and ideas. These are qualities, however, that mark individual differences in the workplace and which employers find desirable. Strong individual initiative and adherence to one's values rank high among the traits and characteristics of a professional.

Acceptance of Responsibility.
A professional worker accepts the responsibilities and restrictions that are inherent in the environment in which he or she operates. When an individual accepts responsibility and the accompanying accountability, this individual is practicing professionalism. Too often, workers cry out that their failures were caused by someone else, luck was against them, and the ball just never bounced in their direction. They are unwilling or emotionally unable to accept responsibility for their errors. They frequently attempt to pass their problems on to others, often with success.

Alicia Pierson is an instructor at Northwest Technical Institute, assigned to teach technical writing. Soon after the schedule for the spring semester was released, Alicia stopped by her department chair's office and said, "We have a problem with my teaching schedule." She went on to explain that the eight o'clock class which she was assigned to teach on Monday, Wednesday, and Friday mornings would require her to leave home by seven-thirty. Alicia further explained that she would have a problem getting her two children to school if she left home before eight o'clock.

---

[4]Kenneth L. Woodward. "Young Beyond Their Years." *Newsweek.* Special Issue, Winter/Spring 1990, 54.

Alicia hoped her department chair would say, "Let me look at the schedule again and perhaps we can switch the assignment." If the department chair responded in this manner, Alicia would have successfully transferred her problem to him. Actually, Alicia had signed a contract to teach classes as assigned. Her ploy, "We have a problem," was an attempt to change the situation from, "I have a problem."

It is not an unusual occurrence for a person to solve a problem by transferring it to another person. Individuals who practice professionalism, however, accept the initiative to resolve their own problems.

Patience. Most professionals have learned that for some problems there are no quick or easy answers. Rather than seize the first possible solution, a professional recognizes the value of examining several alternatives. This applies to personal problems as well as business problems.

David Krupnick, an accounting major, signed up for interviews with three firms at his college's job fair. All three firms, Westin Hotels and Resorts, American Airlines, and the Gillette Company, were reputable firms offering promising career opportunities. Within a week, the recruiter from American Airlines called David and offered him a position in their AAdvantage Department in Dallas. The recruiter asked David if he would like a couple of days to consider the offer. David was excited to finally have an opportunity to launch his career and to be independent. He quickly accepted the offer.

The next morning, David's phone rang again. This time a representative from the Gillette Company presented David with a job offer. The offer was everything that David had dared to dream about—plus, it was in Boston, which would enable David to remain in his home area with his lifelong friends.

Later in the day, David talked with a placement counselor at his college, explaining the dilemma that he now faced. The counselor showed little sympathy to David. "After all, David," she commented, "American Airlines offered you time to consider their offer. If you call now and indicate that you have changed your mind, it is my opinion that you will be acting in an unprofessional and an immature manner."

Lack of patience is a mark of immaturity. A mature individual knows that patience, rather than instant gratification, is a virtue.

Decision-making. In the last scenario, David made a hasty decision which he later regretted. While it is important to search out and examine alternatives and weigh the facts before reaching decisions, there usually comes a time when decisions must be reached. Some people are too indecisive, and their indecisions amount to decisions not to act. Peter Drucker once pointed out, "With regard to the future there can never be certainty, only possibilities."[5] A professional recognizes that to await complete certainty would mean that decisions would never be reached. A calculated risk must be taken.

If people could predict the results of their decisions accurately, they could approximate certainty, which Drucker identifies as the crux of decision-making problems. What they can do is adjust somewhat for uncertainty. Statistical probability may be a useful tool. A life insurance company, for example, uses statistical probability to establish rates. Based upon historical data, the life insurance company can predict, with a high degree of accuracy, the percentage of deaths that will occur over the next five years among people in different age groups. A second tool used to adjust for certainty is the data itself. Most decisions must be based on evidence that is not fully reliable. Reliable evidence simply does not exist. As a result, the decision-maker should try to obtain as complete and as accurate information as possible.

Finally, a professional attempts to catch errors which may be inherent in the decision-making process. For centuries, groups in the Catholic Church have used the "devil's advocate" as a way of testing decisions. The devil's advocate is an individual assigned the task of pointing out weaknesses and errors in a proposed action. The best negative arguments are assembled, and if the decision cannot withstand an attack, action is postponed. Projecting the decision into a detailed plan is another technique for looking at the consequences of a decision in greater detail. A decision about what action to take regarding an employee with a chronic absenteeism problem, for example, may involve more than deciding to retain or fire the worker. The decision-maker looks at different alternatives and projects the possible consequences. If the decision is to fire the employee, will the employee likely file a grievance with a union or labor relations board claiming unfair treatment? If the employee is reprimanded and warned that continued absenteeism will jeopardize employment, is the employee's behavior likely to change? Various alternatives will be examined until the list of alternatives is exhausted. The decision-maker may reach a better decision as a result of such analysis.

Resiliency. Most of us from time to time face adversity. It may be disappointment that we were not chosen for a promotion or selected to serve on an important committee; it may be an injury, pain, illness, or even a brush with death by ourselves, a family member, or a close friend; it may be loss of a job or a demotion. To cope successfully with adversity, we need **resiliency,** that is, the ability to bounce back from whatever negative experience we encounter. A professional never allows setbacks to destroy himself or herself and has the capacity to learn from defeat in order to succeed another time.

Resiliency is characterized by two important traits: achievement and a positive attitude. When an individual knows that he or she has done a good

resiliency-the ability to bounce back from whatever adversity we encounter

[5]Mark B. Siber and V. Clayton Sherman. *Managerial Performance and Promotability.* New York: AMACOM (Division of American Management Association), 1974, 160.

job, this individual experiences one of the most satisfying feelings a person can have. An employee with a good attitude tends to be a better employee and is better liked by other employees. As a result, the person's value to his or her employers is enhanced.

Time Orientation. A professional lives and acts in the present. He or she is not marking time by waiting for that lucky break. Instead, the professional learns from the past and plans for the future. We all know people who are waiting to win the lottery or encounter some stroke of luck that will drastically change their lives. A professional does not wait for tomorrow; he or she acts today.

Procrastination, a major time waster for many people, is prevalent in the workplace. Laziness, a desire to postpone an unpleasant task or undesirable news, and the inability to perform are some of the causes of procrastination. Some people mirror the stance of Scarlett O'Hara's, "I'll worry about it tomorrow," in the movie *Gone With the Wind.* People who procrastinate may lack the drive or energy to accomplish the task at hand, or they may lack the ability or know-how needed to succeed. Most of us, at one time or another, have procrastinated to avoid a difficult or unpleasant task.

It is possible to break out of procrastination modes by establishing personal goals and time lines for achieving the goals.

Rachel Hewlett is enrolled in a business report writing class at New York City Community College. One of the assignments calls for a 25-page research paper to be developed around a contemporary business problem. Rachel is less than enthusiastic about the project; she doesn't enjoy research or writing, and she has conned herself into believing that she is simply too busy with her other classes and her part-time job to prepare the paper which is due in five days. Her friend, Marty Gresham, on the other hand, is putting the finishing touches to her paper. She, too, has a part-time job, and her class load is heavier than Rachel's. "I found a problem that was of interest to me," Marty explained. "I started the project about a month ago and I established a goal of completing seven pages per week— or one page a day. If I didn't meet my goal on a particular day, I made it up the next day."

Another tactic for avoiding procrastination is to calculate the consequences of inaction. If Rachel believed that the cost of procrastination would be failure in the course, she might alter her behavior. Other procrastinators have been able to modify their behaviors by rewarding themselves after a task has been accomplished, or penalizing themselves if the task is not completed. Rachel, for example, might go to a long-awaited movie when the research paper is completed or she might deny herself an outing with friends if she fails to complete the task as planned.

A professional makes good use of time, both on and off the job. Once time has been wasted, it can never be recaptured.

Enthusiasm for Work. A professional usually enjoys his or her work. While work is viewed by some people as necessary for survival, a professional sees work not as drudgery but as challenges, opportunities for creative expression, and opportunities to serve others. Professionalism is characterized by an eager, energetic approach. Such optimism lets others know that the individual is happy in his or her role. A professional also knows that enthusiasm is contagious. It rubs off on coworkers, supervisors, customers and clients, and other business associates.

As indicated earlier, professional status is partly dependent upon special training. According to some behavioral scientists, the higher the level of education beyond high school, the more the employee will put a premium on a job that offers

▶ real challenge

▶ the chance to make a contribution to society

▶ the ability for self-expression

▶ free time for outside interests.[6]

Such employees tend to be self-starters who have a keen interest in their work. While professional workers include both high and low performers, they tend to view their jobs as being interesting and are proud of their professions.

Positive Contributions. Professional employees make valuable contributions to their employers. Their need for achievement is revealed through their desire to accomplish something difficult, reach a high level of

Staying attuned to the importance of little things enables this professional to carry out her job successfully.

[6]Bitel. *What Every Supervisor Should Know,* 565.

success, master complex jobs, and surpass the achievements of others. It is important, however, that such achievements be recognized. As noted earlier in the discussion on needs, recognition is a higher-order need related to esteem and self-actualization. Recognition of contributions should be contingent on the magnitude of the contribution. When recognition is given for a mediocre accomplishment, the employee is being reinforced for performing in a mediocre manner. Care should be exercised in recognizing and rewarding worthy contributions. If an employee feels unappreciated, that employee's future contributions will be adversely affected.

Attention to Little Things. An ancient philosopher is said to have remarked, "The journey of a thousand miles begins with the first step." This wise philosopher reminds us of the importance of staying focused, that is, of breaking big tasks into manageable chunks. The success of programs designed to change human behavior—such as Weight Watchers, Alcoholics Anonymous, Smoke Cessation—is due, in large part, to this philosophy. None insists that participants concentrate on total abstinence for the rest of their lives, even though that may be the participant's goal. Instead, participants may be admonished to stay sober for one day at a time or perhaps to avoid cigarettes for one hour at a time if temptation is severe. The idea is to move the participant off dead-center and to enable this individual to experience a small win. Small wins breed confidence and success and propel people toward the achievement of larger tasks or goals.

Gerald Ristau took a look at the monthly sales goal which Angela Rodrique, sales manager at the Maple Furniture Gallery, had established for him. "I believe that $23,000 is somewhat high for January, considering the Christmas buying season has just ended," Gerald remarked. Ms. Rodrique pointed out that his quota amounted to less than $1,000 per working day, and during the past year his sales had averaged over $1,800 per day.

Looking at the big task in terms of smaller components prevents an individual from being overwhelmed.

A professional is attuned to the importance of little things being an integral part of the big picture. Each detail, trivial task, or small concern is considered and the **4-D formula**—drop, delay, delegate, or do—is applied. In fact, some professionals prepare a list of things to do and review it each day. This prevents them from forgetting to return a telephone call, to answer correspondence, or to take care of other small and seemingly unimportant tasks. Professionals usually have many interruptions and need a plan to ensure that small things are not overlooked. Little things in life and work are important and may enable an individual to reach his or her fullest potential. MasterCard's famous slogan, "Master the Possibilities," typifies how attention to both small and large concerns enables a person to go beyond an ordinary or mediocre performance.

4-D formula-drop, delay, delegate, or do

Good Citizen. Citizenship may be defined as the quality of an individual's response to membership in a community. A professional worker's community includes coworkers, subordinates, supervisors, managers, customers and clients, competitors, vendors and suppliers, professionals in the same line of work, as well as others. How an individual interacts with these people determines the extent to which he or she is judged as a good professional citizen.

Among the ways to demonstrate good professional citizenship is following through on commitments. Keeping commitments and carrying out an acceptable performance enable an individual to be an effective participant in job-related demands. Professional citizenship is further enhanced by the positive outlook and friendly image which one projects. How one treats other people is also reflected in citizenship.

Dr. Charles Sims is recognized as an excellent dentist. Recently, he hired Latonya Shields as a dental hygienist. Latonya has quickly lost respect for Dr. Sims. Being criticized in front of clients and coworkers, Latonya has developed a resentful attitude toward her boss. "He simply does not practice professionalism," she complained to her husband.

Professionalism is practiced when one or more individuals are able to fix the problem, rather than the blame. When this occurs, a win/win strategy is used instead of a win/lose strategy. If Dr. Sims were able to offer constructive criticism in a quiet, nonthreatening, nonhumiliating manner and in private and if Latonya Sims could accept and benefit from the constructive criticism, both would be demonstrating good professional citizenship.

Figure 18.3 contains a summary of the essential elements of professional personal behavior.

Figure 18.3 Essential Elements of Professional Personal Behavior

- ► Self-acceptance
- ► Self-confidence
- ► Self-knowledge
- ► Individualism
- ► Acceptance of Responsibilities
- ► Patience
- ► Decision-making

- ► Resiliency
- ► Time Orientation
- ► Enthusiasm for Work
- ► Positive Contributions
- ► Attention to Little Things
- ► Good Citizen

Equation for Professional Behavior

In the preceding paragraphs, a description of those characteristics, qualities, and traits desired in professional workers have been identified and described. As evident from the discussion, the following equation should provide guidance for individuals wanting to be all that one can become:

Personal Qualities + Social Behavior + Personal Behavior = Professional Behavior

Few people have all the attributes that have been discussed, but the person who is making an effort to develop them is well on the way to becoming a true professional who is noted for professionalism in the workplace.

The Professional at Work

Professions can be divided into two groups: learned (such as business, medicine, engineering, law, and education) and artistic (such as acting, music, and art). We are concerned here with the learned professions.

Professionals work without much direct supervision. Optical technicians polish contact lenses, dental hygienists clean teeth, nurses draw blood samples, computer programmers devise spreadsheets, and teachers prepare lesson plans of their own volitions. These and many other professionals possess specialized knowledge and generally do not require close supervision. When professionals work in teams or groups, however, there is need for mutual adjustment and cooperation.

We is a better pronoun than *I*, according to the chief executive officer at Tech-Tronics. "It is a good idea to present your role to knowledge workers as that of facilitator rather than boss," he told the executive managers who had gathered for an in-service seminar. He continued, "Try to avoid direct confrontations. Don't say 'You're wrong.' Instead, modify your approach by saying something like: 'Perhaps I don't have all the facts that you do. Will you explain your position to me again?'"

Mutual adjustment and cooperation will help avoid direct confrontation.

Professional work is seldom routine or repetitive. Instead, it is frequently investigative in nature. The professional may prepare an actuary table for an insurance company or diagnose the malfunction of a spacecraft, an accounting error, a computer virus, an illness or disease, or a learning problem encountered by a student. Professional work often requires discretion and independent judgment[7]

----

[7]Dale S. Beach. *Personnel: The Management of People at Work.* New York: Macmillan, 1980, 264.

Professional work demands recognized standards of competence in terms of education, training, experience, and human performance. To be designated as a professional in certain fields of endeavor, an aspiring practitioner must prove that he or she has acquired the necessary competencies at levels specified by the standards. Examinations are administered to individuals seeking credentials as certified public accountants, lawyers, doctors, teachers, real estate brokers, and others. It is important to note that such exams typically measure knowledge relating to the field of the test taker. Little has been done to ensure that career aspirants have acquired people skills. Yet, most of us live and work with others every day. Our ability to work harmoniously with others ultimately influences our economic, psychological, and social satisfaction.

Key Points Summary

- Business etiquette, the adherence to certain rules governing business behavior, is one facet of professionalism.

- A profession is a pursuit of an endeavor which requires special training, is characterized by permanence of the occupation, yields both monetary rewards and self-satisfaction rewards, and whose practitioners adhere to ethical practices.

- Minor criteria which are also characteristics of a profession include availability of professional literature and the association of the members of the profession in professional organizations.

- A professional is an individual who has met the requirements to practice a profession, usually as a result of special training and, in some cases, licensing. A professional exhibits loyalty to the profession, experiences professional rewards, adheres to the profession's code of ethics, engages in activities designed to keep himself or herself current in the occupation, and participates in professional associations.

- Individuals who have received special training and who work with professionals in subsidiary or supportive roles are known as *paraprofessionals.*

- Professionalism is the conduct, character, and qualities that mark the behavior expected of a person who engages in the pursuit of a professional career.

- The qualities, characteristics, or attributes which mark the identity of a professional may be classified into three categories: personal qualities, social behavior, and personal behavior.

- Maturity, personal standards or character, and openness are among the personal qualities associated with individuals who practice professionalism.

- Professional social behavior is characterized by acceptance of others, a sense of humor, and adherence to fairness.

- When confidential information is revealed, professional behavior is breached.

- Essential elements of professional personal behavior include self-acceptance, self-confidence, self-knowledge, individualism, acceptance of responsibility, patience, decision-making skills, resiliency, time orientation, enthusiasm for work, positive contributions, attention to little things, and good citizenship.

- A knowledge worker is a person who applies specialized knowledge or information, usually acquired by extended study and considerable experience, to an occupation that requires a high degree of mental effort such as analysis, reasoning, interpretation, and creativity.

- Decision-making may be enhanced by statistical probability, reliable data, the testing of alternatives, and projecting the likely consequences of alternatives.

- Resiliency is the ability to bounce back from whatever adversity we encounter.

- To break out of procrastination modes, an individual should establish personal goals and time lines for achieving the goals.

- According to behavioral scientists, the higher the level of education beyond high school, the more an employee will put a premium on a job that offers (1) real challenge, (2) the chance to make a contribution to society, (3) the opportunity for self-expression, and (4) free time for outside interests.

- The 4-D formula—drop, delay, delegate, or do—should be applied to details, small or trivial tasks, and minor concerns.

- The equation for professional behavior may be stated as follows: Personal Qualities + Social Behavior + Personal Behavior = Professional Behavior.

- Professionals work without much direct supervision, but when working in teams or groups, there is need for mutual adjustment and cooperation.

- Professional work often requires discretion and independent judgment.

- Professional work demands certain recognized standards of competence in terms of education, training, experience, and human performance.

Key Terms

business etiquette	maturity
character	paraprofessionals
fairness	professional
4-D formula	professionalism
injustice	resiliency
knowledge worker	

Discussion Questions

1. Why are individuals holding professional positions more likely to consider their positions as permanent rather than as stepping-stones to other opportunities?

2. Identify an individual whom you consider to be a true professional. Compare that individual's qualities, traits, or characteristics to those identified in this chapter as being the marks of a professional. Which of the marks has the person you identified achieved? Which are missing? Does the individual exhibit other qualities, traits, or characteristics that were not identified in this chapter?

3. Dennis Gordon is a business instructor at Lakeshore Technical Institute where he hopes to receive tenure. Dennis doesn't get along well with his department chair and just received his annual evaluation, which was somewhat negative. Dennis immediately made an appointment with the dean of his division. During his conversation with the dean, Dennis said, "Dr. Baldwin has never liked me, and regardless of how well I perform or how effective I am in the classroom, I will never receive a positive recommendation. I hope you will intercede on my behalf and take steps to ensure fair treatment for me." In your opinion, was Dennis attempting to transfer ownership of the problem? Provide a rationale to support your position.

4. An executive vice president of sales promotion for a leading cosmetics firm recently fired her assistant and provided the following explanation: "Every time I had a tough decision to make and came to her to reinforce my judgment or, if possible, point out ways of improving the decision, she would tear it apart and bring out the most inconsequential and unlikely reasons why it wouldn't work. We don't want or need that kind of negative thinking around here." What advice would you offer to the executive vice president? to the executive vice president's former assistant?

5. Distinguish between business etiquette, business ethics, and professionalism.

6. Which of the characteristics of a profession are likely to undergo modification in the future? Provide a rationale for your response.

Unit 4

APPLICATIONS &CASES

Application 1

Personal and Organizational Values

Mavis Harrison works for the T. J. Gilliam Company, Incorporated, as a sales representative, calling upon druggists and doctors to sell pharmaceutical products. She's good at her job, typically exceeding her sales quotas by a larger margin than other sales reps at Gilliam. Mavis is a dedicated reader and recently read that Germany had banned the sale of a drug manufactured and sold by her company. A governmental agency in Germany has what it believes to be reliable evidence that the drug can cause internal bleeding in younger children.

A few days after reading the news column, Mavis was talking with her supervisor, Marshall Kennworthy, and he mentioned that sale of the drug, Phenomaroxyonal, had not been good in her territory. He asked her to be a bit more aggressive in promoting the drug to her accounts and pointed out that Phenomaroxyonal was rapidly becoming a sales leader in other territories.

Phenomaroxyonal is T. J. Gilliam's name for the drug which was banned in Germany. When Mavis explained the drug banning to Mr. Kennworthy, he smiled and said, "Those dumb foreign doctors don't recognize a medical breakthrough when they see one." He continued by telling her that the firm had sunk a tremendous amount of money into the development and testing of Phenomaroxyonal and that he was under pressure to increase sales of the drug.

The interaction between the two ended when Mr. Kennworthy told Mavis that he expected to see the sale of Phenomaroxyonal soar in her territory. "After all," he remarked, "you have the very best territory. And if you can't produce, we can probably find someone who can."

1. Would you classify Mavis as a whistle blower? If the answer is no, should she become a whistle blower? Explain.
2. Do you believe that organizational values at T. J. Gilliams have been swayed by "what is good for the organization?" Explain.
3. Since Mavis' values and those of her supervisor are in conflict, what are the various alternatives available to Mavis? What would you do if you were in her position?

Application 2

An Office Confrontation

The Deluxe Business Forms Company adopted an affirmative action hiring program about two years ago. The program was formally introduced to company administrators (managers and supervisors) during one of their regularly scheduled bimonthly staff meetings.

Ann Myers, a high-energy, highly visible manager in the customer accounts department, did not view herself as being a particularly prejudiced person; nevertheless, she was somewhat less than enthusiastic about the prospect of hiring minorities to work in her department. Since Robert Knapp, the chief executive officer at Deluxe, embraced the affirmative action program, Ann felt she had no choice but to go along with the new program.

Edward Johnson, a young African-American man who had just graduated from Lakewood Community College where he studied office information systems, was hired as a secretary in Ann's department. Edward was a bright worker who caught on quickly; however, he lacked the years of employment experiences that other secretaries in the department possessed.

Soon after Edward joined the workforce at Deluxe, Ann asked him to prepare a letter to the president of Merchant's National Bank, the firm's largest client. Ann also told Edward to use a specific style of correspondence that she tended to favor.

Edward returned to his work station and carefully prepared the correspondence. After applying the spell-check, Edward meticulously proofread the letter to make sure it measured up to the standards of high quality. As Ann started to sign the letter, she noticed that it was neatly prepared, but it was in a different format than she had specified. Ann was upset and let Edward know she was unhappy. "When I ask for a specific style or format, you had better do it that way," she roared. "Otherwise, you'll be looking for a new job."

Edward, usually slow to react in an angry manner, was visibly upset by Ann's remarks and the tone in which they were voiced. He immediately made an appointment with Mr. Knapp and complained that his supervisor, Ann Myers, was prejudiced against African Americans.

1. Obviously, Ann Myers acted in an unprofessional manner. What advice would you offer her concerning her personal qualities, social behavior, and professional personal behavior?
2. If you were Ann Myers' boss, what steps would you take to ensure that managers and supervisors acquired the ability to accept others?
3. Did Ann Myers assume the role of facilitator or boss in her interactions with Edward Johnson? Explain.
4. What advice would you offer both Ann Myers and Edward Johnson about how to avoid future confrontations?

Application 3

Vying for an Appointment

Deja Shoe, maker of footwear from recycled soda bottles, tires, and "vegetil leather" (based on latex), has rapidly developed a socially conscious reputation. Socially conscious firms strive to do the right thing while at the same time earning a buck.

The two-year-old firm received a major environmental award from the United Nations. The firm's sales have climbed to $2 million, and it makes a unique, positive social contribution by letting workers spend four hours a month on volunteer programs.

To streamline the volunteer program, executives at Deja Shoe hope to appoint an outreach coordinator. Amy Schowalter and Alex Whitman are the two candidates for the position. Both are bright young persons with college degrees from a nearby university. Both have been with the firm for about one year. Amy is extremely well-organized and seems to be effective in almost any role she is asked to assume. Alex has demonstrated effectiveness in interactions with others and he is well-liked. Both have low absenteeism rates, and either one would probably be an outstanding coordinator. Both would like very much to be chosen for the position.

1. Suggest strategies which might be helpful for Amy and Alex to follow in their pursuits of the appointment.
2. What possible barriers might Amy or Alex face in their quest for the appointment? How might such barriers be overcome?
3. What evidence exists to demonstrate that Deja Shoe, as an organization, accepts social responsibilities?

Case 1

Global Competition and Job Security

Early retirements and buyouts, layoffs, plant closings, mergers, and corporate consolidations are sweeping the country and striking panic and fear in workers, many of whom have diligently pursued careers within single companies. Companies use trendy terms like *downsizing* and *rightsizing,* but displaced workers say those are just other ways of saying "You're out of a job." In fact, getting a job with one company and keeping it for 30 years and then collecting a retirement pension and gold watch is an idea about as endangered as a herd of wild horses.

Take Michael L. Cartwright, who now has his own company, as an example. He worked with at least six companies in the last 18 years before establishing his own company in Indianapolis. He wasn't caught in downsizing or layoff. "It's just the nature of the marketing industry for employees to work 18 months or three years and then move on," he said.

At Drake Beam Morin Incorporated, a Manhattan-based firm that specializes in individual and organizational transition, displaced white-collar workers are told up front that any job they get, in any company, should not be expected to last longer than three to five years.

Even jobs that have traditionally been considered secure are not excluded. Jose Martinez, for example, started about 18 years ago as a painter in the Chicago public school system, a seemingly safe and secure employer that never had layoffs. But recently, with the school district in well-publicized trouble, Martinez and coworkers were furloughed for eight months until money was found to put them back to work.

Because of corporate mergers and downsizing, some observers believe that middle management jobs paying $50,000 to $70,000 are disappearing. They point out examples such as locally-based banks being sold to regional banks and the subsequent cuts involving hundreds of jobs as the owners save millions of dollars.

After employers lay off workers, they may hire consultants to do the same jobs, but without health insurance, savings plans, retirement plans, and other long-term benefits provided to full-time employees. The consultants could fill any jobs from janitorial to engineering.

Why, one might ask, are employers instigating continuing programs of cutbacks to reduce their costs? The global economy today is having an impact on all companies—even small service-oriented firms. Global competition, just as domestic competition, means the cheapest price for the highest quality. Labor costs in many countries is cheaper than in the United States. In some countries, employers may not provide the fringe benefits which workers in the United States expect and demand. This means employers must find ways to become more flexible with their workforces.

It is also the reason why eight to ten job changes are predicted for future career seekers. Perhaps that is why Purdue University senior David Lach, who is sending out resumes and looking for a job in civil engineering, remarked, "I don't expect to spend my whole career at one company. I don't think that's plausible in today's society and job market. Most of the people I know say they expect to work for a company about five years and then go to something else, especially if the advancement is not there."

Adapted from: Johnson, Kirk. "Downsizing Launches a Rise in Offices with Leased Workers." (New York Times News Service), The (Louisville, Kentucky) Courier Journal. October 9, 1994, E–4.

Silverstein, Stuart. "Corporate America Escalates Downsizing." (Los Angeles Times), The Indianapolis (Indiana) Star. October 9, 1994, E–1.

Smith, Bruce C. "Flexibility Is Key to New Workplace." The Indianapolis (Indiana) Star. October 12, 1994, E–1.

1. Traditionally, when an individual was hired to work for an employer, it was believed that the employee had an obligation to promote the employer's interests. In view of the fact that the employment contract may be temporary in nature and the employee may never have a vested interest in a retirement plan, should loyalty to an employer be an obligation? Why or why not?

2. Do you agree or disagree with the following statement? "Conflict of values between an employer and employee is more

likely to occur in the future than has been the case in the past as a result of downsizing and rightsizing." Provide a rationale to support your position.

3. As employees find it necessary to make career changes more frequently, what are the implications for human relations?

4. Among the listings of contemporary values that business leaders believe are important are the following:

► Creating an atmosphere of openness and trust.

► Establishing a caring organizational attitude.

► Fostering respect for the individual and for diversity.

► Demonstrating teamwork and mutual support.

Is the current trend toward downsizing and rightsizing a deterrent to the achievement of shared values? Is the trend counter to the above values which business leaders say are important? Provide an explanation.

Case 2

Atlanta's New Top Cop Makes Her Move

When Beverly Harvard joined the Atlanta police force in 1973, the police force was not a warm environment for black or female officers. The city was in a time of racial and political transition, and the tensions of the city were evident in its police department. When Atlanta hired its first black police commissioner in 1974, the white officers were openly defiant at the beginning, even blocking the entrance to the commissioner's office. For years, the department was tied up with race-related lawsuits from both blacks charging discrimination in hiring and promotions, and whites, countering with reverse-discrimination suits.

Female recruits in those years faced rejection by their male counterparts, who insisted that women weren't up to the job and made it clear they didn't want to work with them. There was little support for black women from black male officers as well, whose common ground with their white colleagues was their antipathy toward female cops.

Atlanta came through those painful years with remarkable success, and Harvard, appointed in October 1994, as the city's first woman police chief, stands as proof of the transformation. "We are not void of problems, particularly racial problems, but we are certainly not where we were 20 years ago," said the 43-year-old Macon, Georgia, native. With confirmation by the city council in November 1994, she became the first black woman in America to formally head the police department of a major city.

On the ninth floor of City Hall East, a poster outside Harvard's office door reads, "You can talk about what's wrong with the world or help fix it." With 1,700 officers under her command, Beverly Harvard has won the respect of both men and women on the force, as well as that of Mayor Bill Campbell who named her to the post after watching her serve as acting chief for six months.

If the transition has been relatively smooth, Harvard says, it may be because the real battles were fought more than a decade ago when she first became deputy chief. "Change," she says, "now is easier for the department to accept." Her own success—she has risen from beat cop through a series of administrative and managerial jobs—has paralleled Atlanta's own growth and development from a racially divided southern city to a boomtown attracting national and international business and acclaim. And Harvard has reached the top just in time for one of the city's biggest challenges: the 1996 Summer Olympic Games.

Indeed, the new police chief's first year on the job is likely to be a hectic one. Among other things, she must plan for the security of more than 15,000 Olympic athletes and officials, not to mention the 2 million tourists the games will attract. But Harvard's plans go further than the Olympics. Under her stewardship, the department is increasing emphasis on community policing as a strategy for tackling crime in Atlanta's inner-city neighborhoods. She has initiated community policing training sessions for officers, plans more foot patrols, and is embarking on a round of speeches to community and business groups.

Harvard brings something else new to the job of police chief— the responsibilities of motherhood. She and her husband, Jimmy, a customer-service representative for Delta Air Lines, juggle child-care responsibilities for their six-year-old daughter, Christa. "I'm the choir person; he's the Brownie person," she says. Some Saturdays, Harvard also brings Christa to her office, where both mother and daughter do paperwork, with Christa completing her task with crayons. She is growing up with a radically different view of policing than her mother did, who began by fighting the perception that it wasn't women's work.

Sources: Eddings, Jerelyn. "Atlanta's New Top Cop Makes Her Mark." U.S. News and World Report. vol. 117, no. 25, December 26, 1994/January 2, 1995, 82–87.

1. What barriers to power were encountered by Beverly Harvard?
2. What strategies for acquiring power were likely employed by Beverly Harvard?
3. Is there evidence that Beverly Harvard possesses legitimate or position power? coercive power? personal power? Explain.
4. Does the above case document instances in which political power was directed at opponents? Explain.
5. What characteristics, attributes, or behavior enabled Beverly Harvard to crash through the "glass ceiling?"
6. Based upon information provided in the case, what approach is Beverly Harvard using to communicate values to the Atlanta Police Department's officers?

Unit 4 • Applications & Cases

Case 3

Fall of the Collector

Shirley and Earl McNall knew they had one hot little entrepreneur on their hands. Son Bruce was only five, and he could wipe out everybody on the Monopoly board, building hotels on all the expensive properties, leaving his mom stewing with an empty lot, say, on low-rent Baltic Avenue. Dazzled, the mother, a lab technician, and the father, a biochemistry professor at the University of Southern California, rationed Bruce's television watching and showered him with intellectual goodies.

The pampering paid off. Bruce became a wealthy coin collector while still in his teens. Then he collected a hockey team, collected a football team, collected race horses, collected Rolls-Royces and five residences and a private jet and well-placed friends—collected, all told, a worldwide reputation as an expert in antiquities, a nice guy, a canny businessman and a fine judge of athletes and horses.

Now McNall, 44, stands to collect a prison sentence that could run up to nine years in the worst case. As early as this week, McNall is expected to plead guilty to four federal counts charging him with bank fraud, mail fraud, and conspiracy. Two of his associates have already been accused of defrauding banks and other creditors, fleecing investors of more than $138 million by falsifying financial statements, setting up phony companies to hide assets and securing loans with fictitious collateral. Last month three others pleaded guilty to wire-fraud charges.

What's left of McNall's empire is a shambles. According to bankruptcy-court filings, McNall owes Credit Lyonnais $121 million, the Bank of America $40 million and Merrill Lynch $37 million. What remains of his traceable fortune is in hock. Gone are a couple of his houses, gone his private jet and a few cars, his hockey team, his football team, and his stake in a movie company. His coin business is in legal limbo. Creditors are queuing up to sue him. Soon McNall, the former boy tycoon, may not have an old—or even a plugged—drachma to call his own.

It was his passion for coins that did him in. Early on, his hobby blossomed into a fascination with antiquity. McNall even went so far as to enroll in the graduate program in ancient history at UCLA. But he did not stay long enough to learn how fate exacts a terrible price for greed. Before long, he was traveling the ancient trade routes, striking coup after coup. In 1974, when the record price for an ancient coin was about $100,000, he bought the rarest of them all, the 5th century B.C. Athena decadrachm, for a seemingly outlandish $420,000. But within the week, he sold it for $470,000. That same year, he opened a coin shop on Rodeo Drive in the heart of Hollywood.

McNall began trading in artifacts, many of them stolen by tomb robbers in Turkey, Greece and Italy. To a *Vanity Fair* reporter last spring, he freely boasted of dealing in contraband (at 18, he said, he was smuggling gold coins)—and if caught at it, quickly returning it. "What I don't need to have happen," he explained, "is my academic friends saying, 'You know, deep down morally these things are stolen.' And I do know that . . . I tell all my people, 'If there's a whisper, give it back.'" McNall now prefers not even to whisper to the press.

The money rolled in; McNall rolled on. Here racehorses, there silver trading with Nelson Bunker Hunt. In 1988 McNall bought a money-losing hockey team, the languishing Los Angeles Kings, and boosted ticket sales by luring the great Wayne Gretzky for $15 million. He bought the Toronto Argonauts with Gretzky and comedian John Candy, and for $14 million signed Notre Dame wide receiver Raghib Ismail; this too paid off in attendance and TV contracts.

Meanwhile, McNall was spending drachmas as if he had his own tombful, except that the treasure was not his to spend, belonging as it did to his investors and creditors. "Enjoy it while you can," he said. "I have yet to see a Brink's truck following a hearse." Smitten by his swath and style, bankers fairly begged him to borrow their money; Merrill Lynch created three coin-trading funds for him to manage. McNall set up a bogus horse-appraisal firm, listing his chauffeur as owner and appraiser.

It couldn't last. Lately, his sports enterprises were no longer making big money, and the coin trade was ailing. Creditors called, and McNall scrambled for money. His associates began playing shell games with his various "companies," faking coin sales, borrowing from one bank loan to pay on another. The Merrill Lynch funds crumbled, obliging the company to cough up perhaps as much as $30 million in compensation to 3,500 investors and leading the FBI to investigate the disappearance of $3.3 million in coins from one of the funds. Having learned from the horse's mouth, so to speak, that McNall had a certain familiarity with the smuggling trade, federal officials began looking more broadly into his books and found his tangled web.

From jail the irrepressible faker can be expected to spend his leisure time discoursing to rapt fellow prisoners on his fabulous finagles, the reform policies of the Emperor Augustus and the spellbinding saga of the Honus Wagner baseball card with the $400,000 price tag. Between-times, he can play Monopoly and catch up on his television.

Source: Birnbaum, Jesse. "Fall of the Collector." Time. vol. 144, no. 20, November 14, 1994, 75.

1. Bruce McNall obviously was viewed by many people as a man who had acquired power. What strategies did McNall employ in his quest for power?
2. How was Mr. McNall able to create the impressions of being a powerful, effective businessman?
3. In your opinion, why didn't a whistle blower come forth prior to the FBI investigation?
4. Mr. McNall's associates appeared to share the values adhered to by their boss. These values are in opposition to honesty, openness, and social responsibility. In your opinion, how could such conformance be possible?
5. Which of the marks of a professional did Mr. McNall exhibit? Which appear to be lacking?

Case 4

The Liberated Workplace

Taken together, the various elements of the future workplace form a fascinating picture of a small business truly liberated from space and time. Each of us will have a small personal communicator about the size of a cellular phone that we carry with us wherever we go. It will serve as our telephone, fax machine, modem, and electronic date and note book.

At home, where we spend most of our work time, we will plug it into a workstation that allows us to input with a keyboard, stylus, scanner, and mouse, and deliver output on a printer, a large color screen, and/or a state of the art sound system. When we first plug it in each morning, our electronic secretary will download all the latest information and news we need, letting us print it out or read it on screen.

At the office, where we'll go once a week for our half-day meeting with the staff, we will plug our communicator into a dock in a conference table where we can input via voice, and where we can output into large video conferencing displays screens. Before we leave the office, the company's electronic library will update our personal data bases.

On the road to our car, at an airport, or at a hotel, we'll have access to other docks which let us remain in constant touch with our work.

Far from science fiction, such a scenario is technologically possible today for even the smallest business, and according to most experts, it's likely to be practical in the next decade. And while many who thrive on the latest technology can't wait for it to come, others, including most of the visionaries painting the portrait, aren't so sure it will be a wholly positive development.

"In the liberated workplace of the future, there will be more of a oneness of work life and personal life," says one authority. "For younger people, or for those who are working at what they truly love—like entrepreneurs—that will be wonderful. But for the others it could be incredibly debilitating—they'll have no escape from work."

Futurist and author Faith Popcorn agrees: "As technology gets smaller and more portable, the creeping 'workization' of our lives becomes a psychological and physiological threat. Zones of privacy and work-free spaces may have to be established."

"The liberated small business workplace could lead to depersonalization," another authority believes, "but the flip side is freedom. Employees will still want to get a pat on the back for a job well done, but I don't know if a small business owner will be able to deliver that pat via e-mail to someone's laptop. Of course if we add in truly virtual; reality it could be possible."

"What I find most interesting about this new workplace," another futurist adds, "is that the nature of work changes. Sure it may offer more freedom as to where and when we all do our jobs, but it requires the parameters of what we're doing to be much more strictly drawn. Without continuous human interaction, instructions won't be able to contain as much ambiguity as they do today. That could lead to a real dictatorial type of management. On the other hand, it could lead to a reward system based more on results than appearances. In the future, the incompetent employee in a small business environment won't be able to hide using political and interpersonal skills."

"I think we're in for mixed results," sums up yet another authority. "We could become a society of haves and have nots, in which some have a very rewarding life, but others are forced to work weekends at jobs they hate. It could provide us with tremendous freedom, but at the cost of added responsibilities. Just because it has the potential to enrich our lives doesn't mean it will. We'll have to be careful. Now that we have choices, we'll have to make the right ones."

Source: Pollan, Stephen M., and Mark Levine. "The Liberated Workplace." U.S. News and World Report. vol. 117, no. 19, November 14, 1994.

1. In your opinion, will the development of human relations skills be as important for workers in the liberated workplace as they are today?

2. Which area of study in the interdisciplinary field of human relations—communications, management sciences, psychology and/or sociology—is likely to be emphasized in preparing workers for the liberated workplace? Provide a rationale to support your response.

3. Provide an explanation of what you believe the authority meant by the statement: "In the liberated workplace of the future there will be more of a oneness of work life and personal life."

4. What meaning do you attach to the term, workization, as coined by Faith Popcorn?

5. The liberated workplace calls for self-motivated workers. Do you anticipate difficulty with procrastination when workstations are located in homes?

6. What did the futurist mean when saying, "Without continuous human interactions, a reward system may emerge based more on results than appearances"?

Glossary

absenteeism time away from work

accessions hiring new employees or rehiring former employees

achievement motivation theory McClelland's theory which, like Maslow's, is based on human needs which drives one to fill them

active listener one who is involved in the verbal communication process and lets the sender of the message know that he or she is involved

active listening the counselor listens to a client express feelings and repeats what he or she does not understand until both client and counselor understand the intended meaning

affiliation needs needs to restore a relationship, to console someone, or just be with others

affirmative action employees aggressively seek a more equitable distribution of jobs among minorities in the communities in which they are located

agency shops may offer employment to any qualified worker, but nonunion workers have to pay a fee equal to union dues

alcoholism a problem with medical, social, and economic ramifications

Americans with Disabilities Act a federal civil rights law which makes it illegal to discriminate against individuals with disabilities

arbitrary management decisions and methods based upon discretion rather than reason

arbitration the process of bringing in an impartial third party to render a binding, legally enforceable decision

attendance policy guidelines that state the types and numbers of absences that are acceptable and whether or not employees will be compensated

attitude a mental position one possesses with regard to a fact, issue, or belief

attrition the permanent departure of individuals from an organization

authoritarian management approaches and methods which require workers to submit to the demands of managers

autocratic leader a leader who does not share leadership with others, but makes all decisions and then tells others of the decisions

automation the use of machines to do the work normally done by humans; humans may have to operate and maintain the machines

bar graph display that shows data in the form of bars

barriers impediments to the communication process, such as noise, telephone problems, or a storm that stops mail delivery

body language messages that are sent by body movements

broad-brush EPA's designed to offer help to employees suffering from all kinds of problems

buddy system assigning one person to be in charge of a newcomer's integration into the group (see **peer mentoring**)

bureaucratic organization three layers of authority exist including top managers who are decision makers, middle managers who develop rules and procedures, and workers and supervisors who perform the work

burnout occurs when someone is putting in much more than he or she is getting back from a certain situation or activity

business ethics refers to what is right or wrong, good or bad, human behavior

business etiquette refers to courteous behavior in business settings

caregiver someone who must provide child care or elder care

catharsis the process of obtaining relief from tensions by talking about deeply felt emotions

caveat emptor a Latin term meaning "Let the buyer beware."

centralized control decisions are made by relatively few high ranking officials

chain of command the arrangement of organizational authority which determines who reports to whom

change making something different in a particular way

channel of communication the official route that business or formal communications are expected to follow in an organization

chaos uncomfortable situations where we are not in control

character encompasses one's honor, integrity, constancy, and moral fiber

charisma the power to influence people as a result of magnetic personality traits and characteristic behaviors

child care consortium a group of employers that forms an organization to provide child care for their workers

circular process the process of communications where the sender transmits a message that is interpreted by the receiver who in turn responds to the content of the message to the sender

clique an informal group that is unified by the members' desire to support some "cause"

coaching assisting others to improve performance by giving suggestions and support

code of ethics a compilation of the rules that are supposed to govern the conduct of members of a particular organization or profession

coercive power a form of power used by managers and supervisors to reward or punish workers for compliance or noncompliance

cohesion sticking together or putting the interests of the group over personal interests

collaboration joint endeavors by two or more workers which occur in almost all functions and support areas of today's business environments

collective bargaining   a process of negotiating an employment contract with a firm's owner and/or managers which specifies wages, fringe benefits, and conditions of employment

commission   payment for performance when production occurs or when production quotas are exceeded

commitment   a state of being obligated or emotionally compelled

committee   a group which is given a specific task or assignment

communication   process of creating and sending a message to a receiver who will respond appropriately

communication flow   the routes that communications follow within an organization

compressed workweek   longer work days, but only four days per week

compulsory arbitration   the federal government requires both union and owner/manager representatives to present their unresolved differences to an impartial third party

consumerism   may be defined as the demand that business organizations give proper consideration to consumer wants and needs in reaching their decisions

Contingency Model   leadership theory which describes how the situation influences the relationship between leadership traits and effectiveness

continuous reinforcement   employees with perfect attendance records are paid small bonuses

cooperative counseling   an approach to counseling that blends direct guidance and active listening

coordination   plans to control the timing and sequence of activities

core hours   with flexible scheduling, the specific hours at which the worker must be on the job

corrective counseling   used to change actions because of something the employee does, or to alter the attitude that appears to be at the root of the problem

counseling   the process of formal communication used to assist someone through problems or increase personal effectiveness

counseling session   an attempt to change a worker's behavior and develop them into a productive member of the organization

craft union   an organization of skilled workers who are engaged in a specific trade

critical-incidents technique   an interview technique using job events to determine job satisfaction

decentralization   occurs when decision-making is allowed to filter down to lower ranks of the organization hierarchy

decentralized control   decision-making is allowed to filter down into the lower ranks of the organization's hierarchy

decision maker   someone who has the authority and responsibility to make a decision related to change

demographic characteristics   a study of factors such as population numbers and trends, ages, sex, families, households, incomes, education and geographic location as related to common-interest groups

depressants   drugs that affects the central nervous system that are used as a sedative

developmental counseling   helps employees to grow and fully realize their potential by becoming more effective and more efficient in the workplace

development needs   specific areas of improvement which an interpersonal skills training program should address

deviant   person who strays from accepted norms.

differential knowledge   when some people have access to information and others do not, causing unequal power

directive method   the traditional method of counseling because the counselor directs and controls the counseling session

discharge   releasing an employee who continues to violate attendance policies after being suspended

disciplinary layoff   turnover due to employee performance

distractions   interruptions to the communication processes

diversity   a point of difference

downsizing   a reduction in the number of employees in a company

downward communication   communication that flows from higher to lower levels in the organization

driving forces   supporters of change such as legislation or competition

drug abuse   taking legal and illegal drugs not to induce pleasure but to avoid unpleasant situations

ecology   the relationship between people and the environment

ecosystem distrust   phenomena such as lower interpersonal trust and suspicion of authority figures

efficiency   the measure of how well a worker works

ego trip   an act that enhances and satisfies one's ego

elder care   having the responsibility for an older person

electronic mail   a medium of communication which requires the use of a computer and keyboard terminal where messages are transmitted through electronic networks

e-mail   the shortened name for electronic mail

empathy   the ability to put yourself in someone else's place to understand that person's point of view

emphasis   giving more impact to certain words or phrases to give more force to a message.

employee assistance program   program that provides business and industry with the means to identify employees whose job performance is negatively affected with personal or job related problems

employee coaching   a personalized on-the-job method which is used to develop job skills, knowledge, and attitudes

employee counseling   a means to develop an employee's behavior

employee turnover the number of employees hired as replacements divided by the total number of employees

empowerment the sharing of power at every level within an organization and with everyone

entrepreneur someone willing to take risks, make decisions, and take responsibility for decisions in his or her business

environmental concerns matching workers to the environment in which they work (ergonomics)

Equal Employment Opportunity Commission the federal government agency responsible for enforcing anti-discrimination efforts

equity theory proposes that motivation is influenced by an individual's perception of how equitably he or she is treated on the job

ergonomics matching the worker to the area in which the job is to be completed

esprit de corps common spirit existing among the members of a work group that inspires enthusiasm, devotion, and strong regard for the honor of the group

esteem needs provide motivation related to the goals of feeling a sense of accomplishment, achievement, and respect from others

ethical communications being honest with the person who will receive the communication

ethics moral rules or values governing the conduct of a person or a group

ethnocentrism a belief that one's own group is superior

excessive purchasing on credit abusing credit privileges for nonessential purchases

excused absences time away from work approved by one's employer

expectancy an action-outcome association

expectancy-valence theory suggests that human behavior, to a large extent, is the result of the characteristics of the individual and what the individual perceives to be his or her environment

expert someone who has inordinate knowledge about an issue, the organization, or the change process

externally enacted goals goals that are imposed by someone else

extrinsic reward reward that is external to the workers such as pay and benefits

extrovert an individual who enjoys interacting with others and who enjoys sharing the thoughts and ideas of others

eye contact looking at someone to whom you are communicating

facilitator someone who has no vested interest in the change but is eager to make the process work

fairness implies impartiality and honesty, conformance with established rules, and freedom from self-interest, prejudice, and favoritism

feedback the receiver's response to the sender of a message which informs the sender that the message was received and properly interpreted

feminine style of leadership exercising leadership through strong interpersonal and communication skills

flat organizations many people report to a given supervisor or manager and fewer levels exist within the hierarchy

flexplace the opportunity to choose where work will be completed; most workers work at home, at least part of the time

flex time a policy that allows some employees to adjust their work schedule to some agreed upon set of hours

forced choice a format for performance evaluation where raters are given pairs of descriptors which represent behavior and they must choose the most accurate descriptor

force field analysis a way to look at a change effort without getting emotionally involved

formal communication business communications that takes place in groups, between supervisors and employees, between supervisors, or between employees in a work environment

formal report usually long, presenting information in detail and using tables, charts, graphs, or illustrations to increase the impact of the presentation

free-rein the style that empowers employees to function on their own without mangers being directly involved

4-D formula a process wherein each trivial task or small detail is considered and a decision to drop, delay, delegate, or do is reached

gainsharing the use of pay as a reward for tying individual goals with the goals of the organization which result in improvement in productivity and profitability

gambling putting resources at risk

glass ceiling a limitation of women's ability to advance to upper level management positions

globalization the trend for businesses to operate throughout the world

goals statements of what you want to accomplish

goodwill refers to the favor or prestige that an organization has acquired through relationships with external constituents

grapevine the channels for informal communications in the organization

graphical scale a type of performance evaluation where each descriptor defines a different level of performance

grievance a complaint filed by a worker or workers who believe that owners/managers are violating some provision of the employment contract

group two or more people who interact with each other, are aware of each other, and are working toward some common purpose

group incentive payment plan each person is compensated based upon the performance of a work team

groupthink a process of faulty decision-making

half employee the employee who occasionally drinks to excess also impacts productivity

hallucinogens   drugs that produce mental illusions and impact a person's ability to perceive reality

harassment   unwanted communication that may take many forms

harassment audit   designed to measure the extent to which employees understand harassment policies

Hawthorne effect   a phenomenon wherein employees who are chosen to participate in scientific studies may become more productive because of the attention they receive from researchers

hazing   persecuting or harassing a newcomer with meaningless, difficult, or humiliating tasks

horizontal communications   exchange of information among employees at some level

hostile environment   the atmosphere created by unwelcome and offensive comments, jokes and touching

hotline   an option to employees where they are encouraged to call a particular number to ask for help

human relations   the process of fitting people into work situations in such a manner as to motivate them to work harmoniously achieving high levels of productivity while experiencing economic, psychological, and social satisfaction

hygiene factors   factors that do not cause satisfaction on the job

illustration   usually a picture of some types of data, or contains data within.

imitation   to pattern, follow or copy

inducements   a dinner, gift certificate or a small gift to encourage good work habits

industrial union   an organization made up of all workers in a given industry

inflection   the same as tone of voice, raising and falling of the voice while the message is being stated

informal communication   communications that result from the formation of informal groups; typically not business communications

injunction   a court order which may direct strikers to resume their work, limit the number of pickets that can be used during a strike, or otherwise deal with actions which may be detrimental to the welfare of the state

injustice   a form of unfairness which occurs when cases or subjects are not treated in the same manner

instructive counseling   used as a means to prevent problems rather than solve them after they begin

interactive media   places the trainee in a participatory learning mode in which computer-assisted video hardware and interactive video software are used

interference   barriers that impede the successful delivery of a message

intermediate goals   pursuits that you want to accomplish in one or two years

internally enacted goals   goals you set for yourself

interpersonal conflict   a condition that exists when people possess attitudes, motives, values, and expectations or engage in activities which are incompatible with those of other people

interpersonal relations   interactions which occur among and between people, whether harmonious or conflicting

interpersonal skill training   programs designed to develop or improve skills which are used when dealing with others

interpret   the receiver must decode and understand the message that is received

intrapreneur   someone within a company who takes risks and makes decisions and is responsible for those decisions

intrinsic reward   reward that comes from job satisfaction, pride, or job autonomy

introvert   an individual who is more comfortable with his or her own thoughts and feelings and who prefers not to interact with others

involvement   the degree to which a worker becomes involved with a job

job design   an approach to improving job satisfaction and productivity that is oriented to changing jobs in which workers are engaged

job dissatisfiers   factors such as company policy, interpersonal relationships and working conditions that cause a worker to be dissatisfied

job enlargement   a strategy which involves adding tasks to a job

job enrichment   a strategy which gives workers more tasks within the job and also control and authority over the job

job maintenance factors   factors of the job environment which are necessary to maintain the desired level of worker satisfaction

job performance   how well someone does a job

job rotation   a strategy which allows employees to move from one job to another

job satisfaction   the degree to which someone is happy in a job

job satisfiers   factors such as achievement, recognition, work, responsibility, advancement, and growth that motivate workers

job sharing   a strategy which involves two people assuming one job

kinesics   the scientific name given to body language

knowledge worker   a person who applies specialized knowledge or information, usually acquired by extended study and considerable experience, to an occupation that requires a high degree of mental effort such as analysis, reasoning, interpretation, and creativity

labor unions   a group of workers who have banned together to achieve common goals related to wages, hours, benefits, and working conditions

leader   a person who can influence followers to accomplish goals

leadership   the role of providing direction for others

leadership characteristics   traits which Dr. David Campbell said are descriptive of a leader

Leadership Continuum   illustrates how managers allow subordinates a varied amount of freedom to participate in organizational decision

Leadership Grid® this theory has leadership styles based upon the amount of concern for people versus the amount of concern for production

leadership style the approach used by a leader to influence others

least preferred coworker Fiedler attempted to predict leadership effectiveness based on a trait measurement that resulted in this name

legitimate power a form of power held by people who occupy a higher level position than the people below him

letter the written medium most often used for communications outside of the organization

letterhead professional stationary which contains the name, address, telephone numbers, and logo of the organization

line position designates an employee who is involved in or contributes directly to the main business activity or a firm

listening skill active exercise of hearing a communication

lockouts temporarily closing the business and denying employment to workers in an attempt to thwart labor demands

long-term goals pursuits that you want to accomplish in three or more years

love and belonging need the need for close association with others

lump sum payment when the employee is allowed to take some portion of annual earnings in a larger amount

management by objectives a process in which a manager and worker confer together in determining the goals which the worker will achieve

management tardiness supervisors arriving late for work

managerial incentive plan bonuses or other forms of incentives paid to managers for good performance

Maslow's needs hierarchy one of the earliest and most popular theories of motivation which is based on human needs

maturity a state of becoming the best that an individual can be

measurable outcome a result that readily lets you know your goal is achieved

mediation the process of bringing in a third party to make recommendations for the settlement of differences

medium the method used to send a message which could include a written letter, the telephone, electronic mail (e-mail), or face-to-face verbal messages

memorandum an informal means to send written communications within the organization

merit award an award based upon job performance

merit pay increase increase in wages based on job performance

mirroring restating a client's words to reflect clarity and the client's feelings

misinterpretation a message is not correctly understood by the intended receiver

morale a combination of employee attitudes or inner feelings toward work

motivation a need or absence of something that drives a person to act or react, to behave in a specific way

motivational factors factors that cause a lack of dissatisfaction on a job

motivation-hygiene theory Herzberg's theory which is sometimes called the *two-* or *dual-factor* theory

multicultural leadership providing leadership for people of several races and backgrounds

myths traditional or legendary stories about organizational heroes or events of exceptional character

narcotics drugs that are intended to induce sleep and relieve pain

need for communication before a message is originated and sent, the sender must feel there is a reason for the communication to occur

need for power results in someone who tries to directly influence other people's behavior

Noah's Ark syndrome having every group represented on a team

nondirective method a counseling approach in which a professionally trained counselor does not direct the client with any advice

nonverbal communication messages communicated by one's body

nonverbal messages same as nonverbal communications and body language

norms set standards of parameters within an employee's output must measure and/or expectations to which members or a group are expected to adhere

numerical rating scale a type of performance evaluation where numbers are used to rate the level of performance

objective evaluation when the level of performance is based on easy-to-interpret criteria

off-the-job employee behavior a broad range of employee activities from an employee's political activities to whether or not they smoke

on-the-job employee behavior issues that range from drug testing and use of electronic equipment to track employee's behavior while at work

open shops union membership is voluntary and no fees are paid by nonmembers

oral reprimand when an employee violates a company policy and then is warned verbally

organization two or more people whose combined abilities make the accomplishment of goals possible

organizational chart a picture which shows the hierarchy of personnel within the organization

organizational development a planned strategy designed to improve overall organizational effectiveness

organizational effectiveness refers to human judgments about the desirability of the outcomes of organizational performance from the vantage point of various constituencies directly and indirectly affected by the organization

organizational isolation the setting when a worker is separated from other workers

organizational structure the order of relationships and responsibilities within the organization

organizational value system provides direction for the numerous decisions reached in the workplace

originator the person who normally creates the message and is usually the sender as well

outsourcing an entire department may be taken over by a specialized contractor

overkill changing too much, too soon

paraprofessional a specially trained individual who works along with professionals, but in a subsidiary or supportive role

participative leader a leader who shares the authority to make decisions with others

partnership two or more individual business owners

paternalism a practice wherein an employer attempts to regulate the behavior of employees

payment for production when you are paid for your results

payment for time when you are paid by the hour, day, week, or month

peer assistance a program that trains employees to help coworkers and emphasizes prevention rather than intervention

peer mentoring assigning one person to be in charge of the newcomer's integration into the group (see **buddy system**)

people-oriented leadership building a contented and cooperative work group

performance appraisal the process followed to determine how well an employee works on the job

performance-based payment plans employees are paid based on their performance, like payment for production

personal needs an awareness of "self" in relation to others which actions and reactions are closely linked

personal power a form of power which an individual may possess as a result of knowledge or expertise and/or charisma

personality the totality of complex characteristics including behavioral and emotional tendencies, personal and social traits, self-concept, and social skills

personal space distance allowed between you and another person

Peter Principle this principle states that in a hierarchy, every employee tends to rise to his or her level of incompetence

philanthropy giving funds to charities and/or supporting social causes financially

physiological needs provide motivation related to the goals of obtaining food, shelter, and clothing

physiological response the way one's body reacts to certain situations

picket employees walk around outside the employing organization's premises, often carrying signs, talking with media representatives and the public about injustices they perceive to be occurring

pie chart often shows data segmented like pieces of a pie so relative amounts for different data are easily discernible

piecework payment for the number of pieces a worker can produce

piecework plan when employees are guaranteed a base hourly rate of pay for producing a preset amount but are rewarded for producing more

pitch determines if the voice is deep or if the voice is high

polarization a process which causes a group to adopt a cautious approach to decision-making

policy a general guide to action

politics a term which refers to tactics or strategies used to acquire power

positive stress examples include going on vacation, excelling on an exam, and receiving a promotion

positive you approach keeping the readers in focus throughout the communication in order to make them feel good

posture how individuals position their bodies

power the ability to control anything of value

prejudgment an assessment of a person or situation without the requisite information

prejudice an attitude based partially on ignorance, fear, and cultural patterns

primary boycott the union encourages its members, as well as the general public, to avoid conducting business transactions with a firm involved in a labor dispute

procrastination "Never do today what you can put off until tomorrow."

productivity the measure of output of an individual in the workplace

professional an individual who has met the requirements to practice a profession usually as the result of special training and, in some cases, licensing, and who exhibits loyalty to the profession, experiences professional rewards, adheres to the profession's code of ethics, engages in activities designed to keep himself or herself current in the occupation, and participates in professional associations

professionalism the conduct, character, and qualities that mark the behavior expected of one who engages in the pursuit of a professional career

profit sharing tying absenteeism costs to sharing profits with employees to encourage employees to attend work

programmed instruction a self-teaching method which divides the material to be learned into small capsules of information called *frames*

progressive discipline a process that helps to ensure that the minimum penalty which matches the violation of the rule will be imposed

project team a group created to solve a specific problem, work on a special project, design a plan, or complete some activity (see **taskforce** and **tiger team**)

proposal a bid for funds from another organization such as a government agency, or a bid to complete work for another business

proprietor an individual business owner

proxemics the technical name given to personal space, or the distance you allow between yourself and others

psychographic characteristics a study of factors such as lifestyles, personalities, and self-concepts as related to common-interest groups

public relations a process concerned with activities and communications intended primarily to obtain goodwill or prestige for an organization

quality circles voluntary groups of seven to ten people from the same work area who meet on a regular basis to define, analyze, and solve quality problems and related problems

quality of work life programs which encompass approaches used in making jobs more pleasant for workers

questionnaire the most-used method to determine job satisfaction; a written format distributed to employees

ratified acceptance of a negotiated contract by union members as revealed through votes

reasonable accommodations assistance provided to workers with limitations so they may perform a work task

receiver the recipient of the message that is being sent

redesign a change that seeks to simplify and streamline existing operating procedures

reengineering creates new operating procedures, making radical and innovating changes to business methods

referent power a form of power which a person may hold when he or she possesses charisma to the extent that other people admire and try to emulate personality traits and behaviors

reflexive self the human element that causes us to be aware and reflexive of our being

reliability the consistency of information that is collected

report a presentation of facts to one or more people inside or outside the organization which addresses a specific purpose

resiliency the ability to bounce back from whatever adversity we encounter

resistance to change to withstand the implementation or the effects of an effort to make a situation different

resister someone who likes the status quo and is dubious about proposed changes

restorative counseling an opportunity to prescribe a cure for difficulties which are the cause of the problems

reverse discrimination a sense of unfairness by majority groups when minorities are given preference in hiring and promotions

reward systems prepared with the purpose of providing incentives, or inducements, which will get employees to work more efficiently and productively

right-to-work laws legislation which gives workers a right to determine whether or not to join the union

role behavior oriented to the general expectations of others

safety needs provide motivation related to the goals of job security, protection from physical harm, and avoidance of the unexpected

scabs replacement workers who are willing to fill jobs held by strikers

scapegoat individual who bears the blame for others

scientific management an approach involving the scientific analysis of jobs during which each work task is identified and narrowed to its most elementary function

scientific method analyzing jobs to determine worker tasks and job requirements

secondary boycott the union encourages others not to do business with other firms who are doing business with a firm involved in a labor dispute

selective listening picking parts of a message that one wants to hear or respond to

selectivity selecting the parts of a message you want to hear

self-actualization needs provide motivation related to the goals of fulfillment, living up to one's potential, and for reaching one's fullest potentialities and capabilities

self-directed group a group of workers who to a greater or lesser degree perform roles and make decisions traditionally reserved for management

self-esteem needs the desire for strength, achievement, competence, prestige, and self-confidence

sender the person who transmits a message, usually the originator of the message

sensitivity training a group process in which members learn to be more honest with each other

sentence-completion test a form of written job satisfaction test where employees fill in blanks in statements

separations termination of employment usually subdivided between those who are laid off because of lack of work and those who voluntarily quit

sex discrimination bias based on gender

sexual harassment unwanted attention of a sexual nature

shamrock organization a new structure for employers with the three major components being fewer full time employees, more consultants, and expanded use of temporary employees

shop steward an individual who represents other union members in a specific organization

short report a brief presentation of information and data, often done in the form of a memorandum

short-term goals pursuits that you want to accomplish in a very short period

single-issue programs programs designed to help only employees impaired by drugs and alcohol

social audit monitors the ethical behavior of executives, managers, supervisors, and employees and attempts to discover how well the organization's ethical policies are being followed

social mobility concept the idea that as one subgroup moves up in economic terms, it is replaced by a less fortunate subgroup who is seeking a better way of life

social needs provide motivation related to the goals of gaining acceptance by others and for giving and receiving love

social responsibility an organization's consideration of the social as well as economic effects of its decisions

span of control the number of employees who report to a manager or supervisor

specific measurable outcome indentifiable results which can be observed

staff position positions filled by individuals who perform specialized activities

stakeholder members of the organization and outsiders who have a direct or indirect interest in the organization; someone who has a vested interest in how change oocurs and will likely be called upon to carry out the decision made

standards beliefs or values that come from the culture, religion, and society around us as we grow up

standard time when time per unit rather than units per time is used as the measure of performance

standard time plan a payment plan based upon time needed to complete a task

stereotypes thinking of members of a group as being all the same, without consideration of individual differences

stimulants drugs that act on the central nervous system and are used to keep people awake

stimuli the different needs that drive individuals to make decisions about what they will or won't do

stress the rate of wear and tear on the body

strike workers refuse to show up for work and, in some cases, such actions cause operations to shut down

subjective evaluation when a rater is expected to judge the level of performance of the employee

subordinate power an individual may be able to exert this form of power form lower levels within an organization because of his or her unusual talents

success achieving a goal

successful communication communication that has successfully made it through the complete circular process

suggestion plan an opportunity for employees to suggest ways to improve company operations

supporter someone who has already committed to seeing the change occur and has some ideas about potential changes

suspension barring an employee from his or her job without pay

table a concise way to show data using columns and rows when a detailed explanation is not necessary

tall organizations few people report to each manager and several levels exist within the hierarchy

task force a group created to solve a specific problem, work on a special project, design a plan, or complete some activity (see **project team** and **tiger team**)

task-oriented leadership getting the job done with maximum efficiency

teamwork working together to maximize the strengths of individual group members and minimize their weaknesses

telecommuting performing certain job functions at home on a computer, then transferring the work to the office computer system via modem

temporary employees employees who work for an agency or broker who in turn places them in full- or part-time positions

Theory X leader a leader who doesn't have a lot of confidence in worker's ability to think and act independently

Theory Y leader a leader who places considerable confidence in humans to function as independent individuals

tiger team a group created to solve a specific problem, work on a special project, design a plan, or complete some activity (see **project team** and **task force**)

time lines incremental steps that are set along the way to complete a goal

time log a method to record what you do so you can see how your time is spent

time management how you utilize your time

tinkering changing this or that aspect of a system without realizing the change may not be an improvement

to-do list what must be accomplished during a day

tone of voice the raising and falling of a voice while the message is being stated

Total Quality Management an organizational change concept that suggests planning for change is the preferred action

transactional analysis a method of studying communication by learning of the three ego states of child, adult, and parent

turnover the number of workers hired within a period to replace those leaving the workforce

unexcused absences time away from work not approved by one's employer

unions organizations that have the main goal of representing members in bargaining over job-related issues

union shops establishments in which a worker does not have to be a union member to be hired, but must agree to join the union within a prescribed period of time as a condition of continued employment.

upward communication communications that flow from lower to higher levels of the organization

valence the human/personal orientations toward an outcome

validity the correctness of information that is collected

value conflict occurs when one or more workers' values are in conflict with those of other workers

values beliefs that cause reflection and evaluation of thoughts and feelings and resulting actions

value system consists of what an individual places value on or believes is important

valuing differences programs intended to enhance interpersonal relationships among employees and minimize blatant racism and sexism

verbal communication spoken communication which usually occurs in meetings, or between employees on the same level of the organization

verbal messages oral transmitted messages which are considered to be most effective when face-to-face with the intended receiver

vertical communication communications that are sent either up or down in the organization

vocabulary richness the quality of diversity of one's choice of words which influence impressions formed by others

volume quieter or louder tone of voice

voluntary arbitration both union and owner/manager representatives decide to present their unresolved differences to an impartial third party.

voice mail a system that allows callers to transmit a message which can be restored and listened to

well pay employees receive an extra day's pay for each month in which attendance and punctuality are perfect

whistle blowers people who call attention to the real or imagined misdeeds and unscrupulous behavior of their colleagues or sometimes their supervisors

workaholic a label for someone who is addicted to their work

workplace monitoring a tool to help employers maintain quality control, product security, and customer protection

workplace privacy freedom of unauthorized intrusion from the jobsite

workplace violence harassment, threats, or physical attacks on the job

work team a group of workers assigned to complete a job

written communication a more formal medium of communication which is used extensively by organizations, where messages are usually prepared using a computer or word processor

written warning when the employee's attendance continues to be unsatisfactory, a reprimand in the form of a written warning is given

yellow-dog contract an agreement wherein potential employees agree not to join a union as a condition of employment

Index

A

Absenteeism, 259
  alcohol-related, 284
  connotation of, 300
  controlling, 302-303
    discipline, 304-306
    reward programs, 303-304
  and group efficiency, 300, 301
  reasons for, 300-301
  team management and, 432
ADA. *See* Americans with Disabilities Act
Adams, J. Stacy, 210
Adler, Nancy, 257-58
Affirmative action programs, 123
AFL, 117-18
AFL-CIO, 118
Age Discrimination in Employment Act,
  123, 383
Albrecht, Karl, 109
Alcoholics Anonymous, 320
Alcoholism
  absenteeism and, 284
  identifying, 283-84
  nature of, 282-83
  programs for, 285
Alexander, Roy, 355
Amalgamated Clothing and Textile
  Workers Union, 117
American Airlines, 458, 459
American Assembly of Collegiate Schools
  of Business, 488
American Association of Advertising
  Agencies, 504
American Association of Retired Persons,
  290
American Bar Association, 504
American Civil Liberties Union, 330
American Federation of Labor (AFL),
  117-18
American Management Association, 435,
  479
American Marketing Association, 491-93
American Medical Association, 356, 504
Americans with Disabilities Act (ADA)
  definition of disability, 378-79
  employers' rights and obligations
  under,381
  policing of, 125
  protection of former drug users, 287
  reasonable accommodations provision,
  124
  scope of, 378
Anania, Michael, 150
Angelou, Maya, 448
Arab business customs, 53-54
Aradah, Arkban, 328-29
Arbitrary management, 3
AT&T, 15
Authoritarian management, 3, 4
Automation, 242-43
Avon Products Inc., 372

B

Baby boom generation, 99
Beechhold, Henry F., 161
Beech-Nut Nutrition Corporation, 490
Ben & Jerry's Homemade Incorporated,
  491
Bethlehem Steel, 14
Better Business Bureau, 490
Blackmun, Harry, 67
Blake, Robert, 430, 432, 434
  Leadership Grid®, 430-32
Bloom, David, 126
Boeing, 19
Boesky, Ivan, 35, 126
Born to Win: Transactional Analysis with
  Gestalt Experiments (James and
  Joneward), 115
Bosrock, Mary Murray, 513
Brocka, Bruce, 437
Brocka, Suzanne, 437
Brown, W. Steven, 267
Brown v. Board of Education, 136
Burnout, 317-20
  help for, 319-20
  nature of, 317-18
  symptoms of, 318
Business and Health Magazine, 292
Business ethics. *See* Ethics

C

CalPacific, 396
Cameron, Dan, 261
Campbell, David P., 424
Campbell Leadership Index, 424
Cantoni, Craig, 48
Capitalism and Freedom (Friedman), 495
Carnegie, Dale
  on doing one's best, 66
  How to Win Friends and Influence
  People, 27
Casey, Albert, 455
Catalyst, 371
Caterpillar, 19
Chain of command, 37
Change

costs/benefit analysis of, 392
determining extent of, 397-98
driving and restraining forces in,
  396-97
implementing, 390-92
leader types in, 395
morale and, 391
myths about, 399
at the national and global level, 390
need for, 393-95
at the organizational level, 231-32, 390,
  398
at the personal level, 389-90
and personal values, 479, 482
and reengineering, 408-10
resistance to, 400-404
  chaos, 402-403
  differential knowledge, 403
  increased burdens, 401
  insecurity, 401-402
  lack of benefits, 401
  lack of management support, 401
  lack of ownership, 400
  lack of recognition, 403-404
  superiority, 403
team approach to, 404-408
  knowledgeability, 406
  team composition, 405
  team formation, 405
  team initiation, 406
  resource provision, 406-408
Total Quality Management and, 398-99,
  440
wrong reasons for implementing,
  390-92
  ego trips, 391
  imitation, 391-92
  overkill, 392
  tinkering, 392
Charts, 178
Child care consortium, 289-90
Chinese state-owned company restructuring, 237-38
Chinese protocol and etiquette, 100-101
CIO, 118
Citadel, The, 135-36
Civil Rights Act, 123, 174
Clinton, Hillary, 123
Collaboration, 16
Combination payment plans, 245
Commissions, 275
Communication. *See also* Organizational
  communication
  challenges to
    feelings/emotions, 164-65
    misinterpretation, 164

selectivity, 164
    unpredictable behavior, 165
as circular process, 146
defined, 144-45
in flat organizations, 39
horizontal, 85
and human relations, 25
lack of, as root of organization prob-
    lems, 145
modes of, 148-49
    listening
        as active participant, 163-64
        focused, 162-63
        nonjudgmental, 162
    nonverbal, 150-51
        appearance, 153-53
        body language, 76-77, 151-52
            eye contact, 152, 153
            posture, 152-53
            touch, 153
        space and territory, 154-55
    verbal
        emphasis, 149-50
        intonation pattern, 150
        voice pitch, 149
        voice quality, 149
        voice tone, 149
        voice volume, 149
    written, 155-61
        brief, 157-58
        empathic, 158-60
        specific, 160
        thorough, 156-57
pattern of good, 146-48
steps for good, 25-26, 145
in tall organizations, 39
and teamwork, 37
two-way, 44
in work groups, 85-86
Community relations. *See* Organizations,
    and external groups; Public relations
Compressed workweeks, 241
Congress of Industrial Organizations
    (CIO), 118
Connecticut Community Care Inc., 291
Consumerism, 106-7, 497
Contingency Model, 433-36
    criticism of, 436
    least preferred coworker score in,
        433-34
    situational favorability in, 434-35
Core hours, 241, 357
Corning Inc., 372
*Corporate Dandelions: How the Weed of
    Bureaucracy Is Choking American
    Companies and What You Can Do to
    Uproot It* (Cantoni), 48
Craft union, 117
Customs and traditions
    American culture

eye contact in, 152
on manipulating government
    officials, 473
Arab business customs, 53-54
Chinese protocol and etiquette, 100-101
expatriate failure in American compa-
    nies, 291-92
German business protocol, 480-81
golden rules, 453-54
international résumé, 512-13
international trade, 396-97
Japanese business practices
    commitment to the company, 258
    karoshi (overwork), 206-7
    quality circles, 8, 15-16, 89, 233
    "selling face," 20
    Theory Z, 13, 455
    women's professional role, 318-19
Mexican culture, 82-83
multicultural leadership, 440-43
Singapore's business climate, 466
time management in multicultural
    workplace, 344-45
women in international management,
    258-59

D

"Decade of Downsizing Eases Stigma of
    Layoffs" (Salwen), 231
Deming Prize, 16
Deming, W. Edwards, 16
Department of Defense, 129
Department of Transportation, 287
Derderian, Stephanie, 259
Diamond Star Motors, 37
"Differences in Job Motivation and
    Satisfaction among Female and Male
    Managers" (Forgionne and Peeters),
    226, 227
Direct Foreign Investment, 396
Disciplinary system
    progressive discipline in, 265
    steps in
        changing behavior, 265
        disciplinary actions, 265-66
        employee evaluation, 265
        rule communication, 264-65
        rule establishment, 264
Discrimination
    age, 226-27, 383-84
    disability, 124-25
    gender, 135-36, 225, 370-71
        glass ceiling, 371-72
        sexual harassment as, 374-76
    language, 173-74, 369-70
    legislation against, 35, 123, 124-25, 227
    pay, 118, 123
    prejudice and, 366-70

bases of, 367-69
    racial, 369-70
    wage, 6
Disney Corporation, 57
Diversity
    checking understanding of, 361-63
    growth of, 363
    strength of, in workforce, 360-61
    managing, 360-61, 363-64, 476
    and value conflicts, 476
    valuing differences programs and,
        363-64
Diversity IQ test, 361-63
Downsizing
    and automation, 242-43
    for efficiency, 237-38, 273
    and flattening of organizations, 434
    and layoffs, 230-31, 479
    and middle management, 139, 237-38
    and overqualified workers, 228
    and personal values, 482
Driver, Michael J., 433
Drives, 212-14
Drucker, Peter
    on business ethics, 488
    on certainty, 516-17
    on human development, 112
    and management by objectives, 14
Drug abuse
    drugs involved in, 286-87
    signs of, 285
    testing policies, 286-88

E

EAPs. *See* Employee assistance programs
Eastman Chemical, 440
Economic Policy Institute, 294
EEOC. *See* Equal Employment
    Opportunity Commission
E-mail
    nature of, 185-86
    tampering, 184-85
Employee assistance programs (EAPs)
    confidentiality of, 324
    history of, 320
    nature of, 320
    needs addressed by, 320, 321-22
    service modes of, 323-24
    services offered by, 322-23
Employee coaching
    counseling compared with, 260
    defined, 260, 263
    nature of, 263
Employee counseling
    approaches to, 262-63
    coaching compared with, 260
    defined, 260
    nature of, 260-61

steps in, 261, 298-300
types of
cooperative, 297-98
corrective, 261
developmental, 261
directive, 296
instructive, 261
nondirective, 297
restorative, 261
Employee-management issues
AIDS-related concerns, 118
child care, 118
drug abuse, 118
employee stock ownership plans
(ESOPs), 118
executive compensation, 118
golden parachutes, 118
movement of jobs overseas, 119
pay equity for women, 118
sexual harassment, 118
workplace privacy, 329
Employees
absenteeism of, 259
alcohol-related, 284
connotation of, 300
controlling, 302-303
discipline, 304-306
reward programs, 303-304
and group efficiency, 300, 301
reasons for, 300-301
as ambassadors, 102, 103, 105
attendance policies for, 301
attitudes of, 256-57. *See also* Job performance, attitudes affecting
in bureaucratic organizations, 48
and burnout, 317-20
coaching. *See* Employee coaching
communication style of, 86
compensation plan for, 6
payment for performance, 244-45,
272-73
combination payment plans, 245
group incentive payment plans,
244, 276-77
piecework, 244, 276
payment for time, 243-44
counseling. *See* Employee counseling
disabled, 378-82
and the Americans with Disabilities
Act (ADA), 378-79
assisting, 382
complaints against employers,
380-81
reasonable accommodations for, 379
disciplining. *See* Disciplinary systems
dishonesty of, 22, 74-75, 126-27
discrimination against. *See also*
Discrimination
age, 226-27, 383-84
disability, 124-25

language, 173-74, 369-70
pay, 118, 123
wage, 6
women, 135-36, 225, 370-71
glass ceiling, 371-72
sexual harassment, 374-76
empowerment of. *See* Empowerment
equal treatment of, 267-68
fair evaluation of, 267-68
in female-owned firms, 371
human relations activities of, 17, 106
and inadequate wages, 6
issues with management, 118-19
and job security, 103
and labor unions. *See* Labor Unions
motivating, 8-10, 229. *See also* Human
relations practices
and organizational effectiveness, 50
personal problems of. *See also*
Employee assistance programs
alcoholism
absenteeism and, 284
identifying, 283-84
nature of, 282-83
programs for, 285
drug abuse
drugs involved in, 286-87
signs of, 285
testing policies, 286-88
family
child care, 289, 290, 292
elder care, 290-93
family stress, 293
financial, 293-94
credit problems, 295-96
gambling, 295
health-related, 288-90
at work, 281-82
privacy of, 328-32
as an issue, 329
monitoring in the workplace and,
331-32
off-the-job behavior and, 329, 330
on-the-job behavior and, 329
personal questions and, 330-31
productivity of. *See* Productivity
retaining, 10, 11
rewarding. *See* Performance-based
incentive plans; Reward systems
and rule establishment, 264
stress and. *See* Stress
training. *See* Interpersonal skill training
workaholism among, 91, 219-21
Employee turnover
commitment and, 89
cost of, 307
management and, 307
at *maquiladoras,* 82
minimizing, 307
morale and, 13, 306

nature of, 10, 306
reasons for, 10, 306
team management and, 432
wages and, 6
Empowerment
accountability in, 458-60
cohesion in, 461
esprit de corps in, 463-64
exceptions to, 465
initiating, 458
manager's role in, 456-57
morale in, 462-63
nature of, 456, 458
and participative power, 455-56
teamwork in, 461-62
Entrepreneurship, 238
Equal Employment Opportunity Act
(EEOA), 123
Equal Employment Opportunity
Commission (EEOC)
and age discrimination, 383, 384
creation of, 123
and disability discrimination suits, 380,
381
definition of sexual harassment, 374-75
Guidelines on Harassment Based on
Race, Color, Religion, Gender,
National Origin, Age or Disability,
372-74
harassment prevention guidelines, 365
opposition to English-only rules, 369
Equal Pay Act, 35, 371
Ergonomics, 236-37
Ethics. *See also* Human relations, ethical
dimensions to
breaches of, 489-91
in business, 129, 488, 495-97
codes of, 491, 494
cultivating, 494-95
in communications, 160
defined, 20
and human relations, 20
whistle blowers and, 494
Extrovert, 23

F

Fair Labor Standards Act, 7
Family Support Act, 294
Faulkner, Shannon, 135-36
Federal Age Discrimination Act, 227
Federal Express, 83
Federman, Irwin, 473
Fiedler, Fred
Contingency Model, 433-36
definition of favorable situation, 434
definition of least favorable situation,
436

Filley, Alan, 406
Flexplace, 241
Flextime, 240, 290
Ford, Henry, 6
Ford Motor Company, 14
Forgionne, Guiseppi A., 226, 227
Fortune, 433
Fortune Group, 267
Franklin, Geralyn McCluse, 273
Friedman, Milton, 495
H. B. Fuller, 441
Fuller, R. Buckminster, 398

G

Gainsharing, 276-77
Gantt, Henry L., 6
GATT, 397
Gellerman, Saul W., 494
General Dynamics, 129
General Electric, 482-83
General Foods, 58-59
General Mills
    job enlargement at, 14
    self-directed work groups at, 81, 83
General Motors, 99
General Telephone Company, 115
German business protocol, 480-81
Gilbreth, Frank and Lillian, 6
Glass ceiling, 371-72
Globalization, 99, 344, 396-97
"Global Leadership Competencies:
    Managing to a Different Drumbeat"
    (Lobel), 291
Goals
    determining, 342
    layering, 344-45
    prioritizing, 346-48
    recording, 342-43
    types of
        externally enacted, 343-44
        internally enacted, 344
Goodyear, 81
Gordon, Jack, 72
W. L. Gore and Associates, 433-34
Gore, Wilbert L., 434
Grapevine communication, 182
Graphs, 177-78
Great American Time Squeeze: Trends in
    Work and Leisure 1969-1989
    (Economic Policy Institute), 294
Great Depression, 4
Griffo, Paul, 326
Group incentive payment plans, 244,
    276-77
Guidelines on Harassment Based on Race,
    Color, Religion, Gender, National Ori-
    gin, Age or Disability (EEOC), 372-74

H

Hall, Edward, 154
Harassment
    Equal Employment Opportunity
        Commission guidelines on, 372-74
    forms of, 364
    and hostile environment, 364
    proactive approaches to, 365-66
        creating an inclusive environment,
            366
        no-harassment policy in employee
            handbook, 365
    sexual, 118, 374-76
Harassment audits, 376-78
Harris Bank, 241
Hately, B. J., 356
Hawthorne effect, 7
Hawthorne Studies, 7
Herman v. Western Financial Corporation,
    375
Herzberg, Frederick, 9-10
    on money, 243
    and motivation-hygiene theory, 202-4
Higher Education Research Institute, 127
Hill, Alvin, 344
Home-Office Computing, 161
Horizontal corporation, 440
Howard R. Green Company, 360
How to Win Friends and Influence People
    (Carnegie), 27, 66
Hudson Institute, 363
Huey, John, 433
Hull, Raymond, 49
Human behavior
    mental dimensions of, 18-20
    physical dimensions of, 24
    social dimensions of, 20-23
        attitude, 23, 256-57
        extrovert, 23
        introvert, 23
        personality, 20-22
Human relations
    communication and, 25
    defined, 3
    ethical dimensions to, 20, 21-22
        age discrimination, 226-27
        bank fraud, 208-9
        concerns with time, 356-57
        consequences of decisions and
            actions, 449-50
        corporate image, 490-91
        drug-testing policies, 286-87
        e-mail tampering, 184-85
        employee honesty, 22, 74-75, 126-27
        employee vindictiveness, 435
        equal treatment, 267-68
        ethical ploys, 394-95
        fair evaluation, 267-68
        income inequities, 211-12

offensive writing, 160-61
        pay equity, 35-36, 118
        professional codes of ethics, 503-504
        self-expression, 331-32
        testifying on harassment, 376-77
        workplace turmoil, 435-35
    as field of study, 4, 17
    and internal stakeholders, 51, 57
    movements in. See Human relations
        movements
    need for, in organizations, 33
    professionalism and, 501, 522
    and public relations, 4
    setting for, 3
    in the work environment, 3-4
Human relations movements
    Human Relations, 229, 230
    job satisfaction, 9-10, 229
    labor unions, 7
    morale, 13-16
    motivation, 8-9
    paternalism, 5
    recognition, 7
    scientific management, 6, 234
    worker attitudes, 10-12
Human relations practices, 24
    communication, 25. See also
        Communication
    empathy, 25
    ethical and professional behavior, 27
    motivation, 26
    responsibility, 26
    workplace problem solving, 26-27
Human Resource Executive, 363
Human Side of Enterprise, The
    (McGregor), 426

I

IBM
    job enlargement at, 14
    job security at, 122
Illiteracy, 147-48
Illustrations, 178
Income distribution, 211-12
Industrial revolution
    advantages of, 7
    effect on workplace, 3
Industrial union, 117
In Plain Sight: Obsessions, Morals, and
    Domestic Laughter (Anania), 150
International Society of Primerus Law
    Firms, 503, 504
Interpersonal communication. See
    Communication
Interpersonal relations. See also
    Communication
    body language in, 76-77

defined, 2-3
problem solving, 112-13
settings for, 3
Interpersonal skill training
methods of
new
interactive media, 115
programmed instruction, 115
sensitivity training, 115
transactional analysis, 115
traditional, 111
case studies, 113-14
lectures, 112
on-the-job training, 112
role-playing, 112
simulation, 113
videotapes, 112
written materials, 112
nature of, 111, 116
need for, 111
Introvert, 23

J

James, Muriel, 115
Jansen, Dan, 214
Japanese business practices
commitment to the company, 258
karoshi (overwork), 206-7
quality circles, 8, 15-16, 89, 233
"selling face," 20
Theory Z, 13
women's role in, 318-19
Joanne H. Pratt Associates, 240
Job Descriptive Index, 222
Job design methods, 234-37
Job dissatisfiers, 202, 243
Job enlargement, 14, 45, 236
Job enrichment, 15, 236
Job maintenance factors, 10
Job performance
appraisal of, 259. *See also* Performance
appraisal
attitudes affecting, 257-59
commitment, 258
involvement, 257-58
satisfaction, 258
improving. *See* Job satisfaction, work
environment improvements and
job satisfaction and, 229-31
personal problems and, 281
reinforcing positive, 277-78
rewarding. *See* Reward systems
Job rotation, 14, 235
Job satisfaction
defined, 258
determinants of

employee characteristics
age, 225-26
experience, 227
gender, 224-25
intelligence and education, 228-29
job challenges, 227-28
position, 229
race, 226
job factors, 9-10, 218
determining
critical-incidents technique, 223-24
interviews, 222-23
questionnaires, 222
sentence-completion tests, 224
in female-owned firms, 371
importance of, 219
individual needs and, 218
job titles and, 45
motivated people and, 217
and motivation-hygiene theory, 202-4
and organizational health, 258-59
pay and, 243-45
payment for performance, 244-45
combination payment plans, 245
group incentive payment plans,
244, 276-77
piecework, 244, 275
payment for time, 243-44
performance-based rewards and, 230
positive reinforcement and, 278
self-directed work groups and, 84
team management and, 432
work environment improvements and,
231
ergonomics, 236-37
job enlargement, 14, 45, 236
job enrichment, 15, 236
job rotation, 14, 235
quality of work life, 16, 232-33
scientific method of job design, 234
work teams, 236
worker enhancement programs and, 233
empowerment, 233-34, 434. *See also*
Empowerment
quality circles, 15-16, 89, 233
work group cohesion and, 88
Job satisfiers, 9-10, 202
Job security
benefits to employer, 122
employee concerns over, 231, 482
and Plant Closing Notification Act, 122
success of employer and, 103
Job sharing, 15, 242
Johnson and Johnson, 357
Joneward, Dorothy, 115
Jordan, Michael, 206
Josephson Institute of Ethics, 126
Jury Verdict Research, 226
Justice Department, 385

K

Karoshi, 206-7
Keating, Charles, 126
Kennecott Copper, 320
Kennedy, John F., 497
Kennedy, Joyce Lain, 488
Kiechel III, Walter, 433
Kipper, Barbara Levy, 456
Kirkland v. New York Department of
Correctional Services, 268
Knight, Bob, 448
Knights of Labor, 117
Knowledge workers, 514
Kouzes, James, 407
Krzyzewski, Mike, 448

L

Labor Department, 325, 371
Labor legislation, 120
Labor unions
and agency shops, 120
and arbitration, 121
cooperative relationship with, 121-22,
326
defined, 117
development of, 7, 117-18
and employee-management issues, 118-
19
and Fair Labor Standards Act, 7
government attitudes toward, 120
and grievances, 121
interest in, 118
management tactics against
injunction, 120
lockout, 119-20
scabs, 119
yellow-dog contract, 120
and mediation, 121
and open shops, 120-21
operational procedures of, 120-21
tactics of
collective bargaining, 121
picket, 119
primary boycott, 119
secondary boycott, 119
strike, 119
types of, 117
and union shops, 120
view of management, 121
Leadership
characteristics of, 424-25
effective, 80
and management, 423, 425
multicultural, 440-41
nature of, 423
people-oriented, 84

task-oriented, 84
and Total Quality Management, 437
  approach to change, 398-99, 440
  employee involvement in, 440-41
  overview of, 438-39
  philosophy of, 398
  trends in, 433-34
  variables of, 422-23
Leadership Continuum, 428-29
Leadership Grid®, 430-32
Leadership styles, 425. *See also*
  Management styles
  autocratic, 426, 427-28
  developing, 432-33
  free-rein, 426
  participative, 426, 428, 429, 455-56
  selecting, 429
Leadership theories
  Contingency Model, 433-36
    criticism of, 436
    least preferred coworker score in,
      433-34
    situational favorability in, 434-36
  Leadership Continuum, 428-29
  Leadership Grid®, 430-32
  Theory X, 11, 426-28, 455
  Theory Y, 11-12, 428, 429, 455
  Theory Z, 13, 455
Lincoln, Abraham, 510
Lobel, Sharon, 291
Lowell System, 5

M

McCanse, Anne A., 430
McClelland, David, 205
McGregor, Douglas, 10-11, 434
  Human Side of Enterprise, The, 426
  on leadership variables, 422-23
  Theory X, 11, 426-28, 455
  Theory Y, 11-12, 455
Mackenzie, Alec, 340, 353
Macy's Department Store, 320
Malcolm Baldrige National Quality
  Award, 16
Management by objectives (MBO), 13-14,
  271
Management styles. *See also* Leadership
  styles
  arbitrary, 3
  authoritarian, 3, 4
  feminine, 371
  Japanese, 118
  motivational, 9
  participatory, 277
  scientific, 6
Managerial incentive plans, 276

Managers
  in bureaucratic organizations, 47-48
  in centralized organizations, 40
  and change implementation, 390-92
  coercive power in, 448
  in decentralized organizations, 40
  in directed work groups, 80
  and disabled employees, 382
  and employee attitudes, 257
  and employee empowerment, 234, 434.
    See also Empowerment
  and employee morale, 314
  and employee problems, 313
  and employee productivity, 229, 314
  and employee turnover, 307
  expatriate, 258-9
  in flat organizations, 38-40
  function of, 117, 267, 313
  human relations activities of, 17
  and labor unions. *See* Labor unions
  and leaders, 423, 425
  leadership styles of. *See* Management
    styles
  in maquiladoras, 82
  middle, as endangered species, 139,
    237-38
  in multicultural workplace, 344-45
  and organizational effectiveness, 50
  and parental ego state, 115
  performance appraisal of, 267, 271
  personal power in, 448
  and rule establishment, 264
  and self-directed work groups, 83
  skills of, 17
  and span of control, 39
  in tall organizations, 38-40
  tardiness of, 302
  as teachers, 112, 113
  view of labor unions, 121
  women as international, 258-59
  and workers' achievement needs, 45,
    278
  and workers' interests, 117
  and workers' self-actualization needs,
    448
  and workers' self-expression needs, 46,
    47
  and workers' social needs, 42, 44
  and workers' status needs, 45
Managing People: The Art and Science of
  Business Management (Cameron), 261
Maquiladoras, 82
Maslow, Abraham
  hierarchy of needs, 8, 196
    love and belonging, 8, 197
    physiological, 8, 196-97
    safety and security, 8, 197
    self-actualization, 9, 198-99, 227
    self-esteem, 8-9, 198
  on maturity, 506

motivation theory of, 8
Mayo, Elton, 7
Maytag, 14
Meany, George, 118
Merit pay systems, 274
Metropolitan Life Insurance Company,
  320
Mexican culture, 82-83
Michigan Model, 91
Michigan State University, 127
Milken, Michael, 35
Miller, Rhonda L., 479
Minnesota Satisfaction Questionnaire, 222
Morale
  change and, 391
  cohesive work group and, 89
  defined, 231
  and employee turnover, 13, 306
  as human relations movement
    collaboration, 16
    job enlargement, 14, 236
    job enrichment, 15, 236
    job rotation, 14, 235
    job sharing, 15, 242
    management by objectives, 13-14,
      271
    quality circles, 15-16, 89, 233
    quality of work life, 16, 232-33
    total quality commitment, 16
  Japanese versus American, 462
  planning meetings and, 44
  and productivity, 13, 229
  self-directed work groups and, 83
"More Companies Experiment with
  Workers' Schedules" (Shellenbarger),
  241
Motivation. *See also* Motivation theories;
  Needs
  of employees, 9
  as human relations movement, 8-9
  as human relations practice, 26
  individual differences and, 192
  job challenges and, 227
  as management style, 9
  nature of, 195
  and self, 193
Motivation theories
  achievement motivation theory, 204-9
    and achievement need, 205-7
    and affiliation need, 209
    and power need, 208-9
  equity theory, 210, 244
  expectancy-valence theory, 210-12
  Maslow's, 8, 196, 199-200 *See also*
    Maslow, Abraham
  motivation-hygiene theory, 202-4. *See*
    also Herzberg, Frederick
  values and, 193-95
Mouton, Jane, 430, 432, 434

N

Nader, Ralph, 497
NAFTA, 397
Nantz, Karen, 184
Nanus, Burt, 483-84
National Association of Female
 Executives, 371
National Education Association, 118, 504
Needs
 achievement, 45, 205-7
 affiliation, 209
 and drives, 212-14
 feedback, 207
 individual, 212-14
 love and belonging, 8, 197
 personal responsibility, 205
 physiological, 8, 196-97
 power, 208-9
 safety and security, 8, 197
 self-actualization, 9, 198-99, 227
 self-esteem, 8-9, 198, 235
 self-expression, 46, 47
 social, 42, 44
 status, 45
 values and, 193-95
New York Times, 449-50
Norris-LaGuardia Act, 120
Northwestern National Life Insurance
 Company, 316

O

O'Brien, Patricia, 162
O'Brien, William E., 441
Occupational Safety and Health Act, 123
Occupational Safety and Health
 Administration (OSHA), 8
Older Workers Protection Act, 383
Olsten Corporation, 384
Organizational communication
 in flat organizations, 170-71
 electronic, 182-86
  e-mail, 185-86
  voice mail, 183-85
 formal, 171-75
  horizontal communication, 175
  vertical communication, 171
   downward, 171-72
   upward, 172-75
   verbal or written, 172
 influences on, 168-69
 informal
  example of, 181-82
  grapevine, 182
 organizational groups and, 186-89
  committees and meetings, 188-89
  size of group, 186-87
 problems in

downward communications, 172
 organizational groups, 187-88
 in tall organizations, 171
 written, 175-81
  letters, 175-76
  memorandums, 176
  reports, 176-81
   formal, 180
   graphics in, 177-79
   proposals, 180-81
   short, 179
Organizational chart, 168-69
Organizational effectiveness, 50-57
 goals, 50
 organizational development and, 58-59
 stakeholders, 50-52
  external, 57
  internal, 52-53, 55-56
Organizational environments
 breadth of job assignments, 45
 independence, 46-47
 isolated workers, 42-43
 perceived status, 44-45
 small units, 42
 two-way communication, 44
Organizational politics, 446. See also
 Organizational power
Organizational power
 acquiring, 450-454
  personal political action, 450-51
  political action directed at opponents,
   452-54
  political action involving others, 451-
   52
 charisma and, 448
 coercive, 448
 legitimate, 447-48
 participative, 455-56
 perceptions of, 465-68
 personal, 448-49
 politics and, 447
 referent, 448
 subordinate, 449
Organizational structures
 bureaucratic, 47-49
  concept of, 47-48
  decision-making in, 48
  Peter Principle in, 49
  universities as, 49
 centralized, 40, 41, 42
 decentralized, 40, 41, 42, 232
 defined, 168
 flat, 38-40, 170-71, 434, 440
 job titles in, 45
 shamrock, 389
 tall, 38-40, 171
Organizational theory
 employee unification concepts, 35-38
  common set of goals, 36-37
  coordination of activities, 37

division of labor, 37
 hierarchy of authority, 37-38
 line positions, 33
 staff positions
  defined, 33
  nature of, 34-35
  placement of, 33
Organizations. See also Organizational
 environments; Organizational struc
 tures; Organizational theory
 and child care consortiums, 289-90
 cliques in, 57-58
 communication in, 25. See also
  Organizational communication
 culture created by, 56
 defined, 32
 downsizing of. See Downsizing
 effectiveness of, 50-57
  goals, 50
  organizational development and,
   58-59
  stakeholders, 50-52
   external, 57
   internal, 52-53, 55-56
 employee assistance programs in. See
  Employee assistance programs
 employee empowerment in. See
  Empowerment
 and external groups. See also Labor
  unions
  addressing, 96-97
  building goodwill, 105
  the community, 96-104
   change in
    ghost towns, 98
    globalization of business, 99
    military base closings, 99
    natural disasters, 99
    plant closings, 99
    workforce changes, 99-100
   common-interest groups in, 97-98
    demographic characteristics of,
     98
    psychographic characteristics
     of, 98
   importance of, 97
   interactions with
    employees as ambassadors, 102,
     103, 105
    and employee job security, 103
    and image of organization, 100,
     102-103
   opinion leaders in, 103-5
  consumerism, 106-7, 497
  financial institutions, 116-17
  government, 122-26
   affirmative action programs, 123
   antidiscrimination legislation, 35,
    124-25
   Age Discrimination in

Employment Act, 123, 383
Americans with Disabilities Act
    (ADA)
definition of disability, 378-79
employers' rights and obliga-
    tions under, 381
policing of, 125
protection of former drug users,
    287
reasonable accommodations pro
    vision, 124
scope of, 378
Civil Rights Act, 123, 174
Equal Employment Opportunity
    Act, 123
Equal Pay Act, 35, 371
Federal Age Discrimination Act,
    227
Older Workers Protection Act,
    383
minimum wage, 123
national health insurance, 123-24
roles of, 124-26
investors, 117
the media, 107-9
other firms
    business activities with, 110-11
    need for interpersonal skill train
        ing, 111
    perceptions of organization by, 105-
        6, 111
    self-sabotaging behavior toward,
        128-29
    special groups, 126-27
human relations need in, 33, 51, 57
job norms in, 55-56
myths in, 56
policies in, 55
power in. See Organizational power
progressive discipline in, 265
redesign in, 406
reengineering in, 408-10
settings for, 33
social responsibility of, 495-97
span of control in, 39
Ouchi, William, 13, 455

P

Pan American World Airline, 115
Partnership, 37
Part-time positions, 242
Peeters, Vivian E., 226, 227
Performance appraisal, 259
    defined, 267
    developmental, 268
    forms of, 270-71
        employee objectives, 271
        forced choice format, 270-71

graphical scale, 270
numerical scale, 270
of managers, 266
nature of, 266-67
objective evaluation in, 269
process of, 268-70
purposes of, 267-68
in small businesses, 266-67
subjective evaluation in, 269
team-developed, 273-74
Performance-based incentive plans,
    275-77
for groups, 276
    gainsharing, 276-77
    profit sharing, 277
for individuals
    commissions, 275-76
    managerial incentive plans, 276
    piecework plan, 275
    standard time plan, 276
    suggestion plans, 276
Performance-based payment plans,
    244, 273
    lump sum payments, 274-75
    merit pay systems, 274
Peter, Laurence J., 49
Peter Principle, 49
Peter Principle, The (Peter and Hull), 49
Piecework, 244, 275
Pie charts, 178
Pigatti, Mary, 325
Plant Closing Notification Act, 122
Posner, Barry, 407
Prejudice, 366-67
    bases of, 367-69
    racial, 369-70
    stereotypes and, 367
Privacy, 328-32
    as an issue, 329
    monitoring in the workplace and, 331-32
    off-the-job behavior and, 329, 330
    on-the-job behavior and, 329
Productivity
    cohesive work group and, 88, 89
    company options to improve, 237-43
        automation, 242-43
        restructuring
            downsizing, 237-38
            entrepreneurship, 238
        work schedules, 239-42
            flexible scheduling, 240-41, 290,
                357
            job sharing, 242
            telecommuting, 239-40
    decline of, 230
    defined, 230
    and efficiency, 230
    employee empowerment and, 234
    ergonomics and, 237
    and Hawthorne effect, 7

job norms and, 55
morale and, 13, 229-30
quality of work life and, 232
and self-directed work groups, 83
and social needs, 42, 43
Professional Air Traffic Controllers
    Organization, 118
Professionalism, 501, 522
Professionals
    attributes of, 505
        personal behavior, 511, 514-21
            attentive to details, 520
            citizenship-minded, 521
            contributing, 519-20
            decisive, 516-17
            enthusiastic, 519
            individualistic, 515
            patient, 516
            resilient, 517-18
            responsible, 515-16
            self-accepting, 511
            self-confident, 511, 514
            self-knowledgeable, 514-15
            time-oriented, 518
        personal qualities, 506-507
        social behavior, 507-11
            acceptance of others, 508-509
            fairness, 510-11
            sense of humor, 509-10
    defined, 505
Professions
    behavior in, 522
    characteristics of, 502-505
        permanence, 502-503
        professional ethics, 503-504
        professional rewards, 503
        training, 502
    types of, 522
Profit sharing, 277
Project team, 72
Proprietor, 37
Public relations
    and community changes, 98
    defined, 4
    and external stakeholders, 57
    and human relations, 4

Q

Quality circles
    nature of, 8, 15, 233
    philosophy of, 16
    success of, 89, 233
Quality Management. See Total Quality
    Management
Quality Management: Implementing the
    Best Ideas of the Masters (Brocka and
    Brocka), 437
Quality of work life (QWL), 16, 232-33

R

Reagan, Ronald, 118
Reengineering, 408-10
Renaud, Larry, 140
Reward systems
  for attendance, 303-304
  extrinsic rewards in, 272, 273
  intrinsic rewards in, 272-73
  nature of, 272
  performance-based, 230, 273
Right-sizing. *See* Downsizing

S

"Satisfaction and Performance: Casual
  Relationships and Moderating Effects"
  (Siegel and Bowen), 230
Scanlon, Joseph, 277
Scanlon Plan, 277
Schabacker, Kirsten, 152
Schmidt, Warren, 429
Schnucks Supermarket, 57
Schrag, Dennis, 360
Scientific method of management and job
  design, 6, 234
Scitor Corporation, 289-90
Scott, James, 344
Sculley, John, 463
Sears, 115
Securities and Exchange Commission,
  126
Self, 193
Self-sabotaging behavior, 128-29
Selye, Hans, 312
Sensitivity training, 115
Service America (Albrecht and Zemke),
  109
Service organizations, 109
Shamrock organization, 389
Shaw, George Bernard, 509
Shellenbarger, Sue, 273
Sherrill, Patrick, 326
Singapore's business climate, 466-67
Smith, Dean, 448
Social mobility concept, 367
Social responsibility, 495-97
Society for Human Resource
  Management, 384
Sorensen, Ron, 273
R. I. Spiece Sales Company, 137
Spiece, Tom, 137
Steinem, Gloria, 407
Stereotypes, 367
STP, 396
Stress
  and burnout, 317-20
    help for, 319-20
    nature of, 317-18

symptoms of, 318
defined, 312
employee assistance programs and. *See*
  Employee assistance programs
flextime and, 240-41
impact of, in workplace, 314-16
nature of, 312
solutions to workplace, 316-17
sources of, 312-14, 327
  positive, 313
  supervisor, 314
  work induced, 313-14
success and, 349
and violence in the workplace, 325-28
Success
  defined, 213
  fear of failure and, 214, 349
  measurement of, 213-14
  stress and, 349
Suggestion plans, 276

T

Tables, 177
Taft-Hartley Act
  outlawing closed shops, 120
  outlawing secondary boycotts, 119
  and right-to-work laws, 120
Tannen, Deborah, 162
Tannenbaum, Robert, 429
Task force, 72
Taylor, Frederick, 6, 234
Teamsters, 118
Telecommuting, 239-40, 289
Texas Instruments
  age discrimination suit against, 383-84
  attendance inducement program, 302
Theory of Social and Economic
  Organizations, The (Weber), 47
Theory X, 11, 426-28, 455
Theory Y, 11-12, 428, 455
Theory Z, 13, 455
Tiger team, 72
Timberland Shoes, 396
Time management
  defined, 335
  good, 335
  in multicultural workplace, 344-45
  steps in
    goal setting, 342
    logging activities, 339-42
    priority setting, 346-48
    time analysis, 335-39
    working the plan, 348
  time intrusions and, 349-57
    chatty coworkers, 352-53
    disorganization, 354-55
    inability to say no, 350-51
    meetings, 353-54

paperwork, 355-57
procrastination, 349-50
taking on too much, 351
telephone interruptions, 351-52
time log in, 339-42
  analyzing, 341-42
  keeping, 340-41
Total quality commitment, 16
Total Quality Management
  approach to change, 398-99
  employee involvement in, 440-41
  leadership and, 437
  overview of, 438-39
  philosophy of, 398
"Tough Customers" (Drake), 363
Training , 81
Training programs. *See* Interpersonal skill
  training
Transactional analysis, 115
Tung, Rosalie, 291, 345
21st Century Leadership, 460

U

Ugly American, The, 19
UNESCO, 147
United Auto Workers, 117
United HealthCare Corporation, 325
United Mine Workers Union, 118
United States Chamber of Commerce, 330
United States manufacturing, 19
U.S. Office of Consumer Affairs, 111
U.S. Postal Service, 326
U.S. West Telecommunications
  firing worker over self-expression
  issue, 318-19
  valuing differences program at, 364
United Steelworkers, 117

V

Values
  attitudes and, 472, 477-78
  beliefs and, 477-78
  nature of, 472, 473
  organizational, 482-83
    conflicting, 485-87
    shared, 483-84
  personal
    influences on, 471, 473
      change, 479, 482
      culture and social class, 473-74
      educational experiences, 476
      family, 474
      peer group, 475-75
      television, 477
      work experiences, 476
Valuing differences programs, 363-64
Virginia Military Institute, 136

Voice mail, 183-85
Vroom, Victor, 211, 229

W

Walden, Karen, 74
Wall Street Journal, The
  "Decade of Downsizing Eases Stigma
    of Layoffs," 231
  on employee vindictiveness, 435
  on Japanese managerial women, 258
  "More Companies Experiment with
    Workers" Schedules,î 241
  on telecommuting, 239-40
  on work and family, 273
Wal-Mart, 482
Walton, Sam
  organizational philosophy of, 56
  success of, 9
Weber, Max
  concept of bureaucratic organization,
    47-48
  Theory of Social and Economic
    Organizations, The, 47
Welch, Jack, 482-83
Western Electric, 320
Whistle blowers, 378, 494
Whitehead, Alfred North, 389
Workaholism
  nature of, 219-20
  identifying, 91, 220-21
Worker enhancement programs, 233
Worker Readjustment Program, 122
Workers. See Employees
Work groups
  buddy system (peer mentoring) in, 66
  building effective, 84-91
    cohesion, 88-89
    commitment, 89-91
    communication, 85-86
    conflict resolution, 87-88
  conflict in, 87
  conformity in, 79-80
  directed, 80
  empowering others in, 77-78
  formal, 72
  joining, 64-70
    acceptance versus exclusion, 66
    attaining membership in, 70
    concerns about, 64-65
    coping with undesirable assignments,
      67-69
      being labeled, 67-68
      on fitting in, 68-69
      "paying your dues," 67
    creating a positive impression, 66-67
    reasons for, 64
  participation in, 92-93
  permanent, 72-73

problems in, 86
  conflict, 87
  deviants, 79
  groupthink, 93
  hazing, 69-70
  polarization, 93
  rumors, 85
  scapegoats, 79
  self-serving communication, 86
productivity enhancement of, 88
self-directed, 81, 83-84
size and makeup of, 74-76
social (informal), 71-72
temporary, 73-74
Working conditions
  and employee productivity, 7
  late-19th-century, 7
Working Woman, 152, 162
Work/Life Group of Boston, 293
Work performance. See Job performance
Workplace
  absenteeism in, 259
    alcohol-related, 284
    connotation of, 300
    controlling, 302-303
      discipline, 304-306
      reward programs, 303-304
    and group efficiency, 300, 301
    reasons for, 300-301
  AIDS in, 118
  alcoholism in
    absenteeism and, 284
    identifying, 283-84
    nature of, 282-83
    programs for, 285
  burnout in, 317-20
  changes predicted in, 231-32. See also
  Change
  child care and, 118, 289-90
  cliques in, 57-58
  disabled employees in, 378-82
    and the Americans with Disabilities
  Act (ADA), 378-79
    assisting, 382
    complaints against employers,
      380-81
    reasonable accommodations for, 379
  dishonesty in, 22, 74-75, 126-27
  diversity in
    checking understanding of, 361-63
    growth of, 363
    managing, 360-61, 363-64
    strength of, 360-61
    and value conflicts, 476
    valuing differences programs and,
      363-64
  drug abuse in, 118
    drugs involved in, 286-87
    signs of, 285
    testing policies, 286-88

employee assistance programs in. See
  Employee assistance programs
employee empowerment in. See
  Empowerment
employee stock ownership plans
  (ESOPs) in, 118
employer responsibilities in, 364-66
  no-harassment policy in employee
    handbook, 365
  providing workplace free from
    harassment, 364-65
exclusion in, 366
harassment in
  Equal Employment Opportunity
    Commission guidelines on, 372-74
  forms of, 364
  and hostile environment, 364
  proactive approaches to, 365-66
    creating an inclusive environment,
      366
    no-harassment policy in employee
      handbook, 365
  sexual, 118, 374-76
harassment audits in, 376-78
and industrial revolution, 3, 7
job maintenance factors in, 10
monitoring in, 331-32
movement of jobs from, 119
pay equity for women in, 118
privacy in, 328-32
  as an issue, 329
  monitoring and, 331-32
  off-the-job behavior and, 329, 330
  on-the-job behavior and, 329
problems in, 26-27
stress in. See Stress
violence in, 325-28
  difficult employees and, 327-28
  impact of, 325
  preventing, 326-28
  reducing, 328
  typical profile of, 325
Work teams, 236

X

Xerox Corporation
  Balanced Work Force strategy of, 372
  multidisciplinary teams at, 440-41

Y

You Just Don't Understand (Tannen), 162

Z

Zaharias, Babe, 464
Zemke, Ron, 109

Photo Credits

Chapter 1

Page 3 Courtesy of International Paper Company
Page 7 National Archives Trust
Page 12 Photo by Richard Younker
Page 23 Courtesy of International Business Machines Corporation

Chapter 2

Page 43 Stauffer Chemical Company
Page 46 Photo by Alan Brown/Photonics
Page 55 Howard Grey/Tony Stone Images, Inc.
Page 59 ©Bill Frywire/Masterfile

Chapter 3

Page 71 ©Jim Whitmer
Page 88 Photo by Richard Younker

Chapter 4

Page 99 Courtesy of Schwab Corporation
Page 104 Courtesy of WVXU
Page 114 Courtesy of Newtek
Page 119 United Press International, Inc.

Chapter 5

Page 148 ©Gale Zucker/Stock Boston
Page 155 Courtesy of International Business Machines Corporation
Page 156 Photo by Joe Banks

Chapter 6

Page 183 ©Bill Brooks/Masterfile
Page 187 ©Arthur Grace/Stock Boston

Chapter 7

Page 194 ©H. Armstrong Roberts
Page 198 ©Barbara Alper/Stock Boston
Page 204 ©Michael Dwyer/Stock Boston
Page 213 ©Michael Dwyer/Stock Boston

Chapter 8

Page 220 ©H. Armstrong Roberts
Page 225 Courtesy of the National Air and Space Administration
Page 228 Johnson & Johnson
Page 235 ©Charles Gupton/Stock Boston

Chapter 9

Page 273 Chesebrough-Pond's Inc.
Page 275 Photo by Gary Kessler

Chapter 10

Page 283 Photo by Jeff Greenberg
Page 291 ©Jim Whitmer
Page 300 Photo courtesy of New England Memorial Hospital

Chapter 11

Page 313 ©Jeffry Myers/Stock Boston
Page 317 The Jewish Hospital of Cincinnati
Page 321 ©H. Armstrong Roberts
Page 326 ©Reuters/Bettman

Chapter 12

Page 343 ©Bob Daemmrich/Stock Boston
Page 346 ©H. Armstrong Roberts

Chapter 13

Page 365 Photo by Alan Brown/Photonics
Page 368 ©UPI/Bettman

Chapter 14

Page 391 ©Reuters/Bettman
Page 393 Courtesy of McDonald's Corporation
Page 407 ©UPI/Bettman

Chapter 15

Page 423 ©Wendt WorldWide
Page 438 Photo by Alan Brown/Photonics
Page 442 Courtesy of International Business Machines Corporation

Chapter 16

Page 448 ©UPI/Bettman
Page 456 ©Tony Stone Images, Inc.
Page 459 Courtesy of American Airlines
Page 462 Courtesy of the Boy Scouts of America
Page 463 Photo by Alan Brown/Photonics

Chapter 17

Page 496 Photo Courtesy of Ben & Jerry's Homemade Ice Cream, Inc.

Chapter 18

Page 506 Courtesy of Figgle International

Acknowledgments

Chapter 2

Pages 35–36, Ethical Dimensions to Human Relations
Reprinted by permission of Lynne Joy McFarland, Author of *21st Century Leadership* and Chairman of the LINC Corporation.

"Male Models Earn Half Their Female Counterparts" © 1994 Associated Press. Reprinted by permission.

Nickels, McHugh and McHugh, *Understanding Business,* Richard D. Irwin, Inc., © 1987, pp. 611–613. Reprinted with permission.

Pages 53–54, Customs and Traditions: Watching for the Global Difference
A.J. Almaney and A.J. Alwan, *Communicating with Arabs: A Handbook for the Business Executive,* 1982. Reprinted with permission.

Fernea and Fernea, *The Arab World: Personal Encounters,* © 1985, Doubleday. Reprinted with permission.

From the book THE BUSINESS TRAVELER'S HANDBOOK by F. Minsep, © 1983, Reprinted by permission of Prentice Hall/a Division of Simon & Schuster, Inc.

Page 48, Jan Erickson case
Adapted, with permission of the publisher, from CORPORATE DANDELIONS by Craig J. Cantoni, © 1993 Craig J. Cantoni. Published by AMACOM, a division of the American Management Association. All rights reserved.

Chapter 3

Pages 71–72, Social versus Formal Work Groups; **page 73,** Temporary Groups; **pages 80–81,** Directed versus Self–directed Work Groups; **page 81,** Table 3.2
Reprinted with permission from the Oct. 1992 issue of TRAINING Magazine. Copyright 1992. Lakewood Publications,

Minneapolis, MN. All rights reserved. Not for resale.

Page 72, Roberto Gomez case; **pages 75–76,** Cheryl Wollrab case
Reprinted with permission of JAI Press, Inc., Greenwich Connecticut from Journal of Management, vol. 17, No. 2, (1991)

Pages 74–75, Ethical Dimensions to Human Relations
Hosmer, *Moral Leadership in Business,* Richard D. Irwin, Inc., © 1994, p. 14. Reprinted with permission.

Pages 82–83, Customs and Traditions: Watching for the Global Difference "Culture Shock" and "How Different is Mexico?" by Matt Moffett Reprinted by permission of THE WALL STREET JOURNAL REPORTS © 1992 Dow Jones & Company, Inc. All Rights Reserved Worldwide.

From *Managing Cultural Differences,* by Robert T. Moran and Philip R. Harris. Copyright © 1991 by Gulf Publishing Company, Houston, TX. Used with permission. All rights reserved.

Page 87, Conflict
Hart, *Managing People at Work,* © 1979 McGraw Hill, Inc. Reprinted with permission.

Pages 92–93, Work Group Participation "Applying Small Group Dynamics to Improve Action Team Performance" by Gary Coleman and Eileen VanAken in *Employment Relations Today,* Autumn, 1991. © 1991 John Wiley & Sons, Inc. Reprinted by permission.

Chapter 4

Page 100, Community Interactions
Sharon Brownlee, "The Best of Times for American Women," *U.S. News and World Report,* January 13, 1992, p. 10.

Pages 100–101, Customs and Traditions: Watching for the Global Difference
Adapted, with permission of the publish-

er, from PACIFIC RIM TRADE by Mike Van Horn, © 1989 AMACOM, a division of the American Management Association. All rights reserved.

Page 103, Midway case
Reprinted from *The Pantagraph.*

Page 115, Transactional Analysis
Muriel James and Dorothy Jongeward, BORN TO WIN: TRANSACTIONAL ANALYSIS WITH GESTALT EXPERIMENTS (pg. 36), © 1971 by Addison-Wesley Publishing Company, Inc.

Pages 126–127, Ethical Dimensions to Human Relations
Diane Cole, "Companies Crack Down on Dishonesty." *Managing Your Career,* Spring, 1991, pp. 8–11. Reprinted by permission of the National Business Employment Weekly.

Hoffman and Moore, BUSINESS ETHICS, 2e, © 1989 McGraw-Hill, Inc. Reprinted with permission

Unit 1 Applications & Cases

Page 137, Case 2
Reprinted courtesy *The Indianapolis Star*

Chapter 7

Page 203, Figure 7.4 Factors Affecting Job Attitudes, as Reported in Twelve Investigations
Reprinted by permission of *Harvard Business Review.* An exhibit from "One More Time: How Do You Motivate Employees?" by Frederick Herzberg, (January/February 1968). Copyright © 1968 by the President and Fellows of Harvard College; all rights reserved.

Pages 204–205, Achievement Motivation Theory
Reprinted by permission of *Harvard Business Review.* An excerpt from "Business Drive and National Achievement" by David C. McClelland, (July/August 1962). Copyright © 1962 by the President and Fellows of Harvard College, all rights reserved.